# The Welfare State Reader

# The Welfare State Reader

*Second Edition*

Edited by
Christopher Pierson
and Francis G. Castles

polity

This edition first published in 2006 by Polity Press

Polity Press
65 Bridge Street
Cambridge CB2 1UR, UK.

Polity Press
350 Main Street
Malden, MA 02148, USA



ISBN: 0-7456-3555-5
ISBN: 0-7456-3556-3 (pb)

A catalogue record for this book is available from the British Library.

Typeset in 10 on 12 pt Stempel Garamond
by Servis Filmsetting Ltd, Manchester
Printed and bound in Great Britain
by MPG Books Ltd, Bodmin, Cornwall

For further information on Polity, visit our website: www.polity.co.uk

# Contents

# Acknowledgements

The editors and publishers gratefully acknowledge permission to reproduce copyright material in the following chapters:

Wil Arts and John Gelissen, 'Three Worlds of Welfare Capitalism or More? A State-of-the-Art Report'. From *Journal of European Social Policy*, 12 (2002), by permission of the authors and Sage Publications.

Giuliano Bonoli, 'The Politics of the New Social Policies: Providing Coverage against New Social Risks in Mature Welfare States'. From *Policy and Politics*, 33, 3 (2005), by permission of Policy Press and the author.

Asa Briggs, 'The Welfare State in Historical Perspective'. Abridged from *European Journal of Sociology*, 2 (1961), by permission of Archives Européennes des Sociologies.

Francis G. Castles, 'A Race to the Bottom?' From Francis G. Castles, *The Future of the Welfare State*, Oxford University Press, 2004, by permission of the publisher.

Damien Chalmers and Martin Lodge, 'The Open Method of Co-ordination and the European Welfare State'. Copyright © Damien Chalmers and Martin Lodge. The authors would like to thank the London School of Economics for permission to reproduce this article.

David Coleman, 'Population and Ageing: An Unavoidable Future'. From *Journal of Social Biology and Human Affairs*, 66 (2001), by permission of the author and the publisher.

Commission on Social Justice, 'What is Social Justice?' From Commission on Social Justice, *The Justice Gap*, Institute for Public Policy Research, 1993, by permission of the IPPR.

Nick Ellison, 'Beyond Universalism and Particularism: Rethinking Contemporary Welfare Theory'. From *Critical Social Policy*, 19, 1 (1999), copyright © Journal of Critical Social Policy, 1999, by permission of the author and Sage Publications.

Gøsta Esping-Andersen, 'A Welfare State for the Twenty-First Century'. From Anthony Giddens (ed.), *Global Third Way Debate*, Polity, 2001, by permission of the publisher.

Gøsta Esping-Andersen, 'Three Worlds of Welfare Capitalism'. From Gøsta Esping-Andersen, *The Three Worlds of Welfare Capitalism*, Polity and Princeton University Press, 1990, by permission of the publishers.

Anthony Giddens, 'Positive Welfare'. From Anthony Giddens, *The Third Way*, Polity, 1998, by permission of the publisher.

Colin Hay, 'Globalization, Economic Change and the Welfare State. The "Vexatious Inquisition of Taxation?"'. From R. Sykes, B. Palier and P. M. Prior (eds), *Globalization and European Welfare States*, Palgrave, 2001, by permission of Palgrave Macmillan.

Friedrich von Hayek, 'The Meaning of the Welfare State'. From F. A. Hayek, *The Constitution of Liberty*, Routledge and University of Chicago Press, 1959, by permission of University of Chicago Press and Taylor and Francis Books UK.

Richard Jackson, 'The Global Retirement Crisis'. From *The Global Retirement Crisis*, Washington, DC, Center for Strategic and International Studies, 2002, by permission of the author.

Walter Korpi, 'The Power Resources Model'. From W. Korpi, *The Democratic Class Struggle*, Routledge and Kegan Paul, 1983, reproduced by permission of Taylor and Francis Books UK.

Walter Korpi, 'Welfare-State Regress in Western Europe: Politics, Institutions, Globalization, and Europeanization'. From *Annual Review of Sociology*, 29 (2003), © 2003 by Annual Reviews (www.annualreviews.org), reprinted by permission.

Ruth Lister, 'Investing in the Citizen-Workers of the Future: Transformations in Citizenship and the State under New Labour'. From *Social*

*Policy and Administration*, 37, 5 (2003), by permission of Blackwell Publishing Ltd.

Peter McDonald, 'Gender Equity in Theories of Fertility Transition'. From *Population and Development Review*, 26, 3 (2000), by permission of Blackwell Publishing Ltd.

Mary McIntosh, 'Feminism and Social Policy'. From *Critical Social Policy*, 1 (1981), © Journal of Critical Social Policy 1981, by permission of the author and Sage Publications.

T. H. Marshall, 'Citizenship and Social Class'. From T. H. Marshall, *Citizenship and Social Class and Other Essays*, Cambridge University Press, 1950, originally delivered in Cambridge as the Marshall Lecture in 1949; by permission of Mrs N. Marshall.

Lawrence M. Mead, 'The New Politics of the New Poverty'. From *The Public Interest,* 103 (Spring 1991), by permission of the author.

Charles Murray, 'The Two Wars against Poverty'. From *The Public Interest,* 69 (Winter 1982), by permission of the author.

James O'Connor, 'The Fiscal Crisis of the State'. From the Introduction to J. O'Connor, *The Fiscal Crisis of the State*, Transaction, © 2001, by permission of the publisher.

Claus Offe, 'Some Contradictions of the Modern Welfare State'. From *Critical Social Policy,* 2, 2 (1982), copyright © Journal of Critical Social Policy 1982, by permission of the author and Sage Publications.

Bruno Palier, 'Beyond Retrenchment'. From J. Claesen (ed.), *What Future for Social Security?* Kluwer Law International, The Hague, 2003. Reprinted by permission of the author and Aspen Publishers.

Philippe van Parijs, 'Basic Income and the Two Dilemmas of the Welfare State'. From *Political Quarterly,* 67, 1 (1996), by permission of Blackwell Publishing Ltd.

Carole Pateman, 'The Patriarchal Welfare State'. From Carole Pateman, *The Disorder of Women*, Polity, 1988, by permission of the author and publisher.

Paul Pierson, 'The New Politics of the Welfare State'. From *World Politics,* 48 (1996), copyright © The Johns Hopkins University Press, by permission of the publisher.

Fritz Scharpf, 'Negative Integration and the Loss of Boundary Control'. From G. Marks, F. W. Scharpf, W. Streeck and P. C. Schmitter (eds), *Governance in the European Union*, Sage, 1996, copyright © Sage Publications Ltd 1996, by permission of the publisher.

James H. Schultz, 'The Evolving Concept of "Retirement": Looking Forward to the Year 2050'. From *International Social Security Review,* 55, 1 (2002), by permission of Blackwell Publishing Ltd.

Paul Teague, 'Deliberative Governance and EU Social Policy'. From *European Journal of Industrial Relations*, 7, 1 (2001), copyright © Sage Publications Ltd, by permission of the publisher.

Richard Titmuss, 'Universalism versus Selection'. From R. Titmuss, *Commitment to Welfare*, Allen and Unwin, 1968, by permission of the Literary Estate of Richard Titmuss.

Every effort has been made to trace copyright holders, but if any have been inadvertently overlooked, the publishers will be pleased to make the necessary arrangements at the first opportunity.

# Editors' Note

An ellipsis within square brackets indicates an omission from the original publication, thus: [. . .]. Where more than a paragraph has been excluded, a line space appears above and below such ellipses. Apart from minor amendments (e.g. capitalization, British rather than American spellings and the presentation of reference material), the few editorial interventions necessitated by publishing these extracts in a single volume also appear in square brackets. The authors' opinions are, of course, those held at the time of writing; dates of original publication are reflected in the Notes to each reading.

# Editors' Introduction to the Second Edition

This second edition of *The Welfare State Reader* continues our efforts to produce an introduction to the politics of the welfare state that brings together enduring themes of the literature with up-to-the-minute accounts of the challenges confronting contemporary welfare states. The enduring themes of the literature are ones with a continuing broad resonance across the social sciences. Questions about how best to minimize poverty and promote equality, what sorts of policy intervention produce the best results and the extent to which state intervention for welfare purposes is compatible with other desired goals of modern societies have been central preoccupations of the disciplines of social theory and social policy and have informed a large part of the analytical content of both political science and sociology throughout these disciplines' existence. They are, moreover, questions that have become ever more salient and of ever greater practical policy relevance as the governments of democratic states have responded to popular demands and to new social and economic problems by extending the scope of the caring state. Today, the state spends more on welfare than on all other purposes combined, and long-established programmes like old age pensions, sickness and unemployment benefits and health care have been joined by programmes catering to the care needs of dual-earner families, the residential needs of the frail elderly and income needs of workers whose skills levels do not produce an adequate return in the market economy. An understanding of the main approaches taken to questions relating to the early growth and developmental progress of the welfare state provides an invaluable point of reference for locating the issues raised by contemporary struggles over the state's role as an agency of social amelioration.

While, however, the literature's enduring themes remain hugely relevant to contemporary concerns, the substance of contemporary debates is constantly changing, being continually shaped and reshaped by developments in the wider society and economy and by political responses to those developments. It is because present manifestations of the politics of welfare are in a constant process of transformation that our original conception of a welfare state reader was built around the notion of marrying an exposition of enduring themes with a focus on current challenges. It is because the current challenges of the new century have already begun to change their form and because current scholarship has already begun to conceive those challenges differently that only five years later a new edition of our reader is appropriate. Thus while the main headings of our account are substantially unchanged – welfare regimes, globalization, Europeanization, demographic and political change and the future of welfare – there are only one or two pieces in these sections which have survived from the earlier edition. This is not updating for its own sake. It is updating because the issues are evolving and the scholarly perspectives changing. Illustrative examples treated in this new edition include a reconceptualization of the extent and character of the social policy impact of economic globalization, the emergence of 'Europeanization' as a force undermining the high standards of welfare provision in northern Europe, the evolution of new techniques of social policy decision-making within the European Union and the challenge of declining fertility and other 'new social risks' to the continued viability of the Western welfare state. These issues, along with continuingly important concerns about how we cater to the needs of an ageing population, how far welfare states have been subject to retrenchment in recent decades and the viability of new or 'third way' policy solutions for traditional welfare dilemmas, direct attention to the likely battle lines of welfare state politics and welfare state scholarly debate in coming years.

A minor change in the presentation of this edition compared with the last is that each of the three major parts of the volume is preceded by a brief discussion of the themes and topics treated by the various contributions. It is our hope that this innovation assists readers in following the argument and in locating how each selection fits into the debate. In two far more fundamental ways our approach in this edition remains the same as previously. First, in both editions, we have consciously attempted to overcome the national parochialism that often characterizes welfare state analysis. The emergence of the modern welfare state is an international phenomenon that has taken many forms and which poses challenges that are seen differently by different scholars in different countries. We have tried very hard to give a flavour of this variety, first, by choosing contributions from commentators from many countries and, second, by, wherever possible, selecting those which make reference to differences as well as similarities in the development of and challenges facing modern welfare states. Second, we have been deeply concerned throughout to show that all the issues treated are genuinely matters of debate. These debates are sometimes ideological and/or theoretical, like the debates separating left and right on the appropriate limits to state intervention or the polemics directed by feminist scholars at the patriarchialism of traditional welfare state arrangements. They are also frequently empirical, when, as in debates over the appropriateness of particular models of the welfare state, the extent of welfare retrenchment, the effects of Europeanization and the welfare implications of population ageing, scholars disagree in their analyses and diagnoses of contemporary issues and future welfare state prospects. Whether ideological, theoretical or empirical, such debates are inherently policy relevant because different welfare preferences and diagnoses imply different ways of conceptualizing and tackling pressing social problems. That is why issues concerning the welfare state are inherently political and will always be of passionate concern to scholars and commentators who care about the future of the communities of which they are members.

# Part I

## *Approaches to Welfare*

In this first part, we bring together a series of 'classic' contributions to the literature of the welfare state. Tom Paine is our sole representative of thinking about welfare *before* the rise of the modern welfare state. Writing more than two hundred years ago, many of Paine's thoughts have a strikingly contemporary resonance. His views on the interaction of poverty, criminality, indolence and employment are often simply a more elegant and direct expression of the kinds of arguments that go on today. It is as well to remember that thinking about welfare did not begin in 1945.

It used to be said that we lacked any serious theoretical account of where welfare states came from and what they are for. The business of the welfare state was social administration: the mundane tasks of mopping up poverty and improving public services. This was always, in part, a caricature. There have always been sharp and insightful critics of this dreary-but-worthy view of the welfare state. But we now have a wealth of competing theoretical accounts of the welfare state to choose from and the principal aim of part I of the reader is to offer a representative survey of the best and the most influential of this literature. We begin with a series of writings from the years immediately following the end of the Second World War. These are not, for the most part, the years in which welfare states were founded. The origins of welfare states among most developed states actually lie in the twenty-five years *preceding* the First World War. But the postwar period was one of unprecedented and, at least to some extent, consensual growth in welfare states. It is also the time that gave us the most authoritative and enduring social democratic accounts of welfare and state. Here we have included three 'Classical' statements of the social democratic approach drawn from the work of Asa Briggs, Tom Marshall and Richard Titmuss. The views of social democratic writers on the welfare state have always been vulnerable to misrepresentation, especially as they have so often been glossed as holding a rather simple-minded and wholly benign view of both the state and the human condition, a view which it is difficult to reconcile with a *careful* reading of what they actually said. But certainly these authors stand at the fount of a view of the welfare state which sees it as essentially a 'good thing', capable of forging a new and stable reconciliation between the seemingly competing claims of economic efficiency and social justice. Much of the rest of the literature on the welfare state is a more or less explicit engagement with these positions.

In Perspectives on the Left, we bring this more theoretical approach forward towards our own time. Not all of the contributions here are social democratic. Indeed, O'Connor and Offe are quite explicitly critical of a form of political compromise which they see as unsustainable over the medium term. In slightly differing ways, they argue that capitalist welfare states are vulnerable to a series of deep-seated contradictions which make them politically quite unstable. By contrast, the selections from the Commission on Social Justice and from Walter Korpi represent rather differing attempts to refashion social democratic impulses under the duress of changing (and more difficult) circumstances.

The views represented in Responses from the Right have been extraordinarily influential on welfare debates over the past twenty-five years. Friedrich Hayek probably remains the most sophisticated representative of the view that welfare state institutions are essentially irreconcilable with a social order premised on the value of human freedom. In Hayek's wake have come a vast array of critics who have condemned the welfare state, variously, as uneconomic, unproductive, inefficient, ineffective, despotic and inconsistent with freedom. Two of the most influential spokespeople for a tradition which has always been at its strongest in the Anglo-Saxon world (above all, in North America) are Charles Murray and Lawrence Mead. Murray has become strongly identified with the idea that welfare state institutions tend to produce a social 'underclass' wedded to criminality, while Mead is similarly associated with the idea that welfare generates new forms of poverty and dependency in which the appeal to rights swamps any corresponding sense of social obligations. The views of both authors are given characteristically robust expression in the articles chosen here.

Among the most influential interventions in reshaping the entire debate about the politics of welfare over the past thirty years have been the contributions of feminist authors. Starting (at least in its contemporary form, since there are many precursors) with Elizabeth Wilson's 1977 book *Women and the Welfare State*, the intervening period has seen the growth of a literature which has challenged the very terms on which all previous discussions of state and welfare had proceeded. Although a diverse literature, feminist writers have consistently sought to show how the nature of welfare states and, within them, of the interplay of public and private institutions and of formal and informal labour markets, voluntary and family care and so on, have generated welfare regimes which can be seen to be very clearly gendered in their structures and outcomes. At the same time, they argue that this aspect of gender within the welfare state is effectively concealed, often under the rubric of the universality of citizenship. The two papers in the Feminism section, McIntosh's article on 'Feminism and Social Policy' and Pateman's piece on 'The Patriarchal Welfare State' are outstanding examples of this approach.

# The First Welfare State?

## *Thomas Paine*

[. . .]

When, in countries that are called civilized, we see age going to the workhouse and youth to the gallows, something must be wrong in the system of government. It would seem, by the exterior appearance of such countries, that all was happiness; but there lies hidden from the eye of common observation, a mass of wretchedness that has scarcely any other chance than to expire in poverty or infamy. Its entrance into life is marked with the presage of its fate; and until this is remedied, it is in vain to punish.

Civil government does not consist in executions; but in making that provision for the instruction of youth, and the support of age, as to exclude, as much as possible, profligacy from the one, and despair from the other. Instead of this, the resources of a country are lavished upon kings, upon courts, upon hirelings, impostors and prostitutes; and even the poor themselves, with all their wants upon them, are compelled to support the fraud that oppresses them.

Why is it, that scarcely any are executed but the poor? The fact is a proof, among other things, of a wretchedness in their condition. Bred up without morals, and cast upon the world without a prospect, they are the exposed sacrifice of vice and legal barbarity. The millions that are superfluously wasted upon governments are more than sufficient to reform those evils, and to benefit the condition of every man in a nation, not included within the purlieus of a court.

[. . .]

In the present state of things, a labouring man, with a wife and two or three children, does not pay less than between seven and eight pounds a year in taxes. He is not sensible of this, because it is disguised to him in the articles which he buys, and he thinks only of their dearness; but as the taxes take from him, at least, a fourth part of his yearly earnings, he is consequently disabled from providing for a family, especially, if himself, or any of them, are afflicted with sickness.

The first step, therefore, of practical relief, would be to abolish the poor rates entirely, and in lieu thereof, to make a remission of taxes to the poor of double the amount of the present poor-rates, viz. 4 millions annually out of the surplus taxes. By this measure, the poor will be benefited 2 millions, and the housekeepers 2 millions.

[. . .]

I proceed to the mode of relief or distribution, which is,

To pay as a remission of taxes to every poor family, out of the surplus taxes, and in room of poor-rates, four pounds a year for every child under fourteen years of age; enjoining the parents of such children to send them to school, to learn reading, writing and common arithmetic; the ministers of every parish, of every denomination, to certify jointly to an office, for that purpose, that this duty is performed.

The amount of this expense will be,
For six hundred and thirty thousand children,
at four pounds *per ann.* each, — — — — — — £2,520,000

By adopting this method, not only the poverty of the parents will be relieved, but ignorance will be banished from the rising generation, and the number of poor will hereafter become less, because their abilities, by the aid of education, will be greater. Many a youth, with good natural genius, who is apprenticed to a mechanical trade, such as a carpenter, joiner, millwright, shipwright, blacksmith, &c. is prevented getting forward the whole of his life, from the want of a little common education when a boy.

I now proceed to the case of the aged.

I divide age into two classes. First, the approach of age beginning at fifty. Secondly, old age commencing at sixty.

At fifty, though the mental faculties of man are in full vigour, and his judgement better than at any preceding date, the bodily powers for laborious life are on the decline. He cannot bear the same quantity of fatigue as at an earlier period. He begins to earn less, and is less capable of enduring wind and weather; and in those more retired employments where much sight is required, he fails apace, and sees himself, like an old horse, beginning to be turned adrift.

At sixty his labour ought to be over, at least from direct necessity. It is painful to see old age working itself to death, in what are called civilized countries, for daily bread.

[. . .]

[I propose] To pay to every such person of the age of fifty years, and until he shall arrive at the age of sixty, the sum of six pounds *per ann.* out of the surplus taxes; and ten pounds *per ann.* during life after the age of sixty. The expense of which will be,

| | |
|---|---|
| Seventy thousand persons at £6 *per ann.* | 420,000 |
| Seventy thousand ditto at £10 *per ann.* | 700,000 |
| | £1,120,000 |

This support, as already remarked, is not of the nature of a charity, but of a right. Every person in England, male and female, pays on an average in taxes, two pounds eight shillings and sixpence *per ann.* from the day of his (or her) birth; and, if the expense of collection be added, he pays two pounds eleven shillings and sixpence; consequently, at the end of fifty years he has paid one hundred and twenty-eight pounds fifteen shillings; and at sixty, one hundred and fifty-four pounds ten shillings. Converting, therefore, his (or her) individual tax into a tontine, the money he shall receive after fifty years is but little more than the legal interest of the net money he has paid; the rest is made up from those whose circumstances do not require them to draw such support, and the capital in both cases defrays the expenses of government. It is on this ground that I have extended the probable claims to one third of the number of aged persons in the nation. Is it then better that the lives of one hundred and forty thousand aged persons be rendered comfortable, or that a million a year of public money be expended on any one individual, and him often of the most worthless or insignificant character?

[. . .]

After all the above cases are provided for, there will still be a number of families who, though not properly of the class of poor, yet find it difficult to give education to their children; and such children, under such a case, would be in a worse condition than if their parents were actually poor. A nation under a well-regulated government should permit none to remain uninstructed. It is monarchical and aristocratical government only that requires ignorance for its support.

Suppose then four hundred thousand children to be in this condition, which is a greater number than ought to be supposed, after the provisions already made, the method will be,

To allow for each of those children ten shillings a year for the expense of schooling, for six years each, which will give them six months schooling each year and half a crown a year for paper and spelling books.

The expense of this will be annually £250,000

There will then remain one hundred and ten thousand pounds.

Notwithstanding the great modes of relief which the best instituted and best principled government may devise, there will be a number of smaller cases, which it is good policy as well as beneficence in a nation to consider.

Were twenty shilling to be given immediately on the birth of a child, to every woman who should make the demand, and none will make it whose circumstances do not require it, it might relieve a great deal of instant distress.

There are about two hundred thousand births yearly in England, and if claimed, by one fourth,

The amount would be £50,000

And twenty shillings to every new-married couple who should claim in like manner. This would not exceed the sum of £20,000.

Also twenty thousand pounds to be appropriated to defray the funeral expenses of persons, who, travelling for work, may die at a distance from their friends. By relieving parishes from this charge, the sick stranger will be better treated.

I shall finish this part of the subject with a plan adapted to the particular condition of a metropolis, such as London.

[. . .]

First, To erect two or more buildings, or take some already erected, capable of containing at least six thousand persons, and to have in each of these places as many kinds of employment as can be contrived, so that every person who shall come may find something which he or she can do.

Secondly, To receive all who shall come, without enquiring who or what they are. The only condition to be, that for so much, or so many hours work, each person shall receive so many meals of wholesome food, and a warm lodging, at least as good as a barrack. That a certain portion of what each person's work shall be worth shall be reserved, and given to him, or her, on their going away; and that each person shall stay as long, or as short time, or come as often as he choose, on these conditions.

If each person stayed three months, it would assist by rotation twenty-four thousand persons annually, though the real number, at all times, would be but six thousand. By establishing an asylum of this kind, persons to whom temporary distresses occur would have an opportunity to recruit themselves and be enabled to look out for better employment.

Allowing that their labour paid but one half the expense of supporting them, after reserving a portion of their earnings for themselves, the sum of forty thousand pounds additional would defray all other charges for even a greater number than six thousand.

The fund very properly convertible to this purpose, in addition to the twenty thousand pounds, remaining of the former fund, will be the produce of the tax upon coals, so iniquitously and wantonly applied to the support of the Duke of Richmond. It is horrid that any man, more especially at the price coals now are, should live on the distresses of a community; and any government permitting such an abuse deserves to be dismissed. This fund is said to be about twenty thousand pounds *per annum*.

I shall now conclude this plan with enumerating the several particulars, and then proceed to other matters.

The enumeration is as follows:

First, Abolition of two million poor-rates.

Secondly, Provision for two hundred and fifty-two thousand poor families.

Thirdly, Education for one million and thirty thousand children.

Fourthly, Comfortable provision for one hundred and forty thousand aged persons.

Fifthly, Donation of twenty shillings each for fifty thousand births.

Sixthly, Donation of twenty shillings each for twenty thousand marriages.

Seventhly, Allowance of twenty thousand pounds for the funeral expenses of persons travelling for work, and dying at a distance from their friends.

Eighthly, Employment, at all times, for the casual poor in the cities of London and Westminster.

By the operation of this plan, the poor laws, those instruments of civil torture, will be superseded, and the wasteful expense of litigation prevented. The hearts of the humane will not be shocked by ragged and hungry children, and persons of seventy and eighty years of age begging for bread. The dying poor will not be dragged from place to place to breathe their last, as a reprisal of parish upon parish. Widows will have a maintenance for their children, and not be carted away, on the death of their husbands, like culprits and criminals; and children will no longer be considered as increasing the distresses of their parents. The haunts of the wretched will be known, because it will be to their advantage; and the number of petty crimes, the offspring of distress and poverty, will be lessened. The poor, as well as the rich, will then be interested in the support of government, and the cause and apprehension of riots and tumults will cease. – Ye who sit in ease, and solace yourselves in plenty, and such there are in Turkey and Russia, as well as in England, and who say to yourselves, 'Are we not well off', have ye thought of these things? When ye do, ye will cease to speak and feel for yourselves alone.

[. . .]

## Note

Thomas Paine's *Rights of Man* was first published in London by J. S. Jordan in 1791–2. The same publisher produced several new editions in quick succession. The extract reproduced here is from the Penguin Classics reprint of 1985 (with introduction by Eric Foner and notes by Henry Collins), pp. 218, 240–48.

# ‘Classical’

# The Welfare State in Historical Perspective

## *Asa Briggs*

[...]

A welfare state is a state in which organized power is deliberately used (through politics and administration) in an effort to modify the play of market forces in at least three directions – first, by guaranteeing individuals and families a minimum income irrespective of the market value of their work or their property; second, by narrowing the extent of insecurity by enabling individuals and families to meet certain 'social contingencies' (for example, sickness, old age and unemployment) which lead otherwise to individual and family crises; and third, by ensuring that all citizens without distinction of status or class are offered the best standards available in relation to a certain agreed range of social services.

The first and second of these objects may be accomplished, in part at least, by what used to be called a 'social service state', a state in which communal resources are employed to abate poverty and to assist those in distress. The third objective, however, goes beyond the aims of a 'social service state'. It brings in the idea of the 'optimum' rather than the older idea of the 'minimum'. It is concerned not merely with abatement of class differences or the needs of scheduled groups but with equality of treatment and the aspirations of citizens as voters with equal shares of electoral power.

Merely to define the phrase welfare state in this way points to a number of historical considerations, which are the theme of this article. First, the conception of 'market forces' sets the problems of the welfare state (and of welfare) within the context of the age of modern political economy. In societies without market economies, the problem of welfare raises quite different issues. Within the context of the age of modern political economy an attempt has been made, and is still being made, to create and maintain a self-regulating system of markets, including markets in the fictitious commodities, land, money and labour. The multiple motives lying behind the attempt to control these markets require careful and penetrating analysis.

Second, the conception of 'social contingencies' is strongly influenced by the experience of industrialism. Sickness, old age and death entail hardships in any kind of society. Ancient systems of law and morality include precepts designed to diminish these hardships, precepts based, for example, on the obligations of sons to support their parents or on the claims of charity, *obsequium religionis*. Unemployment, however, at least in the form in which it is thought of as a social contingency, is a product of industrial societies, and it is unemployment more than any other social contingency which has determined the shape and timing of modern welfare legislation. Before the advent of mass unemployment, 'unemployability', the inability of individuals to secure their livelihood by work, was a key subject in the protracted debates on poor law policy. The existence of 'chronic unemployment', structural or cyclical, has been a powerful spur from the nineteenth century onwards leading organized labour groups to pass from concentration on sectional interests to the consideration of 'social rights' of workers as a class; to philanthropic businessmen wishing to improve the 'efficiency' and strengthen the 'social justice' of the business system; and to politicians and governments anxious to avoid what seemed to be dangerous political consequences of unemployment. The memories of chronic unemployment in the inter-war years and the discovery of what it was believed were new techniques of controlling it reinforced welfare state policies in many countries after the Second World War.

Third, the idea of using organized power (through politics and administration) to determine the pattern of welfare services requires careful historical dating. Why not rely for welfare on the family, the church, 'charity', 'self help', 'mutual aid' (guild, trade union, friendly society) or 'fringe benefits' (business itself)? Whole philosophies of welfare have been founded on each of these ideas or institutions: often the philosophies and the interests sustaining them have been inimical to the suggestion that the state itself should intervene. The possibility of using governmental power has been related in each country to the balance of economic and social forces; estimates of the proper functions and, true or false, of the available resources of the state; effective techniques of influence and control, resting on knowledge (including expert knowledge); and, not least, the prevalence (or absence) of the conviction that societies can be shaped by conscious policies designed to eliminate 'abuses' which in earlier generations had been accepted as 'inevitable' features of the human condition.

Not only does the weighting of each of these factors vary from period to period, but it also varies from place to place. It was Bentham, scarcely distinguished for his historical sense, who in distinguishing between *agenda* (tasks of government) and *sponte acta* (unplanned decisions of individuals) wrote that 'in England abundance of useful things are done by individuals which in other countries are done either by government or not at all . . . [while] in Russia, under Peter the Great, the list of *sponte acta* being a blank, that of *agenda* was proportionately abundant.'[1] This contrast was noted by many other writers later in the nineteenth century, just as an opposite contrast between Britain and the United States was often noted after 1945.

If the question of what constitutes welfare involves detailed examination of the nature and approach to 'social contingencies', the question of why the state rather than some other agency becomes the main instrument of welfare involves very detailed examination of a whole range of historical circumstances. The answer to the question is complicated, moreover, by differences of attitude in different countries, to the idea of 'the state' itself. Given these differences, a translation of basic terms into different languages raises difficulties which politicians and journalists may well have obscured. For example, is the term *Wohlfahrtsstaat* the right translation of welfare state? British and German approaches to 'the state' have been so different that they have absorbed the intellectual energy of generations of political scientists. In the nineteenth century there were somewhat similar difficulties (although on a smaller scale) surrounding the translation of the British term 'self help'. A French translator of Samuel Smiles's book of that title (1859) said that the term 'self help' was 'à peu près intraduisible'.

Fourth, the 'range of agreed social services' set out in the provisional definition of 'welfare state' is a shifting range. Policies, despite the finalism of much of the post-1945 criticism, are never fixed for all time. What at various times was considered to be a proper range shifts, as Dicey showed, and consequently must be examined historically. So too must changing areas of agreement and conflict. Public health was once a highly controversial issue in European societies: it still is in some other societies. The 'sanitary idea' was rightly regarded by the pioneers of public health as an idea which had large and far-reaching chains of consequences. It marked an assault on 'fate' which would be bound to lead to other assaults. Public health, in the administrative sphere of drains, sewers and basic 'environmental' services, has been taken outside the politics of conflict in Britain and other places, but personal health services remain controversial. There is controversy, very bitter indeed in the United States, not only about the range of services and who shall enjoy them but about the means of providing them. The choice of means influences all welfare state history. Welfare states can and do employ a remarkable variety of instruments, such as social insurance, direct provision in cash or in kind, subsidy, partnership with other agencies (including private business agencies) and action through local authorities. In health policy alone, although medical knowledge is the same in all countries of the West and the same illnesses are likely to be treated in much the same kind of way, there is a remarkable diversity of procedures and institutions even in countries which make extensive public provision for personal health services.

Fifth, there are important historical considerations to take into account in tracing the relationship between the three different directions of public intervention in the free (or partially free) market. The demand for 'minimum standards' can be related to a particular set of cumulative pressures. Long before the Webbs urged the need in 1909 for government action to secure 'an enforced minimum of civilized life', the case for particular minima had been powerfully advocated. Yet the idea of basing social policy as a whole on a public commitment to 'minimum' standards did not become practical politics in Britain until the so-called 'Beveridge revolution' of the Second World War. The third direction of 'welfare' policy, and the distinctive direction of the welfare state, can be understood only in terms of older logic and more recent history. The idea of separating welfare policy from 'subsistence' standards (the old minima, however measured) and relating it to 'acceptable' standards ('usual work income'), provides an indication of the extent to which 'primary poverty' has been reduced in 'affluent societies'. It may be related, however, to older ideas of equality, some of which would lead direct not to state intervention in the market but to the elimination of the market altogether, at least as a force influencing human relationships. A consideration of the contemporary debate is more rewarding if it is grounded in history. . . .

German experience in the nineteenth century was in certain important respects different from that of Britain. If before 1900 factory legislation was more advanced in Britain than in any other European country, Germany had established a 'lead' in social security legislation which the British Liberal governments of 1906 to 1914 tried to wipe out. Bismarck's reforms of the 1880s – laws of 1882, 1884 and 1889 introducing compulsory insurance against sickness, accidents, old age and invalidity – attracted immense interest in other European countries. Just as British factory legislation was copied overseas, so German social insurance stimulated foreign imitation. Denmark, for instance, copied all three German pension schemes between 1891 and 1898, and Belgium between 1894 and 1903. Switzerland by a constitutional amendment in 1890 empowered the federal government to organize a system of national insurance. In Britain itself a friendly observer noted in 1890 that Bismarck had 'discovered where the roots of social evil lie. He has declared in words that burn that it is the duty of the state to give heed, above all, to the welfare of its weaker members'.[2]

More recently Bismarck's social policy has been described by more than one writer as the creation of a welfare state.[3] The term is very misleading. Bismarck's legislation rested on a basic conservatism which Oastler himself would have appreciated and was sustained by a bureaucracy which had no counterpart in Britain except perhaps in Chadwick's imagination. The Prussian idea and history of the state and the British idea and history of the state diverged long before the 1880s, and it is not fanciful to attribute some of the divergences to the presence or absence a century before of 'cameralism', the idea of the systematic application to government of administrative routines.

Equally important, the history of political economy in the two countries diverged just as markedly. The development of a school of historical economics provided a powerful academic reinforcement in Germany for *Sozialpolitik*. The refusal of historical economists to 'isolate' economic phenomena, including 'economic man', their distrust of 'laws of political economy' covering all ages and all societies, their critique of the motives and institutions of contemporary capitalism and their underlying belief in a 'social order' distinguished them sharply from classical political economists in Britain. Their influence was considerable enough for Schmoller (1838–1917), the most important figure in the history of the school, to argue forcefully that no Smithian was fit to occupy an academic chair in Germany.[4]

Even among the 'precursors' of the historical school and among economists who stayed aloof from Schmoller and his circle, there was a powerful tradition linking social reform with conservative views of society.[5] J. K. Rodbertus (1805–75) was a conservative monarchist who combined dislike of the 'class struggle' and belief in state socialism. Adolf Wagner (1835–1917), who stayed aloof from Schmoller and admired Ricardo as the outstanding economic 'theorist', acknowledged his debt to Rodbertus when he gave a warm welcome to Bismarck's legislation.

According to Wagner Germany had entered a 'new social period', characterized by new economic ideas, new political views and new social programmes. National economy (*Volkswirtschaft*) had to be converted into state economy (*Staatswirtschaft*): the foundation of the new economy would have to be welfare. The idea of regarding 'labour power' as a commodity and wages as its price was 'inhuman' as well as 'unchristian'. Wagner proposed a number of practical measures, some of which went further than those introduced by Bismarck. Schmoller, too, advocated policies aiming at 'the re-establishment of a friendly relation between social classes, the removal or modification of injustice, a nearer approach to the principles of distributive justice, with the introduction of a social legislation which promotes progress and guarantees the moral and material elevation of the lower and middle classes.'[6]

Bismarck, for whom the idea of insurance had a particular fascination both in his domestic and foreign policies, did not envisage a social policy which would go anywhere near as far as some of the 'socialists of the chair' would have wished. He objected, for example, to the limitation by law of the hours of women and children in factories and he was at least as stubborn as any mill-owner of the Manchester School when 'theorists' talked of state officials interfering with private concerns in agriculture or industry. He also disliked extensions of direct taxation. He wanted the state, however, to be actively involved in the financing and administering of the insurance schemes which he proposed and he defended the introduction of these schemes – against both right-wing and left-wing opposition – in terms of 'the positive advancement of the welfare of the working classes'. 'The state', it was laid down in the preamble to the first and unsuccessful bill of 1881, 'is not merely a necessary but a beneficent institution.' Bismarck disagreed with Theodor Lohmann, who drafted his first social insurance legislation, about whether the state should contribute directly to the costs of insurance. Bismarck got his way that it should, but the political parties objected and his first attempts at legislation foundered. It was a measure of his recognition of political realities that the idea of state contributions was dropped in 1884 when his accident insurance bill was introduced. The law of 1889, providing for disability and old age pensions, did entail a flat-rate contribution from the imperial treasury of fifty marks for each person receiving a pension, but this was a small element in the total cost and fell far short of the amount Bismarck had originally envisaged.

Many of Bismarck's critics accused him, not without justification, of seeking through his legislation to make German workers 'depend' upon the state. The same charges have been made against the initiators of all welfare (and earlier, of poor law) policy often without justification, yet it was Bismarck himself who drew a revealing distinction between the degrees of obedience (or subservience) of private servants and servants at court. The latter would 'put up with much more' than the former because they had pensions to look forward to. Welfare soothed the spirit, or perhaps tamed it. Bismarck's deliberate invocation of 'subservience' is at the opposite end of the scale from the socialist invocation of 'equality' as the goal of the welfare state. It is brutally simple, too, when compared with sophisticated liberal attempts to define the conditions in which liberty and equality may be made to complement each other.[7] The invocation was, of course, bound up with conscious political calculation. Bismarck was anxious to make German social democracy less attractive to workingmen. He feared 'class war' and wanted to postpone it as long as possible. His talks with Lassalle in 1863 had ranged over questions of this kind,[8] and in 1884 he argued explicitly that if the state would only 'show a little more Christian solicitude for the workingman', then the social democrats would 'sound their siren song in vain'. 'The thronging to them will cease as soon as workingmen see that the government and legislative bodies are earnestly concerned for their welfare.'[9] It has been suggested that Bismarck was influenced by Napoleon III's successful handling of social policy as an instrument of politics. He certainly spent time seeking an 'alternative to socialism' and it was this aspect of his policy which gave what he did contemporary controversial significance throughout Europe.

His policy also provided a definite alternative to liberalism. During the last years of his life when he was prepared to contemplate insurance against unemployment and when he talked of the 'right to work' as enthusiastically as any Chartist, he was reflecting that sharp reaction against economic liberalism which could be discerned, in different forms, in almost every country in Europe. Disraeli's social policy in his ministry of 1874–80 had somewhat similar features. It also had the added interest of appearing to realize hopes first formulated by Disraeli in the age of Oastler and the Chartists. In 1874 also a royalist and clerical majority in the French National Assembly carried a factory act, limiting hours of work of children below the age of twelve, which went further than a law of 1848 on the same subject. A later and more comprehensive act of 1892 was the work of Conservative Republicans. The nineteenth century closed with a British Moneylenders Act which, Professor Clapham has argued, in effect revived the medieval law of usury, the last remnants of which had been swept away, it was thought for ever, in 1854.[10]

Medieval attitudes to welfare were echoed most strongly in Christian apologetics. Papal encyclicals, notably *Rerum Novarum* (1891), were not only manifestos in crusades against liberalism or socialism but were also important documents in the evolution of *Sozialpolitik*. De Mun, Von Ketteler and Von Vogelsang were writers who advocated particular or general welfare policies: so did Heinrich Pesch, who has been singled out for special treatment by Schumpeter. Among Protestants also there was renewed call for a 'social gospel'. It is not without interest that Lohmann, who had advised Bismarck and went on to advise William II in the formulation of the far-reaching Labour Code of 1891, was a deeply religious man, the son of a Westphalian Lutheran pastor. Canon W. L. Blackley (1830–1902), the pioneer of old-age pensions schemes not only in Britain but in other parts of the world and the founder of the National Providence League, was an honorary canon of Winchester Cathedral. On the Liberal side – and there was a close association in Britain between religious nonconformity and political liberalism – Seebohm Rowntree (1871–1954), one of the first systematic investigators of the facts of poverty, was a Quaker. The whole attack on the limitations of the poor law was guided, though not exclusively, by men of strong religious principles.

The complexity of the nineteenth-century background contrasts at first sight with the simplicity of the twentieth-century story. For a tangle of tendencies we have a 'trend', a trend culminating in greater 'order' and simplification. In fact, however, the twentieth-century story has its own complexities, which are now in the process of being unravelled. Professor Titmuss has shown, for instance, that Lloyd George's national health insurance legislation of 1911, a landmark in 'trend' legislation, was the culmination of a long and confused period in which doctors had been engaged in a 'Hobbesian struggle for independence from the power and authority exercised over their lives, their work and their professional values by voluntary associations and private enterprise.' He has maintained that the legislation of 1911 can only be understood if it is related, as so much else in the twentieth century must be related, to the history of hidden pressures from established interests and a sectional demand for an 'enlargement of professional freedom'.[11] Many of the complexities of twentieth-century history certainly lie buried in the records of the network of private concerns and of professional groups which came into existence in the nineteenth century. There can be no adequate historical explanation which concerns itself in large terms with the state alone. Just as the administration of welfare is complicated in practice and can be understood only in detail, so the outline of welfare state legislation only becomes fully intelligible when it ceases to be an outline, and when it looks beyond parliamentary legislation to such crucial twentieth-century relationships as those between governments and pressure groups and 'experts' and the 'public'.

Yet there are five factors in twentieth-century welfare history (other than warfare, one of the most powerful of factors) which are beyond dispute and dominant enough to need little detailed research. They are, first, the basic transformation in the attitude towards poverty, which made the nineteenth-century poor law no longer practicable in democratic societies; second, the detailed investigation of the 'social contingencies' which directed attention to the need for particular social policies; third, the close association between unemployment and welfare policy; fourth, the development within market capitalism itself of welfare philosophies and practices; and fifth, the influence of working-class pressures on the content and tone of welfare legislation.

The first and second of these five factors can scarcely be studied in isolation. The basis of the nineteenth-century British Poor Law of 1834 was economic logic. That logic was strained when empirical sociologists, like Charles Booth (1840–1916) and Rowntree, showed that a large number of poor people were poor through no fault of their own but because of tendencies within the market system. They pitted statistics against logic by attempting to count how many people were living in poverty and by surveying the various forms that the poverty assumed.[12] Prior to Booth's 'grand inquest', Beatrice Webb wrote, 'neither the individualist nor the socialist could state with any approach to accuracy what exactly was the condition of the people of England'.[13] Once the results of the 'inquest' had been published 'the net effect was to give an entirely fresh impetus to the general adoption of the policy of securing to every individual, as the very basis of his life and work, a prescribed natural minimum of the requisites for efficient parenthood and citizenship.'

Booth's thinking about economics was far less radical than his thinking about welfare, but Rowntree, who drew a neat distinction between 'primary' and 'secondary' poverty, the former being beyond the control of the wage-earner, went on to advocate specific welfare policies, ranging from old-age pensions to family allowances, public-provided housing to supervised welfare conditions in factories. The policies which he urged at various stages of his long life were, indeed, the main constituent policies of the welfare state.[14] Like the welfare state, however, Rowntree stopped short of socialism. He separated questions of welfare from questions of economic power, and remained throughout his life a 'new Liberal'. The main tenet of his liberalism was that the community could not afford the 'waste', individual and social, which was implied in an industrial society divided 'naturally' into 'rich' and 'very poor'. Poverty was as much of a social problem as 'pauperism'. The roots of poverty were to be found not in individual irresponsibility or incapacity but in social maladjustment. Poverty, in short, was not the fault of the poor: it was the fault of society. Quite apart from 'socialist pressure', society had to do something about poverty once it was given facts about its extent, its incidence (Rowntree drew attention to the cycle of poverty in families), its ramifications and its consequences. All facts were grist to the mill. They included facts not only about wages but about nutrition: subsistence levels could only be measured when nutritional criteria were taken into account.

Sharp turns of thought about poverty were by no means confined to people in Britain. There were signs of fundamental rethinking, allied [ . . . ] to 'feeling',[15] both in Europe and the United States at the end of the nineteenth and the beginning of the twentieth century.[16] The survey method, which Booth and Rowntree depended upon, was capable of general applicability.[17] The limitations of systematic 'charity' were noted at least as generally as the limitations of unsystematic charity had been at the beginning of the industrial age. It is no coincidence that in Britain and Sweden, two countries with distinct welfare histories, there was keen debate about the Poor Law at almost exactly the same time. In Sweden the Poor Relief Order of 1871, with its checks on poor relief, was criticized by the Swedish Poor Relief Association which was formed at the first General Swedish Poor Law Congress in 1906. A year later the government appointed a committee to draw up proposals for fresh legislation governing poor relief and the treatment of vagrants. In Britain the Royal Commission on the Poor Laws, which was appointed in 1905 and reported in 1909, covered almost all topics in social policy. The issues were clearly stated and both the social contingencies and the necessary policies of social control were carefully examined. Although new direct legislation was slow to come in both countries, there was much indirect legislation and in both countries there were demands for what Beatrice Webb called 'an enforced minimum of civilized life'.[18]

The main threat to that minimum in the later twentieth century came from 'mass involuntary unemployment'. This, of course, was a world phenomenon which strained poor law and social service systems in most countries and presented a threat – or a challenge – to politicians and administrators. In Britain, which was the first country to introduce compulsory unemployment insurance (1911; greatly extended in 1920), the system of relief broke down under the stresses of the 1930s. Insurance benefits, linked to contributions, were stringently restricted, and while tussles about the 'means test' were leading to extreme differences of outlook between socialists and their opponents, an Unemployment Assistance Board, founded in 1934, was providing a second-line income maintenance service, centrally administered. In Europe there was an extension of unemployment aid schemes, whether by insurance (the Swedes, for example, introduced state-subsidized unemployment insurance in 1934), 'doles' or in certain cases 'positive' state-run schemes of 'public works'. In the United States and Canada, where there had been entrenched resistance to government intervention in welfare provision, new legislation was passed,[19] while in New Zealand, which had long lost its reputation as a pioneer of welfare, there was a remarkable bout of state intervention after the return of a Labour government to power in 1935. The Social Security Act of 1938 contained a list of health services and pensions benefits which, while resting on previous legislation, were everywhere hailed as a bold and daring experiment. The Minister of Finance anticipated later welfare legislators in other countries by arguing unequivocally that 'to suggest the inevitability of slumps and booms, associated as they are with affluence for a limited number during a period, and followed by unemployment, destitution, hardship and privation for the masses, is to deny all conscious progressive purpose.'[20] According to the International Labor Office, the 1938 New Zealand Act 'has, more than any other law, determined the practical meaning of social security, and so has deeply influenced the course of legislation in other countries'.[21]

Twentieth-century social security legislation raises many interesting general issues – the relevance of the insurance principle, for example, the relationship between 'negative' social policy and 'positive' economic policy, and, underlying all else, the nature and extent of the responsibilities of the state. Insurance principles, actuarially unsound though they may be and inadequate though they have proved as instruments of finance at moments of crisis, have been historically significant. They removed the stigma of pauperism from a social service, reconciled 'voluntary' and 'compulsory' approaches to provision, and facilitated 'public approval' of state expenditures which otherwise would have been challenged. They thus served as a link between old ways of thinking ('self help' and 'mutual help') and new. 'Positive' economic policy was in the first instance, as in Roosevelt's America, the child of improvisation: its systematic justification had to await revolutions in political economy (Keynes and after) which accompanied shifts in social power. The difference in tone and content between two books by William Beveridge – his *Unemployment* (1909) and his *Full Employment in a Free Society* (1944) – is one of the best indications of the change in the world of ideas between the early and middle periods of the twentieth century. 'Beveridgism', an important British phenomenon during the Second World War, had sufficient popular appeal to show that the world of ideas and the world of practical politics were not very far apart. For the intellectuals and for the public the magnification of governmental power – and the enormous increase in government expenditure financed from taxation – were taken for granted.

The fourth and fifth factors are also related to each other. In all advanced industrial countries in the twentieth century there has been a movement towards welfare in industry – 'industrial betterment' it was originally called – which has been accompanied by the emergence of philosophies of 'human relations', 'welfare management' and industrial and labour psychology.[22] The movement has to be explained in terms of both economics and politics. A 'managerial revolution', limited though it may have been in its economic effects, has accelerated the tendencies making for 'welfare capitalism'. The need to find acceptable incentives for workers, to avoid labour disputes and to secure continuous production, to raise output in phases of technical change and (more recently) to hold labour 'permissively' in a period of full employment has often driven where 'human relations' philosophies have failed to inspire. Welfare, a word which was often resented by workers, when it was applied within the structure of the firm, was, indeed, used in a business context before it began to be applied to a new kind of state. Within state schemes of welfare employers have made, and are expected to make, sizeable contributions. In France and Italy, in particular, obligatory social charges as a percentage of assessable wages constituted the main source of welfare expenditure.[23] In the United States business rather than the state was, and is, expected directly to provide a network of welfare services. As in all such situations, the provision of welfare varies immensely from one firm (giant businesses are at one end of the scale) to another.

> In contrast to these countries, such as Great Britain, which appear to regard government (for reasons which have been stated above) merely as the most effective of several possible institutions for the administration of income security programs or the provision of services, [ . . . ] a society like the United States that distrusts its government is likely to seek to organize its social security services in such a way as to keep government activity to a minimum.[24]

United States experience, in contrast to the experience described in other countries, shows that this likelihood has been converted into fact.

It is not accidental that the labour movement in the United States has showed little interest in socialism and that its leaders have chosen of their own volition to bargain for 'fringe benefits' at the level of the plant. In most European countries, particularly in Britain and in Scandinavia, there has been a tendency for working-class pressures to lead to greater state intervention. In Britain nineteenth-century patterns of 'mutual dependence' through 'voluntary action', which impressed so many observers from Tocqueville onwards, have become less dominant, except in the field of industrial relations where they have very tenaciously survived.[25]

As we have seen, the demand for state action has been related to the rights of citizenship, to equality as well as to security. During the critical period between the two World Wars, when economic and social conditions were very difficult, welfare measures were demanded and provided 'piecemeal' with varying conditions of regulation and administration, 'a frightening complexity of eligibility and benefit according to individual circumstances, local boundaries, degrees of need and so forth'.[26] The Second World War, which sharpened the sense of 'democracy', led to demands both for 'tidying up' and for 'comprehensiveness'. It encouraged the move from 'minima' to 'optima', at least in relation to certain specified services, and it made all residual paternalisms seem utterly inadequate and increasingly archaic. It was in the light of changes in working-class life within a more 'equal community' that postwar writers noted the extent to which the social services of the earlier part of the century had been shaped by assumptions about the nature of man, 'founded on outer rather than on inner observation', on the 'norms of behavior expected by one class from another'.[27] This period of criticism has already ended. The assumptions which shaped the welfare state have themselves been criticized,[28] and radical political slogans have concentrated more and more on differences of income between 'mature' and 'underdeveloped' countries rather than on differences within 'mature' countries themselves.

It may well be that in a world setting the five twentieth-century factors discussed in this article will be considered less important than other factors – the total size of the national income in different countries, for example, and the share of that income necessary for industrial (as, or when, distinct from social) investment, or even, on a different plane, the nature of family structure. Is not the making of the industrial welfare state in part at least the concomitant of the decline of the large, extended 'welfare family'? How far has the pressure of women (or just the presence of women voters) in industrial societies encouraged the formulation of welfare objectives? The historian does well to leave such large questions to be answered rather than to suggest that all or even the most important part of the truth is already known.

## Notes

From C. Schottland, ed., *The Welfare State*, New York, Harper and Row, 1969, pp. 29–45.

1 J. Bentham, *Works*, ed. J. Bowring, 1843, vol. III, p. 35. Cf. J. M. Keynes's view of the 'agenda' of the state in *The End of Laissez Faire* (1926).

2 W. H. Dawson, *Bismarck and State Socialism* (1890), p. ix.

3 S. B. Fay, 'Bismarck's Welfare State', *Current History*, vol. XVIII (1950).
4 J. A. Schumpeter, *History of Economic Analysis* (1954), p. 765.
5 The pre-history of this approach leads back to Sismondi who has important links with Mill and the English utilitarians. He is a seminal figure in the critique of industrialism and the demand for welfare legislation.
6 A. Wagner, *Rede über die soziale Frage* (1872), pp. 8–9. G. von Schmoller, *Über einige Grundfragen des Rechts und der Volkswirtschaft* (1875), p. 92.
7 For the background of these attempts, see M. Ginsberg, 'The Growth of Social Responsibility', in M. Ginsberg, ed., *Law and Opinion in England in the Twentieth Century* (1959), pp. 3–26.
8 See G. Mayer, *Bismarck und Lassalle* (1927).
9 Dawson, op. cit., p. 35. This remark was made in 1884. Five years earlier the emperor, referring to the anti-socialist law of 1878, had said, 'a remedy cannot alone be sought in the repression of socialistic excesses; there must be simultaneously the positive advancement of the welfare of the working classes' (quoted ibid., p. 110).
10 J. H. Clapham, *An Economic History of Modern Britain*, vol. III (1938), p. 445.
11 R. M. Titmuss, 'Health', in Ginsberg, op. cit., p. 308. Cf. p. 313: 'The fundamental issue of 1911 was not [ . . . ] between individualism and collectivism, between contract and status; but between different forms of collectivism, different degrees of freedom; open or concealed power.'
12 C. Booth, *Life and Labour of the People in London*, 17 vols (1892–1903); B. S. Rowntree, *Poverty: A Study of Town Life* (1901).
13 B. Webb, *My Apprenticeship* (1926), p. 239.
14 For Booth, see T. S. and M. B. Simey, *Charles Booth, Social Scientist* (1960); for Rowntree, see A. Briggs, *Seebohm Rowntree* (1961). See also B. S. Rowntree and G. R. Lavers, *Poverty and the Welfare State* (1951).
15 'In intensity of feeling', Booth wrote, 'and not in statistics, lies the power to move the world. But by statistics must this power be guided if it would move the world aright.' *Life and Labour, Final Volume, Notes on Social Influences and Conclusion* (1903), p. 178.
16 See *inter alia* C. L. Mowat, *The Charity Organisation Society;* K. De Schweinitz, *England's Road to Social Security* (1943); C. W. Pitkin, *Social Politics and Modern Democracies, 2* vols (1931), vol. II being concerned with France; R. H. Bremner, *From the Depths: The Discovery of Poverty in the United States* (1956).
17 See M. Abrams, *Social Surveys and Social Action* (1951); P. V. Young, *Scientific Social Surveys and Research* (1950); D. C. Caradog Jones, *Social Surveys* (1955).
18 The British controversy is well described in U. Cormack, 'The Welfare State', *Loch Memorial Lecture* (1953). For Sweden, see The Royal Social Board, *Social Work and Legislation in Sweden* (1938).
19 J. C. Brown, *Public Relief 1929–39* (1940); E. A. Williams, *Federal Aid for Relief* (1939); P. H. Douglas, *Social Security in the United States* (1939 edn).
20 Quoted in W. K. Hancock, *Survey of British Commonwealth Affairs*, vol. II (1940), p. 275.
21 International Labor Office, *Social Security in New Zealand* (1949), p. 111.
22 See A. Briggs, 'The Social Background', in H. Clegg and A. Flanders, eds, *Industrial Relations in Great Britain* (1955); L. Urwick and E. F. L. Brech, *The Human Factor in Management 1795–1943* (1944); E. D. Proud, *Welfare Work, Employers' Experiments for Improving Working Conditions in Factories* (1916); E. T. Kelly, ed., *Welfare Work in Industry* (1925); PEP, 'The Human Factor in Industry', *Planning* (March 1948).

23 PEP, 'Free Trade and Security', *Planning* (July 1957); 'A Comparative Analysis of the Cost of Social Security', in *International Labour Review* (1953).
24 E. M. Burns, *Social Security and Public Policy* (1956), p. 274.
25 For the nature of the nineteenth-century pattern, see J. M. Baernreither, *English Associations of Working Men* (1893). For industrial relations, see Clegg and Flanders, op. cit.
26 R. M. Titmuss, *Essays on the Welfare State* (1958), pp. 21–2.
27 Ibid., p. 19.
28 See A. Peacock, 'The Welfare Society', *Unservile State Papers* (1960); R. M. Titmuss, 'The Irresponsible Society', *Fabian Tracts* (1960); J. Saville, 'The Welfare State', *The New Reasoner*, no. 3 (1957).

# Citizenship and Social Class

## *T. H. Marshall*

[. . .]

I propose to divide citizenship into three parts. [. . .] I shall call these three parts, or elements, civil, political and social. The civil element is composed of the rights necessary for individual freedom – liberty of the person, freedom of speech, thought and faith, the right to own property and to conclude valid contracts, and the right to justice. The last is of a different order from the others, because it is the right to defend and assert all one's rights on terms of equality with others and by due process of law. This shows us that the institutions most directly associated with civil rights are the courts of justice. By the political element I mean the right to participate in the exercise of political power, as a member of a body invested with political authority or as an elector of the members of such a body. The corresponding institutions are parliament and councils of local government. By the social element I mean the whole range, from the right to a modicum of economic welfare and security to the right to share to the full in the social heritage and to live the life of a civilized being according to the standards prevailing in the society. The institutions most closely connected with it are the educational system and the social services. [. . .]

By 1832 when political rights made their first infantile attempt to walk, civil rights had come to man's estate and bore, in most essentials, the appearance that they have today.[1] 'The specific work of the earlier Hanoverian epoch', writes Trevelyan, 'was the establishment of the rule of law; and that law, with all its grave faults, was at least a law of freedom. On that solid foundation all our subsequent reforms were built.' This eighteenth-century achievement, interrupted by the French Revolution and completed after it, was in large measure the work of the courts, both in their daily practice and also in a series of famous cases in some of which they were fighting against parliament in defence of individual liberty. The most celebrated actor in this drama was, I suppose, John Wilkes, and, although we may deplore the absence in him of those noble and saintly qualities which we should like to find in our national heroes, we cannot complain if the cause of liberty is sometimes championed by a libertine.

In the economic field the basic civil right is the right to work, that is to say the right to follow the occupation of one's choice in the place of one's choice, subject only to legitimate demands for preliminary technical training. This right had been denied by both statute and custom; on the one hand by the Elizabethan Statute of Artificers, which confined certain occupations to certain social classes, and on the other by local regulations reserving employment in a town to its own members and by the use of apprenticeship as an instrument of exclusion rather than of recruitment. The recognition of the right involved the formal acceptance of a fundamental change of attitude. The old assumption that local and group monopolies were in the public interest, because 'trade and traffic cannot be maintained or increased without order and government', was replaced by the new assumption that such restrictions were an offence against the liberty of the subject and a menace to the prosperity of the nation. [ . . . ]

By the beginning of the nineteenth century this principle of individual economic freedom was accepted as axiomatic. You are probably familiar with the passage quoted by the Webbs from the report of the Select Committee of 1811, which states that:

> no interference of the legislature with the freedom of trade, or with the perfect liberty of every individual to dispose of his time and of his labour in the way and on the terms which he may judge most conducive to his own interest, can take place without violating general principles of the first importance to the prosperity and happiness of the community.[2] [ . . . ]

The story of civil rights in their formative period is one of the gradual addition of new rights to a status that already existed and was held to appertain to all adult members of the community – or perhaps one should say to all male members, since the status of women, or at least of married women, was in some important respects peculiar. This democratic, or universal, character of the status arose naturally from the fact that it was essentially the status of freedom, and in seventeenth-century England all men were free. Servile status, or villeinage by blood, had lingered on as a patent anachronism in the days of Elizabeth, but vanished soon afterwards. This change from servile to free labour has been described by Professor Tawney as 'a high landmark in the development both of economic and political society', and as 'the final triumph of the common law' in regions from which it had been excluded for four centuries. Henceforth the English peasant 'is a member of a society in which there is, nominally at least, one law for all men'.[3] The liberty which his predecessors had won by fleeing into the free towns had become his by right. In the towns the terms 'freedom' and 'citizenship' were interchangeable. When freedom became universal, citizenship grew from a local into a national institution.

The story of political rights is different both in time and in character. The formative period began, as I have said, in the early nineteenth century, when the civil rights attached to the status of freedom had already acquired sufficient substance to justify us in speaking of a general status of citizenship. And, when it began, it consisted, not in the creation of new rights to enrich a status already enjoyed by all, but in the granting of old rights to new sections of the population. [ . . . ]

It is clear that, if we maintain that in the nineteenth century citizenship in the form of civil rights was universal, the political franchise was not one of the rights of citizenship. It was the privilege of a limited economic class, whose limits were extended by each successive Reform Act. [ . . . ]

It was, as we shall see, appropriate that nineteenth-century capitalist society should treat political rights as a secondary product of civil rights. It was equally appropriate that the twentieth century should abandon this position and attach political rights directly and independently to citizenship as such. This vital change of principle was put into effect when the Act of 1918, by adopting manhood suffrage, shifted the basis of political rights from economic substance to personal status. I say 'manhood' deliberately in order to emphasize the great significance of this reform quite apart from the second, and no less important, reform introduced at the same time – namely the enfranchisement of women. [ . . . ]

The original source of social rights was membership of local communities and functional associations. This source was supplemented and progressively replaced by a Poor Law and a system of wage regulation which were nationally conceived and locally administered. [ . . . ]

As the pattern of the old order dissolved under the blows of a competitive economy, and the plan disintegrated, the Poor Law was left high and dry as an isolated survival from which the idea of social rights was gradually drained away. But at the very end of the eighteenth century there occurred a final struggle between the old and the new, between the planned (or patterned) society and the competitive economy. And in this battle citizenship was divided against itself; social rights sided with the old and civil with the new. [ . . . ]

In this brief episode of our history we see the Poor Law as the aggressive champion of the social rights of citizenship. In the succeeding phase we find the attacker driven back far behind his original position. By the Act of 1834 the Poor Law renounced all claim to trespass on the territory of the wages system, or to interfere with the forces of the free market. It offered relief only to those who, through age or sickness, were incapable of continuing the battle, and to those other weaklings who gave up the struggle, admitted defeat, and cried for mercy. The tentative move towards the concept of social security was reversed. But more than that, the minimal social rights that remained were detached from the status of citizenship. The Poor Law treated the claims of the poor, not as an integral part of the rights of the citizen, but as an alternative to them – as claims which could be met only if the claimants ceased to be citizens in any true sense of the word. For paupers forfeited in practice the civil right of personal liberty, by internment in the workhouse, and they forfeited by law any political rights they might possess. This disability of defranchisement remained in being until 1918, and the significance of its final removal has, perhaps, not been fully appreciated. The stigma which clung to poor relief expressed the deep feelings of a people who understood that those who accepted relief must cross the road that separated the community of citizens from the outcast company of the destitute.

The Poor Law is not an isolated example of this divorce of social rights from the status of citizenship. The early Factory Acts show the same tendency. Although in fact they led to an improvement of working conditions and a reduction of working hours to the benefit of all employed in the industries to which they applied, they meticulously refrained from giving this protection directly to the adult male – the citizen *par excellence*. And they did so out of respect for his status as a citizen, on the grounds that enforced protective measures curtailed the civil right to conclude a free contract of employment. Protection was confined to women and children, and champions of women's rights were quick to detect the implied insult. Women were protected because they were not citizens. If they wished to enjoy full and responsible citizenship, they must forgo protection. By the end of the nineteenth century such arguments had become obsolete, and the factory code had become one of the pillars in the edifice of social rights. [. . .]

By the end of the nineteenth century elementary education was not only free, it was compulsory. This signal departure from *laissez-faire* could, of course, be justified on the grounds that free choice is a right only for mature minds, that children are naturally subject to discipline, and that parents cannot be trusted to do what is in the best interests of their children. But the principle goes deeper than that. We have here a personal right combined with a public duty to exercise the right. Is the public duty imposed merely for the benefit of the individual – because children cannot fully appreciate their own interests and parents may be unfit to enlighten them? I hardly think that this can be an adequate explanation. It was increasingly recognized, as the nineteenth century wore on, that political democracy needed an educated electorate, and that scientific manufacture needed educated workers and technicians. The duty to improve and civilize oneself is therefore a social duty, and not merely a personal one, because the social health of a society depends upon the civilization of its members. And a community that enforces this duty has begun to realize that its culture is an organic unity and its civilization a national heritage. It follows that the growth of public elementary education during the nineteenth century was the first decisive step on the road to the re-establishment of the social rights of citizenship in the twentieth. [ . . . ]

Citizenship is a status bestowed on those who are full members of a community. All who possess the status are equal with respect to the rights and duties with which the status is endowed. There is no universal principle that determines what those rights and duties shall be, but societies in which citizenship is a developing institution create an image of an ideal citizenship against which achievement can be measured and towards which aspiration can be directed. The urge forward along the path thus plotted is an urge towards a fuller measure of equality, an enrichment of the stuff of which the status is made and an increase in the number of those on whom the status is bestowed. Social class, on the other hand, is a system of inequality. And it too, like citizenship, can be based on a set of ideals, beliefs and values. It is therefore reasonable to expect that the impact of citizenship on social class should take the form of a conflict between opposing principles. If I am right in my contention that citizenship has been a developing institution in England at least since the latter part of the seventeenth century, then it is clear that its growth coincides with the rise of capitalism, which is a system, not of equality, but of inequality. Here is something that needs explaining. How is it that these two opposing principles could grow and flourish side by side in the same soil? What made it possible for them to be reconciled with one another and to become, for a time at least, allies instead of antagonists? The question is a pertinent one, for it is clear that, in the twentieth century, citizenship and the capitalist class system have been at war. [ . . . ]

It is true that class still functions. Social inequality is regarded as necessary and purposeful. It provides the incentive to effort and designs the distribution of power. But there is no overall pattern of inequality, in which an appropriate value is attached, *a priori*, to each social level. Inequality therefore, though necessary, may become excessive. As Patrick Colquhoun said, in a much-quoted passage: 'Without a large proportion of poverty there could be no riches, since riches are the offspring of labour, while labour can result only from a state of poverty . . . Poverty therefore is a most necessary and indispensable ingredient in society, without which nations and communities could not exist in a state of civilization.'[4] [ . . . ]

The more you look on wealth as conclusive proof of merit, the more you incline to regard poverty as evidence of failure – but the penalty for failure may seem to be greater than the offence warrants. In such circumstances it is natural that the more unpleasant features of inequality should be treated, rather irresponsibly, as a nuisance, like the black smoke that used to pour unchecked from our factory chimneys. And so in time, as the social conscience stirs to life, class-abatement, like smoke-abatement, becomes a desirable aim to be pursued as far as is compatible with the continued efficiency of the social machine.

But class-abatement in this form was not an attack on the class system. On the contrary it aimed, often quite consciously, at making the class system less vulnerable to attack by alleviating its less defensible consequences. It raised the floor-level in the basement of the social edifice, and perhaps made it rather more hygienic than it was before. But it remained a basement, and the upper storeys of the building were unaffected. [ . . . ]

There developed, in the latter part of the nineteenth century, a growing interest in equality as a principle of social justice and an appreciation of the fact that the formal recognition of an equal capacity for rights was not enough. In theory even the complete removal of all the barriers that separated civil rights from their remedies would not have interfered with the principles or the class structure of the capitalist system. It would, in fact, have created a situation which many supporters of the competitive market economy falsely assumed to be already in existence. But in practice the attitude of mind which inspired the efforts to remove these barriers grew out of a conception of equality which overstepped these narrow limits, the conception of equal social worth, not merely of equal natural rights. Thus although citizenship, even by the end of the nineteenth century, had done little to reduce social inequality, it had helped to guide progress into the path which led directly to the egalitarian policies of the twentieth century. [ . . . ]

This growing national consciousness, this awakening public opinion, and these first stirrings of a sense of community membership and common heritage did not have any material effect on class structure and social inequality for the simple and obvious reason that, even at the end of the nineteenth century, the mass of the working people did not wield effective political power. By that time the franchise was fairly wide, but those who had recently received the vote had not yet learned how to use it. The political rights of citizenship, unlike the civil rights, were full of potential danger to the capitalist system, although those who were cautiously extending them down the social scale probably did not realize quite how great the danger was. They could hardly be expected to foresee what vast changes could be brought about by the peaceful use of political power, without a violent and bloody revolution. The 'planned society' and the welfare state had not yet risen over the horizon or come within the view of the practical politician. The foundations of the market economy and the contractual system seemed strong enough to stand against any probable assault. In fact, there were some grounds for expecting that the working classes, as they became educated, would accept the basic principles of the system and be content to rely for their protection and progress on the civil rights of citizenship, which contained no obvious menace to competitive capitalism. Such a view was encouraged by the fact that one of the main achievements of political power in the later nineteenth century was the recognition of the right of collective bargaining. This meant that social progress was being sought by strengthening civil rights, not by creating social rights; through the use of contract in the open market, not through a minimum wage and social security.

But this interpretation underrates the significance of this extension of civil rights in the economic sphere. For civil rights were in origin intensely individual, and that is why they harmonized with the individualistic phase of capitalism. By the device of incorporation groups were enabled to act legally as individuals. This important development did not go unchallenged, and limited liability was widely denounced as an infringement of individual responsibility. But the position of trade unions was even more anomalous, because they did not seek or obtain incorporation. They can, therefore, exercise vital civil rights collectively on behalf of their members without formal collective responsibility, while the individual responsibility of the workers in relation to contract is largely unenforceable. These civil rights became, for the workers, an instrument for raising their social and economic status, that is to say, for establishing the claim that they, as citizens, were entitled to certain social rights. But the normal method of establishing social rights is by the exercise of political power, for social rights imply an absolute right to a certain standard of civilization which is conditional only on the discharge of the general duties of citizenship. Their content does not depend on the economic value of the individual claimant. There is therefore a significant difference between a genuine collective bargain through which economic forces in a free market seek to achieve equilibrium and the use of collective civil rights to assert basic claims to the elements of social justice. Thus the acceptance of collective bargaining was not simply a natural extension of civil rights; it represented the transfer of an important process from the political to the civil sphere of citizenship. But 'transfer' is, perhaps, a misleading term, for at the time when this happened the workers either did not possess, or had not yet learned to use, the political right of the franchise. Since then they have obtained and made full use of that right. Trade unionism has, therefore, created a secondary system of industrial citizenship parallel with and supplementary to the system of political citizenship. [ . . . ]

A new period opened at the end of the nineteenth century, conveniently marked by Booth's survey of *Life and Labour of the People in London* and the Royal Commission on the Aged Poor. It saw the first big advance in social rights, and this involved significant changes in the egalitarian principle as expressed in citizenship. But there were other forces at work as well. A rise of money incomes unevenly distributed over the social classes altered the economic distance which separated these classes from one another, diminishing the gap between skilled and unskilled labour and between skilled labour and non-manual workers, while the steady increase in small savings blurred the class distinction between the capitalist and the propertyless proletarian. Secondly, a system of direct taxation, ever more steeply graduated, compressed the whole scale of disposable incomes. Thirdly, mass production for the home market and a growing interest on the part of industry in the needs and tastes of the common people enabled the less well-to-do to enjoy a material civilization which differed less markedly in quality from that of the rich than it had ever done before. All this profoundly altered the setting in which the progress of citizenship took place. Social integration spread from the sphere of sentiment and patriotism into that of material enjoyment. The components of a civilized and cultured life, formerly the monopoly of the few, were brought progressively within reach of the many, who were encouraged thereby to stretch out their hands towards those that still eluded their grasp. The diminution of inequality strengthened the demand for its abolition, at least with regard to the essentials of social welfare.

These aspirations have in part been met by incorporating social rights in the status of citizenship and thus creating a universal right to real income which is not proportionate to the market value of the claimant. Class-abatement is still the aim of social rights, but it has acquired a new meaning. It is no longer merely an attempt to abate the obvious nuisance of destitution in the lowest ranks of society. It has assumed the guise of action modifying the whole pattern of social inequality. It is no longer content to raise the floor-level in the basement of the social edifice, leaving the superstructure as it was. It has begun to remodel the whole building, and it might even end by converting a skyscraper into a bungalow. It is therefore important to consider whether any such ultimate aim is implicit in the nature of this development, or whether, as I put it at the outset, there are natural limits to the contemporary drive towards greater social and economic equality. [. . .]

The degree of equalization achieved [by the modern system of welfare benefits] depends on four things: whether the benefit is offered to all or to a limited class; whether it takes the form of money payment or service rendered; whether the minimum is high or low; and how the money to pay for the benefit is raised. Cash benefits subject to income limit and means test had a simple and obvious equalizing effect. They achieved class-abatement in the early and limited sense of the term. The aim was to ensure that all citizens should attain at least to the prescribed minimum, either by their own resources or with assistance if they could not do it without. The benefit was given only to those who needed it, and thus inequalities at the bottom of the scale were ironed out. The system operated in its simplest and most unadulterated form in the case of the Poor Law and old age pensions. But economic equalization might be accompanied by psychological class discrimination. The stigma which attached to the Poor Law made 'pauper' a derogatory term defining a class. 'Old age pensioner' may have had a little of the same flavour, but without the taint of shame. [ . . . ]

The extension of the social services is not primarily a means of equalizing incomes. In some cases it may, in others it may not. The question is relatively unimportant; it belongs to a different department of social policy. What matters is that there is a general enrichment of the concrete substance of civilized life, a general reduction of risk and insecurity, an equalization between the more and the less fortunate at all levels – between the healthy and the sick, the employed and the unemployed, the old and the active, the bachelor and the father of a large family. Equalization is not so much between classes as between individuals within a population which is now treated for this purpose as though it were one class. Equality of status is more important than equality of income. [ . . . ]

I said earlier that in the twentieth century citizenship and the capitalist class system have been at war. Perhaps the phrase is rather too strong, but it is quite clear that the former has imposed modifications on the latter. But we should not be justified in assuming that, although status is a principle that conflicts with contract, the stratified status system which is creeping into citizenship is an alien element in the economic world outside. Social rights in their modern form imply an invasion of contract by status, the subordination of market price to social justice, the replacement of the free bargain by the declaration of rights. But are these principles quite foreign to the practice of the market today, or are they there already entrenched within the contract system itself? I think it is clear that they are. [ . . . ]

I have tried to show how citizenship, and other forces outside it, have been altering the pattern of social inequality. [ . . . ] We have to look, here, for the combined effects of three factors. First, the compression, at both ends, of the scale of income distribution. Second, the great extension of the area of common culture and common experience. And third, the enrichment of the universal status of citizenship, combined with the recognition and stabilization of certain status differences chiefly through the linked systems of education and occupation. [ . . . ]

I asked, at the beginning, whether there was any limit to the present drive towards social equality inherent in the principles governing the movement. My answer is that the preservation of economic inequalities has been made more difficult by the enrichment of the status of citizenship. There is less room for them, and there is more and more likelihood of their being challenged. But we are certainly proceeding at present on the assumption that the hypothesis is valid. And this assumption provides the answer to the second question. We are not aiming at absolute equality. There are limits inherent in the egalitarian movement. But the movement is a double one. It operates partly through citizenship and partly through the economic system. In both cases the aim is to remove inequalities which cannot be regarded as legitimate, but the standard of legitimacy is different. In the former it is the standard of social justice, in the latter it is social justice combined with economic necessity. It is possible, therefore, that the inequalities permitted by the two halves of the movement will not coincide. Class distinctions may survive which have no appropriate economic function, and economic differences which do not correspond with accepted class distinctions. [ . . . ]

## Notes

Originally delivered in Cambridge as the Marshall Lecture for 1949 and published in *Citizenship and Social Class and Other Essays*, ed. T. H. Marshall, Cambridge, Cambridge University Press, 1950. This version extracted from *States and Societies*, ed. D. Held, London, Open University/Martin Robertson, 1983, pp. 249–60.

1 G. M. Trevelyan, *English Social History* (1942), p. 351.
2 Sidney and Beatrice Webb, *History of Trade Unionism* (1920), p. 60.
3 R. H. Tawney, *The Agrarian Problem in the Sixteenth Century* (1916), pp. 43–4.
4 P. Colquhoun, *A Treatise in Indigence* (1806), pp. 7–8.

# Universalism versus Selection

## *Richard Titmuss*

[ . . . ]

### Universalist and Selective Social Services

In any discussion today of the future of (what is called) 'The Welfare State' much of the argument revolves around the principles and objectives of universalist social services and selective social services.

[ . . . ]

Consider, first, the nature of the broad principles which helped to shape substantial sections of British welfare legislation in the past, and particularly the principle of universalism embodied in such postwar enactments as the National Health Service Act, the Education Act of 1944, the National Insurance Act and the Family Allowances Act.

One fundamental historical reason for the adoption of this principle was the aim of making services available and accessible to the whole population in such ways as would not involve users in any humiliating loss of status, dignity or self-respect. There should be no sense of inferiority, pauperism, shame or stigma in the use of a publicly provided service; no attribution that one was being or becoming a 'public burden'. Hence the emphasis on the social rights of all citizens to use or not to use as responsible people the services made available by the community in respect of certain needs which the private market and the family were unable or unwilling to provide universally. If these services were not provided for everybody by everybody they would either not be available at all, or only for those who could afford them, and for others on such terms as would involve the infliction of a sense of inferiority and stigma.

Avoidance of stigma was not, of course, the only reason for the development of the twin concepts of social rights and universalism. Many other forces, social, political and psychological, during a century and more of turmoil, revolution, war and change, contributed to the clarification and acceptance of these notions. The novel idea of prevention – novel, at least, to many in the nineteenth century – was, for example, another powerful engine, driven by the Webbs and many other advocates of change, which reinforced the concepts of social rights and universalism. The idea of prevention – the prevention and breaking of the vicious descending spiral of poverty, disease, neglect, illiteracy and destitution – spelt to the protagonists (and still does so) the critical importance of early and easy access to and use of preventive, remedial and rehabilitative services. Slowly and painfully the lesson was learnt that if such services were to be utilized in time and were to be effective in action in a highly differentiated, unequal and class-saturated society, they had to be delivered through socially approved channels; that is to say, without loss of self-respect by the users and their families.

Prevention was not simply a child of biological and psychological theorists; at least one of the grandparents was a powerful economist with a strongly developed streak of nationalism. As Professor Bentley Gilbert has shown in his [ . . . ] book *The Evolution of National Insurance: The Origins of the Welfare State*, national efficiency and welfare were seen as complementary.[1] The sin unforgivable was the waste of human resources; thus, welfare was summoned to prevent waste. Hence the beginnings of four of our present-day universalist social services: retirement pensions, the Health Service, unemployment insurance and the school meals service.

The insistent drumming of the national efficiency movement in those far-off days before the First World War is now largely forgotten. Let me then remind you that the whole welfare debate was a curious mixture of humanitarianism, egalitarianism, productivity (as we would call it today) and old-fashioned imperialism. The strident note of the latter is now, we may thank our stars, silenced. The Goddess of Growth has replaced the God of National Fitness. But can we say that the quest for the other objectives is no longer necessary?

Before discussing such a rhetorical question, we need to examine further the principal of universalism. The principle itself may sound simple but the practice – and by that I mean the present operational pattern of welfare in Britain [in the 1960s] – is immensely complex. We can see something of this complexity if we analyse welfare (defined here as all publicly provided and subsidized services, statutory, occupational and fiscal) from a number of different standpoints.

## An Analytical Framework

Whatever the nature of the service, activity or function, and whether it be a service in kind, a collective amenity, or a transfer payment in cash or by accountancy, we need to consider (and here I itemize in question form for the sake of brevity) three central issues:

1 What is the nature of entitlement to use? Is it legal, contractual or contributory, financial, discretionary or professionally determined entitlement?
2 Who is entitled and on what conditions? Is account taken of individual characteristics, family characteristics, group characteristics, territorial characteristics or social-biological characteristics? What, in fact, are the rules of entitlement? Are they specific and contractual – like a right based on age – or are they variable, arbitrary or discretionary?
3 What methods, financial and administrative, are employed in the determination of access, utilization, allocation and payment?

Next we have to reflect on the nature of the service or benefit.

What functions do benefits, in cash, amenity or in kind, aim to fulfil? They may, for example, fulfil any of the following sets of functions, singly or in combination:

1 As partial compensation for identified disservices caused by society (for example, unemployment, some categories of industrial injuries benefits, war pensions, etc.). And, we may add, the disservices caused by international society as exemplified [ . . . ] by the oil pollution resulting from the Torrey Canyon disaster in 1967 costing at least £2 million.[2]
2 As partial compensation for unidentifiable disservices caused by society (for example, 'benefits' related to programmes of slum clearance, urban blight, smoke pollution control, hospital cross-infection and many other socially created disservices).
3 As partial compensation for unmerited handicap (for example, language classes for immigrant children, services for the deprived child, children handicapped from birth, etc.).
4 As a form of protection for society (for example, the probation service, some parts of the mental health services, services for the control of infectious diseases, etc.).
5 As an investment for a future personal or collective gain (education – professional, technical and industrial – is an obvious example here; so also are certain categories of tax deductibles for self-improvement and certain types of subsidized occupational benefits).
6 As an immediate and/or deferred increment to personal welfare or, in other words, benefits (utilities) which add to personal

command-over-resources either immediately and/or in the future (for example, subsidies to owner-occupiers and council tenants, tax deductibles for interest charges, pensions, supplementary benefits, curative medical care, etc.).

7 As an element in an integrative objective which is an essential characteristic distinguishing social policy from economic policy. As Kenneth Boulding has said, '. . . social policy is that which is centred in those institutions that create integration and discourage alienation'.[3] It is thus profoundly concerned with questions of personal identity whereas economic policy centres round exchange or bilateral transfer.

This represents little more than an elementary and partial structural map which can assist in the understanding of the welfare complex [ . . . ]. Needless to say, a more sophisticated (inch to the mile) guide is essential for anything approaching a thorough analysis of the actual functioning of welfare benefit systems. I do not, however, propose to refine further this frame of study now, nor can I analyse by these classifications the several hundred distinctive and functionally separate services and benefits actually in operation in Britain [in the 1960s].

Further study would also have to take account of the pattern and operation of means-tested services. It has been estimated by Mr M. J. Reddin, my research assistant, that in England and Wales today local authorities are responsible for administering at least 3,000 means tests, of which about 1,500 are different from each other.[4] This estimate applies only to services falling within the responsibilities of education, child care, health, housing and welfare departments. It follows that in these fields alone there exist some 1,500 different definitions of poverty or financial hardship, ability to pay and rules for charges, which affect the individual and the family. There must be substantial numbers of poor families with multiple needs and multiple handicaps whose perception [ . . . ] of the realities of welfare is to see only a means-testing world. Who helps them, I wonder, to fill out all those forms?

I mention these social facts, by way of illustration, because they do form part of the operational complex of welfare in 1967. My main purpose, however, in presenting this analytical framework was twofold. First, to underline the difficulties of conceptualizing and categorizing needs, causes, entitlement or gatekeeper functions, utilization patterns, benefits and compensations. Second, to suggest that those students of welfare who are seeing the main problem today in terms of universalism versus selective services are presenting a naive and oversimplified picture of policy choices.

Some of the reasons for this simple and superficial view are, I think, due to the fact that the approach is dominated by the concept or model of welfare as a 'burden'; as a waste of resources in the provision of benefits for those who, it is said, do not need them. The general solution is thus deceptively simple and romantically appealing: abolish all this welfare complexity and concentrate help on those whose needs are greatest.

Quite apart from the theoretical and practical immaturity of this solution, which would restrict the public services to a minority in the population leaving the majority to buy their own education, social security, medical care and other services in a supposedly free market, certain other important questions need to be considered.

As all selective services for this minority would have to apply some test of need–eligibility, on what bases would tests be applied and, even more crucial, where would the lines be drawn for benefits which function as compensation for identified disservices, compensation for unidentifiable disservices, compensation for unmerited handicap, as a form of social protection, as an investment, or as an increment to personal welfare? Can rules of entitlement and access be drawn on purely 'ability to pay' criteria without distinction of cause? And if the causal agents of need cannot be identified or are so diffuse as to defy the wit of law – as they so often are [ . . . ] – then is not the answer 'no compensation and no redress'? In other words, the case for concentrated selective services resolves itself into an argument for allowing the social costs or diswelfares of the economic system to lie where they fall.

The emphasis [ . . . ] on 'welfare' and the 'benefits of welfare' often tends to obscure the fundamental fact that for many consumers the services used are not essentially benefits or increments to welfare at all; they represent partial compensations for disservices, for social costs and social insecurities which are the product of a rapidly changing industrial-urban society. They are part of the price we pay to some people for bearing part of the costs of other people's progress; the obsolescence of skills, redundancies, premature retirements, accidents, many categories of disease and handicap, urban blight and slum clearance, smoke pollution, and a hundred-and-one other socially generated disservices. They are the socially caused diswelfares; the losses involved in aggregate welfare gains.

What is also of major importance [ . . . ] is that modern society is finding it increasingly difficult to identify the causal agent or agencies, and thus to allocate the costs of disservices and charge those who are responsible. It is not just a question of benefit allocation – of whose 'Welfare State' – but also of loss allocation – whose 'Diswelfare State'.

If identification of the agents of diswelfare were possible – if we could legally name and blame the culprits – then, in theory at least, redress could be obtained through the courts by the method of monetary compensation for damages. But multiple causality and the diffusion of disservices – the modern choleras of change — make this solution impossible. We have, therefore, as societies to make other choices; either to provide social services, or to allow the social costs of the system to lie where they fall. The nineteenth century chose the latter – the *laissez-faire* solution – because it had neither a germ theory of disease nor a social theory of causality; an answer which can hardly be entertained today by a richer society equipped with more knowledge about the dynamics of change. But knowledge in this context must not, of course, be equated with wisdom.

If this argument can be sustained, we are thus compelled to return to our analytical framework of the functional concepts of benefit and, within this context, to consider the role of universalist and selective social services. Non-discriminating universalist services are in part the consequence of unidentifiable causality. If disservices are wasteful (to use the economists' concept of 'waste') so welfare has to be 'wasteful'.

The next question that presents itself is this: can we and should we, in providing benefits and compensation (which in practice can rarely be differentially provided), distinguish between 'faults' in the individual (moral, psychological or social) and the 'faults of society'? If all services are provided – irrespective of whether they represent benefits, amenity, social protection or compensation – on a discriminatory, means-test basis, do we not foster both the sense of personal failure and the stigma of a public burden? The fundamental objective of all such tests of eligibility is to keep people out; not to let them in. They must, therefore, be treated as applicants or supplicants; not beneficiaries or consumers.

It is a regrettable but human fact that money (and the lack of it) is linked to personal and family self-respect. This is one element in what has been called the 'stigma of the means test'. Another element is the historical evidence we have that separate discriminatory services for poor people have always tended to be poor quality services; read the history of the panel system under National Health Insurance; read Beveridge on workmen's compensation; Newsom on secondary modern schools; Plowden on standards of primary schools in slum areas; Townsend on Part III accommodations in *The Last Refuge*,[5] and so on.[6]

In the past, poor quality selective services for poor people were the product of a society which saw 'welfare' as a residual; as a public burden. The primary purpose of the system and the method of discrimination was, therefore, deterrence (it was also an effective rationing device). To this end, the most effective instrument was to induce among recipients (children as well as adults) a sense of personal fault, of personal failure, even if the benefit was wholly or partially a compensation for disservices inflicted by society.

## The Real Challenge in Welfare

Today, with this heritage, we face the positive challenge of providing selective, high quality services for poor people over a large and complex range of welfare; of positively discriminating on a territorial, group or 'rights' basis in favour of the poor, the handicapped, the deprived, the coloured, the homeless, and the social casualties of our society. Universalism is not, by itself alone, enough: in medical care, in wage-related social security and in education. This much we have learnt in the past two decades from the facts about inequalities in the distribution of incomes and wealth, and in our failure to close many gaps in differential access to and effective utilization of particular branches of our social services.[7]

If I am right, I think that during the 1960s Britain was beginning to identify the dimensions of this challenge of positive, selective discrimination – in income maintenance, in education, in housing, in medical care and mental health, in child welfare, and in the tolerant integration of immigrants and citizens from overseas; of preventing especially the second generation from becoming (and of seeing themselves as) second-class citizens. We have continued to seek ways and means, values, methods and techniques, of positive discrimination without the infliction, actual or imagined, of a sense of personal failure and individual fault.

At this point, considering the nature of the search in all its ramifying complexities, I must now state my general conclusion. It is this. The challenge that faces us is not the choice between universalist and selective social services. The real challenge resides in the question: what particular infrastructure of universalist services is needed in order to provide a framework of values and opportunity bases within and around which can be developed socially acceptable selective services aiming to discriminate positively, with the minimum risk of stigma, in favour of those whose needs are greatest.

This, to me, is the fundamental challenge. In different ways and in particular areas it confronts the Supplementary Benefits Commission, the Seebohm Committee, the National Health Service, the Ministry of Housing and Local Government, the National Committee for Commonwealth Immigrants, the policy-making readers of the Newsom Report and the Plowden Report on educational priority areas, the Scottish Report, *Social Work and the Community*, and thousands of social workers and administrators all over the country wrestling with the problems of needs and priorities. In all the main spheres of need, some structure of universalism is an essential prerequisite to selective positive discrimination; it provides a general system of values and a sense of community; socially approved agencies for clients, patients and consumers, and also for the recruitment, training and deployment of staff at all levels; it sees welfare, not as a burden, but as complementary and as an instrument of change and, finally, it allows positive discriminatory services to be provided as rights for categories of people and for classes of need in terms of priority social areas and other impersonal classifications.

Without this infrastructure of welfare resources and framework of values we should not, I conclude, be able to identify and discuss the next steps in progress towards a 'Welfare Society'.

## Notes

Lecture delivered at the British National Conference on Social Welfare, London, April 1967, and published in the *Proceedings of the Conference*. This extract from R. M. Titmuss, *Commitment to Welfare*, London, Allen and Unwin, 1968, pp. 128–37.

1 B. B. Gilbert, *The Evolution of National Insurance: The Origins of the Welfare State*, London, Michael Joseph, 1966.
2 *The Torrey Canyon*, Cmnd 3246, London, HMSO, 1967.
3 K. E. Boulding, 'The Boundaries of Social Policy', *Social Work*, vol. 12, no. 1, January 1967, p. 7.
4 This study is to be published by Mr M. J. Reddin as an *Occasional Paper on Social Administration*.
5 P. Townsend, *The Last Refuge*, London, Routledge, 1964.
6 See also R. M. Titmuss, *Problems of Social Policy*, London, HMSO, 1950.
7 See P. Townsend, *Poverty, Socialism and Labour in Power*, Fabian tract, 371, 1967, and R. J. Nicholson, 'The Distribution of Personal Income', *Lloyds Bank Review*, January 1967, p. 11.

# Perspectives on the Left

# What is Social Justice?

## *Commission on Social Justice*

In deciding to develop a conceptual framework for thinking about social justice, the Commission made a big assumption, namely that there is such a thing as 'social justice'. Some people (particularly of the libertarian Right) deny that there is a worthwhile idea of *social* justice at all. They say that justice is an idea confined to the law, with regard to crime, punishment and the settling of disputes before the courts. They claim that it is nonsense to talk about resources in society being fairly or unfairly distributed. The free market theorist Friedrich von Hayek, for example, argued that the process of allocating wealth and property 'can be neither just nor unjust, because the results are not intended or foreseen, and depend on a multitude of circumstances not known in their totality to anybody'.

What libertarians really mean, however, is not that there is no such thing as social justice, but rather that there is only one criterion of a just outcome in society, namely that it should be the product of a free market. But this is not as simple as it may sound, because ideas of fairness (and not merely of efficiency) are themselves used in defining what counts as a free market. While it is often said that a given market competition is not fair because it is not being played 'on a level field', it is not clear what counts as levelling the field, as opposed to altering the result of the match. For example, anti-trust laws can be seen as an interference in a free market, or a device for making the field level.

In fact, people in modern societies *do* have strong ideas about social justice. We all know this from daily conversation, and opinion polls regularly confirm it. We are confident that at least in our belief there is such a thing as 'social justice', we reflect the common sense of the vast majority of people. However, polls are not easy to interpret, and they make it clear that people's ideas about social justice are complex.

There is more than one notion associated with the term social justice. In some connections, for example, justice is thought to have something to do with *equality*. Sometimes it seems to relate to *need:* for example, it can seem notably unfair if bad fortune prevents someone from having something they really need, such as medical care, less unfair if it is something they just happen to want. Yet again, justice relates to such notions as *entitlement*, *merit* and *desert*. These are not the same as each other. For example, if someone wins the prize in the lottery, they are entitled to the money, and it would be unjust to take it away from them, but it has nothing to do with their merits, and they have done nothing to deserve it. Similarly, if talented people win prizes in an activity that requires no great practice or effort, they are entitled to the prize and get it on the strength of their merits (as opposed, for instance, to someone's getting it because he is the son of the promoter), but they may well have not done anything much to deserve it. People who are especially keen on the notion of desert may want there to be prizes only for effort; or, at least, think that prizes which command admiration (as the lottery prize does not) should be awarded only for effort. Humanity has shown so far a steady reluctance to go all the way with this view.

As well as being *complex* in this way, people's views about justice are also *indeterminate*. This means that it is often unclear what the just outcome should be – particularly when various considerations of social justice seem to pull in different directions, as they often do. Most people, for instance, think that inheritance is at least not intrinsically evil, and that parents are entitled to leave property to their children. But no one thinks that one can leave anything one likes to one's children – one's job, for instance – and almost everyone thinks that it can be just for the state to tax inheritances in order to deal with social injustice, or simply to help the common good.

The mere fact that people's ideas about justice are both complex and indeterminate has an important consequence for democratic politics. There is more than one step from general ideas to practical recommendations. There have to be *general* policies directed to social justice, and these are going to be at best an interpretation of people's ideas on such matters. General policies will hope to offer considerations which people can recognize as making sense in the light of their own experience and ideas (this need not exclude challenging some of those ideas). *Specific* policies, however, involve a further step, since they have to express general policies in a particular administrative form. A given scheme of taxation or social security is, in that sense, at two removes from the complex and indeterminate ideas that are its moral roots.

This is not to deny that some administrative practices may acquire a symbolic value of their own. In the 1940s, the death grant was a symbol of society's commitment to end paupers' funerals and ensure for every family the means to offer deceased relatives a proper burial. It is a matter of acute political judgement to decide whether one is dealing with an important example of such a value, as opposed to a fetish (in the more or less literal sense of an inert object that has been invested with value that does not belong to it in its own right). Not every arrangement that has been taken to be an essential embodiment of social justice is, in changing circumstances, really so.

## Theories of Social Justice

There are important theories of social justice. The most ambitious give a general account of what social justice is, explain and harmonize the relations between the different considerations associated with it, do the same for the relations between justice and other goods, notably liberty, help to resolve apparent conflicts between different values, and in the light of all that, even give pointers to practical policies. The most famous such theory in modern discussion is that of John Rawls, which gives a very rich elaboration to a very simple idea: that the fair division of a cake would be one that could be agreed on by people who did not know which piece they were going to get.

Rawls invokes an 'Original Position', in which representatives of various parties to society are behind 'a veil of ignorance' and do not know what role each party will occupy in the society. They are asked to choose a general scheme for the ordering of society. The scheme that they would reasonably choose in these imagined circumstances constitutes, in Rawls's view, the scheme of a just society.

Rawls's theory, and others with similar aims, contains important insights, and anyone who is trying to think about these problems should pay attention to them. But there is an important question – one acknowledged by Rawls himself – of what relation such a theory can have to politics. Rawls thinks that his theory articulates a widely spread sense of fairness, but it is certain that the British public would not recognize in such a theory, or in any other with such ambitions, all its conflicting ideas and feelings about social justice. Even if the Commission, improbably, all agreed on Rawls's or some other such theory, we would not be justified in presenting our conclusions in terms of that theory. The Commission has a more practical purpose.

Our task is to find compelling ways of making our society more just. We shall be able to do so only if we think in ways that people can recognize and respect about such questions as how best to understand merit and need; how to see the effects of luck in different spheres of life; what is implied in saying, or denying, that health care is a morally special kind of good which makes a special kind of demand.

The Commission has to guard against all-or-nothing assumptions. It is not true that either we have a complete top-down theory, or we are left only with mere prejudice and subservience to polls. This particularly applies to conflict. Confronted, as will often be the case, with an apparent conflict within justice, or between justice and some other value, we may tend to assume that there are only two possibilities: the conflict is merely apparent, and we should understand liberty and equality (for instance) in such a way that they cannot conflict; or it is a real conflict, and then it can only be left to politics, majorities, subjective taste, or whatever. This will not do. Reflection may not eliminate all conflicts, but it can help us to understand them, and then arrive at policy choices.

## The Equal Worth of Every Citizen

Social justice is often thought to have something specially to do with equality, but this idea, in itself, determines very little. A basic question is: equality of what? Furthermore, not all inequalities are unjust. For example, what people can do with money varies. Thus disabled people may well need more resources to reach a given quality of life than other people do, and if you are trying to be fair to people with regard to the quality of their life, unequal amounts of money is what fairness itself will demand. What this shows, as the philosopher and economist Amartya Sen has insisted, is that equality in one dimension goes with inequality in another. Since people have different capacities to turn resources into worthwhile activity (for instance because they are disabled), people will need different resources to be equally capable of worthwhile activity.

In fact, virtually everyone in the modern world believes in equality of *something*. All modern states are based on belief in some sort of equality and claim to treat their citizens equally. But what is involved in 'treating people equally'? Minimally, it implies political and civil liberties, equal rights before the law, equal protection against arbitrary arrest, and so forth. These things provide the basis of a 'civil society', a society of equal citizens.

However, these rights and freedoms cannot stand by themselves. More than this formal level of equality is needed if the minimal demands themselves are to be properly met. It is a familiar point that equality before the law does not come to much if one cannot afford a good lawyer. The 'equal freedom' of which modern democratic states boast should amount to more (as Anatole France observed) than the freedom to sleep on park benches and under bridges. Everyone needs the means to make use of their equal freedom, which otherwise would be hollow. Formal equalities have substantive consequences. Perhaps the most basic question about the nature of social justice in a modern society is what those substantive consequences are.

## Meeting Basic Needs

People are likely to be restricted in what they can do with their freedom and their rights if they are poor, or ill, or lack the education which, to a greater extent today than ever before, is the basis of employment opportunities, personal fulfilment and people's capacities to influence what happens to them. These concerns define areas of *need*, and it is a natural application of the idea that everyone is of equal worth that they should have access to what they need, or at least to what they basically need.

Some basic needs are met by providing resources, or by helping people to save or acquire resources. This is the case with paid work; with financial security in old age; and with provisions for dealing with lack of resources, such as benefit in case of unemployment. In the case of health care and education, however, the most appropriate way of meeting needs seems to be not through money, but in kind; we think that someone who is ill has a right to access to treatment for their illness, but not that they have a right to funds which they can choose to spend on treatment or not. One way of expressing this commitment is that the state should itself provide the service. Another is that the state should provide means which command health care or education, but which cannot be converted into money. In the case of health, this may take the form of public insurance, though this can raise basic questions of fairness (with regard to individual risk) as well as of efficiency.

The case of health now raises a fundamental question which was not present fifty years ago. Health care has always seemed a very special good, in relation to social justice as in other respects. It involves our most basic interests, gives great power to certain professionals, and carries heavy symbolic value (brought out, for instance, in Richard Titmuss's famous discussion of blood donation *The Gift Relationship).* Treating health as one commodity, to be bought and sold like any other, is found offensive in most parts of the world (and Americans, though used to that attitude, seem to be turning against it). Our sentiments about health care merge with our sense of some very basic obligations: most people feel that resources should be used to save an identified person (as opposed to a merely statistical casualty) from death.

But today it is a fact that medicine's resources to extend life are expanding at an accelerating rate, and so is their cost. This raises hard questions not only about the distribution of resources devoted to health care (who gets the kidney machine?), but also about the amount of resources that should be devoted to health care at all. These hard questions are questions of justice, among other things. Confronted with the opportunity to save someone in the street from death, we will think that we should stop to save them even if the cost is not taking the children to school, but is it fair to save every saveable person from death at the cost of sending many children to quite inadequate schools?

To answer these questions, the Commission will need to consider what *sort* of goods we take health and health care to be. This was a less pressing question in the past, but it is now harder to avoid the issue of what we are distributing when we distribute medical care, and of what we most want it to do.

Education is also a good to which everyone has a right, because it is so closely tied to basic needs, to personal development, and to one's role in society. But it is also connected to equality in another way. Disadvantage is, notoriously, inherited, and an unfair situation in one generation tends to mean an unfair start for the next. Educational opportunity is still what it always has been, a crucial means for doing something about this unfairness.

This brings out a further point, that the ideal of 'equality of opportunity', which has often been thought by reformers to be a rather weak aspiration, is in fact very radical, if it is taken seriously. The changes required in order to give the most disadvantaged in our society the same life-chances as the more fortunate would be very wide-ranging indeed.

## Opportunities and Life-Chances

Self-respect and equal citizenship demand more than the meeting of basic needs for income, shelter and so on. They demand the opportunities and life-chances central to personal freedom and autonomy. In a commercial society (outside monasteries, kibbutzim, etc.), self-respect standardly requires a certain amount of personal property. As Adam Smith remarked, a working man in eighteenth-century Scotland needed to own a decent linen shirt as a condition of self-respect, even though that might not be true of every man everywhere.

This does not mean that Adam Smith's man should be issued with a shirt. In a commercial society, his need is rather for the resources to buy a shirt of his choice. This is connected with his needing it as a matter of self-respect, which suggests something else, namely that where resources are supplied directly, for instance to those who are retired or who are caring for members of their families, it must be in ways which affirm their self-respect. But most people, for most of their lives, want the opportunities to earn the resources for themselves. The obvious question is whether everyone therefore has a right to a job, or the right to the means to gain a job.

The trouble, clearly, is that it may not be in the power of government directly to bring this about. Having a job, at least as the world is now, is closely connected with self-respect and hence with the equality of citizens, and for this as well as other reasons it must be a high priority for any government to create the circumstances in which there are jobs for those who want them. To insist, however, on a right to work – a right, presumably, which each person holds against the government – may not be the best way of expressing this aim. The Commission will therefore consider not only ways in which employment may be increased, but also what provision social justice demands for those who are unable to do paid work, or who are engaged in valuable unpaid work, or when significant levels of unemployment persist, even for a temporary period. Tackling unemployment is, of course, central to the realization of social justice.

There are questions here of how resources and opportunities can be extended to the unemployed. But there is a wider question as well, that extends to the provision for other needs: how opportunities may be created for the expression of people's autonomy and the extension of their freedom to determine their own lives. There is no doubt that advocates of social justice have often been insensitive to this dimension. The designers of the welfare state wanted to put rights in the place of charity: the idea of *entitlement* to benefit was meant to undercut any notion that the better-off were doing the worse-off a good turn. But the entitlement was often still understood as an entitlement to be given or issued with certain goods and services, the nature of which it was, in many cases, the business of experts to determine. There is a much greater awareness today that what people need is the chance to provide for themselves: [ . . . ] 'there is a limit to what government can do for people, but there is no limit to what they can be enabled to achieve for themselves'.

Relatedly, there is a stronger sense today that the aims of social justice are served not only by redistribution, by bringing resources after the event to people who have done badly. Social justice requires as well that structures should be adapted and influenced in ways that can give more people a better chance in the first place. That is why opportunities, and breaking down barriers to them, are so important.

There are, without doubt, conflicts between these various considerations. You cannot both encourage people's freedom to live their own lives as they choose, and guarantee that they will not suffer if they do not live them well. You cannot both allow people to spend money, if they wish, on their children's education – a right that exists in every democratic country – and also bring it about that everyone gets exactly the same education whether they pay privately for it or not. Here there are questions, too, of how far publicly supported provision to meet need should aim only at a minimal level, available to those without other provision, and how far it should seek to provide a high level of service for everyone. The view of most people is probably that the first answer applies to some needs and the goods and services that meet them, while in the case of health care and education, at least, no one should be excluded by disadvantage from a very high level of provision. Exactly how those different aims should now be conceived, and the extent to which they can realistically be carried out, are central questions for the Commission.

## Unjustified Inequalities

Proponents of equality sometimes seem to imply that *all* inequalities are unjust (although they usually hasten to add that they are not in fact arguing for 'arithmetical equality'). We do not accept this. It seems fair, for instance, that a medical student should receive a lower income than the fully qualified doctor; or that experience or outstanding talent should be rewarded, and so on. Different people may have different views about what the basis of differential rewards should be; but most people accept, as we do, that some inequalities are just. There is, however, a question about the justifiable *extent* of an inequality, even if we accept that the inequality *per se* is not unjust.

Similarly, most people believe that it is fair for people to bequeath their property as they see fit, even though this means that some will inherit more than others. Nonetheless, it is also accepted that society may claim a share of an inheritance through the taxation of wealth or gifts, particularly when the estate is large. It is, after all, offensive to most ideas of social justice that a growing number of people own two homes while others have nowhere to live at all. This does not imply that one person's property should be confiscated to house another; but it does suggest the need for a fundamental reform of housing policy, an issue the Commission will certainly be addressing.

But if some inequalities are just, it is obviously the case that not all are so. It would, for instance, be unjust to allow people to inherit jobs from their parents: employment should be open to all, on the basis of merit. Inheritance of a family title offends many people's views about a classless society, but could not be said to deny somebody else something which they deserved. But inheritance of a peerage, in the UK, carries with it automatic entitlement to a seat and vote in the Second Chamber of Parliament: and that is an inequality of power which seems manifestly unjust.

### *Entitlement and Desert*

Parents can, however, pass on intelligence, talent, charm and other qualities, as well as property or titles. Rawls in his theory rests a lot on the fact that a person's talents, and his or her capacity to make productive use of those talents, are very much matters of luck and are also, in some part, the product of society. Nobody, he has rightly insisted, *deserves* his or her (natural) talents. From this he has inferred that nobody, at a level of basic principle, deserves the rewards of his or her talents. He argues that no one has a right to something simply because it is the product of his or her talents, and society has a right to redistribute that product in accordance with the demands of social justice. 

This is a very strong and surprising claim. Some people might agree that no one deserves a reward that they get on the basis of some raw advantage, without any investment of effort. (Of course, given the existing rules, that does not mean that they are not entitled to it, or that it can merely be taken away from them. It means that it would not necessarily be an injustice to change the rules.) But those who agree to this are very likely to think that people who *do* invest effort deserve its rewards, at least up to a certain point. But Rawls's argument applies just as much to effort as to raw talent. First, it is practically impossible to separate the relative contributions of effort and talent to a particular product. Moreover, the capacity to make a given degree of effort is itself not equally distributed, and may plausibly be thought to be affected by upbringing, culture and other social factors. Virtually everything about a person that yields a product is itself undeserved. So no rewards, in Rawls's view, are, at the most basic level, a matter of desert.

Few people believe this. If someone has taken a lot of trouble in designing and tending a garden, for instance, they will be proud of it and appropriately think of its success as theirs. The same applies to many aspects of life. This does suggest that there is something wrong with the idea that basically people never earn anything by their talents or labours – that in the last analysis all that anyone's work represents is a site at which society has achieved something. Yet, certainly, one does not 'deserve' the talents of birth. It must be true, then, that one can deserve the rewards of one's talents without deserving one's talents. As the American philosopher Robert Nozick forcefully put it, why does desert 'have to go all the way down'?

What the various arguments about entitlement and desert suggest seems to be something close to what many people believe: that there is basic justice in people having some differential reward for their productive activities, but that they have no right to any *given* differential of their reward over others. It is not simply self-interest, or again scepticism about government spending programmes (though that is certainly a factor), that makes people resist the idea that everyone's income is in principle a resource for redistribution; that idea also goes against their sense of what is right. They rightly think that redistribution of income is not an aim in itself.

At the same time, they acknowledge that the needs of the less fortunate make a claim. Luck is everywhere, and one is entitled to some rewards of luck, but there are limits to this entitlement when one lives and works with other people. Even if one is entitled to some rewards from the product of one's efforts and talents, there is the further point that in a complex enterprise such as a company or family, there is rarely a product which is solely and definitely the product of a given person's efforts and talents.

This is no doubt one reason why people are sceptical about vast rewards to captains of industry. It is also a question of the relation of one person's activity to that of others. Few people mind that Pavarotti or Lenny Henry are paid large sums – there is only one of them, and they are undoubtedly the star of the show. But in some cases, one person's reward can be another person's loss. The Nobel Prize winning economist Professor James Meade argued in a submission to the Commission that 'Keynesian full-employment policy. . . . collapsed simply and solely because a high level of money expenditures came to lead not to a high level of output and employment but to a high rate of money wages, costs and prices . . . It is very possible that to absorb two million extra workers into employment would require a considerable reduction in real wage costs.'

This raises a crucial point, concerning the power to determine one's own rewards, and the relationship of that power to questions of justice and desert. In contrast to a simple focus on the distribution of rewards, this raises the question of the *generation* of rewards, the processes whereby inequalities are generated.

Unequal incomes are inherent in a market economy. Even if everyone started off with the same allocation of money, differences would soon emerge. Not all labour commands the same price; not all investments produce the same return; some people work longer hours, others prefer more leisure and so on. The resulting inequalities are not necessarily unjust – although the extent of them may be. In the real world, of course, people start off with very different personal and financial resources. The problem is that too many of these inequalities are exacerbated in the UK's system of market exchange.

But market economies are not all of a piece; different kinds of market produce different outcomes. For instance, Germany, Japan and Sweden all have more equal earnings distributions than the UK, where the gap between the highest and lowest paid is wider today than at any time since 1886. Social justice therefore has a part to play in deciding how a market is constructed, and not simply with the end result.

## *Fair Reward*

Most people have some idea of a 'fair reward'. For example, it is clear to the vast majority of people that disadvantage and discrimination on grounds of sex or race or disability is unjust. However, once one gets beyond the general idea, there is less agreement on what fair rewards should be. Even if there were more agreement about this, it is very difficult, both practically and morally, to impose such notions on a modern economy. The very idea of a society that can be effectively managed from the top on the basis of detailed centralized decisions is now discredited. Moreover, our society does not stand by itself and happily does not have walls around it, and people can go elsewhere.

Ideas of social justice in this area are not, however, necessarily tied to the model of a command economy. It is often clear, at least, that given rewards in a market economy are not fair, because they are not being determined by such things as talent, effort and the person's contribution to the enterprise, but rather by established power relations. Real life does not conform to economic models: people are not paid for the 'marginal product' of their labour. They are paid, among other things, according to social norms. In one sense, such distortions are the product of the market: they are what we get if market processes, uncorrected, are allowed to reflect established structures and habits of power. Examples of this are the huge salaries and bonuses distributed to the directors of some large companies. [ . . . ] These salaries and bonuses are often quite unrelated to the performance of the company concerned, and are sometimes actually inversely correlated with company performance.

In another sense, unjust inequalities are themselves distortions of the market: it is not a fair market in talent and effort if it is not talent and effort that determine the outcome. This is most obviously demonstrated in the case of inequalities of pay between men and women. Although the 1970 Equal Pay Act eliminated overt pay inequities, it had a limited effect on the gap between men's and women's pay, which resulted in the main from job segregation and gender-biased views of what different jobs and different qualities were worth. Hence the concept of 'equal pay for work of equal value', which permits comparisons between two very different jobs performed for the same employer. Although designed to eradicate gender as a consideration in earnings, equal value claims may in practice require a complete transformation in an organization's pay-setting. Equal pay for work of equal value, after all, implies unequal pay for work of unequal value: thus, the basis for differentials has to be made explicit and justified.

Different organizations and people will have different views of what constitutes a fair basis for differentials: it should not be an aim of government to substitute its own view of fair wage settlements. It is, however, a legitimate aim of policy concerned with social justice to develop social institutions (of which equal value laws are one example) which will enable people to express their own ideas of a fair reward.

## The Meaning of Social Justice: A Summary

In arriving at our principles of social justice, we reject the view, so fashionable in the 1980s, that human beings are simply selfish individuals, for whom there is 'no such thing as society'. People are essentially social creatures, dependent on one another for the fulfilment of their needs and potential, and willing to recognize their responsibilities to others as well as claiming their rights from them. We believe our four principles of social justice, based on a basic belief in the intrinsic worth of every human being, echo the deeply held views of many people in this country. They provide a compelling justification and basis for our work:

1 The foundation of a free society is the equal worth of all citizens.
2 Everyone is entitled, as a right of citizenship, to be able to meet their basic needs.
3 The right to self-respect and personal autonomy demands the widest possible spread of opportunities.
4 Not all inequalities are unjust, but unjust inequalities should be reduced and where possible eliminated.

[. . .]

**Note**

From Commission on Social Justice, *The Justice Gap*, London, Institute for Public Policy Research, 1993, pp. 4–16.

# The Fiscal Crisis of the State

## *James O'Connor*

[ . . . ]

Our first premise is that the capitalistic state must try to fulfil two basic and often mutually contradictory functions – *accumulation* and *legitimization*. [ . . . ] This means that the state must try to maintain or create the conditions in which profitable capital accumulation is possible. However, the state also must try to maintain or create the conditions for social harmony. A capitalist state that openly uses its coercive forces to help one class accumulate capital at the expense of other classes loses its legitimacy and hence undermines the basis of its loyalty and support. But a state that ignores the necessity of assisting the process of capital accumulation risks drying up the source of its own power, the economy's surplus production capacity and the taxes drawn from this surplus (and other forms of capital). This contradiction explains why President Nixon calls a legislated increase in profit rates a 'job development credit', why the government announces that new fiscal policies are aimed at 'stability and growth' when in fact their purpose is to keep profits high and growing, why the tax system is nominally progressive and theoretically based on 'ability to pay' when in fact the system is regressive. The state must involve itself in the accumulation process, but it must either mystify its policies by calling them something that they are not, or it must try to conceal them (e.g. by making them into administrative, not political, issues).

Our second premise is that the fiscal crisis can be understood only in terms of the basic Marxist economic categories (adapted to the problems taken up here). State expenditures have a twofold character corresponding to the capitalist state's two basic functions: social capital and social expenses. *Social capital* is expenditures required for profitable private accumulation; it is indirectly productive (in Marxist terms, social capital indirectly expands surplus value). There are two kinds of social capital: social investment and social consumption (in Marxist terms, social constant capital and social variable capital). [ . . . ] *Social investment* consists of projects and services that increase the productivity of a given amount of labour power and, other factors being equal, increase the rate of profit. A good example is state-financed industrial-development parks. *Social consumption* consists of projects and services that lower the reproduction costs of labour and, other factors being equal, increase the rate of profit. An example of this is social insurance, which expands the reproductive powers of the workforce while simultaneously lowering labour costs. The second category, *social expenses*, consists of projects and services which are required to maintain social harmony – to fulfil the state's 'legitimization' function. They are not even indirectly productive. [ . . . ] The best example is the welfare system, which is designed chiefly to keep social peace among unemployed workers. (The costs of politically repressed populations in revolt would also constitute a part of social expenses.)

Because of the dual and contradictory character of the capitalist state, nearly every state agency is involved in the accumulation and legitimization functions, and nearly every state expenditure has this twofold character. For example, some education spending constitutes social capital (e.g. teachers and equipment needed to reproduce and expand workforce technical and skill levels), whereas other outlays constitute social expenses (e.g. salaries of campus policemen). To take another example, the main purpose of some transfer payments (e.g. social insurance) is to reproduce the workforce, whereas the purpose of others (e.g. income subsidies to the poor) is to pacify and control the surplus population. The national income accounts lump the various categories of state spending together. (The state does not analyse its budget in class terms.) Clearly, the different categories cannot be separated if each budget item is not examined.

Furthermore, precisely because of the social character of social capital and social expenses, nearly every state expenditure serves these two (or more) purposes simultaneously, so that few state outlays can be classified unambiguously. For example, freeways move workers to and from work and are therefore items of social consumption, but they also transport commercial freight and are therefore a form of social investment. And, when used for either purpose, they may be considered forms of social capital. However, the Pentagon also needs freeways; therefore they in part constitute social expenses. Despite this complex social character of state outlays we can determine the political-economic forces served by any budgetary decision, and thus the main purpose (or purposes) of each budgetary item. [ . . . ]

The first basic thesis presented here is that the growth of the state sector and state spending is functioning increasingly as the basis for the growth of the monopoly sector and total production. Conversely, it is argued that the growth of state spending and state programmes is the result of the growth of the monopoly industries. In other words, the growth of the state is both a cause and effect of the expansion of monopoly capital. [. . .]

More specifically, the socialization of the costs of social investment and social consumption capital increases over time and increasingly is needed for profitable accumulation by monopoly capital. The general reason is that the increase in the social character of production (specialization, division of labour, interdependency, the growth of new social forms of capital such as education, etc.) either prohibits or renders unprofitable the private accumulation of constant and variable capital. The growth of the monopoly sector is irrational in the sense that it is accompanied by unemployment, poverty, economic stagnation and so on. To ensure mass loyalty and maintain its legitimacy, the state must meet various demands of those who suffer the 'costs' of economic growth. [. . .]

It might help to compare our approach with traditional economic theory. Bourgeois economists have shown that increases in private consumption beget increases in private investment via the accelerator effect. In turn, increases in private investment beget increases in private consumption via the multiplier effect. Similarly, we argue that greater social investment and social consumption spending generate greater private investment and private consumption spending, which in turn generate surplus capital (surplus productive capacity and a surplus population) and a larger volume of social expenses. Briefly, the supply of social capital creates the demand for social expenses. In effect, we work with a model of expanded reproduction (or a model of the economy as a whole) which is generalized to take into account the socialization of constant and variable capital costs and the costs of social expenses. The impact of the budget depends on the volume and indirect productivity of social capital and the volume of social expenses. On the one hand, social capital outlays indirectly increase productive capacity and simultaneously increase aggregate demand. On the other hand, social expense outlays do not increase productive capacity, although they do expand aggregate demand. Whether the growth of productive capacity runs ahead or behind the growth of demand thus depends on the composition of the state budget. In this way, we can see that the theory of economic growth depends on class and political analyses of the determinants of the budget.

This view contrasts sharply with modern conservative thought, which asserts that the state sector grows at the expense of private industry. We argue that the growth of the state sector is indispensable to the expansion of private industry, particularly monopoly industries. Our thesis also contrasts sharply with a basic tenet of modern liberal thought – that the expansion of monopoly industries inhibits the growth of the state sector. The fact of the matter is that the growth of monopoly capital generates increased expansion of social expenses. In sum, the greater the growth of social capital, the greater the growth of the monopoly sector. And the greater the growth of the monopoly sector, the greater the state's expenditures on social expenses of production.

The second basic thesis in this study is that the accumulation of social capital and social expenses is a contradictory process which creates tendencies toward economic, social and political crises. [ . . . ] Two separate but related lines of analysis are explored.

First, we argue that although the state has socialized more and more capital costs, the social surplus (including profits) continues to be appropriated privately. The socialization of costs and the private appropriation of profits creates a fiscal crisis, or 'structural gap', between state expenditures and state revenues. The result is a tendency for state expenditures to increase more rapidly than the means of financing them. While the accumulation of social capital indirectly increases total production and society's surplus and thus in principle appears to underwrite the expansion of social expenses, large monopoly-sector corporations and unions strongly resist the appropriation of this surplus for new social capital or social expense outlays. [ . . . ]

Second, we argue that the fiscal crisis is exacerbated by the private appropriation of state power for particularistic ends. A host of 'special interests' – corporations, industries, regional and other business interests – make claims on the budget for various kinds of social investment. [ . . . ] (These claims are politically processed in ways that must either be legitimated or obscured from public view.) Organized labour and workers generally make various claims for different kinds of social consumption, and the unemployed and poor (together with businessmen in financial trouble) stake their claims for expanded social expenses. Few if any claims are co-ordinated by the market. Most are processed by the political system and are won or lost as a result of political struggle. Precisely because the accumulation of social capital and social expenses occurs within a political framework, there is a great deal of waste, duplication and overlapping of state projects and services. Some claims conflict and cancel one another out. Others are mutually contradictory in a variety of ways. The accumulation of social capital and social expenses is a highly irrational process from the standpoint of administrative coherence, fiscal stability and potentially profitable private capital accumulation.

**Note**

From J. O'Connor, *The Fiscal Crisis of the State*, New York, St Martin's Press, 1973, pp. 6–11.

# Some Contradictions of the Modern Welfare State

## *Claus Offe*

The welfare state has served as the major peace formula of advanced capitalist democracies for the period following the Second World War. This peace formula consists, first, in the explicit obligation of the state apparatus to provide assistance and support (either in money or in kind) to those citizens who suffer from specific needs and risks which are characteristic of the market society; such assistance is provided as legal claims granted to the citizens. Second, the welfare state is based on the recognition of the formal role of labour unions both in collective bargaining and the formation of public policy. Both of these structural components of the welfare state are considered to limit and mitigate class conflict, to balance the asymmetrical power relation of labour and capital, and thus to overcome the condition of disruptive struggle and contradiction that was the most prominent feature of pre-welfare state, or liberal, capitalism. In sum, the welfare state has been celebrated throughout the postwar period as the political solution to societal contradictions.

Until [the 1970s], this seemed to be the converging view of political elites both in countries in which the welfare state is fully developed (e.g. Great Britain, Sweden) as well as in those where it is still an incompletely realized model. Political conflict in these latter societies, such as the USA, was centred not on the basic desirability and functional indispensability, but on the pace and modalities of the implementation of the welfare state model.

This was true, with very minor exceptions, up to the mid-1970s. From that point on we see that in many capitalist societies this established peace formula becomes itself the object of doubts, fundamental critique and political conflict. It appears that the most widely accepted device of political problem-solving has itself become problematic, and that, at any rate, the unquestioning confidence in the welfare state and its future expansion has rapidly vanished. It is to these doubts and criticisms that I will direct my attention in the following remarks. The point to start with is the observation that the almost universally accepted model for creating a measure of social peace and harmony in European postwar societies has itself become the source of new contradictions and political divisions in the 1970s.

Historically, the welfare state has been the combined outcome of a variety of factors which change in composition from country to country: Social Democratic reformism, Christian socialism, enlightened conservative political and economic elites and large industrial unions. They fought for and conceded comprehensive compulsory insurance schemes, labour protection legislation, minimum wages, the expansion of health and education facilities and state-subsidized housing, as well as the recognition of unions as the legitimate economic and political representatives of labour. These continuous developments in Western societies were often dramatically accelerated in a context of intense social conflict and crisis, particularly under war and postwar conditions. The accomplishments, which were won under conditions of war and postwar periods, were regularly maintained; added to them were the innovations that could be introduced in periods of prosperity and growth. In the light of the Keynesian doctrine of economic policy, the welfare state came to be seen not so much as a burden imposed upon the economy, but as a built-in economic and political stabilizer which could help to regenerate the forces of economic growth and prevent the economy from spiralling downward into deep recessions. Thus, a variety of quite heterogeneous ends (ranging from reactionary preemptive strikes against the working class movement in the case of Bismarck, to socialist reformism in the case of the Weimar Social Democrats; from the social-political consolidation of war and defence economies, to the stabilization of the business cycle) adopted identical institutional means which today make up the welfare state. It is exactly its multi-functional character, its ability to serve many conflicting ends and strategies simultaneously which made the political arrangement of the welfare state so attractive to a broad alliance of heterogeneous forces. But it is equally true that the very diversity of the forces that inaugurated and supported the welfare state could not be accommodated forever within the institutional framework which today appears to come increasingly under attack. The machinery of class compromise has itself become the object of class conflict.

## The Attack from the Right

The sharp economic recession of the mid-1970s [gave] rise to a renaissance of neo-*laissez-faire* and monetarist economic doctrines of equal intellectual and political power. These doctrines amount to a fundamental critique of the welfare state, which is seen to be the illness of which it pretends to be the cure. Rather than effectively harmonizing the conflicts of a market society, it exacerbates them and prevents the forces of social peace and progress (namely the forces of the market place) to function properly and beneficially. This is said to be so for two major reasons. First, the welfare state apparatus imposes a burden of taxation and regulation upon capital which amounts to a *disincentive to investment*. Second, the welfare state grants claims, entitlements and collective power positions to workers and unions which amount to a *disincentive to work*, or at least to work as hard and productively as they would be forced to under the reign of unfettered market forces. Taken together, these two effects lead into a dynamic of declining growth and increased expectations, of economic demand overload (inflation) as well as political demand overload (ungovernability) which can less and less be satisfied by the available output.

The reactionary political uses of this analysis are obvious, but it may well be that the truth of the analysis itself is greater than the desirability of its practical conclusions. Although the democratic left has often measured the former by the latter, the two deserve at least a separate evaluation. In my view, at least, the above analysis is not so much false in what it says as in what it remains silent about.

To take up the first point of the conservative analysis: isn't it true that under conditions of declining growth rates and vehement competition on domestic and international markets, individual capitalists (at least those firms which do not enjoy the privileges of the monopolistic sector) have many good reasons to consider the prospects for investment and profits bleak, and to blame the welfare state, which imposes social security taxes and a great variety of regulations on them, for reducing profitability even further? Isn't it true that the power position of unions, which in turn is based on rights they have won through industrial relations, collective bargaining and other laws, is great enough as to make an increasing number of industrial producers unprofitable or to force them to seek investment opportunities abroad? And isn't it also true that capitalist firms will make investment (and hence employment) decisions according to criteria of expected profitability, and that they consequently will fail to invest when long-term profitability is considered unattractive by them, thus causing an aggregate relative decline in the production output of the economy?

No one would deny that there are causes of declining growth rates and capitalists' failure to invest which have nothing to do with the impact of the welfare state upon business, but which are rather to be looked for in inherent crisis tendencies of the capitalist economy such as overaccumulation, the business cycle or uncontrolled technical change. But even so, it still might make sense to alleviate the hardship imposed upon capital and therefore, by definition, upon the rest of society (within the confines of a capitalist society), by dropping some of the burdens and constraints of the welfare state. This, of course, is exactly what most proponents of this argument are suggesting as a practical consequence. But after all, as the fairly compelling logic of the argument continues, who benefits from the operation of a welfare state that undermines and eventually destroys the production system upon which it has to rely in order to make its own promises come true? Doesn't a kind of 'welfare' become merely nominal and worthless anyway if it punishes capital by a high burden of costs and hence everyone else by inflation, unemployment or both? In my view, the valuable insight to be gained from the type of analysis I have just described is this: the welfare state, rather than being a separate and autonomous source of well-being which provides incomes and services as citizen rights, is itself highly dependent upon the prosperity and continued profitability of the economy. While being designed to be a cure to some ills of capitalist accumulation, the nature of the illness is such that it may force the patient to refrain from using the cure.

A conceivable objection to the above argument would be that capitalists and conservative political elites exaggerate the harm imposed upon them by the welfare state arrangements. To be sure, in the political game they have good tactical reasons to make the welfare state burden appear more intolerable than it really is. The question boils down then to what we mean, and how we measure 'reality' in this context. In answering this question we must remember that the power position of private investors includes the power to *define* reality. That is to say, whatever they *consider* an intolerable burden *is* an intolerable burden which will *in fact* lead to a declining propensity to invest, at least as long as they can expect to effectively reduce welfare-state-related costs by applying such economic sanctions. The debate about whether or not the welfare state is 'really' squeezing profits is thus purely academic because investors are in a position to *create* the reality and the effects of 'profit squeeze'.

The second major argument of the conservative analysis postulates that the effect of the welfare state is a disincentive to work. 'Labour does not work!' was one of the slogans in the campaign that brought Mrs Thatcher into power. But again, the analytical content of the argument must be carefully separated from the political uses to which it is put. And again, this analytical argument can, often contrary to the intention of its proponents, be read in a way that does make a lot of empirical sense. For instance, there is little doubt that elaborate labour protection legislation puts workers in a position to resist practices of exploitation that would be applied, as a rule, in the absence of such regulations. Powerful and recognized unions can in fact obtain wage increases in excess of productivity increases. And extensive social security provisions make it easier, at least for some workers for some of the time, to avoid undesirable jobs. Large-scale unemployment insurance covering most of the working population makes unemployment less undesirable for many workers and thus partially obstructs the reserve army mechanism. In sum, the welfare state has made the exploitation of labour more complicated and less predictable. On the other hand, as the welfare state imposes regulations and rights upon the labour-capital exchange that goes on in production, while leaving the authority structure and the property relations of production untouched, it is hardly surprising to see that the workers are not, as a rule, intrinsically motivated to work as productively as they possibly can. In other words, the welfare state maintains the control of capital over production, and thus the basic source of industrial and class conflict between labour and capital; but it by no means establishes anything resembling 'workers control'. At the same time, it strengthens workers' potential for resistance against capital's control, the net effect being that an unchanged conflict is fought out with means that have changed in favour of labour. Exploitative production relations coexist with expanded possibilities to resist, escape and mitigate exploitation. While the *reason* for struggle remained unchanged, the *means* of struggle increased for the workers. It is not surprising to see that this condition undermines the work ethic, or at least requires more costly and less reliable strategies to enforce such ethic.

My point so far has been that the two key arguments of the liberal-conservative analysis are valid to a large extent, contrary to what critics from the left have often argued. The basic fault in this analysis has less to do with what it explicitly states than with what it leaves out of its consideration. Every worthwhile political theory has to answer two questions: first, what is the desirable form of the organization of society and state, and how can we demonstrate that it is at all workable, i.e. consistent with our basic normative and factual assumptions about social life? This is the problem of defining a consistent *model* or goal of transformation. Second, how do we get there? This is the problem of identifying the dynamic forces and *strategies* that could bring about the transformation.

The conservative analysis of the welfare state fails on both counts. To start with the latter problem, it is extremely hard today in Western Europe to conceive of a promising political strategy that would aim at even partially eliminating the established institutional components of the welfare state, to say nothing about its wholesale abolition. That is to say, the welfare state has, in a certain sense, become an irreversible structure, the abolition of which would require nothing less than the abolition of political democracy and the unions, as well as fundamental changes in the party system. A political force that could bring about such dramatic changes is nowhere visible as a significant factor (right-wing middle-class populist movements that occasionally spring up in some countries notwithstanding). Moreover, political opinion research has shown that the fiercest advocates of *laissez-faire* capitalism and economic individualism show marked differences between their *general* ideological outlook and their willingness to have *special* transfers, subsidies and social security schemes abandoned from which they *personally* derive benefits. Thus, in the absence of a powerful ideological and organizational undercurrent in Western politics (such as a neo-fascist or authoritarian one), the vision of overcoming the welfare state and resurrecting a 'healthy' market economy is not much more than the politically impotent daydream of some ideologues of the old middle class. This class is nowhere strong enough to effect, as the examples of Mrs Thatcher and Ronald Reagan demonstrate, more than marginal alterations to an institutional scheme that they had to accept as given when taking office.

Even more significant, however, is the second failure of the conservative analysis, its failure to demonstrate that advanced capitalism *minus* the welfare state would actually be a workable model. The reasons why it is not, and consequently why the neo-*laissez-faire* ideology would be a very dangerous cure, *if* it could be administered, are fairly obvious. In the absence of large-scale state-subsidized housing, public education and health services, and extensive compulsory social security schemes, the working of an industrial economy would be inconceivable. Given the conditions and requirements of urbanization, large-scale concentration of labour power in industrial production plants, rapid technical, economic and regional change, the reduced ability of the family to cope with the difficulties of life in industrial society, the securalization of the moral order, and the quantitative reduction and growing dependence of the propertied middle classes, all of which are well known characteristics of capitalist social structures, the sudden disappearance of the welfare state would leave the system in a state of exploding conflict and anarchy. The embarrassing secret of the welfare state is that, while its impact upon capitalist accumulation may well become destructive (as the conservative analysis so emphatically demonstrates), its abolition would be plainly disruptive (a fact that is systematically ignored by the conservative critics). The contradiction is that while capitalism cannot coexist *with* the welfare state, neither can it exist *without* the welfare state. This is exactly the condition to which we refer when using the concept 'contradiction'. The flaw of the conservative analysis is in the one-sided emphasis it puts on the first side of this contradiction, and its silence about the second one.

This basic contradiction of the capitalist welfare state could of course be thought to be a mere dilemma which then would be solved or managed by a circumspect balancing of the two components. This, however, would presuppose two things, both of which are highly uncertain: first, that there *is* something like an 'optimum point' at which the order-maintaining functions of the welfare state are preserved while its disruptive effects are avoided; and second, if so, that political procedures and administrative practices will be sufficiently 'rational' to accomplish this precarious balance. Before I consider the prospects for this solution, let me first summarize some elements of the contending socialist critique of the welfare state.

## The Critique from the Socialist Left

Although it would be nonsensical to deny that the struggle for labour protection legislation, expanded social services, social security and union recognition which has been led by the working-class movement for over a century now, and which has brought substantial improvements to the living conditions of most wage earners, the socialist critique of the welfare state is nevertheless a fundamental one. It can be summarized in three points which we will consider in turn: the welfare state is said to be (1) ineffective and inefficient, (2) repressive and (3) conditioning a false ideological understanding of social and political reality within the working class. In sum, it is a device to stabilize rather than a step in the transformation of capitalist society.

In spite of the undeniable gains in the living conditions of wage earners, the institutional structure of the welfare state has done little or nothing to alter the income distribution between the two principal classes of labour and capital. The huge machinery of redistribution does not work in a vertical direction but in a horizontal direction, namely *within* the class of wage earners. A further aspect of its ineffectiveness is that the welfare state does not *eliminate the causes* of individual contingencies and needs (such as work-related diseases, the disorganization of cities by the capitalist real estate market, the obsolescence of skills, unemployment, etc.) but *compensates for* some of the *consequences* of such events (by the provision of health services and health insurance, housing subsidies, training and retraining facilities, unemployment benefits and the like). Generally speaking, the kind of social intervention most typical of the welfare state is always 'too late', and hence its *ex post facto* measures are more costly and less effective than a more 'causal' type of intervention would allow them to be. This is a generally recognized dilemma of social policy making, the standard answer to which is the recommendation to adopt more 'preventive' strategies. It is also recognized that effective prevention would mean interference with the prerogatives of investors and management, i.e. the sphere of the market and private property which the welfare state has only very limited legal and *de facto* powers to regulate.

A further argument pointing to the ineffectiveness of the welfare state emphasizes the constant threat to which social policies and social services are exposed due to the fiscal crisis of the state, which in turn is a reflection of both cyclical and structural discontinuities of the process of accumulation. All West European countries [ . . . ] experienced a sharp economic recession in the mid-1970s, and we know of many examples of social policy expenditure cuts in response to the fiscal consequences of this recession. But even if the absolute and relative rise of social policy expenditures continues uninterrupted as a percentage of GNP, it is by no means certain, as Ian Gough and others before him have argued, that increases in the expenditures are paralleled by increases in real 'welfare'. The dual fallacy, known in technical literature as the 'spending service cliché', is this: first, a marginal increase in expenditures must not necessarily correspond to a marginal increment in the 'output' of the welfare state apparatus; it may well be used up in feeding the bureaucratic machinery itself. Second, even if the output (say of health services) *is* increased, a still larger increase in the level of risks and needs (or a qualitative change of these) may occur on the part of the clients or recipients of such services, so as to make the net effect negative.

The bureaucratic and professional form through which the welfare state dispenses its services is increasingly seen to be a source of its own inefficiency. Bureaucracies absorb more resources and provide less services than other democratic and decentralized structures could. The reason why the bureaucratic form of administering social services is maintained in spite of its inefficiency and ineffectiveness must therefore have to do with the social control function exercised by centralized welfare bureaucracies. This analysis leads to the critique of the *repressiveness* of the welfare state, its social control aspect. Such repressiveness, in the view of the critics, is indicated by the fact that in order to qualify for the benefits and services of the welfare state, the client must not only prove his or her 'need', but must also be a 'deserving' client, that is, one who complies to the dominant economic, political and cultural standards and norms of the society. The heavier the needs, the stricter these requirements tend to be defined. Only if, for instance, the unemployed are willing to keep themselves available for any alternative employment (often considerably inferior to the job they have lost) that is made available to them by employment agencies, are they entitled to unemployment benefits; and the claim for welfare payments to the poor is everywhere made conditional upon their conformity to standards of behaviour which the better-to-do strata of the population are perfectly free to violate. In these and other cases, the welfare state can be looked upon as an exchange transaction in which material benefits for the needy are traded for their submissive recognition of the 'moral order' of the society which generates such need. One important precondition for obtaining the services of the welfare state is the ability of the individual to comply with the routines and requirements of welfare bureaucracies and service organizations, an ability which is often inversely correlated to need itself.

A third major aspect of the socialist critique of the welfare state is its *politico-ideological* control function. The welfare state is seen not only as the source of benefits and services, but at the same time the source of false conceptions about historical realities which have damaging effects on working-class consciousness, organization and struggle. The welfare state creates the false image of two separated spheres of working-class life.

On the one side is the sphere of work, the economy, production and 'primary' income distribution. On the other is the sphere of citizenship, the state, reproduction and 'secondary' distribution. This division of the socio-political world obscures the causal and functional links that exist between the two, and thus prevents the formation of a political understanding of society as a coherent totality to be changed. That is to say, the structural arrangements of the welfare state tend to make people ignore or forget that the needs and contingencies which the welfare state responds to are themselves constituted, directly or indirectly, in the sphere of work and production. The welfare state itself is materially and institutionally constrained by the dynamics of the sphere of production, and a reliable conception of social security does therefore presuppose not only the expansion of citizen rights, but of workers' rights in the process of production. Contrary to such insights, which are part of the analytical starting-points of any conceivable socialist strategy of societal transformation, the inherent symbolic indoctrination of the welfare state suggests the ideas of class co-operation, the disjunction of economic and political struggles, and an ill-based confidence in an ever continuing cycle of economic growth and social security.

## The Welfare State and Political Change

What emerges from this discussion of the analysis of the welfare state by the right and the left are three points on which the liberal conservative and the socialist critic exhibit somewhat surprising parallels.

First, contrary to the ideological consensus that flourished in some of the most advanced welfare states throughout the 1950s and 1960s, the welfare state is no longer believed to be the promising and permanently valid answer to the problems of the socio-political order of advanced capitalist economies. Critics in both camps have become more vociferous and fundamental in their negative appraisal of welfare state arrangements. Second, neither of the two approaches to the welfare state could or would be prepared, in the best interests of their respective clientele, to abandon the welfare state, as it performs essential and indispensable functions both for the accumulation process as well as for the social and economic well-being of the working class. Third, while there is, on the conservative side, neither a consistent theory nor a realistic strategy about the social order of a non-welfare state (as I have argued before), it is evident that the situation is not much better on the left where one could possibly speak of a consistent theory of socialism, but certainly not of an agreed upon and realistic strategy for its construction. In the absence of the latter, the welfare state remains a theoretically contested, though in reality firmly entrenched fact, of the social order of advanced capitalist societies.

In short, it appears that the welfare state, while being contested both from the right and the left, will not be easily replaced by a conservative or progressive alternative.

[. . .]

## Note

From *Critical Social Policy*, 2, 2, 1982, pp. 7–14.

# The Power Resources Model

## *Walter Korpi*

*Walter Korpi argues that most modern social scientific accounts of social structure and change have relied upon one of three models: a 'pluralist-industrial' model which emphasizes the emergence in developed industrial societies of a plurality of competing interests and social groupings whose relations are mediated through largely consensual societal institutions; a 'Marxist-Leninist' model which insists that Western societies are still essentially riven by those forms of class struggle originally identified by Marx and in which the state acts in the interests of capital; and a neo-corporatist account in which certain (economically defined) interests have privileged access to the state and in which collective action is negotiated at an elite level between the state and these privileged social actors. Here he offers his own alternative account of a 'power resources model'. (Eds)*

### Power Resources

The stability implied in the pluralist industrial model of society rests on the assumption that the distribution of power resources between various groups and collectivities in the capitalist democracies is potentially equal. Schmitter's assumption of relative stability of neo-corporatist arrangements appears to imply an unequal yet fairly stable distribution of power resources. The Leninist interpretation of Marx similarly implies an unequal but stable power distribution in the capitalist democracies. Such assumptions must be questioned. One way of elucidating the distribution of power is to analyse what instruments and resources of power different groups and collectivities in society have at their disposal in the interaction which takes place between them over long periods of time.

What, then, are power resources? Power resources are characteristics which provide actors – individuals or collectivities – with the ability to punish or reward other actors. These resources can be described in terms of a variety of dimensions. Power resources can thus vary with regard to domain, which refers to the number of people who are receptive to the particular type of rewards and penalties. They can also differ in terms of scope – the various kinds of situation in which they can be used. A third important dimension is the degree of scarcity of a power resource of a particular type. Furthermore, power resources can vary in terms of centrality; i.e. they can be more or less essential to people in their daily lives. They also differ with regard to how easily they are convertible into other resources. The extent to which a power resource can be concentrated is a crucial dimension. Of relevance are also the costs involved in using a power resource and in its mobilization, i.e. in making it ready for use. Power resources can furthermore differ in the extent to which they can be used to initiate action or are limited to responses to actions by others.

It is important to realize that power resources need not be used or activated in order to have consequences for the actions of other people. An actor with the ability to reward or punish need thus not always do so to influence others. Since every activation of power resources entails costs, it actually lies in the interests of power holders to increase efficiency in the deployment of power resources. This can be achieved through what we may call the investment of power resources. Thus, power resources can be invested through the creation of structures for decision-making and conflict regulation, whereby decisions can be made on a routine basis and in accordance with given principles. Investments of power resources can be made in institutions for conflict resolution such as laws, ordinances and bureaucracies, in technologies, in community and national planning, and in the dissemination of ideologies.

Some types of power resource can be described as basic in the sense that they in themselves provide the capacity to reward or to punish other actors. Through processes of investment, from basic power resources actors can derive new types of power resource. These derived power resources, however, ultimately depend on the basic power resources for their effectiveness. The distinction between basic and derived power resources is not easy to make but appears fruitful. It indicates, for instance, that power resources such as ideologies can be seen as ultimately based on resources which provide the capability to apply positive or negative sanctions.

Let us now look briefly at the characteristics of some of the more important basic power resources in Western societies. Among resources familiar to students of power, means of violence have traditionally been considered important. In terms of the aforementioned dimensions, means of violence have a large domain, wide scope and high concentration potential, as well as a relatively high convertibility. Although the legitimate use of violence is typically reserved for the state, resources for violence are not scarce. Their essential drawback is the high costs associated with their use.

Two types of power resource are central and their dimensions important for the theoretical controversy between pluralists and Marxist social scientists. The first type of power resource consists of capital and control over the means of production. The second type is what economists often call 'human capital', i.e. labour power, education and occupational skills. The pluralist approach assumes that persons possessing control over capital and the means of production do not have appreciably greater power resources at their disposal than persons with only human capital. Yet in terms of the aforementioned dimensions, capital and control over the means of production are power resources which differ drastically from human capital, making parity between them extremely problematic.

As power resources, capital and the means of production have a large domain, wide scope and high concentration potential, as well as high scarcity and convertibility. The costs involved in mobilizing and using these resources are relatively low. Furthermore, control over the means of production has high centrality, since it affects people's livelihood. Capital is also typically used to initiate action.

When regarded as a power resource, human capital is characterized by serious limitations. Usually it has a fairly small domain and narrow scope. Since everybody has some of it, human capital is generally not a highly scarce resource. Where labour power is offered on the labour market, its value depends on demand from capital, and its ability to initiate action is limited. Human capital has low convertibility and a low concentration potential. In an era of mass education, formal training beyond a certain level can at times yield diminishing returns. To be effective, the human capital of various individuals and groups must therefore be co-ordinated on a broad basis. This requires investments in organizations for collective action and hence fairly large mobilization costs.

In Western countries, most human capital is utilized in the labour market. Economists often discuss the labour market as one of supply and demand where commodities are bought and sold. But human labour power is a very special commodity, since it is inseparable from its owner. Thus it cannot be sold; that would be slave trade. Labour can be hired only for a certain time, and the buyer acquires the right to make use of the seller's labour capacity during hours of work. Once the employment contract has been concluded, the owner of human capital cannot shed it like an overcoat but must deliver his labour power at the workplace, and on the job must personally subordinate himself to the directives of management. Thus the system of wage labour creates relationships of authority and subordination among people and the basis for a division into classes.

The possibility of increasing the effectiveness of the power resources of individuals through collective action provides a rational explanation for the origin of unions to promote the interests of wage-earners in disputes with employers. It also offers an explanation of why wage-earners organize themselves into political parties. As the growth of 'juristic persons' and corporate actors during the past centuries indicates, other actors also have organized for collective action to increase the efficiency of their power resources. Alongside capital and control over the means of production, organizations to co-ordinate wage-earners' actions – primarily trade unions and political parties – belong to the strategically important power resources in the capitalist democracies.

Are, then, either of these types of strategic power resources – on the one hand control over capital and the means of production, and on the other hand control over human capital co-ordinated through the organizations of wage-earners – dominant in the capitalist democracies? Let us look more closely at the clearest confrontation between them, viz. at the workplace. Control over the means of production forms the basis of management's right of command over labour. It is capital which hires labour, not labour which hires capital. The subordination of labour is, however, a matter of degree inasmuch as the prerogatives of the representatives of capital have been restricted by legislation and by collective bargaining, the effectiveness of which in turn is influenced by the market situation. The prerogatives of management still confirm that, in terms of power resources, the wage-earners in these societies are in a position of inferiority *vis-à-vis* capital. The maintenance of a system of authority and subordination based on control over the means of production is a major problem confronting the dominant groups in the capitalist democracies.

I agree with the pluralist view on power distribution in the capitalist democracies to the extent that in these societies power is probably more widely shared than in other contemporary societies with different political and economic systems. However, I object to the next and crucial step in pluralist thought: that the assumed equal opportunities to mobilize power has generated a distribution of power resources in these societies that is sufficiently equal to no longer warrant our attention. If we view the development of wage-earners' collective organizations as essential for the effectiveness with which their 'human capital' can be applied in the conflicts of interest with capital, it appears evident that the distribution of power resources in Western societies can vary considerably over time as well as between countries. Once we drop the assumptions of the distribution of power resources implicit in the pluralist, neo-corporatist and neo-Leninist models, a host of interesting questions concerning distributive processes, social consciousness and patterns of conflict, as well as institutional functioning and stability, come to the fore.

## Social Change

In Western societies variations in the difference in power resources between labour and business interests, along with their allied groups, can be expected to have a variety of consequences. This difference can influence:

1 the distributive processes in the society;
2 the social consciousness of the citizens;
3 the level and patterns of conflicts in the society; and
4 the shaping and functioning of social institutions.

The processes of distribution in society can be viewed as exchange relations where, for example, the right to control labour power is exchanged for wages. These exchanges, however, need be neither in accordance with principles of equity nor mutually balanced. Instead, we must assume that the distribution of power resources influences the outcomes of the exchange processes and consequently the degree of inequality in society. Stronger groups thus will often get the 'lion's share' of what is to be distributed. Power resources, which can be regarded as stocks of values, thus influence the flow of values between individuals and collectivities.

But the distribution of power resources is also critical for the social consciousness and levels of aspiration of citizens as well as for the way in which they define their interests. Perceptions of what is just, fair and reasonable *vis-à-vis* other groups of citizens are largely dependent upon the power relations between these groups. Weak groups often learn, or are taught to accept, circumstances which stronger groups would consider unjust. Strong actors also tend to develop more long-range definitions of their interests than weaker groups.

The distribution of power resources is of major importance for the levels and patterns of conflict in society. Even if a weak group feels that an exchange relationship is unjust, the group may have to accept the terms of exchange because it lacks better alternatives and opposition may lead to reprisals of various kinds. But when the power resources of actors increase, they can offer resistance in situations which they previously had to accept. They can also attempt to change conditions which they find unjust. The distribution of power resources and its changes thus influences the levels of conflicts in society. Since changes in the distribution of power resources also affect the alternatives for action open to the actors, they can be expected to influence the actors' strategies of conflict and thus the pattern of conflict between them.

From this perspective, changes in the distribution of power resources between different collectivities or classes can thus be assumed to be of central importance for social change. Such changes will affect the levels of aspiration of the actors and their capacity to maintain or to change existing social structures. Social change can be expected to emerge from various types of bargaining, but will sometimes involve manifest conflicts. Since open conflicts are costly to all parties, it is in the interests of the actors to limit their length and frequency. Through settlements following bargaining and/or manifest conflicts, the terms of exchange between the parties are thus moulded.

Where parties are involved in long-term interactions, settlements between them generally tend to involve different types of compromise. Such compromises may lead to the creation of new social institutions or changes in the functioning of existing institutions. Social institutions and arrangements related, for example, to processes of distribution and decision-making can thus be seen as outcomes of recurrent conflicts of interest, where the parties concerned have invested their power resources in order to secure favourable outcomes. Such institutions thus need not be viewed as neutral or objective arrangements for conflict resolution. Instead, the ways in which they were created and function reflect the distribution of power in society. When the distribution of power resources is altered, the form and functioning of such institutions and arrangements are also likely to change.

The distribution of power resources between the major collectivities or classes in society will thus shape people's actions in a variety of ways. These actions, in turn, will affect social structure as well as the distribution of power. A continuous interplay between human action and the structure of society arises. The approach outlined here comes close to the perspective of Marx, according to which structural change is the result of people, through co-operation or conflict, seeking solutions to what they define as important social problems. The definitions of social problems are, however, not objectively given but depend largely on the distribution of power resources in society. The alternative solutions considered and ultimately chosen are also affected by the power distribution.

In this perspective the state can be conceived of as a set of institutional structures which have emerged in the struggles between classes and interest groups in a society. The crucial aspect of this set of institutions is that they determine the ways in which decision-making on behalf of the whole society can legitimately be made and enforced. The state must not, however, be seen as an actor in itself, or as a pure instrument to be used by whichever group that has it under its control. While the institutional structures and the state can be used to affect, for example, distributive processes in the society, these structures also affect the way in which power resources can be mobilized and are, in turn, affected by the use of power resources.

Conflicts of interest between different groups or collectivities continuously generate bargaining, manifest conflicts and settlements. At some points, however, the settlements are the outcomes of important changes in the distribution of power resources and are of such a nature that they significantly affect institutional arrangements and strategies of conflict for long periods of time. In connection with such settlements or 'historical compromises', the patterns and conceptions of 'normal politics' change.

In the capitalist countries, the acceptance of the wage-earners' right to organize in unions and parties and to participate in political decision-making via universal and equal suffrage are examples of such historical settlements. The winning of political democracy was the result of a decrease in the disadvantage of working-class power resources brought about through organization and often through alliances with middle-class groups. It limited the legitimate use of means of repression by the state and opened up legitimate avenues for the citizens to participate in the decision-making of state organs. In many Western countries, the historical settlements concerning political democracy came around the First World War. These institutional changes significantly affected the patterns of interest conflicts in the years to come.

## Societal Bargaining

With the exception of setbacks in countries like Italy, Germany and Spain, during the inter-war period the strength of the unions and working-class parties increased in the Western nations. In the period after the Second World War this trend has by and large continued. Through increasing levels of organization the wage-earners have considerably strengthened their bargaining position in the distributive conflicts in the capitalist democracies. This has affected strategies of conflict and patterns of institutional arrangements. It is my hypothesis that the tripartite 'neo-corporatist' institutional arrangements largely reflect the compromises and settlements generated by the decreasing differences in the distribution of power resources between wage-earners and representatives of capital and allied groups in these countries. The decreasing disadvantage in wage-earner power resources has generated institutional arrangements and practices in reaching settlements involving major interest groups, which we can describe as 'societal bargaining'. The notion of bargaining implies that the outcome of the interaction cannot be predetermined.

The choice of the term 'societal bargaining' to describe arrangements and practices which others have termed 'corporatism' is made not only to avoid a word which many have found hard to swallow. In my view, societal bargaining of the tripartite type that was developed in some countries of Western Europe during the postwar period clearly differs from traditional corporatist arrangements. It is therefore misleading to regard the two as more or less functional equivalents in the way several writers on neo-corporatism have done.

Traditional state corporatism, for example in Italy, Germany and Spain, must be seen as a successful attack on the working class and its organizations in a situation where the power gap between classes was very large. State corporatism was used to widen that gap. The institutional arrangements of societal bargaining, however, have come about in situations where the disadvantage in power resources of the wage-earners is much smaller than where the traditional 'state corporatist' solutions have been practised. Societal bargaining involving the organizations of the wage-earners must, by and large, be seen as reflecting an increasingly strongly organized working class. Whether societal bargaining benefits the wage-earners or not is an empirical question, which cannot be settled through definitions. We must assume, instead, that its long-term as well as the short-term outcomes can vary and are dependent on the distribution of power resources between the parties. From the power resource perspective the institutional arrangements of societal bargaining (i.e. the 'neo-corporatist' institutions) appear as intervening variables between, on the one hand, the distribution of power resources in society and, on the other hand, the pattern and outcome of distributive conflicts.

The spread of societal bargaining in Western nations during the postwar period is the result of an important shift in the lines separating decision-making through markets and politics. Since the breakthrough of political democracy, the relative importance of these two forms of decision-making has been largely dependent on the contest between two different types of power resource: the (at least in principle) equally distributed political resources, and the highly unequally distributed power resources in the markets. By using their votes, wage-earners have been able to encroach upon and to limit the sphere of operations of the markets, where they are more often at a disadvantage. An example of the shift from markets towards politics is the decision-making determining levels of unemployment. Where Keynesian ideas have been accepted, the level of unemployment has come to be seen as a responsibility of the political authorities, and no longer to be left only to market processes. Also, distributive processes have been affected, for example through social policy and taxation.

## A Democratic Class Struggle?

I have suggested above that, in the capitalist democracies, it is fruitful to view politics as an expression of a democratic class struggle, i.e. a struggle in which class, socio-economic cleavages and the distribution of power resources play central roles. In contemporary social science, this view will be challenged from different directions. From a pluralist point of view the primacy which this interpretation gives to class cleavages will be questioned. While accepting the importance of class, those who lean towards the Leninist interpretation of Marxism tend to argue that the major organized interest groups, which presently are the main actors in these conflicts, do not actually represent the interests of the working class. Many writers on neo-corporatism also share such a view. Let us look briefly at the concepts concerned and the counter-arguments made.

The class concept is of relevance, *inter alia*, in attempts to explain social conflict, the distribution of goods and social change. This concept should therefore sensitize us to the many fissures and rents in the social fabric, which may become cleavages delineating the bases upon which citizens will organize themselves into collective action in the conflicts of interest in society. According to my reading of Marx and Weber, the two dominant figures in the theory of class, they both view the class concept in this perspective. Marx no less than Weber recognized a multitude of potential cleavages on the basis of which citizens can combine themselves for collective action. The two differ, however, in the relative importance which they ascribe to different types of bases of cleavage.

Marx assumed that, in the long run, the conflicts of interest rooted in the sphere of production and especially in the economic organization of production would come to dominate over the other potential cleavages, such as those based on market resources and status. Contrary to what is often assumed, the class theory of Marx is not a one-factor theory. Its basic hypothesis is instead that, among the multitude of lines of cleavage and conflicts of interest, the relative importance of those arising from the economic organization of production will increase in the long run.

Weber, however, places class, market resources and status on an equal footing as potential bases for cleavages and assumes that over time their importance will tend to oscillate. The class theory of Weber has also often been misinterpreted, not least by those who regard him as their intellectual standard-bearer. Weber explicitly argued that power must be seen as the generic concept of social stratification, the threefold expressions of which are class, status and party. Yet, pluralist writers have often conceived of power as a separate 'dimension' of social stratification, parallel to, but not included in, 'class' and 'status'. In contrast to Weber's stress on power as the basic independent variable behind social stratification, pluralist writers have therefore tended to conceive of power as restricted to the realm of the political order. While Weber saw 'property' and 'the lack of property' as the basic characteristics of all class situations, the institution of property has received scant attention in pluralist and functionalist analyses of industrial societies.

[. . .]

The Marxian hypothesis that, in the development of capitalism, the relative importance of class will increase at the expense of other possible bases of cleavages has been attacked by generations of social scientists. A recent challenger, Frank Parkin, develops a self-professed bourgeois critique, based on a neo-Weberian approach to stratification which puts power and conflict in a central place. In contrast to the Marxian class theory, which he interprets to be a one-factor theory of distributive conflict, focused exclusively on the positions in the productive system, Parkin argues for a multidimensional approach where control over productive resources, race, ethnicity, religion, sex and so on are viewed as equally important bases for cleavages and the formation of conflict groups. Against the background of developments during the 1960s and 1970s, for example in Northern Ireland, Belgium and the United States, Parkin maintains that, in contrast to Marxian predictions, not class but rather 'racial, ethnic, and religious conflicts have moved towards the centre of the political stage in many industrial societies', and that therefore 'any general model of class and stratification that does not fully incorporate this fact must forfeit all credibility'.[1] Parkin thus explicitly denies the primary role of the sphere of production as a basis for conflict of interest.

Another challenge to the centrality of class in modern Western societies has been made by students of electoral behaviour, who have analysed the relative importance of different bases for party cleavages. While some of them stress the importance of socio-economic factors, others argue that religion and language are more important. Thus in a study of party choice in Belgium, Canada, the Netherlands and South Africa, Lijphart comes to the following conclusions: 'Social class is clearly no more than a secondary and subsidiary influence on party choice, and it can become a factor of importance only in the absence of potent rivals such as religion and language.'[2]

It goes without saying that language, religion and race are easily and frequently seen as introducing a communality of interests and therefore often become bases for collective action. In fact, language and religion are so important bases of cleavages that over the centuries they have helped to generate decision-making units, i.e. states, which tend to be more or less homogenous with respect to these characteristics. Class divisions, on the contrary, occur within decision-making units. In this sense, then, cleavages based on language, religion and ethnicity can be seen as primary to class.

However, a different picture emerges when we look at the cleavages within the present nation-states. Parkin's claim that race, language and religion are of equal or greater importance than the sphere of production in generating social cleavages in industrial society appears to be based on the extent to which different cleavages have generated open or violent conflicts. This, however, is a rather superficial reading of the evidence. While conflicts based on religion, race, ethnicity and also on environmental issues clearly have been the most violent ones during these decades, this fact tells us little about the importance of different cleavages as bases of collective action, which is what is here in question. The power distribution approach outlined above indicates that the extent of manifest conflicts primarily reflects changes in the distribution of power resources between groups or collectivities.

To evaluate the relative importance of different bases of cleavages, we must primarily look not only at the violent conflicts, dramatic as they may be, but also at the more institutionalized conflicts and, above all, at the extent to which these cleavages have served as bases for organizations of interest. In this perspective class organizations in the sphere of production, i.e. unions and employers' (or business) organizations, emerge in the central roles. These organizations have been the key participants in the societal bargaining which has emerged in the Western nations during the postwar period. Only rarely have religious or ethnic groups figured in such contexts. Socio-economic cleavages also remain central bases for the party structures in most Western nations.

As indicated above, many neo-corporatist writers have assumed a major 'goal-displacement' within the organizations purporting to represent the interests of the working class. In neo-corporatism these organizations are assumed to serve largely the interests of the organizational leaderships and to control their members on behalf of the dominant groups in society. Schmitter assumes that this holds for labour unions while, for example, Panitch and Jessop acquit unions and place social democratic parties in the central controlling roles.

While 'goal displacement' within interest organizations is a clear possibility, it is an empirical question to what extent this has occurred in the wage-earner organizations. Assuming rational actors, a high level of voluntary union membership and party support can support the assumption that the union or party furthers the interests of the actors as perceived by them. The claim that unions in the Western nations have largely ceased to represent the interests of their members appears difficult to substantiate. In view of the fact that union members have daily opportunities to evaluate the consequences of leadership decisions at the place of work, such an assumption strikes me as rather absurd.

As far as the left parties are concerned, the variations between them would appear to be greater. Since they are rooted largely in the continuum of social stratification, political parties have a more flexible basis than unions, which reflect class divisions. Therefore goal displacements may occur more easily in left parties than in labour unions. The policy which a left party comes to represent when in government is affected by many factors, and such a party may come to choose a strategy which severely compromises working-class interests. The extent to which this has occurred probably varies considerably between countries. If we assume that unions tend to represent working-class interests more closely than the parties on the left, the closeness of the relationship between a left party and the union movement can be seen as one indicator of the type of policy which the party stands for.

My general hypothesis is that the presence of reformist socialist parties in the government can bring public policies closer to wage-earner interests. Also in this context, the distribution of power resources in society is of crucial importance. In the tripartite societal bargaining between the state, labour and capital, the distribution of power resources and the political composition of the government can affect the pattern of coalition formation in this triad and the outcomes of the bargaining. The smaller the disadvantage in power resources of the labour movement and the stronger the left party hold over the government, the more likely are state representatives to side with labour in the tripartite bargaining. Accordingly, the compromises resulting from societal bargaining can be expected to be more to the favour of wage-earners. There are considerable differences in the power position of the wage-earners between the Western nations.

## Notes

From W. Korpi, *The Democratic Class Struggle*, London, Routledge and Kegan Paul, 1983, pp. 14–25.

1 F. Parkin, *Marxism and Class Theory*, New York, Columbia University Press, 1979.
2 A. Lijphart, 'Language, Religion, Class and Party Choice', in R. Rose, *Electoral Participation*, Beverly Hills, CA, Sage, 1980.

# Responses from the Right

# The Meaning of the Welfare State

## *Friedrich von Hayek*

[ . . . ]

Unlike socialism, the conception of the welfare state has no precise meaning. The phrase is sometimes used to describe any state that 'concerns' itself in any manner with problems other than those of the maintenance of law and order. But, though a few theorists have demanded that the activities of government should be limited to the maintenance of law and order, such a stand cannot be justified by the principle of liberty. Only the coercive measures of government need be strictly limited. [ . . . ] There is undeniably a wide field for non-coercive activities of government and [ . . . ] a clear need for financing them by taxation.

Indeed, no government in modern times has ever confined itself to the 'individualist minimum' which has occasionally been described,[1] nor has such confinement of governmental activity been advocated by the 'orthodox' classical economists.[2] All modern governments have made provision for the indigent, unfortunate and disabled and have concerned themselves with questions of health and the dissemination of knowledge. There is no reason why the volume of these pure service activities should not increase with the general growth of wealth. There are common needs that can be satisfied only by collective action and which can be thus provided for without restricting individual liberty. It can hardly be denied that, as we grow richer, that minimum of sustenance which the community has always provided for those not able to look after themselves, and which can be provided outside the market, will gradually rise, or that government may, usefully and without doing any harm, assist or even lead in such endeavours. There is little reason why the government should not also play some role, or even take the initiative, in such areas as social insurance and education, or temporarily subsidize certain experimental developments. Our problem here is not so much the aims as the methods of government action.

References are often made to those modest and innocent aims of governmental activity to show how unreasonable is any opposition to the welfare state as such. But, once the rigid position that government should not concern itself at all with such matters is abandoned – a position which is defensible but has little to do with freedom – the defenders of liberty commonly discover that the programme of the welfare state comprises a great deal more that is represented as equally legitimate and unobjectionable. If, for instance, they admit that they have no objection to pure-food laws, this is taken to imply that they should not object to any government activity directed toward a desirable end. Those who attempt to delimit the functions of government in terms of aims rather than methods thus regularly find themselves in the position of having to oppose state action which appears to have only desirable consequences or of having to admit that they have no general rule on which to base their objections to measures which, though effective for particular purposes, would in their aggregate effect destroy a free society. Though the position that the state should have nothing to do with matters not related to the maintenance of law and order may seem logical so long as we think of the state solely as a coercive apparatus, we must recognize that, as a service agency, it may assist without harm in the achievement of desirable aims which perhaps could not be achieved otherwise. The reason why many of the new welfare activities of government are a threat to freedom, then, is that, though they are presented as mere service activities, they really constitute an exercise of the coercive powers of government and rest on its claiming exclusive rights in certain fields.

The current situation has greatly altered the task of the defender of liberty and made it much more difficult. So long as the danger came from socialism of the frankly collectivist kind, it was possible to argue that the tenets of the socialists were simply false: that socialism would not achieve what the socialists wanted and that it would produce other consequences which they would not like. We cannot argue similarly against the welfare state, for this term does not designate a definite system. What goes under that name is a conglomerate of so many diverse and even contradictory elements that, while some of them may make a free society more attractive, others are incompatible with it or may at least constitute potential threats to its existence.

We shall see that some of the aims of the welfare state can be realized without detriment to individual liberty, though not necessarily by the methods which seem the most obvious and are therefore most popular; that others can be similarly achieved to a certain extent, though only at a cost much greater than people imagine or would be willing to bear, or only slowly and gradually as wealth increases; and that, finally, there are others – and they are those particularly dear to the hearts of the socialists – that cannot be realized in a society that wants to preserve personal freedom.

There are all kinds of public amenities which it may be in the interest of all members of the community to provide by common effort, such as parks and museums, theatres and facilities for sports – though there are strong reasons why they should be provided by local rather than national authorities. There is then the important issue of security, of protection against risks common to all, where government can often either reduce these risks or assist people to provide against them. Here, however, an important distinction has to be drawn between two conceptions of security: a limited security which can be achieved for all and which is, therefore, no privilege, and absolute security, which in a free society cannot be achieved for all. The first of these is security against severe physical privation, the assurance of a given minimum of sustenance for all; and the second is the assurance of a given standard of life, which is determined by comparing the standard enjoyed by a person or a group with that of others. The distinction, then, is that between the security of an equal minimum income for all and the security of a particular income that a person is thought to deserve. The latter is closely related to the third main ambition that inspires the welfare state: the desire to use the powers of government to ensure a more even or more just distribution of goods. Insofar as this means that the coercive powers of government are to be used to ensure that particular people get particular things, it requires a kind of discrimination between, and an unequal treatment of, different people which is irreconcilable with a free society. This is the kind of welfare state that aims at 'social justice' and becomes 'primarily a redistributor of income'. It is bound to lead back to socialism and its coercive and essentially arbitrary methods.

Though *some* of the aims of the welfare state can be achieved *only* by methods inimical to liberty, *all* its aims *may* be pursued by such methods. The chief danger today is that, once an aim of government is accepted as legitimate, it is then assumed that even means contrary to the principles of freedom may be legitimately employed. The unfortunate fact is that, in the majority of fields, the most effective, certain and speedy way of reaching a given end will seem to be to direct all available resources towards the now visible solution. To the ambitious and impatient reformer, filled with indignation at a particular evil, nothing short of the complete abolition of that evil by the quickest and most direct means will seem adequate. If every person now suffering from unemployment, ill health or inadequate provision for [ . . . ] old age is at once to be relieved of his [or her] cares, nothing short of an all-comprehensive and compulsory scheme will suffice. But if, in our impatience to solve such problems immediately, we give government exclusive and monopolistic powers, we may find that we have been short-sighted. If the quickest way to a now visible solution becomes the only permissible one and all alternative experimentation is precluded, and if what now seems the best method of satisfying a need is made the sole starting-point for all future development, we may perhaps reach our present goal sooner, but we shall probably at the same time prevent the emergence of more effective alternative solutions. It is often those who are most anxious to use our existing knowledge and powers to the full that do most to impair the future growth of knowledge by the methods they use. The controlled single-channel development towards which impatience and administrative convenience have frequently inclined the reformer and which, especially in the field of social insurance, has become characteristic of the modern welfare state may well become the chief obstacle to future improvement.

If government wants not merely to facilitate the attainment of certain standards by the individuals but to make certain that everybody attains them it can do so only by depriving individuals of any choice in the matter. Thus the welfare state becomes a household state in which a paternalistic power controls most of the income of the community and allocates it to individuals in the forms and quantities which it thinks they need or deserve.

In many fields persuasive arguments based on considerations of efficiency and economy can be advanced in favour of the state's taking sole charge of a particular service; but when the state does so, the result is usually not only that those advantages soon prove illusory but that the character of the services becomes entirely different from that which they would have had if they had been provided by competing agencies. If, instead of administering limited resources put under its control for a specific service, government uses its coercive powers to ensure that men are given what some expert thinks they need; if people thus can no longer exercise any choice in some of the most important matters of their lives, such as health, employment, housing and provision for old age, but must accept the decisions made for them by appointed authority on the basis of its evaluation of their need; if certain services become the exclusive domain of the state, and whole professions – be it medicine, education or insurance – come to exist only as unitary bureaucratic hierarchies, it will no longer be competitive experimentation but solely the decisions of authority that will determine what men shall get.[3]

The same reasons that generally make the impatient reformer wish to organize such services in the form of government monopolies lead him also to believe that the authorities in charge should be given wide discretionary powers over the individual. If the objective were merely to improve opportunities for all by supplying certain specific services according to a rule, this could be attained on essentially business lines. But we could then never be sure that the results for all individuals would be precisely what we wanted. If each individual is to be affected in some particular way, nothing short of the individualizing, paternalistic treatment by a discretionary authority with powers of discriminating between persons will do.

It is sheer illusion to think that when certain needs of the citizen have become the exclusive concern of a single bureaucratic machine, democratic control of that machine can then effectively guard the liberty of the citizen. So far as the preservation of personal liberty is concerned, the division of labour between a legislature which merely says that this or that should be done[4] and an administrative apparatus which is given exclusive power to carry out these instructions is the most dangerous arrangement possible. All experience confirms what *is* clear enough from American as

> well as from English experience, that the zeal of the administrative agencies to achieve the immediate ends they see before them leads them to see their function out of focus and to assume that constitutional limitations and guaranteed individual rights must give way before their zealous efforts to achieve what they see as a paramount purpose of government.[5]

It would scarcely be an exaggeration to say that the greatest danger to liberty today comes from the men who are most needed and most powerful in modern government, namely, the efficient expert administrators exclusively concerned with what they regard as the public good. Though theorists may still talk about the democratic control of these activities, all who have direct experience in this matter agree that (as one [ . . . ] English writer put it) 'if the Minister's control . . . has become a myth, the control of Parliament is and always has been the merest fairy tale'.[6] It is inevitable that this sort of administration of the welfare of the people should become a self-willed and uncontrollable apparatus before which the individual is helpless, and which becomes increasingly invested with all the *mystique* of sovereign authority – the *Hoheitsverwaltung* or *Herrschaftstaat* of the German tradition that used to be so unfamiliar to Anglo-Saxons that the strange term 'hegemonic'[7] had to be coined to render its meaning.

## Notes

From F. A. von Hayek, *The Constitution of Liberty*, London, Routledge, 1959, pp. 257–62.

1 Cf., e.g., Henry Sidgwick, *The Elements of Politics*, London, 1891, ch. 4.

2 See on this particularly Lionel Robbins, *The Theory of Economic Policy*, London, 1952.

3 Cf. J. S. Mill, *On Liberty*, ed. R. B. McCallum, Oxford, 1946, pp. 99–100: 'If the roads, the railways, the banks, the insurance offices, the great joint stock companies, the universities, and the public charities, were all of them branches of the government; if, in addition, the municipal corporations and local boards, with all that now devolves on them, became departments of the central administration; if the employees of all these different enterprises were appointed and paid by the government, and looked to the government for every rise in life; not all the freedom of the press and popular constitution of the legislature would make this or any other country free otherwise than in

name. And the evil would be greater, the more efficiently and scientifically the administrative machinery was constructed – the more skilful the arrangements for obtaining the best qualified hands and heads with which to work it.'

4 Cf. T. H. Marshall, *Citizenship and Social Class*, Cambridge, 1958, p. 59: 'So we find that legislation . . . acquires more and more the character of a declaration of policy that it is hoped to put into effect some day.'

5 Roscoe Pound, 'The Rise of the Service State and its Consequence', in *The Welfare State and the National Welfare*, ed. S. Glueck, Cambridge, MA, 1952, p. 220.

6 P. Wiles, 'Property and Equality', in *The Unservile State*, ed. G. Watson, London, 1957, p. 107.

7 See L. von Mises, *Human Action*, New Haven, 1949, pp. 196ff.

# The Two Wars against Poverty

*Charles Murray*

[ . . . ]

When news reports cite percentages of 'people living in poverty', they are drawing from the official definition of the 'poverty line' established in 1964 by a task force in the Social Security Administration. The poverty line is, in effect, set at three times the cost of an adequate diet, and is adjusted for inflation, a variety of family characteristics and one's location (rural or non-rural).

This measure has been attacked as niggardly by some and as overly generous by others. Almost everyone agrees that it fails to capture the important differences in the quality of life between a family living at the poverty line in the South Bronx, for example, and a family with the same income that lives in a less punishing environment. But this measure of poverty has its merits nonetheless. It is widely known, it takes family size and inflation into account, and it provides a consistent measure for examining income over time. I will use it to discuss the history of three different 'types' of poverty: official poverty, net poverty and latent poverty [ . . . ].

The most widely used measure of poverty is the percentage of people with cash incomes that fall beneath the poverty line before taxes, but after taking cash income transfers from government into account. We shall call it *official poverty* because it is the measure reported by the Bureau of the Census.

Conventional wisdom has it that, at least according to this one measure, the 1960s and 1970s brought economic progress for the poor. The most widely shared view of recent events is that the United States entered the 1960s with a large population that had been bypassed during the prosperity of the Eisenhower years. The rich and the middle class gained but the poor did not. Then, after fits and starts during the Kennedy years, came the explosion in the number and size of social programmes under Johnson.

The programmes were perhaps too ambitious, it is widely conceded, and perhaps some of the efforts were misdirected, but at least they put a big dent in the poverty problem; this can be seen, it is said, in the large reduction in poverty that occurred during LBJ's administration and thereafter. The Great Society reforms were seen to have produced results that Eisenhower's 'trickle-down' economics had not.

The essential assertion of this view is that poverty decreased during the War on Poverty and had not been decreasing as rapidly before this period. It is a simple assertion, for which the data are a matter of historical record, and it is only half right.

Poverty did indeed fall during the five Johnson years, from 18 per cent of the population in 1964 to 13 per cent in 1968, his last year in office. Yet this was scarcely an unprecedented achievement. Between 1949 and 1952, poverty had already begun to fall from 33 to 28 per cent. Under Eisenhower it fell to 22 per cent. Under Kennedy and Johnson it dropped to 18 per cent by 1964. In short, the size of the official 'impoverished' population dropped by twenty percentage points in twenty years, of which the five Johnson years accounted for precisely their fair share, five points.[1]

Then, after two decades of reasonably steady progress, improvement slowed in the late 1960s and stopped altogether in the 1970s. A higher percentage of the American population was poor in 1980, in terms of cash income, than at any time since 1968. The percentage dipped as low as 11.1 per cent in 1973, but by 1980 it stood at 13 per cent and was heading upward.

When this history of the official poverty level is placed alongside the history of social welfare expenditures, a paradox appears. Social welfare expenditures had been increasing at a steady rate through the Eisenhower, Kennedy and early Johnson years. But it was not until the budgets of 1967 and 1968 that the Johnson programmes were reaching enough people to have a marked impact on the budget; it was then that social welfare expenditures started to take off. So just at the time when the reforms of the mid-1960s were being implemented, progress in reducing poverty began grinding to a halt!

The paradox is even more pronounced when we remember what it is we are measuring. If the measure were of chronic joblessness, for example, the flattening curve [. . .] would be understandable: it often is harder to fix the last 10 per cent of a problem than the first 90 per cent. But in this case, 'official poverty' is simply a measure of cash income *after* taking government transfers into account. To eliminate official poverty, all we need do is mail enough cheques with enough money to enough people. Starting in the late 1960s, the number of cheques, the size of the cheques and the number of beneficiaries all began to increase. Even if we ignore increased in-kind expenditures such as housing, food stamps and medical care (which are not included in this definition), and discount administrative costs and the effects of inflation, the federal government increased its real cash-benefit payments for income maintenance programmes by more than two-thirds during the 1970s.

Furthermore, the anti-poverty programmes of the 1970s had a much smaller target population than those of earlier, smaller budgets. In 1950 there were an estimated forty-six million people living beneath the poverty line (as it was subsequently defined); in 1960 there were 40 million, and in 1970 only 25 million. Given these conditions – more money and fewer people – progress begun during the 1950s and 1960s should have accelerated in the 1970s instead of slowing, stopping and then reversing.

## Net Poverty

The official poverty statistic is based only on cash income. In-kind assistance – food programmes, housing, medical care – is not included. Yet this assistance has been the fastest-growing component of the social welfare budget, rising from $2.2 billion in 1965 to $72.5 billion in 1980. If the dollar value of these benefits is computed and added to cash income, this new measure may be called *net poverty*: the percentage of the population remaining beneath the poverty level after all resources – cash and in-kind, earned and unearned – are taken into account.[2]

In 1950, in-kind transfers were quite small, so the percentage of official poor (30 per cent) was nearly identical to the percentage of net poor. This situation continued into the early 1960s as net poverty decreased at roughly the same rate as official poverty. By 1968, the gap between official poverty (12.8 per cent) and net poverty (10.1 per cent) was quite small.

Unlike changes in official poverty, however, large decreases in net poverty continued into the early 1970s. Then, from 1972 until 1980, the trendline flattened, just as that for official poverty had a few years earlier. In 1980, net poverty stood at 6.1 per cent of the population, compared with 6.2 per cent in 1972, despite the fact that expenditures on in-kind assistance had tripled (in constant dollars) during the 1970s.

The concept of net poverty is ambiguous. Taken by itself, 6.1 per cent represents a near victory over poverty; it is a very small proportion of the population. But a citizen who lives in a black or Hispanic ghetto, for example, may be forgiven for arguing that poverty has not come within 6.1 percentage points of vanishing. We must consider what it really means to live at or near the poverty level through in-kind support.

It means, to begin with, living in housing projects or other subsidized housing. Given their cost, most of these units ought to provide decent, comfortable housing, but in practice public housing is among the most vandalized, crime-ridden and least livable housing in the country. It means relying on food stamps. In theory, food stamps can purchase the foods necessary for a nutritious diet, but in practice they can be misused in other ways. It also means paying for medical care through Medicaid or Medicare, which have concrete value only if the recipient is sick.

In short, having the resources for a life that meets basic standards of decency is not the same as actually living such an existence. Whether this is the fault of the welfare system or the recipient is not at issue; it is simply a fact that must be kept in mind when interpreting the small, encouraging figure of 6.1 per cent.

But the economic point remains: as of 1980, the many overlapping cash and in-kind benefit programmes made it possible for almost anyone to place themselves above the official poverty level. If the ultimate criterion of social welfare policy is eliminating net poverty, the War on Poverty has very nearly been won.

## Latent Poverty

Of course, eliminating net poverty is not the ultimate criterion. Lyndon Johnson undertook the War on Poverty to end the dole, to enable people to maintain a decent standard of living by their own efforts. As he signed the initial anti-poverty bill he sounded the theme that formed the basis of the consensus for the Great Society:

> We are not content to accept endless growth of relief or welfare rolls. We want to offer the forgotten fifth of our population opportunity and not doles. . . . The days of the dole in our country are numbered.[3]

Johnson was articulating a deeply shared understanding among Americans as to how the welfare system is supposed to work – 'a hand, not a handout' was the slogan. Throughout American history, the economic independence of the individual and the family has been the chief distinguishing characteristic of good citizenship.

To measure progress along these lines we must calculate yet a third statistic. The poverty statistic with which I began, the one used by the government in its analyses, is cash income *after* the cash transfers from the government have been counted. Then I added the value of the non-cash, in-kind transfers in order to measure net poverty. Now I must ask: what is the number of poor before the cash and in-kind transfers are taken into account? How many people *would be* poor if it were not for government help? These may be called the *latent poor*. For practical purposes, they are the dependent population, those who were to be made independent as we eliminated the dole.

Latent poverty decreased during the 1950s. We do not know the precise level of decline, because 1965 is the first year for which the number of latent poor [was] calculated.[4] But we do know that the number of latent poor (pre-transfer poor) can be no smaller than the number of post-transfer poor; therefore, since the number of post-transfer poor stood at 30 per cent of the population in 1950, the percentage of latent poor had to have been somewhat larger (a conservative estimate is 32 per cent). As of 1965, the latent poor were 21 per cent of the population – a drop of about one-third. Put another way, dependency decreased during the years 1950–65. Increasing numbers of people were able to make a living that put them above the poverty level and progress was being made on the long-range goal of eliminating the dole.

The proportion of latent poor continued to drop through 1968, when the percentage was calculated at 18.2, but this [ . . . ] proved to be the limit of our success in the war against economic dependence. At some point during 1968–9, progress stopped; the percentage of latent poor then started to grow. It was 19 per cent by 1972, 21 per cent by 1976, and 22 per cent by 1980.[5] Once again, as in the case of official poverty, the shift in the trendline coincided with the advent of the programmes that were to eliminate poverty.

Again, how could it be that progress against official poverty and net poverty slowed or stopped when so much more money was being spent for cash and in-kind transfers? The data on latent poverty provide one of the most important answers: because latent poverty was increasing, it took more and more money in transfers just to keep the percentage of post-transfer poor stable. The social welfare system fell into the classic trap of having to run faster and faster to stay in the same place. The extremely large increases in social welfare spending during the 1970s were papering over the increase in latent poverty.

The three measures of poverty – official poverty, net poverty and latent poverty – reveal a pattern from 1950 to 1980 that has important implications for the American welfare state. For example, it explains a major element in the budget crisis. As of 1980, roughly the same proportion of people remained above the poverty line through their own earned incomes as did in the early 1960s. But in the early 1960s, our legislated spending obligations to those who earned less than that amount were comparatively small. Whether or not one approves of the spending obligations taken on since then, they cannot be sustained indefinitely in the face of increasing latent poverty. Latent poverty must be turned around, or the obligations must be slashed, or both.

## Rising Tide, Sinking Ships

The poverty trendlines [ . . . ] are not widely publicized. Because it has not been recognized that the implementation of the Great Society reforms coincided with an end to progress in reducing poverty, there has been no debate over why this should be the case.

The best place to begin the debate is to examine the common view that the bright hopes of the 1960s dimmed in the 1970s due to a slowdown in the economy. According to this view, inflation and dislocations brought on by the Vietnam War, along with the revolution in energy prices, made the economy go sour. As the expansionist environment of the 1960s vanished, strategies and programmes of the War on Poverty had to be put aside. It is good that the entitlements and income transfer programmes were in place, runs this line of argument, or else the troubles in the economy would have been even more devastating on the poor.

What, if anything, do the data suggest about the merits of this economic explanation? As in the discussion of poverty, I must start with the simplest, most widely used measure of the state of the economy, growth in the GNP, and examine its relation to changes in the number of people living in poverty. The answer – perhaps surprisingly to those who have ridiculed 'trickle-down' as a way to help the poor – is that changes in GNP have a very strong inverse relation to changes in poverty. As GNP increases, poverty decreases. (The simple correlation coefficient for the period 1950–80 is −.69[6].) The effects of economic growth did indeed trickle down to the lowest economic levels of the society. Economic growth during the 1950s and 1960s was strong, during the 1970s it was weak – and progress in reducing poverty ceased.

So it can be said that the fortunes of the economy explain recent trends in poverty. But the flip side of this finding is that social welfare expenditures did *not* have an effect on poverty. *Once the effects of GNP are taken into account, increases in social welfare spending do not account for reductions in poverty [since the 1950s].* The same analysis that supports the economic explanation for the failure in the 1970s gives scant support to remedies that would boost social welfare spending [ . . . ].

Conservatives generally recognize the role of economic growth in reducing poverty, but some feel this is not a sufficient explanation for the failures of the 1970s. It is not just that the social welfare reforms were ineffective in reducing poverty, they argue, but that the reforms actually made matters worse by emasculating the work ethic and creating 'work disincentives'. As people became less inclined to take low-paying jobs, hold onto them, and use them to get out of poverty, they became dependent on government assistance. The academic treatment of poverty has generally dismissed this conservative explanation out of hand. It has understandably been mistaken for curmudgeonly, mean-spirited and occasionally racist rhetoric. But the trendline for latent poverty – the key indicator of how people are doing without government help – offers a solid reason for concluding that the Great Society reforms exacerbated many of the conditions they sought to alleviate.

It is important to emphasize that the trend in latent poverty did not reverse direction when the economy went bad; it did not even wait until the official poverty and net poverty figures stabilized. Latent poverty started to increase while the other two measures of poverty were still going down. Most strikingly, progress on latent poverty stopped in 1968 while the economy was operating at full capacity (unemployment stood at 3.5 per cent in 1968–9, the lowest rate since the Korean War).

## Welfare and Labour-Force Participation

The second half of the 1960s was a watershed in other ways as well. A number of social indicators began showing strange and unanticipated shifts during those years, and the onset of these changes had no discernible relation to the health of the economy. Together, the evidence is sufficiently provocative to make the conservative interpretation worth looking into.

One such indicator is *participation in the labour force*. By definition, participation in the civilian labour force means either being employed or intending to work, given the opportunity. Among the poor, participation in the labour force 'should' be very high, approaching 100 per cent, for able-bodied adults without childcare responsibilities. Conservatives argue that such participation has dropped because welfare benefits have become more extensive and more easily available. The statistics on labour-force participation – a standard measure calculated by the Bureau of Labor Statistics – are readily available, and they conform quite well to conservative expectations.

Consider the record of two populations of immediate comparative interest: black males, who are disproportionately poor relative to the entire population, and white males, who are disproportionately well off. In 1948 (comparable data for 1950 are not available), the participation rate for both groups was 87 per cent. This equivalence – one of the very few social or economic measures on which black males could claim parity with whites in the 1950s – continued throughout the decade and into the early 1960s. As late as 1965, only a percentage point separated the two groups. But by 1968, a gap of 3.4 percentage points in participation had opened up between black males and white males. By 1972, the gap was 5.9 percentage points. In 1980, 70.5 per cent of black males participated in the labour force compared with 78.6 of white males; the gap had grown to 8.1 percentage points. To put it another way, during the period 1954–67, 1.4 black males dropped out of the labour force for every white male who dropped out; from 1968 to 1980, 3.6 black males dropped out for every white male who did.

The abrupt drop in the labour-force participation of black males cannot easily be linked to events in the economy at large. One of the most commonly cited popular explanations of why poor people drop out of the labour force is that they become discouraged – there are no jobs, so people quit looking. But the gap first opened up during the boom years of 1966–8, when unemployment was at a historic low. The 'discouraged worker' argument cannot be used to explain the drop-out rate during this period. Nor can the opposite argument be substituted: black males did not stop dropping out when the Vietnam boom cooled and unemployment rose. Whether unemployment was high or low, until 1967 black males behaved the same as whites; after 1967 they did not.

One may ask whether this is a racial phenomenon; it is nothing of the kind. Using the 1970 census data, participation for 1970 may be broken down by both race and economic status, and doing so reveals that the apparent racial difference is artificial. For males at comparable income levels, labour-force participation among black males was *higher* than among white males. The explanation of the gap is not race, but income. Starting in 1966, low-income males – white or black – started dropping out of the labour force. The only reason it looks as though blacks were dropping out at higher rates is that blacks are disproportionately poor. If trend-lines are examined showing participation rates by income rather than race, the 1970 census data strongly suggest that middle- and upper-income males participated in the labour force at virtually unchanged rates since the 1950s, while the participation rate for low-income males decreased slowly until 1966, and plummeted thereafter.

This phenomenon needs explanation, for it was a fundamental change in economic behaviour – participation in the labour market itself. Once explanations based on unemployment fail, and once the racial discrepancy is shown to be artificial, the conservative hypothesis has considerable force. Without a doubt, *something* happened in the mid-1960s that changed the incentives for low-income workers to stay in the job market. The Great Society reforms constitute the biggest, most visible, most plausible candidate.

## Welfare and Family Breakup (Revisited)

A second social indicator which links increases in latent poverty to the Great Society reforms is the decline in the intact husband-wife family unit, especially among blacks.

A racial difference in family composition has existed since statistics have been kept, but by the middle of this century the proportions for whites and blacks, while different, were stable. As of 1950, 88 per cent of white families consisted of husband–wife households, compared with 78 per cent of black families. Both figures had remained essentially unchanged since before the Second World War (the figures for 1940 were 86 and 77 per cent, respectively). In the early 1950s, the black proportion dipped slightly, then remained between 72 and 75 per cent until 1965. The figures for white families stayed in the 88 to 89 per cent range between 1958 and 1965, never varying by more than two-tenths of a percentage point from year to year.

The years 1966 and 1967 saw successive drops in the percentage of black husband–wife households, even though it remained in the 72–5 per cent range. Then, in a single year (1968), the percentage dropped to 69, the beginning of a steep slide that has not yet been arrested. By the end of 1980, the proportion of black husband–wife families had dropped to 54 per cent – a drop of 19 percentage points since 1965. The figure for whites dropped by four percentage points in the same period, from 89 to 85 per cent.

From a demographic perspective, a change of this magnitude is extraordinary, nearly unprecedented in the absence of war or some other profound social upheaval. Much is made of the social changes that swept America during the 1960s and 1970s, and discussions of the change in black family composition have discounted the phenomenon as a slightly exaggerated manifestation of this broader social transformation. But the data do not permit such an easy dismissal. In the rest of society the changes in family composition were comparatively modest.

As in the case of labour-force participation, we are witnessing a confusion between race and income, though not as severe. When husband–wife families are examined on the basis of income (using the 1970 census), the percentage of husband–wife families among blacks above the poverty level is found to be 82 per cent, very close to the overall rate for whites. This indicates that data based on income may be expected to show that the precipitous drop in intact families is concentrated among the low-income population, not exclusively (perhaps not even disproportionately) among blacks.

Why did low-income families start to disintegrate in the mid-1960s while higher-income families did not? As in the case of participation in the labour force, there is no obvious alternative to the conservatives' hypothesis: namely, during precisely this period, fundamental changes occurred in the philosophy, administration and magnitude of social welfare programmes for low-income families, and these changes altered – both directly and indirectly – the social risks and rewards, and the financial costs and benefits, of maintaining a husband–wife family. It should surprise no one that behaviour changed accordingly.

This hypothesis is not 'simplistic', as has been charged. It is plausible that the forces which changed welfare policy could have affected family composition even if welfare policy had not been changed. Those forces were surely various and complex. Still, these forces are not enough to explain the extraordinary change in family composition. If in the early 1960s one had foreseen the coming decade of sweeping civil rights legislation, an upsurge in black identity and pride, and a booming economy in which blacks had more opportunities than ever before, one would not have predicted massive family breakup as a result. The revolutionary change in black family composition went *against* the grain of many contemporaneous forces. Casual assertions that 'it was part of the times' are inadequate.

## A Pyrrhic Victory?

The effect of the decline in labour-force participation, and of the breakup of the husband–wife family, were tragic and severe. In the case of the labour market, the nature of the effect is obvious: when low-income males drop out of the labour force and low-income females do not enter it, the size of the latent poor population will grow. This alone could explain why the proportion of latent poor increased even as the proportions of official poor and net poor were still declining.

The effects of family breakup are less obvious, but no less noteworthy. An analysis by the Bureau of the Census indicates that changes in family composition accounted for two million additional poor families in the 1970s.[7] For example, the analysis shows that if black family composition had remained the same as in 1971, the poverty rate for black families would have been 20 per cent in 1980 instead of 29 per cent. Other findings all lead to the same conclusion: the changes in family composition that started in the mid-1960s have raised poverty significantly above the levels that 'would have' prevailed otherwise. The Bureau's analysis actually *understates* the overall effect of the change in family composition on poverty – by 1971, the baseline for the analysis, much of the deterioration had already occurred.

These are some of the reasons behind the paradox of our failure to make progress against poverty in the 1970s despite the enormous increases in the amount of money that the government has spent to do so. There are other reasons as well – the large proportion of the social welfare budget spent on people above the poverty level being perhaps the most notable – but the preceding few will serve to convey a point that is too often missed in the debates over budget cuts in social welfare programmes. It is genuinely an open issue – intellectually as well as politically – whether we should be talking about spending cuts, or whether we should be considering an overhaul of the entire welfare system as conceived in the Great Society. If the War on Poverty is construed as having begun in 1950 instead of 1964, it may fairly be said that we were winning the war until Lyndon Johnson decided to wage it.

### Notes

From *The Public Interest*, 69,1982, pp. 4–16.

1 Data for 1959–79 are taken from the figures published annually in the *Statistical Abstract of the United States*. Figures for 1949–58 are taken from 'Economic Report to the President: Combating Poverty in a Prosperous Economy', January 1969, reprinted in US Department of Health, Education and Welfare, *The Measure of Poverty*, ed. M. Orshansky, Technical Paper I, vol. 1 [n.d.], p. 349, chart 10. The percentage for 1980 was obtained directly from the Poverty Statistics Section of the Bureau of the Census.

2 The figures are taken from Timothy M. Smeeding, *Measuring the Economic Welfare of Low-Income Households and the Antipoverty Effectiveness of Cash and Noncash Transfer Programs*, PhD diss., Department of Economics, University of Wisconsin-Madison, 1975; Smeeding, 'The Antipoverty Effectiveness of In-Kind Transfers', *Journal of Human Resources*, 12, 1977, pp. 360–78; and Smeeding, 'The Anti-poverty Effect of In-Kind Transfers: A 'Good Idea Gone Too Far?', *Policy Studies Journal*, 10, 3, 1982 pp. 499–522.

3 Quoted in the *New York Times*, 21 August 1964, p. 1.

4 The figures for 1965–78 are taken from Sheldon Danziger and Robert Plotnick, 'The War on Income Poverty: Achievements and Failures', in *Welfare Reform in America*, ed. P. Sommers, Hingham, MA, Martinus Nijhoff, 1982, table 3.1, p. 40.

5 It should be noted that the measure of latent poverty excludes social security income. Since families headed by persons over the age of sixty-five make up nearly half of those in latent poverty, the percentages reported here may somewhat exaggerate the extent of the problem among those able to work. (Unfortunately, no figures on this point prior to 1976 have been published.) But even if it were possible to include social security – or exclude the elderly – in calculations over this period, this adjustment would not affect the steep *rise* in latent poverty we have observed. [ . . . ]

6 The variables are the first difference in real GNP per household and the first difference in percentage of population under the poverty line using the official measure of poverty.

7 Gordon Green and Edward Welniak, 'Measuring the Effects of Changing Family Composition during the 1970s on Black–White Differences in Income', unpublished manuscript, Bureau of the Census, 1982.

# The New Politics of the New Poverty

*Lawrence M. Mead*

The poverty of today's underclass differs appreciably from poverty in the past: underclass poverty stems less from the absence of opportunity than from the inability or reluctance to take advantage of opportunity. The plight of the underclass suggests that the competence of many of the poor – their capacity to look after and take care of themselves – can no longer be taken for granted as it could in the past.

The changing nature of poverty has also ushered in a fundamental change in our politics, which formerly focused on class but now emphasizes conduct. Prior to the 1960s, in what I call the era of progressive politics, the overriding issue was how to help ordinary working Americans advance economically. The solutions of liberals and conservatives differed greatly, but both groups agreed that available opportunities would be seized by the poor. They disagreed in locating the barrier to opportunity: liberals blamed the unregulated economy, and conservatives blamed the government. As a result, liberals favoured greater government intervention, while conservatives hoped to reduce it. At issue were class inequalities and the need for economic redistribution: was the inequality meted out by the marketplace acceptable? How desirable were regulations of wages, hours and working conditions, along with the creation of social-insurance programmes to benefit workers and their families?

Anti-poverty strategy and politics differ greatly today, because poverty is rarely found among workers but is common among non-workers. In the new era, characterized by what I call dependency politics, the leading issue is how to handle the disorders of inner-city non-workers: conservatives usually want to enforce civilities, which liberals resist doing. For the most part, we spend less time debating whether the income of the working poor should be larger than we do discussing whether and how we can transform poor non-workers into workers.

Recent disagreements over tax hikes and budget cuts suggest that redistributive conflicts over the economy remain very much with us; economic inequality has increased, and Kevin Phillips's prediction of heightened conflict between rich and poor received much attention [in 1990]. Nevertheless, in the absence of economic collapse serious class conflict is unlikely. The politics of conduct, which focuses on dependency and disorder, is simply more salient than the politics of class. The problems of rising crime, welfarism, homelessness and declining schools (and the tax increases imposed to pay for them) are what chiefly concern most Americans; they worry far less about the income gap separating them from their employers. Most Americans doubt government's ability to solve the new social problems that confront us. Unless government better responds to them, it will receive no new mandate to tackle the older problem of unequal fortunes.

The public's focus on dependency and disorder has obviously damaged the American left, which is more comfortable dealing with issues of economic redistribution. The public's conservatism on social (as opposed to economic) issues largely explains why Republicans have controlled the White House and the national agenda for most of a generation. Democrats in presidential politics have paid a high price for their perceived softness on the question of 'values'. In the 1988 election, Michael Dukakis proposed new benefit programmes of the kind that used to win elections for Democrats. The Bush campaign easily defeated him by speaking of crime and Willie Horton.

But despite its electoral advantages, the anti-government right – like the redistributionist left – is uncomfortable with dependency politics. When the poor behave badly, bigger government becomes indefensible, because many of its beneficiaries are 'undeserving'. But smaller government is also questionable, because many believe that the poor could not cope without the many benefits and services that they receive. Distrust of the dysfunctional poor defeated the most ambitious plans to expand government during the Great Society. But concern for these same poor helps explain why Ronald Reagan was unable significantly to reduce the size of domestic government.

## Working Class to Underclass

This political change was brought about by the appearance of an intractable type of poverty in American cities in the 1960s and early 1970s. Ironically, the same era witnessed the last great victories of old-style progressive politics. The victories were achieved by the civil-rights and feminist movements, which were largely composed of working people seeking expanded economic opportunities. Their demands, like those made in earlier decades by distressed farmers and organized labour, sought to increase the income of workers.

But in the same era, welfare rolls more than doubled, crime soared and riots broke out in the ghettos of major cities. These developments raised issues of order and propriety much more sharply than the earlier movements. By the end of the 1960s, the closely linked problems of poverty, welfare and the inner city dominated the domestic agenda. Since then, the claims of broader groups, including minorities and women, have not gone unnoticed, but they no longer command centre stage. Social-reform efforts now focus on welfare, education and criminal justice, not the economy. Even the recessions of the 1970s and early 1980s, the most serious since the Depression, failed to inspire major new efforts to help workers. Issues of dependency and dysfunction, not opportunity, now preoccupy us.

Some might say that dependency politics is not new, in that controversies about the 'undeserving' poor, and what to do about them, have often marked American history. But if the themes of dependency politics are not new, its prominence as 'welfare politics' before 1960 was largely a local affair. At the national level, the arena was always dominated by groups that were not dependent and were usually employed. Only in the recent era have dependent, mostly non-working groups captured the nation's political attention.

The employment issue, like no other, marks the boundary between the old politics and the new. The movements of the progressive era had weight above all because their members worked, or at least had a job history. The aggrieved might have been destitute, but they could make claims on the basis of desert. The recent poor seldom can do this. They are controversial, above all, because they usually do not work. Only 40 per cent of poor adults had any earnings at all in 1987, and only 9 per cent worked full-time year-round. That initially was why most of them were poor. Work effort among the poor has also dropped sharply. Only 47 per cent of the heads of poor families worked at all in 1987, down from 68 per cent in 1959.

Of course, only about half the poverty population is working-aged, and only about half remains in poverty for more than two years. The underclass, consisting of the poor with the most severe behavioural problems, is quite small: it includes no more than eight million people by various estimates. Yet persistent poverty is highly visible in cities, and it is central to all major urban problems – not only welfare, crime and homelessness, but troubled schools and a decaying economic base. So it gets more policy-making attention than the affairs of the vastly larger working and middle classes.

This new poverty created a new politics because the old politics found no answer to it. Neither of the traditional, competing progressive-era remedies – increasing or decreasing government intervention in the economy – seems an appropriate response to the passive poverty of the inner city. It is true that analysts wedded to progressive-era assumptions – whether liberal or conservative – continue to try to trace passive poverty to some social barrier that must be eliminated: liberals say that poor adults cannot earn enough to make work worthwhile, cannot find jobs or child care, or are barred from jobs by racial bias; conservatives claim that welfare 'pays' dependents not to marry or work. But the hard evidence mostly undercuts these explanations. Liberal claims notwithstanding, jobs usually are available to the unskilled; taking these jobs would generally move families in which both parents worked above the poverty line. The flood of new immigrants entering the job market is one clear sign that opportunity still exists. Working mothers can usually arrange child care informally and cheaply, and discrimination in any overt form has disappeared. But conservative claims notwithstanding, welfare disincentives are also too weak to explain the collapse of the family or the very low work levels typically found in the inner city today.

I do not mean that barriers are totally absent. Differences of opportunity certainly exist in America. Better-educated people, for example, are more likely to succeed. [Since the 1970s] the income disparity between low-skilled and high-skilled workers has increased. The progressive-era debate over whether and how to narrow these differences in wages remains alive.

Unequal opportunities, however, chiefly explain why some workers earn more than others. They usually do not explain the failure of non-workers to work steadily *at all*, which is in turn the cause of most poverty and dependency among working-aged people. Most Americans have responded to stagnant wages by working *more*; only the poor have worked less. Most Americans refuse to believe that society's failure to expand opportunity causes the poverty of non-workers who do not take and hold available jobs.

To explain most entrenched poverty, we must go back to what used to be called the 'culture of poverty'. Non-working adults apparently want to work, but they seldom do so consistently – some because the pay offered is unacceptable, others because they feel overwhelmed by the practical difficulties of employment. These reactions run strongest in the inner city, because of its isolation from workaday society, and among racial minorities who have traditionally faced discrimination. The greatest cause of today's poverty may simply be that the attempts [ . . . ] to equalize opportunity have failed to persuade many blacks and Hispanics that it is worth working.

But if non-work is rooted mostly in the demoralization of the poor, rather than impersonal impediments, then traditional reformism holds no answer for it. Passive poverty has defeated, in turn, the strategies of both larger and smaller governments. The Great Society invented wave after wave of new anti-poverty programmes, only to see the poverty level stagnate and welfare rise. The Reagan administration cut or curbed the growth of these programmes to reinvigorate the economy. But even the longest boom in American history could not reduce poverty below 13 per cent, because the poor are now substantially detached from the economy. Each in its own way, these strategies provided new chances to poor adults, but neither directly addressed the puzzling reluctance of the poor to do more to help themselves.

As a result, social policy has been driven away from structural reforms and towards paternalism. The drift is toward policies that address motivation by seeking to direct the lives of those dependent on government. Public institutions are taking over tutelary functions from weakened families. Social-service agencies are raising children, and schools are organizing the lives of students before and after class as well as during it. Homeless shelters and the criminal-justice system are managing the disordered lives of single men. Above all, recent welfare legislation requires rising numbers of employable recipients to participate in job placement or training on pain of cuts in their grants. Such measures violate the traditional prescriptions of liberals, who want benefits given without conditions, but also those of conservatives, who would prefer to see discipline applied by the private rather than the public sector. But they seem required by the changing nature of the social problem.

These trends are most advanced in the US, but they are appearing in Europe as well. An underclass, largely non-white, has grown up in British cities, while throughout Europe controversy rages over whether immigrants from the Third World are corrupting traditional mores. These racial and ethnic divisions now arouse more passion than the traditional conflicts of labour and business. The behaviour of 'outsiders' is far more controversial than economic claims. Crime, dependency and a failure to learn the national language are at issue, not working-class demands for higher wages and benefits. The West as a whole seems destined for a politics of conduct rather than class.

## The New Agenda

Dependency politics and progressive-era politics differ substantially in content, even though there is much overlap in practice. I exaggerate the contrasts here for emphasis:

*The old issues were economic; the new ones are social.* Progressive-era politics debated the proper organization of society, especially the issue of government control of the economy. Liberals supported higher and more progressive taxation; public regulation of industries; union rights; the minimum wage and other protections for workers; pension, health and unemployment benefits: [ . . . ] [The right sought to] weaken or undo all these steps in the belief that only a revivified free market could really generate 'good jobs at good wages'.

In dependency politics, in contrast, the question is how to deal with the problems of basic functioning among the seriously poor. The social, more than the economic, structure of society is at issue. The focus is on troubled individuals or ethnic groups rather than industry, agriculture, or the relations of labour and management. Social problems are no longer seen to stem directly from injustice, nor are they obviously reformable. So social policy must focus on motivation and order rather than opportunity or equality.

Affluence helped produce this shift. Before the 1960s, working-class incomes were still low enough that many people were poor, even though they worked normal hours. That is much less common today, because the poverty line is constant in real terms while real wages have risen. The poor, who used to work more than the better-off, now commonly work less. Inevitably, the focus of the social agenda has shifted from the low wages that used to impoverish workers to the dysfunctions that keep the non-working poor out of the labour force.

*In progressive-era politics the issue was government control of the economy; in dependency politics it is government supervision of behaviour.* Progressive-era politicians disputed how far government should regulate the free market in the collective interest, how much it should spend on benefit programmes such as Social Security.

In dependency politics, however, the chief question is how far government should control the lives of dysfunctional people in their own interests. Do we require that people stay in school, obey the law, avoid drugs, and so on? Above all, do we require adults to work or prepare for work as a condition of receiving welfare? Proposals to do these things do not much change what government does for people. Rather, they demand that dependants do more for themselves in return.

Formerly it was local authorities who grappled with maintaining social order, while Washington managed the economy. But order issues have become federal, because national programmes are involved in all the key areas – welfare, education and criminal justice. It is now the main domestic challenge of presidents, as of mayors, to reduce crime and dependency and to raise standards in the schools. Presidents Nixon, Carter and Reagan all tried to reform welfare, and George Bush aspired to be an 'education president'.

*The old issues concerned adults; the new issues concern children and youth.* Progressive-era political claims were on behalf of adults, especially workers. The question was how to reorganize government or the economy so that adults could have influence and opportunity. In the dependency era, however, these issues are less salient than people's problems on the road to adulthood – illegitimacy, educational failure and crime. So dependency politics focuses heavily on the formative years. Reformism aims to improve family, neighbourhood and schools rather than the political or economic structure.

Daniel Patrick Moynihan says that social policy has entered a 'post-industrial' age. The main challenge is no longer to expand economic opportunity but to overcome social weaknesses that stem from the 'post-marital' family and the inability of many people to get through school. The inequalities that stem from the workplace are now trivial in comparison to those stemming from family structure. What matters for success is less whether your father was rich or poor than whether you knew your father at all.

A focus on youth is inevitable once the leading social problem changes from the poverty of workers to dysfunctional poverty. For if the source of poverty is behaviour rather than lack of opportunity, remedies must focus on youth, the stage of life at which behaviour is most malleable. Conversely, reform for adults must be structural because it must take personality largely as given.

*The pressures in progressive-era politics arise from self-seeking behaviour; in dependency politics, they arise from passivity.* Progressive-era politics debates the freedom that America allows people to make money and get ahead on their own. To conservatives, this prerogative is a right that government may not limit. To the left, it is a licence that government must restrain in the name of a broader social interest.

The poor and dependent, however, are not exploitative but inert. They are controversial mostly because they do so little to help themselves, not because they hurt others in the pursuit of advantage. Even when violent, they are unable to exert themselves effectively. They are not aggressive so much as *passive* aggressive. So in dependency politics, the issue is whether poor people should have to do more to help themselves. The question is how passive you can be and still be a citizen in full standing.

Formerly, the right defended property and the established order against public controls. Now it is the left that defends the status quo, by justifying passivity among the needy, while the right demands greater activity. Recent measures such as workfare or reformed schools are attempts to stimulate the poor, not to curb the rich. The point is to set a floor under self-advancement, not a ceiling above it. The hope is to make the poor more effectively self-seeking than they are.

*Claims in progressive-era politics derived from strength; those in dependency politics arise from weakness.* The chief players in the progressive era were unions, farmers, businesses and other economic interests that demanded some benefit or protection from government on a basis of desert. They were economically disadvantaged, but their demands were also made from a position of strength, because they had economic and political resources of their own. They could use these resources to get attention from politicians, but they could also survive on their own if rebuffed.

In dependency politics, the claimants usually have no such strength, as they lack any regular position in the economy. They are simply needy. Their main claim is precisely their vulnerability. It is not their own power that gets attention, but politicians' fear of a backlash from the better-off if the needy are left unprotected. Economic groups state their claims by speaking of troubled finances. The very poor state theirs by a disassembly of the personality – by failing to function in embarrassing ways that force society to take responsibility for them.

In dependency politics, the poor claim a right to support based on the injuries of the past, not on anything that they contribute now. Wounds are an asset today, much as a pay cheque was in progressive-era politics. One claims to be a victim, not a worker. The non-white poor, particularly, appeal to historic injustices. Even some policies that aid better-functioning minorities, such as affirmative action, require their beneficiaries to adopt the identity of victimhood to some extent – to exploit an appeal, as Shelby Steele says, based on 'suffering' rather than 'achievements'.

Poverty shifts the agenda from equality to citizenship. The question is no longer what the worst-off members of the community should receive. Now the question is who should be considered a bona fide member of the community in the first place. Who has the moral standing to make the demands for economic redress typically made in the progressive era? When dependency comes to dominate politics, class-oriented issues of equality for workers inevitably move off the agenda, while issues of identity and belonging replace them.

In Europe as well as the US, dependency concerns replaced progressive ones as motives for the reconsideration of the welfare state that began in the 1970s and 1980s. At first, the issues were economic, the fear that excessive spending on income and health programmes was overburdening the economy. Cuts were made to promote economic growth, the step conservatives always recommend in progressive-era politics. [In the 1990s], however, the greater concern has been declining social cohesion, as evidenced by rises in crime, single parenthood and chronic unemployment. The response, in Britain and Sweden as in the US, has been new steps to enforce child support and work effort among the dependent. The shift from the older, redistributive agenda to these new, more behavioural issues ushers in a new political age.

[. . .]

## The Western Tradition

Today's efforts to respond to dependency face serious challenges. They may well not allay our social problems as fully as progressive policies resolved yesterday's economic disputes. The newer, paternalistic social programmes probably will do more to reduce poverty than the less demanding policies of the past: more authoritative schools are producing some results, and workfare programmes have been able to increase work effort (though they have not yet reduced dependency). But it is doubtful that even these programmes can do more than contain the social problem.

Even if they are effective, paternalistic measures raise serious political objections. The new structures reduce disorder, but at a cost to the autonomy of clients. This is particularly true if, as is likely, the chronic poor require direction on an on-going basis, not just temporarily. That is why, even now, government prefers to spend money on the dependent rather than try to tell them how to live. Benefits lack the power of public authority to change behaviour, but they do not violate our notions of a free society.

A more serious problem stems from our political traditions. Anti-dependency policies – and disputes about them – find no basis in the Western political tradition, which assumes that the individuals who compose society are competent to advance their own interests, if not society's. The traditional Western assumption is that politics arises from conflicting interests, as individuals and groups seek economic advantage. Government's task is to resolve these disputes in the general interest. It does not animate society, but rather responds to energy coming from below.

Historically, Western politics has been class-oriented: aristocratic elites, then bourgeois elements, then workers without property have advanced their own conceptions of how government and the economy should be organized. The dominant principles have become more democratic, then more collectivist, as government came to represent the mass of the populace and then to serve its needs. The contending visions may seem radically opposed, but from today's perspective they were remarkably alike: all assumed a working population, competent to advance its own interests.

This tradition is inapplicable to the problems posed by today's dysfunctional poor. But policy makers in [the US] and Europe are prone to respond to these problems by replaying the old scenarios. Today's liberals see history as a grand progression in which the rights of ordinary people have been expanded: first civil liberties, then representative government, then protections against the insecurities of capitalism were attained. Faced with passive poverty, the left can imagine no response other than providing some further entitlement, for example government jobs. The idea that dependants should have to function better seems like an attempt to deny benefits, and is thus anathema.

Anti-government conservatives, for their part, blame poverty on an excess of government, just as the left blames it on the lack of government intervention. They insist that cuts in spending and taxes will somehow liberate the energy of the poor, as they do that of entrepreneurs. The idea that competence is a prior and different problem, requiring perhaps more government rather than less, is unthinkable.

These liberal and conservative responses are doomed to fail. If the seriously poor had the initiative to respond to new opportunities, they would not be poor for very long in the first place. The Great Society and the Reagan era both failed to solve poverty, because each in a different way offered new chances to the poor without confronting the motivation problem. Neither could seriously address competence, because that problem fell outside the Western assumptions underlying their ideas of social reform.

But despite these conceptual failures, government has begun to do something about poverty: a new, paternalistic regime for the poor is emerging. Ronald Reagan's greatest domestic legacy, despite his tax cuts, was not to reduce government; it was to start changing welfare into workfare. But the new regime is accepted grudgingly, if at all. Politicians argue heatedly about the issues of responsibility and competence that it raises, but they seldom do so honestly. They mention the 'underclass' and the need for discipline, but they still talk as if they were offering the poor only 'freedom' or 'opportunity'.

We need a new political language that considers more candidly the questions of human nature that now underlie politics. The political contestants need to defend their positions on a philosophic level, rather than hide behind outmoded theories. Liberals need to show why poor people are blameless, therefore still deserving; conservatives need to show how the poor are competent and why they need to be held accountable, in spite of dysfunction. From such premises they could then erect consistent doctrines of social policy, comparable to the competing theories of economic management that framed the leading issues in the progressive era.

If anyone is writing this theory, it is not philosophers like John Rawls and his critics (who assume a rational economic psychology and thus remain wedded to the competence assumption) but social-policy experts who grapple concretely with poverty. They know too much of the hard evidence about barriers to pretend that nothing has changed. To explain poverty and justify any policy toward it, experts need a psychological doctrine that explains how personal degradation occurs in an affluent and open society.

Differing visions of human nature are what really divide Charles Murray, William Julius Wilson, myself and others. For Murray, poor adults are short-sighted calculators who are tempted into dysfunction by the disincentives of welfare. For Wilson, they are driven into disorder by a changing economy that denies them jobs that could support a family. My own view, articulated in *Beyond Entitlement: The Social Obligations of Citizenship* [1986], is that they are depressed but dutiful, willing to observe mainstream norms like work if only government will enforce them. But none of us has defended these premises in enough depth, or linked them clearly enough to our prescriptions.

Armed with theories like this, the political process might face more squarely the issues raised by dependency politics. It is more important that the positions be candid than that they agree. Progress requires that the fears of both sides be more fully aired, not that one side wins. The debate might finally generate the consensus needed to support the new paternalistic social policy that is already emerging. There could be agreement on the basic civilities that everyone is prepared to enforce. On that basis, the nation could grapple with passive poverty more successfully.

## Note

From *The Public Interest*, 103,1991, pp. 3–20; fuller version in Lawrence M. Mead, *The New Politics of Poverty*, New York, Basic Books, 1992.

# Feminism

# Feminism and Social Policy

## *Mary McIntosh*

During the 1970s, feminists developed a critique of the welfare system that was both sophisticated and damning. It began in a fragmentary way in the early seventies with specific protests about issues like the 'cohabitation rule' and the 'tax credit' proposals. There was a growing awareness that women figure prominently among the clients of social workers, the inmates of geriatric and psychiatric hospitals, the claimants of supplementary benefits – despite the fact that married and cohabiting women are not eligible for many benefits. There was resentment about the degrading way that women are treated when they need state benefits and state services.

The first responses were articulated most clearly by libertarian feminists, who could express vividly what women know of the conditions under which welfare is granted. They know the queues and the forms, the deference, the anger, the degradation, the sense of invisibility and the loss of autonomy. They see the mean, withholding face of the state and can readily take up the negative cry of 'smash the state!' But the cohabitation campaign also raised deeper issues. It was not just that the 'SS' were 'sex snoopers' who prevented women claimants from drawing their benefit if they were suspected of living with a man. They also tried to force women into prostitutional dependence on the men they slept with. This raised the whole question of women's dependence on men and the fact that women were second-class citizens. The Women's Family Allowance Campaign against the Tory government's 1972 tax-credit proposals focused on the same problems. The family allowance paid directly to a mother was preferable to the same, or even a greater, amount paid in tax credits through a father's pay packet. The model of the couple as a financial unit bore little relation to reality as many women experienced it. In the end, after we had defeated this aspect of the tax-credit scheme, the trade unions' reluctance to accept the loss of the child tax allowance that accompanied the improved child benefit only verified what we already knew: that money in a husband's pay packet was not equivalent to a direct payment to his wife.

In the context of the women's liberation movement, the developing awareness of women's relation to the welfare state was crystallized at the national conference in 1974. Elizabeth Wilson's pamphlet *Women and the Welfare State* (1974) was launched there and a new demand, for 'legal and financial independence', was adopted. The new demand, the fifth to be adopted by the movement, recognized clearly the relevance of the state in solving the problem of women's dependence upon men. The other demands (concerned with equal opportunities in jobs and training, equal pay, nurseries, abortion and contraception) all had a bearing on women's independence in their different ways. But this one, as the paper calling for it to be adopted expressed it, 'highlights the links between the state and the family, and the way in which the state systematically bolsters the dependent-woman family' (Gieve et al., 1974). It saw the relevance of state policy not merely to those categories of women who receive or are denied state benefits of various kinds – not merely to mothers and non-mothers, wives and non-wives, earners and non-earners – but to women as a whole category. For it saw how state policies play a part in constructing that category and in constructing the idea of the family in which it exists. All women suffer from the stereotype of the woman as properly dependent upon a man. But all women also suffer in quite practical terms from the fact that there are few viable alternatives to such dependence. (For an argument against this view, see Bennett et al., 1980.)

Since then, this critique of state policy has been detailed and sustained. Academic articles have been published (especially by Hilary Land, 1976, 1977), and so have pamphlets (for instance, Streather and Weir, 1974; Lister and Wilson, 1976). Many a parliamentary select committee and interdepartmental working party has been told of our views by various women's groups. Wider campaigns, like the rousing but in the end rather abortive one on wives' treatment under income tax, have been mounted. What is disappointing is how little this critique has really affected thinking among other radicals about social policy. Goodwill towards feminism expresses itself in manning the crèche, going on the abortion demo and avoiding sexist styles of behaviour. But how many critics of the DHSS review of Supplementary Benefit [in the late 1970s] – apart from women – argued against the aggregation of the income and resources of husband and wife? Yet separate treatment has been our demand ever since the first feminist critiques of the Beveridge Report in the early 1940s (see, for instance, Abbott and Bompas, 1943; Pierce, 1979).

At the same time as this awareness of how the state constructs dependent women, there was a growing awareness of women as state employees. Both the state bureaucracies and the institutions of health, education and welfare employ enormous numbers of women in their lower ranks; often their clients are women; and often they are engaged in classically 'feminine' types of work both in terms of the contents of their tasks and in terms of the social functions they fulfil. In fact, insofar as previously domestic functions like health care, child care and personal services have become socialized, the social tasks are frequently performed by women just as the private ones were. In struggles to improve social services and nurseries, and in struggles to unionize women workers and advance their position, feminist issues and the question of what women in different situations have in common were fought out time and again. 'The patter of tiny contradictions' was how Val Charlton (1974) described a childcare centre started by some women's liberation groups in London.

All of these critical approaches to social policy were the feminist version of the radical and Marxist critiques of the 1960s and 1970s. The burden of these was that the welfare state is nothing of the kind: that it is not redistributive as between the social classes, but makes the working class pay for its own social casualties, that it does not even eliminate poverty at the bottom end of the scale, that it is not the harbinger of socialist provision according to need – neither in its style nor in its effects – and that it is an instrument of bourgeois control, forcing people to work and imposing standards of morality, decency and household management. To this, feminists add that the welfare state is especially oppressive to women, in that it harnesses them into the team that pulls the whole welfare charabanc along.

What was new, though, was that there was a clear recognition at the same time that women need state provision. Faced with a choice between a chancy dependence on a man on the one hand and dependence on the state or exploitation in waged work on the other, feminists opt for the state and the wage.

Personal dependence carries with it a whole baggage of psychological dependence. Lack of autonomy, deference, the need to manipulate personal relations, all tend to stunt women's potential and make us insecure and unadventurous. Indeed the characteristics of femininity which Juliet Mitchell (1974) has explained in terms of the experience of infancy – passivity, masochism and narcissism – could equally be explained by the adult experience of dependence and the practical need to seek support. This explanation would in fact fit better the reality, which is one of public passivity, based on self-repression and often masking an underlying attitude of cynicism and rebellion, similar to that of Franz Fanon's colonized people.

With all their problems, then, the state and the employer can be fought collectively and unlike modern marriage they are not intrinsically patriarchal. And whenever feminists have formulated the demand for the socialization of housework and of personal care, it has been state provision rather than private commercial provision that they have had in mind.

Feminists in [England] have never been for very long attracted to purely anti-statist positions. Such utopian individualism (or even small-scale collectivism) is a possible dream for men who can envisage a world of self-supporting able-bodied people. But women are usually concerned with how the other three-quarters live. They have argued for new forms of interdependence based in the community and not in the family, and these necessarily involve the state at one level or another.

There have been some interesting debates in the women's movement about the development and provision of feminist services. The question has been: should we provide these ourselves or should we demand state provision and then fight about the form that provision should take? Nurseries, playgroups, health care, advice on contraception and abortion, refuges for battered women, rape crisis centres, legal and welfare rights advice – all clearly fall within the ambit of things that we expect to be provided by state agencies. Yet these are either not available or, when they are, are inadequate and unfeminist in their approach. Setting up services like this is a way both of meeting women's needs and also of developing public awareness of the effects of women's oppression, and providing a base for feminist analysis and agitation around the issue (Flaskas and Hounslow, 1980). In Australia and in the United States there has been a great proliferation of feminist health and welfare services and the results have sometimes been disappointing in that the energies of the women involved have been used up in providing a good service so that the more forward-looking political tasks have been neglected. In England, with the notable exception of the network of Women's Aid refuges for battered women, the tendency has been to set up very few feminist agencies but to concentrate on campaigning for state provision. The more developed social and health services in England have made this a more promising direction to work in. It also seems to me to be the right approach, since it can lead to more long-term and more universal provision than any voluntary efforts are likely to do. The character of such campaigns is also different and in some ways more outgoing politically. Instead of the independent and sometimes rather inward-looking group work involved in establishing and running a feminist service, there is the need to make alliances and work in the existing political arena. The struggle to develop the present services in a feminist direction involves work in the unions and professional bodies of the service workers as well as organizing among clients and users.

Making claims on the state thus involves fruitful political work and agitation at many levels and is far from being confined to the politics of Westminster. So in this respect, as in some others, women have been at the forefront of the rethinking of the rather facile radical libertarianism of the 1960s and early 1970s. (The other thing that feminists questioned was the general assumption that decriminalization, decarceration and de-institutionalization were unambiguously progressive. Sometimes they have gone too far as in calling for exceptionally heavy punishments and the suspension of the usual rights of the accused in cases of rape and of violence against women, and in calling for increased state control over pornography. In some spheres we have not yet gone far enough: we should be mounting a much stronger criticism of present ideas of 'community care' and fighting for new forms of institutional care that avoid the problems earlier radicals have pointed to.)

[. . . ] We have to develop ideas and organizations that enable us to engage with social policy as it forms. And this will mean discussing what sort of welfare state we do want, not just sniping at the existing one and waiting for The Revolution to put everything right.

However, for Marxists this cannot mean a Fabian-style formulation of gradual ameliorative goals and means. It must mean taking a very clear class position and working within the labour movement and all organizations that can take up an anti-capitalist position. It means working out what gains can be made in any given situation and what threats most need defending against, not assuming that social policy makers are people of good will who will see reason when a clear and forceful case is put to them. I suggest that at the most general level there are two key points to remember.

(1) The first is that although the dominant factor affecting state policies will always be the long-term interests of the ruling class and although the central interests of the working class and the capitalist class are antagonistic, it is not necessarily the case that their interests will be opposed on every single issue of social policy. The most fundamental reason for this is that, despite the fact that the wage relation is an antagonistic one, workers' and capitalists' interests coincide in requiring the satisfaction of the workers' basic needs, whether through the wage or by other means. The capitalist requires the reproduction of labour power; the worker requires food and clothing. Of course, they will differ widely over what sort of needs should be met and under what conditions: over what constitutes 'adequate' reproduction of labour power; and this is where struggles over social policy come in. The history of the growth of the welfare state and the growth of collective consumption (Grevet, 1976; Castells, 1978) in general in capitalist societies is thus neither a history of cherries snatched from the greedy hands of capitalists by a militant working class, nor is it a history of a crafty capitalist plot to control and enfeeble the workers in the interests of guaranteeing the reproduction of labour power and of the relations of production. It is both. The gains and losses have to be figured partly in terms of some felicific calculus and partly in political terms: are we better placed for the next battle? Has morale improved?

(2) The second key point is that we need to keep in mind the limits that are set on social policy by the capital-labour contradiction. In particular, we need to recognize that the wage system is fundamental to capitalist production and that the primary means of the reproduction of labour power will be the wage. Social security provisions and collective consumption will be designed in such a way as to minimize their interference with the labour market and with the existence of a proletariat obliged to sell its labour power in order to survive.

This means that demands for a 'guaranteed minimum income' have no connection with social policy in capitalist society. The 'guaranteed minimum income' is a demand adopted by the Claimants' Union as a radical solution to their degrading experiences at the hands of the social security officials. They see the problems of the means test, the search for a 'liable relative', and the obligation to sign on for employment as ways in which the working class are harassed and controlled. So they demand their abolition, the right of everyone to a guaranteed income regardless of whether or not they are willing to look for waged work. As a Claimants' Union representative argued in one of the workshops at the 'Crisis in the Welfare State' conference [1980]: 'People who don't have jobs need an income as much as those who do; it is hard work just staying alive in capitalist society.' The demand is thus very different from a demand for a minimum wage coupled with improved social security benefits at the same level. It is a demand that the need to sell one's labour power in order to survive should be abolished. So it is nothing less than a demand that socialism be introduced: but a demand ostensibly made of the capitalist state and a demand that socialism should enter through the back door, the relations of distribution; rather than the front door, the relations of production. It is thus, as its proponents are well aware, an unrealizable demand under capitalism, since it negates the wage relation which lies at the heart of capitalism. Any of their supporters who join the ranks because they think they might actually gain the demand have been sadly deceived. But the existence of such demands can have the depressing effect of making all real current struggles over policy look paltry and reformist by comparison.

Feminists have been very aware of this problem in relation to the demand for 'wages for housework', rejected by the women's liberation movement in England in 1972, but still having a small, vocal following. Effectively this is a demand that women should have a guaranteed minimum income, since the idea that there should be any check on whether they actually do any housework is rejected. It is thus a demand that all women should be lifted out of the proletariat and put on a pension. It, too, can be dispiriting if it has the effect of making current struggles over matters like invalid care allowances or the infamous 'Housewife's Non-Contributory Disability Allowance' seem trivial and reformist.

Though dependence on the wage will continue to be the primary means of support for the working class, we have seen during the twentieth century a notable narrowing of the range of people who are expected to depend upon a wage. A wage-earner is no longer expected to provide the main support for old and disabled relatives, only for his wife and children (or, more rarely, her husband and children). The welfare state has defined whole categories of people out of the labour market – the old, the young, the disabled – enabling the capitalist work process to be intensified and many welfare benefits to be offered unconditionally and apparently benevolently. But there cannot be an infinite extension of such benefits unless the working class is to be de-proletarianized altogether.

These two key points are proposed as basic considerations for the formulation of any socialist strategy for social policy in capitalist societies. But I shall illustrate their importance by looking at the problems of feminist strategy. Women have to consider whether they have gained or lost by the policies accepted by the working class in the past, and how they should relate to working-class political organization for the future. And we have to consider what relation we want women to have to wage labour. Should we become more fully proletarianized or should we seek better conditions of dependence on husbands or on state benefits?

I shall turn now to these more specific questions of feminist strategy. In some ways, the central problem is the same one that has plagued feminism ever since the achievement of the vote left the movement without a central rallying cry. The problem is whether to press for equality with men, usually in terms of legal, political and citizenship rights, or to press for greater support and respect for women in their roles as housewives and mothers: a right to an independent income and a recognition of the importance of their contribution.

The second position was that of the 'new feminists' who emerged after the First World War. So Eleanor Rathbone argued in 1925 that the point had been reached where women could say:

> At least we have done with the boring business of measuring everything women want, or that is offered to them, by men's phraseology. We can demand what we want for women, not because it is what men have got, but because it is what women need to fulfill the potentialities of their own natures and to adjust themselves to the circumstances of their own lives (Rathbone, 1929, quoted in Lewis, 1973).

The argument against the older equalitarianism took the form of a rejection of male definitions of women's work as inferior and a plea for a new dignity and new measures of protection. In some respects it was more progressive than equalitarianism: it sought to change the world, not merely to give women access to the better places in it. But in the end it was less radical because the changes it sought were too shallow. They were designed to ease the suffering where the shoe pinches rather than build a new shoe on a better last. For modern feminists it is easy to see why Rathbone's mountainous ideal of Family Endowment brought forth the rather ridiculous mouse of Child Benefit and why women's dependence is still a key issue today. As Hilary Land put it: 'Eleanor Rathbone laid much emphasis on the unequal economic relationship between husband and wife but had far less to say about the division of responsibilities for child care and housework' (Land, 1980). A deeper analysis would have led her to see the two as inseparable within any wage-based economy. The problem as it was posed then is that of the impossibility either of the equalitarian ideal – which asks for equal treatment for unequal people – or of the 'new feminist' ideal – which asks for women to be treated as different but equal.

It is interesting to ask whether the difference between these two strategies has been transcended by the more recent feminism of the women's liberation movement. Certainly it is not the basis for the main divisions within the movement at present. And the modern movement is characterized much more by methods that have nothing to do with legal changes or state policies and so may appear to sidestep the problems of equalitarianism: cultural politics, the politics of lifestyle and changing household relationships, self-help and self-defence, support for victims of rape and violence, forming international links and (perhaps most distinctively) developing theoretical analyses of women's oppression.

Yet in many fields of work, the choice between those two strategies remains and continues to pose thorny problems. These tend to be the modern versions of the very issues of law and social policy that exercised our feminist grandmothers. The issue of protective legislation, restricting the hours and conditions of women's work in factories, is a conspicuous example. Feminists have been divided over it ever since it was first introduced during the nineteenth century. At that time equalitarianism was the dominant approach and such feminists as took an interest in the question opposed the legislation on the grounds that it infringed women's liberty and put them at a disadvantage in the labour market – a view which I think is justified by the historical evidence (Barrett and McIntosh, 1980; but for the opposite view, see Hutchins and Harrison, 1911; Humphries, 1977, 1981). Later the 'new feminists' attacked this stance and argued that women's functions of home-making and child-rearing could not be carried out properly if they were forced to work long hours and at night outside the home. This is not, of course, a defence that appeals to women's liberationists today.

However, the situation today is not at all comparable to that in the past. For one thing, we have formulated the goal of transforming the processes of home-making and child-rearing, so that if these are to be done privately we want men's factory hours to be limited as well. For another, while the

CBI wants protective legislation ended, the TUC wants it continued and extended to cover men and to cover workers everywhere, not just in factory production. So when the Equal Opportunities Commission (1979) [. . .] recommended abolishing the legislation it was siding with the bosses as well as taking an unhistorical perspective and thinking in terms of immediate equality of treatment (for the unequal) rather than of working to eliminate the underlying inequality.

However, it should be noted that the position that women's liberationists usually adopt on this issue depends upon trusting the TUC. If they are not genuine in their commitment to extend protection to men – or if they have no hope of carrying it through – our position becomes one that simply accepts the present role of women and seeks to protect us from some of its worst penalties. I shall come back later to the questions of political practice that this raises. I want first to say something about strategy in relation to one particular feminist campaign, that for 'disaggregation'. I focus on this campaign because it raises important problems and also because I happen to have been involved in it, rather than because I believe it to be any more or less important than other campaigns. It is obviously just one part of a wider struggle.

Socialist feminists in the women's liberation movement have transcended the old divide in the sense that they have questioned not only masculinity and femininity, not only man's place and woman's place, but also the very existence of social division and difference based on sex. We have firmly located the origin and support for this division in the family. This does not mean that we locate it in individual kin-based households, but in the institution of the family, with its ideology, its imperatives and its constraints, which spread far beyond households themselves and both cause and enable the organization of everything else to be marked by gender division. Women's liberation depends upon the radical transformation of that family. However, although there is much disagreement about the relation of that family system to capitalism, most socialist feminists agree on two things: that the specific character of women's oppression at present is related to the articulation between the family system and the wage system; and that we should start working now towards the transformation of the family system and that it will not automatically arrive along with socialism. Indeed, I would add that the family system is changing and is under great strain at present (and not only because of the resurgence of feminism), so that it is incumbent on us to play a part in determining what form that change takes.

On the whole we choose to campaign for those things that we know will both help the immediate problems of many women and also help to open up possibilities for further and more far-reaching change. The demand for 'disaggregation' in social security, income tax, student grants and so on is a good example. The aggregation of the married couple into a tax unit and into a means-testable unit – however it may be dressed up in unisex clothing – represents women's dependence on their husbands. This is a dependence that is unreliable and degrading when it does exist and which in any case is a less common pattern than is often supposed, since most women are breadwinners (Hamill, 1978). In terms of social security, disaggregation would mean that a married woman who could not get a job could claim supplementary benefit regardless of her husband's income. But it would also mean that a married man would get a single person's benefit with no allowance for the wife; she would have to claim herself and fulfil the usual conditions: unless she was responsible for caring for small children or an invalid or something like that, she would have to sign on for employment.

This is a demand that comes out of our own experience. Several of the group which formulated it had suffered indignities and deprivation at the hands of the social security. Even so, the chief argument for it is not that thousands of women will be better off. It is that all women will have rights to full social security and that all men will lose the right to state back-up for keeping their wives in dependence. We realize that some women, especially older ones who have not had recent experience of going out to work, will be disadvantaged. We realize that forcing women onto the labour-market as it exists for them now is painful. But we believe that married women's dependence is in part responsible for their dreadful position in the labour-market, and the movement is simultaneously fighting for better pay and conditions at work, including the part-time and low-paid jobs that many women are forced to take.

We realize, too, that many who are concerned about poverty will tell us that there are other groups worse off than married women, whose needs should be met first. I think that argument reveals one of the weaknesses of the approach to social policy that focuses on questions of income equality, in terms of the outcome of distributional and redistributional processes, and does not look at the structure of relations involved in producing those outcomes. Our concern is with moving towards a structural change; by unhitching marriage from the social security system we hope to contribute to loosening its ties to the welfare system in general and ultimately to the wage system itself. We do believe that many unemployed married women are in poverty; those who are may benefit from the change. So we think that disaggregation would meet important immediate needs for some women, but more importantly it would help undermine the existing unequal marriage system. (Incidentally, I am not much swayed by the argument that disaggregation would remove one of the few advantages of forming households not based on the heterosexual pair-bond, and so provide another bonus for traditional marriage. For one thing, the argument considers individual types of household rather than the institutions as a whole. But more importantly, it assumes that marriage would be strengthened because more people would be motivated to enter it, or to stay in it, and I doubt whether this would be true for many people.)

In the present situation, the main point of arguing for disaggregation is to get an acceptance of the principle as widely as possible: to get to the point where the chief basis for resistance to it is cost and all the objections on principle have been rejected, both within the labour movement and in official circles. Some of the strongest arguments for it will, of course, be equalitarian ones, not because we want to conceal our real aims, but because equality is indeed an important dimension of the demand and one that people most readily latch on to. [ . . . ]

The day-to-day battles, unfortunately, are much more defensive ones against the cuts. But it is important to give these a feminist dimension, which often means one informed by the perspective of disaggregation, so that we recognize and attack cuts that force women further into dependence as well as those that take away their jobs or give them extra unpaid work. Disaggregation and protective legislation are only two examples. Similar strategic decisions have to be made in relation to almost every field. Should we press for a share of the matrimonial home and adequate maintenance for wives on the breakup of marriage? (Law Commission, 1980) Should we press for cohabitant women to be given rights equivalent to those of married women? (Anne Bottomley et al., 1981) These fields need to be linked and seen as part of the overall strategy for women's liberation, which of course goes far beyond the confines of social policy, even in its broadest sense.

The positions that I have argued for here are adopted in the light of the two key points of guidance for socialist social policy that I outlined earlier. They are based on the belief that there can be significant gains for women and for the working class (real gains for women are also gains for working-class unity) within capitalist society, since not every working-class gain is an immediate capitalist loss. And they are based on the belief that the wage system is fundamental to capitalist society, so that despite all the disadvantages of wage work, the way forward must be through furthering the process of proletarianization of women and rescuing women from pre-proletarian dependence. The struggle to end capitalist wage labour cannot be helped by women opting out and can only be undertaken by a working class that is less divided by male domination than the present one.

I want to end with some remarks about problems of organization in pursuing feminist goals in social policy. I shall not discuss questions of organization for women's liberation in general, though what I shall say clearly reflects certain views on that.

Firstly, I think we have got to develop a feminist presence in all the places where changes in social policy are fought for. This means within the left political parties, within the labour movement, within all the campaigning and lobbying bodies, and as much as possible in the women's organizations. Building up such a presence is often an unattractive activity for contemporary women's liberationists. Once we have experienced the joys and terrors of swimming in structureless movements like the women's liberation movement (if we managed to keep our heads above water), whose favourite forums are the mass meeting in an overcrowded school hall with an inadequate PA system and the small intimate and supportive work-group, we find it hard even to tread water in the structured world of jockeying for office, juggling agendas and bowing to the constraints of representative democracy. But we cannot bypass those organizations; they exist, and each of them has carved out its own space of power. If we are not to be in constant opposition to them we must work within them as well as working in our own ways outside them. Sometimes this means challenging and transforming their styles of work and approach. Often, though, it means forming alliances where we have only a few points of agreement; and often it means compromises: avoiding taking a line that will lose us the support that we need for other more important battles. The question of protective legislation and the TUC, which I discussed earlier, is a case in point. Above all, it means getting in there and arguing our case in the context of on-going work.

The second remark I want to make is about men's relation to feminist social policy and to the Women's Liberation Movement. I think it may be true to say that there is never an entirely acceptable stance for outsiders towards a movement of liberation. I have experienced this as a white person in relation to the black movement in the 1960s and as a Briton in relation to anti-imperialist movements. It is easy to be caught in the double bind of being told simultaneously that we should not interfere, not impose our ideas, not assume we can escape being oppressors by an act of will, leave the oppressed group to constitute its own autonomous movement. But it is easier still to use that double bind as an excuse for doing nothing to support the cause of liberation for carrying on with our own struggles quite unaffected by those of our neighbours. Many men have used that double bind as a way of getting off the hook in relation to women's liberation. They respect the autonomy of the women's movement, wish it well, and there the matter can rest.

But such an easy benevolence is not appropriate to the case. We aim to overthrow men's dominance and remove their privileges as a gender. Our cause cannot just be added on to the list of radical causes. We are not a newly discovered minority group like dyslexics or people whose homes are threatened by road-widening, because our oppression is built into the very structure of production and reproduction. So anyone concerned with social policy must decide what stand to take on the issues we raise and must see the question of women as integral to any analysis of social policy. We have been talking and writing for many years now about the inadequacy of existing analyses. Yet those of us who are teachers still find that our well-meaning male colleagues invite us to give a lecture or two on 'women and welfare', 'women and crime', or whatever. This is done with a modest, 'I am only a man; I can't speak for women'. But I sometimes wonder what they think the other eighteen lectures in their course are about: men? neuters? a gender-free society? The welfare system as it stands (or totters) is utterly dependent upon a specific construction of gender. The Department of Health and Social Security is well aware of that and it is time that critics of social policy were as well.

## Note

This extract, from *Critical Social Policy, 1*, 1981, pp. 32–42, is based on the author's paper given at the Critical Social Policy Conference, 'Crisis in the Welfare State', November 1980.

## References

Abbott, Elizabeth and Bompas, Katherine (1943) *The Woman Citizen and Social Security: A Criticism of the Proposals Made in the Beveridge Reports as they Affect Women*, London, Mrs Bompas.

Allen, Sandra et al. (eds) (1974) *Conditions of Illusion*, Leeds, Feminist Books.

Barrett, Michèle and McIntosh, Mary (1980) 'The Family Wage', *Capital and Class*, no. 11.

Bennett, Fran et al. (1980) 'The Limitations of the Demand for Independence', *Politics and Power*, no. 1.

Bottomley, Anne et al. (1981) *The Cohabitation Handbook: A Woman's Guide to the Law*, London, Pluto Press.

Castells, Manuel (1978) 'Collective Consumption and Urban Contradictions in Advanced Capitalism', reprinted in Castells, *City, Class and Power*, London, Macmillan.

Charlton, Valerie (1974) 'The Patter of Tiny Contradictions', *Red Rag*, no. 5, reprinted in Allen et al.

Equal Opportunities Commission (1979) *Health and Safety Legislation: Should we Distinguish between Men and Women?* London, HMSO.

Flaskas, Carmel and Hounslow, Betty (1980) 'Government Intervention and Right-Wing Attacks on Feminist Services', *Scarlet Woman* (Australia) no. 11.

Gieve, Katherine et al. (1974) 'The Independence Demand', in Allen et al.

Grevet, Patrice (1976) *Besoins populaires et financement public*, Paris, Editions Sociales.

Hamill, Lynn (1978) 'Wives as Sole and Joint Breadwinners', paper presented to the Social Science Research Council, Social Security Research Workshop.

Humphries, Jane (1977) 'Class Struggle and the Persistence of the Working-Class Family', *Cambridge Journal of Economics*, vol. 1, no. 3, pp. 241–58.

Humphries, Jane (1981) 'Protective Legislation, the Capitalist State and Working-Class Men: 1842 Mines Regulation Act', *Feminist Review*, no. 7.

Hutchins, B. L. and Harrison, A. (1911) *A History of Factory Legislation*, London, P. S. King and Son, 2nd edn.

Land, Hilary (1976) 'Women: Supporters or Supported?', in Diana Barker and Sheila Allen, *Sexual Divisions and Society: Process and Change*, London, Tavistock.

Land, Hilary (1977) 'Social Security and the Division of Unpaid Work in the Home and Paid Employment in the Labour Market', in Department of Health and Social Security, *Social Security Research Seminar*, London, HMSO, pp. 43–61.

Land, Hilary (1980) 'The Family Wage', *Feminist Review*, no. 6.

Law Commission (1980) *Family Law: The Financial Consequences of Divorce: The Basic Policy: A Discussion Paper*, Law Com. no. 103, London, HMSO, Cmnd. 8041.

Lewis, Jane (1973) 'Eleanor Rathbone and the New Feminism during the 1920s', mimeograph.

Lister, Ruth and Wilson, Leo (1976) *The Unequal Breadwinner*, London, National Council for Civil Liberties.

Mitchell, Juliet (1974) *Psychoanalysis and Feminism*, London, Allen Lane.

Pierce, Sylvie (1979) 'Ideologies of Female Independence in the Welfare State: Women's Response to the Beveridge Report', paper given at British Sociological Association Annual Conference.

Rathbone, Eleanor F. (1929) *Milestones: Presidential Addresses at the Annual Council Meetings of NUSEC*, London.

Streather, Jane and Weir, Stuart (1974) *Social Insecurity: Single Mothers on Social Security*, Child Poverty Action Group, Poverty Pamphlet no. 16.

Wilson, Elizabeth (1974) 'Women and the Welfare State', *Red Rag*, no. 2.

# The Patriarchal Welfare State

## *Carole Pateman*

[. . .]

Theoretically and historically, the central criterion for citizenship has been 'independence', and the elements encompassed under the heading of independence have been based on masculine attributes and abilities. Men, but not women, have been seen as possessing the capacities required of 'individuals', 'workers' and 'citizens'. As a corollary, the meaning of 'dependence' is associated with all that is womanly – and women's citizenship in the welfare state is full of paradoxes and contradictions. [. . .] Three elements of 'independence' are particularly important for present purposes, all related to the masculine capacity for self-protection: the capacity to bear arms, the capacity to own property and the capacity for self-government.

First, women are held to lack the capacity for self-protection; they have been 'unilaterally disarmed'.[1] The protection of women is undertaken by men, but physical safety is a fundamental aspect of women's welfare that has been sadly neglected in the welfare state. From the nineteenth century, feminists (including J. S. Mill) have drawn attention to the impunity with which husbands could use physical force against their wives,[2] but women/wives still find it hard to obtain proper social and legal protection against violence from their male 'protectors'. Defence of the state (or the ability to protect your protection, as Hobbes put it), the ultimate test of citizenship, is also a masculine prerogative. The anti-suffragists in both America and Britain made a great deal of the alleged inability and unwillingness of women to use armed force, and the issue of women and combat duties in the military forces of the warfare state was also prominent in the [. . .] campaign [of the 1980s] against the Equal Rights Amendment in the United States. Although women are now admitted into the armed forces and so into training useful for later civilian employment, they are prohibited from combat duties in Britain,

Australia and the United States. Moreover, past exclusion of women from the warfare state has meant that welfare provision for veterans has also benefited men. In Australia and the United States, because of their special 'contribution' as citizens, veterans have had their own, separately administered welfare state, which has ranged from preference in university education (the GI bills in the United States) to their own medical benefits and hospital services, and (in Australia) preferential employment in the public service.

In the 'democratic' welfare state, however, employment rather than military service is the key to citizenship. The masculine 'protective' capacity now enters into citizenship primarily through the second and third dimensions of independence. Men, but not women, have also been seen as property owners. Only some men own material property, but as 'individuals', all men own (and can protect) the property they possess in their persons. Their status as 'workers' depends on their capacity to contract out the property they own in their labour power. Women are still not fully recognized socially as such property owners. To be sure, our position has improved dramatically from the mid-nineteenth century when women as wives had a very 'peculiar' position as the legal property of their husbands, and feminists compared wives to slaves. But today, a wife's person is still the property of her husband in one vital respect. Despite recent legal reform, in Britain and in some of the states of the United States and Australia, rape is still deemed legally impossible within marriage, and thus a wife's consent has no meaning. Yet women are now formally citizens in states held to be based on the necessary consent of self-governing individuals. The profound contradiction about women's consent is rarely if ever noticed and so is not seen as related to a sexually divided citizenship or as detracting from the claim of the welfare state to be democratic.

The third dimension of 'independence' is self-government. Men have been constituted as the beings who can govern (or protect) themselves, and if a man can govern himself, then he also has the requisite capacity to govern others. Only a few men govern others in public life – but all men govern in private as husbands and heads of households. As the governor of a family, a man is also a 'breadwinner'. He has the capacity to sell his labour power as a worker, or to buy labour power with his capital, and provide for his wife and family. His wife is thus 'protected'. The category of 'breadwinner' presupposes that wives are constituted as economic dependants or 'housewives', which places them in a subordinate position. The dichotomy breadwinner/housewife, and the masculine meaning of independence, were established in Britain by the middle of the nineteenth century; in the earlier period of capitalist development, women (and children) were wage-labourers. A 'worker' became a man who has an economically dependent wife to take care of his daily needs and look after his home and children. Moreover, 'class', too, is constructed as a patriarchal category. 'The working class' is the class of working *men*, who are also full citizens in the welfare state.

[T. H. Marshall first presented his influential account of citizenship in 1949, at the height of the optimism in Britain about the contribution of the new welfare state policies to social change. He referred specifically to . . . ] the universal, civil right to 'work', that is, to paid employment. The democratic implications of the right to work cannot be understood without attention to the connections between the public world of 'work' and citizenship and the private world of conjugal relations. What it means to be a 'worker' depends in part on men's status and power as husbands, and on their standing as citizens in the welfare state. The construction of the male worker as 'breadwinner' and his wife as his 'dependant' was expressed officially in the census classifications in Britain and Australia. In the British Census of 1851, women engaged in unpaid domestic work were 'placed . . . in one of the productive classes along with paid work of a similar kind'.[3] This classification changed after 1871, and by 1911 unpaid housewives had been completely removed from the economically active population. In Australia an initial conflict over the categories of classification was resolved in 1890 when the scheme devised in New South Wales was adopted. The Australians divided up the population more decisively than the British, and the 1891 Census was based on the two categories of 'breadwinner' and 'dependant'. Unless explicitly stated otherwise, women's occupation was classified as domestic, and domestic workers were put in the dependant category.

The position of men as breadwinner-workers has been built into the welfare state. The sexual divisions in the welfare state have received much less attention than the persistence of the old dichotomy between the deserving and undeserving poor, which predates the welfare state. This is particularly clear in the United States, where a sharp separation is maintained between 'social security', or welfare-state policies directed at 'deserving workers who have paid for them through "contributions" over their working lifetimes', and 'welfare' – seen as public 'handouts' to 'barely deserving poor people'.[4] Although 'welfare' does not have this stark meaning in Britain or Australia, where the welfare state encompasses much more than most Americans seem able to envisage, the old distinction between the deserving and undeserving poor is still alive and kicking, illustrated by the popular bogey-figures of the 'scrounger' (Britain) and the 'dole-bludger' (Australia). However, although the dichotomy of deserving/undeserving poor overlaps with the divisions between husband/wife and worker/housewife to some extent, it also obscures the patriarchal structure of the welfare state.

Feminist analyses have shown how many welfare provisions have been established within a two-tier system. First, there are the benefits available to individuals as 'public' persons by virtue of their participation, and accidents of fortune, in the capitalist market. Benefits in this tier of the system are usually claimed by men. Second, benefits are available to the 'dependants' of individuals in the first category, or to 'private' persons, usually women. In the United States, for example, men are the majority of 'deserving' workers who receive benefits through the insurance system to which they have 'contributed' out of their earnings. On the other hand, the majority of claimants in means-tested programmes are women – women who are usually making their claims as wives or mothers. This is clearly the case with AFDC (Aid to Families with Dependent Children), where women are aided because they are mothers supporting children on their own, but the same is also true in other programmes: '46 per cent of the women receiving Social Security benefits make their claims as wives'. In contrast: 'men, even poor men, rarely make claims for benefits solely as husbands or fathers'.[5] In Australia the division is perhaps even more sharply defined. In 1980–81, in the primary tier of the system, in which benefits are employment-related and claimed by those who are expected to be economically independent but are not earning an income because of unemployment or illness, women formed only 31.3 per cent of claimants. In contrast, in the 'dependants group', 73.3 per cent of claimants were women, who were eligible for benefits because 'they are dependent on a man who could not support them, . . . [or] should have had a man support them if he had not died, divorced or deserted them'.[6]

Such evidence of lack of 'protection' raises an important question about *women's* standard of living in the welfare state. As dependants, married women should derive their subsistence from their husbands, so that wives are placed in the position of all dependent people before the establishment of the welfare state; they are reliant on the benevolence of another for their livelihood. The assumption is generally made that all husbands are benevolent. Wives are assumed to share equally in the standard of living of their husbands. The distribution of income *within* households has not usually been a subject of interest to economists, political theorists or protagonists in arguments about class and the welfare state – even though William Thompson drew attention to its importance as long ago as 1825 [in a book entitled *Appeal of One Half the Human Race, Women, against the Pretensions of the Other Half, Men*] – but past and present evidence indicates that the belief that all husbands are benevolent is mistaken. Nevertheless, women are likely to be better off married than if their marriage fails. One reason why women figure so prominently among the poor is that after divorce, as recent evidence from the United States reveals, a woman's standard of living can fall by nearly 75 per cent, whereas a man's can rise by nearly half.[7]

The conventional understanding of the 'wage' also suggests that there is no need to investigate women's standard of living independently from men's. The concept of the wage has expressed and encapsulated the patriarchal separation and integration of the public world of employment and the private sphere of conjugal relations. In arguments about the welfare state and the social wage, the wage is usually treated as a return for the sale of *individuals'* labour power. However, once the opposition breadwinner/housewife was consolidated, a 'wage' had to provide subsistence for several people. The struggle between capital and labour and the controversy about the welfare state have been about the *family wage*. A 'living wage' has been defined as what is required for a worker as breadwinner to support a wife and family, rather than what is needed to support himself; the wage is not what is sufficient to reproduce the worker's own labour power, but what is sufficient, in combination with the unpaid work of the housewife, to reproduce the labour power of the present and future labour force.

[. . .]

## Women's Work and Welfare

Although so many women, including married women, are now in paid employment, women's standing as 'workers' is still of precarious legitimacy. So, therefore, is their standing as democratic citizens. If an individual can gain recognition from other citizens as an equally worthy citizen only through participation in the capitalist market, if self-respect and respect as a citizen are 'achieved' in the public world of the employment society, then women still lack the means to be recognized as worthy citizens. Nor have the policies of the welfare state provided women with many of the resources to gain respect as citizens. Marshall's social rights of citizenship in the welfare state could be extended to men without difficulty. As participants in the market, men could be seen as making a public contribution, and were in a position to be levied by the state to make a contribution more directly, that *entitled* them to the benefits of the welfare state. But how could women, dependants of men, whose legitimate 'work' is held to be located in the private sphere, be citizens of the welfare state? What could, or did, women contribute? The paradoxical answer is that women contributed – welfare.

The development of the welfare state has presupposed that certain aspects of welfare could and should continue to be provided by women (wives) in the home, and not primarily through public provision. The 'work' of a housewife can include the care of an invalid husband and elderly, perhaps infirm, relatives. Welfare-state policies have ensured in various ways that wives/women provide welfare services gratis, disguised as part of their responsibility for the private sphere. A good deal has been written about the fiscal crisis of the welfare state, but it would have been more acute if certain areas of welfare had not been seen as a private, women's matter. It is not surprising that the attack on public spending in the welfare state by the Thatcher and Reagan governments

[went] hand-in-hand with praise for loving care within families, that is, with an attempt to obtain ever more unpaid welfare from (house) wives. The Invalid Care Allowance in Britain has been a particularly blatant example of the way in which the welfare state ensures that wives provide private welfare. The allowance was introduced in 1975 – when the Sex Discrimination Act was also passed – and it was paid to men or to single women who relinquished paid employment to look after a sick, disabled or elderly person (not necessarily a relative). Married women (or those cohabiting) were ineligible for the allowance.

The evidence indicates that it is likely to be married women who provide such care. In 1976 in Britain it was estimated that two million women were caring for adult relatives, and one survey in the north of England found that there were more people caring for adult relatives than mothers looking after children under sixteen.[8] A corollary of the assumption that women, but not men, care for others is that women must also care for themselves. Investigations show that women living by themselves in Britain have to be more infirm than men to obtain the services of home helps, and a study of an old people's home found that frail, elderly women admitted with their husbands faced hostility from the staff because they had failed in their job.[9] Again, women's citizenship is full of contradictions and paradoxes. Women must provide welfare, and care for themselves, and so must be assumed to have the capacities necessary for these tasks. Yet the development of the welfare state has also presupposed that women necessarily are in need of protection by and are dependent on men.

The welfare state has reinforced women's identity as men's dependants both directly and indirectly, and so confirmed rather than ameliorated our social exile. For example, in Britain and Australia the cohabitation rule explicitly expresses the presumption that women necessarily must be economically dependent on men if they live with them as sexual partners. If cohabitation is ruled to take place, the woman loses her entitlement to welfare benefits. The consequence of the cohabitation rule is not only sexually divided control of citizens, but an exacerbation of the poverty and other problems that the welfare state is designed to alleviate. In Britain today

> when a man lives in, a woman's independence – her own name on the weekly giro [welfare cheque] is automatically surrendered. The men become the claimants and the women their dependents. They lose control over both the revenue and the expenditure, often with catastrophic results: rent not paid, fuel bills missed, arrears mounting.[10]

It is important to ask what counts as part of the welfare state. In Australia and Britain the taxation system and transfer payments together form a tax-transfer system in the welfare state. In Australia a tax rebate is available for a dependent spouse (usually, of course, a wife), and in Britain the taxation system has always treated a wife's income as her husband's for taxation purposes. It is only relatively recently that it ceased to be the husband's prerogative to correspond with the Inland Revenue about his wife's earnings, or that he ceased to receive rebates due on her tax payments. Married men can still claim a tax allowance, based on the assumption that they support a dependent wife. Women's dependence is also enforced through the extremely limited public provision of childcare facilities in Australia, Britain and the United States, which creates a severe obstacle to women's full participation in the employment society. In all three countries, unlike Scandinavia, childcare outside the home is a very controversial issue.

Welfare-state legislation has also been framed on the assumption that women make their 'contribution' by providing private welfare, and, from the beginning, women were denied full citizenship in the welfare state. In America 'originally the purpose of ADC (now AFDC) was to keep mothers out of the paid labor force. . . . In contrast, the Social Security retirement program was consciously structured to respond to the needs of white male workers.'[11] In Britain the first national insurance, or contributory, scheme was set up in 1911, and one of its chief architects wrote later that women should have been completely excluded because 'they want insurance for others, not themselves'. Two years before the scheme was introduced, William Beveridge, the father of the contemporary British welfare state, stated in a book on unemployment that the 'ideal [social] unit is the household of man, wife and children maintained by the earnings of the first alone. . . . Reasonable security of employment for the breadwinner is the basis of all private duties and all sound social action.'[12] Nor had Beveridge changed his mind on this matter by the Second World War; his report, *Social Insurance and Allied Services*, appeared in 1942 and laid a major part of the foundation for the great reforms of the 1940s. In a passage now (in)famous among feminists, Beveridge wrote that 'the great majority of married women must be regarded as occupied on work which is vital though unpaid, without which their husbands could not do their paid work and without which the nation could not continue.'[13] In the National Insurance Act of 1946 wives were separated from their husbands for insurance purposes. (The significance of this procedure, along with Beveridge's statement, clearly was lost on T. H. Marshall when he was writing his essay on citizenship and the welfare state.) Under the act, married women paid lesser contributions for reduced benefits, but they could also opt out of the scheme, and so from sickness, unemployment and maternity benefits, and they also lost entitlement to an old age pension in their own right, being eligible only as their husband's dependant. By the time the legislation was amended in 1975, about three-quarters of married women workers had opted out.[14]

A different standard for men and women has also been applied in the operation of the insurance scheme. In 1911 some married women were insured in their own right. The scheme provided benefits in case of 'incapacity to work', but, given that wives had already been identified as 'incapacitated' for the 'work' in question, for paid employment, problems over the criteria for entitlement to sickness benefits were almost inevitable. In 1913 an inquiry was held to discover why married women were claiming benefits at a much greater rate than expected. One obvious reason was that the health of many working-class women was extremely poor. The extent of their ill health was revealed in 1915 when letters written by working women in 1913–14 to the Women's Cooperative Guild were published. The national insurance scheme meant that for the first time women could afford to take time off work when ill – but from which 'work'? Could they take time off from housework? What were the implications for the embryonic welfare state if they ceased to provide free welfare? From 1913 a dual standard of eligibility for benefits was established.[15] For men the criterion was fitness for work. But the committee of inquiry decided that, if a woman could do her housework, she was not ill. So the criterion for eligibility for women was also fitness for work – but unpaid work in the private home, not paid work in the public market that was the basis for the contributory scheme under which the women were insured! This criterion for women was still being laid down in instructions issued by the Department of Health and Social Security in the 1970s.[16] The dual standard was further reinforced in 1975 when a non-contributory invalidity pension was introduced for those incapable of work but not qualified for the contributory scheme. Men and single women were entitled to the pension if they could not engage in paid employment; the criterion for married women was ability to perform 'normal household duties'.[17]

## Wollstonecraft's Dilemma

So far, I have looked at the patriarchal structure of the welfare state, but this is only part of the picture; the development of the welfare state has also brought challenges to patriarchal power and helped provide a basis for women's autonomous citizenship. Women have seen the welfare state as one of their major means of support. Well before women won formal citizenship, they campaigned for the state to make provision for welfare, especially for the welfare of women and their children; and women's organizations and women activists have continued their political activities around welfare issues, not least in opposition to their status as 'dependants'. In 1953 the British feminist Vera Brittain wrote of the welfare state established through the legislation of the 1940s that 'in it women have become ends in themselves and not merely means to the ends of men', and their 'unique value as women was recognised'.[18] In hindsight, Brittain was clearly overoptimistic in her assessment, but perhaps the opportunity now exists to begin to dismantle the patriarchal structure of the welfare state. In the 1980s the large changes in women's social position, technological and structural transformations within capitalism, and mass unemployment mean that much of the basis for the breadwinner/dependant dichotomy and for the employment society itself is being eroded (although both are still widely seen as social ideals). The social context of Hegel's two dilemmas is disappearing. As the current concern about the 'feminization of poverty' reveals, there is now a very visible underclass of women who are directly connected to the state as claimants, rather than indirectly as men's dependants. Their social exile is as apparent as that of poor male workers was to Hegel. Social change has now made it much harder to gloss over the paradoxes and contradictions of women's status as citizens.

However, the question of how women might become full citizens of a democratic welfare state is more complex than may appear at first sight, because it is only in the current wave of the organized feminist movement that the division between the private and public spheres of social life has become seen as a major *political* problem. From the 1860s to the 1960s women were active in the public sphere: women fought not only for welfare measures and for measures to secure the private and public safety of women and girls, but for the vote and civil equality; middle-class women fought for entry into higher education; and the professions and women trade unionists fought for decent working conditions and wages and maternity leave. But the contemporary liberal-feminist view, particularly prominent in the United States, that what is required above all is 'gender-neutral' laws and policies, was not widely shared. In general, until the 1960s the focus of attention in the welfare state was on measures to ensure that women had proper social support, and hence proper social respect, in carrying out their responsibilities in the private sphere. The problem is whether and how such measures could assist women in their fight for full citizenship. In 1942 in Britain, for example, many women welcomed the passage in the Beveridge Report that I have cited because, it was argued, it gave official recognition to the value of women's unpaid work. However, an official nod of recognition to women's work as 'vital' to 'the nation' is easily given; *in practice*, the value of the work in bringing women into full membership in the welfare state was negligible. The equal worth of citizenship and the respect of fellow citizens still depended on participation as paid employees. 'Citizenship' and 'work' stood then and still stand opposed to 'women'.

The extremely difficult problem faced by women in their attempt to win full citizenship I shall call 'Wollstonecraft's dilemma'. The dilemma is that the two routes toward citizenship that women have pursued are mutually incompatible within the confines of the patriarchal welfare state, and, within that context, they are impossible to achieve. For three centuries, since universal citizenship first appeared as a political ideal, women have continued to challenge their alleged natural subordination within private life. From at least the 1790s they have also struggled with the task of trying to become citizens within an ideal and practice that have gained universal meaning through their exclusion. Women's response has been complex. On the one hand, they have demanded that the ideal of citizenship be extended to them, and the liberal-feminist agenda for a 'gender-neutral' social world is the logical conclusion of one form of this demand. On the other hand, women have also insisted, often simultaneously, as did Mary Wollstonecraft, that *as women* they have specific capacities, talents, needs and concerns, so that the expression of their citizenship will be differentiated from that of men. Their unpaid work providing welfare could be seen, as Wollstonecraft saw women's tasks as mothers, as women's work *as citizens*, just as their husbands' paid work is central to men's citizenship.

The patriarchal understanding of citizenship means that the two demands are incompatible because it allows two alternatives only: either women become (like) men, and so full citizens; or they continue at women's work, which is of no value for citizenship. Moreover, within a patriarchal welfare state neither demand can be met. To demand that citizenship, as it now exists, should be fully extended to women accepts the patriarchal meaning of 'citizen', which is constructed from men's attributes, capacities and activities. Women cannot be full citizens in the present meaning of the term; at best, citizenship can be extended to women only as lesser men. At the same time, within the patriarchal welfare state, to demand proper social recognition and support for women's responsibilities is to condemn women to less than full citizenship and to continued incorporation into public life as 'women', that is, as members of another sphere who cannot, therefore, earn the respect of fellow (male) citizens.

The example of child endowments on family allowances in Australia and Britain is instructive as a practical illustration of Wollstonecraft's dilemma. It reveals the great difficulties in trying to implement a policy that both aids women in their work and challenges patriarchal power while enhancing women's citizenship. In both countries there was opposition from the right and from *laissez-faire* economists on the ground that family allowances would undermine the father's obligation to support his children and undermine his 'incentive' to sell his labour power in the market. The feminist advocates of family allowances in the 1920s, most notably Eleanor Rathbone in Britain, saw the alleviation of poverty in families where the breadwinner's wage was inadequate to meet the family's basic needs as only one argument for this form of state provision. They were also greatly concerned with the questions of the wife's economic dependence and equal pay for men and women workers. If the upkeep of children (or a substantial contribution toward it) was met by the state outside of wage bargaining in the market, then there was no reason why men and women doing the same work should not receive the same pay. Rathbone wrote in 1924 that 'nothing can justify the subordination of one group of producers – the mothers – to the rest and their deprivation of a share of their own in the wealth of a community'.[19] She argued that family allowances would, 'once and for all, cut away the maintenance of children and the reproduction of the race from the question of wages'.[20]

But not all the advocates of child endowment were feminists – so that the policy could very easily be divorced from the public issue of wages and dependence and be seen only as a return for and recognition of women's private contributions. Supporters included the eugenicists and pronatalists, and family allowances appealed to capital and the state as a means of keeping wages down. Family allowances had many opponents in the British union movement, fearful that the consequence, were the measure introduced, would be to undermine the power of unions in wage bargaining. The opponents included women trade unionists who were suspicious of a policy that could be used to try to persuade women to leave paid employment. Some unionists also argued that social services, such as housing, education and health, should be developed first, and the TUC adopted this view in 1930. But were the men concerned, too, with their private, patriarchal privileges? Rathbone claimed that 'the leaders of working men are themselves subsconsciously biased by prejudice of sex. . . . Are they not influenced by a secret reluctance to see their wives and children recognised as separate personalities?'[21]

By 1941 the supporters of family allowances in the union movement had won the day, and family allowances were introduced in 1946 as part of the government's wartime plans for postwar reconstruction. The legislation proposed that the allowance would be paid to the father as 'normal household head', but after lobbying by women's organizations, this was overturned in a free vote, and the allowance was paid directly to mothers. In Australia the union movement accepted child endowment in the 1920s (child endowment was introduced in New South Wales in 1927, and at the federal level in 1941). But union support there was based on wider redistributive policies, and the endowment was seen as a supplement to, not a way of breaking down, the family wage.[22] In the 1970s, in both countries, women's organizations again had to defend family allowances and the principle of redistribution from 'the wallet to the purse'.

The hope of Eleanor Rathbone and other feminists that family allowances would form part of a democratic restructuring of the wage system was not realized. Nevertheless, family allowances are paid to women as a benefit in their own right; in that sense they are an important (albeit financially very small) mark of recognition of married women as independent members of the welfare state. Yet the allowance is paid to women as *mothers*, and the key question is thus whether the payment to a mother – a private person – negates her standing as an independent citizen of the welfare state. More generally, the question is whether there can be a welfare policy that gives substantial assistance to women in their daily lives *and* helps create the conditions for a genuine democracy in which women are autonomous citizens, in which we can act *as women* and not as 'woman' (protected/dependent/subordinate) constructed as the opposite to all that is meant by 'man'. That is to say, a resolution of Wollstonecraft's dilemma is necessary and, perhaps, possible.

The structure of the welfare state presupposes that women are men's dependants, but the benefits help to make it possible for women to be economically independent of men. In the countries with which I am concerned, women reliant on state benefits live poorly, but it is no longer so essential as it once was to marry or to cohabit with a man. A considerable moral panic has developed in recent years around 'welfare mothers', a panic that obscures significant features of their position, not least the extent to which the social basis for the ideal of breadwinner/dependant has crumbled. Large numbers of young working-class women have little or no hope of finding employment (or of finding a young man who is employed). But there is a source of social identity available to them that is out of the reach of their male counterparts. The socially secure and acknowledged identity for women is still that of a mother, and for many young women, motherhood, supported by state benefits, provides 'an alternative to aimless adolescence on the dole' and 'gives the appearance of self-determination'. The price of independence and 'a rebellious motherhood that is not an uncritical retreat into femininity'[23] is high, however; the welfare state provides a minimal income and perhaps housing (often substandard), but childcare services and other support are lacking, so that the young women are often isolated, with no way out of their social exile. Moreover, even if welfare state policies in Britain, Australia and the United States were reformed so that generous benefits, adequate housing, health care, child care and other services were available to mothers, reliance on the state could reinforce women's lesser citizenship in a new way.

Some feminists have enthusiastically endorsed the welfare state as 'the main recourse of women' and as the generator of 'political resources which, it seems fair to say, are mainly women's resources'.[24] They can point, in Australia for example, to 'the creation over the decade [1975–85] of a range of women's policy machinery and government subsidized women's services (delivered by women for women) which is unrivalled elsewhere.'[25] However, the enthusiasm is met with the rejoinder from other feminists that for women to look to the welfare state is merely to exchange dependence on individual men for dependence on the state. The power and capriciousness of husbands is being replaced by the arbitrariness, bureaucracy and power of the state, the very state that has upheld patriarchal power. The objection is cogent: to make women directly dependent on the state will not in itself do anything to challenge patriarchal power relations. The direct dependence of male workers on the welfare state and their indirect dependence when their standard of living is derived from the vast system of state regulation of and subsidy to capitalism – and in Australia a national arbitration court – have done little to undermine class power. However, the objection also misses an important point. There is one crucial difference between the construction of women as men's dependants and dependence on the welfare state. In the former case, each woman lives with the man on whose benevolence she depends; each woman is (in J. S. Mill's extraordinarily apt phrase) in a 'chronic state of bribery and intimidation combined'.[26] In the welfare state, each woman receives what is hers by right, and she can, potentially, combine with other citizens to enforce her rightful claim. The state has enormous powers of intimidation, but political action takes place collectively in the public terrain and not behind the closed door of the home, where each woman has to rely on her own strength and resources.

Another new factor is that women are now involved in the welfare state on a large scale as employees, so that new possibilities for political action by women also exist. Women have been criticizing the welfare state in recent years not just as academics, as activists, or as beneficiaries and users of welfare services, but as the people on whom the daily operation of the welfare state to a large extent depends. The criticisms range from its patriarchal structure (and, on occasions, especially in health care, misogynist practices), to its bureaucratic and undemocratic policy-making processes and administration, to social work practices and education policy. Small beginnings have been made on changing the welfare state from within; for example, women have succeeded in establishing Well Women Clinics within the NHS in Britain and special units to deal with rape victims in public hospitals in Australia. Furthermore, the potential is now there for united action by women employees, women claimants and women citizens already politically active in the welfare state – not just to protect services against government cuts and efforts at 'privatization' (which has absorbed much energy recently), but to transform the welfare state. Still, it is hard to see how women alone could succeed in the attempt. One necessary condition for the creation of a genuine democracy in which the welfare of *all* citizens is served is an alliance between a labour movement that acknowledges the problem of patriarchal power and an autonomous women's movement that recognizes the problem of class power. Whether such an alliance can be forged is an open question.

Despite the debates and the rethinking brought about by mass unemployment and attack on the union movement and welfare state by the Reagan and Thatcher governments, there are many barriers to be overcome. In Britain and Australia, with stronger welfare states, the women's movement has had a much closer relationship with working-class movements than in the United States, where the individualism of the predominant liberal feminism is an inhibiting factor, and where only about 17 per cent of the workforce is now unionized. The major locus of criticism of authoritarian, hierarchical, undemocratic forms of organization since about 1970 has been the women's movement. The practical example of democratic, decentralized organization provided by the women's movement has been largely ignored by the labour movement, as well as in academic discussions of democracy. After Marx defeated Bakunin in the First International, the prevailing form of organization in the labour movement, the nationalized industries in Britain and in the left sects has mimicked the hierarchy of the state – both the welfare and the warfare state. To be sure, there is a movement for industrial democracy and workers' control, but it has, by and large, accepted that the 'worker' is a masculine figure and failed to question the separation of (public) industry and economic production from private life. The women's movement has rescued and put into practice the long-submerged idea that movement for, and experiments in, social change must 'prefigure' the future form of social organization.[27]

If prefigurative forms of organization, such as the 'alternative' women's welfare services set up by the women's movement, are not to remain isolated examples, or if attempts to set them up on a wider scale are not to be defeated, as in the past, very many accepted conceptions and practices have to be questioned. [ . . . ] Debates [during the 1980s] over left alternatives to Thatcherite economics policies in Britain, and over the Accord between the state, capital and labour in Australia, suggest that the arguments and demands of the women's movement are still often unrecognized by labour's political spokesmen. For instance, one response to unemployment from male workers is to argue for a shorter working week and more leisure, or more time but the same money. However, in women's lives, time and money are not interchangeable in the same way.[28] Women, unlike men, do not have leisure after 'work', but do unpaid work. Many women are arguing, rather, for a shorter working day. The point of the argument is to challenge the separation of part- and full-time paid employment and paid and unpaid 'work'. But the conception of citizenship needs thorough questioning, too, if Wollstonecraft's dilemma is to be resolved; neither the labour movement nor the women's movement (nor democratic theorists) has paid much attention to this. The patriarchal opposition between the private and public, women and citizen, dependant and breadwinner is less firmly based than it once was, and feminists have named it as a political problem. The ideal of full employment so central to the welfare state is also crumbling, so that some of the main props of the patriarchal understanding of citizenship are being undermined. The ideal of full employment appeared to have been achieved in the 1960s only because half the citizen body (and black men?) was denied legitimate membership in the employment society. Now that millions of men are excluded from the ideal (and the exclusion seems permanent), one possibility is that the ideal of universal citizenship will be abandoned, too, and full citizenship will become the prerogative of capitalist, employed and armed men. Or can a genuine democracy be created?

The perception of democracy as a class problem and the influence of liberal feminism have combined to keep alive Engels's old solution to 'the woman question' – to 'bring the whole female sex back into public industry'.[29] But the economy has a patriarchal structure. The Marxist hope that capitalism would create a labour force where ascriptive characteristics were irrelevant, and the liberal-feminist hope that anti-discrimination legislation would create a 'gender-neutral' workforce, look Utopian even without the collapse of the ideal of full employment. Engels's solution is out of reach – and so, too, is the generalization of masculine citizenship to women. In turn, the argument that the equal worth of citizenship, and the self-respect and mutual respect of citizens, depend upon sale of labour power in the market and the provisions of the patriarchal welfare state is also undercut. The way is opening up for the formulation of conceptions of respect and equal worth adequate for democratic citizenship. Women could not 'earn' respect or gain the self-respect that men obtain as workers; but what kind of respect do men 'achieve' by selling their labour power and becoming wage-slaves? Here the movement for workplace democracy and the feminist movement could join hands, but only if the conventional understanding of 'work' is rethought. If women as well as men are to be full citizens, the separation of the welfare state and employment from the free welfare work contributed by women has to be broken down and new meanings and practices of 'independence', 'work' and 'welfare' created.

For example, consider the implications were a broad, popular political movement to press for welfare policy to include a guaranteed social income to all adults, which would provide adequately for subsistence and also participation in social life.[30] For such a demand to be made, the old dichotomies must already have started to break down – the opposition between paid and unpaid work (for the first time all individuals could have a genuine choice whether to engage in paid work), between full- and part-time work, between public and private work, between independence and dependence, between work and welfare – which is to say, between men and women. If implemented, such a policy would at last recognize women as equal members of the welfare state, although it would not in itself ensure women's full citizenship. If a genuine democracy is to be created, the problem of the content and value of women's contribution as citizens and the meaning of citizenship has to be confronted.

To analyse the welfare state through the lens of Hegel's dilemma is to rule out such problems. But the history of the past 150 years and the contemporary record show that the welfare of all members of society cannot be represented by men, whether workers or capitalists. Welfare is, after all, the welfare of all living generations of citizens and their children. If the welfare state is seen as a response to Hegel's dilemma, the appropriate question about women's citizenship is: how can women become workers and citizens like men, and so members of the welfare state like men? If, instead, the starting-point is Wollstonecraft's dilemma, then the question might run: what form must democratic citizenship take if a primary task of all citizens is to ensure that the welfare of each living generation of citizens is secured?

The welfare state has been fought for and supported by the labour movement and the women's movement because only public or collective provision can maintain a proper standard of living and the means for meaningful social participation for all citizens in a democracy. The implication of this claim is that democratic citizens are both autonomous and interdependent; they are autonomous in that each enjoys the means to be an active citizen, but they are interdependent in that the welfare of each is the collective responsibility of all citizens. Critics of the class structure of the welfare state have often counterposed the fraternal interdependence (solidarity) signified by the welfare state to the bleak independence of isolated individuals in the market, but they have rarely noticed that both have been predicated upon the dependence (subordination) of women. In the patriarchal welfare state, independence has been constructed as a masculine prerogative. Men's 'independence' as workers and citizens is their freedom from responsibility for welfare (except insofar as they 'contribute' to the welfare state). Women have been seen as responsible for (private) welfare work, for relationships of dependence and interdependence. The paradox that welfare relies so largely on women, on dependants and social exiles whose 'contribution' is not politically relevant to their citizenship in the welfare state, is heightened now that women's paid employment is also vital to the operation of the welfare state itself.

If women's knowledge of and expertise in welfare are to become part of their contribution as citizens, as women have demanded during the twentieth century, the opposition between men's independence and women's dependence has to be broken down, and a new understanding and practice of citizenship developed. The patriarchal dichotomy between women and independence-work-citizenship is under political challenge, and the social basis for the ideal of the full (male) employment society is crumbling. An opportunity has become visible to create a genuine democracy, to move from the welfare state to a welfare society without involuntary social exiles, in which women as well as men enjoy full social membership. Whether the opportunity can be realized is not easy to tell now that the warfare state is overshadowing the welfare state.

## Notes

From C. Pateman, *The Disorder of Women*, Cambridge, Polity Press, 1989, pp. 185–9, 192–209.

1 The graphic phrase is Judith Stiehm's, in 'Myths Necessary to the Pursuit of War', unpublished paper, p. 11.

2 See especially F. Cobbe, 'Wife Torture in England', *The Contemporary Review*, 32, 1878, pp. 55–87. Also, for example, Mill's remarks when introducing the amendment to enfranchise women in the House of Commons in 1867, reprinted in *Women, the Family and Freedom: The Debate in Documents*, ed. S. Bell and K. Offen, vol. 1, Stanford, CA, Stanford University Press, 1983, p. 487.
3 D. Deacon, 'Political Arithmetic: The Nineteenth-Century Australian Census and the Construction of the Dependent Woman', *Signs*, 11(1), 1985, p. 31 (my discussion draws on Deacon); also H. Land, 'The Family Wage', *Feminist Review*, 6, 1980, p. 60.
4 T. Skocpol, 'The Limits of the New Deal System and the Roots of Contemporary Welfare Dilemmas', in *The Politics of Social Policy in the United States*, ed. M. Weir, A. Orloff and T. Skocpol, Princeton, NJ, Princeton University Press, 1988.
5 B. Nelson, 'Women's Poverty and Women's Citizenship: Some Political Consequences of Economic Marginality', *Signs*, 10(2), 1984, pp. 222–3.
6 M. Owen, 'Women – A Wastefully Exploited Resource', *Search*, 15, 1984, pp. 271–2.
7 L. J. Weitzman, *The Divorce Revolution*, New York, The Free Press, 1985, ch. 10, esp. pp. 337–40.
8 J. Dale and P. Foster, *Feminists and the Welfare State*, London, Routledge and Kegan Paul, 1986, p. 112.
9 H. Land, 'Who Cares for the Family?', *Journal of Social Policy*, 7(3), 1978, pp. 268–9. Land notes that even under the old Poor Law twice as many women as men received outdoor relief, and there were many more old men than women in the workhouse wards for the ill or infirm; the women were deemed fit for the wards for the able-bodied.
10 B. Campbell, *Wigan Pier Revisited: Poverty and Politics in the 80s*, London, Virago Press, 1984, p. 76.
11 Nelson, op. cit., pp. 229–30.
12 Both quotations are taken from Land, op. cit., p. 72.
13 Cited in Dale and Foster, op. cit., p. 17.
14 H. Land, 'Who Still Cares for the Family?', in *Women's Welfare, Women's Rights*, ed. J. Lewis, London and Canberra, Croom Helm 1983, p. 70.
15 M. Davis, *Maternity: Letters from Working Women*, New York, Norton, 1978 (first published 1915).
16 Information taken from Land, op. cit. (n. 9), pp. 263–4.
17 Land, op. cit. (n. 14), p. 73.
18 Cited in Dale and Foster, op. cit., p. 3.
19 Cited in Land, op. cit. (n. 3), p. 63.
20 Cited in B. Cass, 'Redistribution to Children and to Mothers: A History of Child Endowment and Family Allowances', in *Women, Social Welfare and the State*, ed. J. Goodnow and C. Pateman, Sydney, Allen and Unwin, 1985, p. 57.
21 Cited in ibid., p. 59.
22 Ibid., pp. 60–1.
23 Campbell, op. cit., pp. 66, 78, 71.
24 F. Fox Piven, 'Women and the State: Ideology, Power, and the Welfare State', *Socialist Review*, 14(2), 1984, pp. 14, 17.
25 M. Sawer, 'The Long March through the Institutions: Women's Affairs under Fraser and Hawke', paper presented to the annual meeting of the Australasian Political Studies Association, Brisbane, 1986, p. 1.
26 J. S. Mill, 'The Subjection of Women', in *Essays on Sex Equality*, ed. A. Rossi, Chicago, University of Chicago Press, 1970, p. 137.

27 See S. Rowbotham, L. Segal and H. Wainright, *Beyond the Fragments: Feminism and the Making of Socialism*, London, Merlin Press, 1979, a book that was instrumental in opening debate on the left and in the labour movement in Britain on this question.

28 See H. Hernes, *Welfare State and Woman Power: Essays in State Feminism*, Oslo, Norwegian University Press, 1987, ch. 5, for a discussion of the political implications of the different time-frames of men's and women's lives.

29 F. Engels, *The Origin of the Family, Private Property and the State*, New York, International Publishers, 1942, p. 66.

30 See also the discussion in J. Keane and J. Owens, *After Full Employment*, London, Hutchinson, 1986, pp. 175–7.

# Part II

## *Debates and Issues*

In part II of the reader, we adopt a more empirical and comparative approach and our focus is unambiguously on *contemporary* developments in the welfare state. The selections here are chosen with three goals in mind. The first is to convey something of the range and variety of welfare state activity as demonstrated in the contemporary practice of advanced, industrial nations. The second is to use the experience of contemporary practice to identify the major challenges, problems and prospects of the advanced welfare state in the coming years of the new millennium. The third is to provide a guide to the major debates and policy issues which have preoccupied scholars from the many disciplines – including sociology, political science, economics and social administration – which see the welfare state and the public sector more broadly as among their central concerns. Since social provision in its many forms is now the predominant activity of the state in all modern societies, these are debates and issues which are clearly pivotal to understanding how such societies function and how they are changing.

Our preference for comparative studies has a double rationale. Partly, we want to avoid the parochialism that comes from identifying any particular welfare state as the template for welfare states in general. More importantly, comparison is a key to better understanding. By the standards of the classic contributors to the welfare state literature discussed in part I, virtually all modern states are welfare states, but that does not mean that they are all the same. Different welfare states achieve different degrees of poverty alleviation, income inequality and risk reduction. Their welfare systems have different implications for welfare dependency and they structure gender inequalities in different ways. Such differences are relevant to both policy goals and normative concerns, because they help us to establish the conditions under which desired social policy objectives may be achieved in practice.

A comparative approach also helps us to locate sources of weakness and strength in welfare state arrangements and institutions. As noted subsequently, a major theme of the contemporary literature is the extent and range of challenges to the viability of the welfare state in recent years. But again there are important differences between countries. Some appear to have coped better with economic and demographic problems than others. In some, support for the welfare state project seems to have remained rock solid, while in others there has been a strong political backlash against at least some forms of public intervention. Locating the reasons why such differences occur may tell us why some welfare states are more vulnerable to attack than others and may even provide us with the knowledge required to redesign welfare state institutions so that they are less vulnerable in future.

All the pieces appearing in part II have been selected in order to present arguments central to major debates in the literature. The first of these debates concerns the ways in which we classify different types of welfare state. The initial section on Welfare Regimes starts out from Gøsta Esping-Andersen's well-known distinction between what he describes as 'liberal', 'conservative/corporatist' and 'social democratic' regime types. This typology has been widely welcomed for at least three reasons. It moves away from expenditure as the sole criterion of welfare effort, replacing it with the more sociological notion of the 'decommodifying' impact of diverse systems of social rights. It suggests that the welfare state is about more than just services and transfers and argues that diverse patterns of social provision are premised on distinctive labour market formations. Finally, it provides plausible connections between the class origins of welfare regimes, their distinctive modes of provision and their consequences for social and economic inequality. The paper by Arts and Gelissen brings this debate up to date. Esping-Andersen's original classification of the three worlds of welfare capitalism sparked off a debate about a whole series of national experiences which (so their observers suppose) point to other worlds of welfare capitalism. There is also a suspicion among some (feminist critics, in particular) that in focusing so strongly on labour market decommodification, Esping-Andersen was looking in the wrong place for a comprehensive explanation of the differences between existing welfare state regimes. Arts and Gelissen offer a comprehensive survey of these critical approaches to the world of differing welfare regimes.

The supposed impact of *globalization* on almost every facet of modern social life has been a ubiquitous feature of discussion in the social sciences for at least a decade. Over time, it has become commonplace to argue that processes of globalization have imperiled all of the major institutional formations in which the welfare state has become condensed in developed capitalist societies. One variant of the argument is that welfare state expansion has reduced economic efficiency and competitiveness and so has become a source of major economic problems, including declining productivity growth and high levels of unemployment. Another is the currently fashionable view that high levels of welfare state spending and highly regulated labour markets are incompatible with the new realities of a globalized economy, which impose heavy constraints on the policy autonomy of the modern state. If nations do not heed the demands of international markets, domestic economic actors will vote with their feet, leaving countries increasingly bereft of supplies of mobile capital and skilled labour. For both variants the bottom line is the same: countries which do not reduce high levels of social spending and taxation are, quite literally, likely to go out of business!

The authors in the Globalization section subject these views to critical scrutiny. In a careful theoretical and empirical review of the existing literature, Colin Hay shows that the impact of 'globalization' is much more ambivalent and uncertain than its more committed admirers (and critics) have supposed. He concludes that under circumstances of real-or-imagined globalization, 'the welfare state is not only a competitive advantage it is a competitive necessity'. Following a brief selection from Fritz Scharpf, which shows why and how heightened transborder economic competition may impact on domestic welfare state settlements, Francis Castles offers a detailed interrogation of the popular idea of a 'race to the bottom' in standards of social provision. His conclusion is that, while some countries have experienced some comparative decline in the standards of their social provision over the last ten to twenty years, the overall evidence suggests that the idea of a welfare 'race to the bottom' is 'a crisis myth rather than a crisis reality'.

One of the most interesting debates of recent years has concerned the extent to which welfare states in Europe have been reshaped by the ongoing process of constitutional change associated with the 'widening and deepening' of the European Union. The first paper in our Europeanization section considers the ways in which changes in Western European welfare states have interacted with the logic(s) of globalization. Walter Korpi is particularly concerned about the effects that globalization and Europeanization have had on the full employment commitments which were an important component of postwar welfare settlements across Western Europe. In his view, the entire postwar social contract is under review (and duress) in contemporary Europe. Paul Teague's paper on 'Deliberative Governance and EU Social Policy' is much more explicitly focused on institutional change at the level of the European Union. Teague surveys the evidence for a distinctive institutional architecture underpinning 'Social Europe' and considers whether we are seeing the emergence of new forms of 'deliberative governance' at the EU level. His conclusion is that, while there are new competences emerging at the EU level, we should be wary of supposing that these are likely to bring us much closer to a 'Social Europe' that replaces traditional national welfare state structures. Finally, in exploring the European dimension of social policy development, Chalmers and Lodge review experience of the 'Open Method of Co-ordination' which has, since the EU Lisbon summit of 2000, been the preferred mechanism for securing the cooperation and coordination of EU member states in transnational public policy-making. They conclude that, as yet, the achievement of these goals is more a matter of policy aspiration than of policy achievement.

Among the most fascinating and intractable problems facing contemporary welfare states are those that arise from changes in the underlying demographic structure of the population. There are certainly some writers (Paul Pierson among them) who remain deeply sceptical about the impact of globalization and yet profoundly concerned about the challenge that societal ageing presents to the integrity of contemporary welfare states. Increasingly this is an issue which is in the news every day as people find that pension entitlements which they had once believed to be secure are legislated away from beneath their feet. In the section on Demographic Challenges to the Welfare State, we look at several issues concerning the changing population structures of modern welfare states. One hugely influential strand of argument has been the view that population ageing combined with excessive state pensions have together seriously compromised the integrity of public finances and that what is required are reforms to reduce basic pension rights and to privatize provision for the middle class. A rather newer concern arises from a seemingly rapid decline in fertility rates and with it a decline in the size of the youthful population which (in developed Western welfare states at least) is going to be called on to support the ever growing pensioner population of the first half of the twenty-first century. Here we include a sober and sensible discussion of the real world of population ageing by David Coleman, an evaluation of prospects over the next fifty years by James Schulz, as well as a rather terrifying account of the coming crisis of pension provision by Richard Jackson. Peter McDonald's paper addresses some of the issues surrounding gender equity and fertility transition. His argument is that unless and until we expand our treatment of gender equity from individual-oriented to family-oriented institutions we shall not reverse (nor should we be able *equitably* to reverse) the transition to extremely low fertility rates.

In the final section of part II, we include two papers that take a very broad perspective on the *political challenges* that now confront the welfare state. Paul Pierson's story is of the emergence of a 'new politics' of the welfare state, in which the natural wish of politicians to avoid blame for unpopular policies has combined with the development of strong constituencies of support for established welfare programmes to make retrenchment an issue of extreme political sensitivity. In Pierson's view, this is ultimately why both Thatcher and Reagan failed in their ideologically driven campaigns against public sector spending. His argument suggests that the challenges, opportunities and constituencies that current practitioners of the politics of welfare confront are quite different from those that faced politicians in the 'classic' years of welfare state growth. Bruno Palier's focus is on the study of the dynamics of welfare state change 'beyond retrenchment'. Retrenchment has been a seemingly universal element in discussions of the welfare state over the past twenty years. But Palier insists that such a focus is too limited and undifferentiated. Even if the overall direction of change has been uniform, this conceals differences of pace in different policy areas, differences between varying welfare regime types and, indeed, moments of innovation and of real change that have been masked by a more general trend of continuity.

# Welfare Regimes

# Three Worlds of Welfare Capitalism

*Gøsta Esping-Andersen*

## What Is the Welfare State?

Every theoretical paradigm must somehow define the welfare state. How do we know when and if a welfare state responds functionally to the needs of industrialism, or to capitalist reproduction and legitimacy? And how do we identify a welfare state that corresponds to the demands that a mobilized working class might have? We cannot test contending arguments unless we have a commonly shared conception of the phenomenon to be explained.

A remarkable attribute of the entire literature is its lack of much genuine interest in the welfare state as such. Welfare state studies have been motivated by theoretical concerns with other phenomena, such as power, industrialization or capitalist contradictions; the welfare state itself has generally received scant conceptual attention. If welfare states differ, how do they differ? And when, indeed, is a state a welfare state? This turns attention straight back to the original question: what is the welfare state?

A common textbook definition is that it involves state responsibility for securing some basic modicum of welfare for its citizens. Such a definition skirts the issue of whether social policies are emancipatory or not; whether they help system legitimation or not; whether they contradict or aid the market process; and what, indeed, is meant by 'basic'? Would it not be more appropriate to require of a welfare state that it satisfies more than our basic or minimal welfare needs?

The first generation of comparative studies started with this type of conceptualization. They assumed, without much reflection, that the level of social expenditure adequately reflects a state's commitment to welfare. The theoretical intent was not really to arrive at an understanding of the welfare state, but rather to test the validity of contending theoretical models in political economy. By scoring nations with respect to urbanization, level of economic growth, and the proportion of aged in the demographic structure, it was believed that the essential features of industrial modernization were properly considered. Alternatively, power-oriented theories compared nations on left-party strength or working-class power mobilization.

The findings of the first-generation comparativists are difficult to evaluate, since there is no convincing case for any particular theory. The shortage of nations for comparisons statistically restricts the number of variables that can be tested simultaneously. Thus, when Cutright (1965) or Wilensky (1975) find that economic level, with its demographic and bureaucratic correlates, explains most welfare-state variations in 'rich countries', relevant measures of working-class mobilization or economic openness are not included. Their conclusions in favour of a 'logic of industrialism' view are therefore in doubt. And, when Hewitt (1977), Stephens (1979), Korpi (1983), Myles (1984) and Esping-Andersen (1985) find strong evidence in favour of a working-class mobilization thesis, or when Schmidt (1982, 1983) finds support for a neo-corporatist, and Cameron (1978) for an economic openness argument, it is without fully testing against plausible alternative explanations.

Most of these studies claim to explain the welfare state. Yet their focus on spending may be misleading. Expenditures are epiphenomenal to the theoretical substance of welfare states. Moreover, the linear scoring approach (more or less power, democracy or spending) contradicts the sociological notion that power, democracy or welfare are relational and structured phenomena. By scoring welfare states on spending, we assume that all spending counts equally. But some welfare states, the Austrian one, for example, spend a large share on benefits to privileged civil servants. This is normally not what we would consider a commitment to social citizenship and solidarity. Others spend disproportionately on means-tested social assistance. Few contemporary analysts would agree that a reformed poor-relief tradition qualifies as a welfare-state commitment. Some nations spend enormous sums on fiscal welfare in the form of tax privileges to private insurance plans that mainly benefit the middle classes. But these tax expenditures do not show up on expenditure accounts. In Britain, total social expenditure [grew] during the Thatcher period, yet this is almost exclusively a function of very high unemployment. Low expenditure on some programmes may signify a welfare state more seriously committed to full employment.

Therborn (1983) is right when he holds that we must begin with a conception of state structure. What are the criteria with which we should judge whether, and when, a state is a welfare state? There are three approaches to this question. Therborn's proposal is to begin with the historical transformation of state activities. Minimally, in a genuine welfare state the majority of its daily routine activities must be devoted to servicing the welfare needs of households. This criterion has far-reaching consequences. If we simply measure routine activity in terms of spending and personnel, the result is that no state can be regarded as a real welfare state until the 1970s, and some that we normally label as welfare states will not qualify because the majority of their routine activities concern defence, law and order, administration and the like (Therborn, 1983). Social scientists have been too quick to accept nations' self-proclaimed welfare state status. They have also been too quick to conclude that if the standard social programmes have been introduced, the welfare state has been born.

The second conceptual approach derives from Richard Titmuss's (1958) classical distinction between residual and institutional welfare states. In the former, the state assumes responsibility only when the family or the market fails; it seeks to limit its commitments to marginal and deserving social groups. The latter model addresses the entire population, is universalistic, and embodies an institutionalized commitment to welfare. It will, in principle, extend welfare commitments to all areas of distribution vital for societal welfare.

The Titmuss approach has fertilized a variety of new developments in comparative welfare state research (Korpi, 1980; Myles, 1984; Esping-Andersen and Korpi, 1984, 1986; Esping-Andersen, 1985, 1987). It is an approach that forces researches to move from the black box of expenditures to the content of welfare states: targeted versus universalistic programmes, the conditions of eligibility, the quality of benefits and services, and, perhaps most importantly, the extent to which employment and working life are encompassed in the state's extension of citizen rights. The shift to welfare state typologies makes simple linear welfare state rankings difficult to sustain. Conceptually, we are comparing categorically different types of state.

The third approach is to theoretically select the criteria on which to judge types of welfare state. This can be done by measuring actual welfare states against some abstract model and then scoring programmes, or entire welfare states, accordingly (Myles, 1984). But this is ahistorical, and does not necessarily capture the ideals or designs that historical actors sought to realize in the struggles over the welfare state. If our aim is to test causal theories that involve actors, we should begin with the demands that were actually promoted by those actors that we deem critical in the history of welfare state development. It is difficult to imagine that anyone struggled for spending *per se*.

## A Re-specification of the Welfare State

Few can disagree with T. H. Marshall's (1950) proposition that social citizenship constitutes the core idea of a welfare state. But the concept must be fleshed out. Above all, it must involve the granting of social rights. If social rights are given the legal and practical status of property rights, if they are inviolable, and if they are granted on the basis of citizenship rather than performance, they will entail a de-commodification of the status of individuals *vis-à-vis* the market. But the concept of social citizenship also involves social stratification: one's status as a citizen will compete with, or even replace, one's class position.

The welfare state cannot be understood just in terms of the rights it grants. We must also take into account how state activities are interlocked with the market's and the family's role in social provision. These are the three main principles that need to be fleshed out prior to any theoretical specification of the welfare state.

## *Rights and De-commodification*

In pre-capitalist societies, few workers were properly commodities in the sense that their survival was contingent upon the sale of their labour power. It is as markets become universal and hegemonic that the welfare of individuals comes to depend entirely on the cash nexus. Stripping society of the institutional layers that guaranteed social reproduction outside the labour contract meant that people were commodified. In turn, the introduction of modern social rights implies a loosening of the pure commodity status. De-commodification occurs when a service is rendered as a matter of right, and when a person can maintain a livelihood without reliance on the market.

The mere presence of social assistance or insurance may not necessarily bring about significant de-commodification if they do not substantially emancipate individuals from market dependence. Means-tested poor relief will possibly offer a safety net of last resort. But if benefits are low and associated with social stigma, the relief system will compel all but the most desperate to participate in the market. This was precisely the intent of the nineteenth-century Poor Laws in most countries. Similarly, most of the early social-insurance programmes were deliberately designed to maximize labour-market performance.

There is no doubt that de-commodification has been a hugely contested issue in welfare state development. For labour, it has always been a priority. When workers are completely market-dependent, they are difficult to mobilize for solidaristic action. Since their resources mirror market inequalities, divisions emerge between the 'ins' and the 'outs', making labour-movement formation difficult. De-commodification strengthens the workers and weakens the absolute authority of the employer. It is for exactly this reason that employers have always opposed de-commodification.

De-commodified rights are differentially developed in contemporary welfare states. In social-assistance dominated welfare states, rights are not so much attached to work performance as to demonstrable need. Needs-tests and typically meagre benefits, however, service to curtail the de-commodifying effect. Thus, in nations where this model is dominant (mainly in the Anglo-Saxon countries), the result is actually to strengthen the market since all but those who fail in the market will be encouraged to contract private-sector welfare.

A second dominant model espouses compulsory state social insurance with fairly strong entitlements. But again, this may not automatically secure substantial de-commodification, since this hinges very much on the fabric of eligibility and benefit rules. Germany was the pioneer of social insurance, but over most of the [twentieth century] can hardly be said to have brought about much in the way of de-commodification through its social programmes. Benefits have depended almost entirely on contributions, and thus on work and employment. In other words, it is not the mere presence of a social right, but the corresponding rules and preconditions, which dictate the extent to which welfare programmes offer genuine alternatives to market dependence.

The third dominant model of welfare, namely the Beveridge-type citizens' benefit, may, at first glance, appear the most de-commodifying. It offers a basic, equal benefit to all, irrespective of prior earnings, contributions or performance. It may indeed be a more solidaristic system, but not necessarily de-commodifying, since only rarely have such schemes been able to offer benefits of such a standard that they provide recipients with a genuine option to working.

De-commodifying welfare states are, in practice, fairly recent. A minimal definition must entail that citizens can freely, and without potential loss of job, income or general welfare, opt out of work when they themselves consider it necessary. With this definition in mind, we would, for example, require of a sickness insurance that individuals be guaranteed benefits equal to normal earnings, and the right to absence with minimal proof of medical impairment and for the duration that the individual deems necessary. These conditions, it is worth noting, are those usually enjoyed by academics, civil servants and higher-echelon white-collar employees. Similar requirements would be made of pensions, maternity leave, parental leave, educational leave and unemployment insurance.

Some nations have moved towards this level of de-commodification, but only recently, and, in many cases, with significant exemptions. In almost all nations, benefits were upgraded to nearly equal normal wages in the late 1960s and early 1970s. But in some countries, for example, prompt medical certification in case of illness is still required; in others, entitlements depend on long waiting periods of up to two weeks; and in still others, the duration of entitlements is very short. [ . . . ] The Scandinavian welfare states tend to be the most de-commodifying; the Anglo-Saxon the least.

## The Welfare State as a System of Stratification

Despite the emphasis given to it in both classical political economy and in T. H. Marshall's pioneering work, the relationship between citizenship and social class has been neglected both theoretically and empirically. Generally speaking, the issue has either been assumed away (it has been taken for granted that the welfare state creates a more egalitarian society), or it has been approached narrowly in terms of income distribution or in terms of whether education promotes upward social mobility. A more basic question, it seems, is what kind of stratification system is promoted by social policy. The welfare state is not just a mechanism that intervenes in, and possibly corrects, the structure of inequality; it is, in its own right, a system of stratification. It is an active force in the ordering of social relations.

Comparatively and historically, we can easily identify alternative systems of stratification embedded in welfare states. The poor-relief tradition, and its contemporary means-tested social-assistance offshoot, was conspicuously designed for purposes of stratification. By punishing and stigmatizing recipients, it promotes social dualisms and has therefore been a chief target of labour-movement attacks.

The social-insurance model promoted by conservative reformers such as Bismarck and von Taffe was also explicitly a form of class politics. It sought, in fact, to achieve two simultaneous results in terms of stratification. The first was to consolidate divisions among wage-earners by legislating distinct programmes for different class and status groups, each with its own conspicuously unique set of rights and privilege which was designed to accentuate the individual's appropriate station in life. The second objective was to tie the loyalties of the individual directly to the monarchy or the central state authority. This was Bismarck's motive when he promoted a direct state supplement to the pension benefit. This state-corporatist model was pursued mainly in nations such as Germany, Austria, Italy and France, and often resulted in a labyrinth of status-specific insurance funds.

Of special importance in this corporatist tradition was the establishment of particularly privileged welfare provisions for the civil service *(Beamten)*. In part, this was a means of rewarding loyalty to the state, and in part it was a way of demarcating this group's uniquely exalted social status. The corporatist status-differentiated model springs mainly from the old guild tradition. The neo-absolutist autocrats, such as Bismarck, saw in this tradition a means to combat the rising labour movements.

The labour movements were as hostile to the corporatist model as they were to poor relief – in both cases for obvious reasons. Yet the alternatives first espoused by labour were no less problematic from the point of view of uniting the workers as one solidaristic class. Almost invariably, the model that labour first pursued was that of self-organized friendly societies or equivalent union- or party-sponsored fraternal welfare plans. This is not surprising. Workers were obviously suspicious of reforms sponsored by a hostile state, and saw their own organizations not only as bases of class mobilization, but also as embryos of an alternative world of solidarity and justice; as a microcosm of the socialist haven to come. Nonetheless, these micro-socialist societies often became problematic class ghettos that divided rather than united workers. Membership was typically restricted to the strongest strata of the working class, and the weakest – who most needed protection – were most likely excluded. In brief, the fraternal society model frustrated the goal of working-class mobilization.

The socialist 'ghetto approach' was an additional obstacle when socialist parties found themselves forming governments and having to pass the social reforms they had so long demanded. For political reasons of coalition-building and broader solidarity, their welfare model had to be recast as welfare for 'the people'. Hence, the socialists came to espouse the principle of universalism; borrowing from the liberals, their programme was, typically, designed along the lines of the democratic flat-rate, general revenue-financed Beveridge model.

As an alternative to means-tested assistance and corporatist social insurance, the universalistic system promotes equality of status. All citizens are endowed with similar rights, irrespective of class or market position. In this sense, the system is meant to cultivate cross-class solidarity, a solidarity of the nation. But the solidarity of flat-rate universalism presumes a historically peculiar class structure, one in which the vast majority of the population are the 'little people' for whom a modest, albeit egalitarian, benefit may be considered adequate. Where this no longer obtains, as occurs with growing working-class prosperity and the rise of the new middle classes, flat-rate universalism inadvertently promotes dualism because the better-off turn to private insurance and to fringe-benefit bargaining to supplement modest equality with what they have decided are accustomed standards of welfare. Where this process unfolds (as in Canada or Great Britain), the result is that the wonderfully egalitarian spirit of universalism turns into a dualism similar to that of the social-assistance state: the poor rely on the state, and the remainder on the market.

It is not only the universalist but, in fact, all historical welfare state models which have faced the dilemma of changes in class structure. But the response to prosperity and middle-class growth has been varied, and so, therefore, has been the outcome in terms of stratification. The corporatist insurance tradition was, in a sense, best equipped to manage new and loftier welfare-state expectations since the existing system could technically be upgraded quite easily to distribute more adequate benefits. Adenauer's 1957 pension reform in Germany was a pioneer in this respect. Its avowed purpose was to restore status differences that had been eroded because of the old insurance system's incapacity to provide benefits tailored to expectations. This it did simply by moving from contribution-to earnings-graduated benefits without altering the framework of status-distinctiveness.

In nations with either a social-assistance or a universalistic Beveridge-type system, the option was whether to allow the market or the state to furnish adequacy and satisfy middle-class aspirations. Two alternative models emerged from this political choice. The one typical of Great Britain and most of the Anglo-Saxon world was to preserve an essentially modest universalism in the state, and allow the market to reign for the growing social strata demanding superior welfare. Due to the political power of such groups, the dualism that emerges is not merely one between state and market, but also between forms of welfare-state transfers: in these nations, one of the fastest growing components of public expenditure is tax subsidies for so-called 'private' welfare plans. And the typical political effect is the erosion of middle-class support for what is less and less a universalistic public-sector transfer system.

Yet another alternative has been to seek a synthesis of universalism and adequacy outside the market. This road has been followed in countries where, by mandating or legislation, the state incorporates the new middle classes within a luxurious second-tier, universally inclusive, earnings-related insurance scheme on top of the flat-rate egalitarian one. Notable examples are Sweden and Norway. By guaranteeing benefits tailored to expectations, this solution reintroduces benefit inequalities, but effectively blocks off the market. It thus succeeds in retaining universalism and also, therefore, the degree of political consensus required to preserve broad and solidaristic support for the high taxes that such a welfare state model demands.

## Welfare State Regimes

As we survey international variations in social rights and welfare-state stratification, we will find qualitatively different arrangements between state, market and the family. The welfare state variations we find are therefore not linearly distributed, but clustered by regime-types.

In one cluster we find the 'liberal' welfare state, in which means-tested assistance, modest universal transfers or modest social-insurance plans predominate. Benefits cater mainly to a clientele of low-income, usually working-class, state dependants. In this model, the progress of social reform has been severely circumscribed by traditional, liberal work-ethic norms: it is one where the limits of welfare equal the marginal propensity to opt for welfare instead of work. Entitlement rules are therefore strict and often associated with stigma; benefits are typically modest. In turn, the state encourages the market, either passively – by guaranteeing only a minimum – or actively – by subsidizing private welfare schemes.

The consequence is that this type of regime minimizes de-commodification effects, effectively contains the realm of social rights, and erects an order of stratification that is a blend of a relative equality of poverty among state-welfare recipients, market-differentiated welfare among the majorities, and a class-political dualism between the two. The archetypical examples of this model are the United States, Canada and Australia.

A second regime-type clusters nations such as Austria, France, Germany and Italy. Here, the historical corporatist-statist legacy was upgraded to cater to the new 'post-industrial' class structure. In these conservative and strongly 'corporatist' welfare states, the liberal obsession with market efficiency and commodification was never pre-eminent and, as such, the granting of social rights was hardly ever a seriously contested issue. What predominated was the preservation of status differentials; rights, therefore, were attached to class and status. This corporatism was subsumed under a state edifice perfectly ready to displace the market as a provider of welfare; hence, private insurance and occupational fringe benefits play a truly marginal role. On the other hand, the state's emphasis on upholding status differences means that its redistributive impact is negligible.

But the corporatist regimes are also typically shaped by the Church, and hence strongly committed to the preservation of traditional familyhood. Social insurance typically excludes non-working wives, and family benefits encourage motherhood. Day care, and similar family services, are conspicuously underdeveloped; the principle of 'subsidiarity' serves to emphasize that the state will only interfere when the family's capacity to service its members is exhausted.

The third, and clearly smallest, regime-cluster is composed of those countries in which the principles of universalism and de-commodification of social rights were extended also to the new middle classes. We may call it the 'social democratic' regime-type since, in these nations, social democracy was clearly the dominant force behind social reform. Rather than tolerate a dualism between state and market, between working class and middle class, the social democrats pursued a welfare state that would promote an equality of the highest standards, not an equality of minimal needs as was pursued elsewhere. This implied, first, that services and benefits be upgraded to levels commensurate with even the most discriminating tastes of the new middle classes; and, second, that equality be furnished by guaranteeing workers full participation in the quality of rights enjoyed by the better-off.

This formula translates into a mix of highly de-commodifying and universalistic programmes that, nonetheless, are tailored to differentiated expectations. Thus, manual workers come to enjoy rights identical with those of salaried white-collar employees or civil servants; all strata are incorporated under one universal insurance system, yet benefits are graduated according to accustomed earnings. This model crowds out the market, and consequently constructs an essentially universal solidarity in favour of the welfare state. All benefit; all are dependent; and all will presumably feel obliged to pay.

The social democratic regime's policy of emancipation addresses both the market and the traditional family. In contrast to the corporatist-subsidiarity model, the principle is not to wait until the family's capacity to aid is exhausted, but to pre-emptively socialize the costs of familyhood. The ideal is not to maximize dependence on the family, but capacities for individual independence. In this sense, the model is a peculiar fusion of liberalism and socialism. The result is a welfare state that grants transfers directly to children, and takes direct responsibility of caring for children, the aged and the helpless. It is, accordingly, committed to a heavy social-service burden, not only to service family needs but also to allow women to choose work rather than the household.

Perhaps the most salient characteristic of the social democratic regime is its fusion of welfare and work. It is at once genuinely committed to a full-employment guarantee, and entirely dependent on its attainment. On the one side, the right to work has equal status to the right of income protection. On the other side, the enormous costs of maintaining a solidaristic, universalistic and de-commodifying welfare system means that it must minimize social problems and maximize revenue income. This is obviously best done with most people working, and the fewest possible living off social transfers.

Neither of the two alternative regime-types espouse full employment as an integral part of their welfare state commitment. In the conservative tradition, of course, women are discouraged from working; in the liberal ideal, concerns of gender matter less than the sanctity of the market.

[ . . . ] Welfare states cluster, but we must recognize that there is no single pure case. The Scandinavian countries may be predominantly social democratic, but they are not free of crucial liberal elements. Neither are the liberal regimes pure types. The American social-security system is redistributive, compulsory and far from actuarial. At least in its early formulation, the New Deal was as social democratic as was contemporary Scandinavian social democracy. And European conservative regimes have incorporated both liberal and social democratic impulses. Over the decades, they have become less corporativist and less authoritarian.

Notwithstanding the lack of purity, if our essential criteria for defining welfare states have to do with the quality of social rights, social stratification and the relationship between state, market and family, the world is obviously composed of distinct regime-clusters. Comparing welfare states on scales of more or less or, indeed, of better or worse, will yield highly misleading results.

## The Causes of Welfare-State Regimes

If welfare states cluster into three distinct regime-types, we face a substantially more complex task of identifying the causes of welfare state differences. What is the explanatory power of industrialization, economic growth, capitalism or working-class political power in accounting for regime-types ? A first superficial answer would be: very little. The nations we study are all more or less similar with regard to all but the variable of working-class mobilization. And we find very powerful labour movements and parties in each of the three clusters.

A theory of welfare state developments must clearly reconsider its causal assumptions if it wishes to explain clusters. The hope of finding one single powerful causal force must be abandoned; the task is to identify salient interaction effects. Based on the preceding arguments, three factors in particular should be of importance: the nature of class mobilization (especially of the working class); class-political coalition structures; and the historical legacy of regime institutionalization.

[ . . . ] There is absolutely no compelling reason to believe that workers will automatically and naturally forge a socialist class identity; nor is it plausible that their mobilization will look especially Swedish. The actual historical formation of working-class collectivities will diverge, and so also will their aims, ideology and political capacities. Fundamental differences appear both in trade unionism and party development. Unions may be sectional or in pursuit of more universal objectives; they may be denominational or secular; and they may be ideological or devoted to business unionism. Whichever they are, it will decisively affect the articulation of political demands, class cohesion and the scope for labour-party action. It is clear that a working-class mobilization thesis must pay attention to union structure.

The structure of trade unionism may or may not be reflected in labour-party formation. But under what conditions are we likely to expect certain welfare state outcomes from specific party configurations? There are many factors that conspire to make it virtually impossible to assume that any labour, or left-wing, party will ever be capable, single-handedly, of structuring a welfare state. Denominational or other divisions aside, it will be only under extraordinary historical circumstances that a labour party alone will command a parliamentary majority long enough to impose its will. [ . . . ] The traditional working class has hardly ever constituted an electoral majority. It follows that a theory of class mobilization must look beyond the major leftist parties. It is a historical fact that welfare state construction has depended on political coalition-building. The structure of class coalitions is much more decisive than are the power resources of any single class.

The emergence of alternative class coalitions is, in part, determined by class formation. In the earlier phases of industrialization, the rural classes usually constituted the largest single group in the electorate. If social democrats wanted political majorities, it was here that they were forced to look for allies. One of history's many paradoxes is that the rural classes were decisive for the future of socialism. Where the rural economy was dominated by small, capital-intensive family farmers, the potential for an alliance was greater than where it rested on large pools of cheap labour. And where farmers were politically articulate and well organized (as in Scandinavia), the capacity to negotiate political deals was vastly superior.

The role of the farmers in coalition formation and hence in welfare state development is clear. In the Nordic countries, the necessary conditions obtained for a broad red–green alliance for a full-employment welfare state in return for farm price subsidies. This was especially true in Norway and Sweden, where farming was highly precarious and dependent on state aid. In the United States, the New Deal was premised on a similar coalition (forged by the Democratic Party), but with the important difference that the labour-intensive South blocked a truly universalistic social security system and opposed further welfare-state developments. In contrast, the rural economy of continental Europe was very inhospitable to red–green coalitions. Often, as in Germany and Italy, much of agriculture was labour-intensive; hence the unions and left-wing parties were seen as a threat. In addition, the conservative forces on the continent had succeeded in incorporating farmers into 'reactionary' alliances, helping to consolidate the political isolation of labour.

Political dominance was, until after the Second World War, largely a question of rural class politics. The construction of welfare states in this period was, therefore, dictated by whichever force captured the farmers. The absence of a red–green alliance does not necessarily imply that no welfare-state reforms were possible. On the contrary, it implies which political force came to dominate their design. Great Britain is an exception to this general rule, because the political significance of the rural classes eroded before the turn of the century. In this way, Britain's coalition-logic showed at an early date the dilemma that faced most other nations later; namely, that the rising white-collar strata constitute the linchpin for political majorities. The consolidation of welfare states after the Second World War came to depend fundamentally on the political alliances of the new middle classes. For social democracy, the challenge was to synthesize working-class and white-collar demands without sacrificing the commitment to solidarity.

Since the new middle classes have, historically, enjoyed a relatively privileged position in the market, they have also been quite successful in meeting their welfare demands outside the state, or, as civil servants, by privileged state welfare. Their employment security has traditionally been such that full employment has been a peripheral concern. Finally, any programme for drastic income-equalization is likely to be met with great hostility among a middle-class clientele. On these grounds, it would appear that the rise of the new middle classes would abort the social democratic project and strengthen a liberal welfare state formula.

The political leanings of the new middle classes have, indeed, been decisive for welfare state consolidation. Their role in shaping the three welfare state regimes described earlier is clear. The Scandinavian model relied almost entirely on social democracy's capacity to incorporate them into a new kind of welfare state: one that provided benefits tailored to the tastes and expectations of the middle classes, but nonetheless retained universalism of rights. Indeed, by expanding social services and public employment, the welfare state participated directly in manufacturing a middle class instrumentally devoted to social democracy.

In contrast, the Anglo-Saxon nations retained the residual welfare state model precisely because the new middle classes were not wooed from the market to the state. In class terms, the consequence is dualism. The welfare state caters essentially to the working class and the poor. Private insurance and occupational fringe benefits cater to the middle classes. Given the electoral importance of the latter, it is quite logical that further extensions of welfare state activities are resisted.

The third, continental European, welfare state regime has also been patterned by the new middle classes, but in a different way. The cause is historical. Developed by conservative political forces, these regimes institutionalized a middle-class loyalty to the preservation of both occupationally segregated social-insurance programmes and, ultimately, to the political forces that brought them into being. Adenauer's great pension reform in 1957 was explicitly designed to resurrect middle-class loyalties.

## Conclusion

We have here presented an alternative to a simple class-mobilization theory of welfare-state development. It is motivated by the analytical necessity of shifting from a linear to an interactive approach with regard to both welfare states and their causes. If we wish to study welfare states, we must begin with a set of criteria that define their role in society. This role is certainly not to spend or tax; nor is it necessarily that of creating equality. We have presented a framework for comparing welfare states that takes into consideration the principles for which the historical actors have willingly united and struggled. When we focus on the principles embedded in welfare states, we discover distinct regime-clusters, not merely variations of 'more' or 'less' around a common denominator.

The historical forces behind the regime differences are interactive. They involve, first, the pattern of working-class political formation and, second, political coalition-building in the transition from a rural economy to a middle-class society. The question of political coalition-formation is decisive. Third, past reforms have contributed decisively to the institutionalization of class preferences and political behaviour. In the corporatist regimes, hierarchical status-distinctive social insurance cemented middle-class loyalty to a peculiar type of welfare state. In liberal regimes, the middle classes became institutionally wedded to the market. And in Scandinavia, the fortunes of social democracy over the past decades were closely tied to the establishment of a middle-class welfare state that benefits both its traditional working-class clientele and the new white-collar strata. The Scandinavian social democrats were able to achieve this in part because the private welfare market was relatively undeveloped and in part because they were capable of building a welfare state with features of sufficient luxury to satisfy the wants of a more discriminating public. This also explains the extraordinarily high cost of Scandinavian welfare states.

But a theory that seeks to explain welfare state growth should also be able to understand its retrenchment or decline. It is generally believed that welfare state backlash movements, tax revolts and roll-backs are ignited when social expenditure burdens become too heavy. Paradoxically, the opposite is true. Anti-welfare-state sentiments [since the 1980s] have generally been weakest where welfare spending has been heaviest, and vice versa. Why?

The risks of welfare state backlash depend not on spending, but on the class character of welfare states. Middle-class welfare states, be they social democratic (as in Scandinavia) or corporatist (as in Germany), forge middle-class loyalties. In contrast, the liberal, residualist welfare states found in the United States, Canada and, increasingly, Britain, depend on the loyalties of a numerically weak, and often politically residual, social stratum. In this sense, the class coalitions in which the three welfare-state regime-types were founded explain not only their past evolution but also their future prospects.

## Note

From *The Three Worlds of Welfare Capitalism*, Cambridge, Polity Press, 1990, pp. 18–34.

## References

Cameron, D. R. (1978) 'The Expansion of the Public Economy: A Comparative Analysis', *American Political Science Review*, 72, 4, pp. 1243–61.

Cutright, P. (1965) 'Political Structure, Economic Development, and National Social Security Programs', *American Journal of Sociology*, 70, pp. 537–50.

Esping-Andersen, G. (1985) 'Power and Distributional Regimes', *Politics and Society*, 14.

Esping-Andersen, G. (1987) 'Citizenship and Socialism', in M. Rein, G. Esping-Andersen and M. Rainwater, *Stagnation and Renewal in Social Policy: The Rise and Fall of Policy Regimes*, New York, Sharpe.

Esping-Andersen, G. and Korpi,W. (1984) 'Social Policy and Class Politics in Postwar Capitalism: Scandinavia, Austria and Germany', in *Order and Conflict in Contemporary Capitalism*, ed. J. Goldthorpe, Oxford, Oxford University Press, pp. 179–208.

Esping-Andersen, G. and Korpi, W. (1986) 'From Poor Relief to Institutional Welfare States: The Development of Scandinavian Social Policy', in R. Erikson et al., *The Scandinavian Model: Welfare States and Welfare Research*, New York, Sharpe.

Hewitt, C. (1977) 'The Effect of Political Democracy and Social Democracy on Equality in Industrial Societies: A Cross-National Comparison', *American Sociological Review*, 42, pp. 450–64.

Korpi, W. (1980) 'Social Policy and Distributional Conflict in the Capitalist Democracies', *West European Politics*, 3.

Korpi, W (1983) *The Democratic Class Struggle*, London, Routledge and Kegan Paul.

Marshall, T. H. (1950) *Citizenship and Social Class*, Cambridge, Cambridge University Press.

Myles, J. (1984) *Old Age in the Welfare State*, Boston, Little, Brown.

Schmidt, M. G. (1982) 'The Role of Parties in Shaping Macro-Economic Policies', in *The Impact of Parties*, ed. F. Castles, London, Sage.

Schmidt, M. G. (1983) 'The Welfare State and the Economy in Periods of Economic Crisis: A Comparative Study of 23 OECD Nations', *European Journal of Political Research*, 11, 1983, pp. 1–26.

Stephens, J. (1979) *The Transition from Capitalism to Socialism*, London, Macmillan.

Therborn, G. (1983) 'When, How and Why does a Welfare State become a Welfare State?', Freiburg, ECPR Workshops.

Titmuss, R. M. (1958) *Essays on the Welfare State*, London, Allen and Unwin.

Wilensky, H. (1975) *The Welfare State and Equality: Structural and Ideological Roots of Public Expenditure*, Berkeley, University of California Press.

# Three Worlds of Welfare Capitalism or More? A State-of-the-Art Report

*Wil Arts and John Gelissen*

[. . .]

## Three Worlds of 'Welfare Capitalism' . . .

The central explanatory questions Esping-Andersen (1990, pp. 4, 105) asks are: Why is the world composed of three qualitatively different welfare-state logics? Why do nations crystallize into distinct regime-clusters? These questions demand a theoretical answer. Since he is of the opinion that the existing theoretical models of the welfare state are inadequate, reconceptualization and retheorization are necessary. In answering these questions he starts with the orienting statement that history and politics matter. Or, more specifically: 'The historical characteristics of states, especially the history of political class coalitions as the most decisive cause of welfare-state variations, have played a determinate role in forging the emergence of their welfare-statism' (1990, p. 1).

What are the historical and political forces behind the regime differences? According to Esping-Andersen (p. 29), three interacting factors are significant: the nature of class mobilization (especially of the working class), class-political action structures, and the historical legacy of regime institutionalization. The provisional answer to his central questions is therefore: If you look at the history of so-called welfare states you find three ideal-typical trajectories, a liberal, a conservative and a social-democratic one. Fortunately, one does not have to go back in history, however, in order to typify 'real' welfare states. We can characterize them, as we have mentioned before, by looking at their positions on two fundamental dimensions of welfare statism:

1 The degree of decommodification, i.e. the degree to which a (social) service is rendered as a matter of right, and the degree to which a person can maintain a livelihood without reliance on the market.
2 The kind of social stratification and solidarities, i.e. which social stratification system is promoted by social policy and does the welfare state build narrow or broad solidarities?

What are the characteristics of the three distinct regime-types to which the historical forces lead? To answer this question, Esping-Andersen (1990, p. 73) argues that although the before-mentioned dimensions are conceptually independent, according to his 'theory' he would expect that there is sufficient covariation for distinct regime-clusters to emerge. In accordance with this theoretical expectation, he succeeds in empirically identifying three closely paralleled models – ideal-types – of regime-types on both the stratification and the decommodification dimension. There appears to be a clear coincidence of high decommodification and strong universalism in the Scandinavian, social-democratically influenced welfare states. There is an equally clear coincidence of low decommodification and strong individualistic self-reliance in the liberal Anglo-Saxon nations. Finally, the continental European countries group closely together as corporatist and étatist, and are also modestly decommodifying (Esping-Andersen, 1990, p. 77).

In spite of anomalies such as the Netherlands and Switzerland, the overall picture is convincing, at least at first glance. This empirical success permits a more extensive description of these three worlds of welfare capitalism. First, there is the liberal type of welfare capitalism, which embodies individualism and the primacy of the market. The operation of the market is encouraged by the state, either actively – subsidizing private welfare schemes – or passively by keeping (often means tested) social benefits to a modest level for the demonstrably needy. There is little redistribution of incomes within this type of welfare state and the realm of social rights is rather limited. This welfare regime is characterized by a low level of decommodification. The operation of the liberal principle of stratification leads to division in the population: on the one hand, a minority of low-income state dependants and, on the other hand, a majority of people able to afford private social insurance plans. In this type of welfare state, women are encouraged to participate in the labour force, particularly in the service sector.

Second, there is a world of conservative-corporatist welfare states, which is typified by a moderate level of decommodification. This regime type is shaped by the twin historical legacy of Catholic social policy,[1] on the one side, and corporatism and étatism on the other side. This blend had three important consequences in terms of stratification. In the first place, the direct influence of the state is restricted to the provision of income maintenance benefits related to occupational status. This means that the sphere of solidarity remains quite narrow and corporatist. Moreover, labour market participation by married women is strongly discouraged, because corporatist regimes – influenced by the Church – are committed to the preservation of traditional family structures. Another important characteristic of the conservative regime type is the principle of subsidiarity: the state will only interfere when the family's capacity to service its members is exhausted (Esping-Andersen, 1990, p. 27).

Finally, Esping-Andersen recognizes a social-democratic world of welfare capitalism. Here, the level of decommodification is high, and the social-democratic principle of stratification is directed towards achieving a system of generous universal and highly distributive benefits not dependent on any individual contributions. In contrast to the liberal type of welfare states, 'this model crowds out the market and, consequently, constructs an essentially universal solidarity in favour of the welfare state' (1990, p. 28). Social policy within this type of welfare state is aimed at a maximization of capacities for individual independence. Women in particular – regardless of whether they have children or not – are encouraged to participate in the labour market, especially in the public sector. Countries that belong to this type of welfare state regime are generally dedicated to full employment. Only by making sure that as many people as possible have a job is it possible to maintain such a high-level solidaristic welfare system.

## . . . or More?

[We have] indicated the tremendous impact of Esping-Andersen's work on comparative social policy analysis (Esping-Andersen, 1990). Since then, several authors have developed alternative typologies or added one or more types to existing classifications for greater empirical refinement. From this vast array of welfare state typologies we have selected six classifications, which we think draw attention to interesting characteristics of welfare states not directly included in Esping-Andersen's classification. All these typologies and their main characteristics are summarized in table 1.

These alternative classifications relate to three important criticisms of Esping-Andersen's classification (for these and other points of critique see Schmidt, 1998; Gough, 2000).[2] First, the misspecification of the Mediterranean welfare states; second, labelling the Antipodean welfare states as belonging to the 'liberal' welfare state regime; and finally, the neglect of the gender-dimension in social policy. In the following sections, we will discuss these criticisms in more detail and present some of the alternative classifications developed by his critics.

**Table 1** An overview of typologies of welfare states

| | Types of welfare states and their characteristics | Indicators/dimensions |
|---|---|---|
| Esping-Andersen (1990) | 1 *Liberal:* Low level of decommodification; market-differentiation of welfare<br>2 *Conservative:* Moderate level of decommodification; social benefits mainly dependent on former contributions and status<br>3 *Social-Democratic:* High level of decommodification; universal benefits and high degree of benefit equality | • Decommodification<br>• Stratification |
| Leibfried (1992) | 1 *Anglo-Saxon (Residual):* Right to income transfers; welfare state as compensator of last resort and tight enforcer of work in the market place<br>2 *Bismarck (Institutional):* Right to social security; welfare state as compensator of first resort and employer of last resort<br>3 *Scandinavian (Modern):* Right to work for everyone; universalism; welfare state as employer of first resort and compensator of last resort<br>4 *Latin Rim (Rudimentary):* Right to work and welfare proclaimed; welfare state as a semi-institutionalized promise | • Poverty, social insurance and poverty policy |
| Castles & Mitchell (1993) | 1 *Liberal:* Low social spending and no adoption of equalizing instruments in social policy<br>2 *Conservative:* High social expenditures, but little adoption of equalizing instruments in social policy<br>3 *Non-Right Hegemony:* High social expenditure and use of highly equalizing instruments in social policy<br>4 *Radical:* Achievement of equality in pre-tax, pre-transfer income (adoption of equalizing instruments in social policy), but little social spending | • Welfare expenditure<br>• Benefit equality<br>• Taxes |
| Siaroff (1994) | 1 *Protestant Liberal:* Minimal family welfare, yet relatively egalitarian gender situation in the labour market; family benefits are paid to the mother, but are rather inadequate<br>2 *Advanced Christian-Democratic:* No strong incentives for women to work, but strong incentives to stay at home | • Family welfare orientation<br>• Female work desirability |

| | | |
|---|---|---|
| | 3 *Protestant Social-Democratic:* True work–welfare choice for women; family benefits are high and always paid to the mother; importance of Protestantism<br>4 *Late Female Mobilization:* Absence of Protestantism; family benefits are usually paid to the father; universal female suffrage is relatively new | • Extent of family benefits being paid to women |
| Ferrera (1996) | 1 *Anglo-Saxon:* Fairly high welfare state cover; social assistance with a means test; mixed system of financing; highly integrated organizational framework entirely managed by a public administration<br>2 *Bismarck:* strong link between work position (and/or family state) and social entitlements; benefits proportional to income; financing through contributions; reasonably substantial social assistance benefits; insurance schemes mainly governed by unions and employer organizations<br>3 *Scandinavian:* social protection as a citizenship right; universal coverage; relatively generous fixed benefits for various social risks; financing mainly through fiscal revenues; strong organizational integration<br>4 *Southern:* fragmented system of income guarantees linked to work position; generous benefits without articulated net of minimum social protection; health care as a right of citizenship; particularism in payments of cash benefits and financing; financing through contributions and fiscal revenues | • Rules of access (eligibility)<br>• Benefit formulae<br>• Financing regulations<br>• Organizational-managerial arrangements |
| Bonoli (1997) | 1 *British:* Low percentage of social expenditure financed through contributions (Beveridge); low social expenditure as a percentage of GDP<br>2 *Continental:* High percentage of social expenditure financed through contributions (Bismarck); high social expenditure as a percentage of GDP<br>3 *Nordic:* Low percentage of social expenditure financed through contributions (Beveridge); high social expenditure as a percentage of GDP<br>4 *Southern:* High percentage of social expenditure financed through contributions (Bismarck); low social expenditure as a percentage of GDP | • Bismarck and Beveridge model<br>• Quantity of welfare state expenditure |

(continued)

**Table 1** (continued)

| | Types of welfare states and their characteristics | Indicators/dimensions |
|---|---|---|
| Korpi & Palme (1998) | 1 *Basic Security:* Entitlements based on citizenship *or* contributions; application of the flat-rate benefit principle | |
| | 2 *Corporatist:* Entitlements based on occupational category *and* labour force participation; use of the earnings-related benefit principle | • Bases of entitlement |
| | 3 *Encompassing:* Entitlement based on citizenship *and* labour force participation; use of the flat-rate and earnings-related benefit principle | • Benefit principle |
| | 4 *Targeted:* Eligibility based on proved need; use of the minimum benefit principle | • Governance of social insurance programme |
| | 5 *Voluntary State Subsidized:* Eligibility based on membership or contributions; application of the flat-rate or earnings-related principle | |

## *The Mediterranean*

One important criticism of Esping-Andersen's classification is that he did not systematically include the Mediterranean countries. Specifically, in *The Three Worlds of Welfare Capitalism* Italy belongs – according to him – to the family of the corporatist welfare state regimes, whereas Spain, Portugal and Greece are not covered by his typology. Although he admits that these countries have some important characteristics in common – i.e. a Catholic imprint (with the exception of Greece) and a strong familialism (Esping-Andersen, 1997, p. 180) – he seems to include them in the continental/corporatist model. His omission of a systematic treatment of the Mediterranean has brought about a lively debate about the existence of a 'Southern' or 'Latin Rim' model of social policy. For example, Katrougalos supports Esping-Andersen's position by arguing that the Mediterranean countries 'do not form a distinct group but rather a subcategory, a variant of the Continental model. They are merely underdeveloped species of the Continental model, welfare states in their infancy, with the main common characteristics being the immaturity of the social protection systems and some similar social and family structures' (1996, p. 43). However, according to other commentators (Leibfried, 1992; Ferrera, 1996; Bonoli, 1997; Trifiletti, 1999) it seems logical to see the South European countries as a separate cluster. They have developed classifications of European welfare states which try to show the existence of a separate 'southern model' of social policy.

Leibfried (1992) distinguishes four social policy or poverty regimes within the countries of the European Community: the Scandinavian welfare states, the 'Bismarck' countries, the Anglo-Saxon countries and the Latin Rim countries. These policy regimes are based on different policy models – modern, institutional, residual and rudimentary – in which social citizenship has developed in different and sometimes incomplete ways. Within these policy regimes, welfare state institutions have a different function in combating poverty. However, it is particularly important that Leibfried adds a fourth category – the 'Latin Rim' countries – to Esping-Andersen's original classification. He emphasizes as an important characteristic of these countries the lack of an articulated social minimum and a right to welfare.

Ferrera also argues explicitly for the inclusion of a 'Southern model' of social policy (1996, p. 4–7). He concentrates on four dimensions of social security systems: the rules of access (eligibility rules), the conditions under which benefits are granted, the regulations to finance social protection and, finally, the organizational-managerial arrangements to administrate the various social security schemes. Based on these dimensions, he makes a distinction between the Scandinavian, Anglo-Saxon, Bismarckian and Southern countries. The Scandinavian countries are characterized by universal coverage for the risks of life. The right to social protection is attributed on the basis of citizenship. The Anglo-Saxon family of welfare states is also characterized by a highly inclusive social security coverage, but only in the area of health care can one speak of fully universal risk coverage. Also flat-rate benefits and means testing play an important role. In the third group of countries, the relationship between social security entitlements, a person's labour market status and role within the family (breadwinner or not) is still clearly visible. Contributions play an important role in financing the various schemes. Almost everybody has social insurance coverage through their own or derived rights. Finally, the social protection systems of Southern countries are highly fragmented and, although there is no articulated net of minimum social protection, some benefits levels are very generous (such as old age pensions). Moreover, in these countries health care is institutionalized as a right of citizenship. However, in general, there is relatively little state intervention in the welfare sphere. Another important feature is the high level of particularism with regard to cash benefits and financing, expressed in high levels of clientelism. The most important features of each type are summarized in table 1.

Bonoli (1997) uses the Mediterranean countries – among others – to develop the final classification we wish to discuss in this section. He is especially critical of the decommodification approach. According to him, it does not allow one to discriminate effectively between the Bismarckian and the Beveridgean approaches to social policy. As an alternative, he combines two approaches to the classification of welfare states. One concentrates on the 'how much' dimension (emphasized in the Anglo-Saxon literature) and the other on the 'how' dimension of social policy (emphasized in the Continental-European or French tradition). As an empirical indicator of the first dimension, he uses social expenditure as a proportion of GDP, and of the second dimension the percentage of social expenditure financed through contributions. These indicators lead him to identify four types of countries: the British countries, the Continental European countries, the Nordic countries and the Southern countries, thus giving credit to the proposal of a 'Southern model'.

Upon examining the combined arguments of Leibfried, Ferrera and Bonoli, as presented in table 1, it appears that a strong similarity exists among their first three types and those of Esping-Andersen. However, all three authors add a fourth – Mediterranean – type of welfare state regime to the original Esping-Andersenian classification. Using empirical evidence, they argue that this is a prototype rather than a subcategory of the continental/corporatist model.

## *The Antipodes*

Esping-Andersen discusses the Antipodean countries (i.e. Australia and New Zealand) as representatives of the liberal welfare state regime. This is because of their marginal commitment to public welfare and strong reliance on means testing. However, according to Castles (1998), Australia and New Zealand have a more particular and a more inclusive approach to social protection than the standard liberal form. Thresholds are set at comparatively high levels, so that a large part of the population receives some means-tested benefits. The result is that the Antipodes exhibit the world's most comprehensive systems of means-tested income support benefits. Redistribution has been traditionally pursued through wage controls and employment security rather than social programmes. Income guarantees, realized by using market regulation, thus play an important role in the institutional set-up of these welfare states. It therefore seems that the Antipodean countries represent a separate social policy model. It led Castles and Mitchell (1993) to question whether 'social spending is the only route to greater income redistribution', implying that there may be other ways than income maintenance by which states may mitigate the effects of market forces.

In a discussion of their study, Hill (1996) points out that Castles and Mitchell's critique of Esping-Andersen's work essentially follows two lines. In the first place, they draw attention to the fact that political activity from the left may have been introduced into those countries in the achievement of equality in pre-tax, pre-transfer income rather than in the pursuit of equalization through social policy. Second, they argue – again about Australia but also with relevance to the United Kingdom – that the Esping-Andersen approach disregards the potential for income-related benefits to make an effective contribution to redistribution. Australian income maintenance is almost entirely means-tested. It uses an approach that neither concentrates on a liberal-type redistribution to the very poor, nor resembles the more universal social-democratic and hierarchical solidaristic conservative ideal-types highlighted in Esping-Andersen's study (Hill, 1996, p. 46). This is the reason why Castles and Mitchell develop an alternative, four-way classification of welfare states: Liberal, Conservative, Non-Right Hegemony and Radical. This utilizes the level of welfare expenditure (i.e. household transfers as a percentage of GDP); average benefit equality; and income and profit taxes as a percentage of GDP.

Other evidence for the exceptional position of the Antipodean countries, specifically Australia, is found when countries are classified according to the typology developed by Korpi and Palme (1998). This is based on institutional characteristics of welfare states. They try to investigate the causal factors which influence the institutional aspects of the welfare state on the one hand, and the effects of institutions on the formation of interests, preferences and identities – as well as on the degree of poverty and inequality in a society – on the other hand. They argue that institutional structures can be expected to reflect the role of conflicts among interest groups, while they are also likely to form important frameworks for the definitions of interests and identities among citizens. They can thereby be expected to influence coalition formation, which is significant for income redistribution and poverty. As the basis of their classification, Korpi and Palme take the institutional structures of two social programmes – old age pensions and sickness cash benefits – which they consider to lie at the heart of the welfare state. The institutional structures of the two programmes are classified according to three aspects: the bases of entitlements, the principles applied to determine benefit levels (to what extent social insurance should replace lost income), and the governance of a social insurance programme (whether or not representatives of employers and employees participate in the governing of a programme). Based on these three aspects, they discriminate among five different ideal-types of institutional structures: the targeted (empirically exemplified by the Australian case), voluntary state subsidized, corporatist, basic security and encompassing model. In table 1, these ideal-types and their most important features are delineated. Again, the Esping-Andersen model stands. However, a number of countries are no longer considered to belong to a subcategory of his three prototypes, but to a new prototype.

## *Gender, Familialism and Late Female Mobilization*

By explicitly incorporating gender, several authors have tried to reconceptualize the dimensions of welfare state variation. Subjecting the mainstream welfare state typologies to an analysis of the differential places of men and women within welfare states would, according to them, produce valuable insights. This does not mean, however, that the characteristics used to construct the typologies are exhaustive (Sainsbury, 1996, p. 41). Gender analysis suggests that there are whole areas of social policy that Esping-Anderson simply misses. What seems to be particularly lacking is a systematic discussion of the family's place in the provision of welfare and care. Not only the state and the market provide welfare, but also families. A further omission is that there is no serious treatment of the degree to which women are excluded from or included in the labour market.[3] Instead of employing the all-or-nothing words 'inclusion' and 'exclusion' to gender differences, it seems sensible to stress the importance of partial citizenship (Bulmer and Rees, 1996, p. 275). Women obtained full civil and political rights a considerable time ago, but with regard to social rights, women are still discriminated against, sometimes formally, and nearly always informally because of different labour market positions, linked to different gender roles. According to many feminist authors, it is the sexual division of paid and unpaid work – especially care and domestic labour – that needs incorporating in the typology (Lewis, 1992; O'Connor, 1993; Orloff, 1993; Sainsbury, 1996; O'Connor et al., 1999).

With respect to another issue, social care, Daly and Lewis (2000, p. 289) argue that different styles of social policy have incorporated the key element of social care differently. They identify certain tendencies concerning care in specific welfare states. For example, the Scandinavian countries form a distinct group in that they have strongly institutionalized care for both the elderly and children. In the Mediterranean welfare states, care tends to be privatized to the family, whereas in Germany it is seen as most appropriately a function of voluntary service providers. In France, a strong distinction is made between care for children and for the elderly, with a strong collective sector in the former and little voluntary involvement. Another form is found in the Beveridge-oriented welfare states – Great Britain and Ireland – where a strong distinction is also made between caring for children and caring for (elderly) adults. In the former – as opposed to the latter – little collectivization has taken place. Although they do not really classify welfare states into actual clusters, Daly and Lewis make a strong case for using social care as a critical dimension for analysing variations.

As far as the gender gap in earnings is concerned, Gornick and Jacobs (1998) found that Esping-Andersen's regime-types do capture important distinctions among contemporary welfare states. Their results showed that the size of the public sector, the extent of the public-sector earnings premium and the impact of the public sector on gender differentials in wages all varied more across regimes than within them. In this way, they showed the fruitfulness of emphasizing the gender perspective in Esping-Andersen's classification of welfare states. Moreover, Trifiletti (1999) incorporated a gender perspective into Esping-Andersen's classification by showing that a systematic relationship exists between the level of decommodification and whether the state treats women as wives and mothers or as workers. The latter is also an important dimension identified by Lewis (1989).

Finally, Siaroff (1994) also argues that the existing literature does not pay enough attention to how gender inequality is embedded in social policy and welfare states. In order to arrive at a more gender-sensitive typology of welfare state regimes, he examines a variety of indicators of gender equality and inequality in work and welfare. He compares the work–welfare choice of men and women (i.e. whether to partake in the welfare state or to engage in paid labour) across countries. This allows him to distinguish among a Protestant Social-Democratic, a Protestant Liberal, an Advanced Christian-Democratic and a Late Female Mobilization welfare state regime. Although the labels suggest otherwise, this typology also shows a strong overlap with the Esping-Andersenian classification. Only the latter type – the Late Female Mobilization welfare state regime – is an addition, which resembles the previously distinguished Mediterranean type of welfare states.

## Ideal and Real-Types

In table 1, we ordered the types discussed above broadly in accordance with the worlds of welfare capitalism as defined by Esping-Andersen. For example, Bonoli's Continental type is very much like Esping-Andersen's Conservative type; in both types contributions play a rather important role. Equally, Castles and Mitchell's Non-Right Hegemony type shows a large amount of congruence with Esping-Andersen's Social-Democratic type, because of the high degree of universalism and equalization in social policy. We could go on, but we would like to raise another issue.

One may wonder whether, if the relationship among the different typologies is as strong as we assume, this close correspondence of types will also be apparent in the actual clustering of countries. Although not every classification developed by these authors covers the same nations, there is a rather large overlap which makes it possible to answer this question. For that purpose, table 2 shows the extent to which the ideal-types – constructed by Esping-Andersen's critics – coincide with his own ideal-types. We then added the ideal-types, proposed by these critics, placing related ideal-types, when possible, under one heading. This results in five – instead of the original three – worlds of welfare capitalism and answers our original question. Next, in table 2 we arranged the real-types according to the different ideal-types, thereby following the suggestions of the different authors.

It appears that, even when one uses different indicators to classify welfare states, some countries emerge as standard examples, approximating certain ideal-types. The United States is, according to everyone's classification, the prototype of a welfare state which can best be denoted as Liberal (with or without the suffix: Protestant, Anglo-Saxon or Basic Security). Germany approaches the Bismarckian/Continental/Conservative ideal-type and Sweden approximates the Social-Democratic ideal-type (Scandinavian/Nordic).

However, consensus seems to end here. For example, according to some, Italy can best be assigned to the second, Corporatist/Continental/Conservative type, but belongs, according to others, along with Greece, Spain and Portugal to a distinctive Mediterranean type. The same holds for Australia, which may either be classified as Liberal or is the prototype of a separate, Radical welfare state. Nevertheless, as far as these countries and types are concerned, consensus is stronger than was initially assumed. One must, however, recognize that discussions are mainly concerned with whether certain types of welfare states are either separate categories or are subgroups of certain main types.

Hybrid cases are a bigger problem. The Netherlands and Switzerland are clear examples of this. If we take, for example, a closer look at the Dutch case, we see that Esping-Andersen (1990) originally assigned the Netherlands to the Social-Democratic type, whereas Korpi and Palme see it as liberally oriented; the Basic Security type. However, most authors place the Netherlands in the second category of Corporatist/Continental/Conservative welfare states. This is also the choice of Visser and Hemerijck (1997), perhaps the foremost specialists on the Dutch welfare state. Curiously enough, this is done using Esping-Andersen's work as a constant, positive reference. If we have another look at Esping-Andersen's work, this is not as surprising as one would expect. It is true that the Netherlands is rated relatively high on social-democratic characteristics, but not exceptionally low on liberal and conservative characteristics. Recently, Esping-Andersen has called the Netherlands the 'Dutch enigma' because of its Janus-faced welfare regime (1999, p. 88). The Netherlands is indeed more a hybrid case than a prototype of a specific ideal-type. If one attaches more importance to certain attributes than to others – and adds other characteristics or substitutes previous ones – then it is easy to arrive at different classifications.

## Empirical Robustness of the Three-Way Classification

Esping-Andersen claims that if we rate real welfare states along the dimensions of degree of decommodification and the modes of stratification, three qualitatively different clusters will appear. Alongside the more fundamental criticism of his three-way classification – that Esping-Andersen employs faulty criteria to demarcate a regime – the empirical fit of his three-way classification has also been questioned. Several authors have tested the goodness-of-fit of the three-way regime typology. In the following, we discuss their findings, which are presented in table 3.

In an effort to evaluate the possible extent to which quantitative techniques – OLS regression and cluster analysis – suggest the same conclusions as alternative qualitative approaches – such as 'BOOLEAN' comparative analysis – Kangas (1994) found some support for the existence of Esping-Andersen's different welfare state regimes. Specifically, cluster analyses of data on characteristics of health insurance schemes in OECD countries in 1950 and 1985 corroborated his conjectures. However, the results also showed the existence of two subgroups within the group of liberal welfare states, which largely accorded with the classification of Castles and Mitchell (1993).

Ragin (1994) also tested Esping-Andersen's claim of a three-world classification. By applying a combination of cluster analysis and 'BOOLEAN' comparative analysis to characteristics of pension systems, he determined which, if any, of Esping-Andersen's three worlds of welfare capitalism each country fitted best. His cluster analysis suggested the existence of a social-democratic cluster, a corporatist cluster and, finally, a rather large 'spare' cluster, which accommodates cases that do not conform to Esping-Andersen's three worlds. On the basis of his findings, Ragin concludes that

**Table 2** Classification of countries according to seven typologies

| | Type | | | | |
|---|---|---|---|---|---|
| | I | II | III | IV | V |
| Esping-Andersen (Decommodification) | *Liberal*<br>• Australia<br>• Canada<br>• United States<br>• New Zealand<br>• Ireland<br>• United Kingdom | *Conservative*<br>• Italy<br>• Japan<br>• France<br>• Germany<br>• Finland<br>• Switzerland | *Social-Democratic*<br>• Austria<br>• Belgium<br>• Netherlands<br>• Denmark<br>• Norway<br>• Sweden | | |
| Leibfried | *Anglo-Saxon*<br>• United States<br>• Australia<br>• New Zealand<br>• United Kingdom | *Bismarck*<br>• Germany<br>• Austria | *Scandinavian*<br>• Sweden<br>• Norway<br>• Finland<br>• Denmark | *Latin Rim*<br>• Spain<br>• Portugal<br>• Greece<br>• Italy<br>• France | |
| Castles & Mitchell | *Liberal*<br>• Ireland<br>• Japan<br>• Switzerland<br>• United States | *Conservative*<br>• West-Germany<br>• Italy<br>• Netherlands | *Non-Right Hegemony*<br>• Belgium<br>• Denmark<br>• Norway<br>• Sweden | | *Radical*<br>• Australia<br>• New Zealand<br>• United Kingdom |
| Siaroff | *Protestant Liberal*<br>• Australia<br>• Canada<br>• New Zealand | *Advanced Christian-Democratic*<br>• Austria<br>• Belgium<br>• France | *Protestant Social-Democratic*<br>• Denmark<br>• Finland<br>• Norway | *Late Female Mobilization*<br>• Greece<br>• Ireland<br>• Italy | |

| | | | | | |
|---|---|---|---|---|---|
| | • United Kingdom<br>• United States | • West-Germany<br>• Luxembourg<br>• Netherlands | • Sweden | • Japan<br>• Portugal<br>• Spain<br>• Switzerland | |
| Ferrera (*Europe only*) | *Anglo-Saxon*<br>• United Kingdom<br>• Ireland | *Bismarckian*<br>• Germany<br>• France<br>• Belgium<br>• Netherlands<br>• Luxembourg<br>• Austria<br>• Switzerland | *Scandinavian*<br>• Sweden<br>• Denmark<br>• Norway<br>• Finland | *Southern*<br>• Italy<br>• Spain<br>• Portugal<br>• Greece | |
| Bonoli (*Europe only*) | *British*<br>• United Kingdom<br>• Ireland | *Continental*<br>• Netherlands<br>• France<br>• Belgium<br>• Germany<br>• Luxembourg | *Nordic*<br>• Sweden<br>• Finland<br>• Norway<br>• Denmark | *Southern*<br>• Italy<br>• Switzerland<br>• Spain<br>• Greece<br>• Portugal | |
| Korpi & Palme | *Basic Security*<br>• Canada<br>• Denmark<br>• Netherlands<br>• New Zealand<br>• Switzerland<br>• Ireland<br>• United Kingdom<br>• United States | *Corporatist*<br>• Austria<br>• Belgium<br>• France<br>• Germany<br>• Italy<br>• Japan | *Encompassing*<br>• Finland<br>• Norway<br>• Sweden | | *Targeted*<br>• Australia |

Underlined countries indicate a prototype.

**Table 3** Empirical robustness of the three-worlds typology

| | Number of clusters and cluster assignment | Method of analysis |
|---|---|---|
| Kangas (1994) | 1 *Liberal:* United States, Canada<br>2 *Conservative:* Austria, Germany, Italy, Japan, the Netherlands<br>3 *Social-Democratic:* Denmark, Finland, Norway, Sweden<br>4 *Radical:* Australia, Ireland, New Zealand, United Kingdom | Cluster analysis |
| Ragin (1994) | 1 *Liberal:* Australia, Canada, Switzerland, United States<br>2 *Corporatist:* Austria, Belgium, Finland, France, Italy<br>3 *Social-Democratic:* Denmark, Norway, Sweden<br>4 *Undefined:* Germany, Ireland, Japan, the Netherlands, New Zealand, United Kingdom | BOOLEAN comparative analysis |
| Shalev (1996) | 1 *Liberal:* United States, Canada, Switzerland, Japan<br>2 *Conservative:* Italy, France, Belgium, Austria, Ireland<br>3 *Social-Democratic:* Sweden, Norway, Denmark, Finland<br>4 *Undefined:* Germany, the Netherlands, United Kingdom, Australia, New Zealand | Factor analysis |
| Obinger & Wagschal (1998) | 1 *Liberal:* United States, Canada, Japan, Switzerland<br>2 *European:* Belgium, Germany, Finland, Ireland, United Kingdom, the Netherlands<br>3 *Conservative:* France, Italy, Austria<br>4 *Social-Democratic:* Denmark, Norway, Sweden<br>5 *Radical:* Australia, New Zealand | Cluster analysis |
| Wildeboer Schut et al. (2001) | 1 *Liberal:* United States, Canada, Australia, United Kingdom<br>2 *Conservative:* France, Germany, Belgium<br>3 *Social-Democratic:* Sweden, Denmark, Norway<br>4 *Undefined:* the Netherlands | Principal component analysis |

the three-worlds scheme does not capture existing diversity as adequately as one would wish.

Shalev (1996) applied factor analysis to fourteen pension policy indicators collected by Esping-Andersen, to test for the presence of liberal, social-democratic and corporatist regime-types. This factor analysis showed that the intercorrelations among these social policy indicators were dependent on two dimensions. The first factor measured the level of social-democratic features, whereas the second dimension measured corporatist features of welfare states. Based on the assignment of factor scores to individual nations, Shalev concluded that his findings were in close correspondence with Esping-Andersen's characterizations of the three welfare state regimes. He admitted, however, that some countries are difficult to classify.

Using cluster analysis, Obinger and Wagschal (1998) tested Esping-Andersen's classification of welfare state regimes using the stratification criterion. After a detailed re-analysis of Esping-Andersen's original data on stratification, they concluded that these data are best described by five regime clusters. In addition to Esping-Andersen's conservative, liberal and social-democratic types, they distinguish a radical and a hybrid European cluster.

The most recent attempt to empirically corroborate Esping-Andersen's classification has been undertaken by Wildeboer Schut et al. (2001). This study examined the actual similarities and differences among the welfare state regimes of the countries originally included in Esping-Andersen's classification. For these countries, fifty-eight characteristics of the labour market, tax regime and social protection system at the beginning of the 1990s were collected. These were submitted to a non-linear principal component-analysis. The results largely confirmed the three-regime typology of Esping-Andersen.

Summing up, Esping-Andersen's original three-worlds typology neither passes the empirical tests with flying colours, nor dismally fails them. The conclusion is, first, that his typology has at least some heuristic and descriptive value, but also that a case can be made for extending the number of welfare state regimes to four, or even five. Second, these analyses show that a significant number of welfare states must be considered hybrid cases: no particular case can ever perfectly embody any particular ideal-type (Goodin et al., 1999, p. 56). Third, if one looks at other social programmes than the ones applied by Esping-Andersen, it becomes clear that they do not conform so easily – if at all – to his welfare regime patterns (Gough, 2000, p. 4).

## Conclusion and Discussion

Before we reach our conclusions, let us examine how Esping-Andersen himself has reacted to the various attempts to amend his typology. The problem is that after considerable discussion it seems impossible for him to make up his mind once and for all. Initially, Esping-Andersen (1997) reacted, for example, positively to Castles and Mitchell's proposal to add a fourth type – a radical welfare state regime – to his typology. He recognized that the residual character and the matter of a means test are just one side of the coin of the Antipodean welfare states. However, he felt that a powerfully institutionalized collection of welfare guarantees, which operate through the market itself, could not be neglected. Later on, however, he argued that the passage of time is pushing Australia, Great Britain and New Zealand towards what appears to be prototypical liberalism (Esping-Andersen, 1999). At first he also partially supported the proposal to add a separate Mediterranean type to his typology (Esping-Andersen, 1996, p. 66; 1997, p. 171). He acknowledged the – sometimes generous – benefits which are guaranteed by certain arrangements, the near absence of social services and, especially, the Catholic imprint and high level of familialism. From the feminist critics he learned not so much the overarching salience of gender as the analytical power that a re-examination of the family can yield. Recently he argued that the acid test of a distinct Mediterranean model depends on whether families are the relevant focus of social aid, and whether families will fail just as markets and states can fail (Esping-Andersen, 1999, p. 90).

All in all, Esping-Andersen is very reluctant to add more regime-clusters to his original three. Against the benefits of greater refinement, more nuance and more precision, he weighs the argument of analytical parsimony, stressing that 'the peculiarities of these cases are variations within a distinct overall logic, not a wholly different logic *per se* (Esping-Andersen, 1999, p. 90).

The answer to the question of whether Esping-Andersen's three-type or a derivative or alternative four-, or five-type typology is preferable depends, however, not only on parsimony and verisimilitude. It also depends on whether these typologies lead to a theoretically more satisfying and empirically more fruitful comparative analysis of welfare state regimes. As far as theory construction is concerned, Baldwin (1996, p. 29) has argued that when asking about typologies, whether of welfare states or anything else, we must ask not just what but also why. Esping-Andersen's tentative answer to the question of why three different welfare state regime types emerged has been sketched earlier on in this paper. Different welfare regimes are shaped by different class coalitions within a context of inherited institutions. This answer is embedded in a power-resources mobilization paradigm. The tentative answer to the question of why regime shifts are scarce is that a national state cannot easily escape its historical inheritance. Institutional inertia is one factor why different welfare state regime types persist, and path dependency is another (Kohl, 2000, p. 125; Kuhnle and Alestalo, 2000, p. 9). Korpi and Palme – and some feminist authors – work in the same power-resources mobilization tradition as

Esping-Andersen. It would be worthwhile to develop a theoretical reconstruction of the different contributions of this paradigm (for an initial impetus to such an endeavour, see Schmidt, 1998, pp. 215–28). Only then could the explanatory value of the typology become apparent.

Whether there is, within the welfare modelling business, an alternative available to Esping-Andersen's power-resource mobilization cum institutional inertia/path dependency theory is difficult to determine. The work of some of the other authors we discussed in this overview has a strong empiricist flavour. However, if we are searching for an underlying theoretical notion, it can be found in the rather general statement that similar causes have similar consequences. Considering the labels these authors have put to the prototypes they distinguish, which are predominantly geographical and ideological in nature, the most important causes are seen to be the pressure of functional exigencies and the diffusion of innovations (Goldthorpe, 2000, p. 54). The first factor could be translated into a 'challenge response' hypothesis. The challenges produced by the force of similar circumstances (characteristics of pre-industrial social structures, political institutions, degree of homogeneity of population, culture, problem perceptions and preferences) lead to comparable welfare state regimes (responses) (Kuhnle and Alestalo, 2000, p. 7). The second factor could be put in terms of learning effects in policy-making. New ideas, new solutions are often a product of a diffusion process. They hit political systems and societies at different points in 'developmental time'. As far as this latter factor is concerned, Boje (1996, p. 15) argues that the fact that most welfare states are confronted with huge social problems has necessitated politicians finding alternative procedures, which may solve these problems more efficiently. Politicians have come to realize that much may be learned from other welfare states.

Castles (1993, 1998) too underscores the importance of both factors. He argues that it is likely that policy similarities and differences among welfare states can be attributed to both the force of circumstances and to diffusion. As far as the latter factor is concerned we can distinguish the institutional arrangements and culture of prototypical welfare states and their transmission and diffusion to other countries. Regarding the former factor, we can observe the immediate impact of economic, political and social variables identified in the contemporary public policy literature. Whether these very general 'challenge response' and 'diffusion' hypotheses will be further developed remains to be seen. For the moment, we can conclude that, given the empiricist nature of the work of the authors who provided alternative typologies, there should be hardly any objection – for the time being – to the incorporation of their findings into a power-resources mobilization paradigm.

Finally, we arrive at the empirical fruitfulness of the typology. In his overview, Abrahamson (1999) concludes that as an organizing principle for comparative studies of welfare states the typologies have proved to be a very robust and convincing tool. Within the power-resources mobilization paradigm (Korpi, 1983; Esping-Andersen and Korpi, 1984; Esping-Andersen, 1990) it has been proposed that the nature of the welfare state regime would decisively influence support for certain forms of social policy. A type that is characterized by universalism would generate the strongest support, whereas arrangements which apply only to minorities would not succeed in winning the support of majorities. Tests of this hypothesis (Papadakis and Bean, 1993; Peillon, 1996; Gelissen, 2000; Gevers et al., 2000) have shown some empirical support, but the evidence is not really encouraging. More encouraging were the results of an effort (Gundelach, 1994) to explain cross-national differences in values with respect to welfare and care using the Esping-Andersenian welfare state regimes. Also, Svallfors's (1997) and Arts and Gelissen's (2001) tests of the hypothesis that different welfare state regimes matter for people's attitudes towards income-redistribution were strongly endorsed. What especially matters to us here is that Svallfors distributive justice and solidarity had included not only Esping-Andersen's regime-types, but also other types and Arts and Gelissen.

It is more difficult to draw a conclusion concerning the influence that welfare state regimes have on social behaviour and their effects. Much of this research has a bearing on the distributive effects of welfare state regimes. Because they are often described in terms of their intended social stratification, a tautological element easily sneaks into the explanations. Positive exceptions are Goodin et al. (1999) and Korpi and Palme (1998). Using panel-data, Goodin et al. (1999) show that welfare state regimes do not only have intended results, but also generate unintended consequences. As intended and expected, the social-democratic regime succeeds best in realizing its fundamental value: minimizing inequality. But this regime is also at least as good in promoting the goals to which other regimes ostensibly attach most importance. Specifically, the social-democratic regime also does very well in reducing poverty – a goal which is prioritized by the liberal welfare state regime – and in promoting stability and social integration, which is the home ground of the corporatist welfare state regime. Korpi and Palme (1998) find that institutional differences lead to a paradox of redistribution: the more benefits are targeted at the poor and the more the creation of equality through equal public transfers to all is a matter of priority, the less poverty and inequality will be reduced. Thus, institutional arrangements characteristic of certain welfare state regimes not only have unintended consequences, but even perverse effects.

All in all, these conclusions provide sufficient impetus to continue the work concerning the resulting welfare state typology. A better formulation of the theory on which it is based deserves priority. Only then can predictions be logically – instead of impressionistically – deduced from theory. Only then is a strict test of the theory possible and only then will the heuristic and explanatory value of the typology become apparent.

## Notes

From *Journal of European Social Policy*, 12, 2, 2002, pp. 137–58.

1 The importance of Catholicism is emphasized by van Kersbergen (1995) in his discussion including Christian-democratic nations such as Germany, Italy and the Netherlands in mainstream welfare state typologies.
2 For reasons of conciseness we refrain from the debate regarding Esping-Andersen's classification of Japan as a liberal welfare state. For a reaction to this critique see Esping-Andersen (1997, 1999). Becker (1996) and Goodman and Peng (1996) are even of the opinion that Japan belongs to a sixth prototype of welfare state regimes, the so-called East-Asian welfare states. We acknowlege the importance of these arguments, but cannot engage with them here (Gough, 2000).
3 Gornick and Jacobs (1998, p. 691) point out that Esping-Andersen himself argues that each regime-type is associated with women's employment levels. Specifically, he (Esping-Andersen, 1990) expects that women's employment rates will be highest in social-democratic countries, whereas in liberal welfare states, moderate levels of female employment will be found. The lowest levels of women's employment will be found in the conservative welfare states.

## References

Abrahamson, P. (1999) The Welfare Modelling Business', *Social Policy and Administration*, 33, 4, pp. 394–415.
Arts, W. A. and Gelissen, J. (2001) 'Welfare States, Solidarity and Justice Principles: Does the Type Really Matter?', *Acta Sociologica*, 44, 4, pp. 283–300.
Baldwin, P. (1996) 'Can We Define a European Welfare State Model?', in B. Greve (ed.), *Comparative Welfare Systems: The Scandinavian Model in a Period of Change*, London, Macmillan, pp. 29–44.
Becker, U. (1996) 'Over de typologie van welvaartsbestellen: Esping-Andersens theorie in discussie', *Beleid & Maatschappij*, 23, 1, pp. 19–30.
Boje, T. (1996) 'Welfare State Models in Comparative Research: Do the Models Describe the Reality?', in B. Greve (ed.), *Comparative Welfare Systems: The Scandinavian Model in a Period of Change*, London, Macmillan, pp. 13–27.
Bonoli, G. (1997) 'Classifying Welfare States: A Two-Dimension Approach', *Journal of Social Policy*, 26, 3, pp. 351–72.
Bulmer, M. and Rees, A. M. (1996) 'Conclusion: Citizenship in the Twenty-First Century', in M. Bulmer and A. M. Rees (eds), *Citizenship Today: The Contemporary Relevance of T. H. Marshall*, London, UCL Press, pp. 269–84.
Castles, F. G. (1993) 'Introduction', in F. G. Castles (ed.), *Families of Nations: Patterns of Public Policy in Western Democracies*, Aldershot, Dartmouth.
Castles, F. G. (1998) *Comparative Public Policy: Patterns of Postwar Transformation*, Cheltenham, Edward Elgar.
Castles, F. G. and Mitchell, D. (1993) 'Worlds of Welfare and Families of Nations', in F. G. Castles (ed.), *Families of Nations: Patterns of Public Policy in Western Democracies*, Aldershot, Dartmouth.
Daly, M. and Lewis, J. (2000) 'The Concept of Social Care and the Analysis of Contemporary Welfare States', *British Journal of Sociology*, 51, 2, pp. 281–98.
Esping-Andersen, G. (1990) *The Three Worlds of Welfare Capitalism*, Cambridge, Polity.

Esping-Andersen, G. (1996) 'Welfare States without Work: the Impasse of Labour Shedding and Familialism in Continental European Social Policy', in G. Esping-Andersen (ed.), *Welfare States in Transition*, London, Sage, pp. 66–87.

Esping-Andersen, G. (1997) 'Hybrid or Unique? The Japanese Welfare State between Europe and America', *Journal of European Social Policy*, 7, 3, pp. 179–89.

Esping-Andersen, G. (1999) *Social Foundations of Post-industrial Economies*, Oxford, Oxford University Press.

Esping-Andersen, G. and Korpi, W. (1984) 'Social Policy as Class Politics in Post-war Capitalism', in J. Goldthorpe (ed.), *Order and Conflict in Contemporary Capitalism*, Oxford, Oxford University Press.

Ferrera, M. (1996) 'The "Southern" Model of Welfare in Social Europe', *Journal of European Social Policy*, 6, 1, pp. 17–37.

Gelissen, J. (2000) 'Popular Support for Institutionalised Solidarity: A Comparison among European Welfare States', *International Journal of Social Welfare*, 9, 4, pp. 285–300.

Gevers, J., Gelissen, J., Arts, W. and Muffels, R. (2000) 'Public Health Care in the Balance: Exploring Popular Support for Health Care Systems in the European Union', *International Journal of Social Welfare*, 9, 4, pp. 301–21.

Goldthorpe, J. H. (2000) *On Sociology: Numbers, Narratives, and the Integration of Research and Theory*, Oxford, Oxford University Press.

Goodin, R. E., Heady, B., Muffels, R. and Dirven, H.-J. (1999) *The Real Worlds of Welfare Capitalism*, Cambridge, Cambridge University Press.

Goodman, R. and Peng, I. (1996) 'The East Asian Welfare States: Peripatetic Learning, Adaptive Change, and Nation-building', in G. Esping-Andersen (ed.), *Welfare States in Transition*, London, Sage, pp. 192–224.

Gornick, J. C. and Jacobs, J. A. (1998) 'Gender, the Welfare State, and Public Employment: A Comparative Study of Seven Industrialized Countries', *American Sociological Review*, 63, 5, pp. 688–710.

Gough, I. (2000) *Welfare Regimes: On Adapting the Framework to Developing Countries*' and 'Welfare Regimes in East Asia and Europe: Comparisons and Lessons', Institute for International Policy Analysis, University of Bath. At www.bath.ac.uk/Faculties/HumSocSci/IFIPA/GSP (accessed 9 Mar. 2001).

Gundelach, P. (1994) 'National Value Differences: Modernization or Institutionalization?', *International Journal of Comparative Sociology*, 35, 1–2, pp. 37–58.

Hill, M. (1996) *Social Policy: A Comparative Analysis*. London, Prentice Hall/Harvester Wheatsheaf.

Kangas, O. E. (1994) 'The Politics of Social Security: On Regressions, Qualitative Comparisons, and Cluster Analysis', in T. Janoski and A. M. Hicks (eds), *The Comparative Political Economy of the Welfare State*, Cambridge, Cambridge University Press, pp. 346–64.

Katrougalos, G. S. (1996) 'The South European Welfare Model: The Greek Welfare State in Search of an Identity', *Journal of European Social Policy*, 6, 1, pp. 39–60.

Kohl, J. (2000) 'Der Sozialstaat: Die deutsche Version des Wohlfahrtsstaates – Überlegungen zu seiner typologischen Verortung', in S. Leibfried and U. Wagschal (eds), *Der deutsche Sozialstaat: Bilanzen- Reformen-Perspectiven*, Frankfurt, Campus, pp. 115–52.

Korpi, W. (1983) *The Democratic Class Struggle*, London, Routledge and Kegan Paul.

Korpi, W. and Palme, J. (1998) 'The Paradox of Redistribution and Strategies of Equality: Welfare State Institutions, Inequality and Poverty in the Western Countries', *American Sociological Review*, 63, 5, pp. 661–87.

Kuhnle, S. and Alestalo, M. (2000) 'Growth, Adjustments and Survival of European Welfare States', in S. Kuhnle (ed.), *Survival of the European Welfare State*, London, Routledge, pp. 3–18.
Leibfried, S. (1992) 'Towards a European Welfare State? On Integrating Poverty Regimes into the European Community', in Z. Ferge and J. E. Kolberg (eds), *Social Policy in a Changing Europe*, Frankfurt, Campus.
Lewis, J. (1989) 'Lone Parent Families: Politics and Economics', *Journal of Social Policy*, 18, 4, pp. 595–600.
Lewis, J. (1992) 'Gender and the Development of Welfare Regimes', *Journal of European Social Policy*, 2, 3, pp. 159–73.
Obinger, H. and Wagschal, U. (1998) 'Das Stratifizierungskonzept in der Clusteranalytischen Überprüfung', in S. Lessenich and I. Ostner (eds), *Welten des Wohlfahrtskapitalismus: Der Sozialstaat in vergleichender Perspektive*, Frankfurt, Campus, pp. 109–35.
O'Connor, J. S. (1993) 'Gender, Class and Citizenship in the Comparative Analysis of Welfare State Regimes: Theoretical and Methodological Issues', *British Journal of Sociology*, 44, 3, pp. 501–18.
O'Connor, J. S., Orloff, A. and Shaver, S. (1999) *States, Markets, Families: Gender, Liberalism and Social Policy in Australia, Canada, Great Britain and the United States*, Cambridge, Cambridge University Press.
Orloff, A. S. (1993) 'Gender and the Social Rights of Citizenship: A Comparative Analysis of Gender Relations and Welfare States', *American Sociological Review*, 58, 3, pp. 303–28.
Papadakis, E. and Bean, C. (1993) 'Popular Support for the Welfare State: A Comparison among Institutional Regimes', *Journal of Public Policy*, 13, 3, pp. 227–54.
Peillon, M. (1996) 'A Qualitative Comparative Analysis of Welfare State Legitimacy', *Journal of European Social Policy*, 6, 3, pp. 175–90.
Ragin, C. (1994) 'A Qualitative Comparative Analysis of Pension Systems', in T. Janoski and A. M. Hicks (eds), *The Comparative Political Economy of the Welfare State*, Cambridge, Cambridge University Press, pp. 320–45.
Sainsbury, D. (1996) *Gender, Equality and Welfare States*, Cambridge, Cambridge University Press.
Schmidt, M. G. (1998) *Sozialpolitik in Deutschland: Historische Entwicklung und internationaler Vergleich*. Opladen, Leske & Budrich.
Shalev, M. (1996) *The Privatization of Social Policy? Occupational Welfare and the Welfare State in America, Scandinavia and Japan*. London, Macmillan.
Siaroff, A. (1994) 'Work, Welfare and Gender Equality: A New Typology', in D. Sainsbury (ed.), *Gendering Welfare States*, London, Sage, pp. 82–100.
Svallfors, S. (1997) 'Worlds of Welfare and Attitudes to Redistribution: A Comparison of Eight Western Nations', *European Sociological Review*, 13, 3, pp. 283–304.
Trifiletti, R. (1999) 'Southern European Welfare Regimes and the Worsening Position of Women', *Journal of European Social Policy*, 9, 1, pp. 49–64.
van Kersbergen, K. (1995) *Social Capitalism: A Study of Christian Democracy and the Welfare State*, London, Routledge.
Visser, J. and Hemerijck, A. C. (1997) *A Dutch Miracle: Job Growth, Welfare Reform and Corporatism in the Netherlands*, Amsterdam: Amsterdam University Press.
Wildeboer Schut, J. M. Vrooman, J. C. and de Beer, P. (2001) *On Worlds of Welfare: Institutions and their Effects in Eleven Welfare States*, The Hague, Social and Cultural Planning Office of the Netherlands.

# Globalization

# Globalization, Economic Change and the Welfare State: The 'Vexatious Inquisition of Taxation'?

*Colin Hay*

## Introduction

It has become something of a popular truism that globalization spells if not quite the passing of the nation-state itself, then the demise of inclusive social provision and with it the welfare state. The competitive imperatives of a borderless world characterized by the near perfect mobility of the factors of production, it is frequently assumed, reveal the welfare state of the postwar period to be an indulgent luxury of a bygone era. Along with Keynesianism, social democracy and encompassing labour-market institutions it must now be sacrificed, if it has not already been sacrificed, on the altar of the competitive imperative – a further casualty of the 'harsh economic realities' summoned by globalization.

Invariably such portentous accounts take the form of a dualistic history: of 'old times' and 'new times', then and now. Once upon a time, when European economies were closed, macroeconomic policy was Keynesian and capital bore a national stamp, the welfare state provided a series of positive externalities, principally wage restraint in return for investment incentives and a social wage. This, in turn, served to establish and sustain a virtuous cycle of high demand, high productivity, high growth. How times have changed. With open economies, a distinctly post-Keynesian ideational environment and heightened capital mobility, positive externalities have given way to negative externalities. The welfare state is now widely held to represent a burden on competitiveness, a burden manifest in punitive levels of taxation and assorted labour-market (and broader supply-side) rigidities. These can only impede the proper functioning of the market and with it the competitive and comparative advantage of the economy (see, classically, Fisher, 1930, 1935; Gilder, 1981; Okun, 1975; for the contemporary centre-left variant, see, for instance, Cerny, 1997; Kurzer, 1993; Scharpf, 1991).

This, at any rate, is the now conventional orthodoxy. It is the wisdom of this view that I question in this chapter.

The near-dominant notion of the corrosive impact of economic globalization on the welfare state might lead one to expect unequivocal and unambiguous evidence of systematic welfare retrenchment across the advanced capitalist economies. Yet the empirical record could scarcely be more difficult to reconcile with the conventional wisdom. For not only is (aggregate) evidence of welfare retrenchment, far less *systematic* welfare retrenchment, quite difficult to find; the positive correlation between social expenditure and economic openness first observed by Cameron (1978) has only strengthened under conditions of globalization (Garrett, 1998; Rodrik, 1997). These are points to which we return in detail below. Suffice it for now to note that they present something of a paradox: a widely accepted conception not only of welfare retrenchment but of the *necessity* of welfare retrenchment which seems to stand in marked contrast to the available empirical evidence. There are at least four potential solutions to this conundrum:

1 That the conventional wisdom on the subject is indeed correct, that the welfare state represents a drain on competitiveness in an era of globalization and the competition state (Cerny, 1990, 1997), but that the institutional and cultural architecture of the welfare state has become so entrenched and embedded as to make its reform and retrenchment an iterative and incremental yet cumulative process down which we are now only slowly embarking (Pierson, 1994, 1996).
2 That the conventional wisdom is simply inaccurate and that far from representing a drain on competitiveness, the welfare state (at least in certain institutional and cultural environments) retains and acquires yet further positive externalities (Barr, 1998; Esping-Andersen, 1994; Finegold and Soskice, 1988; Garrett, 1998; Gough, 1996; Pfaller et al., 1991; cf. Polanyi, 1944).
3 That the aggregate empirical evidence in fact masks the actual degree of retrenchment and that once we control for demographic and other 'welfare inflationary' pressures, observed welfare expenditure is in fact substantially below that we would anticipate (Esping-Andersen, 1996a, 1996b; Rhodes, 1996, 1997).
4 That, once again, the aggregate evidence masks the degree of real retrenchment since the market-conforming nature of that process has served to increase welfare pressures by effectively trading inflation for unemployment. Consequently, although aggregate spending has proved 'sticky', once we control for increased welfare demand we observe both a narrowing of the scope of social provision and retrenchment in terms of the value of benefits to claimants (Ferrera, 1998; Martin, 1997; Rhodes, 1997).

Each of these perspectives, that will be discussed further below, injects a healthy dose of scepticism and some long-overdue theoretical sophistication, analytical clarity and empirical detail into the invariably over-inflated, grossly exaggerated and seldom defended claims of the orthodox view. As we shall see, there is something in each of the arguments briefly sketched above. Moreover, they are by no means incompatible. While one must in the end choose between accounts suggesting that globalization imposes pressures for welfare retrenchment (as in position 1) and those which see a potentially competitiveness-enhancing role for the welfare state (as in position 2), it is important that we acknowledge the attenuating and/or mediating role of institutional factors. Similarly, while authors may differ over the strict composition of welfare inflationary pressures in contemporary societies – with some attributing these to long-term demographic trends (position 3), others to short-term political factors (position 4), and yet others to a combination of the two – it is equally important that we qualify the impression given by the aggregate data of a simple tendency for social expenditure to grow.

In the pages that follow I seek to defend these claims. I argue that:

1 there has indeed been significant welfare retrenchment and reform in recent years in contemporary Europe;
2 such retrenchment has been informed to a considerable extent by impressions of the 'competitiveness-corrosive' qualities of social spending; but
3 such impressions, however paradoxically, have come at a time when evidence of the 'competitiveness-enhancing' qualities of the welfare state have become ever more transparent.

The argument proceeds in four sections. In the first of these I assess the scale of welfare retrenchment in contemporary Europe before moving, in the second, to assess and evaluate the orthodox view in the light of such evidence. In the third section, I attempt to draw up a more balanced assessment of the positive and negative externalities of the welfare state in the competitive environment of the contemporary global political economy. I conclude by considering the prospects for the welfare state in an era of putative globalization. In particular, I focus on the consequences for the form and function of the welfare state of the stark choice currently facing European economies between cost competitive and quality competitive strategies.

## The Scope and Scale of Welfare Retrenchment

However intuitively appealing the familiar argument that globalization drives an inexorable process of welfare retrenchment, it is surely tempting to conclude on the basis of the merest glance at the (aggregate) empirical data that there is simply nothing to explain. For, as table 1 demonstrates, the secular tendency of government expenditure to rise does not appear to have been tempered in recent years. Even in the face of consecutive self-professedly radical neo-liberal regimes set on 'rolling back the frontiers of the state' (as, for instance, in Britain), social expenditure has not only held up rather well, but it now accounts for a greater proportion of national resources than ever before (Pierson, 1994, 1996). A certain degree of caution is nonetheless appropriate before we conclude that globalization has had and is likely to have no impact upon the welfare state. A number of points might here be made.

First, as noted above, we should be somewhat wary of the aggregate nature of this data, for it can give us no picture of the changing *composition of social expenditure*. It may well be that quantitative continuity masks qualitative discontinuity – the welfare state has certainly grown in size yet this in no way excludes the possibility of a quite fundamental transformation in its very form and function (see, for instance, Jessop, 1994). Moreover, even were we prepared to accept on the basis of such evidence that the welfare states which came to characterize the postwar period remain essentially intact today, this need not imply an unambiguous rejection of the globalization thesis.

For, as a number of new institutionalists have noted in recent years (see especially Esping-Andersen, 1990, 1994, pp. 23, 267, 1996a, 1996b, 1999; Pierson, 1994, 1996; Skocpol and Amenta, 1986), welfare states once established become embedded and entrenched. Consequently, while globalization may bring certain pressures for retrenchment to bear upon contemporary welfare regimes, the process by which such pressures are translated into

**Table 1** The secular tendency of state expenditure to rise, 1970–1995 (% of GDP)

| | Government expenditure (% of GDP) | | | | | | | | |
|---|---|---|---|---|---|---|---|---|---|
| | DK | G[a] | F | IRE | I | NL | SW | UK | EU15 |
| 1970 | 36.1 | 32.4 | 33.9 | 30.1 | 28.3 | 36.2 | 36.8 | 31.9 | 31.4 |
| 1975 | 42.4 | 43.1 | 35.4 | 38.8 | 34.7 | 45.4 | 44.6 | 37.6 | 35.4 |
| 1980 | 50.8 | 42.7 | 42.8 | 41.4 | 37.9 | 51.1 | 56.8 | 40.2 | 41.8 |
| 1985 | 55.2 | 43.4 | 49.4 | 47.4 | 45.3 | 53.5 | 61.1 | 41.8 | 45.8 |
| 1990 | 55.5 | 42.0 | 46.5 | 38.5 | 48.6 | 51.5 | 58.4 | 36.6 | 44.4[b] |
| 1995 | 58.2 | 46.3 | 51.0 | 37.4 | 49.2 | 49.0 | 64.7 | 41.0 | 47.6[b] |

[a] West Germany (1970–90).
[b] excluding Luxembourg.
*Source*: European Commission, 1996, pp. 190–1, table 71.

outcomes is itself likely to prove lengthy and protracted, producing iterative yet cumulative directional change (Pierson, 1996, pp. 178–9). By such a view, the effects of globalization are far from being fully realized.

Yet this does not leave the globalization orthodoxy entirely unscathed. For if, as we are so frequently entreated, inclusive welfare regimes can only be sustained at considerable cost to economic competitiveness, then we would expect to see this secular tendency for social spending to rise to be accompanied by an alarming depreciation in economic performance. Globalization, so the argument goes, unleashes a competitive firestorm fuelled by flows of capital in which only the fittest – and leanest – survive. If global markets clear as instantaneously as casual neoclassicists presume, then we would expect current levels of welfare expenditure within the EU to be unsustainable and to precipitate a haemorrhaging of both investment and portfolio capital. Yet again, however, the empirical evidence simply does not support this abstract and neo-Darwinian logic of downward harmonization and competitive deregulation (for more detailed empirical elaboration, see Hay, 1999a, 1999b).

Despite the tendency for social expenditure to rise, however, there may still be reasons for suggesting that welfare retrenchment is under way. Indeed, if we are prepared to relativize the notion of retrenchment so as to take account of fluctuations in demand, then there is in fact fairly unambiguous evidence of retrenchment across the advanced capitalist economies. Two rather separate issues need to be identified. The first relates to the unemployment–inflation trade-off; the second to demographic and other socioeconomic welfare inflationary pressures.

## *The Unemployment–Inflation Trade-Off*

Since the late 1970s something of a paradigm shift in economic policymaking has occurred, associated with the widely perceived crisis of Keynesianism and the growing ascendency of monetarism and supply-side economics (see, for instance, Hall, 1993; Scharpf, 1991). This was associated, in turn, with a much greater emphasis upon inflation-targeting, balanced budgets and fiscal austerity with a consequent respecification of the terms of the postwar social compromise with labour. Accordingly, unemployment throughout the advanced capitalist economies has risen, alarmingly in the case of the northern European economies. This has placed a considerable additional burden upon the welfare state – an ironic and perverse consequence of the marketization and liberalization heralded as a solution to the fiscal crisis of the state in the 1970s. Were it not then for a noticeable tightening of eligibility criteria, a greater emphasis upon benefit targeting and means-testing and the more general development of what might be termed a 'conditional welfare state' stressing the obligations

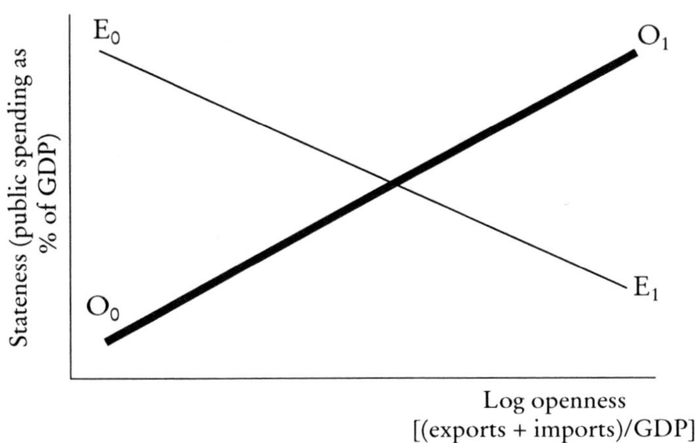


$E_0 - E_1$ expected correlation
$O_0 - O_1$ observed correlation (Cameron, 1978; Rodrik, 1996, 1997)

**Figure 1** Openness and stateness: rhetoric and reality

and duties of claimants, we would expect far more than a merely secular tendency for social expenditure to rise (Esping-Andersen, 1996c; Ferrera, 1998; Hagen, 1992; Jordan, 1998; Ormerod, 1998; Rhodes, 1997; Stephens, 1996; Stephens, Huber and Ray, 1999). The difference between expected welfare expenditure (assuming consistent income replacement ratios and eligibility criteria) and that observed provides a rough index of the extent of effective welfare retrenchment (see figure 1).

A further indication of the degree of welfare retrenchment is provided by *income replacement ratios*. These express the value of welfare entitlements (such as unemployment, sickness and disability benefits) as a percentage of the average net (post-tax) working wage. Throughout the advanced capitalist economies they display a common and marked downward trajectory from a range of start dates (earlier in the liberal countries, later in the social democratic countries) and a variety of initial levels (lower in the liberal regimes, higher in the social democratic regimes) (see, for instance, Clark, 1999; Esping-Andersen, 1996c; Hagen, 1992; Stephens et al., 1999).

## *Endogenous Welfare-Inflationary Pressures*

The increase in the rate of unemployment in Europe since the postwar period is not, however, the only demand-side factor which might account for mounting pressure on the contemporary welfare state. At least three additional and, for the most part, endogenous variables must be considered if we are adequately to assess the extent to which the welfare state is under threat and the precise nature of the challenge it faces. These are: (i) demographic change; (ii) the escalating cost of state-of-the-art health provision; and (iii) the persistence of low rates of economic growth.

(1) *The 'demographic timebomb'* If globalization is a largely intangible and hotly contested factor in the causal mêlée out of which we might account for welfare retrenchment, the same is not the case with demographic change. The problem is simply stated: Europe has a rapidly ageing population due to the inauspicious combination of declining birth rates and greater life expectancy. Accordingly, the ratio of net welfare recipients to net welfare contributors is higher than ever before and rising inexorably. This presents an alarming fiscal predicament likely only to be exacerbated by developments in medical technology and by a projected further fall in the birth rate (see figure 2).

As Rhodes notes, according to EC data, 'in 1995 around 15 per cent of the population of the EU were aged 65 or over, [equivalent] to 23 per cent of the working-age population (15 to 64). By 2005 the over 65s will rise to 26 per cent of the working-age population and to 30 per cent by 2015 [40 per cent in Italy]' (1997, p. 64; see also Taylor-Gooby, 1999). Clearly this represents a significant, escalating and potentially crippling burden on welfare regimes in contemporary Europe.[1]

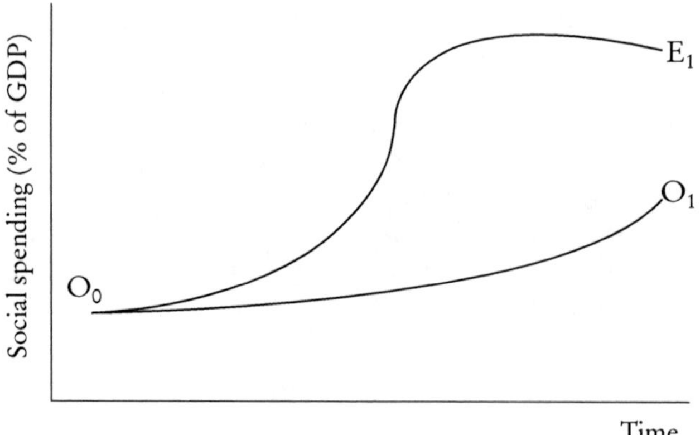


$O_0 - E_1$ expected
$O_0 - O_1$ observed

**Figure 2** Expected welfare expenditure assuming consistent levels of social provision and observed rate of unemployment

(2) *The cost of health provision* A related tendency is that of escalating healthcare demand, a consequence again of an ageing population and a population whose ageing is to a significant extent made possible by expensive and often interventionist medical practices and procedures. According to OECD statistics (Oxley and Macfarlan, 1995), the share of GDP accounted for by health expenditure has doubled since the early 1960s and is set to do so again by 2020. Quite apart from new demands, Rhodes is surely right to note that 'the health care sector, broadly defined, contains its own inflationary dynamic' (1997, p. 64). Yet, were a privatization of health care considered the solution, it should be noted that:

- market provision invariably proves more expensive per capita for a given level of care than public provision (the comparison between Canada and the US is a clear case in point: see Aaron, 1991; Barr, 1998, pp. 277–318); and
- non-mandatory occupational health insurance schemes may impose significant constraints on labour market mobility and hence flexibility.[2]

(3) *The cost of deflation* A third, and equally significant domestic/endogenous factor is simply the combination of low economic growth and high unemployment. Since the 1970s, the advanced capitalist economies have failed to secure the conditions for the high and stable rates of economic growth to which they became accustomed in the early postwar period (1945–70). The resulting low growth–high unemployment environment in which inflation has been held down only by shrinking and deflating the domestic economy renders a welfare state premised upon the principle of full employment extremely costly. Moreover, this cost is born disproportionately by capital which, so conventional wisdom goes, pays a high price for the generosity of welfare provision and the institutionalized rigidity of a comprehensive welfare state once established. As Andrew Martin notes, 'the proposition that the viability of the welfare state is contingent on full employment is familiar and presumably generally accepted – it is hard to think of welfare states as anything but "full employment welfare states" or "Keynesian welfare states"' (1997, p. 6). The ability of the welfare state to respond to escalating demands, particularly those associated with an ageing population, is further compounded by low rates of growth. For, as Gøsta Esping-Andersen notes:

> population ageing does not automatically imply crisis . . . the cost of ageing depends on long-run productivity growth. The OECD estimates that real earnings growth at an annual average rate of 0.5–1.2 per cent (depending on nation) will suffice to finance the additional pension expenditures. (1996a, p. 7)

This may sound simple enough, yet as he goes on to observe in a footnote:

> the earnings performance of many nations in the past decade suggests that such levels of growth may not be so easily attainable. In the United States, for example, real manufacturing earnings declined by an annual average of 0.2 per cent during the 1980s. In Europe, where labour shedding has been much more dramatic, productivity and thus wages have grown at higher rates (1.7 per cent in France, 0.9 per cent in Italy, and 2.4 per cent in Germany). (1996a, p. 28 n6)

Yet labour-shedding merely compounds the fiscal crisis of the welfare state by increasing the ratio of net welfare recipients to net welfare contributors. In the context of such discussions, the global diffusion of neo-liberalism and with it the global depreciation of growth rates (labour-shedding notwithstanding) is a worrying trend. Identifiable theoretically and observable empirically, such a tendency may serve to translate mounting demographic pressure into a pervasive domestic tide of welfare retrenchment. What this also suggests is that far from being the solution, neo-liberalism may itself be part of the problem. The low growth–escalating demand equation is a difficult one to solve; it may well be that the resuscitation of growth may be a condition for the revivification of the welfare state.

## Reassessing the Conventional Wisdom

As the above paragraphs reveal, a quite plausible, compelling and convincing narrative of welfare state retrenchment (or at least of the origins of the pressures for welfare state retrenchment) can be told without reference to exogenous factors so much as to endogenous factors widely experienced (cf. Pierson, 1998). So where does this leave the conventional view so frequently voiced by politicians and academics alike which suggests that it is globalization and the transition from closed to open economies and the flows of capital this has unleashed which have undermined the somewhat indulgent luxuries of the European social model? Is it little more than a convenient alibi, offered as a *post hoc* rationalization for a secular retrenchment already under way and precipitated by rather more immediate and parochial factors?

If we are to assess the impact (if any) of globalization on the viability of the welfare state, it is first essential that we unpack the various logics appealed to and frequently conflated in the claims for incommensurability of inclusive social provision and international competitiveness in an era of deepening economic integration. A series of related, if nonetheless distinct, arguments are frequently invoked, relating to capital mobility, the 'vexatious inquisition of taxation' (Adam Smith) and the need for both flexible labour-markets and a constant supply of cheap malleable labour. It is important that we start by acknowledging what they share. For each exhibits a common analytical-deductive strategy, proceeding on the basis of relatively simple, indeed intuitive, microfoundations through a process of macro-aggregation and extrapolation, to derive a generic tendency (or series of tendencies) for welfare retrenchment. This is an important point. For, arguably, their common structure reveals a common analytical poverty. Enticing and alluring though the logical deduction of, say, the negative externalities of the welfare state may be, there are dangers in extrapolating so presumptuously from invariably pared-down and institutionally unspecified microfoundations (see also Gough, 1996, p. 224; and, for more general critiques of such 'blackboard economics', Fine, 1998; Sen, 1977). Such microfoundations – those concerning the perfect mobility of the factors of production, for instance – are often difficult to square with the empirical evidence. To generalize and extrapolate from such parsimonious premises in this manner may then merely compound the distorting simplicity of the initial assumptions. The prescriptions derived in this manner (such as the harsh necessity of welfare retrenchment) are only as reliable as the premises on which they are based, and these we know to be dubious. It is crucial then that we: (i) isolate such assumptions, (ii) assess their plausibility, and (iii) consider the sensitivity of orthodox predictions to variations in initial assumptions. This I attempt, albeit briefly, in the following section.

## Capital Flight and the 'Vexatious Inquisition of Taxation'

> The . . . proprietor of stock is properly a citizen of the world, and is not necessarily attached to any particular country. He would be apt to abandon the country in which he is exposed to a vexatious inquisition, in order to be assessed a burdensome tax, and would remove his stock to some country where he could either carry on his business or enjoy his fortune at his ease. A tax that tended to drive away stock from a particular country, would so far tend to dry up every source of revenue, both to the sovereign and to the society. Not only the profits of stock, but the rent of land and the wages of labour, would necessarily be more or less diminished by its removal. (Smith, [1776] 1976, pp. 848–9)

The mobility of capital, specifically the mobility of (foreign) direct investors, is crucial to orthodox accounts which seek to derive what they see as the inexorable logic of welfare retrenchment from globalization. What passes in the name of the conventional wisdom here is relatively simply stated (and is not so very different from that elaborated by Adam Smith in the above passage). In the (stylized) closed economies of the initial postwar period, capital enjoyed no exit option. Consequently, governments enjoyed the ability to impose punitive taxation regimes upon unwilling and relatively impotent national capitals with little cost to the domestic economy (except for the tendency for capitalists to accumulate rather than to reinvest their profits). With financial liberalization and the elimination of capital controls under open economy conditions, this is no longer the case. Capital may now exit from national economic environments at minimal cost (indeed, in most neoclassical-inspired models, at zero cost).

Accordingly, by playing off the regulatory regimes of different economies against one another, capital can ensure for itself a higher rate of return on its investment. This it does by seeking out the high growth regimes of newly industrialized countries unencumbered by burdensome welfare traditions, rigid labour-market institutions and correspondingly higher rates of taxation. Similarly, mobile ('footloose') foreign direct investors can seek out low taxation regimes and cheap labour while securing for themselves attractive relocation packages, tax concessions and other subsidies as competitive national economies (and, indeed, local and regional economies) are effectively forced to compete through a process of 'social dumping' and 'competitive deregulation'. This logic threatens to establish a perverse and pathological 'race to the bottom' (Marquand, 1994, p. 18) lubricated by the 'deregulatory arbitrage' of footloose and fancy-free transnational corporations. As Duane Swank notes, for both neo-liberal economists and analytical Marxists alike, the structural power of capital has been increased. This generates a 'prisoner's dilemma' for policy-makers. For, 'in the face of inherent impediments to international policy coordination, governments face incentives to engage in competition for investment' (Swank, 1998, p. 676). The demise of the welfare state is not difficult to derive from such a logic. For, according to such a view, the welfare state represents, quite simply, a cost to capital (in the form of a direct or indirect taxation premium) and hence a drain on national competitiveness. Consequently, centre-left/social democratic administrations, if they are not to precipitate a haemorrhaging of investment and portfolio capital on their election (indeed, in the very anticipation of their election) must convince capital of their fiscal prudence and moderation in advance (Przeworski and Wallerstein, 1988; Wickham-Jones, 1995). It is perhaps chastening at this point to note that, on the basis of such (standard neo-classical) assumptions, the optimal rate of taxation on income from capital in small open economies tends to zero (Razin and Sadka, 1991a, 1991b; Tanzi and Zee, 1997; Tanzi and Schuknecht, 1997).

The policy implications of such an account are painfully clear. As globalization serves to establish competitive selection mechanisms within the international political economy, there is little choice but to cast the welfare state on the bonfire of regulatory controls and labour-market rigidities. Compelling though such an alarming logic may sound, it serves us well to isolate the assumptions which ultimately summon this simple 'logic of no alternative' (see also Hay, 1998; Watson, 1999). They are principally fourfold:

1 That capital invests where it can secure the greatest net return on that investment and is possessed of perfect information of the means by which to maximise this utility.
2 That capital enjoys perfect mobility and that the cost of exit is zero.
3 That capital will invariably secure the greatest return on its investment through minimizing its labour costs by seeking out a captive supply of cheap labour in flexible and deregulated labour markets and by relocating its productive activities in economies with the lowest rates of corporate taxation.

This third assumption leads fairly directly to a fourth and final assumption:

4 That the welfare state (and the taxation receipts out of which it is funded) represent nothing other than lost capital to mobile asset-holders and have no positive (or even potentially positive) externalities for the competitiveness and productivity of the national economy.

Each of these foundational premises is at best dubious, at worst demonstrably false. Consider each in turn. While it may seem entirely appropriate to attribute to capital the sole motive of seeking the greatest return on its investment, the history of specific capitals hardly engenders much confidence in the additional assumption that capital is blessed with perfect information of the means by which to realize that objective. Nonetheless, this is perhaps the least problematic of the assumptions considered here and the least consequential for the present analysis.

The second assumption is demonstrably false – or, at least, demonstrably false for certain types of capital. For while portfolio capital may indeed exhibit almost perfect mobility – its effectively instantaneous flows conducted in the flickering of a cursor and incurring negligible exit costs – the same is simply not the case with *invested* as distinct from (potential) *investment* capital. For, once enticed and attracted to a particular locality, formerly mobile foreign direct investment flows 'bed down', acquiring an array of significant sunk costs (however subsidized by their 'hosts') as virtual/immaterial assets are translated into human and physical capital (Watson, 1997). Consequently, once installed, exit options become seriously depleted and incur significant loss (in terms of irredeemable sunk costs). Thus, while it may be entirely 'rational' for foreign direct investors to proclaim loudly and exaggerate wildly their mobility and their much-vaunted exit options – especially if they can make these sound credible – it is not surprising that the threat of exit is so rarely acted upon (Hay, 1997). What we do witness, however, is the quite predictable phenomenon of what might be termed an 'exit threat business cycle', indicative perhaps of the hollowness of most exit threats.

What this in turn suggests is that the haemorrhaging of invested capital predicted by standard neoclassical models of open economies in which governments fail to internalize the preferences of capital for minimal social protection are grossly exaggerated. They summon a seemingly inexorable logic of welfare retrenchment which is simply unwarranted and whose logic of compulsion can be attributed and traced directly to the implausibility of the initial assumptions. Once we revise such, frankly false, initial premises, a much higher 'burden' of corporate taxation would appear sustainable, consistent with current levels of social expenditure in Europe (Boix, 1998; Locke and Kochan, 1995; Swank, 1998). As Swank again notes, 'contrary to the claims of the international capital mobility thesis . . . the general fiscal capacity of democratic governments to fund a variety of levels and mixes of social protection and services may be relatively resilient in the face of internationalisation of markets' (1999, p. 325). Here it is perhaps instructive to note that despite a marked tendency for direct corporate taxation to fall in recent years in line with the predictions of such neoclassical-inspired models, the overall burden of taxation on firms has in fact remained fairly constant, rising marginally since the mid-1980s (Swank, 1998, 1999).

Yet this does not exhaust the problems of the international capital mobility thesis – not by a long way. For perhaps most problematic of all are assumptions three and four – that capital can only compete in a more intensely competitive environment on the basis of productivity gains secured through tax reductions (whether achieved through domestic political pressure such as the threat of exit, or exit itself) and cost-shedding (through rationalization, downsizing and the proletarianization of labour). This is a distinctly and peculiarly Anglo-US conception of competitiveness, though one ever more intimately associated with the political discourse of globalization (Watson, 1997).

As we shall see, its considerable limitations are clearly exposed if we seek to draw up a balance sheet of the competitive merits and demerits of the contemporary welfare state.

## A Competitive Audit of the Welfare State

Here we can usefully develop, adapt and extend the work of Ian Gough who, in a thorough and perceptive article (1996), assesses the full range of arguments which might be brought to bear upon the complex relationship between the welfare state and international competitiveness (see also Pfaller et al., 1991). Things are considerably more complex than the orthodox globalization thesis would have us believe, for a whole variety of both positive and negative externalities might be identified. At the very least, this suggests that the orthodox account that presents welfare expenditure simply as a drain on competitiveness is a gross and distorting simplification of a far more complex and contingent reality.

## *Negative Externalities: The 'Competitiveness-Corrosive' Consequences of the Welfare State*

As I have been at pains to demonstrate, the conventional orthodoxy tends to posit a simple trade-off between equality and efficiency, such that (redistributive) welfare expenditure comes at a direct cost to economic competitiveness. In addition to the arguments reviewed above, a variety of negative (or 'competitive corrosive') externalities of welfare expenditure – direct and indirect – are identified in this literature. They are summarized in table 2. Due to constraints of space they are not reviewed here (though, for a fuller discussion, see Hay, 1999b). Suffice it to note that the evidence is by no means unequivocal.

At this stage, the economic case for the net competitiveness-corrosive externalities of the welfare state might look impressive. The two most compelling cases are perhaps the first, identifying a tendency for government borrowing to inject inflationary pressures into the economy, and the third, suggesting that the direct and indirect taxation burden associated with social provision increases the cost of labour. Interestingly, however, both of these tendencies are likely to be unevenly distributed among welfare states. For, arguably, the presence of encompassing labour-market institutions and a social democratic tradition of coordinated national wage bargaining

**Table 2** Negative externalities of welfare expenditure

| | Cost/supply of capital | Cost/supply of labour | Productivity of capital and labour |
|---|---|---|---|
| Expenditure/ taxation (indirect effects) | 1 Borrowing crowds out investment<br>2 Social costs encourage capital flight | 3 Direct taxes increase labour cost and reduce supply | — |
| Social programmes (direct effects) | 4 PAYE (pay-as-you-earn) pensions reduce savings | 5 State pensions and unemployment and sickness benefits reduce labour supply | 6 Public sector social provision less efficient |

*Source*: Inspired by and adapted from Gough, 1996, p. 217.

attenuates pressures for wage-push inflation that may be present in more liberal welfare regimes. Moreover, tax-induced additional labour costs tend to have a minimal impact on economies which compete in capital-intensive and quality competitive sectors. For labour costs represent a tiny fraction of the overall production costs and it is quality and innovation rather than cost that is most likely to confer a competitive advantage.

What this in turn suggests is that the balance between competitive-enhancing and competitive-corrosive externalities is likely to be mediated by institutional factors. Principal among these are the degree of encompassment of the wage-bargaining regime and what might be termed the 'regime of competitiveness' of the economy as a whole. For economies competing solely on the basis of cost in low-skill, labour-intensive industries, the welfare state is a clear burden on competitiveness, while for those seeking to pave a high-tech, high-skill route to competitiveness in capital-intensive sectors, any such negative externalities are significantly attenuated. That this is so becomes rather more transparent if we turn from the debit to the credit column of the welfare state's competitiveness audit.

## *Positive Externalities: The 'Competitiveness-Enhancing' Consequences of the Welfare State*

Given the now pervasive orthodoxy, we might expect to find little in the way of hypothesized competitive-enhancing externalities associated with inclusive social provision. Yet what is most striking given the ascendancy of the conventional wisdom is the sheer range and diversity of factors, even in quite mainstream economic analysis, pointing to the potential contribution of the welfare state to competitiveness in export markets. These are presented schematically in table 3 (for a fuller discussion, see Hay, 1999b).

(1) *Macroeconomic stabilization effects* High levels of social expenditure will tend to promote economic stability in so far as they have counter-cyclical economic effects. This is particularly the case with unemployment benefits which (higher underlying rates of structural unemployment notwithstanding) will tend to bolster demand in times of recession. Similarly, transfer payments to the working class are more likely to stimulate consumption (and hence demand) than tax concessions to the middle classes. Consequently, redistributive welfare regimes, particularly those prepared to inject demand into the economy during times of recession, are likely to facilitate macroeconomic stabilization across the economic cycle.

(2) *Public housing provision boosts consumption* The subsidization or direct provision of housing frees capital for consumption, thereby raising the aggregate level of demand within the economy.

**Table 3** Positive externalities of welfare expenditure

| | Cost/supply of capital | Cost/supply of labour | Productivity of capital and labour |
|---|---|---|---|
| Macroeconomic effects | | 1 Macroeconomic stabilization effects | |
| Social programmes (direct effects) | 2 Public social provision boosts consumption | 3 Support for women's employment increases supply of labour | 4 Human capital enhanced through education and training |
| Welfare outcomes (indirect effects) | 5 Social inclusion tempers criminality; crime deters investment | 6 Reduced costs of ill health | 7 Contribution to internal work-place flexibility (trust and reduced transaction costs) |

*Source*: Inspired by and adapted from Gough, 1996, p. 217.

(3) *Support for women's employment increases supply of labour* Quite simply, the provision of nursery places and pre-school care is likely to facilitate access (particularly that of women) to the labour-market and hence to improve the supply of labour with consequent benefits for the productivity of the economy. Moreover, where access to the labour-market can be facilitated in this way (as, for instance, in Sweden in recent years), the ratio of net welfare contributors to net welfare recipients will increase, easing fiscal pressures generated by demographic change.

(4) *Human capital is enhanced through education and training* As Gough notes, most contemporary variants of the competitiveness-enhancing view of the welfare state focus on its supply-side contribution (1996, p. 222). Human capital theory is far the most influential current strand of thought in this area (Allmendinger, 1989; Ashton and Green, 1996; Bosworth et al., 1996, pp. 211–52; Finegold and Soskice, 1988; Lucas, 1988; Prais and Wagner, 1987). In an era of heightened competition, it argues, the skill level of the economy is crucial. Here the welfare state has a central role to play, ensuring flexible high-quality training and reskilling programmes oriented directly towards the delivery of the skills required by the economy. The implications of such a theory are that welfare retrenchment, though frequently couched in terms of competitiveness, may come at a considerable price in terms of the ability of the domestic economy to compete on any basis other than cost alone in international markets.

(5) *Social inclusion tempers criminality; crime deters investment* Consequently, a cost-benefit analysis of welfare retrenchment which fails to take account of the likely cost (both substantive and qualitative) of heightened levels of criminality is wholly inadequate. Costs which must be considered include the expense of incarceration and law enforcement, the cost to child development of crime and social dislocation and the cost to capital of excessive insurance premiums in high crime areas. Once such costs are factored in, the suggestion that competitiveness may be enhanced by welfare retrenchment is rendered, at best, equivocal. The US provides a case in point. For, as recent research demonstrates, if the incarcerated are counted among the ranks of the unemployed, the US male jobless rate rises to a level above the European average for most of the period since 1975 (Western et al., 1998; Western and Beckett, 1998). Moreover, since the job prospects of ex-convicts are significantly eroded such that they invariably leave prison to join the ranks of the long-term unemployed, the impressive employment performance of the US in the 1980s and 1990s has in fact depended in large part on a high and increasing incarceration rate (Western and Beckett, 1999). Moreover, by Bowles and Gintis's calculations, one-quarter of all labour employed in the US is 'guard labour' (1994).

(6) *Reduced costs of ill health* Poor health, arising from under-insurance or non-insurance in a privately financed system, is likely to disrupt production whilst imposing punitive healthcare costs (however funded). Consequently, health – as a public good – is best provided by the state and is most efficient when it contains a significant preventative component. Moreover, a redistributive welfare state contributes significantly to a softening of social stratification (itself closely correlated to poor health) (Wilkinson, 1996). An inclusive state-funded national health service may, then, both decrease the volume of healthcare demand (through preventative medicine) while minimizing the cost of satisfying that demand.

(7) *Welfare enhances flexibility via greater trust and reduced transaction costs* Inclusive welfare states, particularly where associated with encompassing labour-market institutions, encourage relations of cooperation and trust. Significantly, this facilitates internal flexibility – in which workers adapt themselves and their working practices to new demands and new technology – as opposed to external flexibility (i.e. recourse to the labour market). This fosters cooperative relations between managers and labour, with consequent reductions in the rate of labour turnover. This, in turn, is rewarded by higher levels of investment in human capital as workers are less likely to depart with their newly acquired skills (skills acquired at the company's expense) to the competition.

With each of the above observations, the competitiveness balance-sheet of the welfare state moves further into credit.

## Conclusion

What the above discussion serves to suggest is that the relationship between competitiveness and the welfare state is far more complex (and perhaps rather more contingent) than the globalization orthodoxy would have us believe. Nonetheless, this cannot and should not serve to hide the fact that significant welfare retrenchment has occurred and continues apace. That this is so is due, in no small part, to the predominance of a view of the competitiveness-corrosive impact of the welfare state which is at odds with the empirical evidence [ . . . ].

As the analysis of this chapter reveals, however, even this is to present an overly simplified picture. The specific consequences of welfare provision will vary on a case-by-case basis, mediated by a range of institutional and cultural factors. Not the least of these are the scope and scale of welfare provision itself and the 'regime of competitiveness' of the economy as a whole. [ . . . ] Low-cost–low-skill competitiveness in labour-intensive industries places a considerable premium upon externally flexible labour markets and a cheap and voluminous supply of docile (for which read de-unionized and/or demoralized) labour. The welfare state in such a scenario is likely to represent little more than an expensive indulgence – though the social and economic cost of its retrenchment (in terms of the criminalization and marginalization of an underclass) should not be underestimated. Whether out-and-out cost competitiveness represents a viable competitive strategy for any contemporary European economy is debatable. What it does suggest, however, is the stark choice that European economies now face and the significance of that choice for the continued viability of the welfare state. Yet one thing should perhaps be made clear. Europe's most open economies (Britain excepted) have, throughout the postwar period, always sought competitiveness on the basis of quality not cost. They have thus sought to promote internal flexibility within the firm rather than external flexibility in the labour-market, permanent innovation in production as opposed to productivity gains on the basis of hire-and-fire and the elimination of supply-side rigidities, high and stable levels of both human *and* physical capital formation, and inclusive and encompassing labour-market institutions. Within such a model, far from representing a supply-side rigidity, the welfare state is not only a competitive advantage it is a competitive necessity.

## Notes

From R. Sykes, B. Palier and P. M. Prior (eds), *Globalization and European Welfare States*, London, Palgrave, 2001, pp. 38–58.

The author would like to acknowledge the support of the ESRC for research on 'Globalization, European Integration and the European Social Model' (L213252043), research which concentrates on globalization, European integration and welfare/labour market reform in Denmark, Germany, France, Hungary, Ireland, Italy, the Netherlands, Sweden and the UK. I would also like to express gratitude to Pete Alcock, Robert Sykes, Matthew Watson and Daniel Wincott for comments on an earlier version of this chapter.

1 This burden is, however, unevenly distributed and has been responded to differently in different national contexts. For a more extended discussion see Hay (1999b).
2 In the US, for instance, occupationally insured workers are frequently reluctant to move job because of the risk to their eligibility for medical benefits in a context where private provision is likely to prove punitively expensive.

## References

Aaron, H. J. (1991) *Serious and Unstable Condition: Financing America's Health Care*, Washington: Brookings Institution.

Allmendinger, J. (1989) 'Educational Systems and Labour Market Outcomes', *European Sociological Review*, 5, 3, pp. 231–50.

Ashton, D. and Green, F. (1996) *Education, Training and the Global Economy*, London, Edward Elgar.

Barr, N. (1998) *The Economics of the Welfare State*, 3rd edn, Oxford, Oxford University Press.

Boix, C. (1998) *Political Parties, Growth and Equality: Conservative and Social Democratic Economic Strategies in the World Economy*, Cambridge, Cambridge University Press.

Bosworth, D., Dawkins, P. and Stromback, T. (1996) *The Economics of the Labour Market*, Harlow, Longman.

Bowles, S. and Gintis, H. (1994) 'Efficient Redistribution in a Globally Competitive Economy', paper presented to the Colloquium on Social Justice and Economic Constraints, Université Catholique de Louvain, 3 June.

Cameron, D. R. (1978) 'The Expansion of the Public Economy: A Comparative Analysis', *American Political Science Review*, 72, 4, pp. 1243–61.

Cerny, P. G. (1990) *The Changing Architecture of Politics*, London, Sage.

Cerny, P. G. (1997) 'Paradoxes of the Competition State: The Dynamics of Political Globalisation', *Government and Opposition*, 49, 4, pp. 595–625.

Clark, G. L. (1999) 'The Retreat of the State and the Rise of Pension Fund Capitalism', in R. Martin (ed.), *Money and the Space Economy*, New York, Wiley.

Esping-Andersen, G. (1990) *The Three Worlds of Welfare Capitalism*, Cambridge, Polity.

Esping-Andersen, G. (1994) 'The Welfare State and the Economy', in N. J. Smelser and R. Swedberg (eds), *The Handbook of Economic Sociology*, Princeton, Princeton University Press.

Esping-Andersen, G. (1996a) 'After the Golden Age? Welfare State Dilemmas in a Global Economy', in G. Esping-Andersen (ed.), *Welfare States in Transition: National Adaptations in Global Economies*, London, Sage.

Esping-Andersen, G. (1996b) 'Positive-Sum Solutions in a World of Trade-Offs?', in G. Esping-Andersen (ed.), *Welfare States in Transition: National Adaptations in Global Economies*, London, Sage.

Esping-Andersen, G. (1996c) 'Welfare States without Work: The Impasse of Labour Shedding and Familialism in Continental European Social Policy', in G. Esping-Andersen (ed.), *Welfare States in Transition: National Adaptations in Global Economies*, London, Sage.

Esping-Andersen, G. (1999) *Social Foundations of Postindustrial Economies*, London, Sage.

European Commission (1996) *European Economy*, no. 62, Brussels, Directorate-General for Economic and Financial Affairs.

Ferrera, M. (1998) 'The Four "Social Europes": Between Universalism and Selectivity', in M. Rhodes and Y. Mény (eds), *The Future of the European Welfare State: A New Social Contract*? Basingstoke, Macmillan.

Fine, Ben (1998) 'The Triumph of Economics: or, "Rationality" Can be Dangerous to your Reasoning', in J. G. Collier and D. Miller (eds), *Virtualism: A New Political Economy*, Oxford, Berg.

Finegold, D. and Soskice, D. (1988) 'The Failure of Training in Britain: Analysis and Prescription', *Oxford Review of Economic Policy*, 4, 3, pp. 21–53.

Fisher, I. (1930) *The Theory of Interest*, Basingstoke, Macmillan.

Fisher, I. (1935) *The Clash of Progress and Security*, Basingstoke, Macmillan.

Garrett, G. (1998) *Partisan Politics in the Global Economy*, Cambridge, Cambridge University Press.

Gilder, G. (1981) *Welfare and Poverty*, New York, Basic Books.

Gough, I. (1996) 'Social Welfare and Competitiveness', *New Political Economy*, 1, 2, pp. 209–32.

Hagen, K. (1992) 'The Interaction of Welfare States and Labour Markets', in J. E. Kolberg (ed.), *The Study of Welfare State Regimes*, Armonk, NY, M.E. Sharpe.

Hall, P. A. (1993) 'Policy Paradigms, Social Learning and the State: The Case of Economic-Policy Making in Britain', *Comparative Politics*, 25, 2, pp. 275–96.

Hay, C. (1997) 'Anticipating Accommodations, Accommodating Anticipations: The Appeasement of Capital in the Modernisation of the British Labour Party, 1987–1992', *Politics and Society*, 25, 2, pp. 234–56.

Hay, C. (1998) 'Globalisation, Welfare Retrenchment and the "Logic of No Alternative": Why Second-Best Won't Do', *Journal of Social Policy*, 27, 4, pp. 525–32.

Hay, C. (1999a) 'Globalization, Regionalization and the Persistence of National Variation: The Contingent Convergence of Contemporary Capitalism', ESRC One Europe or Several? working paper, University of Birmingham.

Hay, C. (1999b) 'The Vexatious Inquistion of Taxation? Globalization and the Political Economy, of Welfare Retrenchment', ESRC One Europe or Several? working paper, University of Birmingham.

Jessop, B. (1994) 'The Schumpeterian Workfare State', in R. Burrows and B. Loader (eds), *Towards a Post-Fordist Welfare State*, London, Routledge.

Jordan, B. (1998) 'European Social Citizenship: Why a New Social Contract (Probably) Will Not Happen', in M. Rhodes and Y. Mény (eds), *The Future of the European Welfare State: A New Social Contract*? Basingstoke, Macmillan.

Kurzer, P. (1993) *Business and Banking*, Ithaca, NY, Cornell University Press.

Locke, R. and Kochan, T. (1995) 'The Transformation of Industrial Relations? A Cross-national Review of the Evidence', in R. Locke, T. Kochan and M. Piore (eds), *Employment Relations in a Changing World*, Cambridge, MA, MIT Press.

Lucas, R. E .J. (1988) 'On the Mechanics of Economic Development', *Journal of Monetary Economics*, 22, 1, pp. 3–42.

Marquand, D. (1994) 'Reinventing Federalism: Europe and the Left', *New Left Review*, 203, pp. 17–26.

Martin, A. (1997) *What Does Globalization Have to Do with the Erosion of Welfare States? Sorting Out the Issues*, Bremen, Zentrum fur Sozialpolitik.

Okun, A. M. (1975) *Equality and Efficiency: The Big Tradeoff*, Washington, Brookings Institution.

Ormerod, P. (1998) 'Unemployment and Social Exclusion: An Economic View', in M. Rhodes and Yves Mény (eds), *The Future of the European Welfare State: A New Social Contract*? Basingstoke, Macmillan.

Oxley, H. and Macfarlan, M. (1995) 'Health Care Reform: Controlling Spending and Increasing Efficiency', *OECD Economic Studies*, 24, 1, pp. 7–55.

Pfaller, A., Gough, I. and Therborn, G. (eds) (1991) *Can the Welfare State Compete? A Comparative Study of Five Advanced Capitalist Countries*, Basingstoke, Macmillan.

Pierson, P. (1994) *Dismantling the Welfare State? Reagan, Thatcher and the Politics of Retrenchment*, Cambridge, Cambridge University Press.

Pierson, P. (1996) 'The New Politics of the Welfare State', *World Politics*, 48, pp. 143–79.

Pierson, P. (1998) 'Irresistible Forces, Immovable Objects: Post-industrial Welfare States Confront Permanent Austerity', *Journal of European Public Policy*, 5, 5, pp. 539–60.

Polanyi, K. (1944) *The Great Transformation*, Boston, Beacon Press.

Prais, S. J. and Wagner, K. (1987) 'Educating for Productivity: Comparisons of Japanese and English Schooling and Vocational Preparation', *National Institute Economic Review*, 119, pp. 40–56.
Przeworski, A. and Wallerstein, M. (1988) 'Structural Dependence of the State on Capital', *American Political Science Review*, 82, 1, pp. 11–30.
Rao, N. (1996) *Towards Welfare Pluralism: Public Services in a Time of Change*, Aldershot, Dartmouth.
Razin, A. and Sadka, E. (1991a) 'Efficient Investment Incentives in the Presence of Capital Flight', *Journal of International Economics*, 31, 1–2, pp. 171–81.
Razin, A. and Sadka, E. (1991b) 'International Tax Competition and Gains from Tax Harmonisation', *Economic Letters*, 37, 1, pp. 69–76.
Rhodes, M. (1996) 'Globalization and West European Welfare States: A Critical Review of Recent Debates', *Journal of European Social Policy*, 6, 4, pp. 305–27.
Rhodes, M. (1997) 'The Welfare State: Internal Challenges, External Constraints', in M. Rhodes, P. Heywood and V. Wright (eds), *Developments in West European Politics*, Basingstoke, Macmillan.
Rodrik, D. (1996) 'Why Do More Open Economies have Bigger Governments?' NBER working paper no. 5537, National Bureau of Economic Research, Cambridge, MA.
Rodrik, D. (1997) *Has Globalisation Gone Too Far?* Washington, Institute for International Economics.
Scharpf, Fritz (1991) *Crisis and Choice in European Social Democracy*, Ithaca, NY, Cornell University Press.
Skocpol, T. and Amenta, E. (1986) 'States and Social Policies', *Annual Review of Sociology*, 12, pp. 131–57.
Sen, A. (1977) 'Rational Fools: A Critique of the Behavioural Foundations of Economic Theory', *Philosophy and Public Affairs*, 6, 4, pp. 317–44.
Smith, A. ([1776] 1976) *An Inquiry into the Nature and Causes of the Wealth of Nations*, Oxford, Oxford University Press.
Stephens, J. D. (1996) 'The Scandinavian Welfare States: Achievements, Crisis and Prospects', in G. Esping-Andersen (ed.), *Welfare States in Transition: National Adaptations in Global Economies*, London, Sage.
Stephens, J. D., Huber, E. and Ray, L. (1999) 'The Welfare State in Hard Times', in H. Kitschelt, P. Lange, G. Marks and J. D. Stephens (eds), *Continuity and Change in Contemporary Capitalism*, Cambridge, Cambridge University Press.
Swank, D. (1998) 'Funding the Welfare State: Globalisation and the Taxation of Business in Advanced Market Economies', *Political Studies*, 46, 4, pp. 671–92.
Swank, D. (1999) 'Diminished Democracy? Globalisation, Political Institutions and the Welfare State in Developed Nations', author's typescript, quoted with permission.
Tanzi, V. and Schuknecht, L. (1997) 'Reconsidering the Fiscal Role of Government: The International Perspective', *American Economic Review*, 87, 2, pp. 164–8.
Tanzi, V. and Zee, H. H. (1997) 'Fiscal Policy and Long-Run Growth', *International Monetary Fund Staff Papers*, 44, 2, pp. 179–209.
Taylor-Gooby, P. (1999) 'Policy Change at a Time of Retrenchment: Recent Pension Reform in France, Germany, Italy and the UK', *Social Policy and Administration*, 33, 1, pp. 1–19.
Watson, M. (1997) 'The Changing Face of Macroeconomic Stabilisation: From Growth through Indigenous Investment to Growth through Inward Investment', in J. Stanyer and G. Stoker (eds), *Contemporary Political Studies 1997, Volume 2*, Oxford, Blackwell/PSA.
Watson, M. (1999) 'Globalisation and British Political Development', in D. Marsh,

J. Buller, C. Hay, J. Johnston, P. Kerr, S. McAnulla and M. Watson, *Postwar British Politics in Perspective*, Cambridge, Polity.

Western, B. and Beckett, K. (1998) 'The Free Market Myth: Penal Justice as an Institution of the US Labour Market', *Berliner Journal für Soziologie*, 8, 2, pp. 159–82.

Western, B. and Beckett, K. (1999) 'How Unregulated is the US Labour Market? The Penal System as a Labour Market Institution', *American Journal of Sociology*, 104, 4, pp. 1030–60.

Western, B., Beckett, K. and Harding, D. (1998) 'Penal Systems and the American Labour Market', *Actes de la Recherche en Sciences Sociales*, 124, pp. 27–37.

Wickham-Jones, M. (1995) 'Anticipating Social Democracy, Pre-empting Anticipations: Economic Policy-Making in the British Labour Party, 1987–1992', *Politics and Society*, 23, 4, pp. 465–94.

Wilkinson, R. (1996) 'Health, Redistribution and Growth', in A. Glyn and D. Miliband (eds), *Paying for Inequalities*, London, Institute for Public Policy Research.

# Negative Integration: States and the Loss of Boundary Control

## *Fritz Scharpf*

[. . .]

### Negative Integration: The Loss of Boundary Control

In the history of capitalism, the decades following the Second World War were unusual in the degree to which the boundaries of the territorial state had become coextensive with the boundaries of markets for capital, services, goods and labour. These boundaries were by no means impermeable, but transactions across them were nevertheless under the effective control of national governments. As a consequence, capital owners were generally restricted to investment opportunities within the national economy, and firms were mainly challenged by domestic competitors. International trade grew slowly, and since governments controlled imports and exchange rates, international competitiveness was not much of a problem. While these conditions lasted, government interest rate policy controlled the rate of return on financial investments. If interest rates were lowered, job-creating real investments would become relatively more attractive, and vice versa. Thus, Keynesian macroeconomic management could smooth the business cycle and prevent demand-deficient unemployment, while union wage policy, where it could be employed for macro-economic purposes, was able to control the rate of inflation. At the same time, government regulation and union collective bargaining controlled the conditions of production. But since all effective competitors could be, and were, required to produce under the same regimes, the costs of regulation could be passed on to consumers. Hence the rate of return on investment was not necessarily affected by high levels of regulation and union power; capitalist accumulation was as feasible in the union-dominated Swedish welfare state as it was in the American free enterprise system.

During this period, therefore, the industrial nations of Western Europe had the chance to develop specifically national versions of the capitalist welfare state – and their choices were in fact remarkably different. [ . . . ] In spite of the considerable differences between the 'social democratic', 'corporatist' or 'liberal' versions of the welfare state, however, all were remarkably successful in maintaining and promoting a vigorous capitalist economy, while also controlling, in different ways and to different degrees, the destructive tendencies of unfettered capitalism in the interest of specific social, cultural and/or ecological values [ . . . ]. It was not fully realized at the time, however, how much the success of market-correcting policies did in fact depend on the capacity of the territorial state to control its economic boundaries. Once this capacity was lost, through the globalization of capital markets and the transnational integration of markets for goods and services, the 'golden years' of the capitalist welfare state came to an end.

Now the minimal rate of return that investors can expect is determined by global financial markets, rather than by national monetary policy, and real interest rates are generally about twice as high as they used to be in the 1960s. So if a government should now try to reduce interest rates below the international level, the result would no longer be an increase of job-creating real investment in the national economy, but an outflow of capital, devaluation and a rising rate of inflation. Similarly, once the territorial state has lost, or given up, the capacity to control the boundaries of markets for goods and services, it can no longer make sure that all competing suppliers will be subject to the same regulatory regime. Thus, if now the costs of regulation or of collective-bargaining are increased nationally, they can no longer be passed on to consumers. Instead, imports will increase, exports decrease, profits will fall, investment decline and firms will go bankrupt or move production to more benign locations.

Thus, when boundary control declines, the capacity of the state and the unions to shape the conditions under which capitalist economies must operate is also diminished. Instead, countries are forced into a competition for locational advantage which has all the characteristics of a Prisoner's Dilemma game [ . . . ]. The paradigmatic example of this form of 'regulatory competition' was provided, during the first third of the twentieth century, by the inability of 'progressive' states in the United States to regulate the employment of children in industry. Under the 'negative commerce clause' decisions of the Supreme Court, they were not allowed to prohibit or tax the import of goods produced by child labour in neighbouring states. Hence locational competition in the integrated American market prevented all states from enacting regulations that would affect only enterprises within their own state [ . . . ]. In the same way, the increasing transnational integration of capital and product markets, and especially the completion of the European internal market, reduces the freedom of national governments and unions to raise the regulatory and wage costs of national firms above the level prevailing in competing locations. Moreover, and if nothing else changes, the 'competition of regulatory systems' that is generally welcomed by neo-liberal economists [ . . . ] and politicians may well turn into a downward spiral of competitive deregulation in which all competing countries will find themselves reduced to a level of protection that is in fact lower than preferred by any of them.

[ . . . ]

## Note

From G. Marks et al., eds, *Governance in the EU*, London, Sage, 1996, pp. 16–17.

# A Race to the Bottom?

*Francis G. Castles*

## Some Preliminary Considerations

The notion of a 'race to the bottom' in social provision is only a variant of a more general argument: that enhanced international competition is destructive of regulatory standards across the board. The earliest articulation of the argument is to be found in early twentieth-century debates in United States corporate law on the difficulty of regulating corporations under circumstances where they were in a position to escape domestic jurisdiction (see Rieger and Leibfried, 2003). In the contemporary debate, the threat of welfare cutbacks induced by global competition is, in fact, only a relatively minor theme in a debate focusing largely on wages, labour protection laws and environmental standards (see Drezner, 2000). The logic, however, is just the same. In so far as the costs of social provision, better wages and conditions and environmental safeguards fall on business, they lead to high production costs, which, it is argued, will only be endured where business does not have the alternative of removing itself to a more favourable location. Where countries are heavily engaged in international trade and where enterprises cannot be prevented from relocating to countries in which costs are lower, governments are seen as having little option but to accede to the demands of capital for lower taxes, a more flexible labour market and less 'red tape' around health, safety and environmental issues.

The main purpose of this chapter is not to contest the logic of these arguments, but to examine the comparative evidence with a view to establishing how well the 'race to the bottom' hypothesis does actually account for the trajectory of recent social expenditure development. Nevertheless, it is worth very briefly noting a few of the reasons why the logic of international competition might turn out not to have the extreme consequences suggested by these accounts. First, there are reasons for believing that these theories exaggerate the extent of the threat resulting from changes in the international economy. Frequently, they neglect consumption considerations in the determination of locational advantage (i.e. being close to one's market may be as important as minimizing production costs) and offer an exaggerated picture of the likely consequences of capital flight (by the mid-1990s, corporate taxes amounted to somewhat less than 10 per cent of total taxation in OECD countries – see Ganghof, 2000). Second, there are reasons for supposing that the consequences of globalization may be quite different from those presupposed by such accounts. Indeed, rival accounts suggest that exposure to the world economy may actually serve as an incentive for governments to intervene to maintain or even improve regulatory standards in the hope of thereby mitigating some of the adverse consequences of international economic vulnerability (see Cameron, 1978; Ruggie, 1982; Katzenstein, 1985; Rodrik, 1997).

Globalization accounts may also be unrealistic in other ways. A third reason that social expenditures may not have declined as much as predicted is that the extent of change in the international economy in recent years is rather less than is sometimes implied in the crisis literature. In the 1990s, the average level of imports plus exports as a percentage of GDP in OECD countries was only around 5 per cent higher than in the 1980s. Admittedly, over the same period, the average level of foreign direct investment had more than doubled, but this was from a very low base. At the same time, overseas investment flows in OECD countries during the 1980s and 1990s averaged less than 3 per cent of GDP, a figure hardly indicative of overwhelming capital mobility among nations. Finally, these accounts appear totally to misjudge the dynamics of social expenditure change. The implication of the 'race to the bottom' analysis is that countries can rapidly adjust their social expenditure levels in a downward direction, but the prevailing imagery of the policy change literature is of a trajectory of social policy reform strongly shaped by an inertia and irreversibility stemming from a logic of 'increasing returns' and 'path dependent' institutional development (see Pierson, 2000). In Karl Hinrichs's beautiful simile, social security systems are like 'elephants on the move' (Hinrichs, 2001). When they are young, they may stampede ahead, but when they are mature they generally move forward rather slowly. Irrespective of age, turning them around involves much energy and no little persuasive power.

In this chapter, we are looking for signs that such a turnaround has occurred during the course of the past two decades. We assess the extent to which this may have occurred by examining trajectories of social expenditure measured in a variety of ways. Our premise is that, a few minor exceptions apart, it simply does not make sense to talk of a 'race to the bottom' in social provision that is not manifested in social expenditure terms. That is because, in most advanced welfare states, the vast bulk of provision takes the form of income-maintenance schemes and social services funded from various forms of taxation. It is this taxation that business regards as a burden and that it blames for its failure to compete in international markets. For governments persuaded of this diagnosis, there are only two available strategies: to cut benefits and services or to increase borrowing. However, given that the debt interest burden resulting from excessive borrowing is also seen as inimical to the viability of a market economy, the only viable option available to 'responsible' governments is social expenditure cuts. If the theory is correct, there really is 'no alternative'. For countries delivering welfare state provision largely through state-funded benefits and services, a 'race to the bottom' without accompanying expenditure cuts is a contradiction in terms.

## Patterns of Aggregate Spending

The first measures we examine in this chapter are changes in total public social expenditure and total public expenditure, both measured as percentages of GDP. We have already argued that the trajectory of welfare spending in a given period is the key to establishing the reality or otherwise of a 'race to the bottom'. Aggregate social spending as a percentage of GDP is also the most widely used measure of the 'welfare effort' governments make on behalf of their citizens and changes in this measure provide a useful indicator of a nation's continuing commitment to welfare. A focus on total public expenditure provides a context for our discussion of social expenditure trends. It allows us to ask whether trajectories noted as typical of social expenditure development are replicated in other public expenditure arenas and whether expenditures for social policy purposes have become a more or less salient aspect of overall public sector spending over the course of time. Because we seek also to contextualize our discussion in wider historical terms, we provide data not only for the period of our specific analysis from 1980 to 1998, but also for the two preceding decades from 1960 to 1980.

Table 1 provides data for total public social spending as a percentage of GDP in 1960, 1980 and 1998, and for the time periods 1960–80 and 1980–98. These data come from the OECD *Social Expenditure Database* (OECD, 2001c). This source brings together systematic information on thirteen components of social spending for all the long-term member countries of the OECD from 1980 onwards. The data are for twenty-one OECD countries, classified into four 'family of nations' groupings designed to capture affinities and commonalities arising from history, geography, language and culture. The four families – in order of their appearance in this and subsequent tables – consist respectively of English-speaking, Scandinavian, continental Western European and Southern European countries. Two countries – Switzerland and Japan – are difficult

**Table 1** Total public social expenditure as a percentage of GDP in twenty-one OECD countries, 1960, 1980, 1998 and change over time

| | 1960 | 1980 | 1998 | 1960–1980[a] | 1980–1998 |
|---|---|---|---|---|---|
| Australia | 7.4 | 11.3 | 17.8 | 3.9 | 6.5 |
| Canada | 9.1 | 13.3 | 18.0 | 4.2 | 4.8 |
| Ireland | 8.7 | 18.9 | 15.8 | 10.2 | −3.1 |
| New Zealand | 10.4 | 19.2 | 21.0 | 8.8 | 1.8 |
| United Kingdom | 10.2 | 18.2 | 21.4 | 8.0 | 3.2 |
| United States | 7.3 | 13.1 | 14.6 | 5.8 | 1.5 |
| **Family mean** | **8.9** | **15.7** | **18.1** | **6.8** | **2.4** |
| Denmark | 10.6 | 29.1 | 29.8 | 18.5 | 0.8 |
| Finland | 8.8 | 18.5 | 26.5 | 9.7 | 8.0 |
| Norway | 7.8 | 18.6 | 27.0 | 10.8 | 8.4 |
| Sweden | 10.8 | 29.0 | 31.0 | 18.2 | 2.0 |
| **Family mean** | **9.5** | **23.8** | **28.6** | **14.3** | **4.8** |
| Austria | 15.9 | 23.8 | 26.8 | 7.9 | 3.0 |
| Belgium | 13.8 | 24.2 | 24.5 | 10.4 | 0.4 |
| France | 13.4 | 22.7 | 28.8 | 9.3 | 6.1 |
| Germany | 18.1 | 20.3 | 27.3 | 2.2 | 7.0 |
| Netherlands | 11.7 | 27.3 | 23.9 | 15.6 | −3.4 |
| **Family mean** | **14.6** | **23.7** | **26.3** | **9.1** | **2.6** |
| Greece | 7.1 | 11.5 | 22.7 | 4.4 | 11.3 |
| Italy | 13.1 | 18.4 | 25.1 | 5.3 | 6.7 |
| Portugal | – | 11.6 | 18.2 | – | 6.6 |
| Spain | 3.2 | 15.8 | 19.7 | 12.6 | 3.9 |
| **Family mean** | **7.8** | **14.3** | **21.4** | **7.4** | **7.1** |
| Switzerland | 4.9 | 15.2 | 28.3 | 10.3 | 13.1 |
| Japan | 4.1 | 10.1 | 14.7 | 6.0 | 4.6 |
| **Overall mean** | **10.1** | **18.7** | **22.7** | **9.0** | **4.0** |
| **Coefficient of variation** | **38.9** | **31.2** | **22.3** | | |

[a] Because data for 1960 and for 1980 and onwards come from different sources, the figures for change 1960–80 are, at best, approximations.

*Sources*: Data for 1960 from OECD, 1994. In the cases of Denmark, Belgium and Spain, the 1960 figures are the sum of social security transfers plus health spending (data from Castles, 1998). Data from 1980 onwards from OECD, 2001c. Missing data in 1980 for occupational injury spending for Australia and for other contingencies for Denmark, Greece and Italy. 1980 unemployment cash benefits for Austria, France and Ireland interpolated from OECD, 1985. 1998 UK total expenditure reduced by 3.3 per cent of GDP to take account of a definitional change relating to old age cash benefits. All calculated figures subject to rounding errors.

to classify in family of nations terms and data for them are presented separately. In tables 1 to 4, we separately present family of nations means and overall means for all twenty-one cases. This serves as a simple device for assessing the extent of differences among groupings of nations. An overall measure of the similarity of cases is given by the coefficient of variation, which is provided for all measures of expenditure levels, but not for changes over time. Lower values of the coefficient imply a reduction in the overall variation of cases and a consistent downward trend in values suggests a move towards greater convergence in spending patterns.

Looking initially at family of nations patterns in respect of levels of aggregate spending, we note changes in the groupings featuring as welfare state leaders and laggards. Table 1 shows that, in 1960, continental Western Europe was the area making much the greatest welfare effort, with little to choose between the English-speaking and Scandinavian countries in the middle of the distribution, and with Southern Europe, Italy excepted, in the rearguard. By 1980, however, this clear hierarchy of spending had collapsed into two broader groupings, with the Scandinavian and continental Western European countries spending around a quarter of GDP for social policy purposes and the English-speaking and Southern European countries around 15 per cent. Finally, during the course of the period that concerns us here, hierarchy was restored, but along lines rather different from those of the early postwar era. By 1998, the Scandinavian countries had become outright welfare state leaders, with average spending levels of just below 30 per cent of GDP. The countries of continental Western Europe followed close behind, with Southern Europe now somewhat ahead of an English-speaking rearguard. Changes in the welfare state ranking of individual countries were no less dramatic than those of country groupings, with Switzerland moving from the position of being OECD's second lowest spender in 1960 to its third highest in 1998, and with Ireland moving from a position above the OECD mean in 1980 to the third lowest level of spending in 1998. The diversity of expenditure patterns demonstrated in table 1, and the relatively tight bunching of nations sharing close historical, cultural and linguistic affinities, does not seem readily compatible with hypotheses of the kind offered by the crisis literature, suggesting that welfare states everywhere were responding to the same powerful external forces.

Turning now to patterns of expenditure growth, the initial point to note is the substantial contrast between periods. The 1960 to 1980 period was one of consistent and strong social expenditure growth. All the OECD member countries featuring in table 1 experienced increases in spending measured as a percentage of GDP, with Denmark and Sweden leading the way with increases in spending of 18.5 and 18.2 per cent of GDP respectively. For OECD countries in general, expenditure grew by 9 per cent of GDP, which meant a virtual doubling in size of the average OECD welfare state in just two decades. The 1980 to 1998 period was, in comparison, an era of more inconsistent and much reduced spending growth. In the earlier period, there were eight countries which increased their spending by more than 10 per cent of GDP; in the later period, there were just two, Switzerland and Portugal, both of them catching up from the rear of the distribution. In the earlier period, the smallest increase in spending was Australia's 3.9 per cent of GDP; in the later period, there were no fewer than nine countries with expenditure growth of less than 3.9 per cent. Finally, in the second period, the average rate of expenditure growth was more than halved, dropping from nine to four percentage points of GDP. Whether as a consequence of globalization or some other concatenation of forces, there can be no question at all that the pace of welfare state growth had slowed dramatically after 1980.

However, it declined on nothing like the scale hypothesized by the crisis literature. Three sets of figures in table 1 make this abundantly plain. A 'race to the bottom' implies an across-the-board contraction in social spending. However, as the final column of table 1 shows, there were, in fact, only two countries – Ireland and the Netherlands – that experienced any overall cutback in aggregate social expenditure during these years. The second relevant figure is the average 4 per cent increase in spending as a percentage of GDP between 1980 and 1998. Translated into a percentage rise in spending, this means that the average OECD country increased its welfare effort by slightly more than 20 per cent – from 18.7 to 22.7 per cent of GDP – in precisely that period in which the prevailing crisis accounts suggest that expenditure should have been dropping like a stone. The salience of this finding is highlighted by a third set of figures, the consistent downward trend in the coefficients of variation appearing in the final row of table 1, demonstrating a growing similarity of social expenditure levels over a period of almost four decades. The 'race to the bottom' argument implies a sharp break in trend, with a general movement towards higher expenditures in the early postwar years replaced, more recently, by a process of downwards convergence. What table 1 demonstrates is that, throughout the postwar period, increased similarity has been conjoint with increased spending.

We now turn to corresponding patterns of overall public expenditure development. Table 2 presents data on total outlays of general government as a percentage of GDP from OECD *Economic Outlook* (various years) for the same time points and periods as table 1. Table 2, in most respects, tells much the same story as table 1. Total expenditure magnitudes are, of course, much greater than for social spending, with mean levels of total expenditure starting out at a level three times greater than social expenditure and ending up at a level somewhat less than twice as high. By 1998, the OECD mean for total outlays was 43 per cent of GDP, with a high of 55.5 per cent of GDP in Sweden and a low of 30.5 per cent of GDP in the United States. However, despite differences in magnitudes, family of

**Table 2** Total outlays of general government as a percentage of GDP in twenty-one OECD countries, 1960, 1980, 1998 and change over time

| | 1960 | 1980 | 1998 | 1960–1980 | 1980–1998 |
|---|---|---|---|---|---|
| Australia | 21.6 | 31.4 | 33.2 | 9.8 | 1.8 |
| Canada | 28.6 | 38.8 | 40.2 | 10.2 | 1.4 |
| Ireland | 28.0 | 49.3 | 32.2 | 21.3 | −17.1 |
| New Zealand[a] | – | – | 39.5 | – | – |
| United Kingdom | 32.2 | 43.0 | 37.7 | 10.8 | −5.3 |
| United States | 27.2 | 31.4 | 30.5 | 4.2 | −0.9 |
| **Family mean** | **27.5** | **38.8** | **34.8** | **11.3** | **−4.0** |
| Denmark | 24.8 | 56.2 | 54.0 | 31.4 | −2.2 |
| Finland | 26.6 | 38.1 | 48.1 | 11.5 | 10.0 |
| Norway | 29.9 | 43.3 | 46.3 | 13.4 | 3.0 |
| Sweden | 31.0 | 60.1 | 55.5 | 29.1 | −4.6 |
| **Family mean** | **28.1** | **49.4** | **51.0** | **21.3** | **1.6** |
| Austria | 35.7 | 48.1 | 50.3 | 12.4 | 2.2 |
| Belgium | 34.6 | 58.3 | 48.0 | 23.7 | −10.3 |
| France | 34.6 | 46.1 | 49.9 | 11.5 | 3.8 |
| Germany | 32.4 | 47.9 | 46.0 | 15.5 | −1.9 |
| Netherlands | 33.7 | 55.8 | 43.4 | 22.1 | −12.4 |
| **Family mean** | **34.2** | **51.1** | **47.5** | **16.9** | **−3.6** |
| Greece[b] | 17.4 | 30.4 | 42.7 | 13.0 | 12.3 |
| Italy | 30.1 | 41.9 | 47.6 | 11.8 | 5.7 |
| Portugal | 17.0 | 23.8 | 39.8 | 6.8 | 16.0 |
| Spain | – | 32.2 | 40.6 | – | 8.4 |
| **Family mean** | **21.5** | **30.1** | **42.7** | **10.5** | **12.6** |
| Switzerland[a] | – | – | – | – | – |
| Japan | 17.5 | 32.0 | 34.8 | 14.5 | 2.8 |
| **Overall mean** | **27.9** | **42.6** | **43.0** | **15.2** | **0.7** |
| **Coefficient of variation** | **21.8** | **25.0** | **16.6** | | |

[a] Data for New Zealand and Switzerland are not available.

[b] The Greek figure for 1960 is for current disbursements of general government rather than total outlays. For that reason, the figure for change in Greek total outlays for the period 1960–80 should be regarded as an approximation.

*Sources*: Data for 1960 from OECD, 1991; for 1980 from OECD, 1997; for 1998 from OECD, 2001a. All calculated figures subject to rounding errors.

nations patterns were similar, with the single exception that the countries of Southern Europe remained well below the level of public spending of the English-speaking countries in 1980. By 1998, the hierarchy of families of nations in respect of social spending is almost exactly replicated for total outlays. Also, as in the case of aggregate social expenditure, there was a very substantial contrast in growth trajectories in the two periods. In the 1960s and 1970s, average total outlays growth of 15 per cent of GDP was about 60 per cent greater than social expenditure growth in the same period. However, in the period from 1980 to 1998, overall total outlays in the OECD were effectively becalmed, ending up only 0.7 of a percentage point of GDP higher at the end of the period than at its beginning.

This is where the one really significant contrast between total outlays and aggregate social expenditure trends is to be found. Only two out of twenty-one countries experienced social expenditure cutbacks between 1980 and 1998, but no less than eight of the nineteen countries for which we have total outlays data experienced overall public expenditure cuts in the same period. It is also possible to surmise the expenditure trajectories of countries for which data are missing. Given the very substantial expansion of Swiss social spending in this period shown in table 1 and documented in a number of studies (see Lane, 1999; Kriesi, 1999; Armingeon, 2001), it seems reasonable to assume that total outlays in Switzerland increased markedly between 1980 and 1998. By the same token, the relatively small increase in New Zealand's social expenditure shown in table 1, combined with a public sector which, by all accounts, was cut to ribbons in this period (see Kelsey, 1993; Boston and Uhr, 1996; Stephens, 1999), seems likely to have contributed to an overall decline in total outlays in the period after 1980. Given the probability of diverse spending trends in these two countries, it may be concluded that there was some degree of expenditure reduction in nearly half the countries of the OECD. There was also extreme diversity in spending trajectories. Belgium, Ireland and the Netherlands all experienced expenditure cutbacks in excess of 10 per cent of GDP. The public sectors of Finland, Greece and Portugal, on the other hand, grew by similar amounts.

This discrepancy between trends in aggregate social spending and in total public expenditure is extremely interesting. The items of spending included in total outlays which are not also included under the social expenditure head are general public services, public order and safety, defence, education, housing and community services, economic affairs, recreation and culture and a residual other category which includes debt interest payments (see United Nations, 1999). Reading tables 2 and 1 in conjunction suggests that, over the past two decades, these non-social components of public spending have, in aggregate, been subject to greater attrition and downward pressure than has aggregate social spending. Whether these cutbacks are of sufficient magnitude to suggest a possible 'race to the bottom' in respect of total outlays is quite another matter. It certainly seems probable that commentators on the lookout for the influence of globalizing trends on public sector spending would see it as significant that Belgium, Ireland and the Netherlands, the three countries experiencing the greatest cutbacks in total outlays, were simultaneously the three countries which, on most counts, can be seen as the most internationally exposed economies of the 1980–98 period. However, the facts nevertheless remain that the number of countries increasing their overall public spending in this period outweighed the number reducing their public spending and that the average trend of outlays in this period was, however marginally, in an upward direction. Although total spending may have been under greater pressure than aggregate social spending, and although individual country fluctuations in total spending were considerably greater, the evidence for a 'race to the bottom' is simply not there.

## Welfare Salience and Welfare Standards

While data on patterns of aggregate spending clearly contradict the 'race to the bottom' hypothesis, it is perfectly possible that other ways of thinking about recent trajectories of spending might yield findings that provide clues as to the nature of the malaise underlying crisis predictions. In this section, we address two questions with a bearing on such issues. First, we ask whether public spending on welfare has become a more or a less salient part of the public budget in recent decades. Greater salience might itself be a reason magnifying the sense of possible threat. Second, we ask whether increases in aggregate expenditure in these years might actually mask a decline in welfare standards. If governments in Western nations no longer view social protection as a major priority, and if, in consequence, standards of provision are dropping, the notion of a threat to the future of the welfare state becomes far more comprehensible.

Göran Therborn (1983) has argued that in order to qualify as a welfare state, a nation's spending for welfare purposes must exceed its spending for other purposes, and Gøsta Esping-Andersen (1990) has noted that, by this criterion, there were few welfare states in the world until the 1970s. An interesting implication of the 'race to the bottom' hypothesis is that it suggests that any increase in the number of countries qualifying as welfare states as a consequence of expenditure growth in the 'golden age' of welfare state expansion is likely to have been reversed in recent decades. In the 'golden age', captured in our data by the huge increases in social spending occurring in the period between 1960 and 1980, spending on health, pensions, sickness, unemployment and other benefits gradually came to rival the older priorities of state spending for general public services, defence, public order and community services. However, had the 1980s and 1990s really been a period in which cutbacks were concentrated on social programmes, as implied by the 'race to the bottom' hypothesis, the status of welfare as the dominant concern of the modern state would clearly have been in some jeopardy.

In fact, we already know that, in broad terms, such a reversal of the growing salience of the welfare state cannot have occurred. Tables 1 and 2 show that the average rate of growth of social expenditure exceeded that of total outlays in the period after 1980, which can only mean that, on average, the salience of the welfare state in OECD countries was continuing to increase. What we do not know, however, is how individual countries were affected by the expenditure changes taking place in this period. It would, for instance, be quite compatible with the evidence of our analysis so far if we were to discover that some of those countries experiencing cutbacks or relatively small increases in social spending had simultaneously experienced a decline in the ratio of social to non-social spending. While that might not be the same thing as a 'race to the bottom', it could very well explain why welfare elites and welfare recipients in certain countries felt themselves to be under pressure. Table 3, which measures aggregate social expenditure as a proportion of total outlays, provides us with a means of mapping the balance between social and non-social priorities in state spending. It allows us to compare the relative salience of the welfare state in different countries, among different families of nations and at different time points.

An initial point to notice about the figures in table 3 is the massive convergence they demonstrate. In the 1960s, there were very substantial differences in the extent to which individual nations and families of nations prioritized welfare state spending. In that year, Germany was devoting more than 55 per cent of its total spending to welfare, but Japan, Norway and the United States only around 25 per cent. Although not as pronounced as these individual country differences, the gaps between families of nations were also considerable. Initially, patterns were somewhat different from those characterizing aggregate spending. Table 1 reveals that, with the exception of Italy, the countries of Southern Europe were the expenditure laggards of the 1960s, but table 3 suggests, despite incomplete data, that the priority these countries accorded welfare was akin to that of the countries of continental Western Europe, the expenditure leaders of the time. Both in 1960 and 1980, the countries according welfare the lowest priority were to be found largely within the English-speaking family of nations. By the end of the period, individual country differences had diminished appreciably. Germany and Japan remained poles apart in terms of welfare salience, but the gap had decreased from 32.5 to 17.2 percentage points. Gaps between family of nations groups had also diminished and the ordering of family groupings had changed. The salience of welfare spending in the Scandinavian countries had increased hugely over nearly four decades, and these countries' high levels of spending were now matched by

**Table 3** Total public social expenditure as a proportion of total outlays of general government in twenty-one OECD countries, 1960, 1980 and 1998

| | 1960 | 1980 | 1998 |
|---|---|---|---|
| Australia | 34.3 | 36.1 | 53.6 |
| Canada | 31.8 | 34.2 | 44.9 |
| Ireland | 31.1 | 38.4 | 49.0 |
| New Zealand | – | – | 53.1 |
| United Kingdom | 31.7 | 42.3 | 56.7 |
| United States | 27.1 | 41.8 | 47.8 |
| **Family mean** | **31.1** | **38.6** | **50.8** |
| Denmark | 42.7 | 51.7 | 55.2 |
| Finland | 33.1 | 48.6 | 55.2 |
| Norway | 26.1 | 42.8 | 58.3 |
| Sweden | 34.8 | 48.3 | 55.8 |
| **Family mean** | **34.2** | **47.8** | **56.1** |
| Austria | 44.5 | 49.4 | 53.3 |
| Belgium | 39.9 | 41.5 | 51.1 |
| France | 38.7 | 49.2 | 57.8 |
| Germany | 55.9 | 42.3 | 59.3 |
| Netherlands | 34.7 | 48.9 | 55.1 |
| **Family mean** | **42.7** | **46.3** | **55.3** |
| Greece | 40.8 | 37.8 | 53.2 |
| Italy | 43.5 | 44.0 | 52.7 |
| Portugal | – | 48.9 | 45.8 |
| Spain | – | 49.0 | 48.5 |
| **Family mean** | **42.1** | **44.9** | **50.0** |
| Switzerland | – | – | – |
| Japan | 23.4 | 31.6 | 42.1 |
| **Overall mean** | **36.1** | **43.5** | **52.4** |
| **Coefficient of variation** | **22.2** | **13.5** | **9.0** |

*Notes and sources:* Social expenditure data from table 1 expressed as percentages of the total outlays of general government. Sources for total outlays as indicated in table 2. All calculated figures subject to rounding errors.

the high priority they attached to spending of this nature. In 1960, the gap in salience between the top and bottom family groups – continental Western Europe and the English-speaking nations – was 11.6 percentage points. In 1998, the gap between top and bottom – Scandinavia and Southern Europe – was just 6.1 percentage points. Summary statistics tell the same story, with a strongly declining coefficient of variation over time.

The next important point to note is that this process of convergence had occurred as a consequence of more and more countries becoming welfare states according to Therborn's criterion. In 1960, Germany was the only OECD country to devote more resources to welfare than to other purposes. In 1980, Denmark had replaced Germany as the OECD's only welfare state. By 1998, however, fourteen of the twenty countries featuring in table 3 were welfare states by this criterion and Switzerland, the country for which data are missing, would also undoubtedly qualify if the data were available. Finally, and most significantly, this mass shift across the threshold of welfare statehood occurred, not in the golden years between 1960 and 1980, but in the supposedly crisis-ridden years after 1980. In 1980, the average level of welfare salience was 43.5 per cent; by 1998, it was 52.4 per cent. By one reckoning, the OECD area had itself become a giant welfare state, in so far as it was constituted largely by nations spending more on welfare than for all other purposes. By another, there was still some way to go, given that two of the countries yet to become welfare states according to this criterion were the OECD's most populous nations, the United States and Japan.

This analysis has important implications. Over the past two decades, most OECD countries have committed themselves to social policy as their first priority and table 3 provides absolutely no sign that this is a trajectory of change which has exhausted its potential. As we have seen, part of what happened in the 1980s and 1990s was an increase in real spending on welfare, but just as important was a decline in non-social spending. Admittedly, as already noted, the barriers between the categories of spending are far from watertight, but, accepting the distinction as given, what appears to have been happening is that, in a period in which overall expenditure increases have been constrained, policy-makers have been privileging welfare priorities at the margin. This is not what the 'race to the bottom' theorists would have us believe, but clearly finding out why this kind of trade-off is occurring is vital for an understanding of contemporary welfare state dynamics.

A possible explanation that might simultaneously account for a generalized malaise about the future of the welfare state and for an enhanced priority for welfare over other purposes would be if demands or needs for welfare had been increasing over time. This is, in essence, the basis of the account offered in Paul Pierson's book *The New Politics of the Welfare State* (2001). The argument is that expenditure retrenchment is a difficult project for modern governments because they are expected to tackle a wide range of problems from deindustrialization to population ageing and to provide a whole range of new services from drug rehabilitation to services enabling women to combine labour force participation and maternity. Under these circumstances, it is easy to see why commentators interpret what is happening in terms of increased pressure on the welfare state or even of crisis. If governments feel that there are economic and/or political constraints on higher taxing and spending, and if, at the same time, there is an increased demand for welfare services, one of two things must happen: either other expenditure must be cut or existing standards of provision must decline.

We have already seen that there has been some decline in non-social expenditure. In what follows, we discuss briefly what has been happening to standards of welfare provision. Although the 'race to the bottom' argument is essentially a hypothesis about the likely future trajectory of welfare spending, an analogous argument is sometimes encountered about effects on welfare standards. Indeed, for many left-of-centre commentators that is the main concern. Their worry is that capital will press governments to reduce existing standards in order for business to compete in an era of global competition. The arguments are familiar. Enterprises are not competitive when employers must pay huge social security contributions, when generous sickness benefits create mass absenteeism and when unemployment benefits are so high that they diminish the incentive to work. Reducing standards of protection – 'social dumping' – can be presented as the only way for a country to attract new capital or to retain the capital it already has. In effect, this argument concedes that globalization is not the sole factor determining expenditure growth, with increased welfare demand and welfare dependency countering the 'race to the bottom'. The impact of globalization under these circumstances is not to reduce aggregate welfare spending, but rather to reduce individual welfare generosity.

Table 4 provides an admittedly simplistic measuring rod for assessing how well contemporary welfare states have been coping with the increased demands made of them. The two categories of increased welfare need most generally noted in the literature are the impact of population ageing and increasing levels of unemployment. The latter has been highlighted by many commentators as a snare and delusion for those measuring welfare states in purely monetary terms, since increased spending on this count is simply seen as a measure of the welfare state's incapacity to control unemployment (see Esping-Andersen, 1990; Mishra, 1990; Clayton and Pontusson, 1998). All that we do in table 4 is to divide the aggregates of expenditure appearing in table 1 by the percentage of the dependent population, that is, the population aged 65 and over plus the percentage of the civilian population registered as unemployed. The resulting ratio gives a crude measure of welfare generosity, theoretically to be interpreted as the percentage of GDP received in welfare spending for every 1 per cent of the population in need.

There are two obvious deficiencies with this measure. First, it presents an average figure for each country, when we know that benefits to different sections of the population in need in a given country often vary quite markedly. In some countries, and particularly in Southern Europe (see

**Table 4** Welfare state generosity ratio in twenty-one OECD countries, 1980, 1998 and change over time

| | 1980 | 1998 | Change |
|---|---|---|---|
| Australia | 0.73 | 0.89 | 0.16 |
| Canada | 0.78 | 0.88 | 0.09 |
| Ireland | 0.93 | 0.83 | −0.11 |
| New Zealand | 1.61 | 1.10 | −0.51 |
| United Kingdom | 0.88 | 0.98 | 0.10 |
| United States | 0.71 | 0.85 | 0.13 |
| **Family mean** | **0.94** | **0.92** | **−0.02** |
| Denmark | 1.36 | 1.46 | 0.10 |
| Finland | 1.11 | 1.02 | −0.09 |
| Norway | 1.12 | 1.43 | 0.31 |
| Sweden | 1.57 | 1.20 | −0.37 |
| **Family mean** | **1.29** | **1.28** | **−0.01** |
| Austria | 1.35 | 1.36 | 0.01 |
| Belgium | 1.07 | 0.87 | −0.20 |
| France | 1.04 | 1.04 | 0 |
| Germany | 1.08 | 1.05 | −0.03 |
| Netherlands | 1.54 | 1.34 | −0.20 |
| **Family mean** | **1.21** | **1.13** | **−0.08** |
| Greece | 0.72 | 0.81 | 0.08 |
| Italy | 0.89 | 0.86 | −0.03 |
| Portugal | 0.61 | 0.92 | 0.31 |
| Spain | 0.70 | 0.56 | −0.14 |
| **Family mean** | **0.73** | **0.79** | **0.06** |
| Switzerland | 1.09 | 1.52 | 0.43 |
| Japan | 0.91 | 0.72 | −0.19 |
| **Overall mean** | **1.04** | **1.03** | −0.01 |
| **Coefficient of variation** | **29.0** | **25.5** | |

*Notes and sources*: Welfare state generosity ratio calculated by dividing social expenditure data from table 1 by the sum of the percentage of the population aged 65 years and over and the percentage of the civilian population unemployed. Data on both aged population and unemployment from OECD, 2001b. All calculated figures subject to rounding errors.

Ferrera, 1996), a marked insider/outsider differentiation in the labour market is translated directly into the sphere of social security provision, with pension provision for core workers being much more generous than for peripheral workers and the unemployed. Second, it implies that all expenditure is delivered to just two categories of welfare recipient. Ideally, apart from these traditional sources of welfare need, we would have liked to include a proxy for the new kinds of need emerging from a changing family structure (see Orloff, 1993; Daly, 1997; Esping-Andersen, 1999). The percentage of the population constituted by children living in single parent families might have served this purpose, but the information required to calculate such a measure is simply unavailable for the time period covered by this study. The best data available are for eighteen of our twenty-one OECD countries for the period 1986 to 1996 (see Beaujot and Liu, 2002). On the basis of these data, we calculate that the percentage of the population constituted by children living in single parent families increased from an average of 1.8 per cent to 2.4 per cent over this period of ten years. Only in five of these countries – Germany, New Zealand, Sweden, the United Kingdom and the United States – did this lead to an increase in the population in need of more than 1 per cent. In these countries, the trend in welfare generosity is likely to have been somewhat – although not hugely – more adverse than indicated by the figures in the final column of table 4.

Looking at table 4 in conjunction with table 1 shows that taking dependency levels into account really can make a big difference to our comprehension of the relative performance of welfare states. This can be seen by looking at the cases of New Zealand and Switzerland in 1980 and of Greece and Italy in 1998. In the earlier period, New Zealand is close to the expenditure average and Switzerland a complete laggard, but in ratio terms New Zealand turns out to be the OECD's most generous welfare provider of the early 1980s and Switzerland close to the average. This is because, in this period, these countries had much lower levels of dependency than most other OECD countries. The Greek and Italian cases tell the reverse story. In 1998, Greece and Italy were at or around OECD average spending levels, but both were very much below the OECD average in terms of the generosity of provision, because both experienced relatively high levels of dependency. Spain is, undoubtedly, the country in which high and increasing dependency led to the most serious outcomes, with an extraordinarily high level of unemployment producing a level of generosity markedly lower than in any other OECD country.

Where generosity is the criterion, there seems to be a three-tier hierarchy of welfare performance. In both 1980 and 1998, the hierarchy is quite distinct, as demonstrated by a relatively high coefficient of variation that does not decline markedly over time. In both periods, there was a small group of countries with levels of generosity considerably higher than the mean. In 1980, it consisted of New Zealand, Sweden, the Netherlands, Denmark and Austria. In 1998, New Zealand and Sweden had dropped out of this elite group to be replaced by Switzerland and Norway. In both periods, there is a second middling rank of countries constituted almost entirely by

Scandinavian and continental Western European countries, but with New Zealand joining in 1998. At the other end of the distribution, with generosity ratios well below the OECD mean, is a group of Southern European and English-speaking countries together with Japan and, by the end of the period, also Belgium. The relative lack of generosity of these countries stems from different causes. The Southern European countries other than Portugal, but plus Belgium, are around the middle of the distribution in spending terms, but have high levels of dependency. The English-speaking nations, other than New Zealand and the United Kingdom, together with Japan are, by contrast, extremely low spenders, despite quite moderate levels of dependency. These latter are countries, which, one might conclude, are ungenerous by policy choice.

The most important conclusion, however, relates to what was happening to OECD levels of generosity across the board during this period. Between 1980 and 1998, the average level of dependency in OECD countries increased from 17.8 to 22.8 per cent of the population or by just over 25 per cent. What table 4 tells us is that this very substantial increase in need was accommodated with virtually no alteration in the average OECD level of welfare state generosity. Admittedly, standards declined in about half the countries featuring in the table, but, interestingly, most of the really large cuts in generosity – in New Zealand, Sweden and the Netherlands – occurred in those countries where generosity was highest in 1980. Only four countries – Belgium, Ireland, Japan and Spain – experienced sizeable reductions in generosity leaving them well adrift of average OECD standards of provision. That is simply not enough to sustain an argument that increasing exposure to the international economy has fuelled a general trend towards declining welfare standards. The fact, however, that an average 4 per cent increase in social expenditure as a percentage of GDP led to essentially unchanged levels of provision might well be argued as evidence for the proposition that the countries of the OECD have now probably reached the outer limits of welfare state generosity measured in these terms.

## Conclusion

This chapter's main objective has been to use cross-national analysis to establish the validity or otherwise of the 'race to the bottom' hypothesis. If that hypothesis is to have any meaning above and beyond the fact that a minority of countries suffered adverse trends in this period, it must point to some generalized trend towards cutbacks in spending or, in what is, essentially, an extremely watered-down variant of the argument, that there has been some generalized decline in standards of provision. Despite an extensive examination of a wide range of expenditure indicators, no evidence of such trends has been forthcoming and we can only conclude that the 'race to the bottom' is a crisis myth rather than a crisis reality. Despite cutbacks in a number of countries, our analysis demonstrates unequivocally that OECD *average levels* of social expenditure, whether measured as percentages of GDP as generosity ratios, or in real terms, either increased or remained constant between 1980 and 1998. Indeed, given that, during this period, social expenditure was increasing as a percentage of GDP and that non-social categories of expenditure were declining, expenditure for welfare purposes was becoming appreciably more salient with the passing of time.

This enhanced salience combined with a general slowdown in the rate of expenditure growth may, in itself, be part of the explanation of increasing anxiety about the future of the welfare state at a time when all the objective indicators suggest that expenditure levels and standards of provision were being maintained at roughly existing levels. In the 'golden age' of the welfare state, high levels of economic growth made it possible for governments to increase the scope of social spending without cutting back real levels of private consumption and without holding back other public projects. However, in the 1980s and 1990s, new welfare demands could only be satisfied by cutting private consumption or by making trade-offs against other public spending programmes. The welfare state had become simultaneously more salient and more vulnerable on several fronts. Clearly, this has meant that those fighting to extend its frontiers have had to fight harder in recent decades than they did in the years of plenty. Clearly, too, some battles have been lost, making it extremely tempting for those involved to seek compelling explanations of why the forces of 'social progress' are now apparently on the back foot.

This is one of the reasons crisis myths are born. Such accounts generalize from particular reverses and from adverse developments in particular countries in a way that makes such defeats more comprehensible and less blameworthy. When political actors are confronted by forces 'beyond their control', they no longer need excuses for failure. But alibis for failure are only part of the story. Myths also provide excuses for new attacks on the welfare state by its enemies (see Drezner, 2000). Globalization or declining economic growth or some other currently supposed cause of crisis provides a cloak of legitimacy for those seeking to advance plans to cut taxes and spending. Once they have convinced policy-makers that 'there is no alternative', and that the state has no capacity to stand against the economic forces arrayed against it, they have won half the battle. If a 'race to the bottom' is on the cards, clearly it makes sense to be in it, and in it with a vengeance! Crisis myths flourish when opposing sides find that the same abdication of responsibility serves both of their purposes and when neither side seeks to question anecdotal evidence of supposedly general trends. As this chapter demonstrates, the best antidote to myth-making is systematic comparative analysis.

## Note

From Francis G. Castles, *The Future of the Welfare State*, Oxford, Oxford University Press, 2004, pp. 21–46.

## References


Armingeon, K. (2001) 'Institutionalising the Swiss Welfare State', in J.-E. Lane (ed.), *The Swiss Labyrinth: Institutions, Outcomes and Design*, special issue of *West European Politics*, London: Frank Cass, pp. 145–68.

Beaujot, R. and Liu, J. (2002) 'Children, Social Assistance and Outcomes: Cross-national Comparisons', Discussion paper no. 01–20, Population Studies Centre, University of Western Ontario.

Boston, J. and Uhr, J. (1996) 'Reshaping the Mechanics of Government,' F. Castles, R. Gerritsen and J. Vowles (eds), *The Great Experiment: Labour Parties and Public Policy Transformation in Australia and New Zealand*, Sydney, Allen and Unwin, pp. 48–67.

Cameron, D. (1978) 'The Expansion of the Public Economy: A Comparative Analysis', *American Political Science Review*, 72, 4, pp. 1243–61.

Castles, F. (1998) *Comparative Public Policy: Patterns of Post-war Transformation*, Cheltenham, Edward Elgar.

Clayton, R. and Pontusson, J. (1998) 'Welfare State Retrenchment Revisited', *World Politics*, 51, 1, pp. 67–98.

Daly, M. (1997) 'Welfare States under Pressure: Cash Benefits in European Welfare States over the Last Ten Years', *Journal of European Social Policy*, 7, 2, pp. 24–59.

Drezner, D. (2000) 'Bottom Feeders', *Foreign Policy*, 171 (Nov.–Dec.), pp. 64–70.

Esping-Andersen, G. (1990) *The Three Worlds of Welfare Capitalism*, Cambridge, Polity.

Esping-Andersen, G. (1999) *Social Foundations of Post-Industrial Economies*, Oxford, Oxford University Press.

Ferrera, M. (1996) 'The "Southern Model" of Welfare in Social Europe', *Journal of European Social Policy*, 6, 1, pp. 17–37.

Ganghof, S. (2000) 'Adjusting National Tax Policy to Economic Internationalization: Strategies and Outcomes', in F. W. Scharpf and V. A. Schmidt (eds), *Welfare and Work in the Open Economy, Volume II: Diverse Responses to Common Challenges*, Oxford, Oxford University Press, pp. 597–645.

Hinrichs, K. (2001) 'Elephants on the Move: Patterns of Public Pension Reform in OECD Countries' in S. Liebfried (ed.), *Welfare State Futures*, Cambridge, Cambridge University Press, pp. 77–102.

Katzenstein, P. (1985) *Small States in World Markets*, Ithaca, NY, Cornell University Press.

Kelsey, J. (1993) *Rolling Back the State*, Wellington, Bridget Williams Books.

Keohane, R. O. and Milner, H. V. (eds) (1996) *Internationalization and Domestic Politics*, Cambridge, Cambridge University Press.

Kriesi, H. (1999) 'Note on the Size of the Public Sector in Switzerland', *Revue Suisse de Science Politique*, 5, 2, pp. 106–9.

Lane, J.-E. (1999) 'The Public/Private Distinction in Switzerland', *Revue Suisse de Science Politique*, 5, 2, pp. 94–105.

Mishra, R. (1990) *The Welfare State in Capitalist Society*, Toronto, University of Toronto Press.

OECD (1985) *Social Expenditure 1960–1990: Problems of Growth and Control*, Paris, Organization for Economic Cooperation and Development.
OECD (1991) *Historical Statistics, 1960–1989*, Paris, Organization for Economic Cooperation and Development.
OECD (1994) 'New Orientations for Social Policy', *Social Policy Studies*, 12.
OECD (1997) *Economic Outlook*, 61.
OECD (2001a) *Economic Outlook*, 71.
OECD (2001b) *Labour Force Statistics, 1980–2000*, Paris, Organization for Economic Cooperation and Development.
OECD (2001c) *Social Expenditure Database, 1980–1998*, CD-Rom, Paris.
Orloff, A. S. (1993) 'Gender and the Social Rights of Citizenship: The Comparative Analysis of Gender Relations and Welfare States', *American Sociological Review*, 38, pp. 303–28.
Pierson, P. (2000) 'Increasing Returns, Path Dependence and the Study of Politics', *American Political Science Review*, 94, 2, pp. 251–67.
Pierson, P. (ed.) (2001) *The New Politics of the Welfare State*, Oxford, Oxford University Press.
Rieger, E. and Leibfried, S. (2003) *Limits to Globalization: Welfare States and the World Economy*, Cambridge, Cambridge University Press.
Rodrik, D. (1997) *Has Globalisation Gone Too Far?* Washington, DC: Institute for International Economics.
Ruggie, J. (1982) 'International Regimes, Transactions and Change: Embedded Liberalism in the Postwar Economic Order', *International Organization*, 36, 2, pp. 379–415.
Stephens, R. (1999) 'Economics and Social Policy', in D. Milne and J. Savage (eds), *Reporting Economics*, Wellington, New Zealand Journalists Training Organisation, pp. 189–204.
Therborn, G. (1983) 'When, How and Why does a Welfare State become a Welfare State?' ECPR Workshops, Freiburg, Mar.
United Nations (1999) *Classification of Expenditures according to Purpose*, Statistical Papers, Series M, No. 84, New York.

# Europeanization

# Welfare-State Regress in Western Europe: Politics, Institutions, Globalization, and Europeanization

*Walter Korpi*

## Introduction

Once upon a time – not that long ago – there was consensus in Western Europe that the welfare states' full employment and expanding social-citizenship rights inaugurated after the end of World War II had come to stay. This reshaping of the welfare state had emerged in the context of the sea change in power relations, when for the first time in history left parties had come to be either dominant parties in governments or the major opposition parties. In its 1945 election manifesto the British Labour Party made 'jobs for all' and 'social insurance against the rainy day' its primary political objectives and outlined 'the means needed to realise them' (Craig, 1975, pp. 124–5, 130). Labour's unexpectedly great victory set the tone and impressed a lesson that was widely accepted in Europe. Scholars, politicians, and the public came to see the continued existence of such welfare states as ensured by a supportive electorate. In the 1950s this mood was summed up by a leading British Labour politician: 'Any Government which tampered seriously with the full employment welfare state would meet with a sharp reversal at the polls' (Crosland, 1956, p. 28). In the mid-1970s, however, this stability began to evaporate. Before the end of the century Western scholars had shifted their focus from the study of welfare-state expansion to analyses of its regress, welfare-state retrenchment. In the 1990s the study of retrenchment became a growth industry with an outpouring of articles and books.

In scholarly debates on welfare-state retrenchment, one key issue has concerned the extent of retrenchment. On this question the dominant view has been that in Western Europe no sweeping or radical retrenchment has occurred, a view that has recently been questioned. Other central questions have concerned the causes of retrenchment. Here the debate has been rather intensive. In the theoretical discussions key issues have concerned the relative significance of three factors within this context: economic transnationalization, postindustrialism, and distributive conflict as expressed in partisan politics. Debates on economic transnationalization have included not only globalization but also the role of economic and political integration within Europe. On the significance of globalization for retrenchment, views have differed. The major proponent for postindustrial changes as causes for retrenchment has been Paul Pierson. In a series of pioneering and challenging works, Pierson (1994, 1996, 2001a, 2001b, 2001c) staked the claims for what came to be described as 'the new politics of the welfare state'. The new-politics strand of thought rejects the hypothesis that globalization is a main cause of retrenchment, arguing instead that here postindustrialism exerted the major pressures. The new-politics perspective also partly counterposes itself in relation to the power-resources approach to welfare-state development. As is well known, the latter approach views welfare states to a significant extent as outcomes of distributive conflicts involving class-related interest groups and political parties, conflicts where the relative power of actors is significant (Esping-Andersen, 1985, 1990; Huber and Stephens, 2001; Korpi, 1983, 1989; Myles, 1984).

Although Pierson holds that the power-resources approach is very fruitful in explaining welfare-state expansion, he argues that in crucial respects retrenchment is different from expansion. Basic to the new-politics perspective is the hypothesis that, in the retrenchment phase, the major forces driving welfare-state change no longer come from distributive conflicts among socioeconomic interest groups, but rather emanate from postindustrial changes (Pierson, 2001b). Growing service sectors decrease economic growth rates, whereas the greying of populations, changing family patterns, increasing share of women in the public sector labour force, and maturation of government welfare commitments all tend to increase social expenditures. Such postindustrial changes generate intense and persistent pressures on government budgets (Pierson, 2001a). The cold star of permanent austerity therefore guides governments of all political shades to attempt cuts in social expenditures.

A central challenge by the new-politics strand of thought to the power-resources approach is that, in the retrenchment phase, class-related political parties that once drove welfare-state expansion have now largely receded into the background. Thus, although politics still matter, according to the new-politics perspective 'there are good reasons to believe that the centrality of left party and union confederation strength to welfare state outcomes has declined' (Pierson, 1996, p. 151). New-politics supporters view these forces as having been replaced to a large extent by new client groups of benefit recipients generated by welfare states, such as pensioners, healthcare consumers, the disabled, and welfare-state employees.

Because of the size and concentration of interests in such client groups, they have been able to largely resist government attempts at cutbacks. The resilience of the welfare state is further fortified by the new situation in which governments find themselves. In the expansionary period politicians could claim credit for carrying out generally popular reforms, but in the retrenchment phase they have to overcome the negativity bias when strong interest groups are required to forego rights and benefits seen as entrenched parts of the status quo. Pierson thus advanced the hypothesis that for these reasons welfare-state retrenchment is likely to be a limited phenomenon.

In this paper I focus on Western Europe since the mid-1970s and discuss studies of the extent and causes of welfare-state regress or retrenchment. The latter terms are used interchangeably here to refer to policy changes involving or implying cuts in social rights in ways that are likely to increase inequality among citizens. Because of the large number of studies dealing with welfare-state change, this review has to be highly selective, focusing on works that exemplify the various strands of thought concerning the driving forces and extent of retrenchment.[1]

The review begins with a consideration of the definition of the dependent variable in analyses of welfare-state regress and with methodological problems in such analyses. I argue that, although most analyses have focused on social transfers and services, postwar welfare states of Western Europe have typically included full employment as one cornerstone, making unemployment increases an important indicator of welfare-state regress. Furthermore, most comparative studies have been either based on expenditure data and/or focused on one or a few cases. Recent work permitting comparison based on social-citizenship rights, with data for a relatively large number of countries and long time periods, has greatly improved the description of welfare-state regress as well as causal analysis. The next section compares European countries and the United States with respect to the role of full employment in their respective welfare states and their different paths of unemployment development since the end of World War II. The following section describes the extent of retrenchment in social-insurance programmes and discusses the role of welfare-state institutions in this context. Thereafter I discuss the potential role of partisan politics during the period of retrenchment for differences among countries as well as the role of retrenchment for gender inequality. The penultimate section reviews the effects of globalization and of ongoing processes of political and economic integration in Europe on welfare-state regress, differentiating between various aspects of welfare states. The last section discusses the findings in this review. In dealing with theoretical arguments and causal interpretations, I focus attention on a comparison between the new-politics perspective and the power-resources approach.

## Definition and Measurement of Welfare States

In the study of retrenchment the dependent variable, the welfare state, has typically been defined in terms of social transfers and/or social services. Although these two areas, of course, are central, in analyses of retrenchment it is necessary to have a theoretically based definition of the dependent variable. In the power-resources approach scholars view postwar changes in welfare states to a significant extent as reflecting power contests among major interest groups related to the relative role of markets and democratic politics in distributive processes. These conflicts also define and change institutions that set frames for continued distributive conflicts. Such an approach indicates that, although transfers and services are important, here at least one more area must be considered, namely that of unemployment.

In the power-resources perspective unemployment appears as a central variable because for categories of citizens with labour power as their main basic power resource, the efficacy of this resource in distributive conflict and bargaining is to a major extent determined by the demand for labour and by the level of unemployment. In this perspective the maintenance of low levels of unemployment empowers citizens and is an essential preventive part of the welfare state (for example, see Korpi, 1983, p. 188). However, the right to employment is very difficult to establish as a claim right. Yet, in almost all countries of Western Europe in the years after the end of World War II, full employment became what can be called a social protoright in the sense that it was widely expected by citizens and that irrespective of partisan composition most European governments acted so as to maintain full employment

As Blanchflower and Oswald (1994) have shown, the level of unemployment has a clear relevance to wage levels. In local labour markets and industries with high unemployment, wages tend to be lower than where unemployment is low. This empirical fact indicates that the level of unemployment is likely to be both a main bone of contention between employers and employees and a major factor determining outcomes of the positive-sum distributive conflict between them concerning the distribution of firm revenues. The state of the labour market and changes in levels of unemployment must therefore be seen as essential welfare-state indicators and cannot be overlooked in analyses of welfare-state retrenchment.

As in earlier analyses of welfare-state expansion, in the study of retrenchment the typical dependent variable has been welfare-state effort, defined as the size of government social expenditures in relation to the gross domestic product. With basic data available in publications by the International Labour Organization (ILO) and the Organization for Economic Cooperation and Development (OECD), this indicator has been widely used. Unfortunately, however, the well-known problems associated with the welfare-effort indicator become aggravated in the analysis of retrenchment. Thus, for example, international developments and government policies can raise the level of unemployment, thereby increasing public expenditures for the maintenance of the unemployed while also tending to slow down growth in the gross domestic product. Therefore a reliance on the conventional welfare-state effort indicator may make an unemployment crisis appear as an actual increase in welfare-state effort. As argued by Swank (2001, p. 215), with proper control variables some of these problems can be counteracted, yet in this context results based on expenditure changes are likely to remain problematic.

As a complement to studies on welfare-state development based on expenditure data and case studies, within the Social Citizenship Indicator Program (SCIP), alternative measures of welfare-state development are in the process of being created; these measures focus on describing and quantifying the nature of legislated social rights in major social insurance programmes. Preliminary data from this source have been used to analyse retrenchment in social insurance programmes in the 1975–95 period (Korpi and Palme, 2000, 2001, 2003). Since social rights reflect welfare-state development from a different angle than the one expressed in expenditure data, these analyses provide a relevant point of comparison with results from earlier studies.

## The Regress of Full Employment in Europe

As noted above for welfare-state regress, the hypothesis of only limited retrenchment has won rapid and widespread acceptance among Western scholars. This acceptance appears to reflect not so much the weight and depth of the empirical data presented as the symbolic stature of the two cases originally studied by Pierson (1994). Choosing the United States under Ronald Reagan and Britain under Margaret Thatcher as his crucial test cases, Pierson asked, if retrenchment could not be found under such militant anti-welfare state governments, then where else could it be found? In the European context, Pierson's conclusion that the 'British welfare state, if battered, remains intact' was especially persuasive (Pierson, 1994, p. 161). In retrospect it is, however, clear that owing to the pioneering nature of these studies there are many problems associated with the empirical bases upon which these claims have been based. It can be argued that several of these claims are premature and reflect problems in the definition of welfare states, a reliance on case studies of few countries, and the use of social expenditure data as the prime outcome variable. Here I focus on Western Europe since the mid-1970s and discuss studies of the extent and causes of welfare-state regress or retrenchment (Korpi and Palme, 2000, 2001, 2003).

One central problem with most analyses of welfare-state regress is that they have excluded changes in levels of unemployment and have only indirectly dealt with the return of mass unemployment in Europe since the 1970s. In their impressive study Huber and Stephens (2001) brought high unemployment into the analysis in terms of contexts in which retrenchment is likely to occur; however, they did so without analysing the demise of full employment as part of welfare-state regress. Castles (2001) also considers unemployment as a contextual variable in the retrenchment process.

The role of full employment in the welfare state differs greatly between Europe and North America. In almost all democracies of Western Europe the first decades after the end of World War II witnessed a remarkable change in societal power relations when, for the first time in the history of capitalism, left parties emerged as either government parties or major opposition parties and union densities doubled in relation to levels obtained between the world wars. This dramatic change forms the background for the expansionary period of European welfare states. The mobilization of the labour force during the war had proved that in the real world full employment could be achieved. Keynesian ideas showed that also theoretically full employment was possible and that deep recessions such as those appearing between the two world wars could be avoided.

In Western Europe the emergence of full employment as well as the expansion of social transfers and social services thus emerged at approximately the same time. Crosland's (1956) statement about government and full employment (quoted above) indicates that contemporaries saw this triplet as constituting a unity, the full-employment welfare state, where expanding social insurance and services were combined with unemployment rates below the 3 per cent maximum level set by the British social reformer William Beveridge (1944). In Europe the concept of the Keynesian welfare state became widely used (e.g., Offe, 1984). In European countries with an uninterrupted political democracy during the postwar period this type of full-employment welfare state can be seen as an outcome of distributive conflicts and macropolitical bargaining that resulted from the changing relations of power in European societies as noted above. It was a manifestation of what can be called an implicit social contract between the main interest groups in these countries (Korpi, 2002). However, some differences can be found among countries. Ireland and Italy, with the weakest traditions of left government incumbency, retained relatively high levels of unemployment during the 1950s and 1960s. Furthermore, when unemployment levels rose after the first oil shock in 1973, this rise was much more dramatic in the countries of the European Economic Community (EEC) than in the countries of the European Free Trade Area (EFTA), where the rise was delayed for approximately fifteen years.

During the period after World War II Western Europe and the United States had very different histories when it came to levels of unemployment.

In the United States the postwar social contract did not include full employment in the European sense. From 1955 to 1973 US unemployment levels averaged 4.9 per cent (figure 1). In the same period six core countries of the European Economic Community – Belgium, Denmark, France, Germany, Netherlands, and the United Kingdom – had less than half of the US unemployment level, 2.1 per cent. But after the oil shocks in 1973 and 1979, the average unemployment level in these countries quadrupled and was 8.2 per cent during 1982–2000, while changes in the United States were modest. In fact, after World War II and until the end of the century, US unemployment rates have shown essentially trendless fluctuation. In stark contrast Western Europe experienced first the arrival of full employment and thereafter the return of mass unemployment.

Clearly a number of factors were of relevance to the return of mass unemployment to Europe.[2] However, conflicts of interest between major interest groups are likely to have been of significance there. Long-lasting full employment in Europe came to have consequences unwanted by important interest groups. Thus business interests saw with increasing alarm the rising levels of labour-force involvement in industrial conflict as well as the falling share of profits and increasing share of wages in the domestic product. Yet the fear of voter reactions pressed governments of

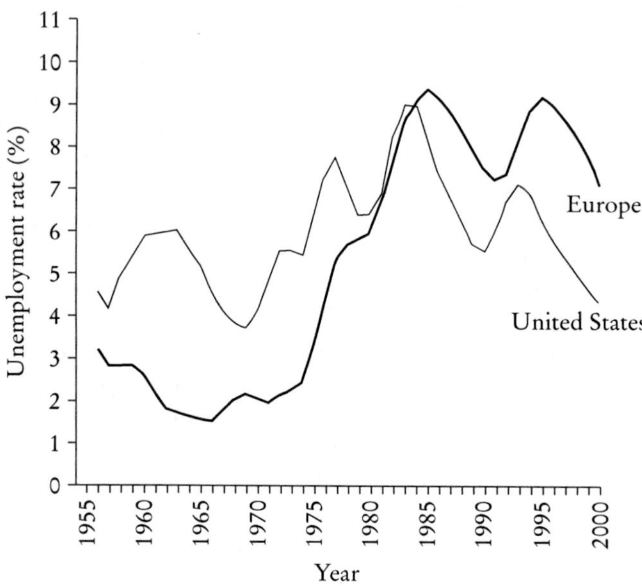


**Figure 1** Unemployment rates (three-year moving averages) 1955–2000 in the United States and in six European countries – Belgium, Denmark, France, Germany, the Netherlands, and the United Kingdom

all political shades to give top priority to full employment in the trade-off between inflation and employment (OECD, 1970). As argued by Rehn (1987), many European governments are likely to have used the window of opportunity created by the oil shocks of 1973 and 1979 to allow levels of unemployment to escalate. In the 1990s US unemployment rates decreased more than the European average.

Within the European perspective, full employment was thus a constitutive part of the welfare state. When judged in relation to the reality prior to 1973, the return of mass unemployment must be seen as a major retrenchment, the eradication of one of the cornerstones of Western European welfare states. However, this radical change has occurred outside the focus of the new-politics approach and has therefore not been conceived as a case of retrenchment.

## Social Insurance, Expenditures, and Institutions

Pierson's pioneering work on welfare-state retrenchment has been followed by a number of interesting studies.[3] Some are comparative and based largely on expenditure data (see Castles, 2001; Clayton and Pontusson, 1998; Hicks, 1999; Huber and Stephens, 2001; Swank, 2001). However, most of them are examinations of a single or a few countries, often in qualitative terms (see Bonoli and Palier, 1998; Green-Pedersen, 2001, 2002; Kautto, 2000; Leibfried, 2001; Levy, 1999; Olsen, 2002; Palier, 2000; Palme, 2002; Palme and Wennemo, 1998). These studies largely agree on the nature of the pressures towards retrenchment faced by modern welfare states: population ageing, changing family patterns, new gender roles, decreasing economic growth rates, technological change, internationalization of the economy, and changing relations between nation-states as a result of the end of the Cold War and political-economic integration in Europe. These studies have also largely agreed that to a remarkable extent European welfare states have been resistant to change. Thus, for example, after a survey van Kersbergen (2000, p. 25) concluded the following: 'The general thesis that may be distilled from the literature is that while the context of welfare state policies has changed, this has not lead to a dismantling of existing welfare state regimes or single programmes.' Green-Pedersen and Haverland (2002, p. 44) note that in the post-Pierson literature 'the expectation of no sweeping retrenchment has largely been confirmed'. Additionally, as the title of his edited book indicates, Kuhnle (2000) and his colleagues observed the *Survival of the European Welfare State*. Furthermore, in the newly redemocratized countries of Western Europe, such as Spain, welfare states have actually expanded (Moreno, 2000). To account for this resilience several of these authors point to the widespread popular support for the welfare state and to the path dependency created by welfare states.

As noted above, although clearly valuable and relevant, many of the studies made on retrenchment are problematic. Apart from overlooking the demise of European full employment, analyses based on expenditure data face other difficulties in disentangling consequences of factors such as increasing levels of unemployment and changes in benefit levels, whereas more qualitatively oriented studies offer rather weak benchmarks for studying change over time and differences between countries. The SCIP database (discussed above) provides preliminary data quantifying social rights in major social-insurance programmes and thereby an alternative empirical basis for the analysis of retrenchment (Korpi and Palme, 2000, 2001, 2003). Here changes in the net replacement rates of three programmes for benefits received as a result of short-term interruptions of work income – that is, benefits during sickness, work accidents, and unemployment – are of particular interest. These programmes are of major importance to government budget deficits. Furthermore in these programmes government decisions on cuts will usually have relatively quick effects on net replacement rates, a circumstance that increases the possibility of relating cuts to political decision making. Thus, these short-term programmes differ from old age pensions, where political decisions may have consequences decades later. Net replacement rates in these programmes give unidimensional variables for studying change over longer time periods and for a relatively large number of countries.

Analyses based on the above social-rights data indicate that in the long perspective starting back in 1930 the average net benefits for thirteen European countries in each of these three programmes have had a monotonic increase with an acceleration that began in 1950 and continued until approximately 1975, followed by a decrease until 1995 (Korpi and Palme, 2003). This downward deviation from the long-increasing trend is an indication of retrenchment. Yet average decreases cannot be described as an overall dismantling of these social-insurance programmes. Unlike the removal of full employment from almost all European welfare states after 1973, in these three social-insurance programmes we find great differences among countries. Here Britain – established as the crucial test case in the earlier literature on the extent and causes of retrenchment – is a relevant example. By 1995, following the coming of the Conservative government in 1979, net replacement rates in these three programmes were cut back below the minimum levels established in the 1946 reform. Replacement rates in sickness insurance were actually reduced to approximately the same level as that in 1930, while unemployment and work-accident insurance benefits plunged to approximately half of their 1930 levels.

Path dependency has often been used as an explanation for welfare-state resilience. Myles and Pierson (2001) have drawn attention to a major mechanism explaining such stability in pay-as-you-go pensions systems: the double payment problem. In countries with well-developed pay-as-you-go pension systems the working generation is paying the pensions for retirees and cannot easily accept also contributing to their own future pensions in a funded system. Mature pay-as-you-go pension systems are therefore difficult to change into funded programmes. It is important that we can explain differences in the extent of path dependency in terms of specific mechanisms that generate more or less resistance to cuts. Often, however, the concept of path dependency is used to label absence of change rather than to explain resistance to change.

As noted above, in the new-politics perspective it is widely assumed that resistance to welfare-state cuts comes primarily from categories of benefit recipients, such as retirees, the unemployed, the handicapped, and health-care consumers. Although such categories are relevant and retirees in particular constitute a significant part of the electorate in most countries, other benefit recipients, for example the unemployed, have traditionally been very difficult to mobilize. It can be argued that of greater relevance here is the much larger constituency of risk-averse citizens, who benefit from insurance in terms of the reduction of risks they are likely to face during the life course. However, in Western societies risk-averse citizens are internally differentiated by a number of potential and partly cross-cutting lines of cleavage, such as occupation, status, income, education, ethnicity, religion, and region. These cleavages also differentiate citizens in terms of lifetime risk as well as in terms of the resources they control to handle these risks. Given these circumstances, reflecting theory formation within the 'new institutionalism', it can be argued that major welfare-state institutions are likely to be of relevance for the formation of values, attitudes, and interests among citizens in ways that are of relevance for patterns of collective action. This is because welfare-state institutions tend to create templates that emphasize some of the lines of cleavage discussed above while downplaying others. The institutional contexts generated by welfare states are therefore likely to affect citizens' coalition formation in terms of the extent of support and resistance that government efforts to cut back social rights are likely to face (Korpi and Palme, 1998; Korpi, 2001). The institutional organization of risk-averse citizens, rather than the number of benefit recipients, is likely to be of main relevance for the degree of path dependency in welfare-state programmes.

To account for differences among countries in terms of welfare-state development, it is fruitful to relate changes in social rights to a welfare-state typology based on the nature of the institutional structures of the main social-insurance programmes in a country (Korpi and Palme, 1998; Korpi, 2001).[4] This typology differentiates social-insurance institutions by using three criteria: basis for claiming benefits, principles for setting benefit levels, and forms of governance of insurance programmes. On the bases of these criteria, it is possible to identify five different types of institutional structures, which historically have existed in Western welfare states. These institutional structures constitute the targeted, voluntary state-subsidized, basic security, state corporatist, and encompassing models. In present-day Europe the latter three models are the most important ones.

The basic-security model is universalistic and gives benefits to all at a flat rate, which typically is rather low. Because of the low benefit rates inherent in this model, it cannot protect accustomed standards of living of better-off citizens, who therefore are likely to gradually develop private solutions such as occupational insurance and savings. In the long run, in this model social-insurance programmes will be a concern primarily for manual workers, whereas private programmes assume main relevance for the middle class. This type of institution provides a context where government attempts to cut public programmes are unlikely to meet widespread or unified resistance and thus are likely to suffer retrenchment. In contrast, the state-corporatist model as well as the encompassing model offer earnings-related benefits. Within these institutional structures, public programmes tend to safeguard accustomed standards of living among the middle class, thereby decreasing the need for private solutions and 'crowding out' different types of private insurance. However, the state-corporatist and the encompassing models affect the middle class within very different contexts. In the state-corporatist model there are several separate occupation-related insurance programmes, differentiated in terms of conditions, financing, and benefits. Each programme is governed by elected representatives of employers and employees, typically from the unions. Within state-corporatist institutions, government attempts at retrenchment are likely to meet resistance from preorganized bodies of risk-averse citizens attempting to safeguard their specific interests. In contrast, in the encompassing model the middle class is included in the same programmes as all other citizens. In the expansion phase this broad constituency was mobilized by political parties and formed a major force in favour of welfare-state expansion. When faced with cutbacks, however, such a heterogeneous assembly of citizens is difficult to mobilize from the inside. In this institutional context the degree of resistance is likely to reflect the extent to which political parties are willing to mobilize voters against cutbacks.

The widely accepted new-politics hypothesis of only limited retrenchment has been called into question by analyses of cutbacks in terms of indicators of social rights, focusing on sickness, work accident, and unemployment insurance programmes (discussed above) and on changes in net replacement levels within thirteen European countries (Korpi and Palme, 2001, 2003). One indicator was based on cuts measured as declines in benefit levels until 1995 from the peak levels reached during 1975–1990. Important differences were found among countries, some part of which can be understood in terms of the structure of their dominant social-insurance institutions.[5] The largest cuts had clearly taken place in countries dominated by basic security institutions. Here Britain was

in class 3/15

clearly in the lead with average net replacement rates that were reduced by almost half. Ireland followed with cutbacks amounting to one-third of peak rates. Denmark had cutbacks of the order of one-fifth of peak rates, while lower rates were found in the Netherlands. Among the basic security countries Switzerland had no major cutbacks.[6] Among the state corporatist countries cuts were, on average, lowest. Thus whereas in Austria, France, Germany, and Italy unemployment insurance programmes had seen significant cuts, sickness and work-accident programmes had largely been spared. An exception here was Belgium, where net benefits decreased markedly in sickness insurance. In the encompassing category, cuts were on the average lower than in countries with basic-security programmes, but both Sweden and Finland had made some important cuts, primarily during the early 1990s when their unemployment levels exploded. Norway with its oil economy largely escaped cuts.

With reliable and comparable empirical data reflecting the character of social rights in a large number of countries over a longer period, we get a perspective on the extent of retrenchment in social-insurance programmes that is quite different from the ones based on expenditure data and qualitative case studies. In at least a handful of European countries, major retrenchment in social-insurance rights now appears. There is no general path dependency; instead the different types of welfare-state institutions in combination with factors such as constitutional veto points appear to play significant roles in terms of path dependency and resistance to cuts.

## Class and Gender

As noted above, a central hypothesis in the new-politics perspective is that, although partisan politics and class-related parties were of major importance during welfare-state expansion, in the retrenchment phase they are of little significance. Although debated, this hypothesis has been accepted by many. Such a view appears to be supported, for example, by observations that in Germany the Christian Democratic–Liberal coalition government was very cautious in attempting to trim its state-corporatist welfare state. This view has received additional support in empirical studies. On the basis of expenditure data, Huber and Stephens (2001) found that over time the role of partisan politics decreased considerably. Similar findings are also reported by Castles (2001). Ross (2000) argues that according to the 'Nixon-goes-to-China' logic, left parties traditionally associated with the welfare-state expansion are likely to have more 'degrees of freedom' to make cuts than have right parties.

On the issue of the role of political parties, we find dissenting voices. Hicks (1999, pp. 220–1) argues that the left–right dimensions remained significant during the retrenchment phase. In a case study of the Netherlands

Green-Pedersen (2001, 2002) analysed the role of the confessional political tendency, which played a major role in all Dutch governments during the twentieth century until 1995. He argued that, because of the pivotal role of the Christian Democratic Party, in the early 1980s this party was able to make the reluctant but relatively weak Social Democratic Party accept cutbacks in welfare benefits. Levy (1999) suggested that, when faced with the necessity to cut, social democratic governments in continental European countries attempted to turn 'vice into virtue' by predominantly cutting, for example, overly lenient pension programmes while improving benefits for the most needy. Kitschelt (2001) as well as Ross (2000) outlined factors in political party systems that are likely to favour possibilities for retrenchment.

In contrast analyses on the role of partisan politics based on SCIP data indicate clearly significant effects of partisan politics on retrenchment in social rights (Korpi and Palme, 2001, 2003). Events of retrenchment were delineated in terms of cuts of at least 10 per cent in net benefit levels in sickness, unemployment, and work-accident insurance during the 1975–1995 period. Taking into account the relative number of cabinet portfolios by different parties and the duration of these cabinets, the relative risk for major cuts was approximately four times higher for the secular centre-right parties than for left parties. Although analyses of welfare-state expansion based on expenditure data has often viewed confessional parties as almost equivalent to social democratic ones, when it comes to retrenchment in social rights they were found to occupy a position between the other two party constellations. This pattern of partisan political effects was also supported by event history analysis and remained when a number of institutional and economic control variables were considered.

Attitudinal studies in several Western European countries indicate that the welfare state has retained widespread public support, a support which continues to be structured by socioeconomic class and the left–right continuum in expected patterns (Taylor-Gooby, 1999; Svallfors, 1999, 2003; Goul Andersen, 1999). Yet changes have also been noted. In Sweden after the conversion by conservative-centrist parties and the employers' confederation to a very critical view of the welfare state, in the early 1990s top-level employees in the private sector became more negative, whereas lower-middle-class employees and workers in private as well as in public sectors largely retained their positive views (Svallfors, 1996). When the conservative-centrist government (1991–4) introduced major cuts in social-insurance programmes, it was unseated by a surge of social democratic support in the 1994 election. In its efforts to decrease large budget deficits, the new Social Democratic government continued to cut replacement rates, cuts contributing to a precipitous fall in the opinion polls. When it comes to welfare-state retrenchment, the Nixon-goes-to-China logic may have a relatively limited sphere of application.

Despite the voluminous writing on welfare-state retrenchment in recent years, one cannot fail to notice the dog that did not bark: little attention has been paid to consequences of regress for gender inequality. This may indicate that retrenchment has not had very serious effects on the position and relative life chances of women. O'Connor et al. (1999, p. 113) note that in the welfare states of Australia, Britain, Canada, and the United States women have been disadvantaged by changes such as strengthened work incentives and increased targeting of programmes, yet 'while retrenchment has occurred, restructuring is perhaps a better overall description of the social policy changes during the last two decades'. Sainsbury (1996, ch. 9) argued that in countries such as Britain and the Netherlands an increasing reliance on means-tested benefits in combination with restricted access to such benefits has increased gender inequality because women rely on such benefits much more than men and because means-tested benefits for wives tend to deter their labour-force participation. Montanari (2000, ch. 3) observes that in Western countries the long-term trend towards an increasing reliance on universal cash benefits in child support was broken in the 1980s when tax concessions increased in importance. Such a development tends to disadvantage single mothers.

In this context, it must also be pointed out that in the Nordic countries with their large public sectors 'manned' largely by women major cuts in the number of employees without a similar decrease in the clients of the public sector have to a significant extent increased the burdens of those remaining there. In continental Europe with relatively low female labour-force participation rates, high unemployment is likely to have slowed the rate of increase in female participation while increasing the role of often insecure part-time jobs.

## Globalization and Europeanization

In the 1990s globalization became a term on everybody's lips and was used to suggest a variety of international challenges facing nation-states and their welfare-state arrangements in particular.[7] Initially threats from globalization against welfare states were often seen as severe, but gradually views have been shifting. For example, although Mishra (1999) saw globalization as a very serious threat to the foundations of welfare states, such views have been questioned by others (e.g., Boyer and Drache, 1996; Garrett, 1998). Many scholars have come to see the effects of globalization as conditional on national institutions and political interventions (Esping-Andersen, 1996; Palier and Sykes; 2001; Swank, 2001). In the processes of globalization international organizations have played significant roles (Deacon et al., 1997). As noted above, Pierson largely dismisses globalization as a source for fundamental welfare-state change. In discussions of the effects of efforts towards economic and political integration within the EU we also find considerable debates (Leibfried and Pierson, 1995; Rhodes, 1996, 2002).

In analysing the role of international political and economic changes for national policy-making, distinguishing between different policy sectors in welfare states is fruitful. One important distinction is found between policies to maintain full employment and social insurance and social services. National policies to maintain full employment are likely to be much more sensitive to, and dependent on, international developments than social-insurance and social-service programmes are. Of relevance here is that, with the exception of the largest economies, most Western countries are markedly export dependent. As Fligstein and Merand (2002) noted, trade growth has been especially pronounced within the E.U. When countries in economic crises decrease their imports, export possibilities in other countries decline and their unemployment problems mount, thereby likely creating a situation that pressures governments to make cuts in social-insurance and social-service programmes. In Europe full employment after the end of World War II was conditioned by Bretton-Woods institutions, giving national governments influence over cross-border capital flows while liberalizing cross-border trade. With the dismantling of cross-border capital controls and increasing economic integration within Europe, if unemployment is allowed to rise in some countries, maintaining full employment becomes very difficult, especially for smaller countries.

A large-scale experiment on the role of economic interdependence and political factors contributing to the rise of unemployment took place in Europe after the two oil shocks in 1973 and 1979. As discussed above, while levels of unemployment increased dramatically in the EEC countries, the EFTA countries (Austria, Finland, Norway, Sweden, and Switzerland), where social democrats had long participated in governments, attempted via various means to avoid the return of mass unemployment. For almost two decades, the EFTA countries were relatively successful in these attempts, but in the early 1990s, especially in Finland and Sweden, unemployment levels converged to the high European average (Korpi, 2002).

Many economists have argued that globalization has interacted with technological developments to increase levels of unemployment in the economically advanced countries. The assumption here is that technological developments in these economies have escalated educational job requirements to levels where the less educated no longer are qualified. At the same time less-qualified production is moved to low-wage countries. In advanced economies job demands are thus assumed to have outrun the educational qualifications of significant sectors of the labour force. Such interpretations are often supported by the observation that levels of unemployment tend to be especially high among workers with low educational qualifications, a correlation interpreted in causal terms. However, a similar correlation existed already during the period of relatively low unemployment. Furthermore, in all Western countries levels of education have been rapidly increasing. Several researchers have found that many employees are educationally overqualified for their present jobs (Åberg, 2003; Borghans and de Griep, 2000; Freeman, 1976). The observed correlation between education and the risk of unemployment may to a significant extent reflect statistical discrimination by employers, who use educational levels as a shorthand when sorting through the increasing numbers of job applicants. An alternative explanation for the increasing levels of unemployment is that overall demand for labour has been depressed and remains low.

In the 1990s economic and political integration in Europe accelerated, with the creation of the EU and the European Monetary Union as important landmarks. In the European Monetary Union we find institutional changes that tend to depress overall demand and thereby counteract decreases in unemployment. In contrast to the Federal Reserve Bank of the United States, which is instructed to consider the effects of its policies on employment and growth as well as on inflation, the new European Central Bank has a very low inflation target as its only goal. Whereas in recent years the Federal Reserve Bank has tended to frequently decrease its prime rates in response to increasing unemployment, European central banks have been steadfast in maintaining high interest levels during long periods, without regard to unemployment levels (Ball, 1999; Carlin and Soskice, 1997). The European Monetary Union and its associated stability pact place strict requirements on economic policies of member countries in terms of low levels of inflation and government debt. It can be argued that in several countries government attempts to achieve and to maintain these criteria have contributed to very high levels of unemployment (Guillén and Álvarz, 2001; Kosonen, 2001).

Yet most of the effects of economic and political integration within the EU on social insurance and social services appear to have been indirect, with high unemployment serving as the main catalyst, whereas direct effects on social policy making have been limited. Most of the interventions of the European Commission in the social-policy arena have been issued not as binding directives but only as recommendations that member countries are free to follow or disregard (Deacon, 2000; Hantrais, 2000; Montanari, 1995, 2001). Based on the SCIP data set, Montanari (1995, 2001) found little evidence for convergence of legislation on social rights within member countries in five main branches of social insurance in the period 1970–90. The European Court of Justice has, however, had direct effects on social policy at the European level by barring some aspects of negative treatment of women in the labour market (Hobson, 2000). In this area, however, future development remains open and to a large extent depends on outcomes of ongoing internal conflicts focused on the issue of if this assembly of countries is to move towards a federal structure implying some form of a European government or if it is to remain a union for cooperation between relatively independent nation-states.

## Discussion

The dramatic changes taking place in the economies of the Western countries during the past three decades have generated a number of important and informative books and articles on the consequences of these changes for welfare states. A review of the rapidly expanding research on welfare-state retrenchment points to the importance of clarifying the nature of the dependent variable, the welfare state. A definition focusing on social expenditures for transfers and services easily invites scholars to consider explanations in terms of general forces related to structural economic change. In the early decades after the end of World War II, scholars widely interpreted welfare-state expansion as a result of the development of industrialism generating universally shared needs for a well-trained and internally differentiated labour force (Kerr et al., 1964). Three decades later, analysts have explained welfare-state retrenchment in terms of postindustrialism, which via demographic and economic changes generates permanent austerity and thereby drives retrenchment. Although it is obvious that both industrialism and postindustrialism significantly change the contexts and conditions for policy-making, the question is to what extent these changes basically alter the nature of distributive conflict in Western societies. In the power-resources approach, viewing welfare states largely as outcomes of distributive conflicts between major interest groups differently endowed in terms of assets to be used in markets and in collective action via politics, conflicts concerning the determination of demand for labour and levels of unemployment emerge as key issues. Government budgetary pressures, the central causal factor driving retrenchment in the new-politics perspective, is to a major extent correlated with the rise in unemployment levels.

The widely shared view that welfare-state regress in Western Europe has been relatively limited partly reflects the fact that many scholars on welfare-state retrenchment have overlooked the return of mass unemployment, a central feature of Western European retrenchment. Furthermore, the widespread reliance on expenditure data has tended to blur the contours of retrenchment. Although the many case studies of a single or a few countries have given very valuable clues to the processes of retrenchment, such information has been difficult to forge into a larger picture of the extent and causes of retrenchment. In this context data on changes in social rights in social-insurance programmes provide a complement to earlier studies, offering limited sets of well-defined comparative measures for a large number of countries and a relatively long time period. Analyses based on such data question earlier interpretations of the extent and causes of retrenchment. Thus since 1975 in a handful of European countries citizenship rights in three main social-insurance programmes have changed in ways that must be described as major retrenchment. Differences in outcomes between earlier analyses and those based on social citizenship rights are especially stark when it comes to Britain, a crucial test case in the discussion on the extent and causes of retrenchment. In the debates on the role of class-related political parties in welfare-state regress, analyses based on social-rights data clearly support the hypothesis of a continued role of partisan politics in the retrenchment phase.

In discussions on the role of globalization and on European integration for welfare-state regress, conflicting hypotheses have been advanced. Here, however, considering different aspects of welfare states and their interactions is necessary. It can be argued that a major part of the effects of globalization and transnational integration on welfare-state retrenchment has been focused on full employment, one of the cornerstones of the postwar European welfare state, the undercutting of which in turn may have effects on social insurance and services. The liberalization of cross-border capital movements has to a significant extent turned the tables to the disadvantage of governments attempting to safeguard full employment. Within the EU, developments limiting the economic policy choices of governments in member countries are also likely to have been significant. In the power-resources perspective, the return of mass unemployment and attempts to make cuts in social-citizenship rights appear as a reworking of the implicit social contract established in Western Europe after the end of World War II.

## Notes

From *Annual Review of Sociology*, 29, 2003, pp. 589–609.

For valuable help in working with this paper the author wants to thank Eero Carroll, Stefan Englund, Ingrid Esser, Tommy Ferrarini, Helena Höög, Tomas Korpi, Ingalill Montanari, Joakim Palme, Ola Sjöberg, and Stefan Svallfors.

1 As pointed out by several authors, welfare states change in a number of ways, only some of which can be described as regress or retrenchment (Ferrera and Rhodes, 2000; Pierson, 2001a). The numerous studies that do not concentrate on retrenchment are not included here. In Eastern Europe developments in the countries of the former Soviet block are so different that they cannot be treated here.

2 For analyses of the arrival, continuation, and demise of full employment in Western countries, see Korpi, 2002.

3 Collective works of significance in this context are volumes by Clasen (2001), Bonoli et al. (2000), Esping-Andersen (1996), Ferrera and Rhodes (2000), Kautto et al. (see Kautto, 1999, 2001), Kuhnle (2000), Pierson (2001c), and Scharpf and

Schmidt (2000a, 2000b). Reviews of selected literature are found in Green-Pedersen and Haverland, 2002, van Kersbergen, 2000, and Lindbom, 2002.

4 In contrast to Esping-Andersen's (1990) influential typology of welfare-state regimes, which is based on a broad set of indicators and therefore fruitful for general descriptive purposes, this typology is focused on welfare-state institutions, which can be seen as intervening variables, relating causes to outcomes. This institution-based typology provides a much more precise basis for differentiation of welfare states, for measuring changes over time, as well as for causal analysis. The social-insurance programmes used for the typology are old age pensions and sickness cash benefits, programmes that are of major relevance for all socioeconomic categories. In almost all these countries sickness cash benefit programmes have the same type of institutional structure as old age pensions.

5 Because of significant correlations between potential causal and contextual variables, such as the number of constitutional veto points, the type of dominant political parties, and the structure of social insurance institutions, separating the different contributions of these factors to retrenchment is difficult.

6 The relative stability in Switzerland is likely to partly reflect the large number of constitutional veto points in its policy-making system.

7 As is well known, the term globalization has many meanings. I use it here to refer to the liberalization of cross-border capital movements and of international trade.

## References


Åberg, R. (2003) 'Unemployment Persistency, Over-education and Employment Chances of the Less Educated', *European Sociological Review*, 19, pp. 199–216.

Ball. L. (1999) 'Aggregate Demand and Long-run Unemployment', *Brookings Papers on Economic Activity*, 2, pp. 189–248.

Beveridge, W. (1944) *Full Employment in a Free Society*, New York, Norton.

Blanchflower, D. G. and Oswald, A. J. (1994) *The Wage Curve*, Cambridge, MA., MIT Press.

Bonoli, G. and Palier, B. (1998) 'Changing the Politics of Social Programmes: Innovative Change in British and French Welfare Reforms', *Journal of European Social Policy*, 8, pp. 317–30.

Bonoli, G., George, V. and Taylor-Gooby, P. (2000) *European Welfare Futures: Towards a Theory of Retrenchment*, Cambridge, Polity.

Borghans, L. and de Grip, A. (eds) (2000) *The Overeducated Worker? The Economics of Skill Utilization*, Cheltenham, Edward Elgar.

Boyer, R. and Drache, D. (eds) (1996) *States against Markets: The Limits of Globalization*, London, Routledge.

Carlin, W. and Soskice, D. (1997) 'Shocks to the System: The German Political Economy under Stress', *National Institute Economic Review*, 159, pp. 57–76.

Castles, F. G. (2001) 'On the Political Economy of Recent Public Sector Development', *Journal of European Social Policy*, 11, pp. 195–211.

Clasen, J. (ed.) (2001) *What Future for Social Security? Debates and Reforms in National and Cross-National Perspective*, The Hague, Kluwer Law Int.

Clayton, R. and Pontusson, J. (1998) 'Welfare State Retrenchment Revisited: Entitlement Cuts, Public Sector Restructuring, and Inegalitarian Trends in Advanced Capitalist Societies', *World Politics*, 51, pp. 67–98.

Craig, F. W. S. (1975) *British General Election Manifestos 1900–1974*, London, Macmillan.

Crosland, A. (1956) *The Future of Socialism*, London, Cape.
Deacon, B. (2000) *Globalization and Social Policy: The Threat to Equitable Welfare*, Geneva, UN Research Institute for Social Development.
Deacon, B., Hulse, M. and Stubbs, P. (1997) *Global Social Policy: International Organizations and the Future of Welfare*, London, Sage.
Esping-Andersen, G. (1985) *Politics against Markets: The Social Democratic Road to Power*, Princeton, Princeton University Press.
Esping-Andersen, G. (1990) *The Three Worlds of Welfare Capitalism*, Cambridge, Polity.
Esping-Andersen, G. (ed.) (1996) *Welfare States in Transition: National Adaptations in Global Economies*, London, Sage.
Ferrera, M. and Rhodes, M. (eds) (2000) *Recasting European Welfare State*, London, Frank Cass.
Fligsten, N. and Merand, F. (2002) 'Globalization or Europeanization? Evidence on the European Economy since 1980', *Acta Sociologica*, 45, pp. 7–22.
Freeman, R. B. (1976) *The Over-educated American*, New York, Academic.
Garrett, G. (1998) *Partisan Politics in the Global Economy*, Cambridge, Cambridge University Press.
Goul Andersen, J. (1999) 'Changing Labour Markets, New Social Divisions and Welfare State Support: Denmark in the 1990s', in S. Svallfors and P. Taylor-Gooby (eds), *The End of the Welfare State? Responses to State Retrenchment*, London, Routledge, pp. 13–33.
Green-Pedersen, C. (2001) 'The Puzzle of Dutch Welfare State Retrenchment', *West European Politics*, 24, pp. 135–50.
Green-Pedersen, C. (2002) *The Politics of Justification: Party Competition and Welfare State Retrenchment in Denmark and the Netherlands from 1982 to 1998*, Amsterdam, Amsterdam University Press.
Green-Pedersen, C. and Haverland, M. (2002) 'The New Politics and Scholarship of the Welfare State', *Journal of European Social Policy*, 12, pp. 43–51.
Guillén, A. M. and Álvarez, S. (2001) 'Globalization and the Southern Welfare States', in B. Palier, P. M. Prior and M. R. Sykes (eds), *Globalization and European Welfare States: Challenges and Change*, Basingstoke, Palgrave, pp. 103–26.
Hantrais, L. (2000) *Social Policy in the EU*, Basingstoke, Macmillan.
Heywood, P., Jones, E. and Rhodes, M. (eds) (2002) *Developments in West European Politics 2*, Basingstoke, Palgrave.
Hicks, A. (1999) *Social Democracy and Welfare Capitalism: A Century of Income Security Politics*, Ithaca, NY, Cornell University Press.
Hobson, B. (2000) 'Economic Citizenship: Reflections through the EU Policy Mirror', in B. Hobson (ed.), *Gender and Citizenship in Transition*, London, Macmillan, pp. 84–117.
Huber, E. and Stephens, J. D. (2001) *Development and Crises of the Welfare State: Parties and Policies in Global Markets*, Chicago, University of Chicago Press.
Kautto, M. (ed.) (1999) *Nordic Social Policy Changing Welfare States*, London, Routledge.
Kautto, M. (2000) *Two of a Kind? Economic Crises, Policy Responses and Well-Being during the 1990's in Sweden and Finland*, Stockholm, Fritzes.
Kautto, M. (ed.) (2001) *Nordic Welfare States in the European Context*, London, Routledge.
Kerr, C., Dunlop, J. T., Harbinson, F. and Meyers, C. A. (1964) *Industrialism and Industrial Man*, New York, Oxford University Press.

Kitschelt, H. (2001) 'Partisan Competition and Welfare State Retrenchment: When Do Politicians Choose Unpopular Policies?', in P. Pierson, *The New Politics of the Welfare State*, Oxford, Oxford University Press, pp. 265–302.

Korpi, W. (1983) *The Democratic Class Struggle*, London, Routledge and Kegan Paul.

Korpi, W. (1989) 'Power, Politics, and State Autonomy in the Development of Social Citizenship: Social Rights during Sickness in Eighteen OECD Countries since 1930', *American Sociological Review*, 54, pp. 309–28.

Korpi, W. (2001) 'Contentious Institutions: An Augmented Rational-Actor Analysis of the Origins and Path Dependency of Welfare State Institutions in the Western Countries', *Rationality and Society*, 13, pp. 235–83.

Korpi, W. (2002) 'The Great Trough in Unemployment: A Long-Term View of Unemployment, Inflation, Strikes and The Profit/Wage Ratio', *Politics and Society*, 30, pp. 365–426.

Korpi, W. and Palme, J. (1998) 'The Paradox of Redistribution and the Strategy of Equality: Welfare State Institutions, Inequality and Poverty in the Western Countries', *American Sociological Review*, 63, pp. 661–87.

Korpi, W. and Palme, J. (2000) 'Distributive Conflict, Political Mobilization and the Welfare State: Comparative Patterns of Emergence and Retrenchment in the Westernized Countries', presented at the annual conference of the American Sociological Association, Washington DC.

Korpi, W. and Palme, J. (2001) 'New Politics and Class Politics in Welfare State Regress: A Comparative Analysis of Retrenchment in Eighteen Countries, 1975–1995', presented at the American Political Science Association, San Francisco.

Korpi, W. and Palme, J. (2003) 'New Politics and Class Politics in the Context of Austerity and Globalization: Welfare State Regress in Eighteen Countries, 1975–1995', *American Political Science Review*, 97, 3, pp. 425–46.

Kosonen, P. (2001) 'Globalization and the Nordic Welfare States', in B. Palier, P. M. Prior and M. R. Sykes (eds), *Globalization and European Welfare States: Challenges and Change*, Basingstoke, Palgrave, pp. 153–72.

Kuhnle, S. (ed.) (2000) *Survival of the European Welfare State*, London, Routledge.

Leibfried, S. (ed.) (2001) *Welfare State Futures*, Cambridge, Cambridge University Press.

Leibfried, S. and Pierson, P. (1995) *European Social Policy: Fragmentation and Integration*, Washington DC, Brookings Institution.

Levy., J. (1999) 'Vice into Virtue? Progressive Politics and Welfare Reform in Continental Europe', *Politics and Society*, 27, pp. 239–73.

Lindbom, A. (2002) 'The Politics of Welfare State Reform', *Journal of European Public Policy*, 9, pp. 311–21.

Mishra, R. (1999) *Globalization and the Welfare State*, Cheltenham, Edward Elgar.

Montanari, L. (1995) 'Harmonization of Social Policies and Social Regulation in the European Community', *European Journal of Political Research*, 27, pp. 21–45.

Montanari, L. (2000) *Social Citizenship and Work in Welfare States: Comparative Studies on Convergence and on Gender*, Stockholm, Swedish Institute for Social Research, Stockholm University.

Montanari, I. (2001). 'Modernization, Globalization and the Welfare State: A Comparative Analysis of Old and New Convergence of Social Insurance since 1930', *British Journal of Sociology*, 52, pp. 469–94.

Moreno, L. (2000) 'The Spanish Development of Southern European Welfare', in S. Kuhnle (ed.), *Survival of the European Welfare State*, London, Routledge, pp. 146–65.

Myles, J. (1984) *Old Age in the Welfare State: The Political Economy of Public Pensions*, Boston, Little, Brown.
Myles, J. and Pierson, P. (2001) 'The Comparative Political Economy of Pension Reform', in P. Pierson, *The New Politics of the Welfare State*, Oxford, Oxford University Press, pp. 305–33
O'Connor, J. S., Orloff, A. S. and Shaver, S. (1999) *States, Markets, Families: Gender, Liberalism and Social Policy in Australia, Canada, Great Britain and the United States*, Cambridge, Cambridge University Press.
OECD (1970) *Inflation: The Present Problem*, Paris, Organization for Economic Cooperation and Development.
OECD (1999) 'Benefit Systems and Work Incentives', Organization for Economic Cooperation and Development, Paris.
Offe, C. (1984) *Contradictions of the Welfare State*, London, Hutchinson.
Olsen, G. M. (2002) *The Politics of the Welfare State: Canada, Sweden and the United States*, Oxford, Oxford University Press.
Palier, B. (2000) 'Defrosting the French Welfare State', *West European Politics*, 23 (special issue), pp. 114–37.
Palier, B. and Sykes, R. (2001) 'Challenges and Change: Issues and Perspectives in the Analysis of Globalization and the European Welfare States', in B. Palier, P. M. Prior and M. R. Sykes (eds), *Globalization and European Welfare States: Challenges and Change*, Basingstoke, Palgrave, pp. 1–16.
Palier, B., Prior, P. M. and Sykes, M. R. (eds) (2001) *Globalization and European Welfare States: Challenges and Change*, Basingstoke, Palgrave.
Palme, J. (ed.) (2002) *Welfare in Sweden: The Balance Sheet for the 1990s*, Stockholm, Fritzes.
Palme, J. and Wennemo, I. (1998) *Swedish Social Security in the 1990s: Reform and Retrenchment*, Valfardsprojektet, Stockholm, Printing Works of the Cabinet Office and Ministries.
Pierson, P. (1994) *Dismantling the Welfare State? Reagan, Thatcher and the Politics of Retrenchment*, Cambridge, Cambridge University Press.
Pierson, P. (1996) 'The New Politics of the Welfare State', *World Politics*, 48, pp. 143–79.
Pierson, P. (2001a) 'Coping with Permanent Austerity: Welfare State Restructuring in Affluent Democracies', in P. Pierson, *The New Politics of the Welfare State*, Oxford, Oxford University Press, pp. 410–56.
Pierson, P. (2001b) 'Post-industrial Pressures on the Mature Welfare States', in P. Pierson, *The New Politics of the Welfare State*, Oxford, Oxford University Press, pp. 80–104.
Pierson, P. (ed.) (2001c) *The New Politics of the Welfare State*, Oxford, Oxford University Press.
Rehn, G. (1987) 'State, Economic Policy and Industrial Relations in the 1980s: Problems and Trends', *Economic and Industrial Democracy*, 8, pp. 16–93.
Rhodes, M. (1996) 'Globalization and West European Welfare States: A Critical Review of Recent Debates', *Journal of European Social Policy*, 6, pp. 305–27.
Rhodes, M. (2002) 'Globalization, EMU and Welfare State Futures', in P. Heywood, E. Jones and M. Rhodes (eds), *Developments in West European Politics 2*, Basingstoke, Palgrave, pp. 37–55.
Ross, F. (2000). 'Beyond Left and Right: The New Partisan Politics of Welfare', *Governance*, 13, 2, pp. 155–83.
Sainsbury, D. (1996) *Gender Equality and Welfare States*, Cambridge, Cambridge University Press.
Scharpf, F. W. and Schmidt, V. A. (ed.) (2000a) *Welfare and Work in the Open*

*Economy: Diverse Responses to Common Challenges*, Oxford, Oxford University Press.

Scharpf, F. W. and Schmidt, V. A. (ed.) (2000b) *Welfare and Work in the Open Economy: From Vulnerability to Competitiveness*, Oxford, Oxford University Press.

Svallfors, S. (1996) *Välfärdsstatens moraliska Ekonomi: Välfärdsopinonen i 90-Talets Sverige*, Umeå, Borca.

Svallfors, S. (1999) 'The Middle Class and Welfare State Retrenchment: Attitudes to Swedish Welfare Policies', in S. Svallfors and P. Taylor-Gooby (eds), *The End of the Welfare State? Responses to State Retrenchment*, London, Routledge, pp. 34–51.

Svallfors, S. (2003) 'Welfare Regimes and Welfare Opinions: A Comparison of Eight Western Countries', in J. Vogel (ed.), *European Welfare Production: Institutional Configuration and Distributional Outcome*, Dordrecht, Kluwer Academic.

Svallfors, S. and P. Taylor-Gooby (eds) (1999) *The End of the Welfare State? Responses to State Retrenchment*, London, Routledge.

Swank, D. (2001) 'Political Institutions and Welfare State Restructuring: The Impact of Institutions on Social Policy Change in Developed Democracies', in P. Pierson (ed.), *The New Politics of the Welfare State*, Oxford, Oxford University Press, pp.197–237.

Taylor-Gooby, P. (1999) 'Hollowing Out versus the New Interventionism: Public Attitudes and Welfare Futures', in S. Svallfors and P. Taylor-Gooby (eds), *The End of the Welfare State? Responses to State Retrenchment*, London, Routledge, pp. 1–12.

van Kersbergen, K. (2000) 'The Declining Resistance of Welfare States to Change?', in S. Kuhnle (ed.), *Survival of the European Welfare State*, London, Routledge, pp. 19–36.

# Deliberative Governance and EU Social Policy

*Paul Teague*

## Introduction

The two main paradigms for analysing European integration have long been intergovernmentalism and neo-functionalism. The former suggests that the Member States control the decision-making process inside the EU and ensure that national sovereignty is as far as possible protected. From this point of view, European integration entails not the creation of a super-state but fostering mutually advantageous political and economic cooperation in a manner that respects national sovereignty. Neo-functionalism normally assumes the opposite, addressing the conditions under which people might shift their loyalty and commitment from national to EU level (Haas, 1958). In explaining just how such a transfer could occur, much use is made of the concept of spillover, a process whereby integration in one functional area obliges closer cooperation between Member States in others.

Although both views still have their robust advocates (Moravcsik, 1999; Strøby Jensen, 2000), it is now widely accepted that neither is able to capture the full complexities of European integration. The new consensus is that while the EU has traits of intergovernmentalism and neo-functionalism, it fully reflects neither one nor the other. It is a political entity that defies such established analytical categories. Multi-level governance is the term now most frequently used to describe its political formation. From this perspective, the EU is not like the traditional nation-state with a tight fit between citizenship, political representation and policy-making. Nor is it a fully fledged supranational body with the capacity to 'steer' the European economy and polity. Rather it is a multi-layered amalgam of national governments and EU institutions, policy networks, independent agencies and interest groups, creating a patchwork governance regime.

The purpose of this article is threefold. The first is to suggest that the consequence of this patchwork form of governance has been to create a dilemma with regard to the institutional organization of economic citizenship – the bundle of rights and procedures used to incorporate people into the world of work – in Europe. On the one hand, EU social policy has been strong enough to create a wedge between economic citizenship and the nation-state – the notion of 'national' industrial relations systems has been destabilized. On the other hand, the institutional system of the EU is too weak to sustain a fully formed model of economic citizenship. Our second aim is to deepen insight into the origins of this dilemma by outlining the institutional dynamics and tensions of key parts of the EU social policy regime. Finally, we argue that EU social policy actors faced with the above dilemma are now designing a new approach, termed deliberative governance, which seeks a more comfortable accommodation of the 'national' and 'European' in the sphere of economic citizenship. It is uncertain whether this new regime can be made fully sustainable.

## The Policy Parameters of Social Europe

According to the multi-level governance thesis, policy-making in the EU oscillates between a number of loosely interconnected institutional layers, and the regulatory impact of EU decisions varies not only across policy arenas but also over time in the same policy area. This is as true for social policy as it is for other aspects of governance. Thus, in the 1970s the Member States attempted to give European integration a 'human face' by enacting employment Directives in tune with economic and social developments on the ground. In the 1980s, social policy took a different institutional twist. On the one hand, the formal political decision-making channels became blocked as the Conservative government in the UK stoutly opposed most interventionist employment policies. On the other hand, the European Court of Justice (ECJ) kept alive the EU presence in labour market governance through a number of important rulings and judgments. A further reorientation in social policy took place in the 1990s when the focus shifted away from employment regulation towards the promotion of policy activity designed to foster job generation. Thus, the institutional drivers behind EU social policy have varied over time as have the aims and objectives of such measures.

This continually mutating policy regime has had an important impact on national employment systems in a number of ways. First of all, an EU-wide interpretative framework for social policy has evolved, that has encouraged a common understanding on both the feasibility and desirability of Europe-wide employment measures. More specifically, it has fostered the view that Europe has a distinctive brand of capitalism which combines social rules with open markets and which is worth protecting. The prolonged and acrimonious battles in the European Council over particular pieces of labour law cannot be dismissed as relatively minor political squabbles. On the whole, they reflect a genuine and continued commitment on the part of large sections of the administrative and political elites in Europe to developing some type of 'third way' capitalism. It is this commitment that explains why most Member States have shied away from the American 'deregulated' labour market model. At the same time, the interpretative framework for Social Europe recognizes that the institutional and political diversity of the Member States places enormous constraints on the adoption of policies to harmonize or centralize employment regulation on an EU basis. Most serious advocates of EU social policy recognize that such a regime will founder if it is not sensitive to the wide variations in national institutional circumstances inside the EU.

Second, the emerging body of European labour law has opened up a regulatory arena for labour market affairs at EU level. Clearly some employment Directives have had a greater impact on domestic employment systems than others. Those on health and safety have probably had the biggest impact, followed by legislation on equality. A distinctive feature of the EU regulatory arena is that while it does not lay down 'tablets of stone' for national labour law regimes, it has nevertheless created important frameworks for the development of domestic employment rules. For example, Marginson (2000) shows that although the European Works Council Directive is weak in several important respects it has opened the door to the Europeanization of national systems of corporate governance.

Third, EU social policy has caused an increase in extra-national forms of policy collaboration and social mobilization. The Amsterdam Treaty made the benchmarking of employment and social policies across the EU a legal obligation. As a result, an essential dimension of national employment policy formation from now on will be lesson-drawing across the Member States. The aim is a convergence in the goals of employment policy in the context of national institutional diversity. A similar but more amorphous process is emerging in relation to the actions of civil associations in the labour market. Trade unions when setting bargaining demands have one eye on domestic circumstances and another on European developments. Equal opportunities groups across the EU are linking up to find the best way to advance the mainstreaming of gender measures in public administration and enterprise practice. Thus a dense web of social and policy connections has emerged as a result of the European integration process, fusing together national administrative and social structures. A loose association, yet to be fully understood, is unfolding between social learning and liberalization inside the EU: a political marketplace has emerged alongside the economic one.

But it is important to recognize that the relationship between the institutional architecture of EU social policy and the European market is far from symmetrical. In many ways, EU social policy has led to an awkward hybrid with regard to economic citizenship in Europe. As suggested earlier, it has been strong enough to loosen the long-established and close association between economic citizenship and the nation-state: the operating institutions of national labour market governance have been opened up to European influences. At the same time, EU social policy is neither sufficiently encompassing nor in-depth to push through a fully developed supranational model of economic citizenship. Thus, while the EU can make important interventions in the labour market, it lacks the *relancement* to build a 'dual' or 'multi-tiered' model of economic citizenship as advocated by Habermas and others (Teague, 1999a).

The prospects of the EU pushing forward and creating a more complete model of economic citizenship are not particularly encouraging, for three reasons. One is that the EU lacks the economic and political competence to build a durable model of economic citizenship. It has virtually none of the attributes of a conventional welfare state: for example, it cannot mount a large-scale redistribution programme through the taxation system. Its policy capacity in important areas such as education and health is weak, and its competence on employment relations matters is carefully circumscribed. For instance, as a result of the legal changes introduced by the Maastricht and Amsterdam treaties it is now well established that wage determination, rules governing strikes and lockouts and the right of association are outside its remit. Second, it is questionable whether there is sufficient popular support for the EU to extend its authority further in the social policy arenas. While talk of a 'legitimacy crisis' may be overplayed, only the most ardent Europhile would claim that a popular base exists for a supranational labour market governance system. Third, it is uncertain whether the institutional drivers behind EU social policy are sufficiently developed to 'carry' a more advanced model of economic citizenship. In the following sections, important components of the EU social policy regime are examined to show just how the EU has arrived at an awkward dilemma with regard to economic citizenship.

## The EU Judicial System and Social Policy

Weiler (1999) has argued that the judicial system of the EU, particularly the workings of the ECJ, has been the key engine behind its political development, even maintaining that it has been responsible for the transformation of Europe. This overstates the role of the EU judicial system in deepening institutional and economic ties between the Member States; nevertheless it has played an influential role across a wide range of policy areas, not least in the labour market sphere. The EU judicial system has advanced intervention in national employment systems in two important ways. One is by developing a body of EU law that has obliged Member States to change in one or another respect domestic labour law regimes. For example, the Equal Pay Directive of 1975 forced them to strengthen sex discrimination legislation. Similarly, the European Works Council Directive has necessitated new legislation on the important matter of employment information and consultation rights. ECJ rulings have also contributed to this process. For example, in the landmark *Barber* case the Court brought the area of pension rights within the competence of (then) Article 119 of the Treaty. Such rulings have had important consequences for national legal regimes in such areas as equal treatment, part-time work and affirmative action. Thus in some instances, EU legal initiatives on employment relations have made national labour law more 'European' in character. In addition, they have promoted a deeper interlocking between domestic and European judicial structures.

The second impact of the EU judicial system on national employment systems is by 'framing' domestic discussions on employment law. For example various ECJ rulings, particularly on sex equality matters, have altered what have been termed 'domestic opportunity structures' (Knill and Lehmkuhl, 1999). In other words, the balance of power and resources between *national* labour market actors alters as a result of a *European* initiative, giving rise to new *domestic* labour market rules that would not otherwise have emerged. For example, the *Barber* ruling had the effect of mobilizing trade unions and equal opportunity groups to search for new test cases to extend the legal reach of both national and European sex equality law. Thus through the process of legal framing the EU can change the domestic labour law agenda. For example, the recent Directive on parental leave has required many Member States to give greater priority to family-friendly employment policies. Framing has caused companies and employees to alter their expectations and preferences about what type of provision should be made on this important issue.

Thus the EU judicial system has made influential interventions into domestic law regimes. But there is a long way from this observation to arguing, as has one distinguished group of academics (Bercusson et al., 1996), that the Member States should transform the EU Social Chapter into a fully fledged Social Constitution. The authors do not fully outline the legal mechanism that would realize their proposal, but they are under no illusion that it would require far-reaching changes. They readily concede, for example, that national legislation governing trade union recognition would have to be reorganized to create a broadly similar European framework for collective rights so as to guarantee common rules of economic and social citizenship. Changes of this kind would demand a closer fit between economic citizenship and representative and decision-making political structures than actually exists. Put differently, enacting a European social constitution would be tantamount to 'federalizing' labour law so that the various tiers of governance with a judicial capacity to intervene in labour market affairs better complement one another.

Formidable obstacles stand in the way of such a constitutionalization of EU social policy. Although the application of national constitutions may vary, the presumption is that each shares the characteristics of promoting equal access and that the law is interpreted and enforced within a common framework of understanding. But are these three attributes – access, interpretation and enforcement – sufficiently developed in the EU judicial system to support a fully fledged EU social policy constitution? For a start, sharply contrasting systems of labour market regulation exist across the Member States. It is common to classify national legal regimes into three categories: Roman-Germanic; Anglo-Saxon; and Nordic (Barnard et al., 1995). In the first, the state has a central and active role in the organization of the labour market; for instance in almost every case there is a law that 'extends' collective agreements to all workers in the relevant sector. In contrast, the Anglo-Saxon system is marked by the relative absence of state intervention in employment relations; for example, the law does not extend the coverage of collective agreements to non-unionized workplaces. The Nordic system lies somewhere between the other two regimes, with comprehensive regulation based on voluntary agreement between strong collective organizations, within the framework of a highly developed welfare state. These national distinctions make it difficult to create a common European framework for the interpretation and enforcement of labour market rules.

Other differences reinforce these core distinctions in national law systems. Thus whereas Germany and the Netherlands use company-based works councils to reinforce employment rights, in France this function is largely the responsibility of government labour inspectorates. In some countries, ordinary courts resolve employment disputes whereas in others it is the responsibility of specially constituted labour or industrial tribunals; more generally, the frameworks of penalties and compensation used to encourage compliance with employment laws differ considerably across the Member States. The use of public agencies to promote and enforce employment legislation, as with equal opportunities or health and safety, is yet another arena of unevenness. All these differences in national labour law traditions and practices make it improbable that an EU social constitution could be enacted.

Consider the issue of subsidiarity. Included in the Amsterdam Treaty is a detailed catalogue of procedures to operationalize subsidiarity as a legislative and policy-making instrument. The Commission now has to show that the Union has the competence to act on a particular matter, explain why EU intervention is preferable to national action in solving the problem, and ensure that the envisaged action is proportional or commensurate to the problem that is being addressed. It is hard to interpret these procedures as anything other than a constraint. Subsidiarity has been grafted onto existing treaties to reassure uneasy Member States that their legal and political distinctiveness would not be threatened by the legal modernization of the EU (Neunreither, 1993).

Subsidiarity has already worked its way into EU social policy-making. Most draft employment Directives are predicated on respecting national legal diversity. For example, Hunt (1999) shows that the revised and updated Acquired Rights Directive is very open-ended, with Member States offered a range of options to implement particular clauses and even the opportunity to opt out from others. Similarly, the Directive on part-time work left it to Member States to determine the enforcement mechanisms and sanctions attached to the law. This trend towards 'light-touch' decentralized labour law is hard to reconcile with the proposal for a European social constitution. At the same time, the EU will continue to play an important role in framing parts of domestic labour law regimes, with a direct impact on particular matters.

## The Commission and EU Social Policy-Making

Traditionally, the functions of the European Commission have been classified as fivefold: administrative; initiating; brokerage; guardian; and representative (Coombes, 1970). It has used each function, with varying degrees of success, to develop EU social policy. The administrative function has been used to obstruct and delay the development of policies which it does not support. An instance of this essentially gatekeeping activity was in the mid-1980s when the British government, after some deft political manoeuvring, persuaded the Council to adopt a labour market flexibility initiative; the Commission was able to thwart the programme through a range of administrative tactics (Teague, 1989).

The strongest Commission influence on labour market affairs is through its capacity to initiate policy. As drafter of proposed Directives and other EU programmes it enjoys considerable freedom in shaping the employment policy agenda. The recent Directives on working time and atypical employment, as well as measures concerning employee information and consultation, have their origins in proposals first made by the Commission nearly two decades ago.

The Commission's brokerage function has been seen to best effect in the social dialogue process. Promoting dialogue between trade unions and employers at European level has been a constant element of social policy, but has been held back by two factors. One is a deep suspicion on the part of employers that they were being press-ganged into a process that did not coincide with their interests. The other has been a lack of clarity on the part of trade unions about what they really want from such a dialogue (Dølvik,

1997). The Commission has made energetic efforts to overcome these hurdles; during the Delors years in particular, it encouraged and cajoled the social partners to enter into meaningful exchanges (Ross, 1995). The first moves came with the Val Duchesse talks which started an open-ended dialogue between the social partners. Both sides (for different reasons) were wary of the initiative, but by assuaging anxieties, resolving disputes and providing administrative back-up, the Commission successfully addressed their concerns. As a result of this brokerage role, more cooperative and purposeful relationships now prevail between the social partners.

As guardian of the Union's legal base, the Commission has the authority to bring cases against Member States considered to be in breach of EU law. Over the years, it has not shunned this responsibility in the social policy field, having made complaints at the ECJ against every Member State for failure to implement properly some piece of EU employment law; the majority of these cases have related to equal opportunities. While action of this kind shows that the Commission is more than willing to fulfil its role as guardian, it also serves to highlight its limited resources to monitor and enforce EU regulation. The Commission is a relatively small bureaucracy unable to police properly the legal relationships between the EU and Member States, that are riven with complexity and lack of transparency (Bercusson, 1996).

The Commission's use of its 'representative function' on labour market matters is relatively undocumented. It has the greatest ability to act autonomously in the area of external trade relationships, as Member States forfeit the right to negotiate their own international trade deals on joining the EU. In the 1970s and 1980s, the Commission used this authority to introduce standards of human rights practices into trading agreements with non-Member States. For instance the Lomé Convention, which gave countries in Africa and the Caribbean preferential access to the European market, committed these countries to enacting a range social and human rights rules. More recently, the Commission has used this representative function to enter the hot debate about connecting international labour standards to world trade agreements. For example, it has supported enabling the World Trade Organization (WTO) to raise concerns about social standards as part of the regulation of the global trading regime. In the future this external dimension of EU social policy is likely to increase in importance as economic liberalization grows apace and other parts of the world form regional economic blocs to strengthen their status and bargaining position in the international trading system.

Characterizing the overall role of the Commission in EU social policy is a matter of some dispute, in line with a wider disagreement about its political status in the integration process. Pollack (1997) argues that the Commission has used the various functions delegated to it by the Member States to carve out a role as a supranational policy entrepreneur with the ability to persuade, mobilize and even manipulate opinion and interest in support of its preferred position. Not everybody concurs with this view. Moravcsik (1999) argues that the capacity of the Commission to influence the policies and programmes of the EU by acting in an entrepreneurial manner has been greatly exaggerated, since it does not have in its armoury the two main instruments which policy entrepreneurs use to influence political decision-making: financial side-payments or credible threats. As a result, it has to rely mostly on the manipulation of the information and ideas to effect authoritative political outcomes; but in these circumstances there must be considerable information asymmetries between the Member States and the EU centre before the Commission is able to punch its weight as a policy enterpreneur. This is not normally the case as each Member State is usually well informed of the others' preferences and strength of opinion, hence the Commission has little room to operate in an entrepreneurial way.

At first glance Moravcsik's argument is persuasive, but on closer examination it contains flaws. Some of his key hypotheses are shaped in a manner that favours his line of argument. Thus he states that 'policy entrepreneurs aim to induce authoritative political decisions that would not otherwise occur' (Moravcsik, 1999, p. 272). In the context of national governments this statement is not particularly contentious, but in relation to the decision-making system of the EU it is less straightforward. It is now widely accepted that in developing policies the EU rarely makes definitive, clear-cut decisions but builds a presence in a policy area through a graduated process of political integration. In this situation, it is difficult to determine when a political decision is genuinely authoritative. The long process from the initiation of a policy proposal to the realization of a tangible EU policy presence increases the opportunities for the Commission to influence the outcome. Considerable evidence exists that it has played an important role in pushing along graduated integration in various policy areas, including labour market affairs (Schmidt, 1998). Thus Moravcsik is simply too trenchant in his argument: the Commission has played a stronger autonomous role in shaping EU governance than he makes out. At the same time, his argument is a timely reminder that the Commission is not some type of supranational policy marauder with the ability to intervene at will in the domestic governance systems of Member States. Important intergovernmental checks and balances inside the EU decision-making system constrain its entrepreneurial freedom.

## *Engrenage* and EU Social Policy

The European Council, Court of Justice and Commission are the institutional bulwarks of the EU, yet the dynamics of its social policy cannot be explained by the activities of these organizations alone. Other factors have played a part in the shaping of employment policies. One such influence is what the French call *engrenage* – the deepening of interactions between national administrative structures and EU institutions (Mény et al., 1996). Although important, these interactions are hard to map and codify as they are mostly played out informally, usually behind closed bureaucratic doors. The literature suggests that the administrative connections between the European and national levels have a Janus-like quality (Hix, 1998). On the one hand, they can be a blockage, hindering the proper transfer of EU laws and programmes within the Member States; on the other, they can operate to extend the scope or deepen the reach of some EU employment policies. To some extent this insight simply accords with the theoretical literature which suggests that institutions can either function to uphold the status quo or be the vehicle for policy innovation (March and Olsen, 1989). At the same time, the way this dual process manifests in the EU is rather distinctive.

Knill (1998) suggests that the decisive factor in determining whether the interplay between the national and European administrative structures takes on a 'negative' or 'positive' character is the 'logic of appropriateness', meaning the degree of symmetry between EU policy and the existing systems of national governance. If EU policy implies far-reaching changes to the core design of national administrative institutions then this logic will be low and there will be considerable resistance to implementing measures in their original form. If the initiative poses no such challenge then the logic of appropriateness will be high, facilitating implementation. Thus EU policies that threaten a pre-existing institutional equilibrium, which balances a range of vested interests, are more likely to meet opposition. Another perspective is that countries with a high propensity for administrative reform are likely to diffuse EU policies more easily: since administrative institutions are adaptable and less embedded, the task of accommodation is more straightforward.

This argument throws light on the implementation process through which EU social measures are diffused into national regulatory frameworks. For instance, the UK has consistently adopted a positive approach to EU health and safety initiatives essentially because it regards its own regulations in this area as more stringent than in most other Member States (Eichner, 1997). Yet in other areas such as the regulation of working time and information and consultation arrangements there is considerable administrative opposition to EU measures, as they conflict with the domestic employment regime. In the Republic of Ireland, to use another example, an inter-administrative 'turf war' has broken out concerning which arm of government should be the gatekeeper for EU social initiatives. The Industrial Development Agency wants a decisive role in the diffusion of EU employment measures so that the country's industrial policy, centred on attracting mobile international investment, is not compromised by over-rigid adherence to new regulations. Other parts of government view this as an unwarranted intrusion into their administrative portfolio. Of course the end result of such administrative tussles is uneven implementation of EU social policy (O'Hagan, 1999). The overall point is that a number of fault-lines can block the administrative linkages between national governance structures and the EU bureaucracy, making the implementation of EU employment measures defective.

The other part of the *engrenage* literature is more upbeat in its interpretation of the administrative connections between the national and European levels. According to this view the interface between the EU and national administration, far from being a drag on the integration process, has actually worked to advance the regulatory competence of the EU (Hix, 1998). The rise of 'comitology' – the use of technical committees and expert policy networks in the EU decision making process – is normally invoked to support this perspective. When setting out to draft a law or regulation the Commission almost always needs 'outside' expert advice and assistance: it is simply too small a bureaucracy to have the necessary knowledge in-house (Joerges, 1997). Thus technical committees are created, consisting mainly of national civil servants and officials from other public and semi-public agencies. Because they meet so regularly to provide possible solutions to identified problems, these committees begin to develop a European policy agenda in their respective fields. Frequently, this policy agenda extends EU regulatory competence or institutional presence in a manner not anticipated at the start of the deliberations. In other words, comitology helps build advanced forms of regulatory cooperation and joint-rule making between the Member States (Wessels, 1997). Another positive spin-off is the Europeanization of national policy officials: committee members obtain greater understanding of different national approaches to problem-solving and become more aware of the need for EU-wide policy solutions. Eichner (1997) gives an authoritative account of how this process has worked in the health and safety area.

Overall the *engrenage* literature points in two different directions at the same time. One emphasizes the administrative failures embedded in the institutional connections between Member States and the EU centre, the other highlights the opportunities these very same connections hold for new forms of pan-European policy collaboration. Since evidence can be mustered to support both views neither can be seen as completely wrong, and certainly the policy community in Brussels is not anguishing over which view is correct. They have simply accepted that the template for policy development has to be promoting EU-wide coordination without overly disrupting existing national regulatory structures.

The recently adopted European employment strategy (EES), frequently referred to as the Luxembourg process, is grounded on this view (Goetschy, 1999). This initiative seeks to mobilize and coordinate policy action across the Member States on four key employment themes or 'pillars': employability, entrepreneurship, adaptability and equal opportunities. A benchmarking procedure has been introduced to improve the connections between national labour market regimes and to upgrade the monitoring and evaluation of employment policy across the Member States (Tronti, 1998). In particular, each Member State is required to submit a national action plan (NAP) setting out policies to advance the four employment priorities and explaining how the effectiveness of a particular programme or suite of measures will be evaluated. The Commission assesses the various NAPs with a view to identifying 'best practice'.

Initial assessments of the EES only confirmed the suspicion that when it came to employment policy formation, each Member State tended to plough its own furrow. Consider the matter of equal opportunities. On the positive side, the benchmarking exercise brought to light some 'best practice' initiatives in Portugal and Spain designed to promote the return of women to work. On the negative side, large gaps were found to exist in domestic regimes for equality in several Member States: for example only Austria, Belgium, Sweden and the UK were found to have adopted 'mainstreaming' equality programmes. In addition, the Commission encountered problems in evaluating the NAPs, finding it hard to establish reliable benchmarks not only because best practice measures were not easy to identity, but also because it proved difficult to make definitive judgements about many schemes as they had only existed for a short period of time. Thus the early indications of the outcome of promoting EU-wide policy convergence of employment policies through a benchmarking mechanism in the context of national institutional diversity were not particularly encouraging.

More recent evaluations of the Luxembourg process are upbeat. In its latest review of the NAPs, the European Commission (2000) refers to Member States developing new structures and institutions for the formation and evaluation of employment policies. In addition, it suggests that most governments are developing open methods of coordination that allow them to learn more from each other, set better targets for individual employment initiatives and assess the potential and weakness of experimental initiatives with greater rigour. Thus from the Commission's standpoint, the rather sobering initial experience of the benchmarking procedure has been left behind. The Luxembourg process is considered to be now yielding positive returns. This evaluation has encouraged the Commission to add new dimensions to the European employment strategy to enforce the four existing pillars: in particular, from now on Member States will be obliged to strengthen the manner in which social partners make an input into employment policy formation and to incorporate the theme of lifelong learning into the benchmarking exercise. Thus the EES seems destined to become the mainstay of EU social policy over the next decade; far from being a 'Euro-watching' exercise it could bring about a closer convergence in employment policies across the Member States (Biagi, 1998). As a result, the *engrenage* process is more likely to stimulate opportunities for coordinated EU action than create barriers to cross jurisdictional learning. Yet at the same time, the connections between the Member States and the EU continue to exhibit fault-lines.

## The Socialization Dynamic and EU Social Policy

The final influence on the shape of EU social policy is the socialization undercarriage of the European integration process. Ever since the early (post-world war) days of European integration, it has been recognized that the process involves a range of influences that would impinge on the 'social glue' that ties national citizens to their particular states. This was very much the concern of the neo-functionalist approach alluded to earlier. But when this approach lost its appeal in the mid-1970s the question of socialization remained on the margins of the European integration literature. Recently it has enjoyed something of a revival, largely as a result of the growing popularity of social constructivist approaches to European integration (Checkel, 1999).

This body of thinking emphasizes the positive feedback loops associated with repeated interactions between national actors and interest groups. European integration is seen as creating a political and social process whereby national actors alter pre-existing preferences, expectations and behaviour as a result of interacting with other European political and economic forces. This process is seen as destabilizing established national frameworks of interpretation and action (Carter and Scott, 1998). On this view, the socialization mechanisms associated with European integration (which some term 'deliberative supranationalism') forge interdependencies between governments, social institutions and civic actors and expose the futility of pursuing purely national courses of action. The advantages of strengthening reciprocal relationships between the Member States and pursuing joint EU action become more apparent. Thus the socialization undercarriage to European integration works to increase the legitimacy of EU social policy. But equally important, it creates 'focal points' that establish the boundaries between acceptable and unacceptable EU-coordinated action in the employment-related field.

These dynamics are evident inside and outside the EU decision-making framework. For instance, the literature on social dialogue and comitology stresses the importance of socialization influences. Through interacting with each other in EU-sponsored committees, the social partners as well as national civil servants have developed a shared understanding about the potential and limits of EU employment policy measures. But socialization dynamics are evident not only inside the 'vertical' institutions of the EU; an unprecedented level of 'horizontal' communication and exchange on employment-related matters occurs across the Member States (Teague, 1999b). Much of this activity seeks to make national industrial relations systems consistent with deeper political and economic integration inside the EU. Monetary union is a striking example of this process. Now that the introduction of the single currency has begun, trade unions are eager to develop greater coordination of wage determination so that trade unions from one Member State do not seek to undercut collective agreements that prevail in other parts of the EU. For the most part, these moves towards Europe-wide coordination have not involved formalized and hierarchical institutional rules or the introduction of American-style pattern bargaining. Instead, coordination is decentralized and horizontal. The motivation is simply to make national collective bargaining institutions compatible with monetary integration so that trade unions do not lose influence in Euroland. In choosing the decentralized route to coordination rather than any other alternative, the trade unions do not appear to have engaged in any profound strategic evaluation: it is as if the national trade unions converged on the decentralized option simultaneously. This can be seen as an instance where the socialization mechanisms of European integration create 'focal points' around which actors almost spontaneously converge. Thus trade unions are increasingly engaging in cross-national learning to weave a European component into their national employment relations strategies.

The general implication is that the socialization influences associated with European integration are finally altering the behaviour of industrial relations actors across the EU: the web of vertical and horizontal employment relations networks spanning the Member States is more dense and meaningful than ever before. In less tangible terms, the interpretative or cognitive frameworks of the separate national employment relations are now much closer to each other. Thus the socialization dynamic to European integration is breaching the sovereignty/supranational dichotomy that has consistently held back deeper forms of policy coordination across the Member States (Taylor, 1996). A common understanding appears to have emerged across the Member States that the important game in town is to invent structures and arrangements that marry established systems of national governance with overarching (but not monolithic) EU regulatory frameworks. This new permissive environment holds out the promise for richer forms of pan-European collaboration on employment relations matters.

However, the argument that socialization dynamics associated with European integration are encouraging cross-jurisdictional learning rests on a fairly distinctive theoretical perspective of how labour markets work. The point of departure of this account is that most market situations exhibit limited information and high transaction costs and that such imperfectly competitive situations encourage imitative behaviour (Grahl and Teague, 1992). Given limited information, market agents have a powerful tendency to take each other's behaviour as an indicator of their own optimal strategy. Mutual imitation of this kind can introduce and sustain social conventions that limit possible distortions arising from market imperfections. On the other hand, the same imitative processes can lead to social contagions that cause and amplify departures from market equilibria. So far the socialization dimension to European integration has worked in a way to create Europe employment relations conventions. But it is equally possible for the very same dynamics to give rise to contagions. In other words, the socialization properties of European integration need ongoing and active management in order to operate in a positive manner.

## Conclusions

The foregoing analysis suggests that the EU lacks the institutional capacity to replicate existing national social systems. It has only sparse competencies in areas such as fiscal redistribution, health and education, social benefits, pensions and even central matters relating to the employment relationship such as pay and industrial action. Because of these limited competencies, talk of the EU building a Social Europe that effectively replaces national social systems is fatuous: the institutional design of the EU always closed off this possibility. At the same time, those accounts that dismiss Social Europe as a sideshow to the market-making activities of European integration are either too negative or assess EU social policy against unrealistic or inappropriate benchmarks. The EU has had an impact on national labour regimes which may be fragmented and contested but which nonetheless cannot be discounted. Overall, EU social policy has evolved in a manner that has raised the prospect of a pan-European form of economic citizenship but at the same time has neither the institutional strength nor political legitimacy to deliver on this promise.

In a sense, European integration has created an acute political dilemma for labour market governance inside the EU. On the one hand, as a result of the deepening institutional and market interdependencies, it is hard to see how purely national social systems in Europe can be economically or institutionally efficient; on the other, the political and institutional foundations are not in place for a fully integrated European model of economic citizenship. It is unlikely that this dilemma will be addressed by a big political 'fix', such as the adoption of a European social constitution or a major transfer of powers relating to redistribution and regulation from the national to the European level. Neither the Member States nor the Commission would support this; instead they have adopted a pragmatic approach to EU social policy in the face of this political dilemma. Social policy has been advanced on a piecemeal basis so that it does not fall foul of the ever-present political and institutional constraints.

An unintended consequence of this pragmatic approach is that the design features of what has been termed deliberative governance are beginning to come into view (Sand, 1998). First, the EU centre, which is made up of the core decision-making organs and the panoply of surrounding committees and interest groups, has a powerful agenda-setting capacity. Commission social policy proposals may go through several burials and resurrections but they tend never to disappear. Directives passed in the 1990s, for instance on European Works Councils and part-time employment, have their origins in proposals first made by the Commission at the start of the 1980s. Through this agenda-setting capacity, the EU is becoming an important 'framing' institution for European employment relations.

Second, a problem-solving style of policy-making is taking root. This has a number of interrelated dimensions. One is that discussions between the social partners at the European-level involve deliberation (preference-changing behaviour) and planning rather than the straightforward bargaining which is more characteristic of interactions between employers and trade unions at national level. A distinctive feature of this deliberative process is reasoned argument in which the social partners find ways to advance certain matters relating to the organization of the labour market, even in the absence of an agreed view on how to solve the particular matter in hand. Deliberation thus enables a procedural consensus to be reached even when there is disagreement about the substantive issues. A further benefit of a deliberative process is that it gives rise to credible commitments through which social partners gain an assurance about each other's behaviour. Where credible commitments prevail, opportunistic behaviour is less likely and trust relations come to the fore. Thus in regard to the European social dialogue the vision is of the various participants seeking to advance their own interests by promoting a common agenda that incorporates the interests and views of others.

Another dimension to problem-solving is the devising of policy packages that are not heavily prescriptive but open-ended and flexible. In the situation where there is such diversity in national labour market institutions it would simply entail policy failure to attempt to over-harmonize employment rules and regulations. Traditional command-and-control type regulations are also unlikely to succeed as the EU lacks the capacity to monitor and enforce such one-size-fits-all policies. Thus a major component of problem-solving in the social policy arena is to accommodate the political demand for a common or converging industrial relations agenda with the hard reality of wide variation in national labour market institutions. In this context, respecting national autonomy through the use of subsidiarity procedures is not a pretext for pushing 'minimalist' social policies but the only credible way of making practical advances towards designated policy goals in circumstances that are not particularly congenial.

The third element to deliberative governance is the use of cross-jurisdictional learning. Europe learning from Europe could be the new motif of EU social policy. Benchmarking is the main policy tool behind such learning activities, an approach which holds out much promise. In the first place, as a policy mechanism it is virtually tailor-made for EU social policy with the heavy emphasis on obtaining policy convergence in the context of institutional diversity. Moreover, cross-jurisdictional learning appears particularly suitable at this time as so many Member States are encouraging experimentation because of widespread dissatisfaction with existing arrangements. Benchmarking, in theory at least, allows the lessons of the best (and presumably the worst) practices arising from experimental labour market programmes to be shared across the EU.

A further feature of this policy approach is that it envisions a pathway to policy change which evolutionary theorists of the firm call recombination (Nelson and Winter, 1982). Particular policy measures or relationships between particular programmes are redesigned through a process of incremental adaptation rather than through large-scale reform. It is not that radical policy initiatives are ruled out or regarded as somehow faulty, but simply as exceptional. Moreover, incremental change is not seen as simple tinkering but, potentially at least, as an ongoing process of internal mutation whereby the overall character and orientation of the policy regime can be radically altered through the culmination of small-scale changes. Cross-jurisdictional learning on social policy matters should thus be seen as a method for devising and diffusing innovatory labour market rules.

Deliberative governance can thus foster much-needed and significant policy reforms. It is this possibility that has led some to claim that deliberative governance is not merely a more efficient and sophisticated form of policy-making but actually constitutes a new form of polyarchy in Europe (Cohen and Sabel, 1997). The inference is that institutional frameworks and procedures are being invented that resolve the governance dilemma with regard to economic citizenship by allowing 'national' and 'European' properties to be conjoined. The analysis presented in this article would suggest that such an interpretation claims too much for deliberative governance practices. To be a functioning polyarchy, deliberative governance must have political foundations very different to those that prevail in most modern parliamentary democracies, where policy programmes are normally considered legitimate because they are enacted by a government, or agents of a government, that has won an electoral contest and which is accountable for its actions in subsequent elections. Political legitimacy is derived for the most part from voting competitions. But such 'majoritarian' principles cannot hold centre stage in a deliberative governance polyarchy as so many policies arise from the work of administrative agencies that are more or less independent of representative political structures. Deliberative governance as a polyarchy needs radically different criteria for political legitimization.

A key conclusion from this article is however that while certain properties of deliberative governance are emerging, most European citizens continue to measure the acceptability and legitimacy of EU actions against the 'majoritarian' principles of parliamentary democracy. Put differently, the political dilemma that EU social policy loosens the close bond between economic citizenship and nation-states without being able to replace it with a fully formed model of European economic citizenship has not abated, even though elements of deliberative governance are evident. Even in terms of a model of policy-making, deliberative governance cannot be considered to have reached full maturity. As argued above, it remains questionable whether the EU centre has yet the full resources and capabilities properly to codify and interpret the information arising from the benchmarking of employment policies. Fault-lines remain between national administrative structures and EU institutions, hampering the coordination of policy measures. Such weaknesses may become more acute as the challenges of stabilizing the Euro zone and completing the enlargement exercise loom ever larger.

Thus we must end this article on a level-headed note. Claims that social policy is playing second fiddle to the main market-making activities of the EU centre, or that it is of a piece with a wider novel political architecture for Europe, must be treated with a fair degree of scepticism. At the same time, the deliberative governance machinery that is beginning to underpin EU social policy is a positive development, although scope exists to make it more effective.

## Note

From *European Journal of Industrial Relations*, 7, 1, 2001, pp. 7–26.

## References

Barnard, C., Clark, J. and Lewis, R. (1995) 'The Exercise of Individual Rights in the Member States of the European Union', Department of Employment Research Strategy Paper 0863924492, Sheffield.

Bercusson, B. (1996) *European Labour Law*, London, Butterworths.

Bercusson, B., Deakin, S., Koistinen, P., Kravaritou, Y., Muckeberger, U., Supiot, A. and Veneziani, B. (1996) *A Manifesto for Social Europe?* Brussels: ETUI.

Biagi, M. (1998) 'The Implementation of the Amsterdam Treaty with Regard to Employment: Co-ordination or Convergence?', *International Journal of Comparative Labour Law and Industrial Relations*, 14, 4, pp. 325–6.

Carter, C. and Scott, A. (1998) 'Legitimacy and Governance beyond the European Nation State: Conceptualising Governance in the European Union', *European Law Journal*, 4, 4, pp. 429–45.

Checkel, J. (1999) 'Social Construction and Integration, *Journal of European Public Policy*, 6, 4, pp. 545–60.
Cohen, J. and Sabel, C. (1997) 'Directly-Deliberative Polyarchy', *European Law Journal*, 3, 4, pp. 313–42.
Coombes, D. (1970) *Politics and Bureaucracy in the European Community: A Portrait of the Commission*, London, Allen and Unwin.
Dølvik, J. E. (1997) *Redrawing Boundaries of Solidarity? ETUC, Social Dialogue and the Europeanisation of Trade Unions in the 1990s*, Oslo, Arena/FAFO.
Eichner, V. (1997) 'Effective European Problem-Solving: Lessons from the Regulation of Occupational Safety and Environmental Protection', *Journal of European Public Policy*, 4, 4, pp. 591–609.
European Commission (2000) *Joint Employment Report 2000*, Brussels, EC.
Goetschy, J. (1999) 'The European Employment Strategy: Genesis and Development', *European Journal of Industrial Relations*, 5, 2, pp. 117–38.
Grahl, J. and Teague, P. (1992) 'Integration Theory and European Labour Markets', *British Journal of Industrial Relations*, 30, 2, pp. 495–514.
Haas, E. B. (1958) *The Uniting of Europe: Political, Social and Economic Forces, 1950–57*, Stanford, Stanford University Press.
Hix, S. (1998) 'The Study of the European Union II: The New Governance Agenda and its Rivals', *Journal of European Public Policy*, 5, 1, pp. 36–65.
Hunt, J. (1999) 'Success at Last? The Amendment of the Acquired Rights Directive', *European Law Review*, 24, 3, pp. 215–30.
Joerges, C. (1997) 'From Intergovernmental Bargaining to Deliberative Problem-Solving: The Constitutionalising of Comitology', *European Law Journal*, 3, 2, pp. 273–99.
Knill, C. (1998) 'European Policies: The Impact on National Administrative Traditions', *Journal of Public Policy*, 18, 1, pp. 1–28.
Knill, C. and Lehmkuhl, D. (1999) 'How Europe Matters: Different Mechanisms of Europeanisation', *European Integration Online Papers*, 3, 7, at http://eiop.or.at/eiop/texte/1998–007a.htm.
March, J. and Olsen, J. (1989) *Rediscovering Institutions: The Organizational Basis of Politics*, New York, Free Press.
Marginson, P. (2000) 'The Eurocompany and Euro Industrial Relations', *European Journal of Industrial Relations*, 6, 1, pp. 9–35.
Mény, Y., Muller, P. and Quermonne, J. -L. (1996) *Adjusting to Europe: The Impact of the European Union on National Institutions and Policies*, London, Routledge.
Moravcsik, A. (1999) 'Supranational Entrepreneurs and International Cooperation', *International Organisation*, 53, 2, pp. 267–306.
Nelson, R. and Winter, S. (1982) *An Evolutionary Theory of Economic Change*, Cambridge, Belknap Press.
Neunreither, K.-H. (1993) 'Subsidiarity as a Guiding Principle for European Community Activities', *Government and Opposition*, 28, pp. 206–20.
O'Hagan, E. (1999) 'Industrial Relations within the Integrating European Union: A Comparative Study of Two Peripheral Economies, Ireland and Hungary', Ph.D thesis, Faculty of Legal, Social and Educational Sciences, Queen's University Belfast.
Pollack, M. (1997) 'Delegation, Agency and Agenda-Setting in the European Community', *International Organisation*, 51, 1, pp. 99–134.
Ross, G. (1995) *Jacques Delors and European Integration*, Oxford, Oxford University Press.

Sand, I.-J. (1998) 'Understanding the New Forms of Governance: Mutually Interdependent, Reflexive, Destabilised and Competing Institutions', *European Law Journal*, 4, 3, pp. 271–93.

Schmidt, S. (1998) 'Commission Activism: Subsuming Telecommunications and Electricity under European Competition Law', *Journal of European Public Policy*, 5, 1, pp. 169–84.

Strøby Jensen, C. (2000) 'Neofunctionalist Theories and the Development of European Social and Labour Market Policies', *Journal of Common Market Studies*, 38, 1, pp. 71–92.

Taylor, P. (1996) *The European Union in the 1990s*, Oxford, Oxford University Press.

Teague, P. (1989) *The European Community: The Social Dimension*, London, Kogan Page.

Teague, P. (1999a) *Economic Citizenship in the European Union: Employment Relations in the New Europe*, London, Routledge.

Teague, P. (1999b) 'Reshaping Employment Regimes in Europe: Policy Shifts alongside Boundary Change', *Journal of Public Policy*, 19, 1, pp. 38–72.

Tronti, L. (1998) 'Benchmarking Labour Market Performances and Policies', *inforMISEP*, 61, pp. 32–43.

Weiler, J. (1999) *The Constitution of Europe*, Cambridge, Cambridge University Press.

Wessels, W. (1997) 'An Ever Closer Union? A Dynamic Macro-Political View on Integration Processes', *Journal of Common Market Studies*, 35, 2, pp. 267–99.

# The Open Method of Co-ordination and the European Welfare State

## *Damian Chalmers and Martin Lodge*

### Introduction

Open Method Co-ordination (OMC) has been treated in the literature as the Lazarus of European integration. Developed at the Lisbon Summit, it has led to the reincarnation of the European Union, both in terms of what it does and how it does it. No longer is the European Union to be centred around the Classic Community Method (CCM) of supranational management of regulation. Instead, it is to be a decentred participatory process, in which national governments are no longer controlled and commanded by the imperatives of EC law, but rather commit themselves to review each other's programmes in the light of a series of mutually agreed standards and of domestic and transnational participatory processes. The European Council and its surrounding machinery is placed at the heart of the Union's policy process, and new types of Union–Member State relations are forged which are centred less around classical legal prescriptions, and more around diffuse national adaptation to a wide array of transnational norms, whose form and origin vary (for initial review, see Hodson and Maher, 2001).

[. . .]

The constitution of the Open Method of Co-ordination was set out at the Lisbon European Council, 23–24 March 2000. The central thrust of this European Council was not regulatory reform, however, but the resurrection of its ambitions and revision of its goals.

> 5. The Union has today set itself a *new strategic goal* for the next decade: *to become the most competitive and dynamic knowledge-based economy in the world, capable of sustainable economic growth with more and better jobs and greater social cohesion.*[1]

Four key policies were to be central to this vision, which, if successful, was to deliver 20 million jobs by 2010.

- Better policies for the information society and research and development (R&D).
- Stepping up the process of structural reform for competitiveness and innovation.
- Completion of the internal market.
- 'Modernization' of the European social model.
- Applying an appropriate macroeconomic policy mix.
- An employment policy with a goal of full employment in a society which is more adapted to the personal choices of men and women.
- A Sustainable Development Strategy.[2]

In terms of policy remit, the Lisbon Strategy was very wide-ranging indeed. As the Commission has noted on its website, it covers nearly all of the Union's social, economic and environmental policies.[3] To that end, a variety of regulatory regimes have been used to implement the Lisbon Strategy. The majority of it is still realized through the Classic Community Method of legislation. In its 2002 Review of the Lisbon Strategy, therefore, the Commission found there were fifty-seven legislative acts or proposals for legislation that fell within classic EC competence, compared with thirty-five initiatives for benchmarking (EC Commission 2002a; *our calculation*). The scale of the tasks, however, meant the development of policies involving not merely the regulatory functions of government, but also those of stabilization, allocation and redistribution. New institutional arrangements were necessary for such fields. Traditional harmonization of laws, in which supranational institutions drew up a corpus of legislation, were perceived as too centralized, too *communautaire* and too rigid. In particular, harmonization was felt to be inappropriate where:

- the area of work was closely connected with national identity or culture, e.g. culture or education;
- the instruments for implementing national policies were so diverse and/or complex that harmonization seemed disproportionate in relation to the objectives pursued, e.g. employment;
- [there was] no political will for EC legislation among the Member States but there was a desire to make progress together. (European Convention Secretariat 2002)

In these areas there was, instead, to be a Europeanization of national policy-making, concerned with securing three values. The first, compatibility, required national policies not to have negative effects for the other Member States or the achievement of the objectives of the Union. The second, consistency, entailed that national policies were to enhance each other's effectiveness. Finally, national government performance was to converge.

Open Method Co-ordination was to provide an institutional framework for securing these values. It was to draw upon the methodologies that had first been applied to the European Employment Pact: co-ordination of economic policy and improvement of the interaction between wage developments and monetary, budget and fiscal policy; improvement of labour market efficiency; and structural reform of the goods, services and capital markets. In addition, the method was to be extended to a number of other fields – the information society, research policy, enterprise, education and vocational training, combating social exclusion, immigration policy, and sustainable development.[4] The institutional frameworks that were to govern these areas were to be marked by the following features:

*The fixing of pan-Union guidelines* Guidelines and targets will be set for each policy sector in which OMC is applied with specific timetables to be set for achieving the goals which they set in the short, medium and long terms.

*The development of national action plans in the light of EU guidelines* National action plans are established setting out specific targets and adopting specific measures in such a way as to translate these EU guidelines into national and regional policies, while retaining the freedom to take into account national and regional differences.

*Regular benchmarking and peer review* Quantitative and qualitative indicators and benchmarks are to be established as a means of comparing best practice. The implementation of national action plans is to be regularly reviewed within the Council in the light of these and the pan-Union guidelines.

*Partnership* Regional and local government, as well as the social partners and civil society, will be actively involved in the development and review of national action plans. Such processes will be carried out in the light of 'best practices on managing change' devised by the European Commission, networking with different providers and users, namely the social partners, companies and NGOs.

*Public–private networking* Implementation of OMC will rely primarily on the private sector, as well as on public–private partnerships. It will depend on mobilizing the resources available on the markets, as well as on efforts by Member States. The Union's role will be to act as an 'enabling State' which acts as a catalyst in this process, by establishing an effective framework for mobilizing and bringing together available resources.

At the Barcelona European Council, held in March 2002, the European Council endorsed a review of the Strategy carried out by the Commission (EC Commission 2002a). Its central points were that:

- delivery of the Lisbon goals depended upon a 3 per cent growth rate, which has proved problematic in the economic climate since September 11th;
- it is early days for most areas of OMC; the Commission was still in the process of formulating draft guidelines;
- progress in some areas, notably structural reform of capital markets – the so-called Cardiff Process – was being held back by a failure to agree legislation at the EC level.

The European Council endorsed this curate's egg of a document. But, if the second-year report of the Commission is 'Slow start, but signs of progress' then there are already ominous signs emerging. The formulation of guidelines has appeared to be more drawn-out and complex than might have been anticipated. The Barcelona European Council expressed impatience and stated that the focus must now move to implementation and away from the simple annual elaboration of guidelines.[5] In December 2002, the Union of Industrial and Employers' Confederations of Europe (UNICE) published a report in which it was heavily critical of the Lisbon Strategy, arguing that it had resulted in little structural reform (UNICE, 2002). Meanwhile, others expressed concern at the lack of progress in addressing welfare reform and the absence of any meaningful strategy in the area (EAPN, 2002).

This was reflected in an increased institutional pessimism about OMC. In its report to the 2003 Spring European Council, the Commission assessment was downbeat across all policy sectors. On employment, the Commission noted that despite five years of the European Employment Strategy (EES) there was little evidence of any significant structural reform. There had been some reform of product service and capital markets in areas covered by EC internal market legislation, but weak implementation overall. The cooperation in knowledge, research and development, and innovation had been weak. Progress on social cohesion was difficult to measure, as there was an absence of clear data. The Sustainable Development Strategy still revolved around legislation rather than economic instruments (EC Commission, 2003). Both the European Socialist Party and the European Social Programme, meanwhile, issued statements indicating that they believed the Lisbon Strategy was focusing insufficiently on jobs, growth, and environmental and social goals (PES, 2003; Social Platform, 2003). The British and Finnish prime ministers issued a joint letter stating that structural reform and economic performance had been modest (United Kingdom government, 2003a). The reasons for this become more apparent if the performance of OMC is broken up into three headings.

*Drawing up of pan-Union guidelines* The most developed and detailed, by some way, are the Broad Guidelines on Economic Policies by the Member States (BEPG). These are individually tailored for Member States, discussed extensively and subject to considerable monitoring.[6] It will be remembered that these draw on a similar methodology to OMC and incorporate many of the criteria developed elsewhere in Lisbon. Their basis lies not in Lisbon, but in the commitment developed at Maastricht in Article 99(2) EC to co-ordinate national economic policy, and in the subsequent commitment made in the Stability and Growth Pact to maintain budgets close to balance or in surplus (Artis and Buti, 2000).[7]

The second category encompasses the guidelines set out in the European Employment Strategy. These are less wide-ranging than the BEPG. They focus on elements of employment policy: improving employability; developing a culture of entrepreneurship; promoting the adaptability of firms; and modernizing work by organizing and strengthening equal opportunities. Yet there is a clearly defined and reflexive strategy which has evolved over time to encompass certain 'horizontal objectives', notably the development of lifelong learning, and a broader policy community by attempting to involve the Social Partners in defining, implementing and evaluating the guidelines. They are less detailed and wide-ranging than the BEPG, and are required to be compatible with the BEPG. While evaluation of national action plans to meet the guidelines takes place, country-specific guidelines are not provided (Article 128 EC). Like the BEPG, the Employment Strategy has a longer lineage than OMC, dating back to the Luxembourg European Council in 1997 (Magnus-Johannsen, 1999).

The third category represents the Sustainable Development Strategy (SDS) adopted at the Göteborg European Council in June 2001. The Strategy involves development of national action plans which not only take account of environmental impacts in decision-making, but also address a series of themes, notably climate change, sustainable transport, public health and management of natural resources. While a series of concrete targets have been set, these are less detailed than under either the EES or BEPG. As yet, indicators have not been developed by the Commission and there are no requirements for Member States to present national action plans for actual discussion. Furthermore, while the Sustainable Development Strategy can be said to be a genuine OMC, unlike the other two discussed, it is misleading to see it as such. The SDS is based upon a mode of governance established in 1993 in the Fifth Action Plan on the Environment and Sustainable Development, and continued in the Sixth Environment Action Plan, which is not dissimilar to OMC in that it sets a series of broad EU targets and guidelines and then commits Member States to involving civil society and market-players in the meeting of these targets. It therefore follows pre-existing trajectories, path dependencies and institutional patterns. What is notable, however, is that it does not build on these. Thus the SDS is really a redescription of the Sixth Action Plan, in that it does not carry any of the features that distinguish OMC from it, notably feedback and review of national policies.

The fourth category contains the OMCs against poverty and social exclusion and those on pensions. A series of objectives have been set. These are, however, very broad. They include facilitating participation in employment and access to all resources; preventing the risks of exclusion; helping the most vulnerable; and mobilizing the relevant bodies. While indicators have been established, no quantitative targets or benchmarks are set. Instead, there is merely a requirement that Member States develop national action plans in these areas.[8]

Fifthly, there are a number of areas which are subject to wide-scale benchmarking. These include e-learning, investment in education, early school-leavers, graduates in mathematics, science and technology, upper secondary education attainment and participation in lifelong learning. In such cases, there is no strategy as such. Rather international excellence and the average of the three 'best performing' states are set as a standard of excellence.[9]

Finally, there is one other area, immigration,[10] where proposals for OMC have been made, but there has been little further development.

*Transformation of national practices in the light of Union guidelines*
Detailed constraints have applied to Member States only in the case of the European Employment Strategy and BEPG. In its Five-Year Report on the European Employment Strategy, the Commission noted that there had been a development of new policy paradigms; there was increased policy convergence and some policy-learning. It also noted, however, that there were few transformative effects in those Member States where there was already either a strong pre-existing convergence or divergence with the guidelines, and that these guidelines had led to some unanticipated effects (EC Commission, 2002c). The position with regard to BEPG was less positive. The Commission assessed national progress in implementing country-specific BEPG across three areas – public finances, labour markets and product markets. It measured progress as either good, some or limited. Only two States, Sweden and Denmark, were considered as having made 'good' progress in more than one of these fields, and none in all three fields. In addition, two Member States, Germany and Austria, were regarded as having made only 'limited' progress in two areas (EC Commission, 2003, p. 39). These results have been confirmed by independent research by the Centre for European Reform, which noted that it was both the OMC elements of the Lisbon Strategy that had hitherto produced the most disappointing results, and that it was the performance by the large economies of France, Germany and Italy that provided most cause for concern (Murray, 2003).

*Participation in government* A central feature of the 'new constitutionalist' praise for OMC are the perceived opportunities it offers for participatory democracy (Gerstenberg, 2002). Here, evidence is particularly disappointing. The Commission notes in its Five-Year Review of the European Employment Strategy – an area with established institutional actors – that participation has generally been weak (European Commission, 2002b). Furthermore, there is little evidence that, since 1993, either the Fifth or Sixth Environment Action Plans have served to mobilize civil society or broaden decision-making.

Responses to this crisis seem disjointed. A number of Heads of State have published communiqués, but the policy responses are disjointed and represent different ideological priorities. The German, UK and French governments issued a joint letter (known in EU circles as the 'three tenors' letter) in which they stated that Europe should not become some form of laboratory for regulation; that there should be some further market liberalization, but nothing that imperils Services of General Economic Interest. Agreement focuses only on the establishment of a High-Level Review Body, paralleling the Hartz Commission in Germany, to review labour markets (United Kingdom government, 2003a). The British and Finnish governments argued for wide-ranging structural reform and market liberalization, as an antidote (United Kingdom government, 2003b). The sheer ephemerality of the measure apart, it also represents a damning indictment on the European Employment Strategy, the predecessor of OMC, to develop a coherent approach after five year's operation.

[. . .]

## Notes

From a paper for the ESRC Centre for Analysis of Risk and Regulation, London School of Economics and Political Science, 2003.

1 Presidency Conclusions (Lisbon European Council), Council of the European Union, SN 100/00, 23–24 Mar. 2000 (emphasis added).
2 This Strategy was introduced not at Lisbon but at the Göteborg European Council, 15 June 2001.
3 At www.europa.eu.int/comm/lisbon_strategy/index_en.html (accessed 16 June 2003).
4 This was added by the Göteborg European Council, 15 June 2001.
5 Conclusions of the Presidency of the European Council, 15 and 16 Mar. 2002; para. 39.
6 For the latest, see Decision 2002/549/EC on the broad guidelines of the economic policies of the Member States and the Community, OJ 2002, L 182/1.
7 Regulation 1466/97, OJ 1997, L 209/1.
8 The most recent outlines are contained in a Communication from the Social Protection Committee to the Committee of Permanent Representatives

(COREPER) on 25 Nov. 2002, Doc 14164/02, Rev 1. EC Commission, 'Joint Report from the Council and the Commission on Adequate and Sustainable Pensions', 17 Dec. 2002.

9 For analysis of these see EC Commission, 'European Benchmarks in Education and Training', COM (2002) 629 final.

10 EC Commission, 'Proposal for Open Method Co-ordination on Immigration', COM (2001) 387.

## References

Artis, M. and Buti, J. (2000). ' "Close to Balance or in Surplus": A Policy-Makers Guide to Implementation of the Stability and Growth Pact', *Journal of Common Market Studies*, 38, 4, pp. 563–92.

EAPN (European Anti-Poverty Network) (2002) 'Response to the Commission Synthesis Report for the Barcelona European Council', 15–16 Mar.

EC Commission (2002a) 'The Lisbon Strategy: Making Change Happen', Commission Staff Working Paper, SEC (2002) 29/2.

EC Commission (2002b) 'Taking Stock of Five Years of the European Employment Strategy', COM (2002) 416.

EC Commission (2002c) 'Streamlining the Annual Economic and Employment Policy Co-ordination Cycles', COM (2002) 487.

EC Commission (2003) 'On the Implementation of the 2002 Broad Economic Policy Guidelines', COM (2003) 4.

European Convention Secretariat (2002) 'Co-ordination of National Policies: The Open Method of Co-ordination', WG VI WD015, Brussels, 26 Sept.

Gerstenberg, O. (2002) 'The New Europe: Part of the Problem – or Part of the Solution to the Problem?' *Oxford Journal of Legal Studies*, 22, 4, pp. 563–71.

Hodson, D. and Maher, I. (2001) 'The Open Method as a New Mode of Governance: The Case of Soft Economic Policy Co-ordination', *Journal of Common Market Studies*, 39, 4, pp. 719–46.

Magnus-Johansson, K. M. (1999) 'Tracing the Employment Title in the Amsterdam Treaty: Uncovering Transnational Coalitions', *Journal of European Public Policy*, 6, p. 85.

Murray, A. (2003) *The Lisbon Scorecard III: The Status of Economic Reform in the Enlarging EU*, London, Centre for European Reform.

PES (Party of European Socialists) (2003) 'EU Social Democrats Launch Campaign for Jobs and Sustainable Growth', 14 Mar., at www.eurosocialists.org.

Social Platform (2003) 'Stability Pact and Lisbon Goals: Foes or Allies? The European Spring Council Ought to Choose', press release, 11 Mar.

UNICE (2002) 'Time is Running Out, Action Needed Now – Lisbon Strategy Status 2003', Union of Industrial and Employers' Confederations of Europe, Brussels.

United Kingdom government (2003a) 'A Message of Confidence in the Future of Europe', 5 Feb., at www.inyourarea.gov.uk/output/page1647.asp (accessed 16 June 2003).

United Kingdom government (2003b) 'Towards Full Employment and Greater Productivity in the EU', 6 Mar., at www.inyourarea.gov.uk/output/page3222.asp (accessed 16 June 2003).

# Demographic Challenges to the Welfare State

# Population Ageing: An Unavoidable Future

## *David Coleman*

### Why Population Ageing is Inevitable

The population of the whole world is getting older and the whole world, sooner or later, will have to manage the consequences. This is happening because birth rates have declined, or are declining, almost everywhere, and additionally because older people are surviving to enjoy longer lives. In most richer countries, birth and death rates started to decline in the nineteenth century or earlier. In the case of Japan, this transition has been particularly rapid and did not begin until the twentieth century. In the poorer countries of the world, rapid declines in birth and death rates have only emerged in the last few decades and in a few the process has not begun. But most demographers believe that eventually the whole world will have few children, but long lives.

When death rates first fell, population started to grow fast. The world increased from 2 to 6 billion people in 100 years, and in the process acquired a newly youthful population with its attendant burdens of dependency. Now as populations mature, we are leaving that behind, the rich countries much sooner than the poor ones. We exchange youthful dependants for elderly ones. If the decline in family size halted so that women continued to have about two children on average (which most women say they want) then with current death rates the proportion of persons aged 65 and over in richer countries would eventually remain constant at about 20 per cent of the total (with 19 per cent aged 15 and under) compared with about 15 per cent at present. Such a population would eventually remain constant in size.

With fertility at no more than the 'replacement' rate of just over two children, population, and the size of the workforce, will eventually cease to grow and would remain constant in size except for the contribution from continued decline in death rates. With fertility below this replacement rate, as it is everywhere in the developed world outside the US, population and workforce will eventually decline in numbers. In some countries where fertility is exceptionally low, as in Italy, Germany, Romania, Russia and a few others, deaths already exceed births. In the case of Italy and Germany, where birth rates have been low for a long time, population is prevented from declining only by continued high immigration (for details see Council of Europe, 2000; Eurostat, 2000.)

Even if population decline is averted by replacement fertility, population ageing is bound to progress further, to an extent dependent on further improvements in survival. The lower the level at which fertility will stabilize, the more aged the eventual population structure will be. At an average family size of 1.8, about the level of the higher fertility European countries such as France and Norway, the percentage aged is about 23 per cent. At 1.6, about the European average, it rises to about 28 per cent. With continued lower fertility, like that seen in Japan and the southern European countries, the proportion would rise to over 30 per cent. Older populations and their problems will be a permanent feature of developed societies, and by the end of this century for the whole world, and thereafter for the whole future of the species.

With constant birth rates (at whatever level), eventually all future population ageing will arise from further declines in mortality; although in those circumstances it seems reasonable to expect that vigorous life would also be extended and the boundaries of old age, and retirement, would need to be moved upwards accordingly, as they already have been. Population ageing through longer survival brings, in part, its own solution, as long as most of the additional years of life are active ones.

Population ageing and its problems are consequences of growing up. They seem even worse than they are, because we are coming to the end of a short and transient period of unusually favourable age-structure. For about fifty years in the later twentieth century, the more developed countries could enjoy the new benefits of low dependency from children together with the relatively low proportion of pensioners. This is because the birth rate had declined in most rich countries as early as the 1930s, while small retired age-groups were inherited from an earlier period. That benevolent phase of population structure, a transitional phase between the youth dependency of the past and the aged dependency of the future, is now going. Resources once needed for dependent children must be transferred to the elderly as a new long-term population system is established. 
In the UK and elsewhere, this system has a similar nominal dependency ratio to the previous one but with a different, less favourable composition.

Richer populations have moved from a position where the average age of consumption, once lower than the average age of production, is now higher, perhaps by four years. The maximum real support ratio arises when the two averages are the same, assuming an equal weighting of needs. The delivery channels of support will also be different. Families, which made and still make the greatest provision for children, will see the burden of transfers eased except in those richer countries where family support is traditionally more important for the elderly, notably southern Europe and Japan. A higher proportion of transfers to the elderly will pass through the state. Those populations which also have a tradition of family care for the elderly will suffer most unless they can change their system (Ermisch and Ogawa, 1994).

## What Can We Do about It?

The first point is to be quite clear that there is no 'solution' to the problem of population ageing. There cannot be one short of a return to high rates of population growth or mass age-specific euthanasia. Immigration cannot solve problems of population ageing except at rates of immigration so high that they would generate economically and environmentally unsustainable population growth rates and permanently and radically change the cultural and ethnic composition of the host population (Coleman, 2000). These answers are already well known to demographers.

Recent population projections by the United Nations have drawn attention to the future decline of population size and ageing of the population which is projected in low-fertility countries. Projections made over such a very long range of fifty years are bound to be substantially in error. Nonetheless, by concentrating exclusively on the possible role of migration in 'solving' such problems they have caused widespread misunderstanding. The analysis focuses on the change in the 'potential support ratio', the ratio of the population of nominal old age dependants (aged 65 and over) to persons in the nominally 'active' population (aged 15–64). This ratio is about 4 or 5 : 1 in most richer countries and is projected to fall to between 2 or 3 : 1 in fifty years.

### *Pensions, Fiscal and Workforce Reforms*

What matters, however, is not demographic abstractions such as the potential support ratio but whether the future costs of dependency are sustainable in the economic and social environment of the future. Fiscal and workforce reforms within the demographic system offer many flexible and promising ways of adapting to population ageing and some of the measures are desirable in their own right. Given the powerful effects of economic growth, pensions reform and workforce change on the viability of economic systems, we may be in danger of missing the point by concentrating too much on the outer demographic structure rather than on the fiscal, economic and workforce structures within it. What matters is whether an affordable system can be developed, not what the 'potential support ratios' are or may be in future.

Labour market, retirement and pension reforms, some already under way, together with future expectations of even modest economic growth and productivity, together offer the prospect of a reasonably effective and affordable management of this burden as long as birth rates are not too low, although definitely not a 'solution' (Daykin and Lewis, 1999). We need to consider first the 'real' support ratios, that is the actual number of taxpayers in relation to aged dependent people. In making such calculations we need to take into account the future reduction of dependency arising from the decline of the youthful dependent population. We need to keep in mind the successful negotiation of substantial population ageing already since the beginning of the century, where in the UK the percentage of persons over age 65 has already tripled from 5 per cent to 15 per cent without economic disaster. We should also recall the reality of actual retirement ages today, which are already substantially below 'official' retirement age. Early retirement, late entry into the workforce and modest workforce participation rates already give us actual support ratios of about 2.5 taxpayers per pensioner, not the nominal 4.1 of the potential support ratio (Government Actuary, 1999), without notable problems.

No one management factor can ameliorate the situation all by itself except with considerable discomfort. We therefore need to address simultaneously as many of these contributing factors as possible. For example the European Commission's Annual Review of the Demographic Situation in Europe in 1995 (European Commission, 1996) recognized the contribution of migration to further population increase but noted that recent immigration, at that time declining, had not been primarily related to economic needs. Unemployment among foreigners is indeed much higher than among the native population. It dismissed the notion that immigration could be an adequate compensation for population ageing, as it would require between 8 and 14 times even the then current high level of net immigration (7 million per year by 2024). Productivity growth required to meet the additional demands on the economy created from pensions would be between 0.1 per cent and 0.3 per cent annually up to 2005, increasing to 0.5 per cent per year by 2025. Such an additional diversion to pensions costs would, for example, reduce a real annual GDP growth rate from (say) 3 per cent to 2.5 per cent. Similar conclusions have been reached by other economists in the US (Lee et al., 1988; Lee, 2000).

In the EU, only 62 per cent of the nominal 'active' population aged 15–64 is economically active. This is the lowest of any major industrial area in the world. An increase of workforce participation rates to the levels already achieved in Denmark, for example, or a return to the levels actually achieved among men in the 1960s, would go a long way to meet adverse future ageing changes. However, improvements in workforce participation rates cannot have a further enhancing effect once they have reached their maximum level, beyond say 2020.

The most effective measures would relate to retirement age. While formal retirement age is 65 in most EU states, actual retirement age is about 58 or 59. Preservation of today's actual support ratio would require the actual retirement age to rise by between five and six years, to between 65 and 66. On that basis, managing the additional costs of elderly dependency simply requires people to stop work when they are 'expected' to, at some time in the future. For the UK itself, the scenarios indicate that an annual increase in work productivity rising to 0.8 per cent by 2025 would be needed to cover additional costs of pensions transfers, in the absence of any other measures.

The incorporation of all dependency (all those not working of all ages, including children) into the equation further ameliorates the expectation of future dependency and future costs. All these measures together could restore the future position to about the current level in most European countries at least up to 2020, according to an analysis published in the Economic Survey of the United Nations Economic Commission for Europe in 1999 (UNECE, 1999).

## *Demographic Measures*

The most 'strategic' responses involve the number of people themselves. Population ageing arises from changes in the birth rate and death rate. Only changes in the birth rate are likely to have any important effect in moderating population ageing without incurring the penalty of unsustainable population growth. Even so, replacement fertility – probably the best that can be hoped for – cannot increase the potential support ratio in mature populations to much more than 3 and would not avert some population decline in counties with long experience of below-replacement fertility. However, much lower birth rates, like those of Japan and southern Europe today, would generate an age structure which would be very difficult to manage with the measures described above. What prospect is there of the birth rate increasing in future?

There is little consensus on this point, despite an extensive literature (see, for example, the papers at a recent IUSSP seminar in Tokyo (IUSSP, 2001). There appear to be no limits to low fertility in the predominantly economic models which attempt to explain the variation of fertility (Golini, 1998). Much of the reduction in the usual measures of fertility, as is well known, is due to the postponement of births. But in most populations the recovery of fertility rates at older ages has so far been insufficient to compensate for the decline in earlier ages, pointing to a fall in completed family size to below two children. Most researchers seem pessimistic about a return of fertility to replacement rates in European countries. Nonetheless, spontaneous recovery of fertility to levels closer to replacement might arise from a number of processes. The delay in childbearing has not yet ended in any country and we cannot foretell what will happen when it does. There may be general population-level tendencies to equilibrium. Enhanced welfare arrangements or other measures which improve the status of women, of the kind being considered by UK government, may remove obstacles to childbearing. There may be fundamental biological reasons why fertility is unlikely to drop permanently to very low levels.

The prospect of higher birth rates is underpinned by the consistent finding, after thirty years of surveys, that women in Europe, at least, wish on average to have about two children (although seldom many more). Furthermore, actual birth rates can go up as well as down. Several Scandinavian countries have experienced rising birth rates since the 1980s, although that of Sweden took a sharp downturn in the mid-1990s. The Total Fertility Rate (TFR) in Denmark has declined from its peak but in Norway it continues at over 1.8 (1.84 in 1999). In Ireland, TFR has remained at about 1.9 after falling below replacement level. Of the fifteen EU countries plus Norway and Switzerland, thirteen out of seventeen had a higher TFR in 1999 than in 1998, although the increases were mostly tiny. Recent French data suggests a more substantial increase to 1.9 in early 2000.

Outside Europe, Australia, Canada, New Zealand and the US, none of which have ever seen low birth rates, increased their fertility from the 1980s. The United States continues at about replacement level, New Zealand a bit less. Although ethnic minority fertility is higher than average in those countries, the non-minority population also continue to have higher birth rates than almost any European countries. In the US TFR in all groups increased further from 1998 to 1999, from 2.059 overall to 2.075. In some populations richer and better educated women now have more children than average; female workforce participation is no longer an impediment to the third child, at least in Scandinavia thanks to state compensation measures. For whatever reason, most national and international projections expect a modest recovery in fertility, although stopping short of replacement level.

If the birth rate does not increase spontaneously, is it responsive to public policy measures? Opinion here is strongly divided. Public policy effects upon the birth rate can be intended or (more usually in the West) unintended. Few Western countries explicitly attempt to increase their birth rate, although many are concerned that it is too low (see United Nations, 2000). Most governments favour welfare policies for the family (welfare payments, workplace and housing policies, etc.) for welfare reasons only. While these might incidentally make it easier for women to have the number of children they say they want, most governments still shy away from overtly 'pronatalist' measures or rhetoric. Evaluation of the effects of welfare policies is difficult because there are so many forms of assistance from which families can benefit. Direct family allowances may play only a modest role. Some studies have found evidence only for a weak effect of welfare and fiscal changes on family size and the pattern of family formation (Gauthier and Hatzius, 1997). Others report somewhat stronger effects. In the early 1980s French pronatalist measures were estimated to add about 0.3 to the average family size. The Swedish case in particular is claimed to be an example of precise, if temporary, response of marriage and birth rates and intervals to changes in relative financial advantage, including the fertility downturn following more recent welfare retrenchment and raised unemployment (Hoem, 2000). It is noteworthy that the only developed countries in the world with relatively high birth rates are those which also have high levels of childbearing outside marriage.

Family subsidies of various kinds, state child care, preferential access to housing in the absence of an open housing market and other measures in the former Communist countries of Eastern Europe attempted simultaneously to promote female workforce participation and the birth rate. Although these policies are often dismissed as having had no more than a transient effect, they appear to have maintained fertility there at close to replacement level until their withdrawal during the post-1990 transition period (UNECE, 1999b). However, these policies operated in a system of universally early marriage, limited access to modern contraception and few social outlets as alternatives to family life.

Elsewhere in the industrial world, there may be tenacious cultural impediments to the development of higher birth rates. Theories of 'gender equity' suggest that very low birth rates arise from unbalanced equality for women (McDonald, 2000). If law, state subsidies and cultural preferences allow women some freedom to engage in work and higher education, but still load them unfairly with expectations to care for children, older relatives and the house by themselves, their time and energies will be so squeezed that childbearing will be very delayed and minimized. Paradoxically, this is likely to happen in societies with a traditional 'familist' culture which considers the care of the elderly to be a family matter, resists state interference and consigns women to unequal domestic roles in which men play little part. The low level of fertility in the familist southern European countries, and in Japan, seems unlikely to be reversed without a broader shift in personal and political culture, as well as fiscal measures to support the family and help women to combine work and child care. Societies with high gender inequality will continue to suffer lower birth rates.

## The Situation in the United Kingdom

The example of UK is somewhat anomalous. There is no tradition of population policy by national government in the United Kingdom. However, some local authorities in southern areas, which are the centres of economic growth and population growth (much of the latter from immigration), consider their areas to be 'full' and resist further house construction. There is much concern over the destruction of the natural environment by the spread of urban areas. However, the present government has announced a controversial re-evaluation of immigration policy, previously restrictive if ineffective. It considers that labour migration should be encouraged further to meet specific current shortages and possibly longer term general needs. Demographic concerns (to do with 'population ageing') have so far only been hinted at, and only rather vaguely.

The UK demographic regime is relatively benign; with a total fertility rate which has been around 1.7–1.8 since the 1970s. Population decline is not projected until after 2035 (partly because of existing high immigration); population projections by the official Government Actuary's department forecast a long-term potential support ratio of around 2.5 (today 4.1), with a median age of 42. To preserve today's potential support ratio would require the formal retirement age (now 65/60) to increase to 72. These results underline the conclusion that substantial population ageing will be impossible to avoid. No plausible demographic change makes a big difference. None of these seem to this author to be obviously catastrophic. In the UK 'demographic time-bombs' only go off in the media, not in real life.

No proposals have been suggested, or even considered, specifically addressed to the issue of increasing the birth rate. They would be controversial and probably counterproductive. In fact the only UK government policy aimed at fertility is a specific target to reduce the (high) teenage conception rate by half by 2010, on welfare grounds (Social Exclusion Unit, 1999). If this were eventually successful in reducing teenage fertility to the EU average, it would bring the UK TFR closer to 1.6 than its current 1.7, which other things being equal would make future ageing trends worse.

The UK family support programmes and other welfare arrangements (such as subsidized 'social' housing) are aimed at welfare and have no demographic intentions, although they may, of course, have unintended demographic consequences. By northern European standards they are relatively modest, but the UK nonetheless maintains a relatively high birth rate. Despite heavier subsidies and an explicitly pronatalist programme, the birth rate of the UK's French neighbours has been much the same as that of the UK for many years. French colleagues have attributed this to an excess of careless, unplanned early childbearing in the UK, encouraged perhaps by specifically (unhelpful) British attitudes towards sex education and perverse incentives in the welfare system. UK birth rates in the 15–19 age-group are certainly anomalously high, four times the EU average and large enough to distort the UK age-specific fertility profile compared with that of most other European countries.

Changes are nonetheless happening, although motivated by welfare concerns for the family and the position of women, not to enhance the birth rate as such. The fortuitous intervention of the European Court, for example, obliged the UK government to equalize its pension entitlement age for men and women on sex equality grounds. Welfare considerations suggested equalization at 60. Demographic imperatives argued otherwise. Retirement age for both sexes will be fixed at 65 from 2010–15, occasioning at least a notional marked improvement in UK dependency ratio trends. Under the UK's 'Foresight' programme launched in 1993, steps are also in hand to discourage unjustified disability-based early retirement and to encourage later working. Tax reliefs are being removed from private pensions taken before age 55, the tax system will make working beyond age 65 easier, legislation is being introduced, on US lines, to make age alone inadequate grounds for not hiring, or for dismissing, labour. Both employers and government are likely to discourage favourable early retirement terms in occupational pension schemes (e.g. through the use of 'defined contribution', not 'defined benefit' schemes). Access to ill-health early retirement is likely to be subject to more stringent criteria. 'Phased retirement' will be encouraged whereby the pensioner continues in part-time work, a response currently discouraged by 'final salary' pension schemes where pension is determined by the last level of salary, not the maximum ever reached. Workforce participation by lone parents (lone parenthood is very high in the UK) is being encouraged as a means of reducing welfare dependency.

While some countries have already started to move their retirement age back from the original fixed limits, to 67 in the US and to 65 in Italy and Japan, the UK has not yet decided on such action. However, it can be said that the UK pensions situation is already much more favourable than that in continental Europe. The necessary shift away from primary dependency on state-run pay-as-you-go pension schemes is already far advanced. The solvency of these unfunded transfer schemes, as is well known, is particularly vulnerable to shifts in the population age structure. Maintaining real pension levels will require substantial increases in payroll taxes. In the UK, state pensions are already linked to prices, not to wages. Furthermore, a high proportion of workers are already members of funded occupational or private pension schemes and government policy aims to extend such coverage to an even higher proportion of the population. While funded schemes cannot entirely evade the consequences of population ageing, they offer many advantages over non-funded state schemes.

Costs of ill-health among the elderly have not received the same attention as pensions. Some calculations, taking into account the reduction of child dependency costs, come to quite modest conclusions about the additional real expenditure, at least for the UK. Sixty per cent of the health expenditure on an individual is concentrated in the twelve months before death; 60 per cent of health expenditure therefore depends on the annual number of deaths, which is projected to increase by 17.5 per cent in the EU by 2025.

## Conclusion

In conclusion, a substantial level of population ageing is here to stay. The 'easy' option of encouraging more immigration to address population ageing is demographically ineffective. It would be a short-term measure which enables hard but necessary decisions to be evaded and would bring serious cultural, social and political difficulties and economic costs. Excessive population ageing can be avoided if excessively low birth rates are avoided. Prudent administrative measures, of the kind noted above, should go hand in hand with policies to make the workplace and the tax and welfare systems more favourable to women, so they can fulfil ambitions, consistently stated in surveys, to have more than one child. But in some low-fertility countries, cultural changes in gender equity in the home, difficult for government to influence, will be essential. In different ways, the US and the Scandinavian countries have shown the way, not for the sake of demographic engineering but to promote equity. Look after women's interests, it may be said, and population will look after itself.

### Note

From *Social Biology and Human Affairs*, 66, 2001, pp. 1–11.

### References

Coleman, D. A. (2000) 'Who's Afraid of Low Support Ratios? A UK Response to the UN Population Division Report on Replacement Migration', Expert Group Meeting on Policy Responses to Population Aging and Population Decline, United Nations, New York, at www.un.org/esa/population/popdecline.htm.

Council of Europe (2000) 'Demographic Developments in the Member States of the Council of Europe', Council of Europe, Strasbourg.

Daykin, C. D. and Lewis, D. (1999) 'A Crisis of Longer Life: Reforming Pension Systems', *British Actuarial Journal*, 5 (part 1), 21, pp. 55–113.

Ermisch, J. and Ogawa, N. (eds) (1994) *The Family, the Market and the State in Ageing Societies*, Oxford, Clarendon.

European Commission (1996) *The Demographic Situation in the European Union 1995*, Luxembourg, Office for Official Publications of the European Communities.

Eurostat (2000) *Demographic Statistics 2000*, Luxembourg, Office for Official Publications of the European Communities.

Gauthier, A. H. and Hatzius, J. (1997) 'Family Benefits and Fertility: An Econometric Analysis', *Population Studies*, 51, 3, pp. 295–306.

Golini, A. (1998) 'How Low can Fertility Get? An Empirical Investigation', *Population and Development Review*, 24, 1, pp. 59–73.

Government Actuary (1999) *National Insurance Fund Long-Term Financial Estimates*, Cm 4406, London, Stationery Office.

Hoem, B. (2000) 'Entry into Motherhood in Sweden: The Influence of Economic

Factors on the Rise and Fall in Fertility 1986–1997', *Demographic Research*, 2, article 4 (17 Apr.), online at www.demographic-research.org/volumes/ vol2/4.

IUSSP (International Union for the Scientific Study of Population) (2001) Seminar on Low Fertility, Tokyo, Mar. 2001, at http://demography.anu.edu.au/ VirtualLibrary/ConferencePapers/IUSSP2001/Program.html.

Lee, R. D.(2000) 'Long-Term Population Projections and the US Social Security System', *Population and Development Review*, 26, 1, pp. 137–43.

Lee, R. D. et al., (eds) (1988) *Economics of Changing Age Distributions in Developed Countries*, Oxford, Clarendon Press.

McDonald, P. (2000) 'Gender Equity in Theories of Fertility Transition,' *Population and Development Review*, 26, 3, pp. 427–40.

Social Exclusion Unit (1999) *Teenage Pregnancy,* Cmnd 4342, London, HMSO.

UNECE (UN Economic Commission for Europe) (1999a). 'Demographic Ageing and the Reform of Pension Systems in the ECE Region', Papers from the ECE Spring Seminar, May 1999, *Economic Survey of Europe 1999*, no. 3, pp. 45–113.

UNECE (UN Economic Commission for Europe) (1999b) 'Fertility Decline in the Transition Economies, 1982–1997: Political, Economic and Social Factors', *Economic Survey of Europe 1999*, no. 1, ch. 4, pp. 181–94.

United Nations (2000) Expert Group Meeting on Policy Responses to Population Aging and Population Decline, New York, United Nations, at www.un.org/esa/ population/popdecline.htm.

# The Evolving Concept of 'Retirement': Looking Forward to the Year 2050

*James H. Schulz*

Almost a half century ago, Eugene Friedmann and Robert Havighurst (1954) pioneers in the field of social gerontology, described retirement:

> Retirement is not a rich man's luxury or an ill man's misfortune. It is increasingly the common lot of all kinds of people. Some find it a blessing; others, a curse. But it comes anyway, whether blessing or curse, and it comes often in an arbitrary manner, at a set age, without direct reference to the productivity or the interest of the individual in his work.

What Friedmann and Havighurst were referring to was the fact that retirement is a product of the industrial revolution. Older people before that historic economic event were not 'retired' people, and there was no retirement role. A big part of the dramatic growth in economic productivity arising from the industrial revolution was a change in the terms of employment – resulting in increased leisure. This increase was particularly marked during a period towards the end of life that became known as 'retirement'.

However, not all workers retired. A few avoided this new opportunity to leave the labour force. Writing about the retirement decision in his book *Chronicles of Wasted Time*, Malcolm Muggeridge (1973) observes: 'Few men of action have been able to make a graceful exit at the appropriate time.' While retirement has been avoided over the years by 'men of action' (a few statespeople and many self-employed farmers and professionals), that is not the interesting part of this historic transformation. Of more importance is the fact that most people do not avoid retirement, do not want to, and in fact retire *as soon as it is economically feasible*. Any list of the most significant developments of the twentieth century should include the dramatic decline in male older worker participation rates over that century and the sharp rise in leisure that went with it.

In recent years, there have been increasing numbers of people predicting that the decline in labour force participation rates has come to an end. And there are many who now argue that the economics of 'population ageing' require people to work longer in the future. It is to this future that this article looks. How is the retirement concept changing throughout the world, and what are the implications for people who reach old age, say, five decades from now? This writer approaches these questions with a crystal ball in one hand and, in the other, thirty-six years of experience doing research on the economics of ageing.

## Economic Growth is the Key to the Retirement of the Future

It is not demography but *economic growth rates* that will determine the future nature of retirement. One of the biggest hoaxes perpetrated in the industrialized world today is the promulgation of the notion that the ageing of population around the world has created a 'crisis'.

What crisis? Is it true that changing demography will place an unsustainable economic burden on nations, given current pension and healthcare programmes? Many argue that unless a radical reduction in retirement benefits occurs, older persons will consume so much of the national output that, as one respected business publication put it, we will end up 'consuming our children' (Chakravarty and Weisman, 1988). Here is an illustrative but typical statement by two economists:

> In every [developed] nation the elderly retire into a world of guaranteed income support and health insurance coverage. And, thus far, the reaction of the developed world to population aging has been to simply increase spending on the elderly . . . Such a reaction to population aging is not sustainable. (Gruber and Wise, 2001)

Such assertions are almost always supported solely by demographic projections of rising 'dependency ratios' and projections of sharply increasing social security tax rates using controversial assumptions. They are rarely supported by sophisticated economic analysis. Analysing the *economic* impact of population changes is a far more difficult challenge than simply presenting demographic dependency ratios (see Easterlin, 1995).

In research that modelled the economic impact of population ageing, we showed that relatively small increases in economic growth rates have the potential to substantially moderate the ill effects of other factors (such as demography) that have a negative impact (Schulz et al., 1991). In fact, the research concluded that, for the United States, the overall support burden pertaining to non-working individuals (both young and old) could be less in the years 2030–50 than it was during the 1950–70 period – assuming a relatively *high rate of economic growth*.[1]

How many years will the future aged be able to spend in retirement? The answer depends fundamentally on the growth of economic output relative to the size of the labour force. The potential impact of demographic ageing on growth has been a major issue for decades in the debate about the roles of public and private pensions. Economists today are virtually unanimous in stressing the need to increase national saving in order to promote economic growth. This emphasis on saving results in part from a long tradition in economics. Both traditional neoclassical growth theory and more recent growth theory give major attention to the role of saving. Economist Robert A. Blecker (1997) points out: 'Since the late 1970s, mainstream macroeconomics has been dominated by a conservative policy consensus, which emphasizes raising national saving rates and avoiding government intervention in financial or labor markets.' But there is a growing literature (discussed in Barr, 2000; Schulz, 1999) that questions this emphasis, especially in connection with pension policy. Recent research suggests that increasing private saving, other factors unchanged, does little to raise private investment. In fact, econometric analysis by Gordon (1995) strongly supports the view of some economists that investment generates saving, not vice versa.

Moreover, there is not just one factor (saving) or two (saving and investment) that are the key determinants of economic growth. While saving and investment are necessary, they are not sufficient to ensure the rate of growth will be adequate to achieve any specified set of goals. There are many other factors that are important – probably more so. These would include the rate of technological change, the willingness of producers to take risks, management organizational and human resource skills, the extent of entrepreneurial drive, and the quality of education and training given to young and old entrants into the labour force.

Therefore, we are left with two conclusions: first, that economic growth is the product of many factors – not just saving and investment in physical capital; and, second, that economic growth is the key to leisure and the primary determinant of potential future leisure.

[. . .]

## Population Ageing: 'Let's Put the Old Folks Back to Work'

[W]ith the approaching retirement of the 'baby boomers' and the consequent demographic ageing, there arise new concerns about retirement policy. As William Jackson (1998) points out: 'A new policy question has arisen: how should we adjust economic and social arrangements to allow for a rising and permanently higher proportion of old people? This question has never been posed or answered before, and its very novelty may provoke alarm.' Population ageing was unknown before the twentieth century. Now there are ageing populations throughout the world (in both industrialized and developing countries). The so-called rising burden of the elderly population in terms of pension and medical costs is a matter of major concern in many countries.

There is a large literature debating the nature of the impact of population ageing and especially its economic ramifications. Much of the focus is on elderly pension and healthcare benefits (and their costs). While there are big differences in views on this question, there seems to be a general consensus that population ageing will require some changes in these two areas – given the projected size of expenditures. Some see a need to *radically* change income provision in old age through privatization of pensions. Others, instead, would *incrementally* reduce pension and health benefits, while also raising taxes by a small amount.

One frequent proposal is to force the elderly population to pay more of the costs and also to encourage older persons who are generally healthy and living longer to work longer; in fact, a number of countries have recently begun to raise the 'normal' age of retirement for full pension benefits. In this regard, Victor Fuchs (2001) argues:

> If health care expenditures for the elderly continue to grow rapidly . . . and if the ability to finance these expenditures by transfers from the young reaches its limit, the only alternative is for the elderly to pick up a large share of the bill. If these payments must come from incomes that grow at only a modest pace, the elderly will become increasingly 'health care poor'. . . . To prevent more and more elderly becoming 'health care poor', they must have additional personal income. They need more income from savings (including pensions and investments) and from earnings, which means they will have to work more both before and after age 65.

But is this feasible based on what we know about past practice and current attitudes? Employers may not need, or be inclined to hire, older workers. Moreover, older people may not want the new jobs, even if they are offered. Without dramatic changes in the ability of countries to moderate business cycles and keep unemployment low over the long run, there may be little change in current provisions that encourage retirement and 'early retirement'. I think that, as in the past, we can expect employers, unions, politicians, and workers themselves to continue supporting mechanisms that encourage older workers to retire at increasingly early ages during periods when unemployment is high.

The issue is further complicated by attitudes of older workers towards work and training. As they grow older, most workers become very choosy about the work they are willing to do – especially if retirement is a financially feasible option through pension benefits. Also, with increasing age comes an understandable reluctance to uproot oneself and make the geographic moves often associated with attractive employment opportunities.

However, there is one factor regarding older worker employment that is often overemphasized: the possible mismatch of older worker skills with future jobs. There is a stereotypical scenario of the job situation in the future which runs something like this. Under the pressure of foreign competition, nations are producing overwhelming numbers of unappealing, low-paying jobs for people of all ages. With the decline in traditional manufacturing industries, more and more workers (both young and old) will be forced in the future to sell 'fast foods' – chicken nuggets and hamburgers at Kentucky Fried Chicken and McDonald's.

Growth in jobs, according to this stereotype, lies in two typical areas: the expansion of eating and drinking establishments and the mushrooming information technology/computer industries. Both areas are seen as poor sources of new jobs for most older workers. Work at McDonald's is tedious and pays poorly, whereas computer jobs are thought to be too demanding in their education and skill requirements. Hence, the argument goes, it will be hard to match the work desires of older workers with the jobs becoming available, unless older workers are ready to settle for 'lousy jobs'.

This potential problem, however, tends to be overdramatized in policy discussions. A closer look at the occupational shifts taking place in industrial countries indicates that most older workers can be matched with appropriate jobs. Most of the new jobs in the future will be in a broad span of industries – including business services, medical services, construction, financial services, and information processing of many types. A large number of the new jobs in these industries are unexotic but often challenging, and can be done by a wide range of workers of any age (Schulz, 1990). Examples are jobs as healthcare specialists, clerks, drivers, salespeople, maintenance personnel, and receptionists.

The problem lies not so much in the nature of the jobs and their skill requirements but in the attitudes of both older workers and their potential employers, in the rigid structure of the workplace, in current hiring practices, in the prevailing wage structure and compensation policies, and in attitudes towards training older workers.

## Attitudes: The Big Barrier to Employment

Without a doubt, the most serious barrier to the re-employment of older workers today is the attitudes of the workers themselves and their potential employers – especially with regard to the issue of productivity and the ability to train older workers. Conventional notions about workers' abilities die hard. Many older workers and most employers truly believe that productivity almost always declines with age and, as the old saying goes, 'old dogs cannot learn new tricks'. Moreover, work environments may remain very rigid with regard to making adjustments to job requirements and remuneration patterns – making it nearly impossible to easily match older workers with existing employment opportunities.

Clearly, there is a need for major changes in employer and union attitudes/practices regarding the training and employment of individuals over the life cycle. As the rate at which young people enter the labour force slows in coming years, businesses will be forced to rethink how they will get the labour necessary for producing their products and services.

However, the outcome of that rethinking is not as predictable as some writers suggest. Firms can respond to demographic changes in the availability of labour in a number of ways; recruiting and hiring different types of workers (such as older workers) is *only one of many ways*. Alternatively, firms can invest in more physical capital that reduces labour needs; or encourage liberalization of immigration policies favouring applicants with needed skills; or encourage more women with children to stay in the labour force by, for example, offering daycare facilities; or shift production processes to developing countries with large labour surpluses and cheap wages.

As a consequence, the new demographic profile evolving in industrialized countries does not necessarily mean there will be serious labour shortages in the future. Nor does it mean that all older workers will find that it is much easier to obtain suitable re-employment after losing or shifting jobs. Hopefully, however, the new demographics do provide an opportunity to devise and promote better policies and programmes for a more efficient use of potential labour force participants. Raising the size and productivity of the labour force through human resource policies is a major alternative to current calls by some for cutbacks in retirement benefits for the old.

Thus, the biggest 'retirement issue' of the new century is likely to be whether both workers and employers see the need and are willing to *modify the retirement 'right'*. Will it be changed to include what each group sees as viable work options in later life to complement the retirement life everyone now expects and almost all enjoy?

## Productive Ageing

In recent years, a number of gerontologists have sought to promote an analytical framework that emphasizes the fact that almost all individuals are engaged in productive activities throughout most of their lives, including the retirement period.[2] The concept of 'productive ageing' has developed in part as a reaction to the limited view of work as defined by economists and the resulting structure of the national income and product accounts which measure the aggregate economic output of the nation. Given present practices, many of the activities and contributions made after (and some before) retirement are not counted in official statistical reckonings of national economic activity.

The productive ageing framework accepts the economic paradigm that focuses on activities that have 'value'. But it seeks to expand the definition of economically valuable activities beyond those whose value is determined by economic markets. Herzog and Morgan (1992), for example, argue that government 'social reporting efforts aimed at monitoring productivity and how it might change as a function of the age of the person are biased by the way productivity is operationalized in most available social statistics'.

In general, the proposed approach to deal with these limitations is to include both traditional market *and* non-market economic activities that result in the production of goods and services. Bass, Caro and Chen (1993), in the introduction to their edited book on productive ageing, expand this view by adding to their definition of productive ageing activities that *develop the capacity* to produce goods and services.

But as Bass, Caro and Chen point out, even with this change, most definitions of productive ageing would exclude 'many important and constructive activities undertaken by the elderly. They exclude, for example, such activities as reflection, worshiping, meditation, reminiscing, reading for pleasure, carrying on correspondence, visiting with family and friends, traveling, and so forth'. Given these exclusions, and others, not everyone agrees with an approach that focuses a discussion of roles in later life almost solely on older persons' *economic* activities and potential.

A different approach is one that seeks to escape from the economic paradigm and looks at the later years of life in primarily non-economic terms. Philosopher Harry Moody (1993) strongly criticizes the productive ageing concept. He argues that:

> By insisting on the productivity of the old, we put the last stage of life at the same level as the other stages. This transposition implicitly sets up a kind of competition or struggle (who can be the most productive?) which the old are doomed to lose as frailty increases. By celebrating efficiency, productivity or power, we subordinate any more claim for the last stage of life in favor of values that ultimately depreciate with meaning of old age.

Moody warns that while the proponents of productive ageing emphasize non-coercion, options, and opportunity, 'productive aging easily can become a subtle means of social control and implies a modification of the "bureaucratized" life course, and in ways that at present remain imponderable'. As Moody points out, productive ageing is more than a matter of semantics. It is a substantive answer to the question: What is later life for?

To me, it seems appropriate to use a framework that is broader than the economic productivity focus. There is a need for a 'wider vision' of late-life 'productivity' that includes altruism, citizenship, stewardship, creativity, and the search for faith. With this broader view, we can see that *retirement is more than stopping paid work and engaging in more leisure activities.* It is a period of life where a variety of special activities compete with the traditional activities of work and leisure for the attention and time of older people.

## Retirement in the Future

We are now ready to draw from the above discussion some of the probable characteristics of retirement in future years. As the World Health Organization has recently stated in a discussion paper for the Second UN World Assembly on Ageing:

> It is time for a new paradigm, one that views older people as active participants in an age-integrated society and as active contributors . . . [The paradigm should challenge] the traditional view that learning is the business of children and youth, work is the business of midlife, and retirement is the business of old age. (WHO, n.d.)

Attitudes towards retirement in the future are likely to move sharply away from the simplistic view of all work before retirement and no work after. Some of the resulting changes we can expect to see are as follows.

*More part-time work* At the same time as rates of retirement have increased, there has also been a large increase in the number of continuing workers who work part-time. Figures 1 and 2 show the increases between 1983 and 1991, averaging the rates for ten countries in the European Union.

A survey of workers in the United States (The Health and Retirement Study) found that nearly three-quarters of the respondents in the first wave of this longitudinal study said that they would 'prefer to phase down from full-time work to part-time work when they retire' (Gustman et al., 1995). Part-time work appeals to many older workers for a variety of reasons. Many see it as a way of escaping from the demands and problems related to their prior full-time work. Part-time work is also growing because of the increased labour force participation of women, since this option has always been a way of their coping with multiple family responsibilities and personal preferences. The UK House of Commons (1999) has pointed out that:

> Two distinct trends can be identified in EU countries' approaches to part-time working. A growing number of countries are developing ways to make part-time work more attractive as a means of promoting the diversity of working choices. On the other hand, strategies in the Nordic countries in par-

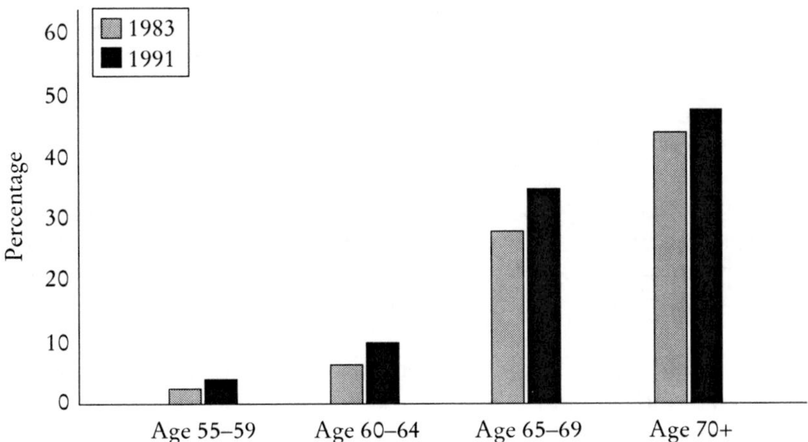


**Figure 1** Part-time male workers in ten European countries (aggregate data), 1983 and 1991
*Source*: Eurostat.

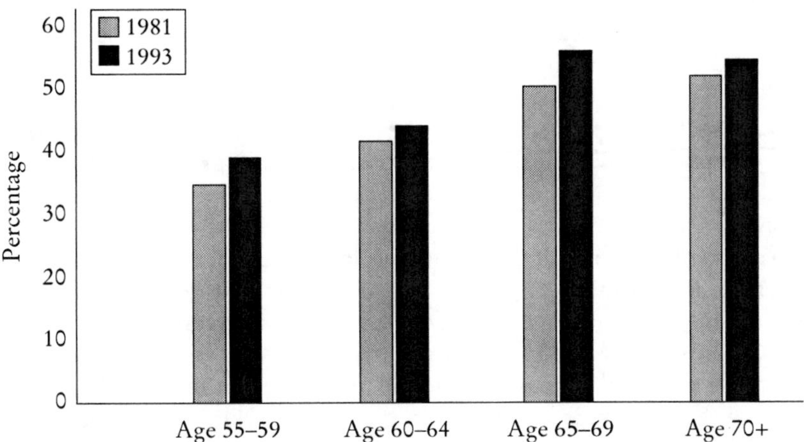


**Figure 2** Part-time female workers in ten European countries (aggregate data), 1981 and 1993
*Source*: Eurostat.

ticular have been based on the full-time norm enabling opportunities for part-time work to be associated with a reduction in full-time hours.

Also, some governments have encouraged part-time work policies as a way of dealing with unemployment problems. For example,

> since 1993, French employees have been entitled to take phased early retirement between the ages of 55 and 65. Early retirement schemes with the principal aim of creating jobs were introduced on an experimental basis in France in 1996, covering both the public and private sectors (House of Commons, 1999).

As we indicated earlier, attitudes towards older workers and different patterns of work in old age are one key to the future. In this regard, the social science literature to date indicates that there is still an unyielding barrier to change regarding work patterns. Regardless of the many advocates of flexible retirement options, real changes will not occur 'unless management becomes more interested in varying work schedules for older workers' (Siegenthaler and Brenner, 2000). Hopefully the changing dimensions of an ageing workforce as the number of young entrants sharply declines will help to encourage this change. And given that workers, employers, and governments find the part-time work option attractive (often for different reasons), the trend towards more part-time employment in the later years is likely to continue.

*Expanded 'citizen participation'* If part-time employment increases in future years, will overall paid labour force participation increase? As indicated above, I do not think that will happen – at least not to any significant extent.

The recent levelling off of labour force participation rates results from a variety of labour market factors, such as the buoyant demand for labour during a record period of economic prosperity. It also results from the fact that the most likely groups to retire early are now doing so. The result is that those still working full-time in old age are few in number. Moreover, many of these workers are not inclined to stop working, given their occupational situations (e.g. farmers).

But two things are likely to happen. First, part-time job opportunities will broaden, given the discussion above and the fact that the demographic decline in new young entrants will encourage employers to respond to the part-time work preference of older workers. Second, there will be an expansion in work not currently counted as 'employment' in the official statistics. Studies show that older persons are not totally opposed to work but often want work that is more rewarding or different from their earlier '9 to 5' jobs. Clearly, for many people the retirement years are becoming an attractive period of exploration and reflection. Relieved of some (or most) of the pressures to work 'to survive', we can expect to see a growth in volunteer work and community and family assistance and involvement, and a rising concern about the environment and the quality of life. Older people in the coming decades will not just sit in their rocking chairs and watch television. They will continue to be active but with a new combination of leisure and work activities – new forms of what might be called 'citizen participation'.

*An older workforce with more training* The composition of the labour force in industrialized countries is undergoing a fundamental change as populations age. Fewer younger people are entering the workforce each year. For example, in the United States, beginning around 1981, there has been a sharp annual decline in the number of new entrants (see figure 3). By the year 2005, the median age of the United States workforce is projected to be over 40 years, compared with 35 years in 1979. In Europe, there is a great deal of concern about labour shortages. One recent estimate (Eberstadt, 2000) is that Europe would need to have sustained net migration at four times its current level in order to satisfy worker demand owing to decline in the working-age population. One option is to retrain older workers.

Up till now, the retraining of older workers has been sporadic at best. 'Lifelong learning' of skills that can be used in new jobs is one of those ideas that many people talk about but few people take seriously.

Why have we paid only lip service to the idea of learning throughout a worker's lifetime? First, there has been a widespread belief that the wonders of science have created a situation where there is no longer enough work for everyone. Technological innovation and modern production methods – such as mass production, new energy sources, complex machines, and

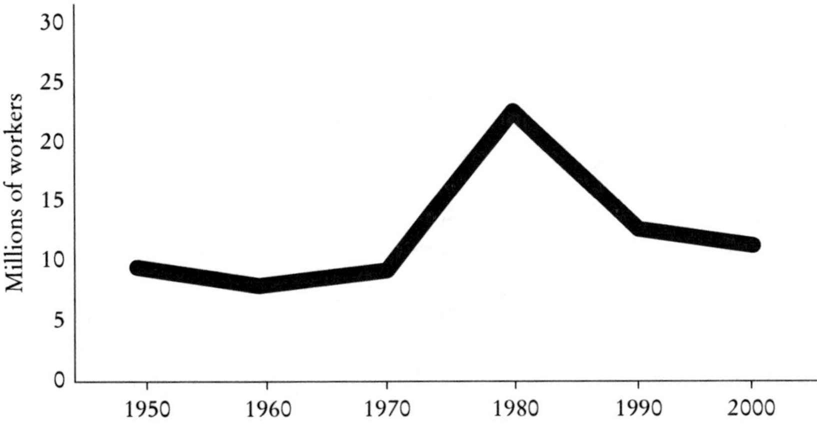


**Figure 3** Entrants to the US workforce (millions of workers)
*Source*: Population Reference Bureau.

robotics – are seen as creating a surplus of workers. Many people argue that nations should recognize the reality of 'surplus labour' and spread the available work around, creating shorter work weeks and earlier retirement. Given the seemingly unlimited desire of people for old and new products and services, economists argue that this view is erroneous – that scarce resources (including labour) will never be sufficient to keep up with growing demand. But the idea of labour surplus as a result of technological revolutions remains strong among many non-economists. In such a world of labour surplus, there would seem to be no need for workers to be retrained, especially as they get older – and also given that there often seems to be no shortage of workers when unemployment is high.

Second, even if a need for labour develops, the view is often that older workers are not as likely to be suitable for the new jobs. This is because it is believed that work performance declines with age. However, this view is not so much the result of research and fact as it is of prejudice and ignorance. To the extent that there has been research, it in large part contradicts the prevailing views of employers. Regarding performance, Sterns and McDaniel (1994) point out that

> an extensive body of research indicates that age and job performance are by no means highly correlated. If performance does anything with age, it improves slightly, but the relationship is very weak. This is true regardless of whether performance is measured by supervisory ratings or through other more objective productivity measurements.

Technological change and robotics have not made human employment unnecessary. Moreover, research shows that most older workers can learn and can be as productive as young workers. In addition, they are able to bring to their new job the insights and wisdom that come with years of experience.

But even if older workers can be retrained, most employers view them as more costly than alternative sources of labour – such as a nation's youth, middle-aged women returning to the workforce, and workers in developing countries. The fact is that up till now unions, government, and business have thought that it is cheaper to terminate workers at early ages than to retrain them for the new jobs being constantly created.

Third, as we have stressed repeatedly in this article, retirement policy to date has been determined over the past sixty years mostly by efforts to deal with chronic unemployment. Why retrain workers, it is argued, when the country cannot even employ the workers already looking for work?

In the future, however, there is likely to be pressure on governments and employers to reverse this lack of interest in retraining. Potential labour shortages in the future are an increasing worry to many industries – despite the current high levels of unemployment in some industrialized countries.

The biggest pressure is likely to come from workers themselves. Over the past couple of decades, job insecurity has risen dramatically among workers at later ages (when job security has traditionally been the highest) and among white-collar workers (again, where job security has historically been relatively high). Many workers have been unable or unwilling to retire as a result of 'downsizing', mergers, employment shifts triggered by global competition, and other results of the new world economic situation. They have had to take what have come to be called 'bridge jobs' – transitional jobs between their prior 'regular' jobs and retirement. Often these jobs are less desirable, given the barriers to 'regular' employment for workers at older ages.

If this bridging phenomenon continues, we can expect workers, and perhaps their unions, to pressure governments and employers to provide retraining. Many governments currently give huge tax subsidies to encourage people to save for retirement and to retire early but give very little in the way of incentives for them to seek out the education and training they need to work longer. Likewise, every country spends huge sums of money on its educational institutions, but those expenditures are almost exclusively for younger people. We can expect to see that imbalance in government resources changed as older workers demand better job opportunities when forced to leave regular employment before retirement.

## Towards a More Flexible Retirement

Pensions were an invention of the twentieth century, designed to provide more secure and more adequate income for various non-working people. They were in large part a reaction to the growing insecurity arising out of the industrial revolution and the inability of families to cope with it by themselves. One almost accidental consequence of creating pensions was a dramatic decline in labour force participation at later ages and the introduction of a new phase of life – retirement.

The first pension schemes were very rigid. Public schemes set a 'normal age of retirement' and often financially penalized workers who deviated from it. Ages of eligibility were relatively high. Employer-sponsored pensions typically rewarded only those workers who stayed with the company, and their provisions were equally rigid.

Eventually this changed. Employers and unions found that pensions could be an important tool in dealing with various labour problems. Initially pensions were used to promote employee loyalty and to deal with special circumstances: physical decline, work accidents, job loss arising from skill obsolescence, and problems arising from cyclical economic instability.

Gradually, however, workers, unions, and governments began to treat retirement through pensions as a 'right'. Workers and unions then pushed for pension benefits that made it possible to retire at a relatively high standard of living. Employers generally acquiesced in this goal. In some cases, they even led the movement to ever earlier retirement. For employers, pensions became an important way of managing their workforce. They saw it as a good way of dealing with the labour force adjustments required by ever changing competitive market conditions.

Much of the rigidity of pensions and the resulting rigidity of retirement policies has disappeared. Pension provisions now allow retirement over a broad span of years without actuarially unfair penalties. Nations have created a variety of mechanisms that provide flexibility and create many 'pathways to retirement' (Kohli et al., 1991).

There has not been a comparable evolution of opportunities with regard to working in the later years. Mandatory retirement provisions, age discrimination practices, lack of retraining opportunities, etc. are still widespread. But looking ahead to the future, we are likely to see the beginning of much greater flexibility in older workers' work and retirement patterns. We are likely to see (a) greater flexibility in hours worked, (b) an expansion in what society considers 'work', and (c) greater opportunities for retraining and new careers in the later years. These changes, together with increases in pension plan normal retirement ages, will no doubt result in a small rise in labour force participation rates among some groups of workers.

However, we should not expect the changes to produce a dramatic upswing in labour force participation. Market-oriented economies will still have to struggle with chronic unemployment problems and, as a result, retirement policy will continue to be influenced by the issue: Who gets the available jobs when full employment does not exist? In addition, for most workers the choice between retirement and work, if income is adequate, is no choice at all: retirement is clearly the preferred status. And if economic growth continues at a reasonable pace, more leisure than we enjoy today will be possible in the future. How that increased leisure will be distributed throughout the life cycle is impossible to predict.

One of the important gains from industrialization has been to fundamentally change the nature of old age. Instead of working (often in unpleasant jobs) till ill-health forces older workers to quit, people now have a meaningful choice between paid work and retirement. Some today would like to roll back those gains and put people back to work – given the so-called pension crisis. Even if the crisis were real (and that is debatable), it is unlikely (I think) that workers would be willing to solve it by significantly decreasing the retirement/leisure period. Time will tell.

## Notes

From *International Social Security Review*, 55, 1, 2002, pp. 85–105.

1 The basic projections were carried out using a real growth rate of 3.0 per cent. Sensitivity testing was then carried out using lower and higher rates, demon-

strating that the burden is very sensitive to the growth rate but not as sensitive to assumptions with regard to either population growth or labour force participation rates.

2 This section is based on material appearing in Schulz (2001).

## References


Barr, N. (2000) '*Reforming Pensions: Myths, Truths, and Policy Choices*', International Monetary Fund Working Paper 00/139, Washington DC.

Bass, S., Caro, F. and Chen, Y. (eds) (1993) *Achieving a Productive Aging Society*, Westport, CT, Auburn House.

Blecker, R. (1997) 'Review of *Macroeconomic Policy after the Conservative Era: Studies in Investment, Saving and Finance*, by G. Epstein and H. Gintis', *Journal of Economic Literature*, 35, 1.

Chakravarty, S. and Weisman, K. (1988) 'Consuming our Children?', *Business Week*, 14 Nov.

Easterlin, R. (1995) 'Economic and Social Implications of Demographic Patterns', in R. Binstock and L. George (eds), *Handbook of Aging and the Social Sciences*, San Diego, CA, Academic Press.

Eberstadt, N. (2000) *Prosperous Paupers and Other Population Problems*, New Brunswick, CT, Transaction.

Friedmann, E. and Havighurst, R. (1954) *The Meaning of Work and Retirement*, Chicago, University of Chicago Press.

Fuchs, V. (2001) 'The Financial Problems of the Elderly: A Holistic Approach', National Bureau of Economic Research Working Paper no. W8236, Cambridge, MA.

Gordon, D. (1995) 'Putting the Horse (Back) before the Cart: Disentangling the Macro Relationship between Investment and Saving', in G. Epstein and H. Gintis (eds), *Macroeconomic Policy after the Conservative Era*, New York, Cambridge University Press.

Gruber, J. and Wise, D. (2001) 'An International Perspective on Policies for an Aging Society', National Bureau of Economic Research Working Paper no. W8103, Cambridge, MA.

Gustman, A, Mitchell, O. and Steinmeier, T. (1995) 'Retirement Measures in the Health and Retirement Study', *Journal of Human Resources* (special issue), 30 5.

Herzog, A. and Morgan, J. (1992) 'Age and Gender in the Value of Productive Activities', *Research on Aging*, 14, 2.

House of Commons (1999) *Education and Employment: Second Report*, London, Stationery Office.

Jackson, W. (1998) *The Political Economy of Population Aging*. Cheltenham, Edward Elgar.

Kohli, M., Rein, M., Guillemard, A. and van Gunsteren, H. (1991) *Time for Retirement: Comparative Studies of Early Exit from the Labor Force*, New York, Cambridge University Press.

Moody, H. (1993) 'Age, Productivity, and Transcendence', in S. Bass, F. Caro and Y. Chen (eds), *Achieving a Productive Aging Society*, Westport, CT, Auburn House.

Muggeridge, M. (1973) *Chronicles of Wasted Time*. London, Collins.

*Productive Aging News* (1993) 'NIA Expert Sees a Revolution in Living for 21st Century', July–Aug.

Schulz, J. (1990) 'What can Japan Teach us about an Aging US Work Force?', *Challenge* (Nov.–Dec.).
Schulz, J. (1999) 'Saving, Growth, and Social Security: Fighting our Children over Shares of the Future Economic Pie?', in R. Butler, L. Grossman and M. Oberlink (eds), *Life in an Older America*, New York, Century Foundation Press.
Schulz, J. (2001) 'Productive Aging – An Economist's View', in N. Morrow-Howell, J. Hinterlong and M. Sherraden (eds), *Productive Aging: Concepts and Challenges*, Baltimore, Johns Hopkins University Press.
Schulz, J., Borowski, A. and Crown, W. (1991) *Economics of Population Aging: The 'Graying' of Australia, Japan, and the United States*, Westport, CT, Auburn House.
Siegenthaler, J. and Brenner, A. (2000) 'Flexible Work Schedules, Older Workers, and Retirement', *Journal of Aging and Social Policy*, 12, 1.
Sterns, H. and McDaniel, M. (1994) 'Job Performance and the Older Worker', in S. Rix (ed.), *Older Workers: How do they Measure Up?* Washington DC, Public Policy Institute, American Association of Retired Persons.
WHO (n.d.) 'Health and Ageing: A Discussion Paper' (1st version), World Health Organization, Department of Health Promotion, Geneva.

# The Global Retirement Crisis

## *Richard Jackson*

[ . . . ]

'Demography is destiny,' demographer Richard Easterlin famously observed. When it comes to public budgets, it certainly is. Rising longevity and falling fertility translate directly into a lower ratio of taxpaying workers to retired beneficiaries, and this in turn translates into a higher cost rate for retirement programmes.

[ . . . ]

[In 2001] the European Commission (EC) and the OECD published long-term projections of the impact of global aging on public budgets. According to these 'official' numbers, spending on public pensions in the typical developed country will grow by 4.4 per cent of GDP by 2050, or from 8.8 to 13.2 per cent of GDP. This represents a 50 per cent increase – and it may be a serious underestimate.

The official projections, in fact, rest on a remarkably optimistic set of assumptions about future economic and demographic developments. They assume that unemployment rates in most countries will fall, that labour force participation rates will rise, and that fertility will rebound back towards the replacement level. All of these developments increase the projected size of the workforce and tax base, and hence decrease the projected pension cost rate. The projections also assume that the historical rate of improvement in longevity will slow. Although this is bad news for people personally, it is good news for government budgets.

[ . . . ]

To assess the potential magnitude of the ageing challenge, the Center for Strategic and International Studies' Global Aging Initiative has developed an alternative projection (see CSIS, 2002). The CSIS projection begins with the official projections, but adjusts key assumptions to more closely reflect historical trends. It assumes that unemployment will continue at its 1990s level, that women's work patterns will not change (except to allow for cohort effects), that fertility will remain constant, and that longevity will grow at its historical pace.

Pension spending under the CSIS 'historical trends' projection grows by 7.0 per cent of GDP between now and 2050 in the typical developed country, or from 8.8 to 15.8 per cent of GDP (figure 1). This is nearly 3 percentage points more than under the official projections – and it is just the average. In some countries, the difference is much more dramatic. In Italy, CSIS projects that pension spending will grow by 4.2 per cent of GDP (rather than 0.3 per cent); in Japan, by 9.6 per cent (rather than 6.3 per cent); and in Spain by 15.8 per cent (rather than 7.9 per cent).

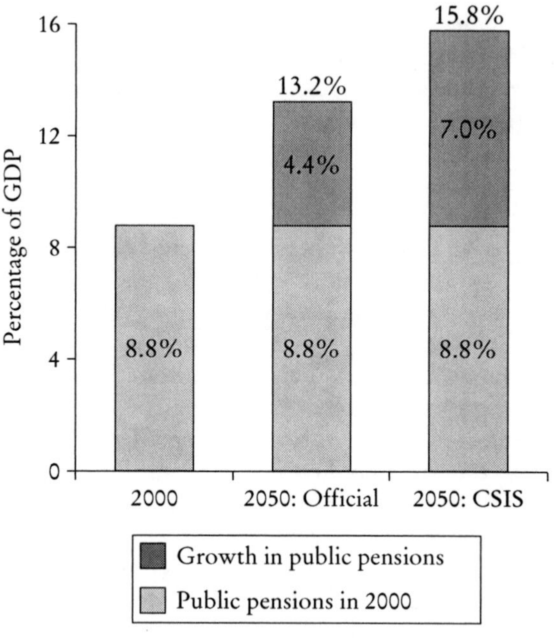


**Figure 1** Spending on public pensions is on track to grow by 7 per cent of GDP in the developed world (spending on public pensions, as a percentage of GDP; developed country (unweighted) average for 2000 and official and CSIS projections for 2050)
*Source*: EC/OECD, 2001, and CSIS, 2002.

The CSIS projection is by no means a worst-case scenario, since it merely assumes that historical trends will continue. If fertility rates fall further or if longevity gains speed up, the bill for public pensions could rise even higher. Like the EC/OECD projections, moreover, the CSIS projection assumes robust productivity growth averaging 1.75 per cent per year. Although this rate is about equal to the developed-country average over the past quarter-century, it could be difficult to sustain. Rates of savings and investment may decline as the developed countries age, and this in turn could lower productivity growth.

The magnitude of the extra pension burden will vary greatly among the developed countries, partly because some are ageing more rapidly and partly because some have earlier retirement ages and more generous benefit formulas (figure 2). Almost everywhere, however, pension costs will begin to ramp up around 2010. And almost everywhere, they will continue to climb rapidly for two to three decades before slowing or plateauing at a higher level. Global ageing is not a temporary challenge. It will bring a permanent shift in the age structure of the developed world's population and will put permanent pressure on public budgets.

Pensions of course aren't the only public costs that are bound to grow as societies age. Health care for the elderly will also be a large burden. In

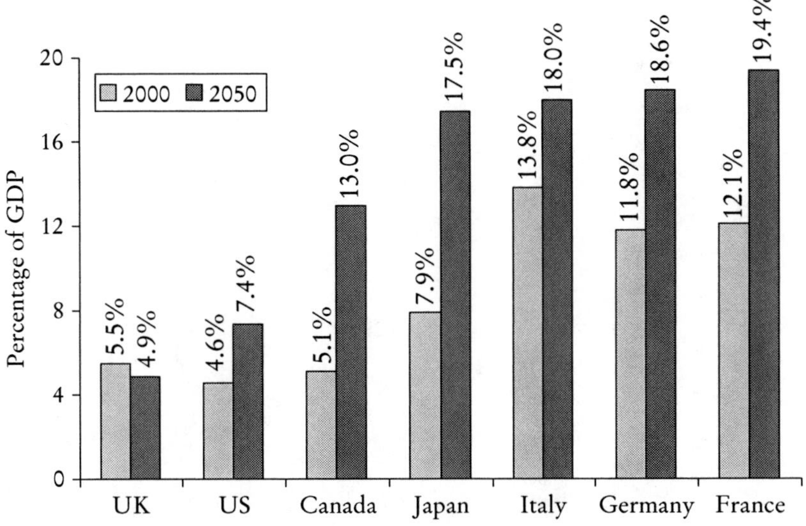


**Figure 2** Behind the averages: the size of the projected pension burden varies greatly among the developed countries (spending on public pensions, as a percentage of GDP; developed country (unweighted) average for 2000 and official and CSIS projections for 2050)
*Source*: EC/OECD, 2001, and CSIS, 2002.

the developed countries, each elder on average consumes three to five times more health care than a younger adult. Moreover, the older elders are, the more costly their care becomes. In the United States, the overall per capita ratio of public healthcare spending on the 'old old' aged 85 and over to spending on the 'young old' aged 65 to 74 is roughly 3 to 1; for nursing home care, the ratio is roughly 20 to 1.

What makes these differentials so ominous is that it is precisely the population of old old that will be growing the fastest. The UN projects that the number of elderly aged 65 to 74 in the developed world will grow by roughly 50 per cent between now and 2050, while the number aged 85 and over will grow by nearly 300 per cent (figure 3). Today, just one out of ten elders in the developed world is 85 or older. By mid-century, the 'ageing of the aged' will push this share up to one out of five.

These demographic multipliers threaten to interact explosively with the rising trend in healthcare costs. Due mostly to the introduction and diffusion of new technologies, per capita public healthcare spending in the developed countries has grown 1.2 percentage points faster than per capita GDP over the past thirty years. The official projections assume that in the future per capita spending will grow no faster than per capita GDP. Even so, the EC and OECD project that public health benefits for the elderly will grow by an average of 2.5 per cent of GDP over the next fifty years, or from 2.1 per cent of GDP today to 4.6 per cent by 2050.

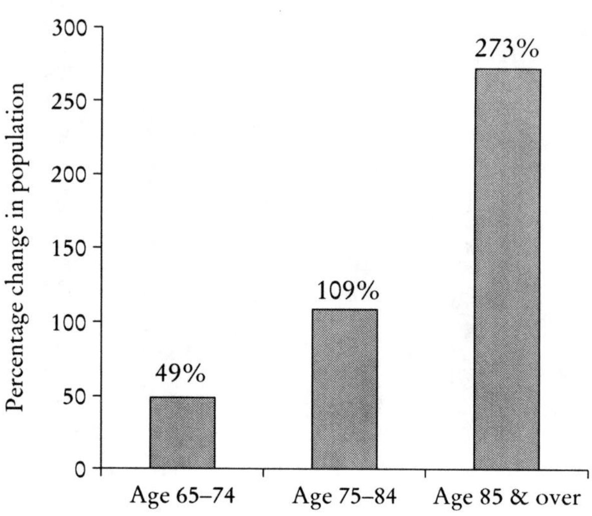


**Figure 3** The 'old old' will be the fastest growing age group (percentage change in the elderly population of the developed world from 2000 to 2050, by elderly age group: UN projection)
*Source*: UN, 2001.

CSIS assumes that healthcare spending will continue to grow 1 percentage point faster than per capita GDP. While this may seem like a small difference, it has a big impact. Under the CSIS projection, public healthcare spending on the elderly in the typical developed country rises by 5.5 per cent of GDP between now and 2050, more than twice what it does under the official projections. Added to the higher growth in pensions under the CSIS projection, this pushes up the projected growth in total public retirement spending to 12 per cent of GDP.

Healthcare costs could rise even faster than CSIS projects. Although some recent studies conclude that the health of the elderly is improving, this does not mean that the historical cost trend will slow. The health of the elderly is improving precisely because society is devoting a high and rising level of real medical resources to their care. And society is doing so because 'good health' is a subjective standard that itself rises over time. As technology and expectations interact, governments may find it harder – not easier – to control spending. This is why a recent panel of experts charged with reviewing the US Medicare projections concluded that a GDP-plus-one-percentage-point growth assumption lies near 'the lower end of the reasonable range' (Technical Review Panel, 2000).

## Facing Up to the Challenge

Altogether, CSIS projects that public retirement spending in the typical developed country will grow from 11 to 23 per cent of GDP by 2050 (figure 4). Part of the additional cost will come due in the form of health benefits rather than pensions. All that matters fiscally and economically, however, is the total burden of public transfers to retired beneficiaries. The fact that public healthcare spending on the elderly is growing too makes the reform of public pensions all the more urgent.

Cost, of course, isn't the only reason public pensions need to be reformed. Most economists agree that unfunded pension benefits substitute for genuine savings, and so reduce capital formation and economic growth. It's easy to understand why: when government promises people future income, they save less on their own. In most countries, retirement rules and benefit formulas also penalize continued work, once minimum eligibility ages or service requirements are met. According to OECD research, a 55-year-old with thirty-five years of employment and a 65-year-old with forty-five years will receive the same benefit in eleven of the developed countries (Vanston, 2000).

As pay-as-you-go systems 'mature', moreover, the deal they offer deteriorates. In the pay-as-you-go model, early cohorts of retirees can receive benefits far in excess of the market value of their lifetime contributions – all paid for by later cohorts of retirees, who necessarily become market losers.

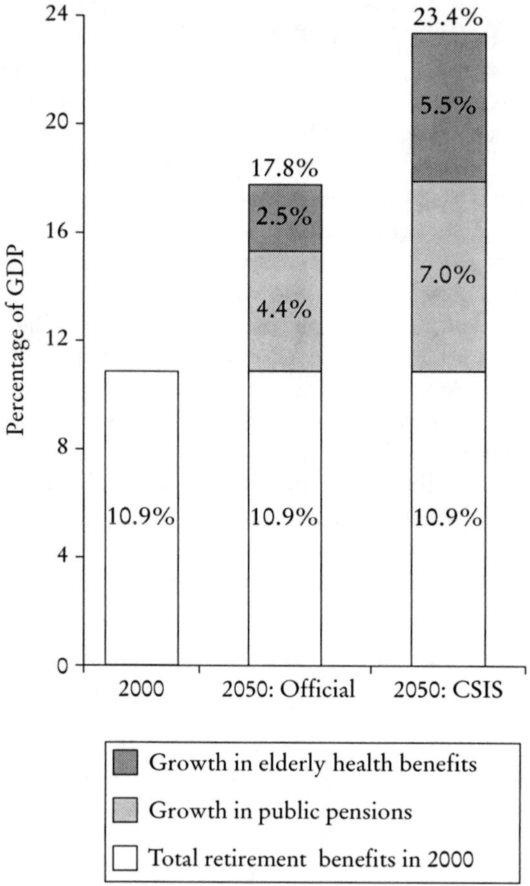


**Figure 4** Total public retirement spending is on track to grow by 12 per cent of GDP in the developed world (spending on public pensions and health benefits for the elderly, as a percentage of GDP; developed country (unweighted) average for 2000 and official and CSIS projections for 2050)
*Source*: EC/OECD, 2001, and CSIS, 2002.

In the United States, according to the Urban Institute, the typical single male retiring in 1960 earned a return of 11.0 per cent on his Social Security payroll taxes; the typical single male retiring in 1980 earned a return of 4.2 per cent (Steuerle and Bakija, 1994). The same worker retiring today can expect a return of just 1.6 per cent. By the time today's college graduates retire, the return will be 1.1 per cent – one-third what they could earn by investing their payroll taxes in risk-free Treasury bonds (figure 5).

For a long time, the advantages of universal pay-as-you-go pensions – social solidarity, poverty relief, and 'windfall returns' – seemed to outweigh

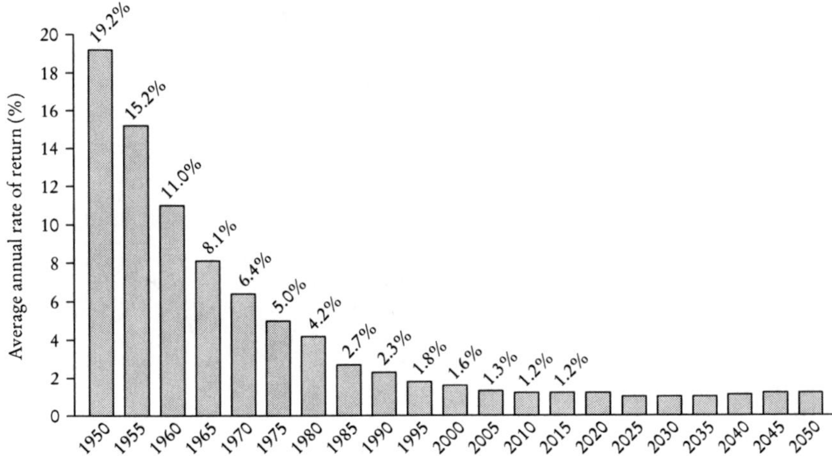


**Figure 5** Today's pay-as-you-go public pensions offer younger workers a poor 'deal' on their lifetime contributions (real annual return on US social security taxes for single male average earners retiring at age 65, 1950–2050)
*Source*: Steuerle and Bakija, 1994.

the drawbacks. Global ageing, however, is changing that calculus. Most governments are coming to understand that today's public pension systems are unsustainable and are beginning to enact reforms, although only a few have faced up to the magnitude of the challenge.

To stabilize spending as a share of GDP, public pension benefits in almost every developed country would eventually have to be cut by 30 to 60 per cent beneath current projections. Yet in almost every country, workers remain highly dependent on public pensions and entirely unprepared for large benefit reductions. In the United States, where public pension benefit levels are modest by developed-country standards, Social Security accounts for roughly 60 per cent of the total income of average-income retirees. In France, Germany, and Sweden, public pensions account for roughly 80 per cent. Among lower-income retirees, the dependence is even more complete.

Only a handful of countries, most of them in the English-speaking world, now have funded private pension systems that cover half or more of the workforce. Just three countries – the United States, the UK, and Japan – possess over 80 per cent of the world's funded pension assets. Nor can the typical retiree fall back on personal savings. Even in the United States, with its traditions of self-reliance, most workers have saved little for retirement. According to a recent survey by the Employee Benefit Research Institute (2000), only 21 per cent of households have accumulated more than $100,000 in retirement savings; 35 per cent say they have accumulated nothing at all.

As societies scale back today's unsustainable public pension promises, they must develop new means of supporting the elderly that do not overburden the economy or overtax the young. Although the generosity of today's pay-as-you-go systems will inevitably be reduced, retirement security can be strengthened – provided reform begins soon.

## Note

Short extract from chapter 1, 'Behind the Projections', of *The Global Retirement Crisis*, Washington, DC, Center for Strategic and International Studies, 2002.

## References

CSIS (2002) *The Global Retirement Crisis*, Washington, DC, Center for Strategic and International Studies.

EC/OECD (2001) 'Budgetary Challenges Posed by Ageing Populations: The Impact of Public Spending on Pensions, Health and Long-Term Care for the Elderly', Economic Policy Committee, EC; and 'Fiscal Implications of Ageing: Projections of Age-Related Spending', Economics Department Working Papers no. 305, OECD.

Employee Benefit Research Institute (2000) *The 2000 Retirement Confidence Survey*, Washington, DC, Employee Benefit Research Institute.

Steuerle, C. E. and Bakija, J. M. (1994) *Retooling Social Security for the Twenty-First Century*, Washington, DC, Urban Institute.

Technical Review Panel (2000) *Review of Assumptions and Methods of the Medicare Trustees' Financial Projections*, Washington, DC, Technical Review Panel on the Medicare Trustees' Reports.

UN (2001) *World Population Prospects: The 2000 Revision*, New York, United Nations.

Vanston, N. (2000) 'Maintaining Prosperity', *Washington Quarterly* (Summer).

# Gender Equity in Theories of Fertility Transition

*Peter McDonald*

The 1994 International Conference on Population and Development placed issues of gender at the centre of discussion of population and development (United Nations, 1995). A leading theme of the conference was that, in less developed countries, higher levels of gender equity are a necessary component in the achievement of lower fertility. In apparent contradiction to this tenet, I have postulated that very low fertility in advanced countries today is the outcome of a conflict or inconsistency between high levels of gender equity in individual-oriented social institutions and sustained gender inequity in family-oriented social institutions (McDonald, 2000a). The implication is that higher levels of gender equity in family-oriented social institutions are necessary to avoid very low fertility. Thus, on the one hand, a higher level of gender equity in social institutions is claimed to lead to lower fertility while, on the other hand, a reorientation of social institutions towards a higher level of gender equity is claimed to prevent very low fertility. Chesnais (1996, p. 733; 1998, p. 83) has described this circumstance variously as 'the essence of a future feminist paradox' and, more recently, as 'the present feminist paradox'. In what follows I address this apparent contradiction or paradox through consideration of a more generalized theory of gender equity in fertility transition.

## What is Gender Equity?

Mason has employed the concept of the gender system, which she defines as 'the socially constructed expectations for male and female behaviour that are found (in variable form) in every known human society. A gender system's expectations prescribe a division of labour and responsibilities between women and men and grant different rights and obligations to them' (Mason, 1997, p. 158). Mason observes that 'studies explicitly concerned with gender systems and their impact on demographic change are relatively new' (ibid.). That this is the case with respect to studies of fertility is lamentable. Indeed, it is almost inconceivable that fertility transition can be studied without considering socially constructed expectations for female behavior.

Mason (1997, p. 159) subdivides the gender system into gender stratification ('institutionalized inequality between male and female members of society') and gender roles (the division of labour between men and women). Gender equity derives from both of these elements of the gender system. Inequality between men and women and the division of labour between them in a particular gender system can be evaluated from the perspective of rights – social, political, and reproductive. Levels of equity in such an evaluation of rights determine the level of gender equity (Fraser, 1994). Thus, gender equity is a value-laden concept that begs the question of whose values should be applied.

In consideration of fertility transition, the obvious answer is that the values of the women and men who are making fertility decisions are important. Do women (or, at least, some significantly sizeable proportion of women) in a particular society consider that existing gender inequality or the existing division of labour is unfair and inequitable? Do the views of men and women coincide? Of course, women and men are unlikely to express themselves in the rarefied language of sociology. Even in the United States, Betty Friedan (1963) could refer to gender inequity only as The Problem That Has No Name. In high-fertility contexts, gender inequity within the family may be experienced by women as, inter alia, a generalized dissatisfaction with the rigours and dangers of a constant round of childbearing and childrearing imposed by spousal, familial, and societal expectations.

The use of the word *system* to describe gender stratification and gender roles may be misleading in that it implies consistency between different social institutions as conceptualized in the classic structural-functional anthropological approach. Essential to my argument is the notion that, in societies undergoing fertility transition, gender stratification and gender roles in different social institutions within a given society can become inconsistent with each other.

## Studies of Gender and Fertility

Mason (1997, pp. 163–72) provides a review of the methodologies that would be required in studies of fertility and the gender system and reports upon the few studies that approximate her standards of evidence. As she points out, the complexity involved in proper studies of the gender system and fertility is challenging. Indeed, it may be argued that despite the logical importance of the gender system to fertility, its lack of centrality in transition theory (until recently) results in no small measure from the poor design of quantitative analyses. To test the relationship between gender equity and fertility, demographers conventionally have studied a sample of women in which there were measures of each woman's 'status' and a measure of her fertility. Typically, a multivariate, cross-sectional analysis is then applied to examine whether a statistically significant relationship exists between women's status and fertility at the individual level. A more sophisticated analysis may add community-level measures of the status of women to the model.

This approach could be described as based on a unidirectional, dichotomous model. As commonly hypothesized, low women's status leads to high fertility; high women's status leads to low fertility. With regard to the fertility transition, this is just one example of several unidirectional, dichotomous models that have been employed in the literature. Some other hypotheses tested by such models are: high education leads to low fertility; higher economic status leads to lower fertility; higher levels of social inclusion lead to lower fertility; lower infant and child mortality leads to lower fertility; higher costs of children lead to lower fertility; lower fertility accompanies lower religiosity; lower fertility is associated with a transition from extended to nuclear families; urbanization leads to lower fertility; and a lower point on the low fertility–ideation scale leads to lower fertility. One also finds 'testing' of the tautology that, other things equal, higher or better use of birth control leads to lower fertility.

In general, the logic of unidirectional, dichotomous models has been criticized because they imply a simple, evolutionary process of social change, universal across all societies, in which progression along the path of the model is always towards a state assessed as superior to the status quo ante (Derrida, 1976; McDonald, 1994). These models have been criticized for not situating fertility within its cultural and institutional context (McNicoll, 1980; Greenhalgh, 1995). The unidirectional, dichotomous model is applied irrespective of, or is only superficially modified by, the social context.[1]

Quantitative studies of the relationship between gender equity and fertility require measures of gender equity. As defined here, gender equity would be evaluated for each social institution on the basis of the assessments of women and, perhaps, men in the society under study. This definition has inherent difficulties with respect to historical studies. In such studies, we would need to rely upon diaries, letters, and published statements of women. On the other hand, much historical research uses these types of sources. An excellent example of such a historical study that provides conclusions supporting the arguments advanced here is Catherine Scholten's (1985) study of childbearing in American society.[2] If gender inequity in contemporary societies is a problem that has no name, it is difficult to obtain measures of the perceptions of gender equity from individual women. Depending upon the social context, social-psychological scales may be useful. Inevitably, however, the degree of gender equity will be measured by the researcher's own assessment of the levels of equity applying in different social institutions, based upon quantitative measures of those institutions. Such measurement will require a sophisticated anthropological knowledge of the society. This is the approach used in the small number of recent quantitative studies cited by Mason (1997, pp. 169–72). The argument that complexity requires the use of qualitative methods is also apposite.

The level of gender equity did not emerge from the influential European Fertility Project as an important determinant of the onset of fertility transition. In this study, a 10 per cent fall in fertility was taken as evidence for the onset of fertility transition (Coale and Watkins, 1986). The focus was on the onset of the decline because the authors concluded that once a fall of 10 per cent had been observed, continuation of the decline was inevitable. The study found that few generalizations could be made across districts of Europe as to the conditions that were contemporaneous with this 10 per cent fall. Given the extent of institutional variation across cultures at the onset of decline, it is not surprising that generalization proved difficult. If consideration is extended to a much larger range of world cultures, this lack of generalization is even more likely to be found. I argue here that the emphasis on the period surrounding the onset of decline may be misplaced. More value may be obtained from studying why fertility continues to decline to low levels after it has commenced to fall. In other words, the scope for theoretical generalization is probably greater in study of the sustained fall of fertility than in study of the commencement of fertility decline. The influence of changes in the level of gender equity may be more evident in this later phase.

## Some Propositions regarding the Relationship between Gender Equity and Fertility

The place of gender equity in fertility transition theory can be approached by considering the following two propositions:

1 Fertility in a society falls as a result of the cumulative actions of individual women and men to prevent births.[3]
2 Sustained lower fertility in any society will lead to fundamental changes in the nature of women's lives.

The first proposition underlies most theories of fertility transition. The implication is that fertility change in a society must be capable of being explained in individual terms. The dimension I highlight here, gender equity, is not an individual characteristic. It is a characteristic of the institutions of society. The first proposition, a truism, says that people, not institutions, change fertility levels. Thus, in proposing a place in fertility transition theory for gender equity, a theory must elaborate upon how the levels of gender equity in social institutions manifest themselves in individual-level decisionmaking. Folbre (1997) has argued that in contemporary market-based economies, the rewards for market production far exceed the rewards for social reproduction, a theme that I have also taken up specifically in relation to low fertility (McDonald, 2000b). It is this imbalance in the reward structure that brings gender inequities in social institutions into the consciousness of individual men and women.

The first proposition also implies that individuals have the knowledge and the social permission necessary to control their births. As I hinted earlier, the notion that the spread of the practice of birth control is a component of fertility transition is tautological. The way in which the idea of birth control is spread, however, is a highly relevant consideration (Watkins, 1986).

The second proposition states that if fertility in a society falls from high to low levels then, inevitably, this will change the nature of the society. In particular, it will change the nature of women's lives. Implicit in the gender system of a high-fertility society is that women devote a great deal of their time and energy to childbearing and childrearing. If fertility falls to lower and lower levels, this in itself is an indication that society no longer places the same emphasis upon this division of labour. Mason (1997, pp. 173–5) mentions the small number of studies that have considered the impact of lower fertility on the gender system, but none of these studies considered the impact of fertility change on women's lives as a component of fertility transition theory. Demographic investigation, as mentioned above, conventionally considers the reverse causal direction of this proposition – that fundamental changes in the nature of women's lives lead to sustained fertility decline. Thus, in the conventional approach, changes in women's lives occur first and then fertility falls. The aim of expressing the proposition in the reverse is to argue that women may elect to have a smaller number of children in order to change the nature of the rest of their lives, not necessarily because those changes have already occurred. A birth is not an event that simply occurs at a moment in time and is explained by circumstances before and about that point in time. In Levinson's (1980) terms, fundamental life events are constructed as part of a transition in people's lives. The decision to have a child (or to avoid having a child) is not independent of the effects upon lives that ensue from that decision. That is, women have a birth or avoid a birth in an effort to shape their futures, not because the decision was preordained by a set of characteristics that they had accumulated prior to the decision (McDonald, 1996). This provides a much more active conception of the role of gender equity in fertility transition. Women in high-fertility societies may choose to have fewer children in the expectation (or vague hope) that to do so will change their futures for the better.[4]

The expectation, of course, may not be realized and this complicates the quantitative study of the issue. A smaller number of children might not mean that a family is economically better off or that a woman is able to pursue paid employment outside the family circle. At an early point in the transition, the statistical evidence may be weak. However, as long as women are able to maintain the expectation that restriction of their fertility will lead to an improvement in their lives, eventually, through successive age cohorts, the expectation will be more often realized.

## Fertility Transition, Gender Equity, and the Institution of the Family

Childbearing is inherent to family reproduction and, as such, it should be impossible to theorize about fertility transition without considering family reproduction and family organization (Seccombe, 1993). Folbre (1983, pp. 267), in addressing conventional theories of fertility transition, has said that 'the failure to incorporate any consideration of changing power relations within the family constitutes what many feminists might consider a fatal error of omission'.

Family organization varies from society to society, and the place of women in that organization is also highly variable. Thus, in this important respect, the starting point of each fertility transition is different. This complicates the use of standard variables across cultures as the social meaning of particular measures will differ. Nevertheless, the following additional propositions can be made:

3 In pretransition societies, high fertility was (is) socially determined, not naturally determined.
4 The transition from high fertility to fertility around replacement level is accompanied by an increase in gender equity within the institution of the family.

There is a large literature on the social supports to high fertility. Typically, social-structural arguments are offered to demonstrate the benefits of high fertility. These principally pertain to the value of children to the family, whatever its structure. (Some studies, of course, also highlight the fact that a degree of control over fertility was exercised in all pretransition societies, that is, the valued number of children was high but below the biological potential.) However, the supports for high fertility in pretransition societies are more than social-structural. High fertility becomes a part of the established family ethos and is supported by the institutions of morality, principally religion.

To argue the point just made would require a long detour; just one evocative example should suffice here:

> 'A mother with a train of children after her is one of the most admirable and lovely Sights in the visible Creation of God,' declared Benjamin Colman as he introduced the text of his sermon 'Fruitful Mothers in Israel' to his Boston congregation. In 1715 the Old Testament injunction 'Be fruitful and multiply', which Colman proceeded to discuss, was familiar to his listeners, and his interpretation of the text was representative of American thought on the purpose of marriage and on women's ordained part as childbearer. (Scholten 1985, p. 8)

Fertility transition requires changes not only to the social-structural supports but also to the moral supports. Here, we would be looking for changes in the morality governing the nature both of the relationship between spouses and of women's ordained role as childrearer. In the West, the assertion of the rights of the individual originating in the Enlightenment may have gradually filtered down to the rights of women within marriage. In the past half-century in developing countries, Westernization has been an increasingly powerful force with which traditional moralities have had to contend. For example, formal education inculcates ideas that empower the individual, allowing for a questioning of traditional morality.

In Western Europe, the decline of parentally arranged marriages and the shift of power over the means of production from the parental generation to the generation of the young couple are indicators of changing rights for women within a modified family organization. These changes extend back into the eighteenth century, predating or contemporaneous with the onset of fertility decline. Seccombe (1993, ch. 5) argues that women in late nineteenth-century and early twentieth-century Europe had a far stronger desire to end the constant cycle of births than men did. The fact that their wishes began to be deferred to by most husbands represented a shift away from patriarchy and towards gender equity in the couple relationship. Prior to the transition, Folbre (1983, p. 270) says, 'women's freedom of reproductive choice is often constrained by forms of patriarchal oppression which are coercively pronatal.' At the same time, throughout the fertility transition in Western Europe, women remained in a subordinate status because of their role within the male-breadwinner model of the family. Only in the past few decades have women in general, but especially married women, been able to assert an independent status outside the family.

Family organization is a vital aspect of cultural identity. Because of this, the family is a conservative institution that normally changes only very slowly. In all societies, family organization is protected from radical change by an idealized family morality, a moral conservatism that is often enshrined in the prevailing religion. Most often, idealized family morality confines women to the hegemony of men. Radical change usually occurs only through changes in political power or through changes in the attitudes of those in power. Otherwise, change is gradual (McDonald, 1992, 1994). Increased gender equity within the family can be a gradual process that does not portend radical family change. Thus, social norms may allow women increased control over their own fertility within what is, in most respects, a male-dominated family system so long as their increased independence does not threaten the prevailing family system.

The contemporary example of the remarkable fall in fertility in Iran may be a case in point. The total fertility rate in Iran fell from 6.2 children per woman in 1986 to 2.5 in 1996 (Abbasi-Shavazi, 2000). During this period, there was no significant change in women's position outside the family. Labour force participation rates for women remain very low and women have a very restricted role in public life. It is arguable, however, that increased levels of education for women provided them with a higher level of equity within the family. Once social permission to practice family planning was provided by the religious leadership in the late 1980s, the country's highly developed public health system was able to provide family planning services to both men and women. More particularly, women were freely able to gain access to these services, providing them with a greater level of reproductive rights and, hence, of gender equity within the family.

Depending upon the cultural or economic setting, various factors may enhance gender equity within the family and hasten the adoption of lower levels of fertility. Where limited fertility control has been practised before the onset of sustained fertility decline, decline may proceed more rapidly because the idea and practice of control is already present in the society. Advances in education for women will attune them to be receptive to non-traditional learning and provide them with the confidence to adopt new ideas. Husbands also may more often defer to the wishes of the educated wife. As more children survive, measures to limit family size may be implemented. Changing cost structures such as generated by compulsory education of children or urban residence may induce changes in fertility. Political regimes that are more socially inclusive may provide access to contraceptive devices and the freedom to use them to a wider range of people. The free movement of information among women in a society and between societies is another factor. The medical profession may become increasingly involved in natal care and warn of the dangers to a woman of having another birth. Advances in contraceptive technology enhance the ease of control over fertility. Finally, government-sponsored family planning programmes may provide social permission and access to contraceptive services. I make no claim here that increased gender equity within families is a sufficient condition for fertility transition; however, it is a necessary condition.

Government-sponsored family planning programmes in the past thirty years have succeeded in part because they addressed their campaigns directly to women, although always within their family context. Conservatism surrounding family organization clearly provided no other option, but the effect has been to raise the levels of gender equity within the family. It has been argued that, in Bangladesh for example, the family planning programme itself has been an agent in improving the status of women within the family. The programme exposes women to the modern outside world, it encourages them to take their own actions with regard to their fertility, it brings them in contact with other women who are not members of their family, and, since the programme's change to a clinic-based delivery system, it allows women to leave their houses unaccompanied by a male family member. This, together with a gradual shift in the power regime within families from the extended to the conjugal unit, has increased gender equity within the family (Simmons, 1996).

In summary, there is a strong case that, where women are provided with greater decision-making power within the family, especially with respect to the right to determine the number of children they have, fertility can fall to low level without major changes in women's lives outside the family. Fertility in the West fell to replacement level by the 1930s even as the male-breadwinner model of the family was rising to its zenith. That is, fertility can fall to low levels while most institutions outside the family are marked by considerable gender inequity. Folbre (1983, p. 276) even argues that the early advance of capitalism may have worsened gender equity in market employment while improving it within the family. Yet as proposed earlier, low fertility will change the nature of women's lives. In time, this will lead to rising demand for greater levels of equity for women in institutions outside the family. Recognition of this outcome lies at the heart of conservative, usually religious, opposition to birth control.[5] In terms of the Cairo agenda, just as women in developing countries have been the beneficiaries of more advanced contraceptive technology than was available during the fertility transition in the West, they are also likely to benefit from a more rapid shift toward a higher level of gender equity in individual-oriented institutions than was the case in the West. Thus, compared to the schematic view of change in the West, depicted in figure 1, gender equity in individual-oriented institutions may be increasing earlier in the fertility transition of contemporary developing countries.

## Gender Equity in Individual-Oriented Institutions

The increasing demand for individual rights and freedoms in the West in the past 200 years has led to the development of strongly individual-oriented institutions. The institutions of democracy, for example, provide

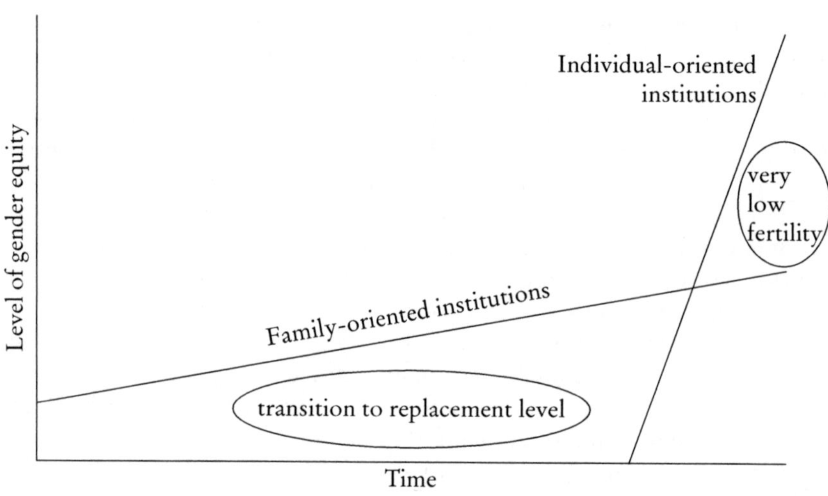


**Figure 1** Conceptual representation of changes in the level of gender equity over time in family-oriented and in individual-oriented institutions in the West and their interaction with the transition from high to very low fertility

individual voting rights, not family voting rights. However, the progress to this situation has passed through a period in which rights and freedoms were extended to individual men, but not to individual women. Effectively, prior to the twentieth century, men exercised the democratic rights of women. Women were educated to the level that would fit them to be suitable wives to the husbands whom they were expected to marry. Education for women was not directed towards future employment in the paid labour force. By the late nineteenth century, a woman was expected to eschew paid employment unless she was single or could not rely upon the earnings of her husband.[6] Thus, individual-oriented institutions were male institutions and, as such, they promoted and protected the male-breadwinner model of the family. A relatively high level of gender equity was a characteristic of women in their family role only.

Women in the West have gradually gained rights also within individual-oriented institutions. The early successes were in the domains of property rights and voting rights. Rights in education grew gradually over a long period of time to the point of broad equality with men today. Rights of women in market employment have risen dramatically in the past few decades. Generally women's remuneration now tends to be guided by the principle of equal pay for equal work and, at least at the non-managerial level, women are now able to compete equitably with men in the labour market. Cumulatively, these changes represent radical or revolutionary change.

At the same time, progress towards gender equity within the family and hence in family-oriented institutions has continued to advance very slowly. While, as argued in the previous section, the change within the family has been sufficient to allow women to have extensive control over their fertility, it has not provided other forms of equity within the family. Full gender equity would be achieved only if gender were not a determinant of which member of the couple undertook the three forms of family work: income generation, caring and nurturing, and household maintenance. In marriages, women remain the predominant providers of care and continue to carry most of the burden of household maintenance. Gender stratification continues to prevail within the contemporary Western family. The same is true in the East Asian developed economies that also now experience low fertility.

## Gender Equity and Very Low Fertility

In advanced economies today, women are able to compete in the labour market as equals so long as they are not constrained by their family roles. Women who value their involvement in individual-oriented institutions are therefore faced with a dilemma if they perceive a potential future family role as inconsistent with their aspirations as individuals. Some women in this circumstance will opt to eschew the family role rather than the individual role, that is, they will not form a permanent relationship or they will elect to have no children or fewer children than they otherwise would have intended (McDonald, 2000a). Most young women today have been educated and socialized to expect that they will have a role as an individual beyond any family role they may have. Thus, a fifth proposition can be advanced:

5 When gender equity rises to high levels in individual-oriented institutions while remaining low in family-oriented institutions, fertility will fall to very low levels.[7]

Cross-national comparisons of contemporary advanced countries provide evidence to support this proposition (Chesnais, 1998; McDonald, 2000a).

## Conclusion

The apparent contradiction stated at the beginning of this article has been addressed through distinguishing two broad forms of gender equity: gender equity in family-oriented institutions and gender equity in individual-oriented institutions. I have argued that the fertility transition from high to low levels has been associated mainly with improving gender equity within family-oriented social institutions, indeed almost exclusively within the family itself. The fall in fertility is associated with women acquiring rights within the family that enable them to reduce the number of their births to more desirable levels. However, change in the institution of the family proceeds slowly because the family system is strongly linked to conservative institutions such as religion. The link is the reification of family as defined by an idealized family morality.

During the twentieth century, a revolution took place in levels of gender equity in individual-oriented institutions in advanced countries. Starting from a point where women had a subordinate status in individual institutions such as formal education and market employment, the century ended with very high levels of gender equity prevailing in these institutions. High levels of equity enjoyed by women as individuals in combination with continuing low levels of equity for women in their roles as wives or mothers mean that many women will end up bearing fewer children than they aspired to when they were younger. The outcome for the society is a very low fertility rate.

The achievement of gender equity in individual-oriented institutions will not be reversed. But in a context of persistent relatively low gender equity in family-oriented institutions, high gender equity in individual-oriented institutions results in very low fertility. The idea is conceptualized in figure 1. Very low fertility rates will persist unless gender equity within family-oriented institutions rises to much higher levels than prevail today. In a context of high gender equity in individual-oriented institutions, higher gender equity in family-oriented institutions will tend to raise fertility.

## Notes

From *Population and Development Review*, 26, 3, 2000, pp. 427–39.
The author benefited from discussions about this article with Hera Cook and Rebecca Kippen.

1 On the other hand, at the opposite extreme, there is a recent fashion to attribute unexplained variation to 'context', adding little or nothing to theory.
2 Other examples are Quiggin (1988) and Seccombe (1993).
3 Maybe including non-marriage or delay of marriage, although, in an early paper, I have argued against this possibility (McDonald, 1981).
4 And, possibly, the futures of their children and of other women. Some altruism may be involved in assuming the role of an innovator.
5 The papal encyclical *Humanae Vitae*, issued in 1968, is a prime example.
6 For some, this idea is still valid, it seems. Mead (1999) argues that in the United States today, mothers in two-parent families should not engage in paid employment while single mothers should.
7 Very low means a total fertility rate below 1.5 births per woman on average.

## References

Abbasi-Shavazi, Mohammad Jalal (2000) 'Effects of Marital Fertility and Nuptiality on Fertility Transition in the Islamic Republic of Iran, 1976–1996', Working Papers in Demography, no. 84, Research School of Social Sciences, Australian National University, Canberra.

Chesnais, Jean-Claude (1996) 'Fertility, Family, and Social Policy in Contemporary Western Europe', *Population and Development Review*, 22, 4, pp. 729–39.

Chesnais, Jean-Claude (1998) 'Below-Replacement Fertility in the European Union (EU-15): Facts and Policies, 1960–1997', *Review of Population and Social Policy*, 7, pp. 83–101.

Coale, Ansley J. and Watkins, Susan Cotts (eds) (1986) *The Decline of Fertility in Europe*, Princeton, Princeton University Press.

Derrida, Jacques (1976) *Of Grammatology*, trans. G. C. Spivak, Baltimore, Johns Hopkins University Press.

Folbre, Nancy (1983) 'Of Patriarchy Born: The Political Economy of Fertility Decisions', *Feminist Studies*, 9, 2, pp. 261–84.

Folbre, Nancy (1997) 'The Future of the Elephant-Bird', *Population and Development Review*, 23, 3, pp. 647–54.

Fraser, Nancy (1994) 'After the Family Wage: Gender Equity and the Welfare State', *Political Theory*, 22, 4, pp. 591–618.

Friedan, Betty (1963) *The Feminine Mystique*, New York, W.W. Norton.

Greenhalgh, Susan (1995) 'Anthropology Theorizes Reproduction: Integrating Practice, Political Economic, and Feminist Perspective', in Susan Greenhalgh (ed.), *Situating Fertility: Anthropology and Demographic Inquiry*, Cambridge, Cambridge University Press, pp. 3–28.

Levinson, Daniel (1980) 'Toward a Conception of the Adult Life Course', in Neil J. Smelser and Erik H. Erikson (eds), *Themes of Work and Love in Adulthood*, Cambridge, MA, Harvard University Press, p. 265–90.

McDonald, Peter F. (1981) 'Social Change and Age at Marriage', in *International Population Conference, Manila, 1981*, Liège, IUSSP, vol. 1, pp. 413–31.

McDonald, Peter F. (1992) 'Convergence or Compromise in Historical Family Change?', in Elza Berquó and Peter Xenos (eds), *Family Systems and Cultural Change*, Oxford, Clarendon Press, pp. 15–30.

McDonald, Peter F. (1994) 'Families in Developing Countries: Idealized Morality and Theories of Family Change', in Lee-Jay Cho and Moto Yada (eds), *Tradition and Change in the Asian Family*, Honolulu, East-West Center, pp. 19–28.

McDonald, Peter F. (1996) 'Demographic Life Transitions: An Alternative Theoretical Paradigm', *Health Transition Review*, 6 (supp.), pp. 385–92.

McDonald, Peter F. (2000a) 'Gender Equity, Social Institutions and the Future of Fertility', *Journal of Population Research*, 17, 1, pp. 1–16.

McDonald, Peter F. (2000b) 'The Shape of an Australian Population Policy', *Australian Economic Review*, 33, 3, pp. 272–80.

McNicoll, Geoffrey (1980) 'Institutional Determinants of Fertility Change', *Population and Development Review*, 6, 3, pp. 441–62.

Mason, Karen Oppenheim (1997) 'Gender and Demographic Change: What Do We Know?', in G. W. Jones et al. (eds), *The Continuing Demographic Transition*, Oxford, Clarendon Press, pp. 158–82.

Mead, Lawrence M. (1999) 'Welfare Reform and the Family', *Family Matters*, 54, pp. 10–17.

Quiggin, Pat (1988) *No Rising Generation: Women and Fertility in Late Nineteenth Century Australia*, Canberra, Australian National University.

Scholten, Catherine M. (1985) *Childbearing in American Society: 1650–1850*, New York, New York University Press.

Seccombe, Wally (1993) *Weathering the Storm: Working-Class Families from the Industrial Revolution to the Fertility Decline*, London, Verso.

Simmons, Ruth (1996) 'Women's Lives in Transition: A Qualitative Analysis of the Fertility Decline in Bangladesh', *Studies in Family Planning*, 27, 5, pp. 251–68.

United Nations (1995) 'Program of Action of the 1994 International Conference on Population and Development Chapters I–VIII', *Population and Development Review*, 21, 1, pp. 187–213.

Watkins, Susan Cotts (1986) 'Conclusions', in A. J. Coale and S. C. Watkins (eds), *The Decline of Fertility in Europe*, Princeton, Princeton University Press, pp. 420–49.

# Political Challenges

# The New Politics of the Welfare State

*Paul Pierson*

## Why the Politics of Retrenchment is Different

This essay's central claim is that because retrenchment is a distinctive process, it is unlikely to follow the same rules of development that operated during the long phase of welfare state expansion. There are two fundamental reasons for this. First, the political *goals* of policy makers are different; second, there have been dramatic changes in the political *context*. Each of these points requires elaboration.

There is a profound difference between extending benefits to large numbers of people and taking benefits away.[1] [After the Second World War] expanding social benefits was generally a process of political credit claiming. Reformers needed only to overcome diffuse concern about tax rates (often sidestepped through resort to social insurance 'contributions') and the frequently important pressures of entrenched interests. Not surprisingly, the expansion of social programmes had until recently been a favoured political activity, contributing greatly to both state-building projects and the popularity of reform-minded politicians.[2]

A combination of economic changes, political shifts to the right, and rising costs associated with maturing welfare states has provoked growing calls for retrenchment. At the heart of efforts to turn these demands into policy have been newly ascendant conservative politicians. Conservative governments have generally advocated major social policy reforms, often receiving significant external support in their effort, especially from the business community.[3] Yet the new policy agenda stands in sharp contrast to the credit-claiming initiatives pursued during the long period of welfare state expansion. The politics of retrenchment is typically treacherous, because it imposes tangible losses on concentrated groups of voters in return for diffuse and uncertain gains. Retrenchment entails a delicate effort either to transform programmatic change into an electorally attractive proposition or, at the least, to minimize the political costs involved. Advocates of retrenchment must persuade wavering supporters that the price of reform is manageable – a task that a substantial public outcry makes almost impossible.

Retrenchment is generally an exercise in blame avoidance rather than credit claiming, primarily because the costs of retrenchment are concentrated (and often immediate), while the benefits are not. That concentrated interests will be in a stronger political position than diffuse ones is a standard proposition in political science.[4] As interests become more concentrated, the prospect that individuals will find it worth their while to engage in collective action improves. Furthermore, concentrated interests are more likely to be linked to organizational networks that keep them informed about how policies affect their interests. These informational networks also facilitate political action.

An additional reason that politicians rarely get credit for programme cutbacks concerns the well-documented asymmetry in the way that voters react to losses and gains. Extensive experiments in social psychology have demonstrated that individuals respond differently to positive and negative risks. Individuals exhibit a *negativity bias*: they will take more chances – seeking conflict and accepting the possibility of even greater losses – to prevent any worsening of their current position.[5] Studies of electoral behaviour, at least in the United States, confirm these findings. Negative attitudes towards candidates are more strongly linked with a range of behaviours (for example, turnout, deserting the voter's normal party choice) than are positive attitudes.[6]

While the reasons for this negativity bias are unclear, the constraints that it imposes on elected officials are not. When added to the imbalance between concentrated and diffuse interests, the message for advocates of retrenchment is straightforward. A simple 'redistributive' transfer of resources from programme beneficiaries to taxpayers, engineered through cuts in social programmes, is generally a losing proposition. The concentrated beneficiary groups are more likely to be cognisant of the change, are easier to mobilize, and because they are experiencing losses rather than gains are more likely to incorporate the change in their voting calculations. Retrenchment advocates thus confront a clash between their policy preferences and their electoral ambitions.

If the shift in goals from expansion to cutbacks creates new political dynamics, so does the emergence of a new *context*: the development of the welfare state itself. Large public social programmes are now a central part of the political landscape. As Peter Flora has noted, 'Including the recipients of [pensions,] unemployment benefits and social assistance – and the persons employed in education, health and the social services – in many countries today almost 1/2 of the electorate receive transfer or work income from the welfare state.'[7] With these massive programmes have come dense interest-group networks and strong popular attachments to particular policies, which present considerable obstacles to reform. To take one prominent example, by the late 1980s the American Association of Retired People (AARP) had a membership of 28 million and a staff of 1,300 (including a legislative staff of more than 100).[8] The maturation of the welfare state fundamentally transforms the nature of interest-group politics. In short, the emergence of powerful groups surrounding social programmes may make the welfare state less dependent on the political parties, social movements, and labour organizations that expanded social programmes in the first place. Nor is the context altered simply because welfare states create their own constituencies. The structures of social programmes may also have implications for the decision rules governing policy change (for example, whether national officials need the acquiescence of local ones) and for how visible cutbacks will be. 'Policy feedback' from earlier rounds of welfare state development is likely to be a prominent feature of retrenchment politics.[9]

In short, the shift in goals and context creates a new politics. This new politics, marked by pressures to avoid blame for unpopular policies, dictates new political strategies.[10] Retrenchment advocates will try to play off one group of beneficiaries against another and develop reforms that compensate politically crucial groups for lost benefits. Those favouring cutbacks will attempt to lower the visibility of reforms, either by making the effects of policies more difficult to detect or by making it hard for voters to trace responsibility for these effects back to particular policy makers.[11] Wherever possible, policy makers will seek broad consensus on reform in order to spread the blame. Whether these efforts succeed may depend very much on the structure of policies already in place.

[...]

To what extent have welfare states undergone retrenchment? What countries and programmes have been most vulnerable to retrenchment initiatives and why? In this section I address these questions by reviewing the evolution of welfare states in four affluent democracies since the late 1970s. The evidence supports a number of claims. (1) There is little evidence for broad propositions about the centrality of strong states or left power resources to retrenchment outcomes. (2) The unpopularity of retrenchment makes major cutbacks unlikely except under conditions of budgetary crisis, and radical restructuring is unlikely even then. (3) For the same reason, governments generally seek to negotiate consensus packages rather than to impose reforms unilaterally, which further diminishes the potential for radical reform. And (4) far from creating a self-reinforcing dynamic, cutbacks tend to replenish support for the welfare state.

Measuring retrenchment is a difficult task. Quantitative indicators are likely to be inadequate for several reasons. First, pure spending levels are rarely the most politically important or theoretically interesting aspects of welfare states. As Esping-Andersen put it in his analysis of welfare state expansion, 'It is difficult to imagine that anyone struggled for spending *per se*'.[12] In particular, rising unemployment may sustain high spending even as social rights and benefits are significantly curtailed. Second, spending estimates will fail to capture the impact of reforms that are designed to introduce retrenchment only indirectly or over the long term. Analysis must focus on qualitative and quantitative changes in programmes and on prospective, long-term changes, as well as on immediate cutbacks. My investigation therefore relies on a combination of quantitative data on expenditures and qualitative analysis of welfare state reforms. Rather than emphasizing cuts in spending *per se*, the focus is on reforms that indicate structural shifts in the welfare state. These would include (1) significant increases in reliance on means-tested benefits; (2) major transfers of responsibility to the private sector; and (3) dramatic changes in benefit and eligibility rules that signal a qualitative reform of a particular programme.[13] The selection of countries to investigate was based on the desire to achieve significant variation on what the welfare state expansion literature suggests are the most plausible independent variables. The cases vary widely in the structure of political institutions, the extent of shifts in the distribution of power resources, the design of pre-existing welfare states, and the severity of budgetary crisis.

Beginning with the quantitative evidence, aggregate measures provide little evidence that any of the four welfare states have undergone dramatic cutbacks. From 1974 to 1990 the expenditure patterns across the four cases are quite similar, despite widely different starting-points. As tables 6 and 7 show, social security spending and total government outlays as a percentage of GDP are relatively flat over most of the relevant period. The exception is the recent surge in Swedish expenditures, which will be discussed below. There is a slight upward trend overall, with fluctuations related to the business cycle. Table 8, which tracks public employment, reveals a similar pattern (although the expansion of Swedish public employment from an already high base stands out). For none of the countries does the evidence reveal a sharp curtailment of the public sector.

Table 9 offers more disaggregated indicators of shifts in social welfare spending among the four countries; spending patterns are reported for what the OECD terms 'merit goods' (primarily housing, education and health care) as well as for various income transfers. The figures suggest a bit more divergence among the cases, with the United States and Germany emerging as somewhat more successful in curbing spending. A very few programme areas – notably British housing and German pensions – experienced

**Table 6** Social security transfers as % of GDP, 1974–90

| | Britain | Germany | Sweden | United States |
|---|---|---|---|---|
| 1974 | 9.8 | 14.6 | 14.3 | 9.5 |
| 1980 | 11.7 | 16.6 | 17.6 | 10.9 |
| 1982 | 14.0 | 17.7 | 18.3 | 11.9 |
| 1984 | 14.0 | 16.5 | 17.6 | 11.0 |
| 1986 | 14.1 | 15.9 | 18.4 | 11.0 |
| 1988 | 12.3 | 16.1 | 19.5 | 10.6 |
| 1990 | 12.2 | 15.3 | 19.7 | 10.8[a] |

[a] 1989.

*Source*: OECD, *Historical Statistics, 1960–1990* (1992), table 6.3.

**Table 7** Government outlays as % of nominal GDP, 1978–94

| | Britain | Germany | Sweden | United States |
|---|---|---|---|---|
| 1978 | 41.4 | 47.3 | 58.6 | 30.0 |
| 1980 | 43.0 | 47.9 | 60.1 | 31.8 |
| 1982 | 44.6 | 48.9 | 64.8 | 33.9 |
| 1984 | 45.2 | 47.4 | 62.0 | 32.6 |
| 1986 | 42.5 | 46.4 | 61.6 | 33.7 |
| 1988 | 38.0 | 46.3 | 58.1 | 32.5 |
| 1990 | 39.9 | 45.1 | 59.1 | 33.3 |
| 1992 | 43.2 | 49.0 | 67.3 | 35.1 |
| 1994[a] | 44.8 | 51.4 | 70.9 | 33.9 |

[a] Projection.

*Source*: OECD, *Economic Outlook* (December 1993), table A23.

**Table 8** Government employment as % of total employment, 1974–90

| | Britain | Germany | Sweden | United States |
|---|---|---|---|---|
| 1974 | 19.6 | 13.0 | 24.8 | 16.1 |
| 1980 | 21.1 | 14.6 | 30.3 | 15.4 |
| 1982 | 22.0 | 15.1 | 31.7 | 15.4 |
| 1984 | 22.0 | 15.5 | 32.6 | 14.8 |
| 1986 | 21.8 | 15.6 | 32.2 | 14.8 |
| 1988 | 20.8 | 15.6 | 31.5 | 14.4 |
| 1990 | 19.2 | 15.1 | 31.7 | 14.4[a] |

[a] 1989.

*Source*: OECD, *Historical Statistics, 1960–1990* (1992), table 2.13.

**Table 9** Government outlays by function as % of trend GDP[a], 1979–90

| | Britain | | | Germany | | | Sweden | | | United States | | |
|---|---|---|---|---|---|---|---|---|---|---|---|---|
| | 1979 | 1990 | 1979–90 | 1979 | 1990 | 1979–90 | 1979 | 1990 | 1979–90 | 1979 | 1989 | 1979–89 |
| Total | 44.9 | 43.2 | −1.7 | 49.9 | 45.8 | −4.1 | 63.2 | 61.4 | −1.8 | 33.2 | 36.9 | +3.6 |
| Public goods[b] | 9.5 | 9.7 | +0.1 | 10.0 | 9.2 | −0.8 | 10.5 | 8.8 | −1.7 | 8.2 | 9.3 | +1.1 |
| Merit goods | 13.6 | 12.2 | −1.4 | 12.3 | 10.9 | −1.4 | 15.9 | 13.4 | −2.6 | 6.1 | 6.0 | −0.1 |
| Education | 5.5 | 5.0 | −0.5 | 5.2 | 4.2 | −1.0 | 6.6 | 5.6 | −1.0 | 4.7 | 4.7 | −0.0 |
| Health[c] | 4.8 | 5.1 | +0.3 | 6.3 | 6.0 | −0.3 | 8.1 | 6.9 | −1.1 | 0.9 | 0.9 | −0.0 |
| Housing and other | 3.4 | 2.1 | −1.2 | 0.8 | 0.7 | −0.1 | 1.2 | 0.8 | −0.4 | 0.5 | 0.4 | −0.1 |
| Income trans. | 12.5 | 13.4 | +0.9 | 20.2 | 18.5 | −1.7 | 24.6 | 26.8 | +2.2 | 11.2 | 11.9 | +0.7 |
| Pensions | 6.7 | 6.5 | −0.2 | 12.7 | 11.2 | −1.5 | 11.0 | 11.5 | +0.4 | 6.9 | 7.0 | +0.1 |
| Sickness | 0.4 | 0.3 | −0.1 | 0.8 | 0.7 | −0.1 | 3.4 | 4.5 | +1.2 | 0.1 | 0.2 | +0.1 |
| Family allowance | 1.7 | 1.6 | −0.0 | 1.2 | 0.8 | −0.4 | 1.6 | 1.3 | −0.3 | 0.4 | 0.4 | −0.0 |
| Unemployment | 0.7 | 0.6 | −0.1 | 0.9 | 1.3 | +0.4 | 0.4 | 0.5 | +0.1 | 0.4 | 0.3 | −0.1 |
| Other income supports | 0.1 | 0.8 | +0.7 | 1.3 | 1.6 | +0.3 | 0.1 | 0.2 | +0.1 | 0.0 | 0.0 | 0.0 |
| Admin. and other spending | 1.4 | 1.6 | +0.3 | 2.6 | 2.4 | −0.2 | 4.9 | 5.2 | +0.3 | 0.6 | 0.6 | −0.0 |
| Add. transfer | 1.4 | 1.8 | +0.5 | 0.5 | 0.4 | −0.1 | 3.2 | 3.7 | +0.6 | 2.7 | 3.5 | +0.8 |

[a] Numbers may not sum to total due to rounding.

[b] Defence and other public services.

[c] For the US, social security related to health spending is included under 'Additional transfers' below.

*Source*: OECD, *Economic Outlook* (December 1993), table 21.

significant reductions. Nonetheless, similarities across countries remain more striking than differences. None of the cases show major rises or declines in overall effort, and there are few indications of dramatic change in any of the subcategories of expenditure.

[. . .]

## The New Politics of the Welfare State

Economic, political and social pressures have fostered an image of welfare states under siege. Yet if one turns from abstract discussions of social transformation to an examination of actual policy, it becomes difficult to sustain the proposition that these strains have generated fundamental shifts. This review of four cases does indeed suggest a distinctly new environment, but not one that has provoked anything like a dismantling of the welfare state. Nor is it possible to attribute this to case selection, since the choice of two prototypical cases of neo-conservatism (Britain and the United States) and two cases of severe budgetary shocks (Germany and Sweden) gave ample room for various scenarios of radical retrenchment. Even in Thatcher's Britain, where an ideologically committed Conservative Party [. . .] controlled one of Europe's most centralized political systems for over a decade, reform [was] incremental rather than revolutionary, leaving the British welfare state largely intact. In most other countries the evidence of continuity is even more apparent.

To be sure, there has been change. Many programmes have experienced a tightening of eligibility rules or reductions in benefits. On occasion, individual programmes (such as public housing in Britain) have undergone more radical reform. In countries where budgetary pressures have been greatest, cuts have been more severe. Over the span of two decades, however, *some* changes in social policy are inevitable; even in the boom years of the 1960s specific social programmes sometimes fared poorly. What is striking is how hard it is to find *radical* changes in advanced welfare states. Retrenchment has been pursued cautiously: whenever possible, governments have sought all-party consensus for significant reforms and have chosen to trim existing structures rather than experiment with new programmes or pursue privatization.

This finding is striking, given that so many observers have seen the post-1973 period as one of fundamental change in modern political economies. A harsher economic climate has certainly generated demands for spending restraint. Additional pressures have stemmed from the maturation of social programmes and adverse demographic trends. Yet compared with the aspirations of many reformers and with the extent of change in fields such as industrial relations policy, macroeconomic policy or the privatization of public industries, what stands out is the relative stability of the welfare state.

I have suggested that to understand what has been happening requires looking beyond the considerable pressures on the welfare state to consider enduring sources of support. There are powerful political forces that stabilize welfare states and channel change in the direction of incremental modifications of existing policies. The first major protection for social programmes stems from the generally conservative characteristics of democratic political institutions. The welfare state now represents the status quo, with all the political advantages that this status confers. Non-decisions generally favour the welfare state. Major policy change usually requires the acquiescence of numerous actors. Where power is shared among different institutions (for example, Germany, the United States), radical reform will be difficult.

As the British and Swedish cases show, radical change is not easy even in a situation of concentrated political power. A second and crucial source of the welfare state's political strength comes from the high electoral costs generally associated with retrenchment initiatives. Despite scholarly speculation about declining popular support for the welfare state, polls show little evidence of such a shift, and actual political struggles over social spending reveal even less. On the contrary, even halting efforts to dismantle the welfare state have usually exacted a high political price. Recipients of social benefits are relatively concentrated and are generally well organized. They are also more likely to punish politicians for cutbacks than taxpayers are to reward them for lower costs. Nowhere is there evidence to support the scenario of a self-reinforcing dynamic, with cutbacks leading to middle-class disenchantment and exit, laying the foundation for more retrenchment. Instead, the recurrent pattern in public-opinion polls has been a mild swing against the welfare state in the wake of poor economic performance and budgetary stress, followed by a resurgence of support at the first whiff of significant cuts.

Nor does the welfare state's political position seem to have been seriously eroded – at least in the medium term – by the decline of its key traditional constituency, organized labour. Only for those benefits where unions are the sole organized constituency, such as unemployment insurance, has labour's declining power presented immediate problems, and even here the impact can be exaggerated.[14] The growth of social spending has reconfigured the terrain of welfare state politics. Maturing social programmes produce new organized interests, the consumers and providers of social services, that are usually well placed to defend the welfare state.

The networks associated with mature welfare state programmes constitute a barrier to radical change in another sense as well. As recent research on path dependence has demonstrated, once initiated, certain courses of development are hard to reverse.[15] Organizations and individuals adapt to particular arrangements, making commitments that may render the costs of change (even to some potentially more efficient alternative) far higher than the costs of continuity. Existing commitments lock in policy makers. Old-age pension systems provide a good example. Most countries operate pensions on a pay-as-you-go basis: current workers pay 'contributions' that finance the previous generation's retirement. Once in place, such systems may face incremental cutbacks, but they are notoriously resistant to radical reform.[16] Shifting to private, occupationally based arrangements would place an untenable burden on current workers, requiring them to finance the previous generation's retirement while simultaneously saving for their own.

Over time, all institutions undergo change. This is especially so for very large ones, which cannot be isolated from broad social developments. The welfare state is no exception. But there is little sign that the last two decades have been a transformative period for systems of social provision. As I have argued, expectations for greater change have rested in part on the implicit application of models from the period of welfare state expansion, which can be read to suggest that economic change, the decline in union power, or the presence of a strong state creates the preconditions for radical retrenchment. I find little evidence for these claims.

## Notes

From *World Politics*, 48, January 1996, pp. 143–79.
I am grateful to the Russell Sage Foundation for financial and administrative support and to Miguel Glatzer for considerable research assistance, as well as helpful comments.

1 R. Kent Weaver, 'The Politics of Blame Avoidance', *Journal of Public Policy*, 6, October–December 1986.
2 Peter Flora and Arnold J. Heidenheimer, eds, *The Development of Welfare States in Europe and America*, New Brunswick, NJ, Transaction, 1982.
3 As recent research has suggested, it would be wrong to treat business as always and everywhere opposed to welfare state programmes. For illuminating studies of the United States, see, for example, Colin Gordon, *New Deals: Business, Labor, and Politics in America, 1920–1935*, Cambridge, Cambridge University Press, 1994; and Cathie Jo Martin, 'Nature or Nurture? Sources of Firm Preference for National Health Reform', *American Political Science Review*, 89, December 1995. Nonetheless, it is clear that *most* business organizations in all the advanced industrial democracies have favoured – often vehemently – cutbacks in the welfare state over the past fifteen years.
4 Mancur Olson, *The Logic of Collective Action: Public Goods and the Theory of Groups*, Cambridge, MA, Harvard University Press, 1965; James Q. Wilson, *Political Organizations*, New York, Basic Books, 1973, pp. 330–37.
5 Daniel Kahneman and Amos Tversky, 'Prospect Theory: An Analysis of Decision under Risk', *Econometrica*, 47, March 1979; idem, 'Choices, Values and Frames', *American Psychologist*, 39 April 1984.
6 Howard S. Bloom and H. Douglas Price, 'Voter Response to Short-Run Economic Conditions: The Asymmetric Effect of Prosperity and Recession', *American Political Science Review*, 69, December 1975; Samuel Kernell,

'Presidential Popularity and Negative Voting: An Alternative Explanation of the Midterm Congressional Decline of the President's Party', *American Political Science Review*, 71, March 1977; and Richard R. Lau, 'Explanations for Negativity Effects in Political Behavior', *American Journal of Political Science*, 29, February 1985.

7 Peter Flora, 'From Industrial to Postindustrial Welfare State?', *Annals of the Institute of Social Science* (University of Tokyo), special issue 1989, p. 154.

8 Christine L. Day, *What Older Americans Think: Interest Groups and Aging Policy*, Princeton, NJ, Princeton University Press, 1990, pp. 25–6.

9 Gøsta Esping-Andersen, *Politics against Markets: The Social Democratic Road to Power*, Princeton, NJ, Princeton University Press, 1985; Paul Pierson, 'When Effect Becomes Cause: Policy Feedback and Political Change', *World Politics*, 45, July 1993.

10 Weaver, op. cit.; Paul Pierson, *Dismantling the Welfare State? Reagan, Thatcher and the Politics of Retrenchment*, Cambridge, Cambridge University Press, 1994, ch. 1.

11 R. Douglas Arnold, *The Logic of Congressional Action*, New Haven, Yale University Press, 1990.

12 Gøsta Esping-Andersen, *The Three Worlds of Welfare Capitalism*, Cambridge, Polity Press, 1990, p. 21.

13 Establishing what constitutes 'radical' reform is no easy task. For instance, it is impossible to say definitively when a series of quantitative cutbacks amounts to a qualitative shift in the nature of programmes. Roughly though, that point is reached when because of policy reform a programme can no longer play its traditional role (e.g. when pension benefits designed to provide a rough continuation of the retiree's earlier standard of living are clearly unable to do so).

14 Indeed, a cross-national comparison of unemployment programmes provides further support for this analysis. The OECD has measured replacement rates for UI (benefits as a percentage of previous income) over time in twenty countries, with data to 1991. These data thus permit, for one programme, a [ . . . ] quantitative appraisal of programme *generosity* rather than simply spending levels. In the majority of cases (twelve out of twenty), replacement rates were *higher* in 1991 than the average rate for either the 1970s or the 1980s, while most of the other cases experienced very marginal declines. Organization for Economic Co-operation and Development, *The OECD Jobs Study: Facts, Analysis, Strategies*, Paris, OECD, 1994, chart 16, p. 24.

15 See Paul David, 'Clio and the Economics of QWERTY', *American Economic Review*, 75, May 1985; and W. Brian Arthur, 'Competing Technologies, Increasing Returns, and Lock-In by Historical Events', *Economic Journal*, 99, March 1989, pp. 116–31. For good extensions to political processes, see Stephen A. Krasner, 'Sovereignty: An Institutional Perspective', in James A. Caporaso, ed., *The Elusive State: International and Comparative Perspectives*, Newbury Park, CA, Sage Publications, 1989; and Douglas North, *Institutions, Institutional Change and Economic Reformance*, Cambridge, Cambridge University Press, 1990.

16 Thus in Germany, Sweden, and the United States the maturity of existing schemes limited policy makers to very gradual and incremental reforms of earnings-related pension systems. More dramatic reform was possible in Britain because the unfunded earnings-related scheme was far from maturity, having been passed only in 1975. Pierson, '"Policy Feedbacks" and Political Change Contrasting Reagan and Thatcher's Persian-Reform Initiatives', *Studies in American Political Development*, 6, Fall 1992.

# Beyond Retrenchment: Four Problems in Current Welfare State Research and One Suggestion on How to Overcome Them

*Bruno Palier*

## Introduction

'Welfare states in transition' (Esping-Andersen, 1996), 'Recasting European welfare states' (Ferrera and Rhodes, 2000), 'Welfare state futures' (Leibfried, 2000), 'Survival of the European welfare state' (Kuhnle, 2000b) and 'The new politics of the welfare state' (Pierson, 2001a) – all of these are among the most important recent publications on the welfare state. Collectively, they indicate that the focus of the academic agenda has moved beyond the crisis of the welfare state and towards an analysis of actual social policy changes which have occurred during the last twenty or twenty-five years. Probably under Anglo-Saxon influence (Reagan and Thatcher pursued explicit anti-welfare agendas) the first analyses of these changes have been phrased in terms of retrenchment (after the 'golden age' of growth). They sought to discover how deep and to what extent governments had reduced social expenditure since the late 1970s. After a couple of decades of debates on the crisis of the welfare state, and countless welfare reforms adopted throughout the industrialized world, many commentators agree on the fact that the welfare state is much more solid and robust than had been assumed and argued in the 1970s. To date, most welfare state analyses have concluded that in the last twenty-five years there has either been stability, little retrenchment or 'path dependent' changes. Even if expenditure on certain programmes has been partially cut back, recent reforms do not change the nature of postwar welfare states.

The idea of only limited changes is particularly linked to continental 'conservative corporatist' welfare states. More precisely, it has often been argued that these welfare states hardly changed at all and the changes which were introduced were counterproductive ('adjusting badly', as Manow and Seils, 2000, put it). In the 'frozen' continental European welfare state landscape (Esping-Andersen, 1996), the French social welfare system in particular has often been regarded as one of the most 'immovable objects' (Pierson 1998, p. 558 n. 8). In France, social expenditure continued to increase rapidly throughout the 1980s, but no fundamental reform seems to have been introduced in health services or in old age pension systems. Attempts to introduce reforms have been fiercely opposed by strikes and demonstrations, especially in 1995 (Levy, 2000).

However, this gloomy picture must be modified. I have argued that during the last twenty-five years, French governments have implemented three different kinds of policies aimed at coping with welfare state problems (Palier, 2000). During the late 1970s and the 1980s, they have responded to social security deficits by mainly raising the level of social contributions; policies which only changed the level of the available instruments. In the early 1990s second order changes appeared with sectorial reforms, such as new medical agreements in health care, a new benefit in unemployment insurance and new modes of calculating retirement pensions. Such moderations introduced new instruments but remained within the traditional (historical and institutional) logic of the French welfare system. However, since these two kinds of changes appeared to be insufficient and since the French welfare system itself appeared to exacerbate economic and social problems (unemployment, social exclusion), governments have also decided to act indirectly by tackling the institutional causes of these problems. The French welfare state was felt to be resistant to change to such a degree that governments decided to introduce structural reforms which would become less easily repealed. These structural reforms, such as new means-tested reinsertion policies (RMI), new financing mechanisms (CSG) and a new role for the state, introduced both new instruments and a new logic of welfare, i.e. structural change which will transform the very nature of the system (Palier, 2000).

The thesis of 'eurosclerosis' or the 'path dependent continuity' argument, commonly found in recent welfare state literature, seem to neglect the latter kinds of reforms, even though they may lead to profound welfare state changes. The structural reforms adopted by French governments in the early 1990s imply the abandonment of some elements of the French (Bismarckian) tradition and a progressive transformation based on the development of means-tested benefits, the growing importance of tax finance and the empowerment of state representatives within the system at the expense of the social partners. Resistance to change may now be progressively overcome, leading to new patterns of social protection in France (Palier, 2001). However, it remains true that, until recently, change has been difficult to implement in France, as in other Bismarckian social insurance welfare systems. There should be a specific comparative analysis of why these countries are more difficult to change than others. As far as France is concerned, Giuliano Bonoli and myself have shown that some of the peculiarities of the French social policy-making system help to explain why major retrenchment has not occurred. In particular, these are a highly popular but particularly fragmented social insurance system which is largely financed by social contributions; numerous divided trade unions, who are particularly eager on keeping their position in the system because of their weakness in industrial relations; and a central state which is relatively weak in this field and thus obliged to negotiate with the other social protection actors (Bonoli and Palier, 1998, 2000).

There might therefore have to be a twofold agenda in comparative welfare state research. On the one hand, we should be able to identify more changes than are usually recognized. On the other, we should be able to understand why continental welfare states are more resistant to change, or at least change differently, than other welfare states. For this, I suggest that we need to draw on and combine public policy analysis and the role of welfare institutions in order to develop and arrive at a more adequate framework of analysis.

With reference to my previous work (Bonoli and Palier, 1998, 2000; Palier, 2000, 2001) and in line with that of others (for instance, Visser and Hemerijck, 1997), I would argue that current research on welfare state changes should go beyond the notion of retrenchment so as to be able to embrace the different kinds of developments which have occurred. Recent European welfare states changes should be analysed by differentiating between both different periods of time and different types of changes introduced by governments. Some reforms may prove to enforce continuity, some others may prove to introduce a new logic in the welfare system. In contrast to the general notion of retrenchment, reforms do not always imply less welfare state. Inspired by general public policy analysis, in this chapter a specific analytic framework is proposed which emphasizes the role of welfare institutions, and distinguishes three types of changes. This framework has been influenced by some dissatisfaction with current research on welfare state changes and in particular with four aspects: the notion of retrenchment, the concept of path dependency, institutionalist approaches of reform, and the analysis of change. Taking each of these four issues in turn, I will conclude with putting forward a proposal for an analytic framework to study recent (and future) social policy changes.

## Beyond Retrenchment

Retrenchment seems to have become one of the most common terms employed to describe recent welfare state developments. The notion lends itself to a stage or functionalist model of analysis of the history of welfare states: emergence (late nineteenth century until 1945) is followed by growth (the golden age, mainly until the 1970s), to limits (or even crisis, the 1980s), and then retrenchment (since the late 1980s). The notion of retrenchment harbours the same problems as those of development, modernization or growth of welfare states. All of these have been criticized for assuming a uniformity of the processes of welfare state development. If all changes which have occurred since the 1980s can be termed retrenchment they would imply shrinking welfare states. Therefore, in this framework, the main question is often to measure how much retrenchment has been applied, with large or small cuts as the dependent variable and a focus on spending. A great deal of academic discussion during the 1990s was aimed at demonstrating that even if expenditure levels were similar, different welfare states spent money differently, under different principles, for different purposes and with different institutions (Esping-Andersen, 1990).

These debates should be kept in mind when focusing on recent changes and it should be taken for granted that different welfare states are changing differently. Even if increasingly similar welfare efforts are made in that sense (Esping-Andersen, 1996; Scharpf and Schmidt, 2000; Pierson, 2001a), there is still a need for a systematic cross-national differentiation of processes of retrenchment, as there has been differentiation between welfare states during their 'golden age' (Esping-Andersen, 1990).

It might perhaps be that retrenchment is not a useful term since some changes in some social protection systems might not be bringing about less generous benefits. Just as the *trente glorieuses* (the thirty years of sustained growth and prosperity that followed the end of the Second World War) could not be analysed merely in terms of more welfare state, current developments are more complex than simply representing less welfare state. Firstly, data show that most of the OECD countries have increased their social spending over the last two decades. Already in the early 1990s Pierson (1994) observed that, if anything, overall welfare spending went up during the years he studied and he concluded that retrenchment efforts had failed. I may propose another point of view. In recognition of new problems which welfare states were confronting, some governments were, or were at least proposing to, spend more rather than less. At least, this applies to many Bismarckian countries in the late 1970s and during the 1980s (Palier, 2000; Manow and Seils, 2000).[1]

Secondly, for governments the question may not be quantitative (of more or less spending) but structural: how can welfare states be transformed in order to promote new principles and to develop new institutions which are more adapted to the current situation? In this case, the measurement of change should not be quantitative (in terms of expenditure, benefit levels, scope of coverage, etc.) but should provide an assessment of the degree of innovation introduced by changes. Typical questions would be whether reforms introduced new institutions or a new logic, or led to the involvement of new actors. However, recent analyses usually focus more on continuity than on change.

## Path Dependency and Continuity

Comparing Reagan's and Thatcher's reform ambitions with actual outcomes, Pierson (1994) emphasized the stability of (American and British) welfare arrangements. He explained this resistance to change by the force of past commitments, the political weight of welfare constituencies and the inertia of institutional arrangements, which all engender a phenomenon of path dependency. Thus, 'any attempt to understand the politics of welfare state retrenchment must start from a recognition that social policy remains the most resilient component of the postwar order' (Pierson, 1994, p. 5). Broadening the scope to other developed countries in order to analyse 'national adaptation in global economies', Gøsta Esping-Andersen came to a similar conclusion, depicting a general 'frozen landscape' and emphasizing the rigidity of continental welfare state arrangements. He concluded that 'the cards are very much stacked in favour of the welfare state status quo' (1996, p. 267). While the conclusion was that, once again, no dramatic changes could be (fore)seen, analyses of developments within different welfare regimes allowed the general notion of retrenchment to be separated out into different processes which are linked to specific institutions within each welfare system.

Nevertheless, among others, John Myles and Jill Quadagno demonstrated subsequently that things were not that fixed. Some changes could be identified, specifically in pension reforms. To put their argument in a caricatured nutshell, retrenchment means targeting instead of universal benefits, reinforcing selectivity and adding conditions to already targeted benefits, and tightening the links between contribution and benefits for contributory benefits (and going from defined benefit to defined contribution) (Myles and Quadagno, 1997, pp. 247–72). Relating these changes to pension policy, Pierson and Myles have recently argued that these changes were always path dependent, demonstrating more continuity than radical changes. While pension reforms often reduce the level of benefits, all are framed by past commitments and specific institutional arrangements. They operate differently and each perpetuates (and sometimes even reinforces) the historical logic in which the pension system has developed (Myles and Pierson, 2001).

Recently, several studies have broadened the scope of comparison beyond pension reforms, pointing out that there are different processes of welfare state adaptation (Scharpf and Schmidt, 2000; Pierson, 2001a). Through their empirical evidence, these comparative analyses of changes seem to confirm the notion of 'three worlds of welfare capitalism' (Esping-Andersen, 1990). In the context of the historical and institutional constraints it seems that there are three paths for welfare state changes. Scharpf and Schmidt (2000) convincingly show that the three worlds do not have the same kind of vulnerabilities in the face of the new global and European environment. Examining the implementation of several policies, Pierson proposes that in each world a specific type of reform is predominantly pursued: commodification in the liberal welfare states, cutbacks in the Nordic countries and recalibration of the Continental systems (Pierson, 2001b).

Very convincingly these analyses provide us with a much better understanding of what is going on than others which simply focus on curtailments. They demonstrate that there are (broadly three) different ways of reforming welfare states and that differences between the welfare regimes explain difference in reforms implemented. However, they still frame their approach in terms of retrenchment or adaptation, as if there has been, within a single country, only one single trend of reform over the last twenty-five years. Clearly, as Visser and Hemerijck (1997) claimed for the Netherlands, there is a need to differentiate between different kinds of reforms within the same country (or welfare regime). Governments have not always implemented the same recipes. They did not display the same behaviour in the late 1970s as during the 1980s or during the 1990s. There is a need for an analytical framework for studying reforms which allows differentiation between countries, but, in accordance with the type or period of reform, also within countries.

Usually, recent comparative studies have concluded that reforms had a limited impact on the structure of the different welfare states, not threatening but preserving the very nature of each system. In fact, reforms are seen as merely reinforcing the logic of each welfare system. Due to the different processes of marketization of their social policies, liberal welfare states have become even more residual and liberal. The social democratic welfare states, thanks to an egalitarian distribution of cuts (around 10 per cent across all benefits) and a rediscovery of the workline, have returned to their traditional road to welfare (Kuhnle, 2000a). Also most of the continental welfare states have remained the same, not only because reforms have reinforced their characteristics but also because of an apparent inability to implement any substantial reform (giving rise to terms such as 'eurosclerosis or 'frozen Fordism'). In short, it seems that fundamental structures of welfare states have remained to a large extent unaltered. The (neo-institutionalist) path dependence approach often leads to the conclusion of prevailing continuity.

## The Role of Welfare Institutions: From Independent to Dependent Variables

In order to explain the kind of continuity revealed by recent research, the impact of institutions is regularly referred to. The emphasis has mainly been put on the variables of general political systems, including constitutional rules, party systems, veto points or players and state structures (federal versus unitary, strong versus weak, etc.). However, the role of welfare state institutions themselves is rarely analysed in any systematic fashion. It might be argued that welfare institutions play a major role in shaping the problems which welfare states face, but they also partly determine the kind of resources which different actors can mobilize, and shape the kind of solutions adopted to face the problems. By welfare institutions, I refer here to the institutionalized rules of the social policy legacy.

## *Explaining Continuity: The Role of Welfare Institutions*

During the last ten years, research has been emphasizing the importance of institutions in understanding the differences in timing in the development of the welfare states, as well as differences in the content of social policies. In order to account for these differences, it is necessary to refer to the general political institution of each country (Bonoli, 2001) as well as to the political orientation of governments (Levy, 1999; Ross, 2000; Huber and Stephens, 2001). With Giuliano Bonoli, I have previously argued that there is a need for more attention to be paid to the institutional dimension of the social protection system itself in order to understand differences in timing and in the content of recent reforms (Bonoli and Palier, 2000).

Drawing on Ferrera (1996, p. 59) in a previous contribution we identified four institutional variables which are helpful in describing social protection systems (Bonoli and Palier, 1998). Accordingly, a welfare state scheme may be characterized by four institutional variables:

- *Mode of access to benefits* For example citizenship, need, work, the payment of contributions, or a private contract.
- *Benefit structure* Benefits can be service-based or in cash. Cash benefits may be means tested, flat-rate, earnings related, or contribution related.
- *Financing mechanisms* This can range from general taxation, to employment-related contributions or premiums.
- *Actors who manage the system* These are those who take part in the management of the system and might include state administration (central and local), social partners (representatives of employers and employees) and the private sector.

These welfare institutions shape the politics of the reform. Institutional factors structure debates, political preferences and policy choices. They affect the positions of the various actors and groups involved. They frame the kinds of interests and resources which actors can mobilize in favour of or against welfare reforms. In part they also determine who is and who is not participating in the political game which leads to reforms. Depending on how these different variables are set, different patterns of support and opposition can be encountered. In general, one may expect these variables to influence the politics of social programmes in the following ways.

*Mode of access* As it delimits the beneficiaries and thus the likely supporters of a scheme, this factor is crucial for shaping the politics of a given social programme. The mode of access also relates to the objectives of a programme, i.e. income maintenance, poverty alleviation or equality. As a result, support for a scheme might come from groups with an ideological orientation congenial to one of these objectives. Generally, left-wing parties have tended towards equality, Christian-Democrats have supported income maintenance and liberal parties have been keener to alleviate poverty (Esping-Andersen, 1990, p. 53).

*Benefit structure* To some extent this variable is related to the previous one, as typically earnings-related benefits are granted on a contributory basis while universal transfers are flat-rate. The nature and the generosity of benefits also determines the kind of support they will receive. Targeted or (low) flat-rate benefits are less likely to be supported by the middle and upper classes than earnings-related benefits. The higher someone's income, the less flat-rate benefits will contribute to his or her living standard. Politically, a flat-rate benefit structure – combined with a low level – might be related to lack of programme support from the middle and upper classes. As earnings inequality increases in many industrial countries, it will become ever more difficult to set a flat-rate benefit which is at the same time affordable and significant for a majority of the population. Targeted benefits are supported mainly for philanthropical reasons or fear, rather than based on material interest, and are thus more readily subjected to criticism. The political support of the benefits is the reverse image of their financial cost. As a consequence, it is more feasible to reduce flat-rate or means tested benefits than earnings-related ones.

*Financing mechanisms* While related to the two previous factors, this variable has some significance in its own right. If the mode of access delineates the beneficiaries of a programme, the financing mechanism determines who is paying for it. The political support for a financing mechanism is likely to be stronger if those who pay for a programme are also those who receive the benefit. The looser the link between benefit and payment, the less legitimate the financing mechanism becomes. As a result, there is a crucial difference between tax- and contribution-financed schemes in their ability to attract public support. Whereas taxation goes to the state, social contributions are perceived as a 'deferred wage' which will return to the insured person at times of sickness, unemployment or retirement. Paying health insurance contributions, for instance, 'buys' a right to health care which guarantees protection during periods of sickness. From a political point of view contributions are raised much more easily than taxes, especially income taxes.

*Actors who manage the system* This dimension determines the accountability and legitimacy of different actors. The more the state controls a system and its generosity, the more the political class is likely to be held responsible for any changes. When benefits are increased, the government is credited; when benefits are reduced, it will be blamed (Pierson, 1996). When management is shared with trade unions and employers, responsibility tends to be diluted, thus diminishing the state capacity to control the development of the social protection system, and particularly levels of expenditure. This variable also determines the range of actors which are regarded as legitimately participating in welfare reform debates. In a state controlled system the debate is confined to political parties. When the management is handed to the social partners, their participation in the debate is legitimized. In the latter case also trade unions are seen as important actors in social policy-making, and widely regarded as defending the current system against retrenching governments. This institutional setting gives rise to tensions over controlling social security between governments on the one hand – often regardless of political persuasion – and trade unions on the other. Union involvement in the management of social security grants unions a de facto veto power against welfare state reforms (Bonoli and Palier, 1996).

## From Independent to Dependent Variable

References to welfare state institutions contribute significantly to the understanding of details regarding both mechanisms of path dependency and differences between welfare regime changes. The institutional shape of the existing social policy landscape poses a significant constraint on the degree and the direction of change. For instance, a comparison between the UK and France, countries with extremely different social policy legacies, show two particular institutional effects. Schemes which mainly redistribute horizontally and protect middle classes well are likely to be more resistant to cuts. Their support base is larger and more influential compared with schemes which are targeted on the poor or are so parsimonious as to be insignificant for most of the electorate. The contrast between the overall resistance of French social insurance against cuts and the withering away of its British counterpart is telling. Also, the involvement of the social partners, and particularly of the labour movement in managing the schemes, seems to provide an obstacle for government-sponsored retrenchment exercises (Bonoli and Palier, 2000).

However, not only social scientists acknowledge the role institutions play in shaping, and sometimes preventing, change. Through learning processes, experts and politicians also recognize this effect – and sometimes therefore decide to change the institutions and thus alter the political game which is blocking reform projects. Two particular institutional features preventing welfare state reform are contribution financing and the involvement of social partners in the management of social security (two characteristics of the Bismarckian welfare systems, widely regarded as the most 'frozen' systems). Some recent reforms, mainly in Bismarckian countries, have been aimed at modifying these institutional arrangements (financing and the management of social security). This is certainly the case in France (Palier, 2000, 2001) but one could also mention reforms introduced in other Bismarckian countries (for example, the introduction of a 'green tax' in Germany replacing some social contribution funding, or the introduction of private employment services in the Netherlands). These developments are not aimed at benefit levels or access and thus cannot be considered as retrenchment (nor as improvement of the generosity of the benefits). Yet they may prove to be extremely important reforms since they could introduce changes in the very nature of national welfare state systems. Thus, what is needed is a framework of analysis which helps to distinguish, identify and assess these kinds of changes.

## Differentiating between Social Policy Changes

Welfare state analyses which focus on the evolution of social policy, or processes of adaptation tend to forget the kind of reform referred to above. Emphasizing the inertia of institutions, they tend to ignore the structural impact which public policies can have. While integrating phenomena of path dependency in welfare state analysis is essential, this should not prevent us from examining the impact of such reforms on social policy. In other words, recent developments within social protection systems are not only due to their own evolutionary dynamic, but also to the implementation of public policies. Incorporating public policy aspects of change into the study of the ways in which social protection systems adapt would allow use to be made of the tools of public policy analysis, and particularly of Peter Hall's approach to change.[2]

### *Social Policy as Public Policy*

Peter Hall (1993, p. 278) proposes that we 'can think of policymaking as a process that usually involves three central variables: the overarching goals that guide policy in a particular field, the techniques or policy instruments used to attain those goals, and the precise settings of these instruments. . . '. According to this approach, it is possible to recast our understanding of welfare regimes in terms of public policies. The instruments of social policy are mainly the four institutional variables mentioned above (the mode of access, the benefit structure, financing mechanisms and management arrangements).

The 'overarching goals' can be related to the three different political logics which are associated with three welfare state regimes (Esping-Andersen, 1990): the centrality of the market in the allocation of resources and residual state intervention in the liberal regime; the centrality of equality, citizenship and 'harmonization' of the population in the social-democratic welfare regime; and the centrality of work, status and occupational identity in conservative-corporatist social insurance systems.

If the above regimes are interpreted as ideal-types rather than precise descriptions of specific realities, three major combinations of these principles, logics and institutional instruments can be derived from the classic typology. These three combinations can be seen as three different repertoires of social policies which are more or less salient in any one specific social protection system. [ . . . ]

While these kinds of categories cannot pretend to describe the reality of any specific social protection system either in its entirety or in detail (because no social protection system would be this consistent, and all combine different logics and instruments to some extent), they are nevertheless useful for the comparative analysis of a specific programme. Each social protection programme is close to one of three goals and presents a specific setting of the four institutional dimensions. Therefore, these categories represent indicators against which changes can be located. In identifying the specific characteristics of a programme (i.e. its goal and the specific combination of the four institutional variables) before and after a reform, objective criteria for assessing changes will have been established. For example, did the reform only lower benefit levels, or did it introduce new modes of access or new rules of calculation – or did the reform set new goals? In other words, it is possible to assess whether a reform did change one or several of the institutional dimensions, and whether it implied a change in the goals.

## *Instrumental, Parametric, or Paradigmatic Changes: Three Orders of Policy Changes*

Elaborating his framework for analysing macroeconomic policy changes, Peter Hall distinguished three different types of changes.

> We can identify three distinct kinds of changes in policy . . . First, [a change of] the levels (or settings) of the basic instruments. We can call the process

> whereby instrument settings are changed in the light of experience and new knowledge, while the overall goals and instruments of policy remain the same, a process of first order change in policy . . . When the instruments of policy as well as their settings are altered in response to past experience even though the overall goals of policy remain the same, [changes] might be said to reflect a process of second order change . . . Simultaneous changes in all three components of policy: the instrument settings, the instruments themselves, and the hierarchy of goals behind policy . . . occur rarely, but when they do occur as a result of reflection on past experience, we can describe them as instances of third order change. (Hall, 1993, pp. 278–9)

This approach helps to differentiate between the different impacts which a reform will have, depending on whether or not it changes the instruments and the overall logic. It provides a grid for assessing the type of change beyond a pure quantitative approach (more or less retrenchment) and a means for judging the degree of innovation introduced by a specific reform. A first order change will not imply profound changes as far as a historical path is concerned. It just implies a change in the instrument settings (such as raising the level of social contributions or lowering benefit levels) without implying a change in the general principles and logic. This type of change might be called instrumental change. Second order changes, often referred to as 'parametric change' in the pension literature, involve the introduction of new instruments (i.e. the introduction of new calculation rules or new entitlement rules). These types of change appear to be path dependent, as Myles and others have shown for pension. They may lead to substantial changes once they have been in place and developed over time.[3] However, more directly, some reforms may involve a change both of the instruments and of the goals (such as changes in the financing mechanisms or in the organization of the management of the system), and thus represent what Hall has termed 'paradigmatic changes'.

## *Policy Learning: The Role of Ideas.*

In addition to identifying different types of change, the aim is also to explain under what conditions changes occur. Peter Hall's approach is based on processes of policy learning. First order changes can be understood as the first response which governments may adopt when faced with a difficulty which at this stage is not perceived as a new problem. By only changing the settings of the usual instruments, 'old recipes' are resorted to, repeating what governments are used to doing. Hall points out that as a response to the first oil shock in the early 1970s, British governments applied 'traditional' Keynesian policies with the aim of boosting demand. Similarly, I have shown that the French government after the mid-1970s merely did what they were used to doing before, i.e. raising social contribution rates in order to finance the growth of social expenditure, rather than reducing social expenditure (Palier, 2000).

However, when something is progressively perceived as a new context, old recipes produce unintended effects or 'anomalies'. Advised by different kinds of experts (among them, at times, social policy comparativists) governments became convinced that they needed to abandon the previous ways of doing things, now perceived to be wrong, and innovate. Two different paths seem available: the introduction of an innovation aimed at preserving the given logic of a system (for example, the so-called 'consolidation' reforms implemented in Germany at the end of the 1980s and during the early 1990s, or the French sectoral reforms, see Palier, 2000, pp. 122–6) or a change of some of the rules of the game, as well as its goals.

An important process here is a change in people's perception of problems and solutions. I have shown that an explanation of the implementation of structural changes in France requires taking account of different intellectual processes. First the idea occurred that former recipes were no longer adequate (such as the Keynesian use of social spending). Second, existing social and economic difficulties were reinterpreted. In the new explanation which emerged in the late 1980s, the position of the social insurance system shifted from one of a victim to one of a cause of the problem.[4] Third, a large majority of the actors concerned about social protection problems agreed with the new measures bringing about structural changes. However, the precise analysis of the different positions which actors adopted towards the new measures shows that the reasons which made them agree with those measures were very different, and sometimes even contradictory. Indeed, an important element for the acceptance of a new measure seems to be its capacity to aggregate different – and even contradictory – interests, based on different, and sometimes contrasting, interpretations. Structural changes are achieved through ambiguous measures rather than via a clear ideological orientation. Finally, these types of change have been introduced gradually but progressively. Fairly marginal at first, they will play a major role within the core of the social protection system to come.

## Conclusion

Analysing all recent reforms of the social protection systems as forms of retrenchment, as it has often been the case, represents a linear reductionist, developmental and purely quantitative view of what is going on. Instead, it is imperative to differentiate between different reform modalities or paths with the help of qualitative analysis. When differentiating between several (usually three) paths of reform, conclusions are often reached that processes are path dependent, but also that outcomes are marked by continuity: that after ten to twenty years of reform different welfare states have apparently remained all but untouched in terms of their own logic and main features. The link, often seen as inevitable, between path dependency and continuity needs to be questioned. [ . . . ] Explaining continuities usually relies on references to the impact of institutions. However, while institutions shape the particular context in which problems, interests and solution are framed, apart from the role played by political institutions, those of the welfare state created by social policy legacies (both as independent and dependent variables) need to be acknowledged more. Emphasizing continuity rarely takes account of public policies, which can have an important impact on welfare state structures. Finally, there is a need for a better differentiation between types of reforms: some reinforce the pattern of a particular system, others introduce structural change. In order to identify the different kinds of reforms, one has to assess whether they merely imply a change in the settings of given instruments, a change of instruments, or a change in both the instruments and in the goals.

With these analytical tools, we will be able to identify more adequately social policy changes which occurred in the recent past and will continue to occur. The analytical framework put forward here confirms that Continental welfare states are more difficult to reform than others. Reference to the impact of welfare states' institutions help us to understand why this is the case. For example, contributory benefits enjoy a particularly high level of legitimacy and are therefore difficult to cut back radically. Transfers are 'paid' for by social contributions, workers assume that they have 'bought' social rights, and benefits are usually generous. In this sense their loss would be more significant than the reduction of a benefit which is already at a low level. Finally, insurance-based transfers are well defended by organized interests, and in particular by trade unions of different branches corresponding to the different professional schemes.

However, this framework of analysis also helps us to realize that structural, paradigmatic changes have occurred, and particularly in Bismarckian countries. In order to cope with structural problems (regarding benefit financing, entitlements and capacities for change), these countries have created new benefit programmes according to new logics (means-tested benefits, privately funded schemes in pension and health systems), they have developed new modes of financing, partly replacing social contributions, and are implementing new management arrangements (privatization of some administrative tasks, empowerment of the state at the expense of the social partners). These changes are the result of a process of policy learning. They have been (or will be) implemented very gradually. Probably because of their marginal scope and because of the fact that they do not directly affect the level of expenditure, few analyses have concentrated on them compared with the more common analyses of welfare state change (and especially of Continental welfare systems) which tend to emphasize path dependency and continuity. However, the increasingly visible impacts of these structural reforms indicate a need for a change in the analytical framework. Social science should not be more resistant to changing their paradigms than, arguably, welfare states themselves!

## Notes

From Jochen Clasen (ed.), *What Future for Social Security? Debates and Reforms in National and Cross-National Perspective*, The Hague, Kluwer Law International, 2003, pp. 105–20. Earlier versions of this chapter were presented at the University of Stirling, the University of Tokyo, the Max Planck Institut in Cologne and to Fellows at Harvard University, Center for European Studies.

The author wishes to thank all the commentators from earlier presentations of this paper, and particularly Olli Kangas, Mari Miura, Fritz Scharpf, Peter Hall and Rosemary Taylor for their very useful comments.

1 'The 1980s were not a time of simple retrenchment. Under the condition where neither federal nor state government was obliged to pay the welfare bill, the door was open for increased benefits or expanded entitlements' (Manow and Seils, 2000, p. 279).

2 An increasing number of scholars are using this framework of analysis for understanding social policy reforms (see for instance Visser and Hemerijck (1997) or Hinrichs (2000)).

3 Myles and Quadagno (1997) illustrate this. Within pension systems, a transition from a defined benefit to a defined contribution scheme implies a change in the mode of pension benefit from deferred wages to savings, for instance.

4 The social insurance system came to be accused of partly causing some economic, social and political problems through three broad mechanisms: the weight of social contributions preventing job creation; the contributory nature of most social benefits reinforcing social exclusion; and the joint management of the system by social partners engendering irresponsibility and a management crisis of the system.

## References

Bichot, Jacques (1997) *Les Politiques sociales en France au 20ème siècle*, Paris, Armand Colin.

Bonoli, Giuliano (2000) *The Politics of Pension Reform: Institutions and Policy Change in Western Europe*, Cambridge, Cambridge University Press.

Bonoli, Giuliano (2001) 'Political Institutions, Veto Points, and the Process of Welfare State Adaptation', in P. Pierson (ed.), *The New Politics of the Welfare State*, Oxford, Oxford University Press, pp. 314–37.

Bonoli, Giuliano and Palier, Bruno (1996) 'Reclaiming Welfare: The Politics of Social Protection Reform in France', in M. Rhodes (ed.), *Southern European Welfare States*, London, Frank Cass, pp. 240–59.

Bonoli, Giuliano and Palier, Bruno (1998) 'Changing the Politics of Social Programmes: Innovative Change in British and French Welfare Reforms', *Journal of European Social Policy*, 8, 4, pp. 317–30.

Bonoli, Giuliano and Palier, Bruno (2000) 'How Do Welfare States Change? Institutions and their Impact on the Politics of Welfare State Reform', *European Review*, 8, 2, pp. 333–52.

Esping-Andersen, Gøsta (1990) *The Three Worlds of Welfare Capitalism*, Cambridge, Polity.

Esping-Andersen, Gøsta (ed.) (1996) *Welfare States in Transition: National Adaptations in Global Economies*, London, Sage.

Ferrera, Maurizio (1996) 'Modèles de solidarité, divergences, convergences. Perspectives pour l'Europe', *Swiss Political Science Review*, 2, 1, pp. 55–72.

Ferrera, Maurizio and Rhodes, Martin (eds) (2000) *Recasting European Welfare States,* Special Issue of *West European Politics*, 23, 2.

Gaxie, Daniel et al. (1990), *Le 'Social' transfiguré*, Paris, PUF.

George, Vic and Taylor-Gooby, Peter (eds) (1996) *European Welfare Policy: Squaring the Welfare Circle*, London, Macmillan.

Hall, Peter (1993) 'Policy Paradigm, Social Learning and the State, the Case of Economic Policy in Britain', *Comparative Politics*, April, pp. 275–96.

Hinrichs, Karl (2000) 'Ageing and Public Pension Reforms in Western Europe and North America: Patterns and Politics', paper presented at the conference What Future for Social Security? Cross-National and Multidisciplinary Perspectives, organized in Stirling by Jochen Clasen, 15–17 June.

Huber, Evelyne and Stephens, John D. (2001) *Political Choice in Global Markets: Development and Crisis of Advanced Welfare States*, Chicago, University of Chicago Press.

Join-Lambert, Marie-Thérèse (1997) *Politiques sociales*, 2nd edn, Paris, Dalloz.

Kuhnle, Stein (2000a) 'The Scandinavian Welfare State in the 1990's: Challenged but Viable', in M. Ferrera and M. Rhodes (eds), *Recasting European Welfare States,* Special Issue of 23, 2, *West European Politics*, pp. 209–28.

Kuhnle, S. (ed.) (2000b) *Survival of the European Welfare State,* London, Routledge.

Leibfried, Stephan (1993) 'Toward a European Welfare State?', in Catherine Jones (ed.), *New Perspectives on the Welfare State in Europe*, London, Routledge, pp. 133–56.

Leibfried, Stephan (ed.) (2000) 'Welfare State Futures', *European Review*, 8, 2.

Levy, Jonah (1999) 'Vice into Virtue? Progressive Politics of Welfare Reform in Continental Europe', *Politics and Society*, 27, pp. 239–73.

Levy, Jonah (2000) 'France: Directing Adjustment?', in F. W. Scharpf and V. A. Schmidt (eds), *From Vulnerability to Competitiveness*, Oxford, Oxford University Press, vol. 2, pp. 308–50.

Manow, Philip and Seils, Eric (2000) 'Adjusting Badly: The German Welfare State, Structural Change and the Open Economy', in F. W. Scharpf and V. A. Schmidt (eds), *From Vulnerability to Competitiveness*, Oxford, Oxford University Press, vol. 2, pp. 264–307.

Myles, John and Pierson, Paul (2001) 'The Comparative Political Economy of Pension Reform', in P. Pierson (ed.), *The New Politics of The Welfare State*, Oxford, Oxford University Press.

Myles, John and Quadagno, Jill (1997) 'Recent Trends in Public Pension Reform: A Comparative View', in K. Banting and R. Boadway (eds), *Reform of Retirement Income Policy: International and Canadian Perspectives*, Kingston, Ontario, Queen's University, School of Policy Studies, pp. 247–72.

Palier, Bruno (2000) '"Defrosting" the French Welfare State', in M. Ferrera and M. Rhodes (eds), *Recasting European Welfare States*, special issue of *West European Politics*, 23, 2, p. 113–36.

Palier, Bruno (2001) 'Reshaping the Social Policy Making Framework: France from the 1980's to 2000', in P. Taylor-Gooby (ed.), *Welfare States under Pressure*, London, Sage.

Pierson, Paul (1994) *Dismantling the Welfare State? Reagan, Thatcher and the Politics of Retrenchment*, Cambridge, Cambridge University Press.

Pierson, Paul (1996) 'The New Politics of the Welfare State', *World Politics*, 48, 1, pp. 143–79.

Pierson, Paul (1998) 'Irresistible Forces, Immovable Objects: Post-industrial Welfare States Confront Permanent Austerity', *Journal of European Public Policy*, 5, 4.

Pierson, P. (ed.) (2001a) *The New Politics of the Welfare State*, Oxford, Oxford University Press.

Pierson, P. (2001b) 'Coping with Permanent Austerity: Welfare State Restructuring in Affluent Democracies', in P. Pierson (ed.), *The New Politics of the Welfare State*, Oxford, Oxford University Press.

Ross, Fiona (2000) 'Interests and Choice in the "Not Quite So New" Politics of Welfare', *West European Politics*, 23, 2, pp. 11–34.

Scharpf, Fritz W. and Schmidt, Vivien A. (eds) (2000) *From Vulnerability to Competiveness: Welfare and Work in the Open Economy*, 2 vols, Oxford, Oxford University Press.

Visser, Jelle and Hemerijck, Anton (1997) *'A Dutch Miracle': Job Growth, Welfare Reform and Corporatism in the Netherlands*, Amsterdam, Amsterdam University Press.

1) beyond retrenchment
361 differenniation in welfare regime changes, structural changes

2) path dependency + continuity
362 targeting, selectivity, added cond. tightening

3) institutions 364-366
benefit-access models, benefit structure financing mechanisms, actors who manage systems

4) analysis of change 368-369
1st order level change - instrumental change
2nd order change of instrument itself parametric change
3rd order change of heirarchy of goals behind the policy - paradigmatic change

# Part III

## *The Futures of Welfare*

Part III on the futures of welfare is comparatively short and is more speculative than those that have gone before. In it, we bring together a number of authors thinking about the 'coming' welfare state. We begin with a short selection from the work of Anthony Giddens. As director of the London School of Economics and thinker-in-residence to Britain's New Labour government especially during its agenda-setting first term, Giddens's thinking on welfare was extraordinarily influential. Drawing on his wider articulation of a 'Third Way', Giddens here discusses the ways in which welfare institutions might be remade in a radically changed social and economic environment to underpin a new form of 'positive welfare' within an 'active welfare state' built on the shifting terrain of the new context set by 'reflexive modernity'. This is followed by a much longer piece in which Giuliano Bonoli considers the emergence of 'new social risks' and considers their impact on the emergence of a 'politics of the new social policies'. The 'new' social risks – reconciling work and family life, coping with single parenthood, dealing with obsolescent skills in mid-career, working outside the formal economy (and its world of welfare) – pose new challenges for both citizens *and* policy-makers. Bonoli considers the ways in which these issues may be addressed. Finally in this first of the concluding sections, we include Nick Ellison's discussion of welfare theory 'beyond universalism and particularism'. Universality – of provision and of citizenship – has traditionally been seen by its architects (or perhaps, social democratic theorists of the welfare state) as one of the key virtues of the modern welfare state. And yet in recent years these claims to universalism have been increasingly challenged by those who have seen the logic of universalism as repressing 'difference' and speaking of and to a privileged majority. Ellison attempts to think his way around the dualism of 'universalism *versus* difference', favouring decentralized and 'deliberative' conceptions of the politics of the social and a greater role for the 'politics of presence', as ways of recasting a social politics that can embrace the virtues of both difference and universality.

The final section contains three more programmatic papers. In 'A Welfare State for the Twenty-First Century', Gøsta Esping-Andersen presents his blueprint for a new welfare regime which is up to all of the challenges (social, economic *and* political) that social policy at the start of the new millennium must meet. His emphasis is on the requirements of a 'social investment state', with a special focus on children and families, lifetime learning, lifelong outcomes and 'life chance guarantees rather than here-and-now equality of all'. Ruth Lister sounds a cautionary note about the parameters and policy implications of the 'social investment state' favoured both by Esping-Andersen and the social policy-makers of New Labour. She is especially concerned that the focus has come to rely so heavily on the iconic status of children as 'citizen-workers of the future' to the neglect of issues of equality and 'child-citizens' in the here and now. In a final, very short but incisive contribution, Philippe van Parijs sketches his ingenious plan to respond to the current crisis of welfare ('the first marriage of justice and efficiency') by jettisoning most of the existing apparatus of the (income transfer) welfare state in favour of a guaranteed Basic Income for every citizen. Even for those who doubt the political practicability of Van Parijs's solution, it is a fascinating and challenging proposal which has provoked a wide-ranging and ongoing debate.

# A New World of Welfare

# Positive Welfare

## *Anthony Giddens*

[. . .]

### Positive Welfare

No issue has polarized left and right more profoundly in recent years than the welfare state, extolled on the one side and excoriated on the other. What became 'the welfare state' (a term not in widespread use until the 1960s and one William Beveridge, the architect of the British welfare state, thoroughly disliked) has in fact a chequered history. Its origins were far removed from the ideals of the left – indeed it was created partly to dispel the socialist menace. The ruling groups who set up the social insurance system in imperial Germany in the late nineteenth century despised *laissez-faire* economics as much as they did socialism. Yet Bismarck's model was copied by many countries. Beveridge visited Germany in 1907 in order to study the model.[1] The welfare state as it exists today in Europe was produced in and by war, as were so many aspects of national citizenship.

The system Bismarck created in Germany is usually taken as the classic form of the welfare state. Yet the welfare state in Germany has always had a complex network of third sector groups and associations that the authorities have depended on for putting welfare policies into practice. The aim is to help these to attain their social objectives. In areas such as child care, third sector groups have almost a monopoly on provision. The non-profit sector in Germany expanded rather than shrank as the welfare state grew. Welfare states vary in the degree to which they incorporate or rely upon the third sector. In Holland, for instance, non-profit organizations are the main delivery system for social services, while in Sweden hardly any are used. In Belgium and Austria, as in Germany, about half the social services are provided by non-profit groups.

The Dutch political scientist Kees van Kersbergen argues that 'one of the major insights of the contemporary debate [about the welfare state] is that to equate social democracy and the welfare state may have been a mistake'.[2] He examines in detail the influence of Christian democracy upon the development of continental welfare systems and the social market. The Christian democratic parties descend from the Catholic parties that were important between the wars in Germany, Holland, Austria and to a lesser degree France and Italy. The Catholic unionists saw socialism as the enemy and sought to outflank it on its own ground by stressing co-determination and class reconciliation. Ronald Reagan's view, expressed in 1981, that 'we have let government take away those things that were once ours to do voluntarily' finds a much earlier echo in Europe in the Catholic tradition. Church, family and friends are the main sources of social solidarity. The state should step in only when those institutions don't fully live up to their obligations.

Recognizing the problematic history of the welfare state, third way politics should accept some of the criticisms the right makes of that state. It is essentially undemocratic, depending as it does upon a top-down distribution of benefits. Its motive force is protection and care, but it does not give enough space to personal liberty. Some forms of welfare institution are bureaucratic, alienating and inefficient, and welfare benefits can create perverse consequences that undermine what they were designed to achieve. However, third way politics sees these problems not as a signal to dismantle the welfare state, but as part of the reason to reconstruct it.

The difficulties of the welfare state are only partly financial. In most Western societies, proportional expenditure on welfare systems has remained quite stable [since the late 1980s]. In the UK, the share of GDP spent on the welfare state increased steadily for most of the century up to the late 1970s. Since then it has stabilized,[3] although the gross figures conceal changes in the distribution of spending and the sources of revenue. The resilience of welfare budgets in the UK is all the more remarkable given the determination of Margaret Thatcher's governments to cut them.

Expenditure on education as a percentage of GDP fell between 1975 and 1995 from 6.7 per cent to 5.2 per cent. Spending on the health service, however, rose over this period. In 1975 it was equivalent to 3.8 per cent of GDP. By 1995 it had risen to 5.7 per cent (a lower percentage than in most other industrial countries). Public housing experienced the greatest cut, declining from 4.2 per cent of GDP in 1975 to 2.1 per cent twenty years later. As happened elsewhere, spending on social security increased most. In 1973–4 it made up 8.2 per cent of GDP. This reached 11.4 per cent by 1995–6. Expenditure on social security went up by more than 100 per cent in real terms over the period. The main factors underlying the increase were high unemployment, a growth in the numbers of in-work poor, and changes in demographic patterns, especially a growth in numbers of single parents and older people.

Much the same developments have affected all welfare systems, since they are bound up with structural changes of a profound kind. They are causing basic problems for the more comprehensive welfare states, such as those in Scandinavia. Nordic egalitarianism has historical and cultural roots rather than being only the product of the universalist welfare state. There is a wider public acceptance of high levels of taxation than in most Western countries. But the benefits system comes under strain whenever unemployment rises, as happened in Finland – this in spite of the fact that the Nordic countries pioneered active labour market policies. Given its relative size, the Scandinavian welfare state is a major employer, particularly of women. Yet as a result the degree of sexual segregation in employment is higher than in most other industrial countries.

The large increase in social security spending is one of the main sources of attack on welfare systems by neo-liberals, who see in it the widespread development of welfare dependency. They are surely correct to worry about the number of people who live off state benefits, but there is a more sophisticated way of looking at what is going on. Welfare prescriptions quite often become sub-optimal, or set up situations of moral hazard. The idea of moral hazard is widely used in discussions of risk in private insurance. Moral hazard exists when people use insurance protection to alter their behaviour, thereby redefining the risk for which they are insured. It isn't so much that some forms of welfare provision create dependency cultures as that people take rational advantage of opportunities offered. Benefits meant to counter unemployment, for instance, can actually produce unemployment if they are actively used as a shelter from the labour market.

Writing against the backdrop of the Swedish welfare system, the economist Assar Lindbeck notes that a strong humanitarian case can be made for generous support for people affected by unemployment, illness, disability or the other standard risks covered by the welfare state. The dilemma is that the higher the benefits the greater will be the chance of moral hazard, as well as fraud. He suggests that moral hazard tends to be greater in the long run than in shorter time periods. This is because in the longer term social habits are built up which come to define what is 'normal'. Serious benefit dependency is then no longer even seen as such but simply becomes 'expected' behaviour. An increased tendency to apply for social assistance, more absence from work for alleged health reasons, and a lower level of job search may be among the results.[4]

Once established, benefits have their own autonomy, regardless of whether or not they meet the purposes for which they were originally designed. As this happens, expectations become 'locked in' and interest groups entrenched. Countries that have tried to reform their pensions systems, for example, have met with concerted resistance. We should have our pensions because we are 'old' (at age sixty or sixty-five), we have paid our dues (even if they don't cover the costs), other people before have had them, everyone looks forward to retirement and so forth. Yet such institutional stasis is in and of itself a reflection of the need for reform, for the welfare state needs to be as dynamic and responsive to wider social trends as any other sector of government.

Welfare reform isn't easy to achieve, precisely because of the entrenched interests that welfare systems create. Yet the outline of a radical project for the welfare state can be sketched out quite readily.

The welfare state, as indicated earlier, is a pooling of risk rather than resources. What has shaped the solidarity of social policy is that 'otherwise privileged groups discovered that they shared a common interest in reallocating risk with the disadvantaged'.[5] However, the welfare state isn't geared up to cover new-style risks such as those concerning technological change, social exclusion or the accelerating proportion of one-parent households. These mismatches are of two kinds: where risks covered don't fit with needs, and where the wrong groups are protected.

Welfare reform should recognize the points about risk made earlier in the discussion: effective risk management (individual or collective) doesn't just mean minimizing or protecting against risks; it also means harnessing the positive or energetic side of risk and providing resources for risk taking. Active risk taking is recognized as inherent in entrepreneurial activity, but the same applies to the labour force. Deciding to go to work and give up benefits, or taking a job in a particular industry, are risk-infused activities – but such risk taking is often beneficial both to the individual and to the wider society.

When Beveridge wrote his *Report on Social Insurance and Allied Services*, in 1942, he famously declared war on Want, Disease, Ignorance, Squalor and Idleness. In other words, his focus was almost entirely negative. We should speak today of *positive welfare*, to which individuals themselves and other agencies besides government contribute – and which is functional for wealth creation. Welfare is not in essence an economic concept, but a psychic one, concerning as it does well-being. Economic benefits or advantages are therefore virtually never enough on their own to create it. Not only is welfare generated by many contexts and influences other than the welfare state, but welfare institutions must be concerned with fostering psychological as well as economic benefits. Quite mundane examples can be given: counselling, for example, might sometimes be more helpful than direct economic support.

Although these propositions may sound remote from the down-to-earth concerns of welfare systems, there isn't a single area of welfare reform to which they aren't relevant or which they don't help illuminate. The guideline is investment in *human capital* wherever possible, rather than the direct provision of economic maintenance. In place of the welfare state we should put the *social investment state*, operating in the context of a positive welfare society.

The theme that the 'welfare state' should be replaced by the 'welfare society' has become a conventional one in the recent literature on welfare issues. Where third sector agencies are not already well represented, they should play a greater part in providing welfare services. The top-down dispensation of benefits should cede place to more localized distribution systems. More generally, we should recognize that the reconstruction of welfare provision has to be integrated with programmes for the active development of civil society.

## Social Investment Strategies

Since the institutions and services ordinarily grouped together under the rubric of the welfare state are so many, I shall limit myself here to comments on social security. What would the social investment state aim for in terms of its social security systems? Let us take two basic areas: provision for old age and unemployment.

As regards old age, a radical perspective would suggest breaking out of the confines within which debate about pension payments is ordinarily carried on. Most industrial societies have ageing populations, and this is a big problem, it is said, because of the pensions time bomb. The pension commitments of some countries, such as Italy, Germany or Japan, are way beyond what can be afforded, even allowing for reasonable economic growth. If other societies, such as Britain, have to some extent avoided this difficulty, it is because they have actively reduced their state pension commitments – in Britain, for example, by indexing pensions to average prices rather than average earnings.

An adequate level of state-provided pension is a necessity. There is good reason also to support schemes of compulsory saving. In the UK the effect of relating pension increases to prices rather than earnings, without other statutory provisions, is likely to leave many retirees impoverished. A man who is fifty in 1998 and leaves the labour market aged sixty-five will receive a government pension amounting to only 10 per cent of average male earnings. Many people don't have either occupational or private pensions.[6] Other countries have come up with more effective strategies. A number of examples of combined public/private sector funding of pensions exist, some of which are capable of generalization. The Finnish system, for example, combines a state-guaranteed basic minimum income and earnings-related pension with regulated private sector provision.

The interest of the pensions issue, however, stretches more broadly than the questions of who should pay, at what level and by what means.

It should go along with rethinking what old age is and how changes in the wider society affect the position of older people. Positive welfare applies as much in this context as in any other: it isn't enough to think only in terms of economic benefits. Old age is a new-style risk masquerading as an old-style one. Ageing used to be more passive than it is now: the ageing body was simply something that had to be accepted. In the more active, reflexive society, ageing has become much more of an open process, on a physical as well as a psychic level. Becoming older presents at least as many opportunities as problems, both for individuals and for the wider social community.

The concept of a pension that begins at retirement age, and the label 'pensioner', were inventions of the welfare state. But not only do these not conform to the new realities of ageing, they are as clear a case of welfare dependency as one can find. They suggest incapacity, and it is not surprising that for many people retirement leads to a loss of self-esteem. When retirement first fixed 'old age' at sixty or sixty-five, the situation of older people was very different from what it is now. In 1900, average life expectancy for a male aged twenty in England was only sixty-two.

We should move towards abolishing the fixed age of retirement, and we should regard older people as a resource rather than a problem. The category of pensioner will then cease to exist, because it is detachable from pensions as such: it makes no sense to lock up pension funds against reaching 'pensionable age'. People should be able to use such funds as they wish – not only to leave the labour force at any age, but to finance education, or reduced working hours, when bringing up young children.[7] Abolishing statutory retirement would probably be neutral in respect of labour market implications, given that individuals could give up work earlier as well as stay in work longer. These provisions won't as such help pay for pensions where a country has overstretched its future commitments, and this perspective is agnostic about what balance should be aimed for between public and private funding. Yet it does suggest there is scope for innovative thinking around the pensions issue.

A society that separates older people from the majority in a retirement ghetto cannot be called inclusive. The precept of philosophic conservatism applies here as elsewhere: old age shouldn't be seen as a time of rights without responsibilities. Burke famously observed that 'society is a partnership not only between those who are living, but between those who are living, those who are dead and those who are to be born'.[8] Such a partnership is presumed, in a relatively mundane context, by the very idea of collective pensions, which act as a conduit between generations. But an intergenerational contract plainly needs to be deeper than this. The young should be willing to look to the old for models, and older people should see themselves as in the service of future generations.[9] Are such goals realistic in a society that has retreated from deference, and where age no longer appears to bring wisdom? Several factors suggest they may be. Being 'old' lasts longer than it used to do. There are far more old people in the population and hence the old are more socially visible. Finally, their growing involvement in work and the community should act to link them directly to younger generations.

The position of the frail elderly, people who need continuous care, raises more difficult questions. There are twenty times more people over eighty-five in the UK today than there were in 1900. Many of the 'young old' may be in quite a different situation from that of those in the same age group a couple of generations ago. It is a different matter for the 'old old', some of whom fare badly.[10] The question of what collective resources should be made available to the frail elderly is not just one of rationing. There are issues to be confronted here, including ethical questions of a quite fundamental sort, that go well beyond the scope of this discussion.

What of unemployment? Does the goal of full employment mean anything any more? Is there a straight trade-off, as the neo-liberals say, between employment and deregulated labour markets – contrasting the US 'jobs miracle' with Eurosclerosis? We should note first of all that no simple comparison between the 'US' and the 'European model' is possible. As economist Stephen Nickell has shown, labour markets in Europe show great diversity. Over the period from 1983 to 1996, there were large variations in unemployment rates in OECD Europe, ranging from 1.8 per cent in Switzerland to over 20 per cent in Spain. Of OECD countries, 30 per cent over these years had average unemployment rates lower than the US. Those with the lowest rates are not noted for having the most deregulated labour markets (Austria, Portugal, Norway). Labour market rigidities like strict employment legislation don't strongly influence unemployment. High unemployment is linked to generous benefits that run on indefinitely and to poor educational standards at the lower end of the labour market – the phenomenon of exclusion.[11]

The position of the third way should be that sweeping deregulation is not the answer. Welfare expenditure should remain at European rather than US levels, but be switched as far as possible towards human capital investment. Benefit systems should be reformed where they induce moral hazard, and a more active risk-taking attitude encouraged, wherever possible through incentives, but where necessary by legal obligations.

It is worth perhaps at this stage commenting briefly on the 'Dutch model', sometimes pointed to as a successful adaptation of social democracy to new social and economic conditions. In an agreement concluded at Wassenaar some sixteen years ago, the country's unions agreed to wage moderation in exchange for a gradual reduction in working hours. As a result, labour costs have fallen by over 30 per cent [since 1988], while the economy has thrived. This has been achieved with an unemployment rate below 6 per cent in 1997.

Looked at more closely, however, the Dutch model is less impressive, at least in terms of job creation and welfare reform. Substantial numbers who would in other countries count as unemployed are living on disability benefit – the country in fact has more people registered as unfit for work than it has officially unemployed. At 51 per cent, the proportion of the population aged between fifteen and sixty-four in full-time work is below what it was in 1970, when it was nearly 60 per cent and well short of the European average of 67 per cent. Of jobs created [since 1988], 90 per cent are part-time. Holland spends the highest proportion of its income on social security of any European country, and its welfare system is under considerable strain.[12]

Strategies for job creation and the future of work need to be based upon an orientation to the new economic exigencies. Companies and consumers are increasingly operating on a world scale in terms of the standards demanded for goods and services. Consumers shop on a world level, in the sense that distribution is global and therefore 'the best' no longer has any generic connection with where goods and services are produced. Pressures to meet these standards will also apply more and more to labour forces. In some contexts such pressures are likely to deepen processes of social exclusion. The differentiation will be not only between manual and knowledge workers, or between high skills and low skills, but between those who are local in outlook and those who are more cosmopolitan.

Investment in human resources is proving to be the main source of leverage which firms have in key economic sectors. One study in the US compared 700 large companies across different industries. The results showed that even a marginal difference in an index of investment in people increased shareholder returns by $41,000.[13] The business analyst Rosabeth Moss Kanter identifies five main areas where government policy can assist job creation. There should be support for *entrepreneurial initiatives* concerned with small business startups and technological innovation. Many countries, particularly in Europe, still place too much reliance upon established economic institutions, including the public sector, to produce employment. In a world 'where customers can literally shop for workers', without the new ideas guaranteed by entrepreneurship there is an absence of competition. Entrepreneurship is a direct source of jobs. It also drives technological development, and gives people opportunities for self-employment in times of transition. Government policy can provide direct support for entrepreneurship, through helping create venture capital, but also through restructuring welfare systems to give security when entrepreneurial ventures go wrong – for example, by giving people the option to be taxed on a two- or three-year cycle rather than only annually.

Governments need to emphasize *lifelong education*, developing education programmes that start from an individual's early years and continue on even late in life. Although training in specific skills may be necessary for many job transitions, more important is the development of cognitive and emotional competence. Instead of relying on unconditional benefits, policies should be oriented to encourage saving, the use of educational resources and other personal investment opportunities.

*Public project partnerships* can give private enterprise a larger role in activities which governments once provided for, while ensuring that the public interest remains paramount. The public sector can in turn provide resources that can help enterprise to flourish and without which joint projects may fail. Moss Kanter points out that welfare to work programmes in the US have sometimes foundered on the problem of transport. Companies offer jobs in areas which those available for them can't easily reach because of lack of adequate transport facilities.

Government policies can enhance *portability*, whether through common standards of education or through portable pension rights. Greater harmonization of educational practices and standards, for instance, is desirable for a cosmopolitan labour force. Some global corporations have already set up standardized entrance requirements, but governments need to take the lead. As in other areas, harmonization is not necessarily the enemy of educational diversity and may even be the condition of sustaining it.

Finally, governments should encourage *family-friendly workplace policies*, something that can also be achieved through public–private collaborations. Countries vary widely in the level of child care they offer, for instance, as do companies. Not only child care, but other work opportunities, such as telecommuting or work sabbaticals, can help reconcile employment and domestic life. The more companies emphasize human resources, the more competition there will be to have the best family-friendly work environments. Governments which help them will also tend to attract inward investment.[14]

Can these strategies produce a return to full employment in the usual sense – enough good jobs to go around for everyone who wants one? No one knows, but it seems unlikely. The proportion of jobs that are full-time and long-term is declining in Western economies. Comparisons between the 'full employment economies', such as the US or the UK, and 'high unemployment' societies, like Germany or France, are less clear cut when we compare not the number of jobs but the hours of work created. Net job creation for skilled work that is secure and well paid over the ten years 1986–96 was the same in Germany as in the US, at 2.6 per cent. Labour productivity doubled in Germany over that period, whereas in the US it rose by only 25 per cent.[15]

Since no one can say whether or not global capitalism will in future generate sufficient work, it would be foolish to proceed as though it will. Is the 'active redistribution' of work possible without counterproductive consequences? Probably not in the form of limits to the working week fixed by government – the difficulties with such schemes are well known. But if we see it in a wider context, we have no need to ask whether redistribution of work is possible. It is already happening on a widespread basis, and the point is to foster its positive aspects. One much-quoted experiment is that at Hewlett Packard's plant in Grenoble. The plant is kept open on a 24-hour cycle seven days a week. The employees have a working week averaging just over 30 hours, but receive the same wages as when they were working a 37.5-hour week. Labour productivity has increased substantially.[16]

Since the revival of civic culture is a basic ambition of third way politics, the active involvement of government in the social economy makes sense. Indeed some have presented the choice before us in stark terms, given the problematic status of full employment: either greater participation in the social economy or facing the growth of 'outlaw cultures'. The possibilities are many, including time dollar schemes [ . . . ] and shadow wages – tax breaks for hours worked in the social economy. As diverse studies across Europe show, 'more and more people are looking both for meaningful work and opportunities for commitment outside of work. If society can upgrade and reward such commitment and put it on a level with gainful employment, it can create both individual identity and social cohesion.'[17]

In sum, what would a radically reformed welfare state – the social investment state in the positive welfare society – look like? Expenditure on welfare, understood as positive welfare, will be generated and distributed not wholly through the state, but by the state working in combination with other agencies, including business. The welfare society here is not just the nation, but stretches above and below it. Control of environmental pollution, for example, can never be a matter for national government alone, but it is certainly directly relevant to welfare. In the positive welfare society, the contract between individual and government shifts, since autonomy and the development of self – the medium of expanding individual responsibility – become the prime focus. Welfare in this basic sense concerns the rich as well as the poor.

Positive welfare would replace each of Beveridge's negatives with a positive: in place of Want, autonomy; not Disease but active health; instead of Ignorance, education, as a continuing part of life; rather than Squalor, well-being; and in place of Idleness, initiative.

## Notes

From *The Third Way*, Cambridge, Polity Press, 1998, pp. 111–28.

1 Nicholas Timmins, *The Five Giants*, London, Fontana, 1996, p. 12.
2 Kees van Kersbergen, *Social Capitalism*, London, Routledge, 1995, p. 7.
3 Howard Glennerster and John Hills, *The State of Welfare*, Oxford, Oxford University Press, 2nd edition, 1998.
4 Assar Lindbeck, 'The End of the Middle Way?', *American Economic Review*, vol. 85, 1995.

5 Peter Baldwin, *The Politics of Social Solidarity*, Cambridge, Cambridge University Press, 1990, p. 292.
6 Stuart Fleming, 'What we'll earn when we're 64', *New Statesman*, 5 June 1998.
7 Will Hutton, *The State We're In*, London, Cape, 1995.
8 Edmund Burke, *Reflections on the Revolution in France* [1790], London, Dent, 1910, pp. 93–4.
9 Daniel Callahan, *Setting Limits*, New York, Simon and Schuster, 1987, p. 46.
10 Ibid., p. 20.
11 Stephen Nickell, 'Unemployment and Labour Market Rigidities', *Journal of Economic Perspectives*, vol. 11, 1997.
12 Dominic Vidal, 'Miracle or Mirage in the Netherlands?', *Le Monde Diplomatique*, July 1997.
13 Rosabeth Moss Kanter, 'Keynote Address', Centre for Economic Performance: Employability and Exclusion, London, CEP, May 1998.
14 Ibid., pp. 65–8.
15 Ulrich Beck, 'Capitalism without Work', *Dissent*, winter 1997, p. 102.
16 Jeremy Rifkin, *The End of Work*, New York, Putnam's, 1995, p. 225.
17 Beck, op. cit., p. 106.

# The Politics of the New Social Policies: Providing Coverage against New Social Risks in Mature Welfare States

*Giuliano Bonoli*

[ . . . ]

## What are New Social Risks?

The concept of new social risks (NSRs) is being used with increasing frequency in the literature on the welfare state (Esping-Andersen, 1999a; Hemerijck, 2002; Jenson, 2002; Taylor-Gooby, 2004). However, a precise definition of what is considered under this label is generally missing. Generally speaking, NSR are related to the socioeconomic transformations that have brought post-industrial societies into existence: the tertiarization of employment and the massive entry of women into the labour force. New social risks, as they are understood here, include the following.

### *Reconciling Work and Family Life*

The massive entry of women into the labour market has meant that the standard division of labour within families that was typical of the *trente glorieuses* or the golden age of welfare capitalism (1945–75) has collapsed. The domestic and childcare work that used to be performed on an unpaid basis by housewives now needs to be externalized. It can be either obtained from the state or bought on the market. The difficulties faced by families in this respect (but most significantly by women) are a major source of frustration and can result in important losses of welfare, for example if a parent reduces working hours because of the unavailability of adequate childcare facilities. As a result, the problem of reconciling work and family life can be labelled as a social risk.

## *Single Parenthood*

Changes in family structures and behaviour have resulted in increased rates of single parenthood across Organization for Economic Cooperation and Development (OECD) countries, which presents a distinctive set of social policy problems (access to an adequate income, child care, relationship between parenthood and work). More generally, it is obvious that difficulties in reconciling work and family life are more serious for single parents than they are for two-parent households.

## *Having a Frail Relative*

As in the case of children, during the *trente glorieuses* care for frail elderly or disabled people was mostly provided by non-employed women on an unpaid, informal basis. Again, with the change in women's patterns of labour market participation, this task needs to be externalized too. The inability to do so (because of lack of services) may also result in important welfare losses.

## *Possessing Low or Obsolete Skills*

Low-skilled individuals have obviously always existed. However, during the postwar years, low-skilled workers were predominantly employed in manufacturing industry. They were able to benefit from productivity increases due to technological advances, so that their wages rose together with those of the rest of the population. The strong mobilizing capacity of the trade unions among industrial workers further sustained their wages, which came to constitute the guarantee of a poverty-free existence. Today, low-skilled individuals are mostly employed in the low value-added service sector or unemployed. Low value-added services such as retail sales, cleaning, catering and so forth are known for providing very little scope for productivity increases (Pierson, 1998). In countries where wage determination is essentially based on market mechanisms, this means that low-skilled individuals are seriously exposed to the risk of being paid a poverty wage (US, UK, Switzerland). The situation is different in countries where wage determination, especially at the lower end of the distribution, is controlled by governments (through generous minimum wage legislation) or by the social partners (through encompassing collective agreements). Under these circumstances, the wages of low-skilled workers are protected, but job creation in these sectors is limited, so that many low-skilled individuals are in fact unemployed (Iversen and Wren, 1998). Overall, the fact of possessing low or obsolete skills today entails a major risk of welfare loss, considerably higher than in the postwar years.

### *Insufficient Social Security Coverage*

The shift to a post-industrial employment structure has resulted in the presence in modern labour markets of career profiles that are very different from that of the standard male workers of the *trente glorieuses*, characterized by full-time continuous employment from an early age and with a steadily rising salary. Yet the social security schemes (most notably pensions) that we have inherited from the postwar years are still clearly based on these traditional assumptions regarding labour market participation. Pension coverage, in most Western European countries, is optimal for workers who spend their entire working life in full-time employment. Part-time work usually results in reduced pension entitlements, as do career interruptions due to childbearing (Bonoli, 2003). The result of the presence of these new career profiles in the labour market may be, if pension systems are not adapted, the translation of the labour market and working poor problems of today into a poverty problem for older people in thirty or forty years' time. From an individual point of view, following an 'atypical' career pattern represents a risk of insufficient social security coverage, and hence a loss of welfare.

These situations are caused by different factors, but have a number of things in common. First they are all 'new', in the sense that they are typical of the post-industrial societies in which we live today. During the *trente glorieuses*, the period of male full employment and sustained economic growth that characterized the postwar years, these risks were extremely marginal, if they existed at all. In addition to newness, new social risks share another feature. They tend to be concentrated on the same groups of people, usually younger people, families with small children, or working women. While it is difficult to set clear borders around the section of the population that bears most NSRs, it is clear that the categories mentioned here are largely overlapping, and that it is possible to identify in every post-industrial society a fairly large minority of the population that struggles daily against the consequences of NSRs.

## From Risk Exposure to Political Mobilization

It is tempting to see parallels between the groups that today are exposed to NSR and industrial workers whose lives were also shattered by social and economic change centuries ago. In so far as industrial workers are concerned, increased exposure to market risks resulted in what has probably been one of the most sustained and successful instances of political mobilization in modern Western history: the creation of labour movements and social democratic parties. These were able to bring workers' concerns to the centre of the political arena and to force through the adoption of labour market regulations, social insurance schemes and universal services, which tremendously improved their living conditions (Stephens, 1979; Castles, 1982; Korpi, 1983; Esping-Andersen, 1985).

To what extent can we draw a parallel between industrial workers in the early days of capitalism and NSR groups today? And in particular, is there any evidence that the political mechanisms that brought traditional welfare states into existence may be in some way replicated in relation to post-industrial social policies? This section looks at empirical evidence on the potential of political mobilization of NSR groups. It focuses on three key dimensions of mobilization: political participation, representation in key democratic institutions, and the policy preferences of members of NSR-exposed groups.

## *Participation*

The key socio-demographic characteristics of NSR groups outlined above are the fact of being young, of possessing low skills and of being a woman. Two of these factors are also the main predictors of voting turnout across Western democracies, and are associated with lower participation. Age is a particularly strong predictor of political participation. Using survey data for seventeen countries, Norris finds that age is by far the best predictor of voting turnout at the micro-level. On average, turnout for the under-25s is just 55 per cent whereas it reaches 88 per cent for the late middle-aged voters (Norris, 2002). It is not entirely clear if the impact of age on turnout reflects a cohort or a life-cycle effect, however. With regard to the US, Putnam provides evidence that political participation of younger generations does not increase as they become older, suggesting that the link between age and turnout reflects a cohort effect (Putnam, 2000). However, other studies reviewed by Norris support the view that in Western Europe the age gap in voting turnout has remained more or less constant over the last thirty years, suggesting instead a life-cycle effect. From the point of view of this article, however, it is not essential to establish whether it is cohort or position in the life-cycle that determines participation. What matters is that those who today have to confront NSRs are less likely to participate in elections.

After age (and together with income), education is the second best predictor of voting turnout, though its impact varies across countries. Education does not successfully predict political participation in most Western European countries, but does so in the US and in Eastern Europe. Finally, gender used to be a powerful predictor of voting turnout, men being more likely to participate in elections than women, but in recent years this is no longer the case (Norris, 2002).

With the exception of women, NSR groups clearly suffer from a participation gap with regard to the rest of society. It is true that education is a strong predictor of turnout only in countries with big educational inequalities (such as the US) or in former communist countries, and not so in Western European countries, on which our analysis concentrates. However, the pre-eminence of age as a determinant of turnout and the fact that it is a key feature of NSR groups suggests that the capacity of this group to influence policy-making via standard democratic channels is likely to be limited.

## Representation

When examining the problem of representation of NSR groups in key democratic institutions, two issues need to be addressed: presence and effective interest representation. Presence refers to whether or not individuals who belong to the social groups that are more exposed to NSRs belong to those institutions. In concrete terms, one needs to find out the extent to which governments, parliaments and labour market-based institutions of representation such as trade unions include among their members women, younger people, low-skilled people and so forth. But presence is arguably not a sufficient condition for effective interest representation. Given the fact that there are no political parties or trade unions that have the explicit function of defending the interests of NSR groups, those who get elected or appointed are unlikely to be under any form of constraint in so far as the interests they represent are concerned. There are reasons to believe the groups exposed to NSR, once elected, will be more sensitive to the demands of other NSR groups, because of empathy or because of the fact that socio-demographically similar people constitute some kind of 'natural' electoral constituency, but, given the absence of clear constraints and accountability relationships between the representatives and the represented, it is difficult to answer this question on a theoretical level, and it probably needs to be settled empirically.

Tables 1 and 2 provide a rough indication of the presence of the social groups identified as most likely to be exposed to NSR in key democratic institutions. Women are a minority in all the parliaments included in table 1, although in some Nordic countries they approach 50 per cent of members. In the rest of Western Europe and in the US, however, the proportion of women in Parliament is between a tenth and a third. Women are seldom represented in government cabinets, again with the exception of some Scandinavian countries (Sweden) where they often represent 50 per cent of cabinet seats (Siaroff, 2000, p. 200). Young people do not have a strong presence in Western parliaments either. The average age of parliamentarians is around 50, with some variation (younger parliaments are found in the Nordic countries, older ones in continental Europe).

Turning to trade unions, a crucial institution in the fields of welfare and employment regulation, these are characterized in most countries by the

**Table 1** Proportion of women in lower houses of parliament (%)

| | 1990 | 2001 |
|---|---|---|
| Sweden | 38.1 | 42.7 |
| Denmark | n.a. | 38.0 |
| Finland | n.a. | 36.5 |
| Norway | 35.8 | 36.4 |
| Netherlands | 21.3 | 34.0 |
| Germany | 20.4 | 31.7 |
| Spain | n.a. | 28.3 |
| Austria | n.a. | 26.8 |
| Switzerland | n.a. | 23.0 |
| UK | 9.2 | 17.9 |
| US | 10.8 | 14.0 |
| France | 5.7 | 10.9 |
| Italy | 12.8 | 9.8 |

*Source*: Inglehart and Norris, 2003.

**Table 2** Average age of Members of Parliament (MPs), spring 2002

| | |
|---|---|
| France | 57 |
| Germany | 54 |
| Italy | 52 |
| Switzerland | 51 |
| UK | 51 |
| Sweden | 49 |
| Finland | 47 |
| Denmark | 47 |

*Source*: Information obtained from individual parliaments.

predominance of older men among their members and leadership (table 3). There are, however, important country variations. In the Nordic countries and in the UK women are more likely to be union members than male workers. In addition, in these countries the age gap in union membership is virtually non-existent, with similar density rates for younger and older employees. In continental European countries, by contrast, there is a clear gender and age gap in unionization rates. It is here that the bias towards higher density among older male workers is stronger. The picture emerging from tables 1, 2 and 3 is one that can be described in terms of underrepresentation of NSR groups in key democratic institutions. Governments, parliaments and trade unions are mostly composed of late-middle-aged men. There are some clear country variations, which, interestingly, go in the same

**Table 3** Net union density for different social groups, 1996

| | Men | Women | Younger workers (up to 34) | Older workers (55 and older) |
|---|---|---|---|---|
| Sweden | 86.9 | 89.9 | 80.6 | 89.9 |
| Norway | 60.8 | 66.6 | 52.7 | 71.3 |
| Germany (West) | 33.9 | 15.1 | 23.2 | 25.3 |
| Germany (East) | 30.1 | 30.4 | 24.0 | 32.4 |
| Italy | 36.9 | 23.2 | 16.1 | 37.7 |
| France | 18.7 | 15.7 | 9.9 | 29.3 |
| Spain | 16.8 | 14.0 | 12.6 | 15.1 |
| Switzerland | 25.9 | 17.5 | 17.7 | 25.5 |
| UK | 34.4 | 35.1 | 35.1 | 25.3 |

*Source*: Ebbinghaus, 2003, on the basis of International Social Survey Project data.

direction. In each of the three tables the presence of NSR groups in key representative outfits is stronger in the Nordic countries, and to a lesser extent in the UK. Their parliaments are younger and more feminized, and their labour movements are more feminized and younger than those found in other Western European countries.

But presence is not a sufficient condition for effective interest representation. What matters is how elected NSR groups vote in their parliaments and the positions they defend. The question of whether members of a given social group tend to represent their fellow members when elected to a position of power is one that, in relation to women, has intrigued feminist political science for several decades.

There is a large corpus of literature on the voting behaviour of women MPs, on their political attitudes, and on their political activities in general. Overall, the message that one gets from this literature is that the presence of women in Parliament matters for decisions on issues that are of particular concern to women, such as childcare policy or equal opportunities (Norris and Lovenduski, 1989, 2003; Tramblay, 1998; Sawer, 2000). If we can rely on several studies on the behaviour of women acting as elected officials, we know much less about other social groups likely to be more strongly exposed to NSR, such as the young or the low-skilled. One study of British parliamentary candidates' attitudes found that support for gender equality measures was stronger among younger women (Norris and Lovenduski, 2003), suggesting that age might have an impact on issues that are of relevance to the lives of NSR groups. But we certainly need more empirical research on this issue if it is to be settled satisfactorily.

The available evidence suggests that, when elected, individuals belonging to NSR-exposed groups are likely to be more sensitive to the needs and demands of this social group than other elected officials, and that this trend may be on the increase. This finding goes in the direction of more political influence for NSR groups, as in spite of the lack of dedicated representative outfits, they seem capable of making themselves heard through the existing channels. However, the evidence reviewed is sketchy, and should be weighed against the presence gap outlined above before concluding that NSR groups have real opportunities to influence policy-making in parliaments and in labour market institutions.

## Preferences

The third condition that needs to be fulfilled for NSR groups to be able to influence policy to their advantage is some degree of distinctiveness and homogeneity of their political preferences. Do NSR groups tend to express political preferences that are different from those of other voters? Are these shared by all NSR-exposed individuals? The last two decades have seen an interesting and rather puzzling development in the voting behaviour of women. Throughout the 1950s and the 1960s women's voting patterns were consistently slightly more right-wing than men's. More recently, first in the US and then in a majority of advanced democracies, women voters tend to prefer left-wing parties to a larger extent than their male counterparts. This shift has been explained with reference to a mix of structural and cultural factors: labour market participation, secularization, social support for gender equality and so forth (Inglehart and Norris, 2003).

The shift to the left of female electorates fits in well with the NSR perspective put forward in this article. Women, especially younger ones, who have become exposed to NSR only in the last few decades, are more likely to turn to left-wing parties in so far as they tend to promote the kind of policies that can improve their quality of life (child care, parental leave, etc.). As a matter of fact, the gender gap in voting behaviour is stronger in countries which have a higher female employment rate: the more women are exposed to NSR the more they tend to mobilize for left-wing parties.[1] Perhaps the clearer cases of gender-based cleavages in voting behaviour are the Scandinavian countries, where women are considerably more likely than men to support the Social Democrats (Esping-Andersen, 1999b).

Distinctive patterns of voting among those who are exposed to NSR emerge also from voting behaviour in referendums on age-related social policies in Switzerland. In a study of nineteen referendums on decisions with a different impact according to age group, age turned out to be a significant predictor of voting behaviour in fourteen. Policies for the younger groups, such as paid maternity leave, more funds for universities, better employment protection or unemployment compensation, were generally opposed by older voters. Improvements in the pension system, by contrast, were supported more strongly by older voters (Bonoli, 2004a).

Similar cleavages on age-related social policy issues can be observed also in opinion polls in virtually all countries (Esping-Andersen, 1999b, p. 312; Armingeon, 2004), but voting behaviour in referendums is certainly a more reliable indicator of political opinions. Note that public opinion data suggest the cleavage to be one-sided: older respondents do not support policies for the young, but there is no clear age-related distinction in support for retirement pensions and other policies for older people. This is also confirmed by surveys on referendum voting on old-age issues in Switzerland.

The overall impression is that there is some distinctiveness in the political preferences expressed by NSR groups but the correlations are usually rather weak. In addition, the defining socio-demographic features of NSR groups (age, gender, skill level, family configuration) tend to be less strong a predictor of policy and political preferences than the traditional determinants of class and religion: two factors that intersect the cleavage between traditional welfare state clienteles and welfare groups investigated in this study.

### *Limited Power Resources*

This overview of patterns of political participation, representation and preferences of NSR groups paints a mixed picture in so far as their ability to influence policy is concerned. Low participation, internal divisions and the lack of dedicated representative outfits can be formidable obstacles to successful political mobilization. On the other hand, distinctiveness in political preferences and effective interest representation of elected officials are political assets for NSR groups. On balance, and especially if we compare the situation of NSR groups to that of industrial workers during the twentieth century, the evidence reviewed here suggests that, at least for the time being, the 'power resources' of NSR groups remain largely insufficient to impose the kind of policies that would serve their interests through the democratic game. The Nordic countries, and to a lesser extent the UK, however, may represent an exception here. It is there that, according to the data presented in this article, NSR groups have a stronger presence in democratic and labour market institutions and, as far as the Nordic countries are concerned, it is also where one finds the most developed policies for them. In other countries, especially in continental European nations, if policies providing coverage against NSR are being developed, this must be as a result of some different mechanism than through imposition in the political arena.

The political weight of new social risks groups is not insignificant. It is probably insufficient to bend the political system to their advantage, but it can still influence adaptation. New social risks groups, if unable to change the world on their own, may nonetheless represent an interesting constituency for vote-seeking politicians. At the same time, if capable of striking the right alliances with other groups in society, NSR groups may obtain at least some policies that protect their interests.

## New Patterns of Social Policy-Making for New Social Risks

The particular nature of NSRs and of the policies aimed at addressing them generates a distinctive set of opportunities for policy-making that did not exist, or did not exist to such an extent, during the construction phase of postwar welfare states. Traditional social policies had among their key objectives the decommodification of wage earners and, in this respect, they were bound to develop in the context of an opposition between wage earners and employers, the latter trying to resist high levels of decommodification that could be detrimental to business profitability. Policies that cover NSRs do not decommodify workers; they just make their condition more attractive. If anything, they represent an additional incentive to work for those groups of the population who have traditionally been excluded from paid employment, especially women. One of the consequences of better NSR coverage is to increase labour supply. In the current context of population ageing and, in some countries, population decline combined with difficulties in integrating immigrant populations, an increase in domestic labour supply is likely to be welcomed by business.

The new social policies discussed here distinguish themselves from the traditional ones also in terms of cost. Generally speaking, to provide a service to a section of the population only, say working parents, is less costly than to set up a universal pension scheme. A quick comparison of expenditure figures in social programmes covering old and new risks shows very clearly that the latter come much cheaper. The biggest spenders on family services and on active labour market policies have outlays on these programmes not exceeding 2 per cent of GDP, whereas typical figures for programmes like health care and pensions are in the region of 10 per cent of GDP. The comparatively low cost of providing coverage of NSRs may reduce the opposition against it from those who have to foot the bill.

These key features of NSR coverage policies open up a set of new opportunities for policy-making that have been exploited, especially in continental European countries. By understanding the mechanisms that are behind policy decisions in this broad field, we may be better able to account for developments in countries where the political mobilization and representation of NSR groups are particularly weak, and which lack a tradition of social intervention in this area of policy, or where political institutions do not allow the unilateral imposition of government policy.

## *Turning Vice into Virtue*

This mechanism for the modernization of conservative welfare states has been identified by Jonah Levy. It is an approach that 'targets inequities within the welfare system that are simultaneously a source of either economic inefficiency or substantial public spending', and generates savings that can be used to 'pursue a variety of virtuous objectives: redistributing income toward the poor . . . facilitating the negotiation of far-reaching, tripartite social pacts' (Levy, 1999, p. 240). Levy provides a few examples: in the Netherlands, reductions in public spending on disability pensions, a scheme that was widely abused in the 1980s, made it possible for the government to introduce tax breaks targeted on low-income households. In Italy, pension privileges for some workers (civil servants) were abolished but at the same time the reform introduced flexible retirement age, and inequities between occupational groups have been done away with.

These (and other) instances of policy-making based on 'turning vice into virtue' have in common the fact that they originate in the context of budget austerity that makes intolerable expenditure that is widely regarded as inefficient. The funds generated by reducing this kind of expenditure can be used to finance new initiatives. In fact, the prime objective of reform being cost containment, it is only a small part of the funds freed by the austerity measures that are assigned to the new programmes.

## *Modernizing Compromises*

A similar mechanism, but with a stronger political dimension, has been observed especially in countries characterized by fragmented political institutions or by countries temporarily ruled by weak governments. Typically the compromise takes the shape of the inclusion, within a single reform, of measures of cost containment or retrenchment, and of improvements in provision. The cost containment measures generally concern policies that provide coverage for 'old risks', while the improvements and expansion concern NSR coverage. That is why these reforms can be qualified as 'modernizing compromises'.

Switzerland is probably the clearest case of such compromises. In the 1995 pension reform, an increase in women's retirement age was traded against contribution credits for carers and contribution sharing between spouses. The two measures were supported and opposed by important sections of the population. The inclusion of both in a single piece of legislation made the reform stronger in parliament and with voters. It survived the referendum obstacle and is now law. Similarly, the 1995 unemployment insurance reform combined a two-year time limit on passive benefits with increased spending on active labour market policies. Again, it was a compromise that contained measures strongly supported by the right (the time limit on benefits) and by the left (active labour market policies) and that was as a result able to attract the support of a large section of the political spectrum. It too is now law (Bonoli, 2001).

A modernizing compromise took place also in the Swedish pension reform of the 1990s. On the one hand, the reform reduced pension entitlements for some occupational groups. The main losers were white collar employees and managers, or those who start working relatively late after a long period spent in education, but overall about 80 per cent of the population is likely to lose between 7 and 8 per cent of their pension as a result of changes introduced (Anderson, 2001)[2]. On the other hand, in order not to penalize women but also as a compensation for white collar workers who had lost out because of the change in the pension formula, the reform introduced generous contribution credits for several categories of non-employed people. These are granted for career interruptions due to childrearing, periods of unemployment, study, military service and sickness. With regard to childrearing, if a parent reduces working hours in the four years following the birth of a child, contributions are credited to his or her pension account on the basis of previous earnings. If he or she stops working completely, then the contribution credit will be based on 75 per cent of the average wage. The Swedish reform combined overall retrenchment in pensions with the introduction of one of the most generous systems of contribution credits for carers. Swedish contribution credits, unlike those in most other countries, apply not only to the state pension, but also to private individual retirement accounts. In this way, the reform package was able to attract the support of a sufficient number of political actors to guarantee its adoption.

Modernizing compromises seem a promising avenue to achieve advances in the coverage of NSRs. Supporters of welfare retrenchment and of increased coverage for NSRs usually belong to different political camps, and if they do join forces on a single reform initiative, they are likely to form an extremely strong coalition in the political arena. This mechanism is more likely to exist in countries where political institutions, because of their fragmentation, encourage the formation of large coalitions around given policy proposals. Here the incentive for political actors to compromise is strongest (the alternative being stalemate). Paradoxically, one may thus expect countries with fragmented political institutions to move faster in the development of policies that cover NSRs.

## *Convergence of Interests with Employers*

Some of the key features of NSR coverage policies make them particularly attractive to employers. As seen above, these policies do not provide decommodification, they are generally not as costly as the more traditional forms of social intervention, and they have a clearly favourable impact on labour supply. This is the case especially of child care and other policies aimed at making it easier for families to reconcile work and family life. As a result of their introduction, one can expect the labour supply of women to increase significantly (Daly, 2000). Active labour market policies (ALMPs) can have a similar impact, by encouraging the transition from non-employment to employment of individuals belonging to various groups of non-working people, most notably youth and long-term unemployed people, older working-age persons, and some disabled people. ALMPs have a positive impact on labour supply not only in quantitative but also in qualitative terms, and can contribute to matching labour supply and demand.

These sorts of policies would obviously present a clear interest for employers under any set of circumstances, but the ongoing process of population ageing makes them essential measures. In virtually all industrial countries, all other things being equal, population ageing will lead to a reduction of the working-age population and, as a result, of labour supply. This could translate into labour shortage in some economic sectors, a development already observed in the late 1990s and early 2000s, and as a result lead to wage increases that could be detrimental to business profitability. Many countries are turning to immigration as a solution to the labour market problems that may be generated by population ageing and decline. However, especially in the conservative welfare states of continental Europe, this strategy is met with scepticism by large sections of the population who, on many occasions, have contributed to the success of extreme right-wing populist political parties.

This situation is resulting in an increasing tendency among employers to look for solutions to the ageing-induced labour market problems domestically, and particularly among the groups whose employment rates are lower: above all women, but also older working-age people and some disabled people. This may be needed in order to strike the necessary alliances with the rest of the political right, which, under pressure from anti-foreigner extreme right parties, seems to be clearly turning away from immigration as the solution to the contraction of labour supply. In policy terms, this translates into support for childcare subsidies and ALMPs.

An example of this mechanism is provided by a recent bill, voted by the Swiss parliament, which makes provision for a substantial increase in subsidies for day care centres. The bill was supported by a coalition that included the left (Social Democrats), the Christian Democrats and a section of the Free Democrats, a Liberal party that closely represents employers' interests. The director of the Swiss employers' association publicly supported the bill. Swiss employers' attitude towards childcare policy contrasts sharply with their open opposition to any form of additional social expenditure, and with the position they took a few years ago on a paid maternity leave scheme, which they successfully fought (Ballestri and Bonoli, 2003).

Convergence of interests between working women and employers arguably played a big role in the expansion of publicly subsidized child care in other countries as well. In France, [while] an extensive pre-school system was organized as early as the late nineteenth century, the expansion of provision for the 0–3 year old group goes back to the early 1970s amid concerns for labour shortage (Morgan, 2001, pp. 26–9). In Sweden, employers' support for publicly subsidized child care goes back to the late 1950s and 1960s, a period also characterized by labour shortage (Naumann, 2001). The economic consequences of NSR coverage are such that they favour the formation of cross-class alliances between NSR groups, mostly represented by left-of-centre parties, and employers. The resulting coalition can be politically very influential and succeed in pushing through reform.

## *Affordable Credit Claiming for Post-Socialist Left-Wing Parties*

The late 1990s saw the return to power of left-of-centre parties in twelve out of fifteen European Union member states. Often, this happened after long periods of time spent in the opposition (UK, Germany, Italy). As a result, the accession to government was met with strong expectations by the traditional and new constituencies of these progressive parties. Left-of-centre governments, however, were moving under tight constraints. Economic internationalization meant that it was extremely difficult to levy the funds needed to (re-)expand the traditional elements of the welfare state, such as pensions, health care and unemployment insurance. This problem was compounded by the fact that population ageing, welfare state maturation and the transformation of labour market and family structure were imposing increasing costs on the welfare state. The fact that several of these left-ruled countries were also candidates for the European Monetary Union further reduced their room for manoeuvre in designing new policies or expanding existing ones.

The combination of electoral pressures to adopt policies that would be noticeably different from those of their predecessors, and the economic constraints that were externally and internally imposed upon them, pushed several governments towards the adoption of policies providing coverage against NSRs. If the social democratic parties that ruled most of Europe in the late 1990s were unable to respond to the expectations of their traditional electorates (who, in several cases, turned to more left-wing parties), they still could do something different from their predecessors that would 'speak' to a new potential constituency – NSR groups. Because of their lower cost, these policies were not incompatible with the economic constraints outlined above. Their attractiveness for employers meant that this group, whose support or at least acquiescence was essential for the social democratic governments of the 1990s, would probably refrain from openly fighting their policies.

Often under the label of 'third way', a move towards a new orientation in social policy has happened in virtually all European Union member countries. Active labour market policies and measures designed to help parents reconcile work and family life were introduced across Western Europe in the 1990s. The UK has been at the forefront in this development, but other countries like Germany, Italy or the Netherlands have taken significant steps towards improving the protection against the new social risks discussed in this article. Often this has been the result of brand new policies, but on many occasions reform has consisted of improvement or adaptation of existing provision (Bonoli, 2004b).

It is interesting to note, however, that this move did not generally pay off in electoral terms, as by 2002 most of these governments had suffered substantial electoral losses. In many cases, the strategy of focusing social policy on NSR groups has failed to gain the social democrats new votes. This may be explained with reference to the overall low levels of political participation of NSR groups. The fact that in the 1970s, contrary to the 1990s, political parties found child care to be a vote winner (for instance in France and Sweden) may reflect changes in political attitudes but also in the age composition of electorates. The proportion of the population aged 65 or more in France and Sweden in the 1970s was between 13 and 14 per cent. In contrast, in the late 1990s, in Italy and Germany, two countries where third way social democratic parties have suffered major electoral losses, the same figure is between 16 and 19 per cent. While the difference (between three and six percentage points) may not look dramatic, one needs to take into account that because of the participation gap between different age groups, it underestimates the increase in the political influence of older voters.

## Conclusion

In a majority of OECD countries social programmes providing protection against new social risks are still at an embryonic stage, but virtually everywhere these issues are being discussed in public debates. There are big country variations in the extent to which NSR coverage has been developed, with the Nordic countries being at the forefront. However, even in those countries lagging behind in the adaptation of their social protection systems, essentially the conservative welfare state of continental and southern Europe, some steps in this direction have been taken.

This article has tried to put forward hypotheses capable of accounting for the observed patterns of policy-making. Political explanations developed for the postwar years, in fact, cannot be transposed to the post-industrial age. The low levels of participation, the weak representation and the existence of internal cleavages among those exposed to NSRs means that strong mobilization capable of obtaining protective legislation is unlikely. The power resources available to NSR groups are simply not comparable to those of industrial workers during the heyday of the industrial society. However, there is evidence that, on occasion, issues that are of interest to NSR groups are picked up by politicians and are, rightly or wrongly, believed to be vote winners. Under such circumstances the social groups exposed to NSRs can still exert political influence via democratic institutions, albeit of a different kind from the one deployed by labour movements during the twentieth century. Nonetheless, given the low level of participation among younger voters and the ageing of Western electorates, it is unlikely that political competition to attract the votes of NSR groups will be a sufficient force to restructure welfare states. The analysis of instances of policy-making that have resulted in improved coverage against NSRs suggests that this part of the process of welfare state adaptation will be characterized by mechanisms of political exchange, compromise and cross-class alliances. As the political weakness of NSR groups makes unilateral imposition of policy impossible, the only path to effective reform is to strike compromises and form alliances with other political forces. Ironically, these deals are most likely with those political actors that have been most inimical to the welfare state: retrenchers and employers. Alliances between NSR groups and the former can be made on the basis of what has been referred to above as a modernizing compromise, or the combination within a single piece of legislation of cuts in provision with improvements in the coverage of NSRs. Employers may also be interested in joining forces with NSR groups, especially when protection against NSRs means easier labour market participation. From the employers' point of view this means increased labour supply and a more efficient labour market, a goal for which it may be worth investing some public money.

## Notes

From *Policy and Politics*, 33, 3, 2005, pp. 431–49. Earlier versions of this article have been presented at the Nordic Social Policy Research Meeting, Helsinki, 22–24 Aug. 2002; at the American Political Science Association annual meeting, Boston, 29 Aug.–1 Sept. 2002; at the annual meeting of the Swiss Political Science Association, Fribourg, 9 Nov. 2003; and at the conference on The Politics of New Social Risks, Lugano, 25–27 Sept. 2003. It is based on research financed by the Swiss Office for Education and Science (grant 00.0438) in the context of the EU Framework 5 project WRAMSOC.

The author would like to thank Karen Anderson, Klaus Armingeon, Maurizio Ferrera, Silja Hausermann, Peter Taylor-Gooby and Martin Rein for their comments.

1 As a matter of fact there is a fairly strong and statistically significant correlation among OECD countries between the size of the gender gap in voting and the female employment rate (r = 0,534, sig. 0.049, two-tailed).
2 This loss should, however, be compensated by the income stream resulting from newly introduced individual private pensions, although this will depend to a significant extent on the returns on the invested capital, and is as a result unpredictable.

## References

Anderson, K. M. (2001) 'The Politics of Retrenchment in a Social Democratic Welfare State: Reform of Swedish Pensions and Unemployment Insurance', *Comparative Political Studies*, 34, 9, pp. 1063–91.

Armingeon, K. (2004) 'Reconciling Competing Claims of the Welfare State Clientele', paper presented at the American Political Science Association annual meeting, Chicago, 2–4 Sept.

Ballestri, Y. and Bonoli, G. (2003) 'Létat social suisse face au nouveaux risques Sociaux', *Swiss Political Science Review*, 9, pp. 3, 35–58.

Bonoli, G. (2001) 'Political Institutions, Veto Points, and the Process of Welfare State Adaptation', in P. Pierson (ed.), *The New Politics of the Welfare State*, Oxford, Oxford University Press, pp. 238–64.

Bonoli, G. (2003) 'Two Worlds of Pension Reform in Western Europe', *Comparative Politics*, 35, 4, pp. 399–416.

Bonoli, G. (2004a) 'Generational Conflicts over Resource Allocation: Evidence from Referendum Voting on Social Policy Issues in Switzerland', paper presented at the conference on Erosion or Transformation of the Welfare State?, University of Fribourg, Switzerland, 15–16 Oct.

Bonoli, G. (2004b) 'Social Democratic Party Policies in Europe: Towards A Third Way?', in G. Powell (ed.), *Social Democratic Party Policies in Contemporary Europe*, London, Routledge, pp. 197–213.

Castles, F. G. (1982) *The Impact of Parties: Politics and Policies in Democratic Capitalist States*, London/Beverly Hills, CA: Sage Publications.

Daly, M. (2000) 'A Fine Balance: Women's Labor Market Participation in International Comparison', in F. V. Schmidt (ed.), *Welfare and Work in the Open Economy*, Oxford, Oxford University Press, vol. 2, pp. 467–510.

Ebbinghaus, B. (2003) 'Trade Union Movements in Post-industrial Welfare States', paper presented at the conference on The Political Regulation of New Social Risks', Lugano, 23–25 Sept.

Esping-Andersen, G. (1985) *Politics against Markets: The Social Democratic Road to Power*, Princeton, Princeton University Press.

Esping-Andersen, G. (1999a) *Social Foundations of Post-industrial Economies*, Oxford, Oxford University Press.

Esping-Andersen, G. (1999b) 'Politics without Class? Post-industrial Cleavages in Europe and America', in H. Kitschelt, P. Lange, G. Marks and J. D. Stephens (eds), *Continuity and Change in Contemporary Capitalism*, Cambridge, Cambridge University Press, pp. 293–316.

Hemerijck, A. (2002) 'The Self-Transformation of the European Social Model(s)', in G. Esping-Andersen (ed.), *Why we Need a New Welfare State*, Oxford, Oxford University Press, pp. 173–214.

Inglehart, R. and Norris, P. (2003) *Rising Tide: Gender Equality and Cultural Change*, Cambridge, Cambridge University Press.

Iversen, T. and Wren, A. (1998) 'Equality, Employment, and Budgetary Restraint: The Trilemma of the Service Economy', *World Politics*, 50, pp. 507–46.

Jenson, J. (2002) 'From Ford to Lego: Redesigning Welfare Regimes', paper presented at the American Political Science Association annual meeting, Boston, 31 Aug.–3 Sept.

Korpi, W. (1983) *The Democratic Class Struggle*, London, Routledge and Kegan Paul.

Levy, J. (1999) 'Vice into Virtue? Progressive Politics and Welfare Reform in Continental Europe', *Politics and Society*, 27, 2, pp. 239–73.

Morgan, K. (2001) 'Conservative Parties and Working Women in France', paper presented at the American Political Science Association annual meeting, San Francisco, 30 Aug.–2 Sept.

Naumann, I. (2001) 'The Politics of Child Care: Swedish Women's Mobilization for Public Child Care in the 1960s and 1970s', ECSR Summer School on Family, Gender and Social Stratification, Stockholm, 23–25 Aug.

Norris, P. (2002) *Democratic Phoenix: Reinventing Political Activism*, Cambridge, Cambridge University Press.

Norris, P. and Lovenduski, J. (1989) 'Women Candidates for Parliament: Transforming the Agenda?', *British Journal of Political Science*, 19, 1, pp. 106–15.

Norris, P. and Lovenduski, J. (2003) 'Westminster Women: The Politics of Presence', *Political Studies*, 51, 1, pp. 84–102.

Pierson, P. (1998) 'Irresistible Forces, Immovable Objects: Post-industrial Welfare States Confront Permanent Austerity', *Journal of European Public Policy*, 5, 4, pp. 539–60.

Putnam, R. D. (2000) *Bowling Alone: The Collapse and Revival of American Community*, New York, Simon and Schuster.

Sawer, M. (2000) 'Parliamentary Representation of Women: From Discourses of Justice to Strategies of Accountability', *International Political Science Review*, 21, 4, pp. 361–80.

Siaroff, A. (2000) 'Women's Representation in Legislatures and Cabinets in Industrial Democracies', *International Political Science Review*, 21, 4, pp. 197–215.

Stephens, J. (1979) *The Transition from Capitalism to Socialism*, Urbana, Illinois University Press.

Taylor-Gooby, P. (2004) 'New Risks and Social Change', in P. Taylor-Gooby (ed.), *New Risks, New Welfare?* Oxford, Oxford University Press, pp. 1–27.

Tramblay, M. (1998) 'Do Women MPs Substantively Represent Women? A Study of Legislative Behaviour in Canada's 35th Parliament', *Canadian Journal of Political Science*, 31, 3, pp. 435–65.

# Beyond Universalism and Particularism: Rethinking Contemporary Welfare Theory

*Nick Ellison*

The universalist impulse has long been a founding principle of modern welfare theory, particularly in Britain. Marshall's 'Citizenship and Social Class' (1963) is usually regarded as the paradigm account of a theory of social rights that held that individuals belonging to a defined community (typically a national community) were entitled, through their status as citizens, to a range of social goods guaranteed by the central state designed to meet their basic needs (food, shelter, education, health, etc.). Richard Titmuss, writing in the tradition of Tawney, provided an ethical socialist version of these ideas (Titmuss, 1963). Unlike Marshall, for whom welfare provision was a means of correcting but not replacing the inegalitarian bias of the market, Titmuss's ambition was none other than the substitution of capitalist society for one based on egalitarian fellowship (Ellison, 1994) – solidaristic social integration. To this end he consistently sought to maximize the role of the state in the interests of greater social equality, most obviously in the area of social security (Titmuss, 1963), while simultaneously promoting the ideals of altruism and reciprocity (Titmuss, 1970) as key features of a 'welfare society' in which the effects of the competitive marketplace were severely reduced, if not entirely eliminated.

These ideas were taken up by many commentators (see, for example, contributors to Bosanquet and Townsend, 1972; Townsend, 1979) and effectively provided the normative basis of welfare theory – and indeed policy-making – in the postwar period. They stand as evidence of an abiding conviction that social equality was a realizable goal and that the central (nation) state was the most appropriate vehicle to guide society towards this objective. During the 1980s, however, this 'welfare collectivist' perspective came to be questioned (Le Grand, 1982, 1989; Glennerster, 1983). In an era of rapid economic change, high unemployment and welfare state retrenchment, the faultlines of postwar paternalistic universalism became increasingly clear as existing levels of social protection were reduced. The effect on marginal or vulnerable groups – women and minority ethnic communities, the old and the sick – was to exacerbate difficulties that had always characterized their relationship with the welfare system. Often not eligible for contributory benefits because of gaps in their employment record, women, particularly single mothers, were subjected to the increasing incidence of means-tested and discretionary payments as income support levels were cut (Millar, 1994). Cuts in health care and the 'privatization' of community care particularly affected women, both as carers and as those (especially older women) who needed to be cared for (Baldwin, 1994). Again, evidence of 'institutional racism' in the allocation of scarce public housing and other services (Skellington, 1992; Mason, 1995; Solomos and Back, 1996) led to a growing conviction that 'universalism', far from treating those with the same needs in like fashion, in fact further marginalized the already marginal.

This scepticism has been echoed in a rather different manner by feminists and others who, as part of a wider movement against existing Western intellectual and social frameworks, were challenging 'humanly inclusive problematics, concepts, theories, objective methodologies' (Harding, quoted in Di Stefano, 1990, p. 73) in the name of 'difference'. In its effort to subsume all aspects of social provision under the universalist rubrics of 'citizenship' and 'social justice', the welfare state was held from this pluralist standpoint to have created a false uniformity which eliminated, or reduced, 'the diversity of identity, experience, interest and need in welfare provision' (Williams, 1992, p. 206–7). The pluralist position has been best characterized by those like Iris Young (1989, 1990) and Seyla Benhabib (1996b) who argue that broad, all-inclusive notions of 'citizenship', social justice and so on effectively mask power relations which operate to the benefit of dominant groups. In Young's view (1989, p. 258), 'persons from one perspective or history can never completely understand and adopt the point of view of those with other group-based perspectives and histories'. So where a particular set (or sets) of interests already predominate, efforts to assimilate others, even where these may be well-intentioned, are likely to fail because these entrants come 'into the game after it has already begun, after the rules and standards already have been set' (Young, 1990, p. 164). These inherent differences of power, perspective and experience suggest that new groups will have to prove themselves according to existing rules and standards, their interests being likely to suffer as a result. The difficulty of attending properly to women's interests in the context of a supposedly universal welfare state is a case in point (Walby, 1990; Lister, 1990, 1993), but the same could be said of the position forced upon minority ethnic populations and other vulnerable groups.

## Debating the Universalist–Particularist Divide

There is a dichotomy here which runs to the heart of contemporary social policy analysis. On one side stands the universalist plea for greater social justice and equality, a 'fair' allocation of social goods to mitigate the inegalitarian effects of the market and generate social cohesion; on the other, demands for the recognition of diversity and 'difference' sustain the view that universalism can, paradoxically, be socially exclusive. A number of commentators have recently attempted to resolve this divide by suggesting that it is either less significant, or less rigid, than it appears. As we shall see, one strand of thought wants to play down the significance of difference entirely, while others want to discover a means of reconciling the universalist–particularist duality, the aim being to develop a set of principles which, by taking greater account of difference and plurality, can provide not so much an enduring normative base as an acceptable standard for deciding allocatory issues.

Peter Taylor-Gooby provides a good example of those who continue to place their faith in universalism, arguing that the particularist challenge is less significant than it appears. He initiated a rather belated debate among social policy academics (Taylor-Gooby, 1994) about the potential impact of 'postmodern' thinking on the discipline in an effort to discredit, if not the epistemological assumptions, then certainly what he considers to be the practical implications of postmodernist perspectives. Although his definition of postmodernism is none too specific (Hillyard and Watson, 1996; Penna and O'Brien, 1996) – Taylor-Gooby (1994, p. 387) tends to associate postmodern thinking simply with an 'emphasis on diversity and pluralism in views of what is desirable' – the point is to dispel the idea that distributional decisions can be based upon notions of fragmentation and difference. Such an emphasis he holds to be misguided. While acknowledging that contemporary social policy clearly encompasses a greater plurality of provision, reflecting a greater diversity of needs, than was the case in the postwar era, Taylor-Gooby's main concern is that, in a world where the practice and ideology of free market liberalism has triumphed over competing ideologies, the postmodern stress on particularism 'may obscure one of the great reversals for the most vulnerable groups in a cloud of detail, may ignore the wood through enthusiasm for bark-rubbing' (Taylor-Gooby, 1994, pp. 388–9). Inequalities in living standards and the 'stricter regulation of the lives of some of the poorest groups may fail to attract the appropriate attention if the key themes of policy are seen as difference, diversity and choice' (Taylor-Gooby, 1994, p. 403). So, although trends towards pluralism should not be discounted entirely, too much attention to these 'postmodern' concerns will risk subverting efforts to combat the rising poverty and inequalities associated with the now-hegemonic free market, which can best be accomplished by embracing the ethic of welfare state universalism traditionally associated with the creation of the socially just society.

This is an extreme position, judged by contemporary standards, and is vulnerable to the kind of criticisms voiced by 'difference pluralists' like Young. Moreover, in the face of all available evidence, it continues to place faith in the prospect of a socialist alternative to the postwar 'Keynesian' welfare state, which could somehow reorganize welfare provision in the collective interest. The danger with this pro-state line of argument is that, in the current socioeconomic climate, welfare state institutions are more likely to continue to hostage citizens to capitalist fortunes, as Marxists criticized them for doing in the past (Gough, 1979; Offe, 1984), rather than act as bulwarks for the protection of the vulnerable. Events since 'new' Labour's recent success at the polls would seem to confirm this trend (Ellison, 1997a). Put bluntly, the postwar 'Keynesian' welfare state failed to maintain any redistributive momentum in the colder economic and political climate of the post-1975 period and, far from embracing a socialist alternative, national governments in the majority of advanced industrial societies have been engaged in sustained attempts to reorganize their welfare systems the better to favour the requirements of global capitalism (Esping-Andersen, 1996). While Taylor-Gooby plainly understands the negative consequences of capitalist triumph for the worst off, it is difficult to see how this undoubted victory can be squared with his continued faith in welfare state universalism.

Other attempts to discuss the relationship between universalism and particularism give greater credence to the pluralist turn than Taylor-Gooby allows, if in certain cases only reluctantly. Spicker (1996, p. 229), for instance, confesses to an ambivalence about particularism, being 'both attracted and appalled' by the implications of 'postmodern' diversity. The difficulty, for him, lies in the realization that neither approach can be taken too far. In particularist vein Spicker (1996, p. 223) argues, for example, that:

> the recognition of duties at the personal level, duties which usually far exceed those required from universal principles like human rights or altruism, is fundamental to much moral conduct . . . I suspect that we would feel that there was something morally wrong with someone whose commitment for the Third World was so great that he or she subordinated all responsibility to family, friends and community to it.

It is important, in other words, to recognize the needs and demands of particular interests, but at the same time acknowledgement of difference must have limits. What we need to do in Spicker's view 'is to find a way of appealing to [particularist] values like "community" and "solidarity" which does not leave room for exclusion and injustice' (Spicker, 1996, p. 230). The solution is thought to lie in a notion of 'moderate particularism' (see Jones, 1990) which takes seriously the need to empower disadvantaged groups but which, in adjudicating amongst different interests, would also take cognizance of the relative weight of advantage and disadvantage, especially where this affects freedom and choice over available resources. Spicker (1996, p. 231) contends that

> if principles like 'community' and 'solidarity' are advocated as a means of empowerment and the removal of disadvantage, there does not have to be any inconsistency. But this means that they must be treated as secondary rather than primary values; universal claims like freedom and equality have priority.

The particular claims of distinct communities or solidarities cannot, then, be pushed too far for fear of undermining universalist goals.

This view clearly acknowledges that the socially excluded might have legitimate concerns about the levels of social protection afforded under the universalist principle but it does not move the argument very much beyond Taylor-Gooby's more forthright position. If universal values like freedom and equality have primacy over particularist demands, whose interests ultimately define the nature of these values? One of the most persuasive aspects of Young's position is precisely that powerful groups define 'universal' values in ways that are ultimately to their own benefit – but the argument can also be pursued in a different but equally convincing manner.

Even if we were to accept, *pace* Young, that appropriate social goods and services could be provided for the worst off by well-intentioned elites, inequality and discrimination will not necessarily be eliminated from the picture. In order to understand why this is so, it is important to recognize, with Yeatman, that a duality exists at the heart of welfare state 'discourse'. In her view (Yeatman, 1994, p. 85), universalizing notions like citizenship are 'predicated on a dualism of independence and dependency'. Some individuals are able to achieve independent status by freely contracting in the marketplace, meeting their needs with the proceeds of market transactions while, for a variety of reasons, others cannot achieve this status without resorting to public provision, for the receipt of which they are duly stigmatized. Although an emphasis on 'empowerment' might allow certain groups to escape the worst effects of this 'welfare tutelage', it is unclear how far the claims of difference and diversity could be taken in an environment where the application of certain 'universal' understandings of freedom and equality effectively 'coerce' welfare recipients into relations of subordination even as they claim to be favouring them.

One means of advancing beyond the boundaries of the above debate, which displays all the hallmarks of theoretical stalemate, is to claim that the universalist–particularist divide, though significant, is not as rigid as it might appear. In a manner that echoes Spicker's concerns but attempts to transcend the position he outlines, Thompson and Hoggett make clear their dissatisfaction with what they regard as the false divide between universalist and 'postmodern'/particularist perspectives. In their opinion:

> the choice of either universalism or particularism is misconceived. Any justifiable universalism, or egalitarianism must take particularity and difference into account; and any legitimate particularism or politics of difference must employ some universal or egalitarian standard. (Thompson and Hoggett, 1996, p. 23)

The way forward is to distinguish between universalism and the associated notion of positive selectivism, on the one hand, and particularism, or the claims of difference, on the other. This conceptual clarification, according to Thompson and Hoggett, makes it possible to treat universalist and particularist perspectives not only in less dichotomous terms but, more positively, as a mutually reinforcing duality.

Their argument suggests that welfare universalism, even where this incorporates an element of positive selectivism, can create relations of tutelage with the state on the lines of Yeatman's analysis (positive discrimination or 'quotas' would be examples). It is consequently important to move beyond 'forms of selectivism that only manage to redress certain inequalities in terms of the dominant understanding of what equality requires' – and it is here that Thompson and Hoggett (1996, p. 30) introduce an element of particularism, arguing that 'particularist principles aim to attend to specific differences between particular individuals – differences which make a *moral* difference' (original emphasis). They have in mind the kinds of affiliation that Spicker mentions, affiliations that stress 'social diversity rather than commonality and thereby give emphasis to particular needs, moral frameworks and social expectations of different groups'.

There are, of course, limits to this line of thought, but it is here that the universalist and particularist perspectives can be construed as mutually supportive. Thompson and Hoggett reiterate the often-made point that particularist positions ultimately depend on certain universalist principles for their coherence: the most obvious examples occur where interest group demands for fairer or more equal treatment are made in accordance with underlying universalist assumptions about what constitutes 'fairness', 'equality' and so on. In support of this point of view, they argue that it is not really logical to define 'difference' as sheer otherness; there is a condition of (human) relatedness even if this reduces merely to the necessary condition of linguistic communication across the spaces that divide us – and in practice the amount of common ground is likely to be greater than this. In this way it is possible to presuppose at least a degree of common understanding about what constitutes the 'rules of the game', even where aspects of these rules may be contested. Endorsement for such an approach comes from Young (1989, p. 263), who recognizes that even those wishing to champion difference need to acknowledge and subscribe to agreed principles of justice if all claims are ultimately to be settled.

Returning to the terrain of welfare, it seems plausible, in the light of these comments, to suggest that universalist nostrums need to be sensitive to the differences among particular cases, while recognizing that too great an emphasis on particularism will risk a collapse into 'an untenable relativism' if actors remain unwilling to seek out comparison with others in the interests of a wider universalism (Thompson and Hoggett, 1996, p. 35). In social policy terms it is certainly feasible to imagine the prescription of universalist goals – for instance the right of all citizens to equal levels of health care – within which the needs and interests of particular groups can be accommodated. It might be necessary to underpin universalist provision by incorporating elements of positive selectivism to ensure, for example, that health authorities in deprived areas have a greater value of resource in order to meet proportionately greater needs to match the general goal of universal care – similar to the educational priority areas of the late 1960s. But *particularist* needs may also be met by, say, matching specific types of service to the needs of specific groups, so introducing a distinctly pluralist dimension into the account.

How might these concerns be reflected institutionally? The apparatus required to incorporate the range of issues Thompson and Hoggett discuss needs to have both centralized and decentralized elements, and the authors refer to Hirst's (1994) concept of associational democracy to illustrate how (universal) basic needs and (differentiated) specific needs might be reconciled. While basic needs could be met by a form of guaranteed minimum income paid by the central state, associations could cater for specific needs either by seeking automatic entitlement where the nature of provision is determined by a citizen's general status (e.g. the category of child or older person), or through the creation of specific contracts with the central state where needs are highly particular and the right quality of user-specific provision needs to be ensured, as they may be in the case of certain forms of disability or mental ill-health (Thompson and Hoggett, 1996, p. 38).

This depiction of a decentralized welfare system potentially more sensitive to particular needs is in many ways compelling and appears to leave us on the cusp of a different, less normatively driven, approach to social policy. The underlying thrust of the argument advanced by Thompson and Hoggett suggests that they are willing to play down the significance of attempting to find points of normative agreement about the nature of 'equality', 'liberty' and so on in favour of more pragmatic questions about how available resources may best be allocated to meet a wide range of differently constituted needs. Recognizing that inequalities can often best be addressed through attention to the particular as opposed to the universal, this approach apparently gives ground to pluralist perspectives in a way that the positions advanced by Taylor-Gooby or Spicker do not – but there are difficulties nevertheless.

On closer analysis, the precise balance to be struck between universalist and particularist forms of provision remains opaque. Although Thompson and Hoggett clearly want to see greater space for particularism, they still want to subsume the particular within the universal. The authors continue to rely, for example, upon a 'sophisticated universalism' which 'accepts' certain forms of selectivism and 'elements of particularism' (Thompson and Hoggett, 1996, p. 32), arguing that 'universalism seeks to provide a fair standard by which to treat particular cases, and . . . particularism derives its moral force from an underlying universalism' (Thompson and Hoggett, 1996, p. 34). But this understanding seems to require particularist interests to demonstrate that their demands are in fact consistent with universalist definitions of 'justice'. Although it would be wrong to dismiss this recognition of particularism as insincere or reducible in any easy sense to a dominant universalism, the formulation is insufficiently specific – the consequence being that it is impossible to know quite how this attempt to reframe the universalist–particularist paradigm would work out in practice.

Two problems are particularly evident. First, while Thompson and Hoggett add theoretical weight to their position by continuing to employ principles of 'equality', 'fairness' and 'justice', these principles remain only vaguely defined. If liberal notions of 'fairness as impartiality' appear too abstract and consequently too implicated in universalist conceptions of the good easily to fit the complex framework Thompson and Hoggett advance, conceptions directed towards the 'concrete' as opposed to the 'generalized' other (Gilligan, 1982; Benhabib, 1986; White, 1991) clearly want to promote a qualitatively different, and not necessarily 'equal', division of resources which may tip the balance too far in a particularist direction. Although these considerations are central to their position, Thompson and Hoggett neither define these principles themselves, nor indicate how agreement about the content of such ideas may be arrived at.

Second, there is the more practical issue of competing claims. Although associationalism provides an example of how universal and particular interests may be treated, the authors do not take sufficient account of the problem of scarce social resources and do not consider how *competing* claims might be resolved (Benhabib, 1996a, p. 35). Here there is a danger of the reassertion of the universalist–particularist divide. Universalists would argue that the state should have ultimate responsibility for adjudicating among competing demands in the interests of the greater good and may legitimately ask whether a 'thin' associationalist state could counter, or even moderate, the claims of powerful interests (Amin, 1995). On the other hand, any greater centralization of allocational power would activate particularist scepticism about the emancipatory potential of universalist solutions.

These difficulties suggest not only that Thompson and Hoggett have failed to resolve the universalist–particularist dichotomy as successfully as might initially have appeared, but that the attempt to discover a means of reconciling these opposing perspectives might in fact be misguided. For it seems that efforts to prescribe formulae for integrating universalist and particularist values will always be vulnerable to inherent centrifugal impulses, both at the level of theory, where the epistemological status of proposed distributional principles is open to challenge from either viewpoint, and at the level of practice, where specific patterns of resource allocation are likely to be contested on the grounds that they favour one or other set of interests.

The remainder of this article argues that it is possible to move beyond the constraints imposed by the universalist–particularist paradigm without entirely losing our sense of the importance of having universal allocatory principles for social provision but that, in order to do so, universalist ambitions must be reduced in favour of a greater recognition of the claims of specific interests. We need to advance on two fronts. Theoretically, it is important to strip away the conceptual dualism that characterized the above discussion. While there is a need to retain a sense of principled allocation which continues to address issues of 'fairness' and 'justice' there is no reason why this should depend too heavily on universalist prescriptions. Indeed, it will be argued below that the only 'universal' elements needed to underpin claims to particular patterns of distribution are those procedural requirements, agreed by all participants in the public sphere, which underpin agreed norms of communicative behaviour. With these elements in place, outcomes could be elaborated according to decentralized, essentially pragmatic, processes of 'deliberation' as parties to particular debates negotiate on the strength of their claims.

Certain aspects of 'deliberative democracy' are explored below but before moving on to consider this issue it is important to see how a greater appreciation of postmodern ideas can sharpen our understanding of the contemporary social and political context that deliberative theories will need to address. In an increasingly complex and fragmented social world, claims to resources become intimately connected to perceptions of identity and difference, and these in turn are accompanied by dilemmas of social inclusion and exclusion which threaten efforts to mount coherent demands because they introduce a genuine ambivalence about the nature of social belonging into distributional debates. Postmodern thinking can help to illuminate our perceptions of the difficult, ambiguous nature of identity and difference in contemporary societies. In so doing, and even where their logic is not accepted entirely, postmodern insights can enhance our appreciation of the forms that deliberative institutions will need to take if they are to facilitate agreement about the (particularist) distribution of social goods and services and, by extension, the nature of social inclusion itself.

## Beyond Universalism and Particularism? Social Policy and Postmodern Critique

Much of the recent social policy literature which addresses issues of universalism and particularism tends to treat the latter as somehow 'postmodern', but this is a misnomer. Difference pluralism has been embraced by many scholars who, like Young, Benhabib or Carole Pateman, cannot be described as postmodern thinkers. For a variety of reasons postmodernists may be suggesting rather more than that patterns of political accountability, social provision and so on should be more responsive to a plurality of demands. In fact, the postmodern challenge is not so much concerned with particularist diversity or the claims of difference as with the ways in which the *identities* which give voice to such claims are constituted.

If, for the moment, we accept with those like Judith Butler that identity and difference are pure social construction, the self having no predetermined 'essence', then it becomes difficult to sustain a view of particularity or difference that is in any sense 'fixed'. According to this radical postmodernist/poststructuralist perspective we exist as fragmented subjects whose identities are not preconfigured, our 'agency' being constituted purely in specific actions. As Butler states, 'there need not be a "doer behind the deed" . . . the "doer" is invariably constructed through the deed' (cited in Evans, 1995, p. 134). Particularisms will emerge and recede as identities are constructed (and deconstructed) within prevailing discourses of power in ways which defy any final sense of integration or resolution. On this reading, there is no longer, as Honig (1996, p. 258) puts it:

> a place called home, a place free of power, conflict and struggle, a place – an identity, a form of life, a group vision – unmarked or unriven by difference and untouched by the power brought to bear upon it by the identities that strive to ground themselves in its place.

The prospect, then, is one of permanent struggle, both within and among different identities, to achieve transitory forms of belonging, permanently threatened by disruption, as these fragile constructions fracture under both internal and external pressures.

Construing this postmodernist identity politics in the social and political language of fairness and social justice is clearly an ambitious task, but one which postmodern radical democrats like Chantal Mouffe are currently attempting. In Mouffe's (1996, p. 24) words, 'a radical pluralist approach, informed as it is by a non-essentialist politics, acknowledges the impossibility of a fully realised democracy and of the total elimination of antagonisms'. But Mouffe thinks it possible that a radical pluralist politics might create 'a chain of equivalence among the democratic demands found in a variety of groups . . . around a radical democratic interpretation of the political principles of the liberal democratic regime' – an equivalence that could eventuate in a common radical democratic identity for all citizens. Of course, according to Mouffe such an outcome is only feasible if we retain the idea of a decentred subject because it is only by so doing that it becomes possible to eliminate universalizing notions of inclusion – and hence domination. The point is to destroy 'subject positions' or discourses of power (racism, sexism, ageism) while being clear that these are never synonymous with social and political actors themselves, for the latter are always constituted by a range of shifting 'subjectivities' which cut through the individual, allowing her simultaneously to be dominant in some social contexts while subordinate in others.

At first sight this version of postmodern theorizing seems compelling. Critical of the 'essentialism' which underpins attempts to mount theoretical justifications for existing definitions of 'fairness' or 'justice', it questions the status of the principles governing resource allocation in liberal and social democratic societies in ways which appear to reduce the salience of the universalist–particularist divide, thus allowing us to move on. After all, if identities are as fractured as postmodernists suggest this must effectively eliminate any hope of discovering an agreed theoretical foundation on which to base allocatory practices and in the process remove any vestige of universalist principles and policies in favour of a potentially infinite range of particular identity claims.

But this solution to the theoretical stalemate is bought at a high cost, for one of the apparent strengths of Mouffe's postmodernist perspective – the perceived distinction between social actors and subject positions – disguises a severe weakness. Mouffe hopes to avoid obvious charges of endorsing an unlimited relativism through her notion of a chain of equivalence which will somehow 'select in' certain subject positions while 'selecting out' others. The difficulty, however, is that, if subject positions are 'fungible' (Benhabib, 1996a), which is to say infinitely constructible and thus 'replaceable', it is hard to see how they can be so only to the degree that they open possibilities for the construction of particular (i.e. radical) positions and not other less palatable alternatives. Fraser (1996, p. 205) criticizes those she refers to as 'deconstructive anti-essentialists' for failing to distinguish between 'emancipatory and oppressive identity claims, benign and pernicious differences'. Applied to Mouffe's notion of a chain of equivalence, how plausible is it to assume that all challenges to subject positions will contribute to the liberating project of radical democracy? Might not decentred subjects challenge power discourses from perspectives which are not necessarily compatible with liberating or emancipatory principles?

At this point the full-blown postmodern project retreats into incoherence. An approach which denies the validity of attempts to justify certain principles of fairness and social justice, whatever their precise theoretical foundation, not only risks an anarchy of competing claims from a variety of combinations of subject positions while offering no means of deciding among them, but also raises questions about how we can deal with those who seek to maintain, or alter, distributional outcomes at the expense of others. However, this criticism does not imply that postmodernist thinking has no worthwhile contribution to make for, conceptually shaky though this line of thought may be, postmodern theorists are surely correct to 'problematize' liberal or social democratic universalist reasoning. By drawing attention to the difficulties facing attempts to develop and justify universalist principles, it has been pointed out that postmodernism's primary role is 'to politicise the nature and identity of the political community on which these traditions have depended' (Yeatman, 1994, p. 90). In this way postmodern thinking stands in critical, but not necessarily oppositional, relation to modernist ideas, acting as an analytical aid which, by opening up new ways of thinking about rights and social justice, 'is not to be understood as supplanting but as entering into relationship with the distinctive rights talk of both liberalism and social democracy' (Yeatman, 1994, p. 90).

This formulation of the relationship between postmodernist and modernist approaches is helpful for two reasons. First, as intimated, it acknowledges the danger of unqualified relativism which, at its most extreme, postmodernist thinking embraces. Second, and more importantly for present purposes, treating postmodern theorizing as an analytical device facilitates an understanding of the complexities involved in deciding allocatory claims because the postmodernist characterization of the fragmented nature of identity has a certain presence in the ambivalent character of demands for social inclusion and in so doing illuminates the ambiguities that cut through the universalist–particularist divide. A clear aspect of the new, fractured world of social policy is precisely that vulnerable or marginal groups want 'social inclusion' while simultaneously demanding social and political changes which challenge the nature of what it means to be included. In this way the desire for inclusion (in the sense of gaining access to the social rights, resources and opportunities available to others) frequently exists contiguously with demands for the alteration of, inter alia, the basis of social 'membership', the principles informing resource allocation and the means of access to resources themselves.

So, while radical postmodernist assumptions about the deracinated nature of decentred subject positions raise many more difficulties than they solve, the 'postmodern element' in the present discussion is manifested in the following ways. First, the burgeoning presence of 'difference' in contemporary social policy suggests that the prospect of *permanent* agreement about principles of resource allocation is chimerical. As suggested earlier, there is nothing necessarily 'postmodern' about accepting a lack of permanence in allocatory arrangements, but the potential degree of fragmentation in social politics lends this characterization a certain postmodern colour (Ellison, 1997b). Second, this colour is enhanced by the recognition that social actors, while not purely constructed through action – and possessing a grounded sense of identity as Fraser and others would have it – nevertheless live in a contingent world and therefore are likely actively to embody the ambivalence which pervades claims for inclusion. Not only will this mean that they will stand in critical relation to the very structures, theoretical and institutional, to which they wish to belong, or from which they wish to draw particular resources, but in view of the rapid and extensive changes currently affecting industrial societies in general and their welfare systems in particular, the further suggestion is that actors will pursue their demands in different ways depending on the specific manner in which change affects them. Because of the difficulties any one interest, or set of interests, would encounter in claiming priority for preferred allocational principles in this fractured social universe, the result is likely to be a highly complex series of debates where neither the identities involved, nor the parameters of the discussions themselves, are permanently fixed.

Framed in this manner, the best method by which different and competing interests can reach agreement about access to goods and services arguably must be through extensive processes of deliberation. All parties whose interests are affected by the pattern of distribution in a particular policy area should have the opportunity to further their claims in negotiations about resource allocation. At first sight such a tentative formulation may appear weak. It is vulnerable, for example, to the accusation that clear and defensible (if nonetheless contestable) allocational principles have been jettisoned in favour of a vague, hand-to-mouth approach which seeks to judge each claim, at best, according to the preconceptions of the parties involved in a particular area of debate. Such a dialogic perspective, it may be argued, betrays little sense of the fundamental issues at stake in debates about the distribution of resources where the claims of difference may need to be judged against other, more pressing, considerations about the effects of, say, increasing poverty and inequality.

These points would have more force if they could counter the arguments against Taylor-Gooby's defence of welfare universalism mentioned above. As they stand, however, they have come to be regarded, even it seems by Taylor-Gooby himself, as 'second best theory' (Taylor-Gooby, 1997). In the light of these criticisms, the deliberative option deserves attention for, if it is impossible to agree upon universalist procedures for adjudicating the complexities of competing claims for scarce resources, the allocation of goods in particular policy areas will only be regarded as legitimate where each and every party to each and every area of debate is recognized and given voice.

## Deliberative Democracy and a Politics of Presence

Space does not permit a full discussion of the various possible approaches to deliberative democracy (see, for example, Cohen, 1989; Fishkin, 1991; Rawls, 1993; Young, 1993; Habermas, 1995). For present purposes, it is important to develop a deliberative account that can speak to the fragmentary, complex social politics which informs contemporary debates about social policy, so the ideas of theorists such as Rawls and Habermas, both of whom perceive deliberation in overly formal and rationalistic terms (Bohman, 1996, pp. 44–5), will not be drawn upon here.

To accomplish this task we need to be aware of the significance of 'informal' sites of social and political interaction as 'transformative spaces' in which the clash of competing interests can lead to potentially new and unheralded outcomes. As Anne Phillips has written, 'the common core that characterises theories of deliberative or communicative or discursive democracy is that political engagement can change initial statements of preference or interest'. Indeed, the point 'that deliberative democracy insists on . . . is the capacity for formulating new positions in the course of discussion with others' (Phillips, 1995, p. 149). There is a flexible quality to this conception which is further developed by Bohman (1996, p. 57) who argues that deliberation should be based upon 'dialogue' rather than more formal or regulative types of discourse which may require 'specific epistemic expertise', hence:

> dialogue is the mere give and take of reasons. It does not necessarily aim to produce well-justified claims; rather it aims to produce claims that are wide enough in scope and sufficiently justified to be accountable to an indefinite public space of fellow citizens.

Taken together, these perspectives are attractive because they contain a capacity for reflexivity which is essential if deliberative theory is to address the ambivalence associated with social inclusion/exclusion discussed in the previous section. The significant point about public deliberation, as Bohman (1996, p. 58) comments, is precisely that 'it takes place within a framework of accountable social interaction that is reflexively called into question as it is being used'.

An important additional dimension to this depiction of a reflexively ordered public space lies in Phillips's attempt to augment the idea of deliberative democracy by reference to a 'politics of presence'. While some deliberative theorists are chary of a politics which gives too much leeway to disparate interest groups, believing that factionalism will undermine deliberative processes, others like Sunstein (1991) and Phillips argue that it is important to ensure the 'presence' of the widest possible range of interests. They attempt to reduce the prospect of endemic factional strife by arguing that group 'representatives', rather than merely playing the role of mandated functionaries, should behave as autonomous actors, being prepared to change their positions if convinced by the arguments of others. 'Democracy', on this reading, becomes less a vehicle for giving each group 'a piece of the action' (Sunstein, quoted in Phillips, 1995, p. 152) and more a method for testing existing preferences against the views and perceptions of others. The hope is that, with the continuing emphasis on dialogue, increased understanding of the position of others will help resolve seemingly entrenched conflicts.

This approach goes some way towards providing the theoretical outline of an institutional framework sufficient to provide the 'transformative space' in which the complex debates which characterize contemporary social politics can be played out. How might such a framework be constituted in practice and how might it avert the recidivistic return towards the universalist–particularist dichotomy in social policy?

What follows provides only the briefest outline of how a deliberative social politics might operate in the area of welfare. While this account owes a good deal to the spirit of Hirst's (1994, 1998) conception of an associational welfare system, it nevertheless differs from his vision in two important ways. First, in practical terms, although Hirst's (1994, p. 167) view that associationalism 'publicises civil society and pluralises the state' is broadly endorsed, the institutional mechanisms are quite different. The decentralized 'social policy communities' discussed later do not conform to the autonomous, self-governing voluntary agencies of the associationalist vision, nor is the central state as 'thin' as associationalist accounts would have it. Second, without wanting to push the analysis towards too full an acceptance of postmodern reasoning, both the principles governing communication and allocation, *and* the social actors themselves who are involved in debates about needs, services and resource allocation, will need to be less 'ontologically grounded' than they appear to be in the associationalist model.

It is important, in the first place, to distinguish among three levels of governance and between two types of decision-making represented in the first and third levels. The first level – that of central democratic institutions – should be primarily concerned with fashioning decision-making *procedures*, particularly those designed to regulate communicative behaviour and other 'rules of the game' including those rules governing discussions about social justice and, by extension, the division of available resources. Local authorities comprise the second level of governance, their main role being an adminstrative rather than a decision-making one, while debates about policy proposals, *substantive* decisions about which proposals to pursue and associated debates about the prioritizing of resource claims are the province of the third level, composed of a range of decentralized 'social policy communities'.

It is in the nature of this deliberative vision that these decision-making levels will be characterized by a high degree of fluidity, responding to the ebb and flow of group influence as collective actors are confronted by the pressures of social change. In this connection, it is particularly important to understand that the principles of communication, distribution and social justice developed within the first level of central democratic institutions are *mutable*. Agreement about such principles will be subject to reappraisal according to the play of different interests in the context of a prevailing politics of presence where all potential constituencies are represented, but where, following Phillips, representatives are not directly mandated.

The key feature of this level is the stress which needs to be placed on presence in conditions of what Benhabib (1986, p. 30) has called a 'historically self-conscious universalism'. This refers to a process of 'reflective equilibrium' by which it is possible to arrive at a '"thick description" of the moral presuppositions of the cultural horizon of modernity' which is likely to (but might not) include principles of universal respect and egalitarian reciprocity not as transcendental principles of communicative ethics but as contingent features of social and political discourse upon which all parties have duly reflected. Of course, this process can only be perceived as legitimate if the full range of social groups have voice and minority or marginal interests are properly engaged in drawing up agreement about communicative principles and procedures, as well as the practical procedures for resource allocation (for a discussion about the numbers necessary to achieve effective engagement see Kymlicka, 1995, pp. 144–9).

Local authorities, comprising the second, administrative, level, would need to be organized functionally, mirroring the pattern of decentralized interests below. With senior staff appointed by independent panels made up from a cross-section of policy community members and others nominated by the centre, individual local authority departments would act as conduits channelling demands up from, and resources down to, policy community level – but this role needs to be augmented in two important ways. First, the departments should have an advisory capacity, providing information to policy communities about available resources, furnishing expert opinion where required and suggesting methods for optimizing the returns on budget allocations. Second, existing separately from the functional departments, but appointed in the same way, local authority budget committees should act as 'budget brokers' using information provided by the departments to make the case to central institutions for the resources demanded by the policy communities but also policing subsequent allocations coming from above.

The diffuse nature of the third, substantive level makes it more difficult to describe in detail. Above all, it would need to be characterized by a decentralized, deliberative politics designed to give voice to the demands of myriad interests, with deliberative procedures conforming to the communicative rules agreed by central democratic institutions. This sphere is likely to be one of 'mutually interlocking and overlapping networks and associations of deliberation, contestation and argumentation' (Benhabib, 1996b, p. 74) which, taken together, exhibit a form of 'public conversation'. Deliberative activity here carries no necessary condition of presence so long as the parties whose interests are liable to be affected by change in a particular policy arena have an equal opportunity to participate in debates about the goods and services they most need, as well as in the framing of policy proposals relevant to the realization of their demands. It is of course possible that individual citizens will be active in more than one social policy community, advancing different, even contradictory, claims in different places. In this way the postmodern dimension finds expression at the level of human action because the identities and demands of social actors, though not necessarily split among different *subject* positions, will nevertheless fragment across different policy spaces, exemplifying the endemic contingency of identity and so highlighting the ambiguous nature of human action in the face of persistent dilemmas of social inclusion and exclusion.

At this general level, it becomes possible to see how this brief account of a deliberative social politics could abrogate the universalist–particularist divide. By privileging particularist engagement at the level of decentralized policy debate and formulation, but in the prevailing context of a centralized politics of presence in which all agreements about principle are open to negotiation and change, the universalist–particularist paradigm collapses. Policy proposals will now inevitably reflect particularist concerns for, by definition, they will be rooted in difference – a formulation which echoes Calhoun's (1995, p. 72) 'two cheers to particularism'. The remaining cheer is reserved for disembedded 'universal' principles of communication and social justice which, however mutable, give shape to the deliberative process.

Such is the broad outline of a possible deliberative democracy, but how might it work in practice? The final task is to put a little social policy flesh on these admittedly bare theoretical bones. Any social policy community – the education community, for instance – will inevitably contain producer and user interests including those concerned about the nature of delivery systems and existing resource levels, as well as others interested in reforming specific areas of provision the better to service particular needs. The community is also likely to be divided into different functional sections producing proposals for, say, teaching and learning needs (including special needs), buildings and equipment, educational opportunities and access, and so on. Taken as a whole, however, the community's task would be to decide policy priorities, reaching internal agreement about necessary goods and services, and the resources required to deliver them, before channelling its demands for resources through the relevant local authority department.

How this process might work in practice needs further elaboration on at least two counts. First, how is the membership of a social policy community to be decided? Second, how is competition for inevitably limited resources among policy communities *within* local authority areas and, more generally, *among* local authorities themselves to be managed?

## Membership

Because policy community members will not simply debate choices presented to them but actively *develop* policy alternatives in ways which evoke Barber's (1984, p. 200) conception of 'strong democracy', it is vital that all those who wish to be involved 'feel able to contribute to ongoing debates'. As suggested, membership of social policy communities would be likely to reflect a functional mix with individuals desiring different levels of involvement according to the (changing) depth of interest and the nature of the issues involved. The main concern is how this complex membership can be honed into a reasonably sophisticated policy-making body. Here it is helpful to invert Stewart's (1996, p. 31) point that participatory democratic processes can actively strengthen representative democracy for, conversely, there is every reason to believe that particular forms of decentralized representation can enhance the wider deliberative process. If, for example, individuals were to be elected by standing policy community 'fora' (formally constituted bodies but open to all those able to demonstrate a direct interest) to develop proposals for the community's consideration, these policy-making committees could be placed under a duty both to disseminate detailed information about their proposals and to invite counter-proposals. Naturally, these would need to be debated and ultimately endorsed by the full forum, with opportunities being provided for the expression of dissenting views and recommendations for possible alternatives, but this prefiguration of forum discussions would help to develop fairly sophisticated knowledge of relevant issues, so ensuring a high standard of deliberation.

Of course, some of the difficulties commonly associated with deliberative democracy (see Johnson, 1998) – monopoly of discussion by powerful interests, the undue influence of those who speak last – could well emerge if the above model, or something like it, was operationalized. These are complex issues, to be sure, and satisfactory solutions cannot be fully developed here, but it is possible to imagine certain basic safeguards that could help to offset these problems. We have already seen that policy community discussions must conform to standards of debate and procedure agreed by the central state, where membership is characterized by a politics of presence, but further conditions could be added. In order to prevent elected policy-makers succumbing to the temptations of power, individuals should hold their posts for relatively short periods of time, say three years; again, in an effort to avoid the dangers of permanent exclusion, specific consideration of minority social and political needs could be made a fundamental requirement of all policy discussions.

Smaller but nonetheless significant concerns about the order of speaking in debates, procedures for 'summing up' and so on would need to be dealt with by agreed procedural rules which could, for example, allow minority interests a final right of reply, or dissenting positions greater amounts of time to present their case. It is important to remember, however, that the decentralized and fragmented nature of the deliberative process, *taken as a whole*, should mean that those finding themselves in a majority position over a specific issue in a particular policy community could well find themselves in a minority elsewhere. The point of the process is not to eliminate 'policy winners' but to ensure that the full range of interests have equal access to debates and that 'winners' should not consistently be drawn from the same social groups in all circumstances.

## *Managing Competition for Resources*

Issues of membership and conduct aside, the model outlined (see figure 1) raises another potentially unpalatable prospect. Critics may fairly point out that political, administrative and financial chaos could be the likely result of deliberative democracy where policy communities *within* particular local authorities and *across* local authorities as a whole demand consistently high resource levels to implement widely differing proposals. To minimize these risks, decentralized, 'particularized' policy formulation needs to be balanced against more centralized resource allocation mechanisms. Where intra-authority competition is concerned, initial budgetary control could be exercised by local authority budget committees allocating fixed sums for each policy community predicated on amounts anticipated from central government and additional sums raised by local taxes. What is still likely to remain a disorganized process, however, could be further rationalized by the advisory role played by local authority departments. Teams of policy specialists, augmented where necessary by co-opted experts, would work closely with each policy community forum advising on the implications of adopting particular policies, including budgetary implications, and the nature of possible alternatives.

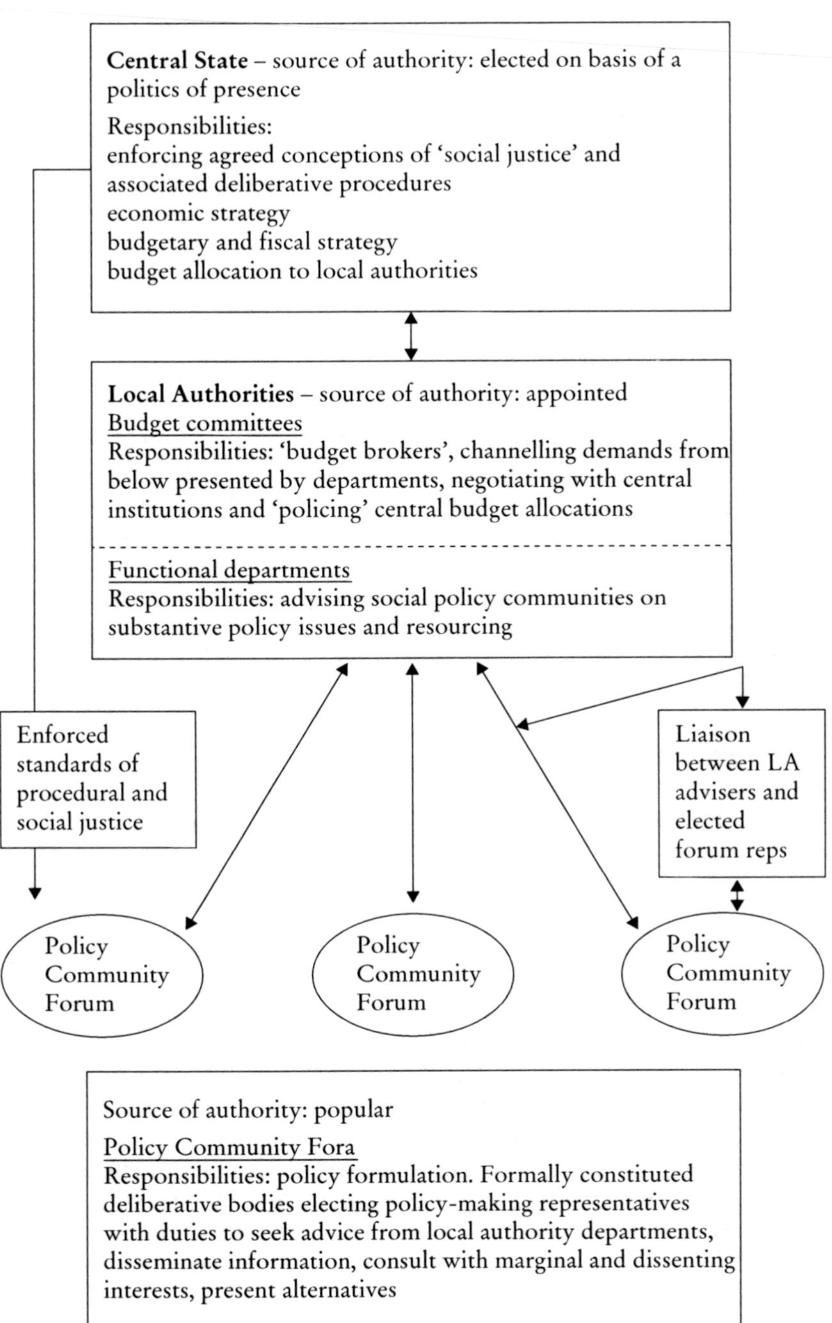


**Figure 1** Model for a deliberative social policy

At inter-authority level the state must be centrally involved in overseeing budget allocation and, in order to dissuade policy communities from advancing constantly overinflated demands, central institutions would need to be a good deal thicker than Hirst, for example, envisages. Though playing no direct policy-making role, the state nevertheless would have an important part to play as an economic manager and overall budget controller. Responsibility for supply-side policies designed to secure economic efficiency in a broadly free market context, together with responsibility for the tax-raising powers necessary to provide resources for social goods and services, would exist alongside the final power to decide the total available budget for distribution through local authority budget committees to policy communities. Resources would need to be allocated partly on a (egalitarian) bloc basis to ensure basic levels of funding across all categories of need and partly on the basis of differentiated need according to the nature of demands expressed by the policy communities themselves. Where resourcing is concerned, the fact that central democratic institutions must conform to criteria of communication and allocation agreed in debates characterized by a politics of presence is important. Because particular interests are engaged (though not mandated) at this level, all social groups will be party to decisions about the size of the 'social budget' and budget allocation, and, by extension, to deliberations about the resourcing of particular claims. To be sure, each community may not get precisely what has been demanded and policies may need to be adjusted to accord with current economic realities, but appeal mechanisms could take account of contested decisions and, because policy-making is firmly lodged at policy community level, the decentralized, particularistic nature of the enterprise remains intact.

## Conclusion

This article has questioned the utility of the universalist–particularist paradigm in contemporary welfare theory. It has argued that current attempts either to reject its significance or to harmonize its two constituent elements have not proved successful and that we need to move beyond the confines imposed by this duality by exploring the possibilities offered by deliberative conceptions of democracy. As a first step, it is important to acknowledge the ways in which postmodern thinking can help us to break loose from attempts to develop and justify immutable principles of justice on which the respective merits of 'universality' and 'difference' can be founded, allowing space to frame a more variegated understanding of the increasingly fractured nature of contemporary social politics. While this need not – indeed should not – imply complete endorsement of postmodern reasoning in which social actors are reduced to fragmented 'subject positions' in the context of an impossible relativism, the suggestion here is that it is important to take account of the ways in which actors' identities are likely to be split among different, and increasingly complex, policy arenas as they struggle to deal with the persistent demands of change.

The brief outline of a decentralized deliberative politics included here stands as an initial attempt to sketch how this emergent complexity might take institutional form. Certainly, if we are to take seriously the degree of social fragmentation which increasingly characterizes late modern societies, and the implications this holds for efforts to retain a universalist perspective in social policy, then we must continue to discuss and elaborate conceptions of this kind. The most significant point, however, is also the most paradoxical. Generations of welfare theorists have assumed that social inclusion is best achieved through state-directed, universal social policy outputs. It is time to shift our attention from a concern with outputs to the view that increased participation in developing policy inputs is likely to prove considerably more socially inclusive. In fact, achieving equality of, or inclusion in, outputs is not really the issue. A deliberative approach to social policy, by encouraging *all* social groups to participate in framing and pursuing policy proposals through access to deliberative institutions, would make for a much greater degree of inclusion – and hold out the prospect of a greater degree of social equality – than traditional universalist welfare ideals managed to achieve.

## Note

From *Critical Social Policy*, 19, 1, 1999, pp. 57–85.

## References

Amin, A. (1995) 'Beyond Associative Democracy', Discussion Paper TI 1-95-220, Tinbergen Institute, Amsterdam/Rotterdam.

Baldwin, S. (1994) 'The Need for Care in Later Life: Social Protection for Older People and Family Caregivers', in S. Baldwin and J. Falkingham (eds), *Social Security and Social Change: New Challenges to the Beveridge Model*, Hemel Hempstead, Harvester Wheatsheaf.

Barber, B. (1984) *Strong Democracy: Participatory Politics for a New Age*, Berkeley, University of California Press.

Benhabib, S. (1986) *Situating the Self: Gender, Community and Postmodernism in Contemporary Ethics*, Cambridge, Polity.

Benhabib, S. (1996a) 'From Identity Politics to Social Feminism: A Plea for the Nineties', in D. Trend (ed.), *Radical Democracy: Identity, Citizenship and the State*, London, Routledge.

Benhabib, S. (1996b) 'Introduction', in S. Benhabib (ed.), *Democracy and Difference: Contesting the Boundaries of the Political*, Princeton, Princeton University Press.

Bohman, J. (1996) *Public Deliberation: Pluralism, Complexity and Democracy*, Cambridge, MA, MIT Press.

Bosanquet, N. and Townsend, P. (1972) *Labour and Inequality*, London, Fabian Society.

Calhoun, C. (1995) *Critical Social Theory: Culture, History and the Challenge of Difference*, Oxford, Blackwell.

Cohen, J. (1989) 'Deliberation and Democratic Legitimacy', in A. Hamlin and P. Pettit (eds), *The Good Polity: Normative Analysis of the State*, Oxford, Clarendon Press.

Di Stefano, C. (1990) 'Dilemmas of Difference', in Linda J. Nicholson (ed.), *Feminism and Postmodernism*, London, Routledge.

Ellison, N. (1994) *Egalitarian Thought and Labour Politics: Retreating Visions*, London, Routledge.

Ellison, N. (1997a) 'From Welfare State to Post-Welfare Society? Labour's Social Policy in Historical and Contemporary Perspective', in B. Brivati and T. Bale (eds), *New Labour in Power: Precedents and Prospects*, London, Routledge.

Ellison, N. (1997b) 'Towards a New Social Politics: Citizenship and Reflexivity in Late Modernity', *Sociology*, 31, pp. 697–717.

Esping-Andersen, G. (1996) 'After the Golden Age? Welfare State Dilemmas in a Global Economy', in G. Esping-Andersen (ed.), *Welfare States in Transition: National Adaptations in Global Economies*, London, Sage.

Evans, J. (1995) *Feminist Theory Today: An Introduction to Second-Wave Feminism*, London, Sage.

Fishkin, J. (1991) *Democracy and Deliberation: New Directions in Democratic Reform*, New Haven, Yale University Press.

Fraser, N. (1996) 'Equality, Difference and Radical Democracy: The United States Feminist Debates Revisited', in D. Trend (ed.), *Radical Democracy: Identity, Citizenship and the State*, London, Routledge.

Gilligan, C. (1982) *In a Different Voice*, Cambridge, MA, Harvard University Press.

Glennerster, H. (ed.) (1983) *The Future of the Welfare State: Remaking Social Policy*, London, Heinemann.

Gough, I. (1979) *The Political Economy of the Welfare State*, London, Macmillan.

Habermas, J. (1995) 'Reconciliation through the Public Use of Reason: Remarks on John Rawls' Political Liberalism', *Journal of Philosophy*, 52, pp. 109–31.

Hillyard, P. and Watson, S. (1996) 'Postmodern Social Policy: A Contradiction in Terms?', *Journal of Social Policy* 25: 321–46.

Hirst, P. (1994) *Associative Democracy*, Cambridge, Polity.

Hirst, P. (1998) 'Social Welfare and Associative Democracy', in N. Ellison and C. Pierson (eds), *Developments in British Social Policy*, London, Macmillan.

Honig, B. (1996) 'Difference, Dilemmas and the Politics of Home', in S. Benhabib (ed.), *Democracy and Difference: Contesting the Boundaries of the Political*, Princeton, Princeton University Press.

Johnson, J. (1998) 'Arguing for Deliberation: Some Skeptical Considerations', in J. Elster (ed.), *Deliberative Democracy*, Cambridge, Cambridge University Press.

Jones, P. (1990) 'Universal Principles and Particular Claims: From Welfare Rights to Welfare States', in A. Ware and R. R. Goodin (eds), *Needs and Welfare*, London, Sage.

Kymlicka, W. (1995) *Multicultural Citizenship*, Oxford, Clarendon Press.

Le Grand, J. (1982) *The Strategy of Equality*, London, Allen and Unwin.

Le Grand, J. (1989) 'Markets, Welfare and Equality', in J. Le Grand and S. Estrin (eds), *Market Socialism*. Oxford, Clarendon Press.

Lister, R. (1990) 'Women, Economic Dependency and Citizenship', *Journal of Social Policy*, 19, pp. 445–68.

Lister, R. (1993) 'Tracing the Contours of Women's Citizenship', *Policy and Politics*, 21, pp. 3–17.

Marshall, T. (1963) 'Citizenship and Social Class', in *Sociology at the Crossroads*, London, Heinemann.

Mason, G. (1995) *Race and Ethnicity in Modern Britain*, Oxford, Oxford University Press.

Millar, J. (1994) 'Lone Parents and Social Security Policy in the UK', in S. Baldwin and J. Falkingham (eds), *Social Security and Social Change: New Challenges to the Beveridge Model*, Hemel Hempstead, Harvester Wheatsheaf.

Mouffe, C. (1996) 'Radical Democracy or Liberal Democracy?', in D. Trend (ed.), *Radical Democracy: Identity, Citizenship and the State*, New York, Routledge.

Offe, C. (1984) *Contradictions of the Welfare State*, London, Hutchinson.

Penna, S. and O'Brien, M. (1996) 'Postmodernism and Social Policy: A Small Step Forwards?', *Journal of Social Policy* 25, pp. 39–61.

Phillips, A. (1995) *The Politics of Presence*, Oxford, Clarendon Press.

Rawls, J. (1993) *Political Liberalism*, New York, Columbia University Press.

Skellington, R. (1992) *'Race' in Britain Today*, London, Sage.

Solomos, J. and Back, L. (1996) *Race, Politics and Social Change*, London, Routledge.

Spicker, P. (1996) 'Understanding Particularism', in D. Taylor (ed.), *Critical Social Policy: A Reader*, London, Sage.

Stewart, J. (1996) 'Innovation in Democratic Practice in Local Government', *Policy and Politics*, 24, 1, pp. 29–41.

Sunstein, C. (1991) 'Preferences and Politics', *Philosophy and Public Affairs*, 20, 1, pp. 3–34.

Taylor-Gooby, P. (1994) 'Postmodernism and Social Policy: A Great Leap Backwards?', *Journal of Social Policy*, 23, pp. 385–404.

Taylor-Gooby, P. (1997) 'In Defence of Second-Best Theory: State, Class and Capital in Social Policy', *Journal of Social Policy*, 26, pp. 171–92.

Thompson, S. and Hoggett, P. (1996) 'Universalism, Selectivism and Particularism: Towards a Postmodern Social Policy', *Critical Social Policy*, 46, pp. 21–43.

Titmuss, R. (1963) 'The Social Division of Welfare', in *Essays on the Welfare State*, London, Allen and Unwin.

Titmuss, R. (1970) *The Gift Relationship*, London, Allen and Unwin.

Townsend, P. (1979) *Poverty in the United Kingdom*, Harmondsworth, Penguin.

Walby, S. (1990) 'Is Citizenship Gendered?' *Sociology*, 28, pp. 379–95.

White, S. K. (1991) *Political Theory and Postmodernism*, Cambridge, Cambridge University Press.

Williams, F. (1992) 'Somewhere Over the Rainbow: Universality and Diversity in Social Policy', in N. Manning and R. Page (eds), *Social Policy Review 4*, Canterbury, Social Policy Association.

Yeatman, A. (1994) *Postmodern Revisionings of the Political*, London, Routledge.

Young, I. M. (1989) 'Polity and Group Difference: A Critique of the Ideal of Universal Citizenship', *Ethics*, 99, pp. 250–74.

Young, I. M. (1990) *Justice and the Politics of Difference*, Princeton, Princeton University Press.

Young, I. M. (1993) 'Justice and Communicative Democracy', in R. Gottlieb (ed.), *Tradition, Counter-Tradition, Politics: Dimensions of Radical Democracy*, Philadelphia, Temple University Press.

# Ways Ahead?

# A Welfare State for the Twenty-First Century

*Gøsta Esping-Andersen*

[ . . . ]

What I present here is [ . . . ] an attempt to construct a welfare edifice that is in [ . . . ] harmony with the kind of economy, employment, and family that is in the making. [ . . . ] The challenge is immense because the revolutions in both employment and family structure are creating massive new opportunities but also new social risks and needs. Changing technologies, intensified global integration, and our capacity to adapt, occupy centre-stage as far as competitiveness is concerned; the service sector will overdetermine as far as employment is concerned. Although it is evident that high-end services will dominate job-trends, both the new family needs and a full employment scenario will imply a sizeable share of low-end, low-productivity jobs in social and personal services. It will, accordingly, be difficult to avoid new dualisms. A knowledge-intensive economy will produce new skill-based cleavages with, possibly, polarization. How to deal with the losers is one major challenge. A knowledge-intensive economy necessitates not just expertise among producers, but also among consumers. Therefore, unless we succeed in broadly strengthening the cognitive capacities and resource base of citizens, the long-term scenario might very well be a smattering of 'knowledge islands' in a great sea of marginalized outsiders. This poses the first-order challenge of how to democratize skills. [ . . . ] And it poses the second-order challenge of how to redesign social policy. The most simple-minded 'third way' promoters believe that the population, via education, can be adapted to the market economy and that the social problem will, hence, disappear. This is a dangerous fallacy. Education, training or lifelong learning cannot be enough. A skill-intensive economy will breed new inqualities; a full-employment service economy will reinforce these. And if we are unwilling to accept low-end services, it will be difficult to avoid widespread unemployment. In any case, education cannot undo differences in people's social capital.

The new family and life course pose an equally formidable challenge. Greater instability and the rise of 'atypical' households mean also potential polarization. At one end, divorce, separations, and single parenthood create severe risks of poverty. At the other end, the trend towards dual-earner households strengthens families' resource base. We must assume strong marital homogamy, and therefore a widening gap between strong and weak households.

The standard male breadwinner model that once guaranteed adequate welfare and high fertility is declining both numerically and in its capacity to effectively prevent child poverty. Indeed, the conventional family may increasingly constitute an obstacle to flexibility and adaptation since the welfare of too many depends on the job and income security of one person. And with family revolution is emerging new life course patterns, much less linear, homogeneous, and predictable. The upshot is that new risks and resource needs are bundling heavily among youth and in child families. The challenge, again, is to redefine social policy so that it nurtures strong and viable families and protects those most at risk. If those most at risk happen to be children and youth, the urgency of reform is so much greater because it is today's children who will be tomorrow's productive base – or, in the case of failure to reform, tomorrow's expensive social problems.

As was always the case, access to paid work is families' single best welfare guarantee. The difference today is that emerging family types face new and severe trade-offs between employment and family obligations; trade-offs that are better resolved by access to services than traditional income maintenance. Postwar 'welfare capitalism' functioned well because labour markets and families themselves were the principal source of welfare for most citizens, most of their lives. Presently, both labour markets and families create widespread insecurity, precariousness, and often social exclusion and this means obviously added burdens on public social protection schemes. The single greatest challenge we face today is how to rethink social policy so that, once again, labour markets and families are welfare optimizers and a good guarantee that tomorrow's adult workers will be as productive and resourceful as possible.

The emerging risk and needs structure is in stark contrast with the existing, highly aged-biased, emphasis of most contemporary European welfare states. Our social policy challenge implies a rethinking of the life cycle, of the balance between income transfers and services and, more generally of the guiding principles of social justice and equality. If Europe aims to maximize its competitive position in the world economy and, at the same time, commit itself to full employment, new inequalities will be difficult to avoid. The burning question is, what do we do about them? The most fundamental conclusion that emerges is that we must re-think the concept of social rights. The existing principle of guaranteeing maximum welfare and equality 'for-all-here-and-now' cannot be consistent with the emerging economic imperatives. If relatively low incomes, bad jobs, or precarious employment cannot be avoided (and might arguably even merit encouragement), there is the issue of how to soften their welfare effects in the short run. However, the core welfare issue must focus on long-run dynamics, on citizens' life chances. Low wages or bad jobs are not a threat to individuals' welfare if the experience is temporary; they are if individuals become trapped. In brief, the core principle of social rights should be redefined as effective guarantees against entrapment, as the right to a 'second chance'; in short, as a basic set of *life chance guarantees*.

## The Diversity of European Welfare Regimes

These challenges to social protection are not equally severe across all European welfare systems. We must avoid two errors. One is to ignore the great diversity of European welfare systems. A second is to remain too narrowly preoccupied with just the welfare state. Society's total welfare package combines inputs from the welfare state proper, markets (and especially labour markets), and families. Many view the welfare state as overburdened, inefficient, threatened or, simply, malfunctioning. Some advocate that it be radically slimmed, others that it be strengthened, and still others that it be overhauled. Whatever opinions are put forth, there is an implicit view of what, alternatively, ought to be the role of markets and families. Those who advocate 'decentralization' basically suggest a greater responsibility to families and the 'local community'; those who champion privatization assign welfare to the cash-nexus but, in practice, the result would also be a greater burden on many families. To capture the interplay of state, family, and market, it is useful to cast our analysis in terms of *welfare regimes.*

Turn the clock back to the postwar decades, and we would identify two distinct European welfare regimes. The Nordic-cum-British was largely general revenue financed, stressing universal, flat-rate benefits. The other, prevalent in Continental Europe, emphasized contribution financed and employment-based social insurance. As social protection systems evolved and matured by the 1970s, differences emerged much more clearly. The Nordic countries branched out into a unique model, first by adding an earnings-related component to flat-rate 'citizens' benefits and, secondly, by shifting the emphasis from income transfers towards servicing families, stressing employment-activating policies and, above all, women's integration in the labour market. The Nordic model may be famous for its generosity and universalism, but what really stands out is its employment-bias and its 'de-familialization' of welfare responsibilities. Britain, in contrast, gradually moved towards more targeting and income testing, assigning more welfare responsibilities to the market – thus converging with North America. The hallmark of most Continental European countries is how little has changed. They remain firmly wedded to employment-based, contributory social insurance but have extended coverage to residual groups via ad hoc income-tested programs (like the RMI in France or the *pensione sociale* in Italy). A second defining feature of Continental European, and especially Mediterranean, social protection systems is their strong *familialism*, i.e. the idea that families hold the principal welfare responsibility for their members, be it in terms of sharing incomes or in terms of care needs. Hence, these countries are uniquely committed to protecting the male breadwinner (via insurance and job protection), highly reliant on social contributions for financing, and comparatively very underdeveloped in social services.

Such differences mean that we cannot forge general strategies for social reform at an abstract pan-European level. It also follows that we shall err terribly if we limit our attention solely to *governments'* welfare role. I believe it is futile to discuss whether we should reduce public social commitments without considering what effects such might have on family and market welfare delivery. A strategy of 'decentralizing' welfare to community and family may sound appealing to many, but how will it affect women's double role as workers and care-givers? Alternatively, a scenario of more markets may appear more efficient, but if this means that large populations will be priced out of the welfare market, do potential efficiency gains clearly outweigh potential welfare losses? Reforming European welfare commitments for the coming century implies *regime change*, that is reordering the welfare contributions of markets, families and state so that the mix corresponds better to the overall goals we may have for a more equitable and efficient social system.

## The Transformation of the Social Risk and Needs Structure

Most European social protection systems were constructed in an era with a very different distribution and intensity of risks and needs than exists today. With the main exception of Scandinavia (and Britain), the allocation of welfare responsibilities between state, market, and families has not changed dramatically over the past fifty years. What has changed, however, is the capacity of households and labour markets to furnish those basic welfare guarantees that once were assumed. Indeed, both now generate new risks and, equally importantly, also new needs.

The postwar model could rely on strong families and well-performing labour markets to furnish the lion's share of welfare for most people, most of their lives. Until the 1970s, the norm was stable, male breadwinner-based families. With few interruptions, the male could count on secure employment, steady real earnings growth, and long careers – followed by a few years in retirement after age 65. Women would typically cease to work at first birth, and were thus the main societal provider of social care for children and the frail elderly. Unemployment and poverty were limited among prime-age households, and the main social risks were concentrated at the two 'passive' tail-ends of the life cycle: in large child families, and among the aged. Hence, besides health care, European welfare states came to prioritize income maintenance and, *par excellence*, pensions.

The problem behind the new risk configuration is that it stems primarily from weakened families and poorly functioning labour markets. As a consequence, the welfare state is burdened with responsibilities for which it was not designed. A well-functioning welfare state for the future must, accordingly, be recalibrated so that labour markets and families function more optimally.

## *Family Risks*

Families today have far fewer children, yet child poverty is rising. Ongoing changes in labour markets and families affect young households most severely. The reasons are well-documented: Firstly, unemployment and insecurity are concentrated among youth and the low-educated (males in particular). The incidence of 'no-work households' is sometimes alarmingly high, and this is one symptom of an emerging new polarization: Homogamy means that unemployment, precariousness, and poverty 'comes in couples'. Youth often face serious delays in 'getting started', in making a smooth transition from school to careers, or in forming independent families; southern European youth can often anticipate three years' unemployment and this, obviously, is one cause of falling birth rates. The consequences of youth precariousness vary nonetheless depending on social policy approach. The unemployed – particularly youth – face severe revenue problems in many EU countries. Southern Europe's 'familialism' implies that most unemployment is absorbed by parents, but this is not the case in northern Europe. Where, as in Denmark, unemployed youth are typically entitled to social benefits, poverty is modest; where, as elsewhere, they rely primarily on assistance, poverty is widespread.

The new risks are also a function of the rise of 'non-standard' households. [ . . . ] Two types have, in particular, become prominent: the 'no work-income' and the single parent household. Both run high risks of income poverty. No-work households are generally transfer dependent, often relying on social assistance. Except in Scandinavia, child poverty is alarmingly high in lone parent families. Yet, across all kinds of child families – in two-adult families as well as in single parent households – the strikingly best safeguard against poverty is that mothers work. The low levels of single-parenthood poverty in the Nordic countries are, in fact, less due to generous social transfers than to adequate work incomes made possible by child care. Simply put, mothers' employment is a very effective antidote to the risks that come with family instability and labour market precariousness. If this is the case, the single most pressing social policy issue has less to do with income maintenance and much more to do with servicing working mothers.

The new distribution of life cycle risks is most evident when we contrast younger and older households. The economic well-being of child families has been eroding while, concomitantly, it has improved among the elderly. High incomes have allowed the elderly to live independently and, coupled to rising longevity, this implies that the chief needs among the aged have shifted towards caring services. And herein lies one of the key epochal transformations: the main welfare needs within young and aged households have less to do with improved income transfers and more to do with access to services. Among the ultra-aged in particular, the pressing need is for home-help services and care centers. Within child families, poverty can best be stemmed by enhancing parents' labour market prospects and earnings capacity.

Notwithstanding, most European welfare states remain uniquely biased in favour of the aged rather than youth; in favour of income maintenance rather than services. The Nordic countries are an exception as far as servicing is concerned; and with Ireland, they remain the exception in prioritizing young families.[1] Put differently, society may be overspending on passive maintenance and underinvesting in the kinds of resources that strengthen citizens' capacities.

Services can, besides government, be provided by the market or families themselves. In Europe, however, marketed family services, such as private day care, are generally priced out of the market.[2] In brief, where government provision (or subsidization) is absent, as in most of continental and especially southern Europe, families themselves must shoulder most of the caring burden of children and the elderly. The upshot of familialism is of course to worsen women's incompatibility between family responsibilities and paid work and, indirectly, to weaken families' capacity to autonomously combat poverty. But since, in effect, young cohort women today do work, traditional familialism mainly provokes another perverse result, namely a *de facto* low-fertility equilibrium!

## Welfare Asymmetries across Generations and the Life Course

We should be careful to avoid a simple zero-sum trade-off between the welfare of the aged and the young. There exists, of course, some evidence that the rising welfare of retirees occurs at the expense of youth and children, at least in countries (like the U.S. or Italy) where improvements in aged welfare have not been accompanied by an upgrading of family policies. Also, it is clear that income distribution trends in most countries favour the aged. The median retired household can usually count on a disposable income of at least 80 per cent of the national median.[3]

Certainly there remain pockets of poverty among the aged, typically concentrated among widows and persons with problematic contribution histories. Old-age poverty tends to be higher in countries which, until recently, had large rural populations (Greece, Italy, and Spain, for example). It is also well known that retirement income declines somewhat with age. Nonetheless, all indications are that the large mass of pensioners in most countries have sufficient (and sometimes perhaps 'excess') incomes, especially in light of reduced consumption and household capital expenditures, and because an often very large proportion (the EU average is 75 per cent) of the elderly own their home outright. What is more, in many countries retirees enjoy preferential tax treatment and are generally exempt from social contributions.

The economic well-being of today's elderly is the result of a unique combination of factors that produced high retirement income and lifetime asset accumulation.[4] [ . . . ] The average household at age 65 possesses wealth that equals 4–5 times its annual income stream. And, although we have only scattered nation-specific evidence, there are indications of pension overprovision in some countries. My own analyses of Italian family expenditure data indicate a 30 percentage point excess of income over expenditure in the average retiree household. A recent study by Kohli on intra-family money streams indicates a huge dominance of transfers from the aged (70+) to their children and grandchildren: 24 per cent of income is transferred to their children; almost 15 per cent to their grandchildren.[5]

Such downward intra-family redistribution surely varies by income decile and by nation. Moreover, excess revenues reflect not just pension generosity but also home ownership, private assets, and lower consumption needs. Still, where it exists the redistributive effect must be considered perverse if the welfare of youth is becoming a function of the riches of their retired forebears. Indeed, it is doubly perverse in the sense that pay-as-you-go pensions are financed by the working age population. The welfare state was presumably built in order to even the playing field, but here is a case where it helps re-establish inherited privilege.

Any debate on reforming pensions must consider the life course specificities of past, current and *especially* future retiring cohorts. If current retirement cohorts are generally well-off it is because they are the main beneficiaries of Golden Age capitalism. Firstly, most of their careers spanned decades of strong productivity and earnings growth with low unemployment among prime-age males. Secondly, with the regulation of seniority rights and the emergence of efficiency wage systems, the age–wage profile was decoupled from productivity – hence rising earnings even when productivity declines with age.[6] Thirdly, today's pensioners are the chief beneficiaries of pension upgrading in the 1960s and 1970s. Fourthly, although there has been a decline in real earnings growth in recent decades, the financial returns on investments have risen.

A major reform of present pension systems confronts the dilemma that future retirement cohorts are unlikely to amass similar lifetime assets, either through individual initiative (work and savings) or through the redistributive mechanisms of public pension schemes. Or, more likely, future retirement cohorts will, if uncorrected, become far more dualistic, possibly even polarized in terms of life chances. Today's youth often face serious delays in passing to stable employment: besides longer schooling, a large proportion can anticipate protracted and maybe frequent unemployment combined with more precarious employment. This correlates with skills and education. Secondly, as deregulation weakens the security of the prime-age 'insider' workforce, career interruptions and redundancies are increasingly likely, among the less skilled in particular.[7] Thirdly, today's young cohorts are unlikely to benefit from decades of powerful real earnings growth and, if productivity bargaining becomes increasingly decentralized, seniority-based wage systems may weaken. Again, there is a clear trend towards more inequality in skills-based earnings power. Fourthly, these are the cohorts which will fully experience the impact of ongoing pension reform in EU member countries, with the shift towards more individualized and actuarially based entitlement calculations. And, yet again, this will favour the strongest workers in the labour market.

If *de facto* retirement age will remain at 59–60, today's young cohorts will be hard put to cumulate a minimum of, say, thirty-five contribution years towards the basic pension. There cohort-specific disadvantages are, nonetheless, offset by three key factors: One, their higher educational attainment and superior cognitive skills imply greater adaptability and ability for retraining across their careers. As they age, an investment in retraining may appear more logical than, simply, early retirement. The stronger is the skills and educational base of young workers today, the greater will be the pay-off when they eventually age. Two, each new retirement cohort shows sharp improvements in health and longevity, and all indications are that this will continue. Already today, the typical 65-year-old male can expect another eight to ten disability-free years. Those who are young now will be able to count on many more disability-free years. Three, the ongoing growth of women's lifetime employment implies that future retirement households will be able to double up pension savings or, in the case of divorce, women will increasingly have independent pension entitlements.

A strategy of resolving the looming pension crisis by radically reducing pension entitlements today would be counterproductive in the long run if, as is very possible, future retirees will look more like their forebears in the 1940s or 1960s. If, now, pensioner households have too much income, it would be a more equitable, and certainly more prudent, policy to simply tax away the excess.[8] If, then, a major reduction of public pensions is a suboptimal long-run strategy, our attention must shift to an alternative policy. As virtually all agree, the key to long-term sustainability lies in population growth and, more realistically, in raising participation rates.[9]

[...]

## The Link to Labour Markets

The new welfare policy priorities that emerge from the preceding analysis boil down to one basic issue, namely that social policy must maximize citizens' productive resources and life chances. It is important to recognize that any 'work-friendly' policy must align itself to the dynamics of a services-led economy.

The service economy is tendentially dualistic, combining knowledge-intensive professional and technical jobs with low-end, low value-added, and labour intensive, servicing. The former are concentrated in business and some social services (teachers, doctors); the latter in sales, consumer, and also some social services (restaurant workers, home helpers, nursing assistants). Europe, like North America, is very dynamic as far as business services are concerned. Europe's development of social services is, excepting Scandinavia, sluggish. And European private consumer services are stagnant if not actually in decline.

Contrary to popular belief, services are *everywhere* biased in favour of skilled and good jobs. The dilemma, nonetheless, is that a significant amelioration of mass unemployment means stimulating also low-productivity services, and this means that we must rely also on personal consumer services and social services. The good news is that these are sheltered from international trade competition; the bad news is that they compete directly with unpaid household 'self-servicing'. The problem is that many services are extremely price sensitive. They will grow if, as in the United States, wages and costs are relatively low, and thus affordable, or if, as in Scandinavia, they are subsidized by government.[10]

Herein lies the great European policy dilemma. The task of forging a more equitable and efficient social protection system, as outlined above, pales in comparison to the trade-offs involved in stimulating employment-intensive services. *Yet, no solution exists unless we realize that social protection and service employment are directly linked.* The gist of the problem is simple, namely that strong service growth implies more taxation if we emphasize public services or, alternatively, more wage inequality (and lower fixed labour costs) if we emphasize market services.

Most European welfare states and industrial relations systems have committed themselves for decades to a degree of security for the prime age (male) worker, and a degree of earnings and income equality, that is not compatible with a large, low-end service economy. Moreover, the existing financial pressures on most European welfare states today make it difficult to replicate the Nordic countries' social service expansion twenty years ago.

This dilemma is now well recognized within EU member states. Witness the extension of targeted wage subsidies (usually aimed at youth and contingent on training), and recent EU-level proposals to stimulate labour intensive services through a reduction of the VAT.[11] There is virtually universal agreement that strong wage compression, a high tax wedge (especially through mandatory contributions) and, perhaps, overly rigid employment regulation block lower-end services. The great dilemma, though, is that the kind of *tout court*, American-style, deregulation that would fuel such jobs is unacceptable to European policy-makers.[12]

The stagnation of low-end services in Europe is directly linked to the nexus between families and social protection. On one hand, employment-based social insurance systems impose very high fixed labour costs whose marginal effect is especially strong in low-wage, low-productivity jobs: a high tax-wedge *de facto* prices them out of the market. On the other hand, the lion's share of such service jobs compete with households' own internal servicing capacity. So, where women's employment rate is low, households service themselves; where most women work, households' demand for outservicing increases. In brief, the double earner family externalizes its servicing needs and creates jobs.[13]

As discussed above, dual earner families require services to begin with and herein lies the gist of a win-win policy scenario, namely that more social care services are a key instrument in combating poverty *and* a potentially very effective employment multiplier. Markets cannot generally guarantee affordable, high-quality care for small children or the aged, and high-quality day care is crucial if our aim is to optimize the life chances of children. In other words, public subsidies or direct public delivery is basically a first precondition. Here, in other words, is a prime rationale for shifting welfare priorities in favour of servicing families. An investment in women's ability to work is also an investment in family welfare and in job creation.

Since the traditional welfare state defined its obligations primarily in terms of income maintenance for those unable to work, social protection has been viewed as 'unproductive' consumption and problematic redistribution. This 'income maintenance' philosophy has, by and large, been carried over in addressing contemporary social problems. Yet, I have tried to make a strong case that servicing families is the single most effective policy against poverty, welfare dependency, and also an investment in human resources at the same time. In brief, family services should be regarded not as merely 'passive consumption', but also as active investments which yield a long-run return.

[. . .]

The social advantages of a low-end labour market are clear: it provides easy-entry jobs for youth, immigrants, low-skilled workers, and returning women. Whereas in much of Europe now, the transition from school to work can last for years, and where immigrant workers have difficulty integrating themselves into the official economy, and where low-skilled workers are increasingly condemned to unemployment, low-end services could play a very positive function *if*, that is, they do not become lifelong traps. A brief spell of low earnings and unrewarding work will not, by definition, harm people's life chances – to the contrary if they provide bridges into the labour market or help supplement income. The criteria by which we must judge the costs and benefits of low-end jobs cannot be based on snapshot notions of equality for all, here and now. The only reasonable benchmark is life course dynamics.

[. . .]

A low-end labour market need not be incompatible with a new welfare state scenario. Indeed, one might restate the point in this way: *no win-win welfare model for Europe will be possible unless we accept a different notion of equality.* We have become accustomed to an overly static, here-and-now concept of redistributive justice: the welfare state must assure that all citizens are protected always. A far more realistic principle would be that our future welfare state accepts, perhaps even sanctions, inequalities here and now in order to maximize better life chances for all. If the 'knowledge society' and the modern family create inequalities, the most effective social policy would be one that guarantees that citizens will not become trapped into social exclusion, poverty, or marginality across their life course.

## A European Welfare State for the Twenty-First Century

[. . .]

The issue before us has to do with the long term, with the kind of society that our children will live in. And if this means redefining welfare priorities, we cannot escape the need for some common, basic criterion of what is desirable, given known constraints. What are the common goals to be reached? What do we seek to accomplish? What are the first principles that must guide policy-making? What, in brief, can be our common yardstick of justice, of equality, of collective guarantees and individual responsibility? And, once agreed upon, how can our commitments to equity be best put to use in order to maximize efficiency?

## *Basic Criteria for Policy Choice*

We must probably assume that most EU countries have reached their maximum limits of public expenditure and taxation. In fact, convergence towards the Maastricht criteria compels expenditure reductions, not bold and expensive reform vistas. The need for restrictive policy already limits the degree to which nations can promote the knowledge society, be it investments in infrastructure, education, training, or in improved social welfare.

The resource dilemma worsens considerably when we take into account the new inequalities and social risks that knowledge-based economies inevitably provoke. The evidence is by now clear that the social opportunity structure, rewards, and life chances create new winners and losers and, most likely, a deepening gulf between those with skills and those without. The new service economy can create jobs, but it *cannot* guarantee good wages and jobs for all. The fabric of our social protection systems will therefore be put to a severe test in terms of nurturing efficiency while securing social cohesion, welfare and equity. We must probably accept two ground rules for policy-making. We are compelled to re-prioritize the allocation of our existing welfare package. One, we cannot pursue too one-dimensionally a 'learning society', a human capital-based strategy, in the belief that a tide of education will lift all boats. Such a strategy inevitably leaves the less endowed behind and, equally importantly, it requires that we redistribute resources and welfare to families and, especially, to children. The modern family is an integral part of the new economic scenario, and its welfare risks are mounting. Children's ability to make the best out of schooling depends not just on the quality of schools, but also on the social conditions in their families; women are today often more educated than males but will have difficulty putting this to maximum use without generous leave programs and care services.

The second ground rule is that new social policy challenges cannot be met by additional taxation or spending as a percent of GDP. We must accordingly concentrate on how to improve upon the status quo. Entitlement conflicts and equity issues are easily subdued when the total pie grows. When, instead, we must divide the pie up differently, a clash of interests is hard to avoid.

[ . . . ]

## *Principles of Reform: Towards a Social Investment Bias*

Contemporary policy slogans such as work-friendly or women-friendly benefits, lifelong learning and social investment strategies, or the popular distinction between active and passive measures, all have in common an implicit distinction between policies that somehow enhance or diminish citizens' self-reliance and capacities, economies' efficiency and productivity. Such slogans reflect a growing unease with the existing bias of compensating the losers of economic change with passive income maintenance, of reducing labour supply, or of parking surplus workers on public benefits. The new policy vocabulary mirrors a growing consensus that social policy must become 'productivist', to coin an expression traditionally used in Swedish policy-making. That is, social policy should actively mobilize and maximize the productive potential of the population so as to minimize its need for, and dependence on, government benefits. [ . . . ]

Some policies can be regarded as an investment in human resources, capabilities and self-reliance; others, while welfare enhancing, are clearly passive income maintenance. Obviously, such a distinction is – and must be – ambiguous. Unemployment benefits appear 'passive', but they *do* aid workers in their search for new employment, and they do improve the labour-matching process. Similarly, child allowances add to families' consumption power but they do also diminish poverty and thus enhance children's future life chances. *The important point to stress here is that contemporary policy fashion tends to stress far too narrowly the wonders of 'activation' policies while ignoring income maintenance.* The need for 'passive' measures will not disappear even in the best designed, productivist welfare state: there will always be people and groups that must depend primarily on redistribution, and activating citizens' productive potential often necessitates income subsidies. Regardless, a first principle of any win-win strategy must be that it prioritizes social investment over passive maintenance.[14] A second, derivative principle is that highest priority should go to social investments in children – who are our future productive potential.

## Towards a New Welfare State Design

[ . . . ] The preceding analysis points to a set of concrete policy priorities:

- *maximizing mothers' ability to harmonize employment and children*
- *encouraging older workers to delay retirement*
- *socializing the cost of children mainly by prioritizing investments in children and youth*
- *redefining the mix of work and leisure across the life cycle*

- *reconceptualizing 'equality' and basic social rights as being primarily a question of life chance guarantees*

This will, in the most general terms, imply a greater emphasis on protecting young households, and a stronger emphasis on servicing families.

## The Limits of a Learning Strategy

Accelerating the pace towards a knowledge- and skill-intensive economy implies heavy investments in education, training and cognitive abilities. Those with low human and social capital will inevitably fall behind and find themselves marginalized in the job and career structure. The problem is a double one because such an economy requires not only highly skilled producers, but also users, of knowledge. It is accordingly imperative that educational investments be as broad-based as possible. As so much recent research has shown, concrete expertise may be less salient than possessing the essential cognitive abilities required to learn, adapt and be trainable in the first place. Activation measures, such as training or retraining, will have a low payoff if workers' initial cognitive capacities are low. They are much more likely to pay off if they are designed around a more comprehensive and individualized 'activation package'.

One pervasive problem across Europe today is that the stock of low-educated and low-skilled 'excess' workers can be very high – in part because of delayed agricultural decline, in part because of heavy job losses in traditional, low-skill industries, and in part because of an often wide gulf in education between generations of workers. A massive investment in learning will probably reap most of its benefits among younger cohort workers. The dilemma, then, is how to manage the present stock of mostly older, low-skilled males. Early retirement has, so far, been the leading policy and it may have been the only realistic policy so far. Lifelong education is an attractive alternative, but may be overly costly and ineffective if the main clientele are older, low-skilled workers. A third policy would be to deregulate job protection and seniority wage systems so as to align wages closer to productivity differentials – as is generally American practice. This would cause the incomes of youth and older workers to decline, possibly sharply so.

There exists no ready-made formula for a win-win policy in this regard – largely because the problem varies dramatically from country to country. An obvious first step is to assure that future generations of workers will have a sufficient skill and cognitive base so that the dilemma eventually evaporates. The problem is the second step, namely what to do with the existing stock. If we are assured that early retirement in the past decades has succeeded in managing what was a transitory glut of elderly low-skilled workers, the dilemma resolves itself and the process of curtailing early retirement can be accelerated. If not, we are left with a mix of continued early retirement, possibly retraining, or downward wage adjustments (or re-employment). The social partners are clearly unwilling to accept across-the-board deregulation of job security and wages, but it might be an efficiency gain to prolong the employability of older workers by subsidizing part of their wage bill. This is especially the case if, as often occurs, retired workers return to work in the undeclared shadow economy. Just as in the case of youth workers, very high fixed labour costs help price them out of the market.

A lifelong learning strategy can be effective when the basic cognitive skills are already present, and this means that we need to make sure that coming generations have the resources required to benefit from investments in training and education across their lifetime. In many EU countries, the existing generational gap is enormous and it is, therefore, imperative that this is not reproduced in the future.

## *Equitable retirement*

The principal problem in today's overly aged-biased welfare systems is that they provide incentives with inequitable results. Workers easily collude with employers to retire early because they will gain little or nothing by postponing exit. At the same time, the pay-as-you-go nature of pension schemes means that retirement at high benefits is heavily financed by the active workforce. Reinstating actuarial incentives to delay retirement would clearly be more equitable and efficient, and it would vastly improve upon the transparency of costs involved in retiring out older workers.

Since workers can expect to be disability-free until age 75, raising and flexibilizing retirement age to 65 in the medium-term, and possibly 70 in the long term, via incentives can be positive for individual workers and also for welfare state finances. Abolishing mandatory retirement age and developing flexible mechanisms of gradual exit could be pursued immediately. Longevity implies that the share of ultra-aged (80+) just about doubles every two decades. And this means costly and intensive servicing and care needs. If, as I have suggested, retirement households often enjoy 'excess' income and wealth which, if *not* taxed, generates perverse redistribution, an incentive-neutral and far more equitable policy would be to earmark taxation of pensioners to their own collective caring needs. Such a taxation mechanism, even if highly progressive, is also likely to be distributionally neutral across pensioner households (the rich generally live longer).

Altering the welfare and work nexus among the aged cannot be an end in itself, but is primarily a means to achieve more intergenerational equity

and a more efficient utilization of public resources. [ . . . ] There are really only two genuinely effective policies to combat the long-term financial consequences of aging: sharply reducing pension entitlements, or raising participation levels. Reducing entitlements means stimulating private pension plans for large parts of the population. The problem with a private-dominated pension mix is that it replicates life course inequalities, and the more that private plans grow, the more is it likely that we shall see downward pressures on public benefits targeted to low-income households. Even if a system dominated by private schemes augments national savings rates (and thus 'efficiency'), they will possibly lead to non-Paretian outcomes: the weakest may end up worse off. Identifiable trends in labour markets also threaten the viability of a predominantly private pension structure since declining job security and more intense inequalities will negatively affect workers' capacity to accumulate individual savings.

## *Harmonizing Family Welfare and Labour Markets*

Postindustrial, service-dominated labour markets cannot avoid producing new inequalities. One source of dualisms comes from systems of strong protection of stably employed 'insiders' with a possibly growing clientele of 'outsiders', such as precariously employed temporary workers or the unemployed. Insider–outsider cleavages tend to affect youth and women workers most negatively. A second source of new inequalities comes from the rising relative wage premium of skills. And a third will emerge if, and once, labour-intensive consumer services grow. The standard trade-off between jobs and inequality, epitomized by the US–Europe comparison, is far too simplistic, but it is difficult to imagine a return to full employment in Europe unless also low-paid and often low-quality service jobs are encouraged.

European industrial relations systems and welfare policy are generally premised on a commitment to wage equality and job security. Hence wage minima, contractual regulations, and high fixed labour costs are difficult to touch. There are two prevailing arguments against a 'low-wage labour market' through deregulation. The first, and most convincing, is that US-style deregulation not only creates huge inequalities, but also that it threatens the basic fabric of trust and cooperation built into European models of social partnership. Europe's tradition of broadly negotiated 'efficiency wage' arrangements is, to a great degree, its comparative advantage. The second, and far less convincing, argument is that a low-wage service economy poses a direct threat to families. The defence of existing regulatory practice is often premised on the traditional assumption that families' welfare depends almost exclusively on the wages, job security, and accumulated entitlements of the male breadwinner.

This family model is in rapid extinction. Unfortunately, some of its latter-day successors, like single parent households, are at high risk, but much less so if the parent is able to work. Two-income families enlarge the tax-base and minimize the welfare lacunae that prevail when wives' entitlements are derived from the husband. And the dual-earner family is the single best strategy to minimize child poverty. Two earners are moreover an effective household buffer in the eventuality of employment interruptions. It follows that a knowledge-society strategy premised on investments in education *must* be coupled to a recast family policy, the cornerstones of which must be guarantees against child poverty. Such guarantees must centre on affordable child and aged care, on adequate child benefits, and on maternity and parental leave arrangements that minimize mothers' employment disruption and maximize their incentive to have children. In the long run, therefore, the most persuasive 'win-win' strategy is to redirect resources to child families if our goal is to sustain our long-term welfare obligations towards the aged while effectively combating social exclusion.

Whether the externalization of family care is placed in the market or directly furnished by public agencies is unimportant, as long as standards and affordability are guaranteed. [ . . . ] There [is] a strong case for prioritizing high standard childcare services to the weakest families since optimal quality care may offset inequalities that stem from uneven social capital within families.

## *Life Chance Guarantees rather than Here-and-Now Equality for All*

Any assessment of the pros and cons of heightened labour market inequalities must be premised on a dynamic, life chances perspective and not, as is typically the case, on a static view of fairness and equality. Low-end, low-paid jobs, even at near-poverty wages, are not by definition a welfare problem. The acid test of egalitarianism and justice is not whether such jobs exist or what share of a population is, at any given moment, low-paid. Low-end employment would be compatible with '*Rawlsian*' optimization if it does not affect negatively people's life chances. The issue here is entrapment and mobility chances.

On this score, unfortunately, research has not yet provided much undisputable evidence. We do know that a sizeable minority of low-wage workers in the USA remain trapped for many years (a higher rate than is the case in Europe where, comparably, low-wage jobs are much rarer). And those most likely to become trapped are the low-skilled. We also have fairly good evidence that, net of family origins, skills and education constitute the single best guarantee of mobility. Hence, expanding low-wage service jobs in tandem with heavy investment in skills would, for the majority, constitute a win-win policy. The problem lies in the risks of entrapment among the minority which, perhaps, is 'untrainable' or, for various other reasons excluded from mobility. It is precisely for this reason that a 'learning strategy' needs to be accompanied with a basic income guarantee strategy.[15]

Nonetheless, the problem of inequality would disappear if the welfare state extends a basic life chances guarantee to citizens: a guarantee of job mobility via education or, alternatively, a guarantee that condemnation to a life of low wages does not imply income poverty throughout the life course.[16]

At the risk of repetition, the greater is the investment in social resources among children, the greater will be the later pay-off in terms of lifelong learning abilities and readjustment, and the smaller will be the burden of compensating the 'losers'.

## *Leisure and Work*

The kind of 'win-win' scenario presented above appears heavily biased towards work. Notwithstanding sluggish growth, European GDP *per capita* is now 50 per cent greater than before the 1970s oil shocks. And such wealth ought to translate into more leisure time. [ . . . ]

Contemporary European political debate is dominated by the controversy over the 35-hour week, promoted for its purported positive effects on job-creation. If, indeed, its main goal is to stimulate employment, the strategy is at best controversial and, at worst, self-defeating. If the goal is to extend leisure time, the question that few have posed is, why focus on weekly or monthly, rather than on life-time distributions of leisure and work?

The irony is that the call for a shorter work-week follows several decades of significant work-time reductions on a yearly and a life-cycle basis. The typical EU member country's annual working hours is now down to 1,600–1,700 hours, mainly attributable to the spread of part-time work, vacations, holidays, and paid leave arrangements, and – unfortunately – also to unemployment and exclusion from the labour market. Much more dramatic are reductions in lifetime employment. The average (male) worker in 1960 would work for roughly forty-five years; his contemporary equivalent will work perhaps thirty-five years. It is not altogether clear to what extent more leisure is voluntary and desired, and to what extent it reflects inability to attain gainful employment. In the case of women, most leisure is often unpaid housework.

Should we favour more leisure on all accounts? Fewer weekly hours, annual hours *and* lifetime hours? If so, do we agree on the associated economic opportunity cost? Is it equitable if the cost of leisure for some is shifted onto the shoulders of others? Do our leisure-time arrangements adequately maximize our productive potential? Can we envision alternative, more equitable and efficient, distributions between leisure and work? These are questions that almost no one raises in the current social policy debate, but they are crucial for any consideration of a new welfare order.

To some extent, the prevailing leisure–work mix is due to intended policy effects, like maternity or parental leave. But, to a large extent, it is also due to unintended consequences of policies designed to (or unable to) solve completely different problems. Early retirement and unemployment are obvious examples. Leaving aside 'unwanted' leisure, do we in fact have an adequate understanding of what would be citizens' optimal leisure–work preferences? I think not. Early retirees may be individually content to exit prematurely, given constraints and incentives. But if these incentives are societally harmful and were thus removed, would the desire to exit remain? Would Italian women's employment rates follow Holland's if restrictions against part-time work were eliminated? Or would Dutch women's working hours approach full-time if, as in Scandinavia, affordable day-care were available?

The chief problem is that past policy has resulted in overly rigid leisure–work arrangements that permit individual workers little choice as to how to optimize their own mix. At the same time, work-leisure incentives for some groups are gained at a cost to others. Basically, existing practice reflects a social order that is no longer dominant. We have, so far, bundled free time within the working week, within stipulated vacations and holidays, and at the tail end of our lives. If our goal is to optimize life chances in a dynamic sense, such an order may not be compatible with the exigencies of an evolving knowledge society.

Emerging trends in family and labour market behaviour suggest that citizens' demand for leisure and work may be spaced out across the life cycle in a radically different manner than so far. The case of paid maternity and parental leave is one of the few examples of policy that seeks to address emerging incompatibilities. A full-fledged 'lifelong learning' model will require similar arrangements, namely paid education or training leaves. There is a strong case to be made in favour of the idea floated within Nordic social democracy in the 1970s [ . . . ] to rethink the work-leisure mix in terms of life-time 'leisure accounts', that citizens (after a minimum number of contribution years) can draw upon their retirement savings accounts at will, be it for purposes of education, family care-giving, or pure vacation. There is, in principle, no reason why retirement should be concentrated in older ages. A radical version of the win-win scenarios developed above would, in fact, call for the abolition of retirement as we know it and redefine it as an issue of pacing individuals' life course. If some are more risk averse, they will opt for educational leaves or minimal career interruptions; if some are more drawn towards leisure, they will favour interruptions. The bottom line is that citizens have much greater individual command over how to design their own life course, over how to mix work, education, family, and free time. If the financial consequences are transparent, an individual will be able to rationally decide whether the choice of time off at age 35 against one year less of retirement is advantageous or not.

[ . . . ]

## Notes

Extract from 'Ageing Societies, Knowledge Based Economies, and the Sustainability of European Welfare States', report prepared for the Portuguese Presidency of the European Union, Spring 2000; reprinted in this version in Anthony Giddens (ed.), *The Global Third Way Debate*, Cambridge, Polity, 2001, pp. 134–56.

1 Social transfers account for only a third of working single mothers' total income in Scandinavia.
2 My own estimates suggest that due to high fixed labour costs and wage compression, full-time, full-year day care in countries such as Germany or Italy costs about half of what an average full-time employed mother can expect to earn. A significant reduction of relative servicing costs can only realistically occur on the backdrop of a radical deregulation of wages and reduction of fixed labour costs.
3 We usually define the poverty line as less than 50 per cent of median (adjusted) disposable income.
4 Public transfers account for the lion's share of total disposable income in countries like France, Germany and Sweden (70–90 per cent), but far less in others (such as the UK or the USA, where private pension plans and accumulated savings play an important role). Earnings (often undeclared) can play an important role in pensioner income packages. This may be especially pronounced in cases, such as Italy, where early retirement is prevalent and where there exist strong incentives to supply and demand workers who do not incur fixed labour costs. Pension schemes are, in some cases, clearly subsidizing the informal economy.
5 In some countries, young families' access to housing depends heavily on intergenerational capital transfers of this kind. M. Kohli: 'Private and Public Transfers between Generations', *European Societies*, 1, 1999, pp. 81–104.
6 To illustrate the point, workers at age (ca) 60 earn 100 per cent of average wage in Denmark and the UK, a full 140 per cent in France, but only 80 per cent in the USA:

Estimated age–wage relativities for males, 1990 (average = 100)

| | At age *c*.20–25 | At age *c*.50 | At age *c*.60 |
|---|---|---|---|
| Denmark | 85 | 105 | 100 |
| France | 70 | 120 | 140 |
| UK | 80 | 125 | 100 |
| USA | 65 | 105 | 80 |

*Source*: OECD.

7 The OECD estimates that workers with less than secondary education can expect five to seven years of unemployment over their lifetime in the UK, Finland and Spain, and between three and five years in Ireland, Germany, Sweden, France, Belgium, Denmark, and Canada.
8 The same argument holds for privatizing pensions. Just like public insurance schemes, private plans work well for workers with long stable and well-paid careers. Coverage is low among employees in atypical (such as part-time or temporary) employment, and traditional employer occupational pension plans are eroding as a result of the decline of large firms. Encouraging private pensions

for the top half of the labour market and limiting public pension commitments to the bottom half of the population is certainly one possible long-term scenario. I assume, however, that such a scenario is not on the political agenda in the large majority of EU countries. Targeting public pensions only to the poor would reduce the public expenditure burden dramatically, but to put it bluntly: why should we construct inequalities in the future when it is not necessary? Privatization will never qualify as a Paretian welfare improvement. As far as taxing retirement income is concerned, one should clearly avoid too much taxation since this may produce negative savings incentives among pre-retirement workers. If there is inequity in the distribution of resources between the aged and the young, a system of taxing excess incomes among the aged would be acceptable (and more incentive-neutral) if it were earmarked to cover other risks among the elderly (such as disabilities and intensive care needs).

9 Forecast simulations suggest that a move to strictly targeted public pensions (covering the bottom third only) would bring most countries' pension finances into balance by 2050.

10 In the Nordic countries, up to a third of total employment is in the public sector, fuelled by social service growth. There, as across the European continent, private consumer services are generally 'priced out of the market' – indeed, they have been declining over the past decades.

11 Individual countries, like Denmark, have experimented with alternative subsidization schemes to induce more consumption of service labour. Often such subsidies are an attempt to avoid lower-end services ending up in the black economy.

12 And, that such deregulation would almost surely have adverse consequences across the entire labour market, not to mention that it would by necessity imply a major roll-back of existing welfare guarantees.

13 Hence, women's average weekly hours of unpaid domestic labour is almost twice as high in Spain as in Denmark.

14 Contemporary national accounts systems are unable to distinguish between social expenditures that play an 'investment role' and those that do not. Parallel to the distinction between capital and consumption accounts, some social expenditures arguably enhance a nation's capital stock and reap a dividend. The actual task is daunting and full of ambiguities, but this is also the case in conventional national economic accounts (should a tank or a jeep for the military be classified as investment or consumption?).

15 Whether such an income guarantee be designed around the Anglo-Saxon formula of work-conditional income supplements or along more traditional social assistance lines is left open.

16 It is very important to distinguish this 'life chances' guarantee from conventional 'guaranteed citizen income' plans that many advocate. Above all, the life chances guarantee is meant to be premised on work and not, like the latter, on the assumption that there will not be sufficient work available. Indeed, the main principle here is to reward the incentive to work. This is not the place to discuss the practical design of such life chance guarantees. Clearly, active training and learning policies will come to play a core role. One might consider a variant of the American 'earned income credit' subsidy, or similar 'negative income tax' models, as a means to guarantee welfare for those who end up trapped in inferior employment.

# Investing in the Citizen-Workers of the Future: Transformations in Citizenship and the State under New Labour

*Ruth Lister*

## Introduction

In a recent scientific report, commissioned by the Belgian Presidency of the European Union in 2001, Gøsta Esping-Andersen and colleagues presented 'a set of building blocks' for the creation of a 'new welfare architecture'. The architecture's foundation stone is 'a child-centred social investment strategy' (Esping-Andersen et al., 2002, pp. 6, 26)[1] The foundation stone is, in fact, already being laid in some countries – most notably the liberal-oriented welfare states of Canada and the UK. This paper offers a critical analysis of the strategy's genesis and implications in the UK, in the context of a brief overview of the more general transformations of citizenship and the state under New Labour. The paper focuses in particular on the emergent 'social investment state''s construction of children – its main beneficiaries – as citizen-workers of the future.

## Transformations in Citizenship and Governance

'No rights without responsibilities', described by Anthony Giddens as 'a prime motto' for third-way politics, sums up New Labour's position on citizenship (1998, p. 65).[2] It is reflected in a range of social policies designed to regulate behaviour (Deacon, 2002). These include use of the benefits system not merely to promote the paid work ethic in the name of social inclusion but also to discourage and punish anti-social behaviour. In the words of Alistair Darling (when Work and Pensions Secretary):

> there is no unconditional right to benefit . . . It's not only possible, but entirely desirable that we should look at making sure the social security

> system and the benefits system are matched by responsibility . . . It is right that we should ask ourselves if there is a role for the benefits system as part of the wider system in asserting the values we hold and asserting the kind of behaviour that we want to see. (Address to the Parliamentary Press Gallery, reported in the *Independent*, 16 May 2002)

'Citizenship for the twenty-first century' is how Tony Blair (2002b) has described New Labour's governance model of partnership between the individual and the state. This model of governance represents a further development of the managerial state inherited from the Conservatives (Clarke and Newman, 1997; Clarke et al., 2000; Lister, 2002). With partnership 'out goes the Big State. In comes the Enabling State' (Blair, 2002b, 2002c). The enabling state is a leaner state, in which brokerage and regulating, as well as enabling, are emphasized over providing (Miliband, 1999). Partnership, while not a novel idea, is, in its multifarious guises and new suits of clothing, the linchpin of New Labour's modernizing governance agenda (Newman, 2001).[3] Although frequently associated in the governance literature with the 'hollowing out' of the state, Janet Newman suggests an alternative interpretation of partnerships:

> that they can be viewed as a further dispersal and penetration of state power. The spread of an official and legitimated discourse of partnership has the capacity to draw local stakeholders, from community groups to business organisations, into a more direct relationship with government and involve them in supporting and carrying out the government's agenda . . . Labour's emphasis on holistic and joined-up government, and its use of partnerships as a means of delivering public policy, can be viewed as enhancing the state's capacity to secure political objectives by sharing power with a range of actors, drawing them into the policy process. (Newman, 2001, p. 125)

The 'joined up government' to which Newman refers, with its slogan of 'joined up solutions for joined up problems', particularly in tackling social exclusion (Mulgan, 1998, p. 262; Miliband, 1999), is combined with a problem-solving, technocratic approach under which 'what matters is what works' (Blair, 1998a, p. 4). This 'dogmatic pragmatism' (Clarke, 1999, p. 85) diverts attention from the need for more systemic structural change (Lister, 2001).

If partnerships are the linchpin of the new governance, managerialism, another element in New Labour's inheritance, can be seen as the 'organizational glue' that holds it together (Newman, 1998; Clarke and Hoggett, 1999, p. 15; Clarke et al., 2000).[4] It is embodied in the government's enthusiasm for target-setting and its plans to 'root out waste and inefficiency' and to 'provide efficient and modern public services' (HM Treasury, 1998, p. 1). Increases in public spending carry a managerialist price tag of value for money, reform, audit and targets. In his 2002 Spending Review statement, the Chancellor emphasized that

> in each area of service delivery . . . we are tying new resources to reform and results, and developing a modern way for efficient public services, which includes setting demanding national targets; monitoring performance by independent and open audit and inspection; giving front-line staff the power and flexibility to deliver; extending choice; rewarding success; and turning around failing services. (Brown, 2002b, col. 22)

## The Social Investment State

Brown presented his Spending Review as addressing 'past decades of chronic underinvestment in education, health, transport and housing'. The 'role of Government', he declared, 'is – by expanding educational, employment and economic opportunity, and by encouraging stronger communities – to enable and empower people to make globalization work for their families and their future' (2002b). With the exception of the absence of any explicit reference to children, this sums up pretty well the main elements of the 'social investment state'.

The term was coined by Giddens in his articulation of the third way. The guideline, he argues, 'is investment in *human capital* wherever possible, rather than direct provision of economic maintenance' (1998, p. 117, emphasis in original). An earlier template was provided by the Commission on Social Justice in its vision of an 'Investors' Britain'. Its central proposition was that 'it is through investment that economic and social policy are inextricably linked'. 'High investment – in skills, research, technology, childcare and community development – is the last and first step' in a 'virtuous circle of sustainable growth' (Commission on Social Justice, 1994, pp. 97, 103). The emphasis was on economic opportunity in the name of social justice as well as of economic prosperity and the achievement of security through investment in and redistribution of 'opportunities rather than just . . . income' (1994, p. 95).

Although the Commission's report was seen by many as promoting a 'modernizing' agenda, within a year of publication (after the death of John Smith, its instigator), its report had effectively metamorphosed from a symbol of New Labour to one of old, as the juggernaut of accelerated modernization rolled over it. Nevertheless, the influence of its model of an 'Investors' Britain' is clear, if unacknowledged. New Labour has rejected the traditional egalitarian model espoused by the Labour Party for a paradigm and discourse of lifelong opportunity and social inclusion (Lister, 2000a, 2001, 2002). This is linked to 'a new supply-side agenda for the left'. The agenda emphasizes 'lifetime access to education and training' as part of the necessary investment in 'human capital'. It is complemented by 'an active labour market policy for the left' in which 'the state must become an active agent for employment, not merely the passive recipient of the casualties of economic failure' (Blair and Schröder, 1999, pp. 31, 35).[5] Both exemplify Bob Jessop's formulation of the post-Fordist 'Schumpetarian workfare state' in which 'redistributive welfare rights take second place to a productivist reordering of social policy' in the name of international competitiveness and the need to equip the population to respond to global change (Jessop, 1994, pp. 24; 2000; see also Holden, 1999).

As well as investment in 'human capital', the social investment state is concerned to strengthen *social* capital: 'investors argue that investment in social institutions is as important as investment in economic infrastructure' and that 'the moral and social reconstruction of our society depends on our willingness to invest in social capital', which is both 'a good in itself' and 'also essential for economic renewal' (Commission on Social Justice, 1994, pp. 306, 308). New Labour has launched a 'national strategy action plan' for neighbourhood renewal animated by the 'vision that, within 10 to 20 years, no one should be seriously disadvantaged by where they live' (Social Exclusion Unit, 2001, p. 8). According to Blair, a 'central goal' and 'a key task for our second term is to develop greater coherence around our commitment to community, to grasp the opportunity of "civil renewal". That means a commitment to making the state work better. But most of all, it means strengthening communities themselves' (Blair, 2002a, pp. 9, 11; 2002c). The appeal to community has played a key role in the third-way differentiation of New Labour from the new right and old left, for it posits 'an alternative to both the untrammelled free market (of neo-liberalism) and the strong state (of social democracy)' (Levitas, 2000, p. 191).

## Children

For the Commission on Social Justice (CSJ), families and children were critical to the strengthening of both social and human capital. 'Children are 100 per cent of the nation's future' it declared, and it argued that 'the best indicator of the capacity of our economy tomorrow is the quality of our children today' (1994, p. 311). A similar message emerges from Esping-Andersen's sketch of a 'new welfare architecture', in which he emphasizes that 'a social investment strategy directed at children must be a centrepiece of any policy for social inclusion' (Esping-Andersen et al., 2002, p. 30).

Children emerged as key figures in New Labour's nascent social investment state early in 1999. In his Beveridge Lecture, the Prime Minister pledged the government to eradicate child poverty in two decades, explaining that 'we have made children our top priority because, as the Chancellor memorably said in his Budget, "they are 20 per cent of the population but they are [echoing the CSJ] 100 per cent of the future"' (Blair, 1999, p. 16). Around the same time, the Treasury published a document, *Tackling Poverty and Extending Opportunity*, which emphasized the impact of poverty on children's life chances and opportunities (HM Treasury, 1999).

Although the pledge to end child poverty was made by Blair, much of the policy impetus on children has come from the Treasury, which under Brown has become a key actor in the development of social policy (Deakin and Parry, 2000). Brown has described child poverty as 'a scar on Britain's soul', arguing that 'we must give all our children the opportunity to achieve their hopes and fulfil their potential. By investing in them, we are investing in our future' (Brown, 1999, p. 8). He has developed these themes in a series of speeches, together with the argument that 'tackling child poverty is the best anti-drugs, anti-crime, anti-deprivation policy for our country' (Brown, 2000a). In his foreword to the pre-2002 Budget report, he states that 'our children are our future and the most important investment that we can make as a nation is in developing the potential of all our country's children' (Brown, 2001, p. iv). While this report does acknowledge that 'action to abolish child poverty must *improve the current quality of children's lives* as well as investing to enable children to reach their full potential as adults' (HM Treasury, 2001, p. 5, emphasis added), the point is not developed.[6] Brown went on to present his 2002 Budget as:

> building a Britain of greater enterprise and greater fairness, and nothing is more important to an enterprising, fairer Britain than that, through education and through support for the family, we invest in the potential of every single child in our country. (Brown, 2002a, col. 586)

## *New Investment in Children*

Brown also announced 'one of the biggest single investments in children and families since the welfare state was formed in the 1940s' (2002a, col. 587). He was referring primarily to additional investment in an evolving tax credits system that reflects the influence of the Canadian and Australian models and represents what Sylvia Bashevkin has described as an increasingly 'fiscalized social policy' (2000, p. 2). Means-tested benefits for children are being replaced by a child tax credit (CTC), which 'will provide a single, seamless system of income-related support for families with children' paid direct to the caring parent with the universal child benefit (HM Treasury, 2002a, para. 5.17).[7] In addition, a new working tax credit will incorporate a childcare element (payable to the caring parent). These tax credits represent a further shift in the balance of financial support towards means-testing in the name of the principle of 'progressive universalism', i.e. 'giving everyone a stake in the system while offering more help to those who need it most' (HM Treasury, 2002, para. 5.5).[8]

Prior to the introduction of the CTC, the amount of money available for the children of both employed and non-employed parents has already been increased significantly. This includes a phased improvement in the social assistance rates for children so that by October 2002 the real value of assistance for under-11-year-old children had virtually doubled. This improvement deviates from the third way in welfare as initially articulated by New Labour: improvements in out-of-work benefits were dismissed as 'dependency' – inducing 'cash handouts' to be rejected in favour of 'a modern form of welfare that believes in empowerment not dependency' (DSS, 1998, p. 19). It has therefore not been trumpeted as loudly as other policy developments, so much so that many people are still unaware of it. It is an example of a wider phenomenon: 'redistribution by stealth'. Redistribution of resources, as opposed to redistribution of opportunities, does not fit the New Labour template. When pressed on the issue, Brown has therefore described it as redistribution based on 'people exercising responsibilities' to work and bring up children in contrast to old forms of redistribution based on 'something for nothing' (*Today Programme*, BBC Radio 4, 29 Mar. 1999).

More consistent with the New Labour template has been the piloting and planned introduction of means-tested educational maintenance allowances to encourage young people from low-income families to stay on at school and a commitment to an experiment in 'asset-based welfare' with a universal 'child trust fund' under which every new-born child would be given a modest capital sum, accessible only when they reach 18 (Kelly and Le Grand, 2001). Indeed, assets-based welfare has itself been characterized as representing a transition to a social investment state (Sherraden, 2002). The New Labour template also informs a series of service-based initiatives. Of particular significance is Sure Start, which was inspired by the American Head Start programme (see HM Treasury, 2001). Sure Start is to be combined with early years education and child care within a single interdepartmental unit with an integrated budget. A further injection of funds into the national childcare strategy is promised, in the face of evidence that the policy is flagging. This will involve the creation of children's centres and of an additional 250,000 childcare places by 2005–6 (Strategy Unit, 2002).

For all its weaknesses, the national childcare strategy represents a breakthrough in British social policy. It represents the first time that government has accepted that child care is a public as well as a private responsibility. Birte Siim has argued that 'from the point of view of social policies towards women and children, Britain . . . represents an exception to the rule of European social policies', particularly in the area of childcare services (Siim, 2000, p. 92). This, she suggests, reflects the dominant liberal philosophy of the separation of public and private spheres and (partial) non-intervention in the latter (see also Lewis, 1998; O'Connor et al., 1999).

This philosophy has framed general policy towards children other than those deemed at risk of abuse or neglect. Despite the introduction of family allowances and their extension and replacement by child benefit, children have been the subject of public neglect. The UK has been described as 'a serious contender for the title of worst place in Europe to be a child' (Micklewright and Stewart, 2000, p. 23). Arguably, this reflects not only the liberal strand in the dominant social welfare philosophy but also ambivalence in British attitudes towards children (Lister, 2000b). A tendency to sentimentalize and idealize children has existed alongside a reluctance to accommodate their presence in the adult world and an element of hostility and fear, as reflected in the recent demonization of 'feral children'.[9] In addition, during the Thatcher years there was an increasingly strongly expressed view that having children is 'essentially a private matter', akin to other expensive consumer goods (Beenstock, 1984, cited in J. Brown, 1988). Such claims tap deep-rooted attitudes put most crudely in the (male) expression – 'why should I pay for another man's pleasure?'

This sentiment underlies some of the hostility that has always existed towards family allowances/child benefit and the fact that child poverty has not been a popular cause in the UK. Keith Banting's analysis, for instance, suggests that, although family poverty became an important issue for the 1964–70 Wilson Labour government (partly thanks to pressure from the newly formed Child Poverty Action Group), it was a key concern for neither organized labour nor the wider electorate (Banting, 1979). As the former Conservative Chancellor observes, approvingly, in his memoirs, 'the moral sense of the nation' is more sympathetic to pensioner than child poverty (Lawson, 1992, p. 595). Such attitudes may help to explain signs of disappointment among some government ministers that 'the pledge to end child poverty has not generated the expected political returns', particularly in the 'Labour heartlands' (Barnes, 2000, p. 1). One consequence has been the bizarre spectacle of the Chancellor calling for an 'alliance for children' to put the kind of pressure on him that Jubilee 2000 did with regard to debt eradication in the South. He envisaged 'a movement based on faith in the future, a crusade for nothing less than the kind of society our children will inherit' (Brown, 2000b). In response, the End Child Poverty Campaign has been set up by a number of children's charities.

## *Children as Citizen-Workers of the Future*

We are witnessing a genuine, unprecedented, attempt to shift the social priorities of the state and nation to investing in children. What are the implications for citizenship? Jane Jenson, writing in the Canadian context, has suggested that, in the social investment state, children have become the 'model citizens' but they are so symbolically because, as minors, they cannot be full citizens able 'to employ the force of democratic politics to insist on social reform in the name of equality' (2001, pp. 122, 125). In a more recent paper with Denis Saint-Martin she traces a shift in the 'ideal-typical representation of citizen' from 'citizen-worker' in the 'social rights' citizenship regime to 'the child as citizen-in-becoming' in the 'social investment' regime (Jenson and Saint-Martin, 2001, table 2).

In the UK, as argued above, the 'citizen-worker' is still centre stage. In so far as s/he is being joined there by the child, it is the child as 'citizen-*worker*-in-becoming' or 'citizen-*worker* of the future'. It is the future *worker*-citizen more than *democratic*-citizen who is the prime asset of the social investment state. Moreover, the future orientation and discourses of the social investment state encourage not just the elision of demands for equality in the here-and-now,[10] but also, paradoxically, the partial disappearance of childhood and of the child *qua* child, including the child as a rights-bearer (under the UN Convention on the Rights of the Child). The child as cipher for future economic prosperity and forward-looking modernization overshadows the child as child-citizen.[11]

In many ways, the discourse of social investment in children reflects that deployed by organizations and individuals, in the UK and elsewhere, making the case for better state financial support and services for children.[12] As such, it has arguably proved its utility in persuading politicians. In turn, it may also represent a politically astute discourse for politicians to use in a culture unsympathetic to children and alongside a rhetoric hostile to cash benefits. However, there are also dangers: as Sanford F. Schram has cautioned in the US context, the deployment of the economistic discourse of investment represents 'a slippery politics' (1995, p. 24). Valerie Polakow warns that if children are seen to 'matter instrumentally, not existentially', expenditure on them will only be justifiable where there is a demonstrable pay-off, so that there is no room for 'expenditure which merely contributes to the well-being or enjoyment of children as children' (1993, p. 101).

In the UK, while there is strong support for the commitment to eradicate child poverty, there is also an emergent critique of the social investment paradigm from a child-centred perspective as well as ongoing criticism of the government's patchy record on children's rights. According to Alan Prout, the central focus of policy 'is on the better adult lives that will, it is predicted, emerge from reducing child poverty. It is not on the better lives that children will lead as children' (2000, p. 305). Fawcett et al. contrast this focus with what has been called a 'new paradigm' of childhood:

> For governments, children symbolise 'the future', 'social renewal', 'survival of the nation' or equivalent sentiments. Such a view is at odds with alternative approaches which counsel the importance of seeing *children as 'beings' rather than 'becomings'*, as people to be valued in their own right in the present rather than assessed primarily in terms of how well they will construct the future. (Fawcett et al., 2004, emphasis added)

Prout does not reject the discourse of investment in children but warns that, 'on its own a focus on futurity is unbalanced and needs to be accompanied by a concern for the present well-being of children, for their participation in social life and for their opportunities for human self-realisation' (2000, p. 306). As the Children's Forum declared in their official statement to the UN General Assembly, 'you call us the future, but we are also the present' (cited in Stasiulis, 2002, p. 508).

This assertion of their agency as children is supported by a study of childhood poverty from within the new paradigm of childhood. Its author, Tess Ridge, criticizes the focus 'on children as "adults to be", as future investments, rather than as children with their own voices and agency, their own experiences and concerns' (Ridge, 2002b, p. 12; 2002a; see also Roche, 1999). Goals and targets are future-oriented rather than focused 'on the quality of children's lives – goals of achieving childhoods that are, as far as possible, happy, healthy and fulfilled' (Piachaud, 2001, p. 453; see also Thomas and Hocking, 2003). Likewise, in the target-filled world of the managerial state, education is reduced to a utilitarian achievement-oriented measurement culture of tests and exams, with little attention paid to the actual educational experience.

The state is, however, not monolithic and there are spaces within it where children *are* valued as 'beings' and not just 'becomings'. For instance, Fawcett et al. (forthcoming) suggest that, on the ground, programmes such as Sure Start do often engage with 'quality of life issues in the here-and-now as well as investing in the future'. Of particular significance is the Children and Young People's Unit (CYPU) established by the government in 2000 within the Department for Education and Skills. In 2001 it published a consultation document, *Building a Strategy for Children and Young People*. This set out a vision and set of principles that pays attention to the present as well as the future and that treats children and young people as social actors whose views should be taken into account. An imaginative consultation process was designed to maximize children and young people's own participation. The Unit has also published a guidance document on children and young people's participation in decisions that affect their lives at every level from their own lives to national policy-making.

'Promoting citizenship and social inclusion' is one of the arguments put in favour of such an approach (CYPU, 2001, p. 6). This conjures up what Daiva Stasiulis calls the 'imaginary of the child citizen as an active participant in governance', personified in and promoted by an emergent international children's movement (2002, p. 509; see also Roche, 1999).[13] This imaginary does not, however, have very deep roots in government thinking about children and children's rights, as codified in the UN Convention on the Rights of the Child.

Children's right to express their views and have them taken seriously in all matters affecting them is enshrined in Article 12 of the Convention on the Rights of the Child. Gerison Lansdown (2002) has argued that 'it is far from adequately implemented in respect of children in the UK'. Her view and that of many children's rights activists is that the appointment of a Children's Rights Commissioner is crucial to the protection and promotion of the human rights of children (Children's Rights Alliance for England, 2002; Willow, 2002). [14] Hitherto, the government has resisted such calls for an English Commissioner, despite acceptance in the devolved administrations and many other countries and a commitment in Labour's 1992 Election Manifesto (subsequently dropped by Blair) (Lansdown, 2002). This was the subject of criticism in the second UK report of the UN Committee on the Rights of the Child, which highlighted the extent to which the government's approach to children's rights has been piecemeal and partial (CRC, 2002). A particular focus of criticism in the report is the 'unequal enjoyment of economic, social, cultural, civil and political rights' by vulnerable groups of children including asylum and refugee children (CRC, 2002, para. 22). There has, for instance, been a reluctance to extend to the children of asylum-seekers the welfare and educational rights enjoyed by other children (Maternity Alliance, 2002; Sale, 2002; see also Stasiulis, 2002).

More generally, New Labour has been more willing to countenance rights for children who do not live with their parents than to intervene in the private sphere of the family of those who do. This is most notable in the refusal to remove parents' right to hit their children, again strongly criticized by the UN Committee as constituting 'a serious violation of the dignity of the child' (CRC, 2002, para. 35). As Fawcett et al. (forthcoming) observe, the government thereby 'allies itself with older discourses around "children as property" and sets itself firmly against moves to democratize the family more fully, a rather curious positioning in view of its much-vaunted claims to be "modern" and its assumptions about gender equality'.

Jenson and Saint-Martin (2001) warn that neglect of gender equality issues may be one consequence of the future-oriented social investment state. There is a danger that children's poverty is divorced from that of their mothers and more generally that 'questions of gender power . . . are more and more difficult to raise, as adults are left to take responsibility for their own lives' (Jenson, 2001, p. 125). In Canada, the discourse of child poverty has dominated policy-making on poverty for longer. A Status of Canada Women report argues that the discourse has served to make the structural causes of poverty less visible; to encourage a response motivated by pity for the helpless child; and to displace women's issues generally and women's poverty specifically (Wiegers, 2002; Stasiulis, 2002).

A focus on children and social investment does not, however, necessarily have to mean the displacement of gender issues. Esping-Andersen, for instance, makes the somewhat instrumentalist case for treating the development of 'women-friendly' policies as themselves 'a social investment'. He justifies this position on the grounds that 'in many countries women constitute a massive untapped labour reserve that can help narrow future age dependency rates and reduce associated financial pressures' and that 'female employment is one of the most effective means of combating social exclusion and poverty' (Esping-Andersen et al., 2002, p. 94).

It would be wrong to say that New Labour has ignored the issue of gender equality but the consensus is that it has accorded it relatively low priority, despite the establishment of a Women and Equality Unit and a number of specific policies that will improve women's lives. New Labour's avoidance of a systematic gendered analysis and strategy is not, however, simply a function of its child-oriented priorities. It also reflects its association of feminism with 'yesterday's politics' (Coote, 2002, p. 3) and a related reluctance to acknowledge structural inequalities and conflicts of interest in a concern to promote consensus and cohesion (Franklin, 2000a, 2000b; McRobbie, 2000; Coote, 2001). That said, a focus on the child is one way of side-stepping social divisions, even though these frame and shape children's opportunities and adult outcomes: 'because the figure of the child is unified, homogeneous, undifferentiated, there is little talk about race, ethnicity, gender, class and disability. Children become a single, essentialized category' (Dobrowolsky, 2002, p. 67).

## Conclusion

The design of the new welfare architecture in the UK involves the changing construction of both citizenship and the state. With regard to citizenship, in return for the promise of investment in economic opportunity by the state, increased emphasis is being placed on the responsibilities of citizens, most notably: to equip themselves to respond to the challenges of economic globalization through improved employability; to support themselves through paid work; to invest in their own pensions; and to ensure the responsible behaviour of their children.

The changing construction of the state has been analysed here from the perspective of both governance and its role. In terms of *governance*, the emergent state can be characterized as 'the enabling, managerial, partnership state', a partial inheritance from the previous Conservative government. In terms of *role*, the notion of 'the social investment state' captures its essence, both analytically and normatively. While there are some differences of detail and emphasis in the various formulations of the social investment state, broadly its key features are as set out in box 1.

Box 1 *Key features of the social investment state*

- Investment in human and social capital: children and community as emblems.
- Children prioritized as citizen-workers of the future.
- Future-focused.
- Redistribution of opportunity to promote social inclusion rather than of income to promote equality.
- Adaptation of individuals and society to enhance global competitiveness.
- Integration of social and economic policy, but with the latter still the 'handmaiden' of the former.

From a normative perspective, as investment in 'human' and social capital becomes a primary function of the social investment state, the child and the community have become its emblems. The child in particular takes on iconic status. However, it is the child as 'citizen-worker' of the future rather than the 'citizen-child' of the present who is invoked by the new discourse of social investment. Thus, despite the prioritizing of children, the quality of their childhood risks being overshadowed by a preoccupation with their development as future citizen-workers. At the same time, the poverty of today's citizens of working age is marginalized. Moreover, despite a strong emphasis on the need to integrate economic and social policy, integration has not challenged the traditional subordinate 'handmaiden' relationship of the social to the economic (Titmuss, 1974, p. 31; see also Beck et al., 1997).

From an analytical perspective, it is difficult to make sense of current developments using only traditional welfare regime analysis. In some ways the UK is shifting further towards a liberal welfare regime, as conventionally articulated, with increased reliance on means-tested and private forms of welfare provision (Lister, 2000a, 2002). In other ways, most notably in relation to child care, it is inching in the direction of more institutionalized Continental and Nordic welfare states, as the state finally acknowledges that child care is a public as a well as a private responsibility. The idea of the 'social investment state' may therefore provide a more helpful analytic framework for understanding the emergent new welfare architecture. Indeed, the suggestion is that it may represent a transformation of some liberal regimes, most notably the UK and Canada, into a rather different – hybrid – animal from that described in Esping-Andersen's original analysis (Dobrowolsky and Saint-Martin, 2002; Jenson and Saint-Martin, 2002).[15]

It may be tempting, therefore, to interpret all policy developments in terms of the social investment state template. We need, though, to be careful. First, not all policy shifts are necessarily *reducible* to the template, even if they are consistent with it. Thus, for instance, New Labour's preoccupation with citizenship responsibility and the obligations associated with the paid work ethic needs to be analysed in its own right as well as simply as an expression of the social investment state. Indeed, it helps us to understand better the true complexion of the model-citizen in that state. Likewise, shifts in governance, characterized here as the emergence of the 'managerial, partnership state', cannot simply be subsumed under the rubric of social investment, even if they are associated with it in practice. Second, the state is not a monolith and it is dangerous to assume 'unity or integration' or to flatten out complexity (Pringle and Watson, 1992, p. 63; Clarke, 2000). New Labour itself has been described as 'essentially ambiguous and Janus-faced', reflecting the 'often contradictory and conflicting traditions of social democracy, social conservatism, Thatcherism and pragmatism' upon which it draws (Smith, 2001, p. 267; Lister, 2001). Such ambiguities mean that there are spaces, such as around childhood and poverty, that civil society actors can exploit to argue for a more genuinely child-focused and also more egalitarian approach. Thus, from both a normative and analytic perspective, even if we are witnessing a genuine paradigm shift, analysts and activists need to remain alert to complexities and possible inconsistencies within the specific policy configurations to be found in emergent social investment states.

## Notes

This paper was first given at the American Political Science Association annual meeting in 2002 and then published in this revised form in *Social Policy and Administration*, 37, 5, 2003, pp. 427–43. It engages with the work of a team of political scientists led by Jane Jenson of Montreal University.

1 A revised version of the report has been published as Esping-Andersen et al., 2002. See also 'A Welfare State for the Twenty-First Century' in this volume.

2 Interestingly, Amitai Etzioni has dismissed this formulation as a 'grave moral error' on the grounds that 'basic individual rights are inalienable, just as one's social obligations cannot be denied': the relationship between the two is complementary not conditional (2000, p. 29). For a more detailed exposition of the construction of citizenship under New Labour see, for instance, Dwyer, 1998, 2000; Lister, 1998; Heron and Dwyer, 1999; Rose, 1999.

3 In New Zealand also, partnerships have been identified as a key element in 'a post-welfarist, post-neoliberal form of social governance' (Larner and Craig, 2002, p. 4).

4 Under the Tories, managerialism cast welfare subjects as customers and consumers rather than citizens (Clarke, 1997, 1998; Hughes and Lewis, 1998). New Labour has attempted to marry the two in the person of 'the demanding, sceptical, citizen-consumer' who expects improved standards from public services in line with those in the private sector (DSS, 1998, p. 16). There is the same emphasis on individual customer service and user- rather than provider-led welfare as under the Conservatives (a model which was not necessarily realized in practice and which had more purchase in some arms of the welfare state than others). At the same time, though, there is something of a more collective and democratic approach: examples include the introduction of citizens' juries and various fora for 'listening to' particular groups such as

women and older people, as well as resident participation in the neighbourhood renewal action plan. Yet, when Blair (1998b) tells us that 'in all walks of life people act as consumers and not just citizens' the suspicion is that it is the consumer rather than the citizen who represents the ideal New Labour welfare subject (see also Gamble and Kenny, pp. 1999).

5 Fairclough criticizes New Labour's use of the 'human capital' discourse, with its 'reification of people' and its translation of learning into an 'economic rather than an educational process' (2000, pp.49, 75).

6 The November 2002 Pre-Budget Report does acknowledge that poverty 'excludes children from the everyday activities of their peers' (HM Treasury, 2002b).

7 A higher children's tax credit will be paid during the year of a child's birth as part of a package to improve support in the early years of a child's life (see HM Treasury, 2002a).

8 The government did implement a significant increase in the universal child benefit in its first term, but all the indications are that this will not be repeated. There is considerable criticism of the heavy reliance on means-testing, not least from the former minister Frank Field, who has described tax credits as 'a form of permanent serfdom' (Field, 2002).

9 The 'feral child' figured prominently in a number of newspaper reports of the acquittal of the young people tried for the murder of the black child Damilola Taylor. See, for instance, the *Daily Mail,* 26 Apr. 2002, and Anderson, 2002, and, for a critical account of its wider use, Hari, 2002.

10 See Jenson, 2001; Jenson and Saint-Martin, 2001; Dobrowolsky and Saint-Martin, 2002.

11 According to one participant, when ministers were asked at a seminar in 1998 why they were focusing on children, the response was that 'children are the future; we are not interested in the past' (Seminar for Hilary Land, 25 Mar. 2002, London). A similar future orientation can be found in Esping-Andersen's exposition in which he argues, for instance, 'minimizing child poverty now will yield an individual and social dividend in the future. And in the far-off future, it should diminish the risks of old age poverty' (Esping-Andersen et al., 2002, p. 55).

12 See, for instance, J. Brown, 1988; England and Folbre, 1999; Esping-Andersen et al., 2002; European Forum for Child Welfare, 2002. Indeed, I have used the argument myself, particularly in my former role as director of the Child Poverty Action Group.

13 The movement was made visible as children took to the streets in March 2003 to protest against war with Iraq.

14 The case has also been made by Cherie Booth QC in the 2002 Barbara Kahn Memorial Lecture in which she criticized the government for being 'half-hearted' about children's rights (*Guardian*, 25 Sept. 2002).

15 Esping-Andersen himself suggests a bifurcation between 'youth-oriented' liberal regimes and a group that is 'ever more aged-biased and service-lean' (1999, p. 166). He includes the UK in the latter (with the USA), but this was before the emergence of New Labour's social investment state.

## References

Anderson, B. (2002) 'The Time for Sentimentalism is Over: Let Us Tame these Feral Children', *Independent*, 29 Apr.

Banting, K. (1979) *Poverty, Politics and Policy*, Basingstoke, Macmillan.

Barnes, M. (2000) 'Editorial: Keeping up the Pressure', *Poverty*, 106, p. 1.

Bashevkin, S. (2000) *Road-testing the Third Way: Welfare Reform in Canada, Britain and the United States*, Jerusalem, Hebrew University of Jerusalem.

Beck, W., van der Maesen, L., and Walker, A. (eds) (1997) *The Social Quality of Europe*, The Hague, Kluwer Law International.

Beenstock, M. (1984) 'Rationalising Child Benefit', paper given at Policy Studies Institute seminar, London, June, cited in J. Brown, *Child Benefit*, London, Child Poverty Action Group, 1988.

Blair, T. (1998a) *The Third Way: New Politics for the New Century*, London, Fabian Society.

Blair, T. (1998b) 'The Government's Strategy', in *The Government's Annual Report 97/98*, London, Stationery Office.

Blair, T. (1999) Beveridge Lecture, Toynbee Hall, London, 18 Mar., reproduced in R. Walker (ed.), *Ending Child Poverty*, Bristol, Policy Press.

Blair, T. (2002a) 'New Labour and Community', *Renewal*, 10, 2, pp. 9–14.

Blair, T. (2002b) Speech to Labour Party Conference, Blackpool, 1 Oct. at www.labour.org/uk/tbconfspeech/.

Blair, T. (2002c) 'My Vision for Britain', *Observer*, 10 Nov.

Blair, T. and Schröder, G. (1999) 'Europe: The Third Way/Die Neue Mitte', reproduced in *The Spokesman*, 66, pp. 27–37.

Brown, G. (1999) 'A Scar on the Nation's Soul', *Poverty*, 104.

Brown, G. (2000a) Speech to the Children and Young Person's Unit conference, Islington, London, 15 Nov.

Brown, G. (2000b) Speech to the CPAG Child Poverty conference, Our Children are our Future, London, 15 May.

Brown, G. (2001) 'Foreword', in HM Treasury, *Tackling Child Poverty*, at www.hm-treasury.gov.uk.

Brown, G. (2002a) Budget Statement, *House of Commons Hansard*, 17 Apr.

Brown, G. (2002b) Spending Review, *House of Commons Hansard*, 15 July.

Brown, J. (1988) *Child Benefit: Investing in the Future*, London, Child Poverty Action Group.

Children's Rights Alliance for England (2002) Report to the Pre-sessional Working Group of the Committee on the Rights of the Child, London: CRAE, at www.crights.org.uk.

Clarke, J. (1997) 'Capturing the Customer', *Self, Agency and Society*, 1, 1, pp. 55–73.

Clarke, J. (1998) 'Consumerism', in G. Hughes (ed.), *Imagining Welfare Futures*, London, Routledge.

Clarke, J. (1999) 'Coming to Terms with Culture', in H. Dean and R. Woods (eds), *Social Policy Review 11*, Luton, Social Policy Association.

Clarke, J. (2000) 'Governing Welfare Systems: Subjects and States', paper presented at the Social Policy Association annual conference, Roehampton.

Clarke, J. and Hoggett, P. (1999) 'Regressive Modernisation? The Changing Patterns of Social Services Delivery in the United Kingdom', in H. Wollmann and E. Schröter (eds), *Comparing Public Sector Reform in Britain and Germany*, Aldershot, Ashgate.

Clarke, J. and Newman, J. (1997) *The Managerial State*, London, Sage.

Clarke, J., Gewirtz, S. and McLaughlin, E. (eds) (2000) *New Managerialism, New Welfare?* London, Sage.

Commission on Social Justice (1994) *Social Justice: Strategies for National Renewal*, London, Vintage.

Coote, A. (2000) 'Introduction', in A. Coote (ed.), *New Gender Agenda*, London, Institute for Public Policy Research.

Coote, A. (2001) 'Feminism and the Third Way: A Call for Dialogue', in S. White (ed.), *New Labour: The Progressive Future?* Basingstoke, Palgrave.

CRC (UN Committee on the Rights of the Child) (2002) 'Concluding Observations of the Committee on the Rights of the Child: United Kingdom of Great Britain and Northern Ireland', Geneva, Office of the High Commissioner for Human Rights, at www.unhchr.ch.

CYPU (Children and Young People's Unit) (2001) *Learning to Listen: Core Principles for the Involvement of Children and Young People*, Nottinghamshire, DfES Publications.

Deacon, A. (2002) *Perspectives on Welfare*, Buckingham, Open University Press.

Deakin, N. and Parry, R. (2000) *The Treasury and Social Policy*, Basingstoke, Macmillan.

Dobrowolsky, A. (2002) 'Rhetoric versus Reality: The Figure of the Child and New Labour's Strategic "Social Investment State" ', *Studies in Political Economy* (Autumn), pp. 43–73.

Dobrowolsky, A. and Saint-Martin, D. (2002) 'Agency, Actors and Change in a Child-Focused Future: Problematizing Path Dependency's Past and Statist Parameters', paper prepared for the Canadian Political Science Association annual meeting, University of Toronto, 29 May–1 June.

DSS (Department for Social Security) (1998) *New Ambitions for our Country: A New Contract for Welfare*, London, Stationery Office.

Dwyer, P. (1998) 'Conditional Citizens? Welfare Rights and Responsibilities in the Late 1990s', *Critical Social Policy*, 18, 4, pp. 493–517.

Dwyer, P. (2000) *Welfare Rights and Responsibilities*, Bristol, Policy Press.

England, P. and Folbre, N. (1999) 'Who should Pay for the Kids?', *Annals of the American Association of Political and Social Science*, 563, pp. 194–207.

Esping-Andersen, G. (1999) Social *Foundations of Postindustrial Economies*, Oxford, Oxford University Press.

Esping-Andersen, G., with Gallie, D., Hemerijck, A. and Myles, J. (2002) *Why We Need a New Welfare State*, Oxford, Oxford University Press.

Etzioni, A. (2000) *The Third Way to a Good Society*, London, Demos.

European Forum for Child Welfare (2002) 'Eradicating Child Poverty: Fact or Fiction' at www.efcw.org.

Fairclough, N. (2000) *New Labour, New Language?* London, Routledge.

Fawcett, B., Featherstone, B. and Goddard, J. (2004) *Contemporary Child Care Policy and Practice*, London, Palgrave.

Field, F. (2002) 'Gordon Brown's Invention: A Form of Permanent Serfdom', *Daily Telegraph*, 11 June.

Franklin, J. (2000a) 'After Modernisation: Gender, the Third Way and the New Politics', in A. Coote (ed.), *New Gender Agenda*, London, Institute for Public Policy Research.

Franklin, J. (2000b) 'What's Wrong with New Labour Politics?', *Feminist Review*, 66, pp. 138–42.

Gamble, A. and Kenny, M. (1999) 'Now We are Two', *Fabian Review*, 111, 2, pp. 10–11.

Giddens, A. (1998) *The Third Way: The Renewal of Social Democracy*, Cambridge, Polity.

Hari, J. (2002) 'Yah Boo to a Daily Mail Myth', *New Statesman*, 23 Sept., pp. 24–5.

Heron, E. and Dwyer, P. (1999) 'Doing the Right Thing: Labour's Attempt to

Forge a New Welfare Deal between the Individual and the State', *Social Policy and Administration*, 33, 1, pp. 91–104.
HM Treasury (1998) *Modern Public Services for Britain: Investing in Reform* (Pocket Guide), London, HM Treasury.
HM Treasury (1999) *Tackling Poverty and Extending Opportunity*, London, HM Treasury.
HM Treasury (2001) *Tackling Child Poverty: Giving Every Child the Best Possible Start in Life*, London, HM Treasury, at www.hm-treasury.gov.uk.
HM Treasury (2002a) *Budget Report*, London, HM Treasury.
HM Treasury (2002b) *Pre-Budget Report*, London, HM Treasury.
Holden, C. (1999) 'Globalization, Social Exclusion and Labour's New Work Ethic', *Critical Social Policy*, 19, 4, pp. 529–38.
Hughes, G. and Lewis, G. (1998) *Unsettling Welfare*, London, Routledge.
Jenson, J. (2001) 'Rethinking Equality and Equity: Canadian Children and the Social Union', in E. Broadbent (ed.), *Democratic Equality, What Went Wrong?* Toronto, University of Toronto Press.
Jenson, J. and Saint-Martin, D. (2001) 'Changing Citizenship Regimes: Social Policy Strategies in the Investment State', paper prepared for workshop on Fostering Social Cohesion: A Comparison of New Political Strategies, Université de Montréal, 21–22 June.
Jenson, J. and Saint-Martin, D. (2002) 'Building Blocks for a New Welfare Architecture: From Ford to LEGO', paper prepared for the American Political Science Association annual conference, Boston, 29 Aug.–1 Sep.
Jessop, B. (1994) 'The Transition to Post-Fordism and the Schumpeterian Workfare State', in R. Burrows and B. Loader (eds), *Towards a Post-Fordist Welfare State?* London, Routledge.
Jessop, B. (2000) 'From the KWNS to the SWPR', in G. Lewis, S. Gewirtz and J. Clarke (eds), *Rethinking Social Policy*, London, Sage.
Kelly, G. and Le Grand, J. (2001) 'Assets for the People', *Prospect*, Dec.
Lansdown, G. (2002) 'Children's Rights Commissioners for the UK', in B. Franklin (ed.), *The New Handbook of Children's Rights*, London, Routledge.
Larner, W. and Craig, D. (2002) 'After Neoliberalism? Local partnerships and Social Governance in Aotearoa New Zealand', paper presented at the American Political Science Association annual meeting, Boston, 28 Aug.–1 Sep.
Lawson, N. (1992) *The View from No. 11*, London, Bantam Press.
Levitas, R. (2000) 'Community, Utopia and New Labour', *Local Economy*, 15, 3, pp. 188–97.
Lewis, J. (ed.) (1998) *Gender, Social Care and Welfare State Restructuring in Europe*, Aldershot, Ashgate.
Lister, R. (1998) 'Vocabularies of Citizenship and Gender: The UK', *Critical Social Policy*, 18, 3, pp. 309–31.
Lister, R. (2000a) 'To RIO via the Third Way: Labour's "Welfare" Reform Agenda', *Renewal*, 8, 4, pp. 9–20.
Lister, R. (2000b) 'The Politics of Child Poverty in Britain from 1965 to 1990', *Revue Française de Civilisation Britannique*, 11, 1, pp. 67–80.
Lister, R. (2001) 'New Labour: A Study in Ambiguity from a Position of Ambivalence', *Critical Social Policy*, 21, 4, pp. 425–47.
Lister, R. (2002) 'Towards a New Welfare Settlement?', in C. Hay (ed.), *British Politics Today*, Cambridge, Polity.
McRobbie, A. (2000) 'Feminism and the Third Way', *Feminist Review*, 64, pp. 97–112.

Maternity Alliance (2002) 'A Crying Shame: Pregnant Asylum Seekers and their Babies in Detention', briefing paper, London, Maternity Alliance.

Micklewright, J. and Stewart, K. (2000) 'Child Well-Being and Social Cohension', *New Economy*, 7, 1, pp. 18–23.

Miliband, D. (1999) 'This is the Modern World', *Fabian Review*, 111, 4, pp. 11–13.

Mulgan, G. (1998) 'Social Exclusion: Joined Up Solutions to Joined Up Problems', in C. Oppenheim (ed.), *An Inclusive Society: Strategies for Tackling Poverty*, London, Institute for Public Policy Research.

Newman, J. (1998) 'Managerialism and Social Welfare', in G. Hughes and G. Lewis (eds.), *Unsettling Welfare* London, Routledge.

Newman, J. (2001) *Modernising Governance*, London, Sage.

O'Connor, J. S., Orloff, A. S. and Shaver, S. (1999), *States, Markets, Families: Gender, Liberalism and Social Policy in Australia, Canada, Great Britain and the United States*, Cambridge, Cambridge University Press.

Piachaud, D. (2001) 'Child Poverty, Opportunities and Quality of Life', *Political Quarterly*, 72, 4, pp. 446–53.

Polakow, V. (1993) *Lives on the Edge: Single Mothers and their Children in the Other America*, Chicago, University of Chicago Press.

Powell, M. (ed.) (1999) *New Labour, New Welfare State?* Bristol, Policy Press.

Pringle, R. and Watson, S. (1992) '"Women's Interests" and the Post-structuralist State', in M. Barrett and A. Phillips (eds), *Destabilizing Theory: Contemporary Feminist Debates*, Cambridge, Polity.

Prout, A. (2000) 'Children's Participation: Control and Self-Realisation in British Late Modernity', *Children and Society*, 14, pp. 304–15.

Ridge, T. (2002a) *Childhood Poverty and Social Exclusion: From a Child's Perspective*, Bristol, Policy Press.

Ridge, T. (2002b) 'Listening to Children: Their Contribution to Anti-poverty Policies', *Poverty*, 111, pp. 10–13.

Roche, J. (1999) 'Children: Rights, Participation and Citizenship', *Childhood*, 6, 4, pp. 475–93.

Rose, N. (1999) 'Inventiveness in Politics', *Economy and Society*, 28, 3, pp. 467–93.

Sale, A. U. (2002) 'News analysis', *Community Care*, 20–26 June, p. 20.

Schram, S. F. (1995) *Words of Welfare: The Poverty of Social Science and the Social Science of Poverty*, Minneapolis, University of Minnesota Press.

Sherraden, M. (2002) 'From a Social Welfare State to a Social Investment State', in C. Kober and W. Paxton (eds), *Asset-based Welfare and Poverty*, London, National Children's Bureau.

Siim, B. (2000) *Gender and Citizenship: Politics and Agency in France, Britain and Denmark*, Cambridge, Cambridge University Press.

Smith, M. J. (2001) 'Conclusion: The Complexity of New Labour', in S. Ludlam and M. J. Smith (eds), *New Labour in Government*, Basingstoke, Macmillan.

Social Exclusion Unit (2001) *A New Commitment to Neighbourhood Renewal*, London, Cabinet Office.

Stasiulis, D. (2002) 'The Active Child Citizen: Lesson from Canadian Policy and the Children's Movement', *Citizenship Studies*, 6, 4, pp. 507–38.

Strategy Unit (2002) *Delivering for Children and Families*, London, Cabinet Office.

Thomas, G. and Hocking, G. (2003) *Other People's Children*, London, Demos.

Titmuss, R. M. (1974) *Social Policy*, London, Allen and Unwin.

Wiegers, W. (2002) *The Framing of Poverty as 'Child Poverty' and its Implications for Women*, Ottawa, Status of Women Canada.

Willow, C. (2002) 'Lagging Behind?', *Community Care*, 12–18 Sept., p. 30.

# Basic Income and the Two Dilemmas of the Welfare State

*Philippe van Parijs*

Can we avoid a social tragedy? Can we help entering the next century with our welfare states in disarray, with labour's hard-won conquests under deadly threat, and with a growing minority of citizens losing all hope of ever getting a decent job and securing a decent standard of living throughout their existence? I believe we can, but also that it won't be easy. We shall badly need intelligence and will, to come to terms with two central dilemmas.

## First Dilemma: Fighting Exploitation versus Fighting Exclusion

Improving the incomes and working conditions of the poorest workers – whether directly through a statutory minimum wage and other aspects of labour law or indirectly through improving the levels of the replacement incomes granted to those out of work – has long been a central objective of our welfare states. But because exclusion from paid work is also a major form of deprivation, another central objective must be to fight against unemployment. The tension between these two objectives generates our first dilemma. Under a number of (un-Keynesian) assumptions that have become realistic enough, the more you do to improve the material situation of the poorest among the workers, the scarcer the jobs become, and the more people there are who are deprived of the privilege of having one. Thus the two objectives potentially pull in opposite directions; and as soon as unemployment ceases to be a marginal phenomenon, this leads to an acute dilemma.

This dilemma can be highlighted by starting from the dramatic explosion of inequalities in gross earnings that has been observed in much of the Western world [since the early 1980s]. The exact pattern of causation is disputed. But it is bound to include such factors as worldwide outlet expansion, increased competition on both labour and goods markets and the nature and distribution of the skills made more crucial by the computer revolution. In both the US and Western Europe, the higher gross earnings have risen considerably; but at the bottom end, there is a striking difference. Owing precisely to the better social protection of both the employed and the unemployed, what has led in the US to a sizeable fall in the lower categories of earnings has led in Europe to a considerable permanent increase – across cycles – in the proportion of people excluded from gainful employment. The very success (however partial) of Europe's fight against exploitation is making exclusion the dominant form of social injustice. Is there a way out of this painful dilemma between the fight against exploitation and the fight against exclusion, between our concern with poverty and our concern with unemployment? Yes, there is.

Along with a growing number of people across Western Europe,[1] I have been arguing that any realistic and desirable solution to this dilemma must involve the introduction of a comprehensive minimum income guarantee that takes the form, *not* of a means-tested safety net in which people get stuck – as illustrated by the UK's basic social security, Germany's *Sozialhilfe*, France's *revenu minimum d'insertion*, etc. – but of a genuine unconditional floor. Under various names – basic income, social dividend, *Grundeinkommen, reddito di cittadinanza, allocation universelle*, etc., this idea is being proposed as a key component of the backbone of a positive progressive project for a post-neo-liberal, post-communist Europe. Of course, because of the principled though partial disconnection between labour and income it implies, this proposal calls for some quite radical rethinking – not least in those parties whose very name makes it clear that they regard (paid) labour as central. But contrary to what is sometimes said, it does not rely on some absurdly optimistic assumption of abundance. Nor does it give up the aim of full employment, at any rate in the important sense of trying to give everyone the possibility of doing meaningful paid work. Indeed, something like a basic income is part of any realistic strategy for achieving it.

Ever wider circles of people are beginning to see some sense in this bold claim, as they start realizing the narrow limits of what can be expected from such alternative policies as general working time reduction or active labour market policies, and as they start sharing the following crucial insights. Coupled with a corresponding reduction in all other benefits and in the net minimum wage, basic income can be viewed as an employment subsidy given to the potential worker rather than to the employer, with crucially distinctive implications as to the type of low-productivity job that is thereby made viable. Secondly, because it is given irrespective of employment status, the introduction of a basic income abolishes or reduces the unemployment trap, not only by making more room for a positive income differential between total idleness and some work, but even more by providing the administrative security which will enable many people to take the risk of accepting a job or creating their own. Thirdly, basic income can be viewed as a soft strategy for job-sharing, by providing all with a small unconditional sabbatical pay, and thereby making it more affordable for many either to relinquish their job temporarily in order to get a break, go self-employed or retrain, or to work durably on a more part-time basis.

The combined effect of these three processes should lead to a far more flexible working of the labour market, with significantly more stepping-stone, training-intensive, often part-time jobs. Such jobs must be paid little because they represent a risky investment on the part of the employer in a free human being who could leave at any time; and they could acceptably be paid little because the pay would supplement an income to which the workers are unconditionally entitled and which therefore enables them to filter out the jobs that are not sufficiently attractive in themselves or in terms of the prospects they offer.

Of course, the size of this effect will be very sensitive to the level of the basic income and to the package of labour-market and tax-and-benefit institutional adjustments that will need to accompany its introduction. But if embedded in an appropriate package, even a modest basic income could put a halt to the growing dualization and demoralization of our socio-economic system. Under present conditions, the indignation of the jobless who are morally and legally expected to keep looking for what many know they will never find is matched by the outrage of those who subsidize with their social security contributions the idleness of people who are overtly transgressing the rules of the game. Once it stops being Utopian to believe that all those who wish to work can find a job which earns them (when added to the unconditional part of their income) enough to live on, the conditions attached to supplementary entitlements – typically, unemployment benefits restricted to active job-seekers – can more realistically and more legitimately be expected to be enforced. The introduction of an unconditional basic income would thereby also make it possible to rehabilitate the social insurance aspect of our welfare systems. Consequently, whereas a well-intentioned gradual increase in the real level of the safety net could rightly be feared further to disturb the working of the labour market, a well-embedded gradual lifting of the floor can be expected to address both the poverty and the unemployment problem.

## Second Dilemma: Economic Capacity versus Political Capacity

Whether or not one is willing to introduce a basic income and make it a central component of our welfare states, one seems faced with a second dilemma which was neatly, though shockingly, illustrated by a full-page advert published some time ago in Belgian newspapers on behalf of the (socialist) president of the Walloon government. The advert starts with a copy of a number of large cheques made out by various companies which had decided to settle or expand in Wallonia. The headline, and the punchline of the message, reads: 'What unites us today is no longer charity but business.'

Here is, then, our second dilemma. *Either* you try to formulate and implement your ideal of social justice in one region or in one nation, but then you soon find out that, for a number of mutually reinforcing reasons, the potential mobility of savings, investment, skilled labour and consumer demand is now such in Europe that the only aim you can afford in all areas of policy – social, educational, environmental and so on – is none other than 'business', as the advert put it. The economic constraints are so powerful that you are compelled to run the state as if it were a firm and to make competitiveness your paramount concern. *Or* you try to give yourself some leeway by attempting to formulate and implement your ideal of social justice on a large scale – typically, [. . .] the European Union – but then you are soon faced with the powerful obstacles that stem from a widespread distrust of highly centralized institutions, from a lack of identification and hence of spontaneous solidarity between residents of the various areas, and from the difficulty of generating a common public debate across national and linguistic boundaries about the extent and shape of the solidarity you advocate.

Is there a way out of this second dilemma? Once again, I think there is, and one in which basic income has some role to play. I shall here make no attempt even to sketch the broad outlines of what I believe [would be] an adequate solution. Let me just state two firm convictions to which I have been led by a close observation of the debate around the regional aspect of redistribution in Europe and in my own country [Belgium], whose very existence is contingent upon the preservation of a nationwide social security system. One is that a high level of structural redistribution across the borders of broadly autonomous political entities can be sustained only if it takes the form of an interpersonal transfer system, rather than of grants to the governments of the beneficiary entities. The other conviction is that, especially if the political entities involved are culturally and linguistically very different, such a system can be sustained only if on both the contribution and the benefit sides it can operate using extremely simple and uncontroversial information. Fatal resentment is far less likely to arise, for example, if all that needs checking on the benefit side is whether [particular individuals exist] and how old they are, rather than whether they really need psychiatric treatment or truly are involuntarily unemployed.

Because of the conjunction of these two convictions, I strongly believe not only that basic income does have a central role to play in solving the first dilemma of our European welfare states, but also that it has a significant role to play in tackling the second one, between the economic unsustainability of a generous national welfare state and the political unsustainability of a generous transnational welfare state. The argument sketched here would need to be elaborated and qualified along many dimensions. But I predict that as more and more people start realizing the full extent and exact nature of the two big dilemmas we face, basic income will be transformed from the pet idea of a handful of cranks who believe abundance has been reached at long last to a key weapon in the struggle for the preservation of social solidarity and the promotion of social justice.[2]

## Notes

From *Political Quarterly*, 67, 1, 1996, pp. 63–6.

1 The Basic Income European Network, founded in 1988, gathers together individuals and organizations from fourteen countries. [ . . . ]

2 Several aspects of the argument sketched here are developed in Philippe van Parijs, *Real Freedom for All: What (if Anything) Can Justify Capitalism?*, Oxford, Oxford University Press, 1995.

# Index

CPSIA information can be obtained at www.ICGtesting.com
Printed in the USA
LVOW030838301211

261674LV00010B/4/P